IN CONCERT

Reading and Writing

SECOND EDITION

KATHLEEN T. McWHORTER
Niagara County Community College

PEARSON

Boston Columbus Hoboken Indianapolis New York San Francisco
Amsterdam Cape Town Dubai London Madrid Milan Munich Paris Montreal Toronto
Delhi Mexico City São Paulo Sydney Hong Kong Seoul Singapore Taipei Tokyo

Executive Acquisitions Editor: Matthew Wright
Program Manager: Anne Shure
Senior Development Editor: Gillian Cook
Product Marketing Manager: Jennifer Edwards
Senior Field Marketing Manager: John Meyers
Executive Digital Producer: Stefanie Snajder
Content Specialist: Anne Leung
Project Manager: Donna Campion
Project Coordination, Text Design, and Electronic Page Makeup: Lumina Datamatics, Inc.
Program Design Lead/Cover Design: Beth Paquin
Cover Image: gudinny/Shutterstock
Senior Manufacturing Buyer: Roy L. Pickering, Jr.
Printer/Binder: RR Donnelley/Kendallville
Cover Printer: Phoenix

Acknowledgments of third-party content appear on pages 599–600, which constitute an extension of this copyright page.

Library of Congress Cataloging-in-Publication Data
McWhorter, Kathleen T.
In concert : reading and writing / Kathleen T. McWhorter, Niagara County Community College.—Second edition.
pages cm
Includes index.
ISBN 978-0-13-395653-5—ISBN 0-13-395653-9
1. English language—Rhetoric—Study and teaching. 2. Report writing—Study and teaching. 3. Critical thinking—Study and teaching. I. Title.
PE1404.M396 2015
808'.04207—dc23 2014039842

---

1 16

www.pearsonhighered.com

Student Edition ISBN 10: 0-13-459088-0
Student Edition ISBN 13: 978-0-13-459088-2

A la Carte ISBN 10: 0-13-464538-3
A la Carte ISBN 13: 978-0-13-464538-4

Brief Contents

Detailed Contents iv

Preface to the Instructor xiv

PART ONE INTRODUCTION TO READING AND WRITING 1

Chapter 1 An Overview of the Reading Process (with Writing) 1
Chapter 2 An Overview of the Writing Process (with Reading) 37

VOCABULARY WORKSHOPS 68

PART TWO READING, WRITING, AND ORGANIZING PARAGRAPHS 89

Chapter 3 Topics, Main Ideas, and Topic Sentences 89
Chapter 4 Details, Transitions, and Implied Main Ideas 115
Chapter 5 Organization: Basic Patterns 151
Chapter 6 Organization: Additional Patterns 181
Chapter 7 Strategies for Revising Paragraphs 215

PART THREE READING AND WRITING ESSAYS 238

Chapter 8 Reading, Planning, and Organizing Essays 238
Chapter 9 Drafting and Revising Essays 270
Chapter 10 Reading and Writing Essays with Multiple Patterns 297
Chapter 11 Writing Essays Using Sources 321

PART FOUR CRITICAL THINKING, READING, AND WRITING 342

Chapter 12 Critical Thinking: Making Inferences and Analyzing the Author's Message 342
Chapter 13 Critical Thinking: Evaluating the Author's Techniques 368
Chapter 14 Critical Thinking: Reading and Writing Arguments 391

PART FIVE THEMATIC READER: WRITING IN RESPONSE TO READING 423

PART SIX REVIEWING THE BASICS 497

Credits 599

Index 601

Detailed Contents

Preface to the Instructor xiv

PART ONE INTRODUCTION TO READING AND WRITING 1

Chapter 1 An Overview of the Reading Process (with Writing) 1

WHAT IS ACTIVE READING? 2

WHAT IS THE READING PROCESS? 3

PRE-READING STRATEGIES 4

Preview Before Reading 4

Examining Professional Writing *"Secrets for Surviving College and Improving Your Grades," Saundra K. Ciccarelli and J. Nolan White 5*

Make Predictions 9 ■ Connect Reading to Prior Knowledge and Experience 10 ■ Form Guide Questions 10

DURING READING STRATEGIES 11

Highlight and Annotate 11 ■ Map 14 ■ Outline 16
Figure Out Unfamiliar Words 17 ■ Analyze Visuals 19
Use Textbook Learning Aids 21 ■ Use the SQ3R System for Learning from Textbooks 22

POST-READING STRATEGIES 23

Paraphrase 24 ■ Summarize 26 ■ Use Learning and Recall Strategies 28

THINK CRITICALLY 30

The Benefits of Critical Thinking 30 ■ Critical Thinking Is Active Thinking 31 ■ Think Critically About Information in Textbooks 32

Read and Respond: A Textbook Excerpt *"Secrets for Surviving College and Improving Your Grades," Saundra K. Ciccarelli and J. Nolan White 33*

SELF-TEST SUMMARY 35

Chapter 2 An Overview of the Writing Process (with Reading) 37

WHAT IS GOOD WRITING? 38

CONNECT THE READING AND WRITING PROCESSES 39

Examining Professional Writing *"The Flight from Conversation," Sherry Turkle 40*

THE SIX STEPS IN THE WRITING PROCESS 44

Examining Student Writing 45

Jake's First Writing Assignment 46 ■ Jake's Second Writing Assignment 46

GENERATE IDEAS 47

When to Use Which Technique 48 ■ Sorting Usable Ideas 48 ■ Choosing Your Own Topic 49

ORGANIZE YOUR IDEAS 50

Using an Idea Map to Organize Your Ideas 51

CONSIDER YOUR AUDIENCE AND PURPOSE 52

Considering Your Audience 52 ■ Writing for a Purpose 54

WRITE A FIRST DRAFT 55

THINK CRITICALLY ABOUT INCORPORATING VISUALS INTO YOUR WRITING 56

REVISE AND REWRITE DRAFTS 57

Peer Review 58

PROOFREAD YOUR FINAL DRAFT 59

Read and Respond: A Student Essay *"The Romance of Technology," Jake Frey* 61

Read and Respond: A Professional Essay *"The Flight from Conversation," Sherry Turkle* 63

SELF-TEST SUMMARY 66

Vocabulary Workshops 68

WORKSHOP 1 Expanding Your Vocabulary 68

WORKSHOP 2 Using Context Clues 74

WORKSHOP 3 Using Word Parts 80

PART TWO READING, WRITING, AND ORGANIZING PARAGRAPHS 89

Chapter 3 Topics, Main Ideas, and Topic Sentences 89

WHAT IS A PARAGRAPH? 90

Examining Professional Writing *"Greed, Cancer, and Pink KFC Buckets," John Robbins* 91

Examining a Paragraph 93

IDENTIFYING AND SELECTING TOPICS 95

Reading: Locating the Topic of a Paragraph 95 ■ Writing: Selecting a Topic 98

Examining Student Writing *"The Russian and U.S. School Systems," Kate Atkinson* 98

Writing: Refining Your Topic 100

READING AND WRITING TOPIC SENTENCES 101

Reading: Locating Topic Sentences 102 ■ Reading: Placement of Topic Sentences 102 ■ Writing: Developing Effective Topic Sentences 105 ■ Writing: Broad Versus Narrow Topic Sentences 106

THINK CRITICALLY ABOUT TOPIC SENTENCES 109

Read and Respond: A Student Essay *"The Russian and U.S. School Systems," Kate Atkinson 110*

Read and Respond: A Professional Essay *"Greed, Cancer, and Pink KFC Buckets," John Robbins 111*

SELF-TEST SUMMARY 113

Chapter 4 Details, Transitions, and Implied Main Ideas 115

WHAT ARE DETAILS, TRANSITIONS, AND IMPLIED MAIN IDEAS? 116

Examining Professional Writing *"Among Dorms and Dining Halls, Hidden Hunger," Kate Robbins 117*

READING: IDENTIFY SUPPORTING DETAILS 119

Types of Supporting Details 124 ■ Thinking Critically About Details 128

Examining Student Writing *"From Bullet to Blue Sky," Yesenia De Jesus 129*

WRITING: SELECT AND ORGANIZE DETAILS TO SUPPORT YOUR TOPIC SENTENCE 132

Selecting Relevant Details 132 ■ Including Sufficient Details 134 ■ Types of Supporting Details 135 ■ Organizing Details Effectively 135 Using Specific Words 138

USE TRANSITIONS TO GUIDE YOUR READING AND WRITING 140

READING: IDENTIFY IMPLIED MAIN IDEAS 143

Read and Respond: A Student Essay *"From Bullet to Blue Sky," Yesenia De Jesus 147*

Read and Respond: A Professional Essay *"Among Dorms and Dining Halls, Hidden Hunger," Kate Robbins 148*

SELF-TEST SUMMARY 150

Chapter 5 Organization: Basic Patterns 151

WHAT ARE PATTERNS OF ORGANIZATION? 152

Examining Professional Writing *"Cairo Tunnel," Amanda Fields 153*

READING AND WRITING TIME SEQUENCE: CHRONOLOGICAL ORDER, PROCESS, AND NARRATION 154

WHAT IS TIME SEQUENCE? 154

READING CHRONOLOGICAL ORDER AND PROCESS 155

Thinking Critically About Time Sequence 156

Examining Student Writing *"The End of the Road: A Guide to Break Ups," Leila Kaji 157*

WRITING PROCESS PARAGRAPHS 159

Types of Process Paragraphs 160 ■ Writing a Topic Sentence for a Process Paragraph 160 ■ Explaining the Steps in a Process 161 ■ Organizing a Process Paragraph 161

READING NARRATION 161

WRITING NARRATION PARAGRAPHS 163

Writing a Topic Sentence for a Narrative Paragraph 164 Including Sufficient Details 165 ■ Organizing a Narrative Paragraph 165

READING AND WRITING DESCRIPTION 165
WHAT IS DESCRIPTION? 165
READING DESCRIPTION 166
Thinking Critically About Description 167
WRITING DESCRIPTIVE PARAGRAPHS 168
Writing a Topic Sentence for a Descriptive Paragraph 169
Organizing a Descriptive Paragraph 170
READING AND WRITING EXAMPLE 170
WHAT IS AN EXAMPLE? 170
READING EXAMPLE 171
Thinking Critically About Example 172
WRITING EXAMPLE PARAGRAPHS 174
Writing a Topic Sentence 174 ■ Choosing Appropriate Examples 175 ■ Organizing an Example Paragraph 176
Read and Respond: A Student Essay *"The End of the Road: A Guide to Break Ups," Leila Kaji 176*
Read and Respond: A Professional Essay *"Cairo Tunnel," Amanda Fields 177*
SELF-TEST SUMMARY 179

Chapter 6 Organization: Additional Patterns 181
WHAT ARE ADDITIONAL PATTERNS OF ORGANIZATION? 182
Examining Professional Writing *"E-Waste and E-Waste Recycling," Jay Withgott and Scott Brennan 183*
READING AND WRITING DEFINITION 184
WHAT IS DEFINITION? 184
READING DEFINITION 186
Combining Definition and Example 187 ■ Thinking Critically About Definition 187
WRITING DEFINITION PARAGRAPHS 188
Writing a Topic Sentence 189 ■ Adding Explanatory Details 189 ■ Organizing a Definition Paragraph 189
READING AND WRITING CLASSIFICATION 190
WHAT IS CLASSIFICATION? 190
READING CLASSIFICATION 191
Thinking Critically About Classification 191
WRITING CLASSIFICATION PARAGRAPHS 193
Deciding on What Basis to Classify Information 193
Writing a Topic Sentence 194 ■ Explaining Each Subgroup 194 ■ Organizing a Classification Paragraph 195
READING AND WRITING COMPARISON AND CONTRAST 195
WHAT ARE COMPARISON AND CONTRAST? 195
READING COMPARISON AND CONTRAST 195
Comparison 196 ■ Contrast 197 ■ Thinking Critically About Comparison and Contrast 197

WRITING COMPARISON OR CONTRAST PARAGRAPHS 198

Writing a Topic Sentence 198 ■ Developing Points of Comparison or Contrast 198 ■ Organizing a Comparison or Contrast Paragraph 199

Examining Student Writing *"Benefits of Joining the Military," Jessica Nantka 201*

READING AND WRITING CAUSE AND EFFECT 203

WHAT ARE CAUSE AND EFFECT? 203

READING CAUSE AND EFFECT 203

Thinking Critically About Cause and Effect 205

WRITING CAUSE AND EFFECT PARAGRAPHS 207

Distinguishing Between Cause(s) and Effect(s) 207 ■ Writing a Topic Sentence 208

Read and Respond: A Student Essay *"Benefits of Joining the Military," Jessica Nantka 211*

Read and Respond: A Professional Essay *"E-Waste and E-Waste Recycling," Jay Withgott and Scott Brennan 211*

SELF-TEST SUMMARY 214

Chapter 7 Strategies for Revising Paragraphs 215

WHAT IS REVISION? 216

READ CRITICALLY TO REVISE 217

Examining Student Writing *217*

FIRST DRAFT *217*

WRITING: CONSIDER YOUR PURPOSE AND AUDIENCE 219

READING AND WRITING: EXAMINE YOUR IDEAS 219

Relevant and Sufficient Detail 220 ■ Logical Organization of Ideas 222 ■ Revising for Specific and Vivid Language 224

First Revision—Showing Changes in Ideas *"My Unexpected Addiction," Elizabeth Lawson 225*

EDIT FOR CORRECTNESS 226

What Errors to Look For 226 ■ Keeping an Error Log 228

Read and Respond: A Student Essay *228*

Second Revision—Showing Editing and Proofreading *"An Unexpected Addiction," Elizabeth Lawson 229*

Read and Respond: A Professional Reading *Students Vulnerable to Computer Gaming Addiction 231*

SELF-TEST SUMMARY 237

PART THREE READING AND WRITING ESSAYS 238

Chapter 8 Reading, Planning, and Organizing Essays 238

WHY READ AND WRITE ESSAYS? 239

Examining Professional Writing *"Mind Your Own Browser," Simson L. Garfinkel 240*

READ ESSAYS TO BUILD COMPREHENSION AND RECALL 242

Reading: Understanding the Structure of an Essay 242 ■ Reading for Retention, Recall, and Response 247 ■ Thinking Critically About Essays 248

WRITE ESSAYS TO EXPRESS IDEAS 249

Examining Student Writing *"Relationship. 2.0: Dating and Relating in the Internet Age," Ted Sawchuck 249*

CHOOSE A TOPIC 251

Working with Assigned Topics 251 ■ Choosing Your Own Topic 253

GENERATE IDEAS ABOUT YOUR TOPIC 254

Narrowing Your Topic Further 255

CONSIDER AUDIENCE, PURPOSE, AND TONE 256

Considering Your Audience 256 ■ Considering Your Purpose 257 ■ Deciding on an Appropriate Tone 258

WRITE A THESIS STATEMENT 260

Grouping Your Ideas to Discover a Thesis Statement 260 ■ Writing an Effective Thesis Statement 262

PLAN AND ORGANIZE YOUR ESSAY 263

Using Outlining and Idea Mapping 263 ■ Obtaining Complete and Correct Information 264 ■ Organizing Your Essay 264

Read and Respond: A Student Essay *"Relationship. 2.0: Dating and Relating in the Internet Age," Ted Sawchuck 265*

Read and Respond: A Professional Essay *"Mind Your Own Browser," Simson L. Garfinkel 266*

SELF-TEST SUMMARY 268

Chapter 9 Drafting and Revising Essays 270

WHAT IS A DRAFT? 271

READ WHILE DRAFTING 272

WRITE AND REVISE THE BODY OF AN ESSAY 272

Drafting Body Paragraphs 272

Examining Student Writing *272*

Supporting Your Thesis with Substantial Evidence 273

Using Transitions to Make Connections 276

WRITE THE INTRODUCTION, CONCLUSION, AND TITLE 278

Writing the Introduction 278 ■ Writing the Conclusion 279 Selecting a Title 279

THINK CRITICALLY ABOUT AND REVISE YOUR DRAFT 280

Examining Your Ideas 280 ■ Examining Content and Structure 282 ■ Revising Thesis Statements 283 Revising Paragraphs 284 ■ Revising Sentences and Words 285

EDIT AND PROOFREAD 286

Common Errors to Avoid 287 ■ Using Spell-Checkers and Grammar Checkers 287 ■ Using a Proofreading Checklist 287 Presenting Your Essay 287 ■ Revision and Proofreading Checklists 288

Read and Respond: A Student Essay *"Relationships. 2.0: Dating and Relating in the Internet Age," Ted Sawchuck 289*

Read and Respond: A Professional Essay *"You're Under Surveillance," Julia Angwin 289*

SELF-TEST SUMMARY 295

Chapter 10 Reading and Writing Essays with Multiple Patterns 297

WHAT IS A MULTI-PATTERN ESSAY? 298

Examining Professional Writing *"What Is the High Art of Competitive Eating?," Gabriel Muller 299*

RECOGNIZE MULTIPLE PATTERNS WHEN READING 303

Identifying the Primary Pattern of Organization in a Multi-Pattern Essay 304 ■ Identifying Secondary Patterns of Organization in a Multi-Pattern Essay 305

Examining Student Writing *"Gang Life: Better from the Outside," Dejohn Harris 306*

WRITE A MULTI-PATTERN ESSAY 308

Generating and Organizing Ideas About Your Topic 308 ■ Selecting Primary and Secondary Patterns 309 ■ Writing a Thesis Statement that Reflects Your Primary Pattern 312 ■ Drafting an Introduction 313 ■ Drafting Body Paragraphs 314 ■ Using Transitions to Help Readers Follow Your Thought Patterns 315 ■ Drafting a Conclusion 315

Read and Respond: A Student Essay *"Gang Life: Better from the Outside," Dejohn Harris 316*

Read and Respond: A Professional Essay *"What Is the High Art of Competitive Eating?" Gabriel Muller 317*

SELF-TEST SUMMARY 320

Chapter 11 Writing Essays Using Sources 321

WHAT IS AN ESSAY THAT USES SOURCES? 322

Examining Student Writing *"Weighing the Consequences of Censorship in Media," Adam Simmons 322*

READING: FIND AND RECORD APPROPRIATE SOURCES 326

Tips for Finding Appropriate Sources 326 ■ Recording Sources to Avoid Plagiarism 327

WRITING: USE SOURCES TO SUPPORT YOUR THESIS AND DEVELOP YOUR ESSAY 328

CRITICAL THINKING: SYNTHESIZE SOURCES 331

How to Compare Sources to Synthesize 331 ■ How to Develop Ideas About Sources 332

DOCUMENT SOURCES USING MLA OR APA STYLES 334

Documentation 335 ■ An Overview of the MLA Style 335 ■ An Overview of the APA Style 337

Read and Respond: A Student Essay *"Weighing the Consequences of Censorship in Media," Adam Simmons 339*

SELF-TEST SUMMARY 340

PART FOUR CRITICAL THINKING, READING, AND WRITING 342

Chapter 12 Critical Thinking: Making Inferences and Analyzing the Author's Message 342

HOW DOES CRITICAL THINKING APPLY TO READING AND WRITING? 343

Examining Professional Writing *"A Brother Lost," Ashley Womble 344*

MAKE INFERENCES 346

Reading: How to Make Inferences 347 ■ Writing: Thinking Critically About Inferences 349

ASSESS THE SOURCE AND AUTHOR QUALIFICATIONS 349

Reading: Considering the Source 350 ■ Reading: Considering the Author's Credentials 350 ■ Reading: Evaluating Internet Sources 351 ■ Writing: Thinking Critically About Source and Authority 353

DISTINGUISH BETWEEN FACT AND OPINION 354

Writing: Thinking Critically About Fact and Opinion 355

EVALUATE EVIDENCE AND OMISSIONS 356

Reading: What Evidence Has the Author Provided? 356

Reading: What Information Has the Author Omitted? 357

Writing: Thinking Critically About Evidence 358

ANALYZE TONE 358

Writing: Thinking Critically About Tone 361

Read and Respond: A Student Essay *"The Role of Sports in Life," Chase Beauclair 361*

Read and Respond: A Professional Essay *"A Brother Lost," Ashley Womble 364*

SELF-TEST SUMMARY 366

Chapter 13 Critical Thinking: Evaluating the Author's Techniques 368

WHY EVALUATE THE AUTHOR'S TECHNIQUES? 369

Examining Professional Writing *"Sweatshops at Sea," Virginia Sole-Smith 370*

UNDERSTAND CONNOTATIVE AND FIGURATIVE LANGUAGE 373

Reading Connotative Language 373 ■ Writing: Using Connotative Language Carefully 374 ■ Reading Figurative Language 374 ■ Writing: Using Figurative Language Effectively 377

ANALYZE ASSUMPTIONS 377

Writing: Making Reasonable Assumptions 379

EVALUATE GENERALIZATIONS 380

Writing: Making Generalizations Based on Sufficient Evidence 381

IDENTIFY BIAS 381

Writing: Handling Bias Openly 385

Read and Respond: A Student Essay *"TV's Bloody Obsession: Why Vampire Television is Dangerously Appealing," Aurora Gilbert 385*

Read and Respond: A Professional Essay *"Sweatshops at Sea," Virginia Sole-Smith 388*

SELF-TEST SUMMARY 390

Chapter 14 Critical Thinking: Reading and Writing Arguments 391

WHAT IS AN ARGUMENT? 392

THE PARTS OF AN ARGUMENT 393

Examining Professional Writing *"Who Are the Animals in Animal Experiments?," Aysha Akhtar, MD, MPH 396*

READ AN ARGUMENT EFFECTIVELY 399

Recognizing Types of Supporting Evidence 399

THINK CRITICALLY ABOUT ARGUMENTS 402

Evaluating Evidence 402 ■ Examining Opposing Viewpoints 404 ■ Considering Emotional Appeals 405 ■ Identifying Errors in Reasoning 407

Examining Student Writing *"Marijuana: An Argument for Legalization," Quinne Sember 408*

WRITE ARGUMENT ESSAYS 414

Analyzing Your Audience 414 ■ Writing a Thesis Statement 414 ■ Researching Your Topic 416

Providing Adequate Supporting Evidence 416

Read and Respond: A Student Essay *"Marijuana: An Argument for Legalization," Quinne Sember 419*

Read and Respond: A Professional Essay *"Who Are the Animals in Animal Experiments?," Aysha Akhtar, MD, MPH 419*

SELF-TEST SUMMARY 422

PART FIVE THEMATIC READER: WRITING IN RESPONSE TO READING 423

Theme 1: Crime in the 21st Century: Technology and Trafficking 424

READING 1: "Technology and Crime," Frank Schmalleger 424

READING 2: "Why Human Trafficking is Called Modern Day Slavery," Phillip Martin 436

READING 3: "Human Traffic: Exposing the Brutal Organ Trade," Nancy Scheper-Hughes 442

READ AND RESPOND TO THE THEME 455

Theme 2: Journalism: A Changing Field in a Digital Age 456

READING 1: "An Inside Look at Today's News Media," John Vivian 456

READING 2: "The Media Need to Stop Inspiring Copycat Murders. Here's How," Zeynep Tufekci 462

READING 3: "Photojournalism in the Age of New Media," Jared Keller 467

READ AND RESPOND TO THE THEME 474

Theme 3: Sports and Society 475

READING 1: "Drug Abuse Among Athletes," Michael D. Johnson 476

READING 2: "The National Brain-Damage League," Shankar Vedantam 481

READING 3a: (Opinion Piece: PRO) "Should College Football Student Athletes Get Paid?," Zachary Fegely 485

READING 3b: (Opinion Piece: CON) "College Athletes Already Have Advantages and Shouldn't Be Paid," Paul Daugherty 490

READ AND RESPOND TO THE THEME 494

Theme 4: Issues Facing College Students 495

READING 1: "Secrets for Surviving College and Improving Your Grades," Saundra K. Ciccarelli and J. Nolan White, Chapter 1, p. 5

READING 2: "Among Dorms and Dining Halls, Hidden Hunger," Kate Robbins, Chapter 4, p. 117

READING 3: "Students Vulnerable to Computer Gaming Addiction," Chapter 7, p. 231

READ AND RESPOND TO THE THEME 496

PART SIX REVIEWING THE BASICS 497

A. UNDERSTANDING THE PARTS OF SPEECH 498

B. UNDERSTANDING THE PARTS OF SENTENCES 517

C. AVOIDING SENTENCE ERRORS 534

D. WRITING EFFECTIVE SENTENCES 563

E. USING PUNCTUATION CORRECTLY 580

F. MANAGING MECHANICS AND SPELLING 591

Credits 599

Index 601

Preface to the Instructor

Looking at *In Concert* Through a New Lens

The first edition of *In Concert* was received with enthusiasm by many instructors teaching integrated reading and writing classes. They applauded my efforts to combine reading and writing skills, but, at the same time, called for more integration of skills. Looking at *In Concert* with this goal was a challenging task. What changed my perspective, and radically changed the book, was the concept of moving the student and professional essays up to the front of the chapters and using them as the basis for instruction, illustration, and practice, mirroring the growing movement toward writing from reading.

Everything changed with this new focus. Examples that before had been drawn from many unrelated sources now mainly come from one source that students have already previewed, thought about, and connected to their prior experience. Discussions of writing techniques primarily relate to a single source, so students can connect what they have just read to what they are learning; they have seen the technique in practice, now it is being called out and discussed, and next they are going to apply it in their own writing. Although some exercises still require that students apply skills to new content, many now relate directly to the student and professional readings, providing a coherent, focused approach to teaching reading and writing in tandem.

In addition, it became clear there was a lot of repetition. Combining chapters, reducing information into easy-to-read charts, and line editing throughout, has cut over 80 pages, allowing me to include an all-new thematic reader, and providing a briefer, more streamlined and accessible text. For further details of this comprehensive revision, read the following list of new features.

New To The Second Edition

Each of the following changes and new features moves the second edition of *In Concert* further toward providing integrated instruction.

- **NEW! Stronger integration of reading and writing in all chapters.** Chapter 1, "An Overview of the Reading Process (with Writing)," combines content from the previous Chapters 1 and 3 to present the steps in the reading process (pre-, during, and post-) and show students how to use writing while reading to identify (highlight, annotate) and organize (map, outline) key information. It also shows students how to use writing to condense, summarize, and recall information after reading (paraphrase, summarize, review). The chapter is built around a professional reading, which is used to both demonstrate skills and provide students with practice in applying them.

Chapter 2, "An Overview of the Writing Process (with Reading)," outlines the six steps in the writing process and shows how the reading and writing processes complement and interact with each other. It integrates reading and writing beginning with a professional essay, that is annotated to show the major elements of good writing, and then tracking a student writer as he works through each step of the writing process.

All of the remaining chapters have been extensively revised to more effectively tie reading and writing together by moving either the student essay and/or the professional essay earlier in the chapter, allowing students deconstruct it to determine how the author created it, what he she wanted to convey, and how they might use similar techniques in their own writing.

- **NEW! Thematic Reader.** For the growing numbers of instructors who teach writing in the context of reading, this edition includes a thematic reader that consists of four themes—crime in the twenty-first century, news coverage and journalism, American sports, and issues facing college students—each containing three readings, one of which is a textbook excerpt. The readings range in length from two to ten pages and are followed by exercises and activities. Synthesis activities and essay writing assignments follow each theme. Readings for the fourth theme are interspersed throughout the book, but an introduction to them, synthesis questions, and integrative writing assignments appear within the Thematic Reader.
- **NEW! Streamlined, reader-friendly chapters.** The second edition has been carefully edited to deliver chapter content in the clearest, most expeditious manner. The chapters contain more bulleted lists, more tables that concisely present information, and more annotations that show rather than tell students what they need to learn.
- **NEW! Streamlined coverage of MLA and APA documentation.** Because ample information is presented online and numerous documentation preparation tools are available for student use, the MLA and APA documentation sections in Chapter 11 have been condensed into tabular format.
- **NEW! Coverage of how to use visuals in student writing.** The content in Chapter 4, "Reading and Evaluating Visuals," from the first edition has been pared down and revised—to more closely align visuals with both the reading and writing processes—and integrated into Chapter 1, which focuses on analyzing and interpreting visuals, and Chapter 2, which shows students how to select and integrate visuals into their own writing.
- **NEW! Seven professional readings.** In general, the professional essays new to this edition are longer, somewhat more challenging, and more representative of readings that might be assigned in academic courses. New essay topics include college survival skills, animal experimentation, eating contests, gaming addiction, surveillance, food scarcity among college students, and the effects of technology on interpersonal communication.
- **NEW! Four student essays.** The new student essays are longer than in the first edition and are more representative of the level of writing instructors want their students to strive toward. New essay topics include the role of sports in life, vampire TV, breaking up relationships, and online romance.
- **NEW! Coverage of writers' techniques.** A new section of exercises and activities following the professional readings, "Reading and Writing: An Integrated Perspective," guides students in analyzing the strategies and techniques the writer used in the essay, and include questions about visuals that accompany the reading.

Features

In Concert teaches both reading and writing skills by demonstrating how they work together and complement one another in every chapter and through using all of the features listed below.

- **Extensive Coverage of Critical Thinking** To be prepared for freshman composition classes, students need to be able to think critically and respond in writing to what they have read. **Part Four** addresses critical thinking skills for both reading and writing, including coverage of reading and writing arguments. Each professional reading is followed by a "Thinking and Writing Critically section" and many chapters contain a section "Thinking Critically About . . ." that links chapter skills with related critical thinking skills.
- **Metacognitive Approach to Reading and Writing** Both reading and writing are approached as thinking processes—processes in which students read, write, and assess their performance of the task. They are encouraged to be aware of, control, assess, and adjust how they are reading and writing.
- **Emphasis on Textbook Reading and Writing** Chapter 1 includes skills for reading textbook chapters and describes the SQ3R system. Students learn recall strategies and use writing to highlight, annotate, map, outline, paraphrase, and summarize ideas they read. Numerous textbook excerpts appear throughout the text; several function as in-chapter professional readings.
- **Visual Literacy** Students learn to read and interpret various types of visuals, integrate text and visuals, and think critically about visuals.
- **Vocabulary Coverage** Vocabulary building skills are emphasized throughout the book: Chapter 1 presents an introduction to vocabulary (dictionary usage and strategies for figuring out unfamiliar words); three Vocabulary Workshops provide instruction on how to use context clues and word parts, expand vocabulary, and learn specialized terms; and a "Strengthening Your Vocabulary" section after each professional reading helps students learn new words.
- **Multimodal Essay Chapter** This chapter recognizes that writers often rely on several methods of development in a single essay and offers strategies for combining and integrating two or more rhetorical modes.
- **Introductory Material on Reading and Writing Using Sources** As Chapter 11 offers an overview of research, synthesis, and documentation of sources and features a student essay annotated to highlight MLA formatting.
- **Part Five, A Thematic Reader: Writing in Response to Reading** This new addition to the text contains thirteen readings, organized by four themes, and each accompanied by exercises, activities and synthesis questions (Readings for Theme 4 are drawn from chapter readings.).
- **Part Six, Reviewing the Basics** is a handbook that provides a simple, clear presentation of forms and rules of English usage with examples and exercises. In addition, MySkillsLab has been updated to match the presentation of skills in the text, providing ample online practice opportunities.

Chapter Features

- **Visual and Engaging Chapter Openers** Each chapter opens with a photograph or other image that is intended to capture students' attention, generate interest, connect the topic of the chapter to their experience, and get students writing immediately about chapter-related content.

- **Learning Objectives Tied to Interactive Summaries** Learning objectives at the beginning of each chapter identify what students can expect to learn and correspond directly to the interactive summaries at the end.
- **Reading and Writing Connections** Examples of everyday, academic, and workplace situations are presented to demonstrate the relevance and importance of chapter skills.
- **Examining Professional Writing** In a number of chapters, students start by reading and thinking about a professional article, essay, or textbook excerpt. They study the professional reading as an effective writing model, and it is also used for instruction in and practice with the reading strategies taught in the chapter.
- **Examining Student Writing** Many chapters begin the writing instruction by asking students to read and analyze a student essay, which is then deconstructed over the course of the chapter to explain and illustrate key writing skills and is also used for practice. In other chapters, students follow a student writer as he or she uses the reading and writing processes to draft and revise an essay and answer questions about the final product.

MySkillsLab®

- **MySkillsLab** Almost all the exercises that follow the professional readings in Parts One to Four and all of the writing assignments that follow the professional readings in Part Five can be completed online at MySkillsLab. These exercises can be easily identified, as the MySkillsLab logo is integrated into their titles. Students can go online to a chapter-specific module, click on the appropriate exercise, and complete and submit it.
- **Linked Writing Exercises** Writing in Progress exercises guide students step-by-step through the writing process.
- **Visualize It!** Many chapters contain idea maps that show how paragraphs and essays are organized from both a reading and a writing perspective.
- **Self-Test Summary** Included at the end of each chapter is a Self-Test Summary that corresponds to the learning goals stated at the beginning of the chapter. This summary allows students to test their recall of chapter content and mastery of each learning goal.
- **Reading Levels in Annotated Instructor's Edition** A **Lexile® measure**—the most widely used reading metric in U.S. schools—provides valuable information about a student's reading ability and the complexity of text. It helps match students with reading resources and activities that are targeted to their ability level. Lexile measures indicate the reading levels of content in MySkillsLab and the longer selections in the Annotated Instructor's Editions of all Pearson's reading books. See the Annotated Instructor's Edition of *In Concert* and the *Instructor's Manual* for more details.
- **Online Multiple-Choice Comprehension Questions for Professional Readings** These questions provide a quick assessment of students' literal comprehension and recall of the chapter goals in Chapters 1–14 and of the readings in Part 5. These question sets are useful for students needing more guidance with literal comprehension skills as well as for verifying that students have read the assigned chapters and readings.

Instructor Support and Professional Development

Pearson is pleased to offer a variety of support materials to help make teaching reading and writing easier for instructors and to help students excel in their coursework.

Annotated Instructor's Edition for *In Concert* (ISBN 9780133956672/ 0133956679) The *AIE* offers in-text answers to all exercises, practice sets, and reading/writing assignments. It also indicates which activities are offered simultaneously in MySkillsLab. It is a valuable resource for experienced and first-time instructors alike.

Online Instructor's Resource Manual for *In Concert* (ISBN 9780133956603 / 0133956601) The material in the *IRM,* written by Mary Dubbé, is designed to save instructors time and provide them with effective options for teaching the integrated reading/writing course. It offers suggestions for setting up their course; provides sample syllabus models; provides lots of extra practice for students who need it, and is an invaluable resource for adjuncts.

Test Bank for In Concert (ISBN 9780133956566 / 0133956563) An abundance of extra practice exercises are included in the *Test Bank for In Concert.* The *Test Bank*, created by Jeanne Jones, can also be used to create tests in Pearson's MyTest (9780133956597 / 0133956598) test creation tool.

PowerPoint Presentation for In Concert (ISBN 0133956571 / 9780133956573) Mary Dubbé has created PowerPoint presentations to accompany each chapter of *In Concert* and consists of classroom ready lecture outline slides, lecture tips classroom activities, and review questions.

Answer Key for In Concert (ISBN 9780133956658 / 0133956652) The Answer Key contains the solutions to the exercises in the student edition of the text.

Professional Development

Pearson offers a variety of professional development programs and resources to support full- and part-time instructors. These include Pedagogy & Practice, an open-access digital resource gallery [http://pedagogyandpractice.pearsonhighered.com/], and our Speaking About English online conference series, featuring scholar/ educators addressing pedagogical topics via web-based presentations. These conferences are held twice a year and are free of cost to attend. Information about future conferences, as well as archives of past sessions, can be found on the conference website [http://www.pearsonhighered.com/speakingabout/english/]. Updated information about any and all of these Partnership Programs can always be found on our catalog page [http://www.pearsonhighered.com/english/].

MySkillsLab®

MySkillsLab™ www.myskillslab.com

Efficiently blending the market-leading and proven practice from MyWritingLab and MyReadingLab into a single application and learning path, MySkillsLab offers a wealth of practice opportunity, additional instruction/content support, and extensive progress tracking for integrated reading/writing courses.

- **Reading** MySkillsLab improves students' mastery of 23 reading skills via mastery-based skill practice and improves students' reading levels with the Lexile®

framework (www.Lexile.com) to measure both reader ability and text difficulty on the same scale and pair students with readings within their Lexile range.

- **Writing** MySkillsLab offers skill remediation in grammar and punctuation, paragraph development, essay development, and research, and improves students' overall writing through automatic scoring by Pearson's proven Intelligent Essay Assessor (IEA).

MySkillsLab®

A Deeper Connection Between Print and Media

Pearson's MySkillsLab (www.myskillslab.com) is deeply integrated into the assignments, practice sets, and reading selection activities in *In Concert*. Students can complete and submit various exercises and activities within the eText/ MySkillsLab course and some of the results flow right to the Instructor Gradebook.

Acknowledgments

I wish to express my gratitude to the many instructors who reviewed *In Concert* for their excellent ideas, suggestions, and advice on preparing this text:

Shaunte Allen, Cedar Valley College; Regina (Gina) Barnett, Tidewater Community College–Virginia Beach; Craig Barto, Southern University; Robyn Browder, Tidewater Community College–Virginia Beach; Sandi Buschmann, Cincinnati State; Maureen Cahill, Tidewater Community College–Virginia Beach; Sharon M. Cellemme, South Piedmont Community College; Helen Chester, Milwaukee Area Technical College; Mattie Coll, John Tyler Community College; Karen Cowden, Valencia College; Amber Cristan, Kinonen Bay College; Christopher Deal, Piedmont Community College; Margaret DeSalvo, Kingsborough Community College; Genevieve Dibua, Baltimore City Community College; Joanne Diddlemeyer, Tidewater Community College–Norfolk; Barbara Doyle, Arkansas State University– Jonesboro; Mary Dubbe, Thomas Nelson Community College; Kim Edwards, Tidewater Community College–Chesapeake; Jennifer Ferguson, Cazenovia College; Lisa Ferrell, Arkansas State University; Mindy Flowers, Midland College; Tarasa Gardner, Moberly Area Community College; Susan Givens, Northern Virginia–Manassas; Sharon Green, Niagara University; Beth Gulley, Johnson County Community College; Clinton Hale, Blinn College–Brenham College; Barbara Hampton, Rend Lake College; Tom Hargrove, Tidewater Community College–Chesapeake; Curtis Harrell, North West Arkansas Community College; Carlotta Hill, Oklahoma City Community College; Wayne Johnson, Odessa College; Frank Lammer, Northeast Iowa Community College; Erlinda Legaspi, City College of San Francisco; Alice Leonhardt, Blue Ridge Community College; Glenda Lowery, Rappahannock Community College; Maureen Maas-Feary, Finger Lakes Community College; Agnes Malicka, Northern Virginia–Alexandria Campus; Jennifer McCann, Bay College; Margaret McClain, Arkansas State University; Chante McCormick, City College of San Francisco; Brenda Meisel, Northern Virginia Community College–Woodbridge; Nancy S. Morrison, J. Sargeant Reynolds Community College; Robbi Muckenfuss, Durham Technical Community College; Debbie Nacquin, Northern Virginia Community College; Erin Nelson, Blinn College; Carl Olds, University of Central Arkansas; Debbie Ousey, Penn State University– Brandywine; Michelle Palmer, Pulaski Technical College; Catherine Parra, Northern Virginia–Loudoun; Pat Pierce, Pulaski Technical College; Elizabeth Price, Ranger College; Betty Raper, Pulaski Technical College; Joan Reeves, Northeast Alabama Community College; Linda Robinett. Oklahoma City Community College; Tony Rogers, Benjamin Franklin Institute of Technology; Dianna Rottinghaus, Johnson County Community College; Charis Sawyer, Johnson County Community College; Susan Silva, El Paso Community College; Syble Davis Simon, Houston

Community College; Benjamin Sloan, Piedmont Virginia Community College; Catherine Swift, University of Central Arkansas; Shari Waldrop, Navarro College; Colleen Weeks, Arapahoe Community College; Michelle Zollars, Patrick Henry Community College

I wish to thank Kathy Tyndall, retired department head of the Pre-Curriculum Department at Wake Technical Community College, who has worked with me as a consultant on the project. She is an experienced teacher of integrated reading and writing courses, and she was able to provide me with fresh insights and new perspectives about integrating reading ad writing instruction within a textbook format. Mathew Wright, executive editor, deserves special thanks for offering advice on the scope and depth of the revision and providing resources for the book's development. I also thank Eric Stano, executive editor, for the opportunity to revise the book and for his support throughout the revision process. I also wish to thank Jeanne Jones for her valuable assistance in drafting, revising, and preparing the manuscript and Janice Wiggins, development editor, for helping me locate stimulating professional essays. Gillian Cook, senior development editor, deserves special recognition for encouraging me to reshape my thinking to create a more integrated book. Our day-to-day collaboration, discussions, and brainstorming stimulated my creativity and resulted in a fresh new approach to many chapters.

I would also like to thank the following students who provided samples of their writing for the student essays:

Kate Atkinson; Yesenia De Jesus; Dejohn Harris; Leila Kaji; Jessica Nantka; Quinne Sember; Chase Beauclair; Aurora Gilbert; Jacob Frey; Elizabeth Lawson; Ted Sawchuck; Adam Simmons

I also value the professional and creative efforts of Melissa Sacco and her team at Lumina Datamatics, Inc.

Kathleen T. McWhorter

1 An Overview of the Reading Process (with Writing)

LEARNING GOALS

Learn how to . . .

- **GOAL 1** Read actively
- **GOAL 2** Use the reading process
- **GOAL 3** Preview, predict, question, and connect to prior knowledge (pre-reading)
- **GOAL 4** Identify, organize, and understand key information (during reading)
- **GOAL 5** Paraphrase, summarize, and recall information (during and post-reading)
- **GOAL 6** Think critically about what you read

THINK About It!

Why is the student in the photograph so obviously overwhelmed? What reading, writing, and study strategies would help him cope with the heavy reading and study workload of college? This chapter focuses on the reading process and the reading and writing strategies that can help you to become an active reader. You will learn how to preview a text and discover what you already know about the topic; how to identify what is important to learn, using highlighting and annotating, and how to organize it, using mapping and outlining; and how to use post-reading strategies, including paraphrasing and summarizing, to organize and recall information. All of these skills will also help you to prepare for writing essays and taking exams.

Reading and Writing Connections

EVERYDAY CONNECTIONS

- **Reading** You read an article in the newspaper about a proposed high-rise development in a historically significant part of town.
- **Writing** You write a letter to the editor arguing against the proposed development and proposing the area be listed in the National Register of Historic Places.

ACADEMIC CONNECTIONS

- **Reading** You read a section of a world history text titled "China's Golden Age: The Tang and Song Dynasties."
- **Writing** In an essay exam question for the same class, you are asked to describe events that led to the end of the Tang Dynasty and the rise of the Song Dynasty.

WORKPLACE CONNECTIONS

- **Reading** You read in the company newsletter that a new management training program is being offered for existing employees.
- **Writing** You write a summary of your qualifications and your history with the company so that you can be considered for the management training program.

What Is Active Reading?

■ GOAL 1
Read actively

Active readers are involved with what they are reading. They interact with the author and his or her ideas. Table 1-1 contrasts the active strategies of successful readers with the passive ones of less successful readers. Throughout the remainder of this chapter and this book, you will discover specific strategies for becoming a more active reader and learner. Not all strategies work for everyone; experiment to discover those that work for you.

TABLE 1-1 ACTIVE VERSUS PASSIVE READING

Active Readers . . .	Passive Readers . . .
Tailor their reading strategies to suit each assignment.	Read all assignments the same way.
Analyze the purpose of a reading assignment.	Read an assignment because it was assigned.
Adjust their reading speed to suit their purposes.	Read everything at the same speed.
Question ideas in the assignment.	Accept whatever is in print as true.
Skim the headings or introduction and conclusion to find out what an assignment is about before beginning to read.	Check the length of an assignment and then begin reading.
Make sure they understand what they are reading as they go along.	Read until the assignment is completed.
Read with pencil in hand, highlighting, jotting notes, and marking key vocabulary.	Simply read.
Develop personalized strategies that are particularly effective.	Follow routine, standard methods.

EXERCISE 1-1 Reading Actively

Directions: Rate each of the following items as either helpful (H) or not helpful (NH) in reading actively. Then discuss with a classmate how each of the items marked NH could be changed to be more helpful.

_____ **1.** Beginning to write an essay without reviewing the chapter in which is it assigned

_____ **2.** Giving yourself a maximum of one hour to write an essay

_____ **3.** Using different techniques to read different types of essays

_____ **4.** Highlighting important new words in an essay

_____ **5.** Rereading an essay the same way as many times as necessary to understand it

What Is the Reading Process?

■ GOAL 2
Use the reading process

Reading is much more than moving your eyes across a page. It is a multi-step process that involves numerous strategies to use before, during, and after reading that will help you understand and remember what you read and prepare you to write in response to what you read. Figure 1-1 will help you visualize the reading process.

FIGURE 1-1 THE READING PROCESS

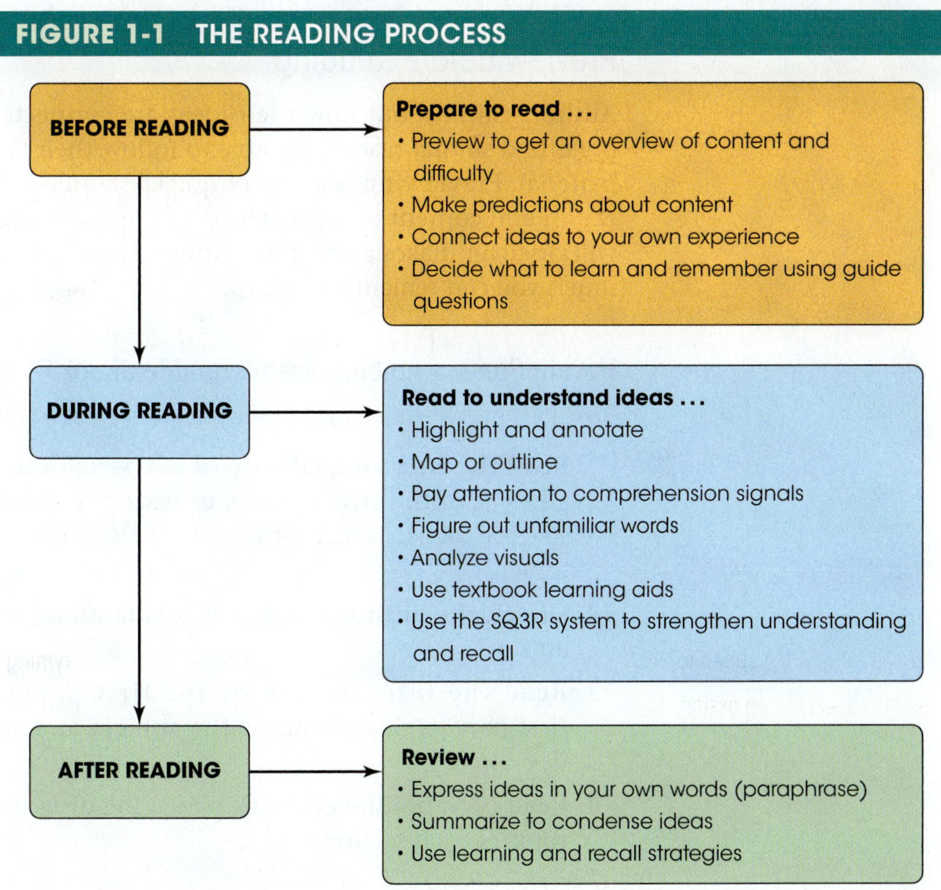

NOTE: Critical thinking is an essential part of the reading process; readers need to interpret, evaluate, and react to the ideas presented, connect them to their own ideas, and express them clearly in writing.

Reading is also more than just understanding what an author says. It involves thinking critically about what you are reading and have read. Think of reading as a process of interacting with the author—questioning, commenting, interpreting, and evaluating what is said. You will learn more about critical reading and thinking in this chapter as well as in Chapters 12, 13, and 14.

Reading is not a lock-step process that you follow from beginning to end. Instead, plan to move back and forth within the reading process. Plan to reread, perhaps more than once. If you have trouble understanding a passage, you may need to go back and get an overview of how it fits within the whole article, for example. And you are really never finished reading. New thoughts, responses, and reactions may occur to you long after you have read and reviewed the material.

Reading involves many related skills, such as learning new words, identifying what is important, determining how a reading is organized, understanding how ideas are connected, both within individual paragraphs and in essays, articles, and textbooks. Chapters 3–11 will help you polish these skills.

Pre-Reading Strategies

■ GOAL 3
Preview, predict, question, and connect to prior knowledge

Just as you probably would not jump into a pool without checking its depth, you should not begin reading an article or textbook chapter without knowing what it is about and how the author organized it. This section will show you how to preview, ask questions, and discover you what already know about what you will read.

Preview Before Reading

Authors think about how their ideas are connected and how they can best be organized so that readers are able to follow their thoughts and understand their material. **Previewing** is a way of quickly familiarizing yourself with the organization and content of a chapter or article *before* beginning to read it, which you will discover makes a dramatic difference in how effectively you read and how much you can remember.

How to Preview Articles, Essays, and Textbook Chapters

Think of previewing as getting a sneak peek at what a reading will be about.

1. **Read the title and subtitle of the selection.** The title provides the overall topic of the article, essay, or textbook chapter. The subtitle suggests the specific focus, aspect, or approach the author will take toward the overall topic.
2. **Check the author's name.** If it is familiar, what do you know about the author?
3. **Read the introduction or the first paragraph.** The introduction or first paragraph introduces the subject and suggests how the author will develop it.
4. **Read each boldfaced (dark print) heading.** Headings announce the major topic of each section.

5. **Read the first sentence under each heading, which often states the central thought of the section.**
6. **If the reading lacks headings, read the first sentence of each of a few paragraphs on each page to discover main ideas.**
7. **Note any graphic aids.** Graphs, charts, photographs, and tables often suggest what is important in the selection, as they have been chosen to support the author's message. Be sure to read the captions for photographs and the legends on graphs, charts, or tables.
8. **Read the last paragraph or summary.** This may provide a condensed view of the selection, often reviewing key points, or it may draw the reading to a close. If the last paragraph is lengthy, read only the last few sentences.

EXAMINING PROFESSIONAL WRITING

The following textbook excerpt, "Secrets for Surviving College and Improving Your Grades," is taken from the introductory section of *Psychology*, fourth edition, by Saundra K. Ciccarelli and J. Nolan White. It offers a variety of strategies for learning from and studying college textbooks. This excerpt will be used throughout this chapter to demonstrate techniques and give you practice in reading and learning from college textbooks.

Thinking Before Reading

Study the highlighted parts of the essay and, using the "How to Preview Articles, Essay, and Textbook Chapters" section above, see if you can explain why each of the sections/sentences is highlighted.

After you have previewed the essay, connect the reading to your own experience by answering the following questions:

a. Do you wish reading and studying were easier?

b. Do you spend time reading and studying but not get the grades you feel you deserve?

Secrets for Surviving College and Improving Your Grades

1 *I want to make better grades, but sometimes it seems that no matter how hard I study, the test questions turn out to be hard and confusing and I end up not doing very well. Is there some trick to getting good grades?*

2 Many students would probably say that their grades are not what they want them to be. They may make the effort, but they still don't seem to be able to achieve the higher grades that they wish they could earn. A big part of the problem is that despite many different educational experiences, students are rarely taught how to study.

STUDY METHODS: DIFFERENT STROKES FOR DIFFERENT FOLKS

WHAT ARE SOME DIFFERENT METHODS OF STUDYING?

3 Most college students, at one point or another in their educational experiences, have probably run into the concept of a *learning style,* but what exactly is it? In general, a learning style is the particular way in which a person takes in, or absorbs, information.

4 We learn many different kinds of things during our lives, and one method of learning probably isn't going to work for everyone. Some people seem to learn better if they can read about a topic or put it into their own words (verbal learners). Others may find that looking at charts, diagrams, and figures help them more (visual learners). There are those who learn better if they can hear the information (auditory learners), and there are even people who use the motion of their own bodies to help them remember key information (action learners). While instructors would have a practical nightmare if they tried to teach to every individual student's particular learning style, students who are aware of their own style can use it to change the way they study. So instead of focusing on different learning styles, this section will focus on different *study methods.* Take the opportunity to try them out and find which methods work best for you. Table A lists just some of the ways in which you can study. All of the methods listed in this table are good for students who wish to improve both their understanding of a subject and their grades on tests. See if you can think of some other ways in which you might prefer to practice the various study methods.

WHEN AND WHERE DO YOU FIT IN TIME TO STUDY? WHAT ARE SOME STRATEGIES FOR TIME MANAGEMENT?

5 One of the biggest failings of college students (and many others) is managing the time for all the tasks involved. Procrastination, the tendency to put off tasks until some later time that often does not arrive, is the enemy of time management. There are some strategies to defeating procrastination (The College Board, 2011):

- Make a map of your long-term goals. If you are starting here, what are the paths you need to take to get to your ultimate goal?
- Get a calendar and write down class times, work times, social engagements, everything!
- Before you go to bed, plan your next day, starting with when you get up and prioritizing your tasks for that day. Mark tasks off as you do them.
- Go to bed. Getting enough sleep is a necessary step in managing your tasks. Eating right and walking or stretching between tasks is a good idea, too.
- If you have big tasks, break them down into smaller, more manageable pieces. How do you eat an elephant? One bite at a time.
- Do small tasks, like answering emails or writing the first paragraph of a paper, in those bits of time you might otherwise dismiss; riding the bus to school or work, waiting in a doctor's office, and so on.
- Build in some play time—all work and no play pretty much insures that you will fail at keeping your schedule. Use play time as a reward for getting tasks done.

TABLE A MULTIPLE STUDY METHODS

Verbal Methods	Visual Methods	Auditory Methods	Action Methods
• Use flash cards to identify main points or key terms. • Write out or recite key information in whole sentences or phrases in your own words. • When looking at diagrams, write out a description. • Use "sticky" notes to remind yourself of key terms and information, and put them in the notebook or text or on a mirror that you use frequently. • Practice spelling words or repeating facts to be remembered. • Rewrite things from memory.	• Make flash cards with pictures or diagrams to aid recall of key concepts. • Make charts and diagrams and sum up information in tables. • Use different colors of highlighter for different sections of information in text or notes. • Visualize charts, diagrams, and figures. • Trace letters and words to remember key facts. • Redraw things from memory.	• Join or form a study group or find a study partner so that you can discuss concepts and ideas. • While studying, speak out loud or into a digital recorder that you can play back later. • Make speeches. • Record the lectures (with permission). Take notes on the lecture sparingly, using the recording to fill in parts that you might have missed. • Read notes or text material into a digital recorder or get study materials recorded and play back while exercising or doing chores. • When learning something new, state or explain the information in your own words out loud or to a study partner. • Use musical rhythms as memory aids, or put information to a rhyme or a tune.	• Sit near the front of the classroom and take notes by jotting down key terms and making pictures or charts to help you remember what you are hearing. • While studying, walk back and forth as you need out loud. • Study with a friend. • While exercising, listen to recordings you have made of important information. • Write out key concepts on a large board or poster. • Make flash cards, using different colors and diagrams, and lay them out on a large surface. Practice putting them in order. • Make a three-dimensional model. • Spend extra time in the lab. • Go to off-campus areas such as a museum or historical site to gain information.

- If your schedule falls apart, don't panic—just start again the next day. Even the best time managers have days when things don't go as planned.

Time saved or time wasted?

6 Another problem that often interferes with time management is the enduring myth that we can effectively multitask. In today's world of technological interconnectedness, people tend to believe that they can learn to do more than one task at a time. The fact, however, is that the human mind is not meant to multitask and trying to do so not only can lead to car wrecks and other disasters, but also may result in changes in how individuals process different types of information, and not for the better. One study challenged college students to perform experiments that involved task switching, selective attention, and working memory (Ophir et al., 2009). The expectation was that students who were experienced at multitasking would outperform those who were not, but the results were just the opposite: the "chronic multitaskers" failed miserably at all three tasks. The results seemed to indicate that frequent multitaskers use their brains less effectively, even when focusing on a single task.

7 Another study found that people who think they are good at multitasking are actually not (Sanbonmatsu et al., 2013), while still another study indicates that video gamers, who often feel that their success at gaming is training them to be good multitaskers in other areas of life such as texting or talking while driving, are just as unsuccessful at multitasking as nongamers (Donohue et al., 2012). In short, it's better to focus on one task and only one task for a short period of time before moving on to another than to try to do two things at once.

READING TEXTBOOKS: TEXTBOOKS ARE NOT MEATLOAF

HOW SHOULD YOU GO ABOUT READING A TEXTBOOK SO THAT YOU GET THE MOST OUT OF YOUR READING EFFORTS?

8 No matter what the study method, students must read the textbook to be successful in the course. (While that might seem obvious to some, many students today seem to think that just taking notes on lectures or slide presentations will be enough.) This section deals with how to read textbooks for understanding rather than just to "get through" the material.

9 Students make two common mistakes in regard to reading a textbook. The first mistake is simple: Many students don't bother to read the textbook *before* going to the lecture that will cover that material. Trying to get anything out of a lecture without having read the material first is like trying to find a new, unfamiliar place without using a GPS or any kind of directions. It's easy to get lost. This is especially true because of the assumption that most instructors make when planning their lectures: They take for granted that the students have already read the assignment. The instructors then use the lecture to go into detail about the information the students supposedly got from the reading. If the students have not done the reading, the instructor's lecture isn't going to make a whole lot of sense.

10 The second mistake that most students make when reading textbook material is to try to read it the same way they would read a novel: They start at the first page and read continuously. With a novel, it's easy to do this because the plot is usually interesting and people want to know what happens next, so they keep reading. It isn't necessary to remember every little detail—all they need to remember are the main plot points. One could say that a novel is like meatloaf—some meaty parts with lots of filler. Meatloaf can be eaten quickly, without even chewing for very long.

The SQ3R method

WHAT IS THE SQ3R METHOD?

11 With a textbook, the material may be interesting but not in the same way that a novel is interesting. A textbook is a big, thick steak—all meat, no filler. Just as a steak has to be chewed to be enjoyed and to be useful to the body, textbook material has to be "chewed" with the mind. You have to read slowly, paying attention to every morsel of meaning. (See page 22–23 for an explanation of the SQ3R method.)

12 So how do you do that? Probably one of the best-known reading methods is called SQ3R, first used by F. P. Robinson in a 1946 book called *Effective Study*.

13 Some educators and researchers now add a fourth R: *Reflect*. To reflect means to try to think critically about what you have read by trying to tie the concepts into what you already know, thinking about how you can use the information in your own life, and deciding which of the topics you've covered interests you enough to look for more information on that topic. For example, if you have learned about the genetic basis for depression, you might better understand why that disorder seems to run in your best friend's family.

After reading a chapter section, take time to reflect on what the information means and how it might relate to real-world situations.

14 Reading textbooks in this way means that, when it comes time for the final exam, all you will have to do is carefully review your notes to be ready for the exam—you won't have to read the entire textbook all over again. What a time-saver! Recent research suggests that the most important steps in this method are the three

R's: Read, Recite, and Review. In two experiments with college students, researchers found that when compared with other study methods such as rereading and note-taking study strategies, the 3R strategy produced superior recall of the material.

EXERCISE 1-2

Evaluating Your Previewing of "Secrets for Surviving in College"

Directions: Answer each of the following questions based on what you learned by previewing "Secrets for Surviving in College and Improving Your Grades."

1. Why do many students not achieve the grades they want?
2. What does the term *learning style* mean?
3. What is one of the biggest failings of college students?
4. What is the SQ3R method?

This exercise tested your recall of some of the important ideas in the article. Check your answers by referring back to the article. Did you get most or all of the items correct? This exercise demonstrates, then, that previewing helps you learn the key ideas in a selection before actually reading it.

Make Predictions

Predictions are educated guesses about the material to be read. For example, you might predict an essay's focus, a chapter's method of development, or the key points to be presented within a chapter section. Table 1-2 presents examples of predictions that may be made from a heading and an opening sentence in "Secrets for Surviving College."

You make predictions based on your experience with written language, your background knowledge, and your familiarity with a subject. While previewing a reading assignment, make predictions about its content and organization, and anticipate what topics the author will cover and how the topics will be organized using these questions:

- What clues does the author give?
- What will this material be about?
- What logically would follow next?

TABLE 1-2 SAMPLE PREDICTIONS

Heading	Prediction
Where and When Do You Fit in Time for Study?	The author will provide tips on how to find time to study.
Opening Sentence	**Prediction**
Most college students, at one point or another, have probably run into the concept of a *learning style*, but what exactly is it?	The author will define the term *learning style*.

Connect Reading to Prior Knowledge and Experience

After previewing your assignment, you should take a moment to think about what you already know about the topic—this is your **prior knowledge**. For example, a student was asked to read an article titled "Growing Urban Problems" for a government class. His first thought was that he knew very little about urban problems because he lived in a rural area, but then he remembered a recent trip to a nearby city where he saw homeless people on the streets. This led him to recall reading about drug problems, drive-by shootings, and muggings.

Activating your prior knowledge aids your reading in three ways: (1) it makes reading easier, because you have already thought about the topic; (2) the material is easier to remember, because you can connect it with what you already know: and (3) topics become more interesting if you can link them to your own experiences. Here are some techniques to help you activate your background knowledge, using "Secrets for Surviving College" as an example.

- **Ask questions and try to answer them.** What have I learned in the past about improving my grades? What do I already know about study methods?
- **Draw on your own experience.** What have I done in the past that improved my grades? What are my friends who are successful in school doing that results in their being successful in class and in taking exams?
- **Brainstorm.** Jot down or type everything that comes to mind about doing well in college and improving your grades. List facts and questions, or describe cases you have recently heard or read about.

At first, you may think you know very little—or even nothing—about a particular topic, but by using one of these techniques, you will find that you almost always know something relevant.

Form Guide Questions

Did you ever read an entire page or more and not remember anything you read? Guide questions can help you overcome this problem. You develop **guide questions** to answer while or after you read. Most students form them mentally, but you can jot them in the margin if you prefer.

The following tips can help you form questions to guide your reading. It is best to develop guide questions *after* you preview but *before* you read.

Tips for Developing Guide Questions

- **Turn each major heading into a series of questions.** The questions should ask something that you feel it is important to know.
- **As you read a section, look for and highlight the answers to your questions.**
- **When you finish reading a section, stop and check to see whether you can recall the answers.** Place check marks by those you cannot recall. Then reread.
- **Avoid asking questions that have one-word answers, like *yes* or *no*.** Questions that begin with *what, why*, or *how* are more useful.

Here are some headings with examples of the kinds of questions you might ask about them.

HEADING	QUESTIONS
Reducing Prejudice	How can prejudice be reduced? What type of prejudice is discussed?
The Deepening Recession	What is a recession? Why is it deepening?
Newton's First Law of Motion	Who was Newton? What is his First Law of Motion?

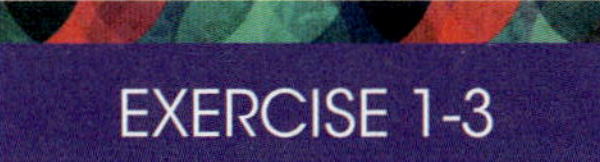

EXERCISE 1-3

Writing Guide Questions

Directions: Write two guide questions for each of the following headings that appear in "Secrets for Surviving College and Improving Your Grades."

HEADING	QUESTIONS
1. Study Methods: Different Strokes for Different Folks	1. ______________________________
2. The SQ3R Method	2. ______________________________

EXERCISE 1-4

Practicing Previewing and Predicting

Directions: Based on your previewing of "Secrets for Surviving In College and Improving Your Grades" on pages 5–9, answer the following questions to sharpen your previewing skills and strengthen your recall of what you read.

1. How difficult is the material?
2. How has the author organized the material?
3. What type of material is it (for example, practical, theoretical, historical background, or a case study)?
4. Where are the logical breaking points where I might divide the assignment into portions?
5. At what points should I stop and review?

During Reading Strategies

■ GOAL 4
Identify, organize, and understand key information

You can read textbooks and other college assignments more effectively, remember more of what you read, and review more efficiently if you interact with the text through highlighting and annotating, take notes, create graphic organizers, learn vocabulary, and use textbook aids. Writing *as you read* and writing *in response to reading* increases comprehension and recall and aids you in connecting what you are learning to what you already know.

Highlight and Annotate

Highlighting and annotating important facts and ideas as you read are effective ways to keep track of information. They are also big time-savers. If it takes you four hours to read an assigned chapter in sociology and you do not highlight or annotate it, a month later when you need to review it to prepare for an exam, you will have to spend another four hours rereading it.

Highlighting to Identify What to Learn

Here are a few basic suggestions for highlighting effectively:

1. **Read a paragraph or section first.** Then go back and highlight what is important.
2. **Highlight key portions of any topic sentence.** Also highlight any supporting details you want to remember (see Chapter 4).
3. **Be accurate.** Make sure your highlighting reflects the ideas stated in the passage.
4. **Highlight the right amount.** If you highlight too little, you may miss valuable information. On the other hand, if you highlight too much, you are not zeroing in on the most important ideas, and you will wind up rereading too much material when you study. As a general rule of thumb, highlight no more than 20 to 30 percent of the material.

Read the following paragraph (para. 4) from the textbook excerpt "Secrets for Surviving College and Improving Your Grades." Notice that you can understand its meaning from the highlighted parts alone.

> We learn many different kinds of things during our lives, and one method of learning probably isn't going to work for everyone. Some people seem to learn better if they can read about a topic or put it into their own words (verbal learners). Others may find that looking at charts, diagrams, and figures help them more (visual learners). There are those who learn better if they can hear the information (auditory learners), and there are even people who use the motion of their own bodies to help them remember key information (action learners). While instructors would have a practical nightmare if they tried to teach to every individual student's particular learning style, students who are aware of their own style can use it to change the way they study.
>
> —Ciccarelli and White, "Secrets for Surviving College and Improving Your Grades," *Psychology*, PIA-4–5

EXERCISE 1-5 Using Highlighting

Directions: Read and then highlight paragraph 6 from "Secrets for Surviving College and Improving Your Grades" on page 7. Use the questions that follow to guide your highlighting.

1. What is the topic sentence of this paragraph?
2. According to the writer, is the human mind meant to multitask?
3. In addition to car accidents and other disasters, what may result from trying to multitask?

4. What three types of tasks were involved in the study by Ophir?
5. What did the results of the study seem to indicate?

Annotating to Record Your Thinking

Annotating is a way to keep track of your impressions, ideas, reactions, and questions *as you read*. In contrast to highlighting, annotating is a way of recording *your* thinking about the key ideas you have identified. It allows you to interact with the reading as a critical reader, almost as if you are having a conversation with the writer—questioning, challenging, agreeing with, disagreeing with, or commenting on what he or she is saying. There is only one rule of annotating: **Read with a pen or pencil in your hand, and make notes in the margin as you read.**

Let's consider an example of a student writer and how she used annotations to record her ideas and impressions as she read. In her mass-media course, Lin was given an assignment:

> Write an essay on how the media, such as TV, radio, and magazines, shape people's thinking.

In a textbook, she found a section on how the media portray men and women differently. As Lin read the discussion carefully, highlighter in hand, all kinds of questions and thoughts came to mind. By annotating as she read, she was able to record her questions and reactions—all of which would help her when it came time to write her essay. Here is the excerpt Lin read, along with her marginal annotations.

Excerpt from Reading

All Media?

Media images of men and women also differ in other subtle ways. In any visual representation of a person-such as a photograph, drawing, or painting-you can measure the relative prominence of the face by calculating the percentage of the vertical dimension occupied by the model's head. When Dane Archer and his colleagues (1983) inspected 1,750 photographs from *Time, Newsweek*, and other magazines, they found what they called "face-ism," a bias toward greater facial prominence in pictures of men than of women. This phenomenon is so prevalent that it appeared in analyses of 3,500 photographs from different countries, classic portraits painted in the seventeenth century, and the amateur drawings of college students.

Who selected them? Were they selected randomly?

Aren't men's faces larger?

Stereotyping?

Why is the face more prominent in pictures of men than of women? One possible interpretation is that face-ism reflects historical conceptions of the sexes. The face and head symbolize the mind and *intellect*—which are traditionally associated with men. With respect to women, more importance is attached to the heart, emotions, or perhaps just the body. Indeed, when people evaluate models from photographs, those pictured with high facial prominence are seen as smarter and more assertive, active, and ambitious—regardless of their gender (Schwarz & Kurz, 1989). Another interpretation is that facial prominence signals power and *dominance*.

Stereotyping
Why?

-Brehm and Kassin, *Social Psychology, p. 239*

Many readers develop their own style of annotating, using underlining, asterisks, exclamation points, and other marks to express their ideas, as shown in the following box.

Ways to Annotate Text

- Underline or highlight key ideas
- Mark key terms or definitions with a star *
- Number key supporting points (1, 2, 3 . . .)
- Circle and define unfamiliar words
- Indicate useful examples with brackets [ ]
- Mark useful summary statements with an asterisk (*)
- Draw arrows ↔ connecting ideas
- Highlight statements that reveal the author's feelings, attitudes, or biases
- Indicate confusing statements with a question mark (?)
- Argue with the author by placing an exclamation point (!) next to assertions or statements with which you disagree

In recording your responses in the margin, you might include the following:

Questions	Why would . . . ?
Challenges to the author's ideas	If this is true, wouldn't . . . ?
Inconsistencies	But the author earlier said . . .
Examples	For instance . . .
Exceptions	This wouldn't be true if . . .
Disagreements	How could . . . ?
Associations with other sources	This is similar to . . .
Judgments	Good point . . .

EXERCISE 1-6

Practicing Annotating

Directions: Annotate the textbook excerpt "Secrets for Surviving College and Improving Your Grades" on pages 5–9. Did you find yourself creating your own system of symbols and marginal annotations?

Map

An **idea map** is a visual picture of the organization and content of a paragraph, essay, or textbook chapter. It is a drawing that enables you to see what is included in a brief outline form. Idea maps are used throughout this book for both reading and writing. For reading, you can use them to help you understand a selection—discover how it is organized and study how ideas relate to one another. For writing, an idea map can help you organize your own ideas and check to be sure that all the ideas you have included belong in your essay. Some students prefer mapping to outlining because they feel it is freer and less tightly structured.

Maps can take many forms. You can draw them in any way that shows the relationships between ideas either by hand or using a computer. Use the following tips and refer to the sample map.

Tips for Mapping

1. **Identify the overall topic or subject.** Write it in the center or type it at the top of the page.
2. **Identify major ideas that relate to the topic.** Write or type the major ideas, and connect each one to the central topic.
3. **As you discover supporting details that further explain an idea already mapped, connect those details to that idea.**

Once you are skilled at drawing maps or generating them using a computer, you can be more creative, developing different types of maps to fit what you are reading. For example, you can draw a *time line* to show historical events in the order in which they occurred. A time line starts with the earliest event and ends with the most recent.

Another type of map is one that shows a process—the steps involved in doing something. When you study chronological order and process in Chapter 5, you will discover more uses for these kinds of maps.

EXERCISE 1-7 Understanding Maps

Directions: Read paragraphs 2 and 3 from the textbook excerpt "Secrets for Surviving College and Improving Your Grades" on pages 5–6, and complete the map that follows, filling in the writer's main points in the spaces provided.

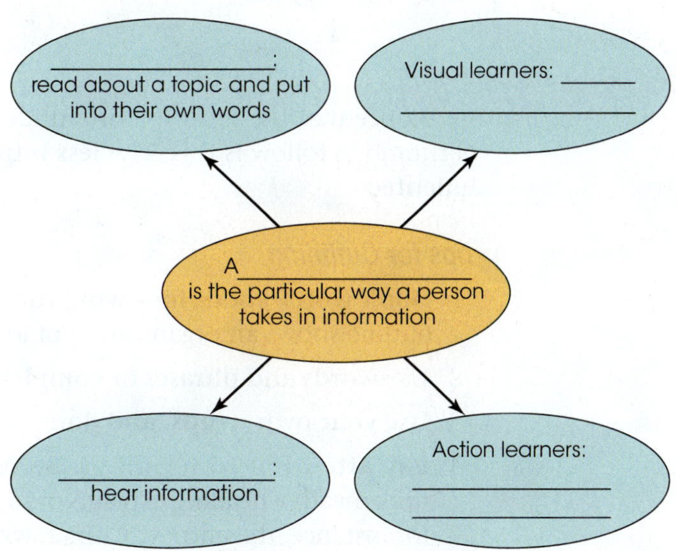

EXERCISE 1-8

Creating Maps

Directions: Read paragraph 4 from the textbook excerpt "Secrets for Surviving College and Improving Your Grades" on page 6, and create your own map of the paragraph on a separate sheet of paper. Be sure to include the writer's main points as well as some supporting details.

Outline

Making an outline is another good way to keep track of what you have read. **Outlining** involves listing major and minor ideas and showing how they are related. When you make an outline, follow the writer's organization. An outline usually follows a format like the one on the left below. An outline of an essay about a vacation in San Francisco is shown on the right. Look at both carefully to see how outlining works in practice.

I. Major topic
    A. First major idea
        1. First key supporting detail
            a. Minor detail or example
            b. Minor detail or example
        2. Second key supporting detail
            a. Minor detail or example
            b. Minor detail or example
    B. Second major idea
        1. First key supporting detail
            a. Minor detail or example
            b. Minor detail or example
        2. Second key supporting detail
II. Second major topic
    A. First major idea

I. Favorite places
    A. Chinatown
        1. Restaurants and markets
            a. Fortune cookie factory
            b. Dim sum restaurants
        2. Museums
            a. Chinese Culture Center
            b. Pacific Heritage Museum
    B. Fisherman's Wharf
        1. Pier 39
            a. Street performers
            b. Sea lions sunning themselves on the docks
        2. Ghirardelli Square

Notice that the most important ideas are closer to the left margin. The rule of thumb to follow is this: **The less important the idea, the more it should be indented.**

Tips for Outlining

1. **Don't worry about following the outline format exactly.** As long as your outline shows an organization of ideas, it will work for you.
2. **Use words and phrases or complete sentences,** whichever is easier for you.
3. **Use your own words, and don't write too much.**
4. **Pay attention to headings.** Be sure that all the information you place underneath a heading explains or supports that heading. In the outline above, for instance, the entries "Chinatown" and "Fisherman's Wharf" are correctly

placed under the major topic "Favorite Places." Likewise, "Pier 39" and "Ghirardelli Square" are under "Fisherman's Wharf," since they are located in the Wharf area.

EXERCISE 1-9 Using Outlines

Directions: After rereading the textbook excerpt "Secrets for Surviving College and Improving Your Grades" on pages 5–9, fill in the missing information in the outline that follows.

I. Different methods of studying

  A. ______________________________

  B. Study methods

II. ______________________________

  A. Strategies to defeat procrastination

  B. Multitasking is not effective

    1. Human mind is not meant to multitask

    2. Studies show that:

      a. ______________________________

      b. ______________________________

      c. Video gamers are just as unsuccessful at multitasking as nongamers

    3. ______________________________

III. Textbook reading

  A. ______________________________

    1. They don't read before the lecture

    2. ______________________________

  B. The SQ3R method

    1. Some add fourth R: Reflect

    2. ______________________________

Figure Out Unfamiliar Words

A print and/or online dictionary is a crucial tool for locating meanings, learning correct pronunciation, learning about word origins, and finding synonyms. Two popular dictionaries available in print and online are the Merriam Webster (http://www.m-w.com) and American Heritage (http://www.ahdictionary.com), both of which provide an audio component.

As you read, circle or highlight new words, and use the following tips to learn their meanings. Notice that the first step is not to look them up in a dictionary but to use other strategies that can help you determine meaning and keep reading.

How to Figure Out Unfamiliar Words

1. **Pronounce the word.** Often, by "hearing" the word, you will recall its meaning.
2. **Try to figure out the word from its context—the words and sentences around the unfamiliar word.** Often there is a clue in the context that will help you figure out a meaning.

   Example: During her lecture, the **ornithologist** described her research on western spotted owls as well as other species of birds.

   The context reveals that an ornithologist is a person who studies birds.

   Be sure to look for clues to meaning after the word, as well as before it.

   Example: The elderly man walked with the help of a **prosthesis**. He was proud that his artificial limb enabled him to walk without assistance.

   The context reveals that a prosthesis is an artificial limb. Refer to Vocabulary Workshop #2 (p. 74) for more practice using context clues.
3. **Look for parts of the word that are familiar.** You may spot a familiar root (for example, in the word *improbability* you may see a variant spelling of the word *probable*), or you may recognize a familiar beginning (for example, in the word *unconventional*, knowing that *un-* means "not" lets you figure out that the word means "not conventional"). Refer to Vocabulary Workshop #3 (p. 80) for more practice using word parts.
4. **If you still cannot figure out the word, mark it and keep reading, unless the sentence does not make sense without knowing what the word means.** If it does not, then stop and look up the word in a print or online dictionary.
5. **When you finish reading, look up all the words you have marked.**
6. **After reading be sure to record, in a vocabulary log notebook or computer file, the words you figured out or looked up so you can review and use them frequently.**

READING AND WRITING IN PROGRESS

Analyzing Words

Directions: List any words in "Secrets for Surviving College and Improving Your Grades" on pages 5–9 for which you did not know the meaning. Write the meaning for each and indicate what method you used to figure it out (context, words parts, or dictionary).

Word	Meaning	Method
1. ______	______	______
2. ______	______	______
3. ______	______	______

Analyze Visuals

Writers include visuals in many forms of writing, including textbooks, articles and essays, research reports, manuals, and magazines and newspapers. They help writers present complex information in a simple, readable format that readers can easily understand and to clarify or emphasize important concepts. Table 1-3 summarizes some of the different types of visual aids and how writers use them.

Because graphics clarify, summarize, or emphasize important facts, concepts, and trends, you need to study them closely. The list of tips on page 20 will help you get the most out of graphic elements that you encounter in your reading.

TABLE 1-3 TYPES OF VISUAL AIDS

TYPE OF GRAPHIC	Bar graphs	Circle graphs (Pie charts)	Line graphs
WRITERS USE THESE TO ...	Compare quantities or amounts using bars of different lengths.	Show whole/part relationships or how parts of a unit have been divided or classified.	Plot information along a horizontal axis (line) and a vertical axis, with one or more variables plotted between the two axes. The line graph connects all these points, thus showing a progression.
EXAMPLE			
TYPE OF GRAPHIC	**Maps**	**Diagrams**	**Infographics**
WRITERS USE THESE TO ...	Show the exact positions of physical objects such as cities, states, or countries; provide statistical or factual information about a particular area or region.	Explain an object, idea, or process by outlining parts or steps or by showing the object's organization.	Combine several types of visual aids into one, often merging photos with text, diagrams, or tables.
EXAMPLE			

TYPE OF GRAPHIC	Tables	Charts	Cartoons
WRITERS USE THESE TO . . .	Display facts, figures, statistics and other data in a condensed orderly sequence for clarity and convenient reference.	Display quantitative (numbers-based) or cause and effect relationships.	Make a point quickly or simply; lighten the text by adding a touch of humor; often help to make abstract concepts more concrete or real.
EXAMPLE	**TABLE 1-2 SAMPLE** **Heading** Where and When Do You Fit in Time for Study? **Opening Sentence** Most college students, at one point or another, have probably run into the concept of a *learning style*, but what exactly is it?	ORGANIZATIONAL CHART A D B C E F I G H	"I'm sending you to a job hunting seminar. Trust me when I say you're going to need it."

Tips for Reading Visuals

1. **Read the title or caption and legend.** The title tells you what situation or relationship is being described. The legend is the explanatory caption that may accompany the visual, and it may also function as a key, indicating what particular colors, lines, or pictures mean.
2. **Determine how the visual is organized.** If you are working with a table, note the column headings. For a graph, notice the labels on the vertical axis (the top-to-bottom line on the left side of the graph) and the horizontal axis (the left-to-right line at the bottom of the graph).
3. **Determine what variables (quantities or categories) the visual is illustrating.** Identify the pieces of information that are being compared or the relationship that is being shown. Note any symbols and abbreviations used.
4. **Determine the scale or unit of measurement.** Note how the variables are measured. For example, does a graph show expenditures in dollars, thousands of dollars, or millions of dollars?
5. **Identify any trends, patterns, or relationships the visual is intended to show.**
6. **Read any footnotes and identify the source.** Footnotes are printed at the bottom of a graph or a chart. They indicate how the data were collected, explain what certain numbers or headings mean, and describe the statistical procedures used. Identifying the source is helpful in assessing the reliability of the data.
7. **Make a brief summary note.** In the margin, jot down a brief note about the key trend or pattern emphasized by the visual. Writing will crystallize the idea in your mind, and your note will be useful when you review it.

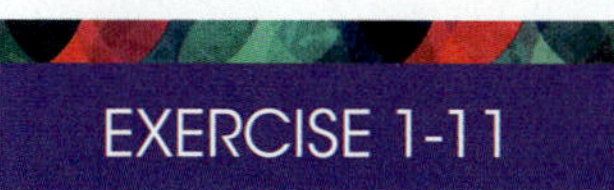

EXERCISE 1-11 Interpreting Visuals

Directions: Using the visuals in "Secrets for Surviving College and Improving Your Grades" on page 7, answer each of the following questions:

1. Describe the visuals.
2. What are you supposed to learn from these visuals and the caption?
3. Why did the author include the visuals with the reading?
4. On what topic do the visuals provide more detail or further explanation?

Use Textbook Learning Aids

Because textbooks are written by teachers, they contain numerous features to help you learn. Table 1-4 below summarizes these features and explains how to use each.

TABLE 1-4 TEXTBOOK AIDS TO LEARNING

Feature	How to Use It
Preface or "To the Student"	■ Read it to find out how the book is organized, what topics it covers, and what learning features it contains.
Chapter Opener (may include chapter objectives, photographs, and chapter outlines)	■ Read it to find out what the chapter is about. ■ Use it to test yourself later to see whether you can recall the main points.
Marginal Vocabulary Definitions	■ Learn the definition of each term. ■ Create a vocabulary log (in a notebook or computer file) and enter words you need to learn.
Photographs and Graphics	■ Determine their purpose: what important information do they illustrate? ■ For diagrams, charts, and tables, note the process or trend they illustrate. Make marginal notes. ■ Practice redrawing diagrams without referring to the originals.
Test Yourself Questions (after sections within the chapter)	■ Always check to see whether you can answer them before going on to the next section. ■ Use them to check your recall of chapter content when studying for an exam.
Special Interest Inserts (can include profiles of people, coverage of related issues, critical thinking topics, etc.)	■ Discover how the inserts are related to the chapter content: what key concepts do they illustrate?
Review Questions/Problems/Discussion Questions	■ Read them once *before* you read the chapter to discover what you are expected to learn. ■ Use them after you have read the chapter to test your recall.
Chapter Summary	■ Test yourself by converting summary statements into questions using the words *Who? Why? When? How?* and *So What?*
Chapter Review Quiz	■ Use this to prepare for an exam. Pay extra attention to items you get wrong.

EXERCISE 1-12 Evaluating Textbook Learning Aids

Directions: Using this textbook or a textbook from one of your other courses, use Table 1-4 to analyze the features the author includes to guide your learning. Identify particularly useful features, and decide how you will use each when you study.

Use the SQ3R System for Learning from Textbooks

Instead of reading now and studying later when an exam is scheduled, the **SQ3R method** enables you to integrate reading and learning by using the five steps listed below. By using SQ3R, you will strengthen your comprehension, remember more of what you read, and need less time to prepare for an exam. Don't get discouraged if you don't see dramatic results the first time you use it. It may take a few practice sessions to get used to the system.

Feel free to adapt the SQ3R method to suit how you learn and the type of material you are studying. For example, if writing helps you recall information, you might add an *Outline* step and make the *Review* step a *Review of Outline* step. Or if you are studying a course in which terminology is especially important, such as biology, then add a *Vocabulary Check* step.

Steps in the SQ3R System

Survey Become familiar with the overall content and organization of the material using the steps for previewing on page 4.

Question Ask questions about the material that you expect to be able to answer as you read. As you read each successive heading, turn it into a question.

Read As you read each section, actively search for the answers to your guide questions. When you find the answers, underline or mark the portions of the text that concisely state the information.

Recite Probably the most important part of the system, "recite" means that after each section or after each major heading you should stop, look away from the page, and try to remember the answer to your question. If you are unable to remember, look back at the page and reread the material. Then test yourself again by looking away from the page and "reciting" the answer to your question.

Review Immediately after you have finished reading, go back through the material again, reading headings and summaries. As you read each heading, recall your question and test yourself to see whether you can still remember the answer. If you cannot, reread that section. Once you are satisfied that you have understood and recalled key information, move toward the higher-level thinking skills. Ask application, analysis, evaluation, and creation questions. Some students like to add a fourth "R" step—for "Reflect."

EXERCISE 1-13

Examining a Textbook Excerpt Using SQ3R

Directions: Apply the SQ3R system to an article or a section in a textbook chapter you are currently reading. List your questions in the margin or on a separate sheet of paper, and highlight the answers in the article or textbook. After you have finished, write a paragraph evaluating how well SQ3R worked for you, and note how you might adapt it.

The professional readings in this text are intended to be challenging, and even using all the strategies described above, you may still encounter difficulties reading them. Use the following suggestions to help you approach these types of assignments:

Tips for Understanding Difficult Assignments

1. **Analyze the time and place in which you are reading.** If you've been working for several hours, mental fatigue may be the source of the problem. If you are reading in a place with distractions or interruptions, you might not be able to understand what you are reading.
2. **Rephrase each paragraph in your own words.** You might need to approach complicated material sentence by sentence, expressing each in your own words.
3. **Read aloud sentences or sections that are particularly difficult.** Reading out loud sometimes makes complicated material easier to understand.
4. **Reread difficult or complicated sections.** In fact, sometimes several readings are appropriate and necessary.
5. **Slow down your reading rate.** On occasion, simply reading more slowly and carefully will provide you with the needed boost in comprehension.
6. **Write a brief outline of major points.** This will help you see the overall organization and progression of ideas.
7. **Highlight key ideas.** After you have read a section, go back and think about and highlight what is important. Highlighting forces you to sort out what is important, and this sorting process builds comprehension and recall.

Post-Reading Strategies

■ GOAL 5
Paraphrase, summarize, and recall information

As a college student, you are expected to learn large amounts of textbook material. Rereading to learn is *not* an effective strategy. Writing *is* an effective strategy. In fact, writing is an excellent means of improving both your comprehension and your retention.

Writing during and after reading has numerous advantages:

1. **Writing focuses your attention.** If you are writing as well as reading, you are forced to keep your mind on the topic.
2. **Writing forces you to think.** Highlighting or writing forces you to decide what is important and understand relationships and connections.

3. **Writing tests your understanding.** One of the truest measures of understanding is your ability to explain an idea in your own words. When an idea is unclear or confusing, you will be at a loss for words.
4. **Writing facilitates recall.** Research studies indicate that information is recalled more easily if it is elaborated on. Elaboration involves expanding and thinking about the material by drawing connections and associations, seeing relationships, and applying what you have learned. Writing is a form of elaboration.

Paraphrase

A **paraphrase** is a restatement, in your own words, of a paragraph, passage, or reading selection. It is a condensed (shortened) rewording of each sentence or key idea in the order in which it appears in a reading. Why is paraphrasing such a useful skill for so many college courses?

- **It is a way to record an author's ideas for later use.** Sometimes your paraphrase can be incorporated directly into a paragraph or essay. Remember, however, that although you have changed the wording, you are still working with someone else's ideas. It is, therefore, necessary to document the source at the end of your essay. (For further information about documentation, see Chapter 11.)
- **Paraphrasing helps you clarify an author's ideas.** When you paraphrase, you are forced to work with each idea individually and see how the ideas relate to one another.
- **Paraphrasing is a useful study and learning strategy.** When you paraphrase a reading, you think through and learn the information it contains.
- **Because a paraphrase requires you to use different words from those in the reading, writing paraphrases helps you develop your vocabulary.**
- **By paraphrasing, you are practicing your own writing skills.**

Writing a paraphrase involves two skills: (1) substituting synonyms and (2) rewording and rearranging sentence parts, as detailed in the following box.

Writing a Paraphrase

1. **Substitute synonyms.** A **synonym** is a word that has the same general meaning as another word. For example, *thin* and *lanky* are synonyms. When selecting synonyms, use the following guidelines:
   - **Make sure the synonym you choose fits the context (overall meaning) of the sentence.** Suppose the sentence you are paraphrasing is "The physician attempted to *neutralize* the effects of the drug overdose." All of the following words are synonyms for neutralize: *negate, nullify, counteract.* However, *counteract* fits the context, but *negate* and *nullify* do not. *Negate* and *nullify* suggest the ability to cancel, and a drug overdose, once taken, cannot be canceled. It can, however, be counteracted.
   - **Refer to a dictionary.** Use a print or online dictionary to check the exact meanings of words; refer to a thesaurus (a dictionary of synonyms) to get ideas for alternative or equivalent words.

- **Do not try to replace every word in a sentence with a synonym.** Sometimes a substitute does not exist. In the sentence "Archaeologists study fossils of extinct species," the term *fossils* clearly and accurately describes what archaeologists study. Therefore, it does not need to be replaced.
- **Consider connotation.** A word's *connotation* is the feelings it invokes. Some words have positive connotations, while others have negative connotations. When writing a paraphrase, select words with connotations that mirror the original. For instance, if the original reading uses the word *adorable*, which has a positive connotation, do not paraphrase with the word *sticky-sweet*, which has a negative connotation.
- **Be sure to paraphrase—that is, do not change only a few words.**

2. **Reword and rearrange sentence parts.** When rearranging sentence parts, use the following guidelines:
   - Split lengthy, complicated sentences into two or more shorter sentences.
   - Be sure you understand the author's key ideas as well as related ideas, and include both in your paraphrase.

A Sample Paraphrase

Marcie was writing an essay on animal communication for her biology class. In a reading, she found one passage that contained exactly the information she needed. To help herself remember both the author's main point and the details, she decided to paraphrase. Here is an excerpt from the reading, followed by Marcie's paraphrase:

Communication in the Animal Kingdom

Animal species have complex forms of. Ants send chemical signals secreted from glands to share communication information about food and enemies with other members of the colony. When honeybees discover a source of nectar, they return to the hive and communicate its location to the other worker bees through an intricate dance that signals both direction and distance. Male songbirds of various species sing in the spring to attract a female mate and also to warn other males to stay away from their territory to avoid a fight. Dolphins talk to each other at great depths of the ocean by making a combination of clicking, whistling, and barking sounds.

—Kassin, *Psychology*, p. 252

Marcie's Paraphrase of "Communication in the Animal Kingdom"

According to Kassin (252), animals have complicated ways of communicating. Ants can tell one another about food and enemies by secreting chemicals from their glands. Honeybees tell others in their hive that they have found a source of nectar by a detailed dance that indicates both where the nectar is located and how far away it is. In the spring, male songbirds sing to draw females and to warn other males to stay away so as to avoid a dispute. Using clicks, whistles, and barking sounds, dolphins communicate with one another.

Look closely at Marcie's paraphrase and the original reading, noticing how she substituted synonyms. For example, in the first sentence, she substituted *complicated* for *complex*, *ways* for *forms*, and so forth. She also included all of the author's important main ideas and supporting details.

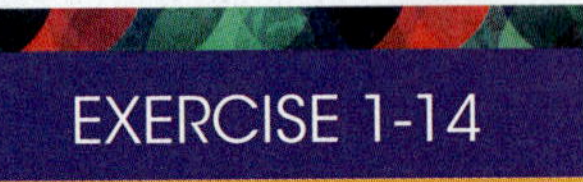

EXERCISE 1-14

Writing a Paraphrase

Directions: Working with a classmate, reread paragraphs 8–10 from the textbook excerpt "Secrets for Surviving College and Improving Your Grades" on page 8. Working sentence by sentence, write a paraphrase. Then compare your work and combine both of your paraphrases to produce a revised paraphrase.

Summarize

A **summary** is a brief statement of the major points of a reading, and it is always shorter than the original. Unlike a paraphrase, a summary does not attempt to cover all of the reading's key points and details. Usually a summary is about one-fifth the length of the original or less.

Writing summaries has four main benefits:

1. **Writing a summary improves your grasp of a writer's ideas** because you must identify key ideas and explain how they relate to one another.
2. **Writing a summary saves you time when you are reviewing or studying for an exam.**
3. **College instructors across the disciplines—not just writing instructors—assign summaries.** For example, you may be asked to write a plot summary of a short story or a summary of your findings for a science laboratory experiment.
4. **Summarizing is an important workplace skill.** You might be asked to summarize a meeting, condense a lengthy report, or briefly describe the outcomes of a sales conference you attended.

To write an effective summary, follow these guidelines:

Writing a Summary

1. **Complete the reading before writing your summary.** Feel free to highlight and/or annotate as you read.
2. **Review the reading.** Review your highlighting and/or annotations, or use your review to highlight and annotate for the first time.
3. **Write an opening sentence that states the author's thesis or main point.** For a review of thesis statements, see Chapter 8, page 246.
4. **Explain the author's most important supporting ideas.** Be sure to express the author's main ideas in your own words; don't copy phrases or sentences. If you can't express an idea in your own words, you

probably don't fully understand it, so reread, talk to someone about the passage, or seek other information about the passage to clarify its meaning.

5. **Include restated definitions of key terms, important concepts, procedures, or principles.** Do not include examples, descriptive details, quotations, or anything not essential to the main point. Do not include your opinion.
6. **Present the ideas in the order in which they appear in the original source.**
7. **Reread your summary to determine whether it contains sufficient information.**
8. **Ask yourself this question:** If someone had not read the article, would your summary be a good substitute that covers all the author's main points? If not, revise your summary to include additional information.
9. **Indicate the source of the material you summarized.** See Chapter 11, page 334 for more information on how to cite sources.

Evaluating Summaries

Directions: Reread the textbook excerpt "Secrets for Surviving College and Improving Your Grades" on pages 5–9. Working with a classmate, compare the two sample summaries below and decide which is better. Explain your choice.

Sample Summary 1

Students commonly make two errors when reading textbooks. First, many students do not read the textbook before going to a lecture about the material. Most instructors assume students have read the assignment and then use the lecture to provide details; students won't understand the lecture if they haven't read the assignment. Second, students try to read textbook material like a novel, starting at the first page and reading continuously. Textbook material should be read slowly with attention paid to meaning.

Sample Summary 2

Students have to read textbooks to succeed in a course; taking notes on lectures or slide presentations is not enough. Students make two common mistakes regarding textbooks. Their first mistake is not bothering to read the textbook before going to class. This is like trying to find a new place without any directions. It's especially important because most instructors assume students have read the assignment. Their lectures are used to go into detail about the textbook information, so if you haven't read the material, you won't understand the lecture.

The second mistake students make is trying to read textbook material as if it were a novel with an interesting plot and lots of "filler." Textbook material may be interesting but it has no "filler." Textbook material must be read slowly and with attention given to every morsel of meaning.

Writing a Summary

Directions: Using the steps listed in the "Writing a Summary" box on page 26, write a summary of paragraphs 11–13 of the textbook excerpt "Secrets for Surviving College and Improving Your Grades" on page 8. Swap your summary with that of a classmate and together compare and discuss your summaries.

Use Learning and Recall Strategies

In order to get good grades, you have to plan when to study and use the right techniques to get the most out of the time you spend. Use the following strategies.

1. **Immediate Review** Review new information as soon as possible after you hear or read it to fix it in your mind by doing the following:
   - Review your lecture notes as soon as possible after taking them.
   - Review a textbook chapter as soon as you finish reading it by rereading each chapter heading and the summary.
   - Review all new course materials at the end of each day of classes to make the information stick in your mind.
2. **Periodic Review** Briefly review previously learned material on a regular basis (every three weeks or so), so you will not forget it. For example, you will not remember material from the first two weeks of a course if you do not review it regularly, which means you will have to relearn it for the final exam.
3. **Final Review** Briefly review material as close in time as possible before a test or exam to fix it in your mind.
4. **Building an Intent to Remember** Very few people remember things that they do not intend to remember. Before you begin to read an assignment, define as clearly as possible what you need to remember, depending on the type of material, why you are reading it, and how familiar you are with the topic. For instance, if you are reading an essay for a class discussion, plan to remember not only key ideas but also points of controversy, applications, and opinions with which you disagree. However, if you are reviewing a chapter for an essay exam, look for important ideas, trends, and significance of events.

   As you read a text assignment, sort important information from that which is less important by asking and answering questions such as
   - How important is this information?
   - Will I need to know this for the exam?
   - Is this a key idea or is it an explanation of a key idea?
   - Why did the writer include this?
5. **Organizing and Categorizing** Information that is organized is easier to remember than material that is randomly arranged. One effective way to organize information is to *categorize* it, to arrange it in groups according to similar characteristics. Suppose, for example, that you had to remember the following list of items to buy for a picnic: *cooler, candy, 7-Up, Pepsi, napkins, potato chips, lemonade, peanuts, paper plates*. The easiest way to remember this list would be to divide it into groups.

DRINKS	SNACKS	PICNIC SUPPLIES
7-Up	peanuts	cooler
Pepsi	candy	paper plates
lemonade	potato chips	napkins

By putting similar items together, you are learning three shorter, organized lists rather than one long, unorganized one.

If you were reading an essay on discipline in public high schools, instead of learning one long list of reasons for disruptive student behavior, you might divide the reasons into groups such as peer conflicts, teacher–student conflicts, and so forth, which are easier to remember.

6. **Associating Ideas** Association involves connecting new information with previously acquired knowledge. For instance, if you are reading about divorce in a sociology class and trying to remember a list of common causes, you might try to associate each cause with a person you know who exhibits that problem. If one cause of divorce is lack of communication, for instance, you might remember this by thinking of a couple you know whose lack of communication has caused relationship difficulties.
7. **Using a Variety of Sensory Modes** Your senses of sight, hearing, and touch can all help you remember what you read, as the more senses you use the easier it is to recall information. Activities such as highlighting, note taking, and outlining involve your sense of touch and reinforce your learning, while repeating the information out loud or listening to someone else repeat it is also effective.
8. **Visualizing** Visualizing, or creating a mental picture of what you have read, often aids recall when you are reading about events, people, processes, or procedures. Visualization of abstract ideas, theories, philosophies, and concepts can be more difficult, although you may be able to create a visual picture of the relationship of ideas in your mind or on paper.
9. **Using *Mnemonic* Devices** Memory tricks and devices, often called **mnemonics**, are useful in helping you recall lists of factual information. You might use a rhyme such as "Thirty days hath September, April, June, and November . . ." to memorize months or make up a word or phrase in which each letter represents an item you are trying to remember: ***Roy G. Biv,*** for example, helps you remember the colors in the light spectrum—**r**ed, **o**range, **y**ellow, **g**reen, **b**lue, **i**ndigo, **v**iolet.

EXERCISE 1-17 Using Recall Strategies

Directions: Four study-learning situations follow, based on the textbook excerpt "Secrets for Surviving College and Improving Your Grades." Indicate which of the strategies described in this section—organization/categorization, association, sensory modes, visualization, and mnemonic devices—might be most useful in each situation.

1. For an essay test, you will be expected to give examples of each of the different study methods listed in Table A. How might you remember each study method and corresponding examples for the test?

____

2. For a class discussion, you are expected to be familiar with the strategies to defeat procrastination discussed in paragraph 5. What retention aid(s) could help you remember them?

____

3. You are expected to explain and discuss the information about multitasking in paragraphs 6 and 7, including the three studies cited in these paragraphs. How could you learn this information easily?

____

____

4. You know that you will be tested on different aspects of the SQ3R method (paragraphs 11–13) on the next exam. What could you do as you review to help yourself remember details about the SQ3R method?

____

____

Think Critically

■ GOAL 6
Think critically about what you read

The biggest difference between high school and college is the difference in your instructors' expectations of how you should *think*. High school classes focus on developing a basic foundation of knowledge, often built through memorization. In college, however, you are expected not only to learn and memorize new information, but also to *analyze* what you are learning—to be a **critical thinker**.

Critical does not mean "negative." Critical thinking means evaluating and reacting to what you read, rather than accepting everything as "the truth." Thinking critically sometimes requires you to consult multiple sources of information to develop perspective on a topic. For example, when writing an essay on how post-traumatic stress disorder affects returning veterans, you might read several accounts written by vets and consult several research studies, gleaning ideas from each.

The Benefits of Critical Thinking

The ability to think critically offers many benefits. In your college courses, critical thinking allows you to

- Do well on essay exams, particularly those that ask for analysis.
- Write effective essays and term papers.
- Distinguish good information from incomplete, inaccurate, or misleading information.

In everyday life and in the workplace, a good set of critical-thinking skills will help you

- Make informed, reasonable decisions.
- Spend money wisely and make good financial choices.
- Understand issues in the news, including business and political issues.
- Expand your interests beyond "passive entertainment" (such as watching TV or movies) to active entertainment that engages your mind and creativity.

Critical Thinking Is Active Thinking

Critical thinking is essential to effective reading. For example,

- When reading a college textbook, you might ask yourself if the author is trying to influence your opinions.
- When reading a newspaper, you might ask yourself if the article is telling the full story or if the journalist is leaving something out.
- When reading an advertisement, you might ask yourself what message the ad is sending to get you to buy the product.

To help you strengthen your critical reading skills, Chapters 12–14 are devoted entirely to critical thinking.

EXERCISE 1-18

Understanding Critical Thinking

Directions: Indicate whether each of the following statements is true (T) or false (F) based on your understanding of critical thinking.

_____ **1.** Thinking critically about a reading selection means finding ways to criticize it and show all the ways it is wrong.

_____ **2.** Critical reading is not necessary unless the instructor specifically assigns some sort of "critical-thinking" exercise to go along with the reading.

_____ **3.** While textbooks offer good opportunities for critical reading, so do other reading materials, such as magazines and Web sites.

_____ **4.** Critical-thinking skills are important in college but do not have much relevance in the "real world."

_____ **5.** Engaging in critical thinking sometimes requires you to consult additional sources of information beyond what you are currently reading.

EXERCISE 1-19

Thinking Critically

Directions: The passage below is a brief excerpt from a sociology textbook chapter. Read the paragraph and answer the questions that follow.

> Modern medical technology is marvelous. People walk around with the hearts, kidneys, livers, lungs, and faces of deceased people. Eventually, perhaps, surgeons will be able to transplant brains. The costs are similarly astounding . . . our national medical bill is approaching $3 trillion a year. This is even more than the total amount that the country raises in income taxes (Statistical Abstract 2013: Table 468).
>
> —Henslin, *Sociology: A Down-to-Earth Approach*, p. 174

(Hint: Think analytically and critically to answer the following questions.)

1. The author states that "modern medical technology is marvelous." What indication is there that he might not totally believe this?

____

____

2. Why does the author suggest that surgeons might be able to transplant brains in the future?

____

3. The author writes, "People walk around with the hearts, kidneys, livers, lungs, and faces of deceased people." What might the wording of this sentence indicate about the author's attitude toward transplanted organs?

____

____

____

____

Think Critically About Information in Textbooks

We live in a society bombarded with information. Everywhere you look, you will see written materials, from newspapers and magazines to billboards and Web sites. Numerous experts estimate that the amount of information available to society is increasing by over 50 percent every year.

That's a lot of information for a person to take in. So how do you cut through the clutter to find and learn the information you need? Here are some suggestions.

Tips for Finding Relevant Information

- **Practice selective reading.** You do not have to read everything you see. (College assignments are the exception, of course.) Learn to quickly skim material to see if it interests you, and then read the material that does.
- **Understand the goal of what you are reading.** Is it to educate you or to convince you of something? In advertising, lovely words and images are used to make products seem desirable. In the news, politicians rant and rave about the issues. Evaluate the purpose of what you are reading by asking yourself what the writer's goal is.
- **Adjust your reading speed to match the task.** If you are reading an article in *People* magazine, you probably can skim through it quickly. However, if you are filling out paperwork for financial aid or medical claims, you will want to read the forms slowly and carefully to make sure you are doing everything right.
- **Read the "fine print."** When dealing with important paperwork, look to see if important information is buried in large amounts of text or in small print so that you'll be less likely to read it. Never sign anything without reading it completely first.

EXERCISE 1-20

Thinking Critically About Information

Directions: Read the passage and then answer the question that follows.

Hidden Information

Banks and credit card companies make a huge amount of money each year by charging interest to their customers. When you use a credit card, you are actually borrowing money from the credit card company. Unless you pay the borrowed amount back within one month, you start paying interest charges. By law, credit card companies are required to tell you on your credit card statement how much interest they are charging you.

Have you ever looked at your credit card statement? It is filled with information and can have pages of "fine print" (that is, very small print) with the information required by law. How many people take the time to read this information? Not many. The credit card companies have effectively buried important information that they don't want you to know.

The back side of your credit card statement is filled with tiny print. Somewhere in the middle it says, "You are not responsible for paying for any purchases made if your credit card is stolen." You receive a phone call from the credit card company offering you "protection against unauthorized use of your card." If you pay them $99 a year, they will cover any purchases that are made if your card is stolen. Should you pay the $99 for the protection plan? Why or why not?

____

____

____

READ AND RESPOND: A TEXTBOOK EXCERPT

Secrets for Surviving College and Improving Your Grades

Saundra K. Ciccarelli and J. Nolan White

The questions and activities below refer to the textbook excerpt "Secrets for Surviving College and Improving Your Grades" on pages 5–9. You have been working with this excerpt throughout the chapter and have mastered much of its content. Now you are ready to examine it, integrate and apply ideas, and write in response to reading it.

As you read the professional readings throughout the remainder of this book, be sure to use the skills you have learned in this chapter: previewing, highlighting, annotating, mapping, outlining, paraphrasing, and summarizing. You now have a valuable repository of skills that you can use to help you understand, analyze, and respond to the reading. Be sure to use them!

Writing in Response to Reading

Strengthening Your Vocabulary MySkillsLab®

Identify at least five words used in the reading that are unfamiliar to you. Using context, word parts, or a dictionary, write a brief definition of each word.

Reading and Writing: An Integrated Perspective

1. How would you describe your learning style? What type of instruction works best for you in the classroom?
2. In your daily life, are you a multitasker? Write a journal entry describing the types of tasks you attempt to do at the same time. Do you think you are effective when you multitask? Why or why not?
3. How do the authors capture the reader's attention? Evaluate the title and the introduction of the selection.
4. What techniques do the authors use to introduce ideas and let the reader know what is important?

THINKING VISUALLY

5. Evaluate Table A (p. 7). How effectively does the table present the information about study methods?
6. What do the photos accompanying this selection add to the material? What other photos or illustrations would be effective for this subject?

Thinking and Writing Critically

1. How would you describe the authors' attitude toward this subject? Evaluate how well their tone matches the material.
2. Write a sentence describing the authors' purpose and their intended audience.
3. Which one of the time management strategies seems most useful? Which seems least useful? Explain your reasons.
4. What piece of information or advice in this selection was most helpful to you? What other information do you wish the authors had addressed about studying or learning?
5. The authors report that the three Rs in the SQ3R method (Read, Recite, and Review) may be the most important steps. Apply this to your own experience; do you agree? Do you use the fourth R—Reflect—when you are reading?

Writing Paragraphs MySkillsLab®

1. Write a paragraph explaining how you would answer the question, "Is there some trick to getting good grades?" Include your own strategies as well as any from the selection that sound especially effective to you.

2. Write a paragraph addressing the idea of multitasking. Why do the authors call it an "enduring myth"? Were you surprised to read about the study results showing the ineffectiveness of multitasking? Why or why not?

3. The authors advise you to use play time as a reward for getting tasks done. What other rewards do you use when you complete a task? Write a paragraph exploring how play time and other rewards can improve your performance or effectiveness.

Writing Essays MySkillsLab®

4. Identify at least four study methods in Table A that work for you and four new ones that you are willing to try. Write an essay describing how you will apply these methods as you study specific subjects.

5. One of the time management strategies described in this selection involves making a map of your long-term goals. Create such a map for yourself, and then write an essay answering the author's question: "What are the paths you need to take to get to your ultimate goal?"

SELF-TEST SUMMARY

To test yourself, cover the Answer column with a sheet of paper and answer each question in the left column. Evaluate each of your answers as you work by sliding the paper down and comparing your answer with what is printed in the Answer column.

QUESTION	ANSWER
■ GOAL 1 Read actively What is active reading?	*Active reading* is a way to get involved and interact with ideas presented in a reading.
■ GOAL 2 Use the reading process What is involved in the reading process?	The *reading process* involves using strategies before, during, and after you reading that will help you understand, organize, and remember what you read and prepare you to write about it.
■ GOAL 3 Preview, question, and connect the reading to prior knowledge (pre-reading) Why are previewing, questioning, and connecting to prior knowledge helpful?	*Previewing* allows you to becoming familiar with a reading's content and structure before reading. *Questioning* involves creating questions that will guide your reading. *Connecting to prior knowledge* enables you to discover what you already know about the topic and helps you remember the new material.

(continued)

(*continued*)

QUESTION	ANSWER
■ GOAL 4 Identify, organize, and understand key information (during reading) What techniques help you identify, organize, and understand key information?	1. Highlight important parts of topic sentences as well as key supporting details, be accurate, and highlight the right amount. 2. Use mapping to show how ideas in a paragraph or chapter are related. 3. Use outlining to list major and minor ideas and to show how they related. 4. Read and interpret visuals. 5. Use textbook learning aids to discover what is important and help you learn. 6. Apply the SQ3R method to learn from textbooks as you read. 7. Follow the tips on page 23 for reading difficult assignments.
■ GOAL 5 Paraphrase, summarize, and recall information (during and post-reading) Why are paraphrasing and summarizing useful; what does recalling information involve?	*Paraphrasing*—a restatement in your own words of a paragraph, passage, or reading selection—is a good way to ensure you have understood an author's ideas. *Summarizing*, writing a brief statement of the major points of a reading, is an effective way to condense ideas. *Learning and recall strategies* include immediate review, periodic review, final review, building an intent to remember, organizing and categorizing, association, using a variety of sensory modes, visualization, and mnemonic devices.
■ GOAL 6 Think critically about what you read What is critical thinking, and how do you think critically about information?	*Critical thinking* means evaluating and reacting to what you read, rather than accepting everything as "the truth." To find and learn the information you need in textbooks, practice selective reading, understand the goal of what you are reading, adjust your reading speed to match the task, and read the "fine print."

MySkillsLab®

Visit **Chapter 1, "An Overview of the Reading Process with Writing,"** in MySkillsLab to test your understanding of chapter goals.

2

An Overview of the Writing Process (with Reading)

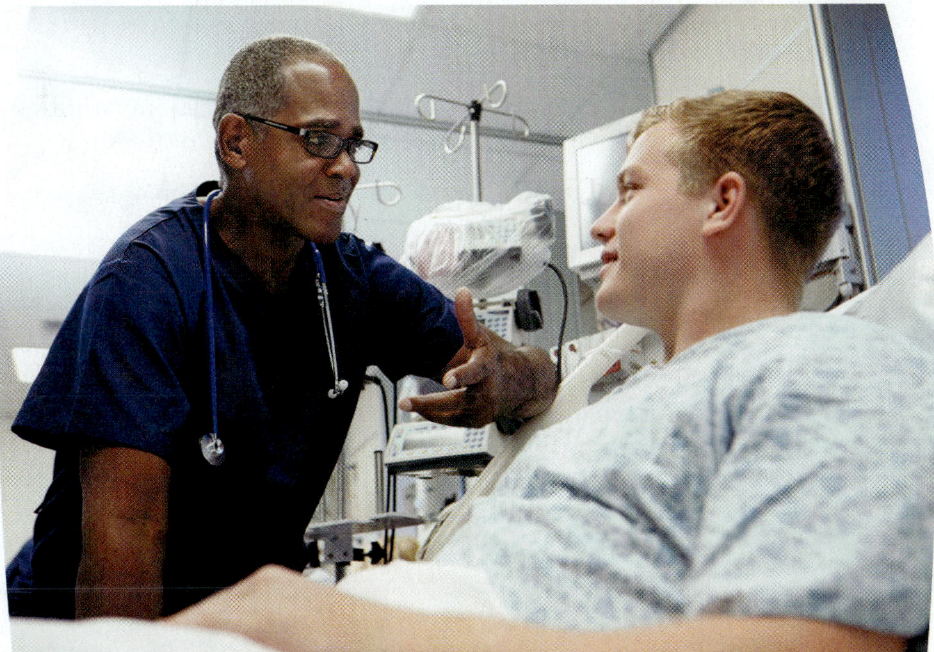

THINK About It!

Study the photograph above showing a triage nurse working with a patient being admitted to a hospital emergency room for treatment. In admitting the patient, the nurse follows a process—a series of steps taken in a particular order. First, he asks the patient to describe symptoms. Then he takes a brief medical history, including recent surgeries and medications taken. Next, he assesses the patient's physical condition by measuring vital signs. Using all of the information collected, the nurse determines the severity of the patient's condition. Based on this determination, he assigns the patient an order of treatment placement and communicates this to the doctor in charge. In much the same way as a nurse assesses a patient, writers must also follow a series of steps—which usually include reading—when writing a paragraph or an essay.

This chapter will explain the writing process and show you how to follow it to become a more successful writer. In Chapter 1 you saw that reading is a process—not just a matter of picking up a book and starting to read. Likewise, writing is a process—not just a matter of sitting down in front of a computer and starting to type but involving steps to follow before, during, and after you have written your first draft.

LEARNING GOALS

Learn how to . . .

- GOAL 1 Recognize good writing
- GOAL 2 Compare the reading and writing processes
- GOAL 3 Use the writing process
- GOAL 4 Generate ideas
- GOAL 5 Organize ideas
- GOAL 6 Consider your audience and purpose
- GOAL 7 Write a first draft
- GOAL 8 Think critically about incorporating visuals into your writing
- GOAL 9 Revise and rewrite
- GOAL 10 Proofread for correctness

Reading and Writing Connections

EVERYDAY CONNECTIONS

- **Reading** You read the summary on a police report describing an auto accident that you were involved in.
- **Writing** You plan, write, and revise a letter to your auto insurance company explaining how the police report supports your account of the accident.

ACADEMIC CONNECTIONS

- **Reading** You read an assigned short story in American literature.
- **Writing** You plan, write, and revise a plot summary of the short story.

WORKPLACE CONNECTIONS

- **Writing** You plan, write, and revise your yearly self-evaluation letter for your job performance review.
- **Reading** You read the performance appraisal your manager prepared about you for your review.

What Is Good Writing?

■ GOAL 1
Recognize good writing

To the question "What is good writing?" many students answer, "Correct grammar, spelling, and punctuation—no errors." Actually, good writing involves much more than not making errors. Think about pieces of writing that you have enjoyed reading or found helpful. What made them satisfying?

- **Good writing requires thinking.** Good writing is a thinking process. As you read this book, you'll see that writers do a great deal of work before they actually begin writing. They think about their audience and topic, develop ideas and supporting material, and plan how best to say what they want to say. Once they have written a draft, they reevaluate their ideas to see if there is a better way to express them.
- **Good writing involves revision.** Finding the best way to express your ideas involves experimentation and change. This process is called *revision*. When you revise, you rethink ideas and improve what you have said and how you have said it. All good writers revise, sometimes many times.
- **Good writing expresses ideas clearly.** Good writers communicate with their readers in a direct and understandable way, making their main points clearly and supporting these points with details, facts, reasons, and examples. Good writers also arrange their main points logically. This book contains a variety of techniques to help you arrange ideas logically.

- **Good writing is directed toward an audience.** Suppose you were going to an interview for a job. Would you wear the same clothes you wear to stop by a friend's apartment? Of course not; you modify your appearance in keeping with the situation and the people you will be seeing. Similarly, when you write, you must consider your audience. Ask yourself: Who will be reading what I write? How should I express myself so that my readers will understand what I write? Considering your audience is essential to good writing. You will learn more about this process in the "Consider Your Audience and Purpose" section later in the chapter.
- **Good writing achieves a purpose.** In written communication, you write for a specific reason or purpose. Sometimes, in college, you write for yourself: to record an assignment, to take notes in class, or to help yourself learn or remember information for an exam. Many other times, you write to communicate information, ideas, or feelings to a specific audience. You will learn more about writing for a purpose later in the chapter.
- **Good writing requires using three basic building blocks.** To improve your writing, you need to practice using the three basic building blocks of written language: the sentence, the paragraph, and the essay. A **sentence** expresses one or more complete thoughts. A **paragraph** expresses one main idea and is usually made up of several sentences that explain or support that idea. An **essay** consists of multiple paragraphs that explain related ideas, all of which support a larger, broader idea. This text focuses on writing paragraphs and essays. However, Part Six, "Reviewing the Basics," will help you write more effective sentences by answering your questions about grammar, mechanics, and punctuation. The chart that follows shows how the parts of paragraphs are very much like the parts of an essay.

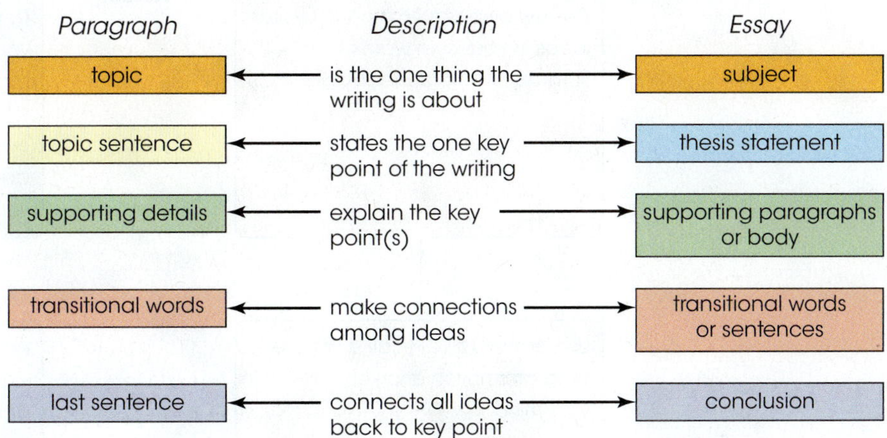

Connect the Reading and Writing Processes

■ GOAL 2
Compare the reading and writing processes

In college, much of what you write will be in response to what you read. The reading and writing processes complement each other, as shown in Figure 2-1 on the next page. Active reading, in which you interact with the text, annotate and highlight, take notes, and organize what you learn, is crucial to the writing process, and using the two together is what produces strong, clear, well-organized writing. In addition, both reading and writing involve critical thinking; readers evaluate the ideas of others, while writers evaluate their own ideas.

FIGURE 2-1 THE SIMILARITIES BETWEEN THE READING AND WRITING PROCESSES

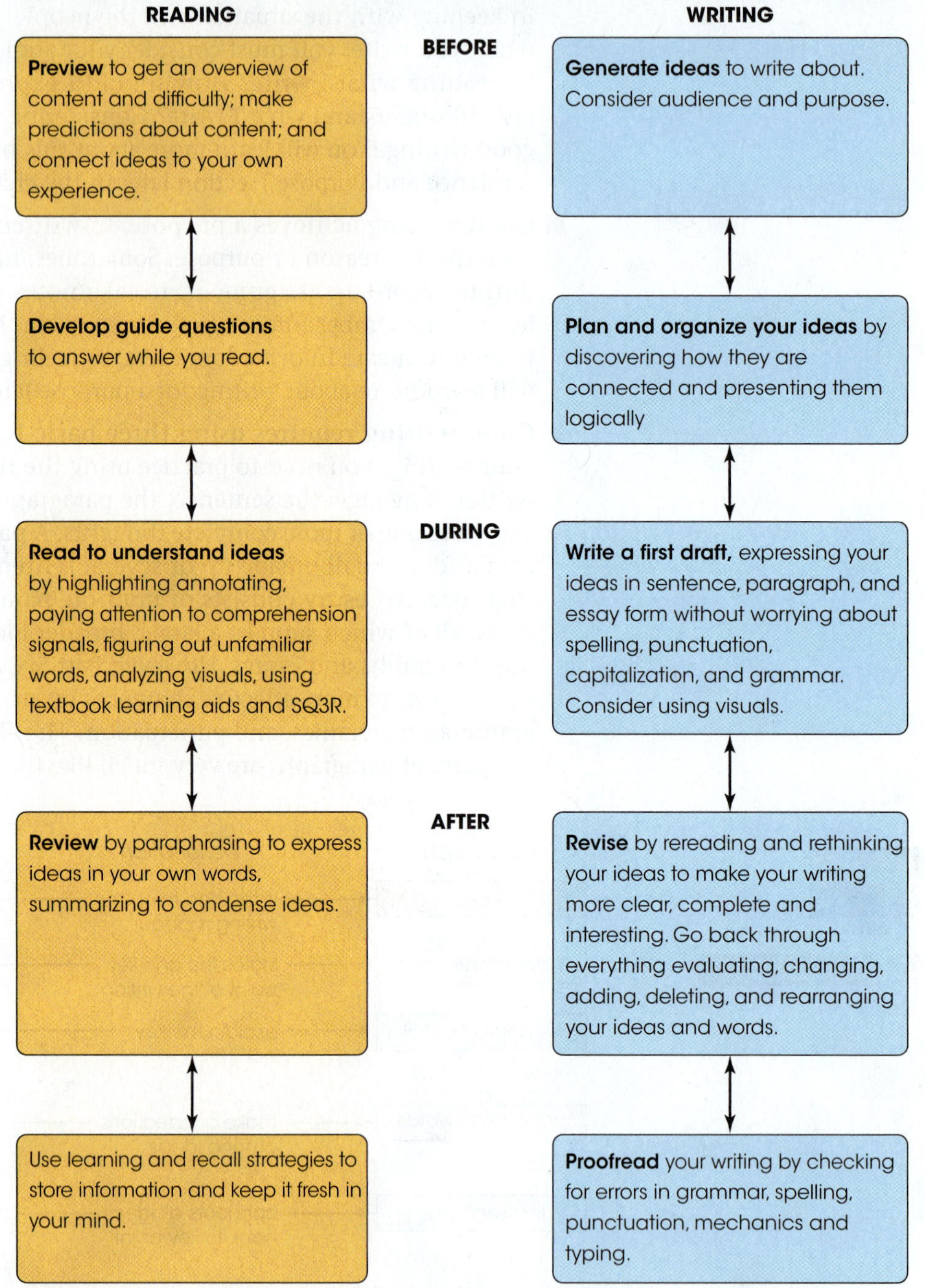

	READING	WRITING
BEFORE	**Preview** to get an overview of content and difficulty; make predictions about content; and connect ideas to your own experience.	**Generate ideas** to write about. Consider audience and purpose.
	Develop guide questions to answer while you read.	**Plan and organize your ideas** by discovering how they are connected and presenting them logically
DURING	**Read to understand ideas** by highlighting annotating, paying attention to comprehension signals, figuring out unfamiliar words, analyzing visuals, using textbook learning aids and SQ3R.	**Write a first draft,** expressing your ideas in sentence, paragraph, and essay form without worrying about spelling, punctuation, capitalization, and grammar. Consider using visuals.
AFTER	**Review** by paraphrasing to express ideas in your own words, summarizing to condense ideas.	**Revise** by rereading and rethinking your ideas to make your writing more clear, complete and interesting. Go back through everything evaluating, changing, adding, deleting, and rearranging your ideas and words.
	Use learning and recall strategies to store information and keep it fresh in your mind.	**Proofread** your writing by checking for errors in grammar, spelling, punctuation, mechanics and typing.

NOTE: Reading and writing involve critical thinking at all stages of both processes.

EXAMINING PROFESSIONAL WRITING

Good writing helps both readers and writers. By examining how ideas are expressed clearly, logically, and concisely, you will learn how to improve your own writing. The professional writing below is an example of good writing. As you read the article, look closely at the marginal annotations that highlight the basic structure of an essay. This structure enables the author to effectively communicate her message to her readers.

Thinking Before Reading

Before you read "The Flight from Conversation," connect the reading to your own experience by answering the following questions:

1. Do you own a cell phone? If so, how often and for what reasons do you use it during a normal day?
2. In an average day, what is your dominant mode of communication? Face-to-face contact or technological contact?
3. Have you ever accidentally left your cell phone at home? How did it make you feel?

The Flight from Conversation

The title suggests the thesis.

Sherry Turkle

The visual supports the thesis.

1 We live in a technological universe in which we are always communicating. And yet we have sacrificed conversation for mere connection.

The author presents introductory information to capture the reader's attention.

2 At home, families sit together, texting and reading e-mail. At work executives text during board meetings. We text (and shop and go on Facebook) during classes and when we're on dates. My students tell me about an important new skill: it involves maintaining eye contact with someone while you text someone else; it's hard, but it can be done.

The thesis statement states the one key point of the essay.

3 Over the past 15 years, I've studied technologies of mobile connection and talked to hundreds of people of all ages and circumstances about their plugged-in lives. I've learned that the little devices most of us carry around are so powerful that they change not only what we do, but also who we are.

Body paragraphs support the thesis and explain the key point(s).

4 We've become accustomed to a new way of being "alone together." Technology-enabled, we are able to be with one another, and also elsewhere, connected to wherever we want to be. We want to customize our lives. We want to move in and out of where we are because the thing we value most is control over where we focus our attention. We have gotten used to the idea of being in a tribe of one, loyal to our own party.

Each body paragraph contains a topic sentence that relates to the thesis.

Details within the paragraph support the topic sentence.

5 Our colleagues want to go to that board meeting but pay attention only to what interests them. To some this seems like a good idea, but we can end up hiding from one another, even as we are constantly connected to one another. A businessman laments that he no longer has colleagues at work. He doesn't stop by to talk; he doesn't call. He says that he doesn't want to interrupt them. He says they're "too busy on their e-mail." But then he pauses and corrects himself. "I'm not telling the truth. I'm the one who doesn't want to be interrupted. I think I should. But I'd rather just do things on my BlackBerry." A 16-year-old boy who relies on texting for almost everything says almost wistfully, "Someday, someday, but certainly not now, I'd like to learn how to have a conversation."

6 In today's workplace, young people who have grown up fearing conversation show up on the job wearing earphones. Walking through a college library or the campus of a high-tech start-up, one sees the same thing: we are together, but each of us is in our own bubble, furiously connected to keyboards and tiny touch screens. A senior partner at a Boston law firm describes a scene in his office. Young associates lay out their suite of technologies: laptops, iPods and multiple phones. And then they put their earphones on. "Big ones. Like pilots. They turn their desks into cockpits." With the young lawyers in their cockpits, the office is quiet, a quiet that does not ask to be broken.

7 In the silence of connection, people are comforted by being in touch with a lot of people—carefully kept at bay. We can't get enough of one another if we can use technology to keep one another at distances we can control: not too close, not too far, just right. I think of it as a Goldilocks effect.

8 Texting and e-mail and posting let us present the self we want to be. This means we can edit. And if we wish to, we can delete. Or retouch: the voice, the flesh, the face, the body. Not too much, not too little—just right. Human relationships are rich; they're messy and demanding. We have learned the habit of cleaning them up with technology. And the move from conversation to connection is part of this. But it's a process in which we shortchange ourselves. Worse, it seems that over time we stop caring, we forget that there is a difference.

9 We are tempted to think that our little "sips" of online connection add up to a big gulp of real conversation. But they don't. E-mail, Twitter, Facebook, all of these have their places—in politics, commerce, romance and friendship. But no matter how valuable, they do not substitute for conversation. Connecting in sips may work for gathering discrete bits of information or for saying, "I am thinking about you." Or even for saying, "I love you." But connecting in sips doesn't work as well when it comes to understanding and knowing one another. In conversation we tend to one another. (The word itself is kinetic; it's derived from words that mean to move, together.) We can attend to tone and nuance. In conversation, we are called upon to see things from another's point of view.

10 Face-to-face conversation unfolds slowly. It teaches patience. When we communicate on our digital devices, we learn different habits. As we ramp up the volume and velocity of online connections, we start to expect faster answers. To get these, we ask one another simpler questions; we dumb down our communications, even on the most important matters. It is as though we have all put ourselves on cable news. Shakespeare might have said, "We are consum'd with that which we were nourish'd by." And we use conversation with others to learn to converse with ourselves. So our flight from conversation can mean diminished chances to learn skills of self-reflection. These days, social media continually asks us what's "on our mind," but we have little motivation to say something truly self-reflective. Self-reflection in conversation requires trust. It's hard to do anything with 3,000 Facebook friends except connect.

11 As we get used to being shortchanged on conversation and to getting by with less, we seem almost willing to dispense with people altogether. Serious people muse about the future of computer programs as psychiatrists. A high school sophomore confides to me that he wishes he could talk to an artificial intelligence program instead of his dad about dating; he says the A.I. would have so much more in its database. Indeed, many people tell me they hope that as Siri, the digital assistant on Apple's iPhone, becomes more advanced, "she" will be more and more like a best friend—one who will listen when others won't.

12 During the years I have spent researching people and their relationships with technology, I have often heard the sentiment "No one is listening to me." I believe this feeling helps explain why it is so appealing to have a Facebook page or a Twitter feed—each provides so many automatic listeners. And it helps explain why—against all reason—so many of us are willing to talk to machines that seem to care about us. Researchers around the world are busy inventing sociable robots, designed to be companions to the elderly, to children, to all of us.

13 One of the most haunting experiences during my research came when I brought one of these robots, designed in the shape of a baby seal, to an elder-care facility, and an older woman began to talk to it about the loss of her child. The robot seemed to be looking into her eyes. It seemed to be following the conversation. The woman was comforted. And so many people found this amazing. Like the sophomore who wants advice about dating from artificial intelligence and those who look forward to computer psychiatry, this enthusiasm speaks to how much we have confused conversation with connection and collectively seem to have embraced a new kind of delusion that accepts the simulation of compassion as sufficient unto the day. And why would we want to talk about love and loss with a machine that has no experience of the arc of human life? Have we so lost confidence that we will be there for one another?

14 We expect more from technology and less from one another and seem increasingly drawn to technologies that provide the illusion of companionship without the demands of relationship. Always-on/always-on-you devices provide three powerful fantasies: that we will always be heard; that we can put our attention wherever we want it to be; and that we never have to be alone. Indeed our new devices have turned being alone into a problem that can be solved. When people are alone, even for a few moments, they fidget and reach for a device. Here

connection works like a symptom, not a cure, and our constant, reflexive impulse to connect shapes a new way of being.

15 Think of it as "I share, therefore I am." We use technology to define ourselves by sharing our thoughts and feelings as we're having them. We used to think, "I have a feeling; I want to make a call." Now our impulse is, "I want to have a feeling; I need to send a text." So, in order to feel more, and to feel more like ourselves, we connect.

Transitional words/phrases make connections among ideas.

16 But in our rush to connect, we flee from solitude, our ability to be separate and gather ourselves. Lacking the capacity for solitude, we turn to other people but don't experience them as they are. It is as though we use them, need them as spare parts to support our increasingly fragile selves. We think constant connection will make us feel less lonely. The opposite is true. If we are unable to be alone, we are far more likely to be lonely. If we don't teach our children to be alone, they will know only how to be lonely.

17 I am a partisan for conversation. To make room for it, I see some first, deliberate steps. At home, we can create sacred spaces: the kitchen, the dining room. We can make our cars "device-free zones." We can demonstrate the value of conversation to our children. And we can do the same thing at work. There we are so busy communicating that we often don't have time to talk to one another about what really matters. Employees asked for casual Fridays; perhaps managers should introduce conversational Thursdays. Most of all, we need to remember—in between texts and e-mails and Facebook posts—to listen to one another, even to the boring bits, because it is often in unedited moments, moments in which we hesitate and stutter and go silent, that we reveal ourselves to one another.

In her concluding paragraph, the author connects all the ideas she has discussed back to her key point.

18 I spend the summers at a cottage on Cape Cod, and for decades I walked the same dunes that Thoreau once walked. Not too long ago, people walked with their heads up, looking at the water, the sky, the sand and at one another, talking. Now they often walk with their heads down, typing. Even when they are with friends, partners, children, everyone is on their own devices. So I say, look up, look at one another, and let's start the conversation.

Sherry Turkle is a psychologist and professor at M.I.T. and the author, most recently, of *Alone Together: Why We Expect More From Technology and Less From Each Other.*

The Six Steps in the Writing Process

■ GOAL 3
Use the writing process

You will often write in response to something you have read, using the following six steps. You first *generate ideas*, and then you explore various ways of *organizing* them. Two important factors you should consider when planning any writing are *your audience* and *your purpose*, which will influence both what you say and how you say it. A fourth step is to *write a first draft*. As part of drafting, you may consider whether you want or need to include visuals to effectively communicate your ideas. Once you have written a first draft, be sure to spend time *revising and rewriting*. Reading your paragraph or essay carefully and critically, and taking time to reorganize, rewrite, add and delete content is crucial to successful writing. Finally, *edit and proofread* your paragraph or essay for correctness. The steps in the writing process are shown in Figure 2-2.

FIGURE 2-2 STEPS IN THE WRITING PROCESS

1. Generating ideas	Finding ideas to write about
2. Organizing your ideas	Discovering how ideas are connected and presenting them logically
3. Considering audience and purpose	Identifying the most appropriate way to communicate with your audience and clarifying your purpose for writing
4. Writing a first draft	Expressing your ideas in sentence, paragraph, and essay form without worrying about spelling, punctuation, capitalization, and grammar Considering using visuals
5. Revising	Rereading and rethinking your ideas to make your writing more clear, complete, and interesting. Going back through everything evaluating, changing, adding, deleting, and rearranging your ideas and words to improve your writing
6. Proofreading	Checking for errors in grammar, spelling, punctuation, mechanics and typing

NOTE: Critical thinking is an important part of this process; writer's need to continually evaluate their own ideas and those of the authors they read and discover connections among them.

EXAMINING STUDENT WRITING

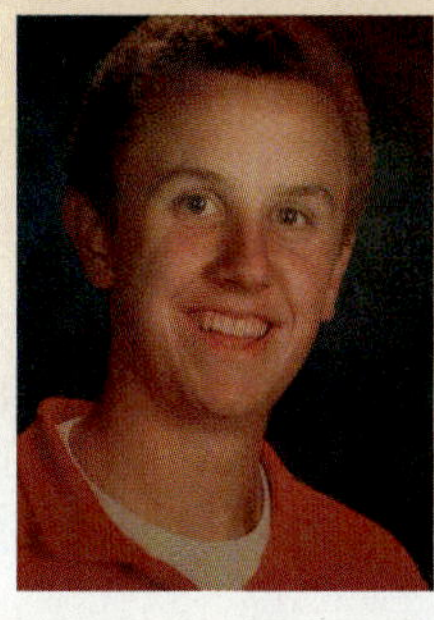

Jake is a student at Virginia Tech University in Blacksburg, Virginia. He is majoring in mechanical engineering.

A good way to learn to read and write essays is to study the work of other student writers. In this chapter, we will follow Jake Frey as he responds to two writing assignments. For the first one, he did not approach writing as a process, which led to an unsuccessful paper. For his second assignment, written in response to the reading "The Flight from Conversation" on page 41, he learned from his mistakes, and you will see how he applied each step in the writing process to produce the final essay shown on page 61.

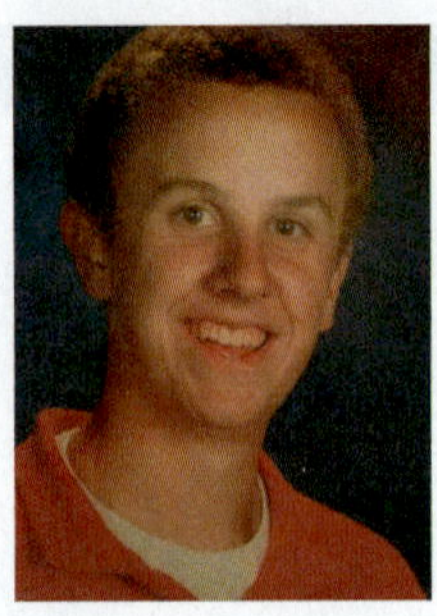

Jake's First Writing Assignment

For his first writing assignment, Jake was asked to write an essay about some aspect of reality TV. At first, he thought this assignment would be an easy one, but he had so many ideas floating around in his head that he was unable to bring any one idea into focus. Finally, on the night before the first draft was due, Jake sat down at his computer and typed the following sentence:

> Reality TV can be fun to watch, but there are so many things wrong with it.

At that point Jake was in trouble; he didn't know what to say next. Realizing that he *had* to write something, he tried to describe a few reality TV shows and their features. His thoughts were all over the place, but time was short, and he had other work to do, so he put the paper away and moved on. On the next day, he handed the paper in and hoped for the best. When the professor returned the papers, Jake was disappointed when he saw his grade. The instructor's note said, "I know you tried. Next time, though, plan out your essay, write a draft, and then revise it." Jake thought, "I really tried. This is really disappointing. I need to learn a different way to go about writing!"

Where did Jake go wrong? Actually, he made several mistakes, but they all stem from a larger problem. He was viewing writing as a single-step activity instead of a multi-step process. Writing is a series of steps in which you **generate ideas** on what to say, **plan** how you will organize your ideas, and then **write**, **revise**, and **proofread** what you have written. Figure 2-2 (p. 45) summarizes the steps in the writing process.

Jake neither thought nor planned before he began writing; consequently, he had trouble knowing what to say. Then, in desperation, he ended up simply rambling about the topic, without placing his observations into a unifying framework. Once he finished writing, he put the assignment away and did not look at it again. When he handed in his assignment, he had not reread it even once to see how he could improve it, nor had he proofread for errors. In this chapter, and throughout this book, you will learn to approach writing as a process and avoid making Jake's mistakes.

When writing, people frequently find that some of the steps overlap or that some circling back to earlier steps is necessary. For example, you may continue to organize your ideas while writing your first draft, or you may need to generate more ideas while revising. This circling back is fine; the writing process does not always go in a straight line.

If you use each of these steps, you will find that writing will be easier and more successful for you than it was for Jake. You will not find yourself frustrated, staring at a blank sheet of paper, or writing something that doesn't seem to hang together or say much. Instead, you will feel as if you are developing and focusing your ideas, shaping them into words, and making a point that will hold and interest your reader. You will be well on your way to producing a good paper.

Jake's Second Writing Assignment

For his second writing assignment, shown below, Jake learned from his mistakes and approached writing as a multi-step process. Throughout the remainder of the chapter, we will follow Jake as he writes an essay in response to the following assignment.

> **Assignment:** Read the article "The Flight from Conversation," and write an essay on some facet of technology or communication that relates to the thesis of the article.

Generate Ideas

■ GOAL 4
Generate ideas

Before you begin to write a paper, the first step is to generate ideas about your topic. There are a number of different ways to generate ideas. Four good techniques you can use to generate ideas are

- freewriting.
- brainstorming.
- branching.
- questioning.

These techniques can help you overcome the feeling that you have nothing to say. They can unlock ideas you already have and help you discover new ones.

Since each of these four techniques provides a different way to generate ideas, feel free to choose from among them. At times, you may use several at different points in your writing process, or you may need to use only one of them for a particular writing assignment. Jake chose to generate ideas by brainstorming, the first example in Table 2-1, but you might have chosen a different technique. Be sure to experiment to see what works best for you. Study Table 2-1 to see how Jake could have generated ideas for the topic of communication and technology using other techniques.

TABLE 2-1 TECHNIQUES FOR GENERATING IDEAS

Technique	How to Do It	Example
Brainstorming	1. List all ideas about your topic that come to mind. 2. List words and phrases, observations, and thoughts without attention to correctness. 3. Give yourself a time limit; then stop, review, and repeat as necessary.	• No real relationships • Relationships—lose meaning • Fast • Convenient • Talk constantly and wear out conversation • Break up and get back together without seeing each other in person • Complications in relationships • Romantic—really? • No escape—can keep tabs on each other all the time • Easy access • Meaningless event • Hide behind screen • No personal contact—no practice at being with others • Can happen any time • Can tweet and text personal feelings at any time • Can revise or delete • Can arrange dates easily • Many "friends"—really few friends
Freewriting	1. Write nonstop about your topic. 2. Write whatever comes to mind without concern about correctness. 3. Give yourself a time limit; then stop, review, and repeat as necessary.	Technology, it is everywhere, and it is used by almost everyone. People at one time stopped and asked for directions now they have GPS for that. People at one time had to write letters now there is texting and even video chatting, so people are never really out of reach. And don't forget Instagram. Technology, in the form of phones, has really made communication easier and has almost even taken the social aspect out of life. Two people may be in the same room, but they do not have to look at each other to talk because of texting. Love used to be gestures in the form of letters and written affection as well as grand gestures of flowers and big date nights. While the grand gestures may still be intact the letters have become nonexistent and have been replaced by incessant talking through texting and tweeting and chatting online. Bullying has even become easier because people can stay anonyms online but say some crude things and attack people. Technology also seems to distinguish people's social status with it becoming a race to see who can own the newest gadgets and this only feeds the companies who have a new model every few months. Teens seem to use technology for romance because they have grown up with technology and rely on technology to have a relationship. There are couples that never stop talking minute after minute texting from the morning till night. Teen's text constantly in the presence of anyone and anywhere. People meet on Facebook, get phone numbers, announce they are dating over Twitter and then two months later break up over text and may have possibly never actually went on a date, and this whole process is called love.

(continued)

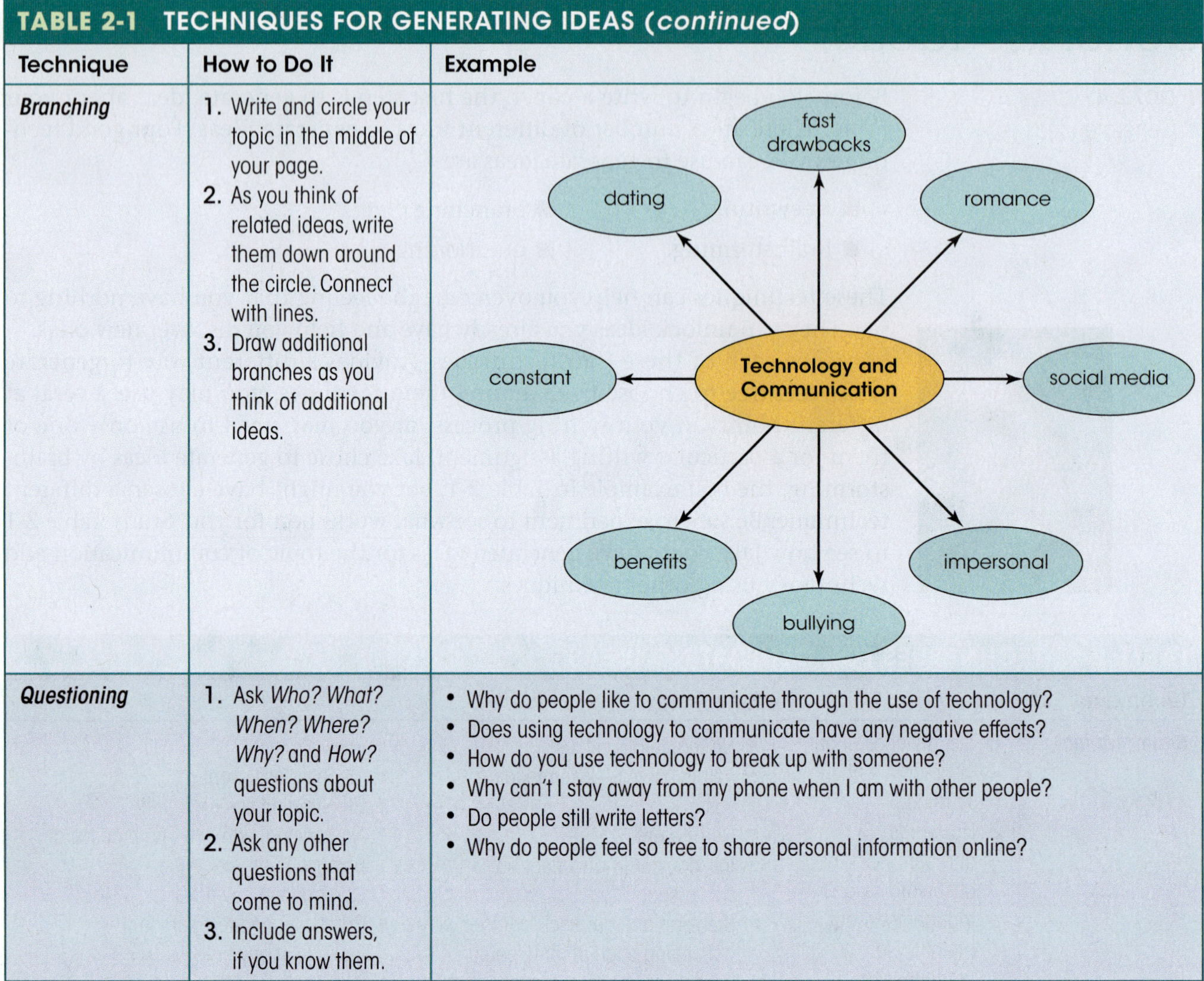

TABLE 2-1 TECHNIQUES FOR GENERATING IDEAS (*continued*)

Technique	How to Do It	Example
Branching	**1.** Write and circle your topic in the middle of your page. **2.** As you think of related ideas, write them down around the circle. Connect with lines. **3.** Draw additional branches as you think of additional ideas.	Technology and Communication fast drawbacks romance social media impersonal bullying benefits constant dating
Questioning	**1.** Ask *Who? What? When? Where? Why?* and *How?* questions about your topic. **2.** Ask any other questions that come to mind. **3.** Include answers, if you know them.	• Why do people like to communicate through the use of technology? • Does using technology to communicate have any negative effects? • How do you use technology to break up with someone? • Why can't I stay away from my phone when I am with other people? • Do people still write letters? • Why do people feel so free to share personal information online?

When to Use Which Technique

Now that you have learned about freewriting, brainstorming, branching, and questioning, you are probably wondering when to use each technique. In general, there are no rules to follow. The best advice is to give them all a good chance and use the technique, or techniques, with which you are most comfortable.

You may also find that for certain topics, one technique works better than the others. For example, suppose you decide to write a paragraph about your mother's sense of humor. While it might be difficult to think of questions, freewriting might help you remember humorous events from your life with her. Suppose, however, that you are studying types of discrimination in your sociology class. Your instructor has assigned a paper that requires you to explain the effects of one type of discrimination. Asking questions about the specific topic is likely to produce useful ideas to include in your paper.

Sorting Usable Ideas

Freewriting, brainstorming, branching, and questioning each produces a wide range of usable ideas. You will need to sort through them to decide which ones you can put together and expand upon to produce a paper that is unified and interesting to your reader.

Choosing Your Own Topic

When your instructor assigns a topic or provides a choice of topics, part of your paper, in a sense, has been done for you. You may not like the topic(s), or you may need to narrow the topic down to make it more manageable, but at least you have a point from which to start. If your instructor directs you to choose a topic, you have greater freedom, but sometimes your first reaction may be "I don't know what to write about!"

Don't be tempted to grab just any topic in order to get on with writing. Remember that the most important element in clear writing is clear *thinking*. Invest your time in thinking about what you want to write. Use one—or more—of the four techniques you just learned for generating topics—freewriting, brainstorming, branching, or questioning. You can also generate ideas by reacting to the world around you. Here are some suggestions to get you involved in your world:

Tips for Generating Topics

1. **Think of an interesting topic that was discussed in one of your classes or a topic that relates to your major.** Nursing students might, for example, think of genetic counseling for prospective parents, and accounting students of new computer software.
2. **Think of activities you have participated in over the past week.** Going to work or to church, playing softball, taking your child to the playground, shopping at a mall, or seeing a horror film could produce the following topics: communication patterns among co-workers; why attendance at church is rising (or falling); the problem with pitchers; how toddlers develop language skills; the mall as an adult playground; the redeeming value of horror films.
3. **Look around you or out the window.** What do you see? Perhaps it is the television, a dog lying at your feet, traffic, or children playing tag. Possible topics are the influence of television on what we buy, pets as companions, cars as noise polluters (or entertainment), and play as a form of learning.
4. **Think of the time of year.** Think about what you do on holidays or vacation, what is happening around you in the environment, or what this season's sports or upcoming events might mean to you.
5. **Use a writing journal.** A writing journal is a notebook or computer file in which you record your thoughts and ideas on a regular basis. Many students try to write daily and find that a journal is a useful way to spur their thinking and become a more effective writer.
6. **Think of a controversial topic you have read about, heard about on the radio or on television, or argued about with a friend.** A political candidate up for reelection, a terminally ill patient's right to euthanasia, and reforms in public education are examples.
7. **As you read, listen to the news, or go about your daily life, be alert for possible topics and write them down.** Keep the list and refer to it when your next paper is assigned.

If you choose a topic that interests you, one that you know something about or are willing to read about, you will feel more like writing. You will also find that you have more to say and that what you write will be more engaging and memorable for your reader.

EXERCISE 2-1

WRITING IN PROGRESS

Evaluating Techniques for Generating Ideas

Directions: Select one of the topics listed below. Try all four techniques—freewriting, brainstorming, branching, and questioning—on the same topic.

Topics

1. Is violence a necessary part of sports?
2. What is the best gift you have ever given or received?
3. What role does technology play in your life?
4. How can people eat well without spending a lot of money?
5. What should a person do (or not do) when he or she is laid off?
6. Why is it so difficult to save money?
7. What annoying bad habit do you wish you could break?
8. What changes would you like to make in your life?

When you have tried all four techniques, read the list of ideas produced by using each one. Mark the usable ideas. Then write short answers to the following questions:

Questions

1. Which technique produced the most usable ideas?
2. Which technique were you most comfortable using?
3. Which technique were you least comfortable using? Why?

Organize Your Ideas

■ GOAL 5
Organize ideas

Once you have generated ideas about your topic, the next step is to decide how to organize them. Ideas in a paragraph or essay should progress logically from one to another. Group or arrange your ideas in a way that makes them clear and understandable to your reader.

Jake reviewed his brainstorming list (shown in Table 2-1, p. 47) and saw three major themes: technology and romance, loss of social skills, and the benefits of communicating with technology. He rearranged his list, using those headings, as shown below.

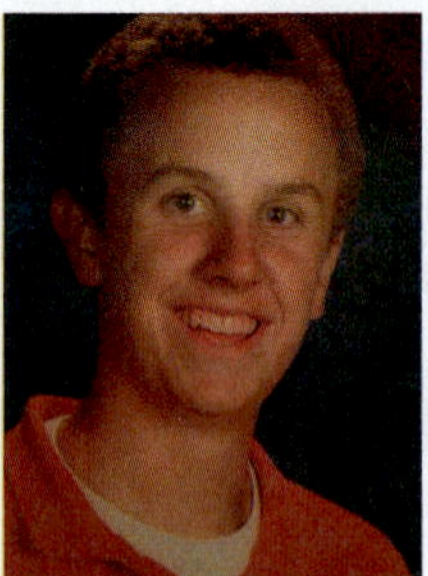

Technology and Romance

Relationships—lose meaning
Talk constantly and wear out conversation
Break up and get back together without seeing each other in person
Complications in relationships
Can tweet and text personal feelings at any time
Can arrange dates easily
Convenient
No escape—can keep tabs on each other all the time
Romantic—really?
Meaningless event

Loss of Social Skills
Hide behind screen
Many "friends"—really few friends
No real relationships
No personal contact—no practice at being with others

Benefits of Communicating with Technology
fast
can happen any time
easy access
can revise or delete

As Jake reviewed his brainstorming ideas, he realized that the aspect of technology and communication that he was most interested in was romance. He brainstormed a few more ideas and decided the best way to organize his ideas was to focus on three negative effects that technology has had on romantic relationships.

Using an Idea Map to Organize Your Ideas

One effective way to organize your ideas is to draw an idea map, a visual picture of the organization and content of an essay. When you are beginning to write, an idea map can help you organize your ideas into paragraphs and see how paragraphs fit together to form essays. Here is an idea map that Jake drew for his essay on romance and technology. He developed his ideas further as he drew the map.

VISUALIZE IT!

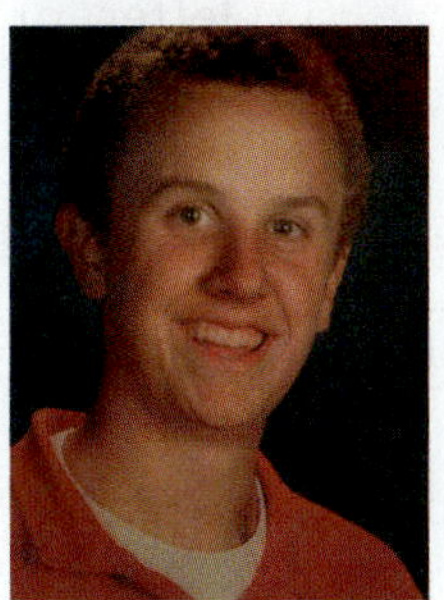

Jake's Idea Map

Technology has changed romance and dating into a meaningless event.

- No personal contact
  - Communicate constantly by phone
  - Use Google for romantic poems
  - Text ILY
- Expedited life cycle of relationship
  - Start relationship in morning and finish by end of school day
- Robbing kids of childhood
  - Kids with access to social media
  - Learn from what teens and adults model
  - Should be concerned with childhood pleasures, not dating

EXERCISE 2-2

WRITING IN PROGRESS

Arranging Ideas Logically

Directions: Use the topic that you generated ideas for in Exercise 2-1. Determine which ideas are usable and interrelated, and arrange them in a logical order.

Consider Your Audience and Purpose

■ GOAL 6
Consider your audience and purpose

In an earlier section of the chapter, you saw that among the characteristics of good writing are "Good writing is directed toward an audience" and "Good writing achieves a purpose."

Considering Your Audience

When you write, ask yourself: Who will be reading what I write? How should I express myself so that my readers will understand what I write?

Considering your audience is essential to good writing. What is appropriate for one audience may be inappropriate for another. For example, if you were writing about a car accident that you were involved in, you would write one way to a close friend (casual and personal with lots of details) and another way to your professor (more businesslike and direct with a focus on the impact on your coursework rather than on your feelings).

Writers make many decisions based on the audience they have in mind. As you write, consider the following:

- How many and what kinds of details are appropriate
- What format is appropriate (for example, paragraph, essay, letter, or memo)
- How many and what types of examples should be used
- How formal the writing should be
- What kinds of words should be used (straightforward, technical, or emotional)
- What tone the writing should have; that is, how it should sound to readers (for example, friendly, distant, knowledgeable, or angry)

Audience is as important in the workplace as it is in personal and academic writing. You would write differently to a manager within your company than you would to a customer outside it, as the following two e-mail messages show.

E-mail Message 1: Salesperson to Customer

From: Jim Watts [Jwatts@pcs.net]
Sent: Wednesday, April 04, 2015 9:46AM
To: Tim Rodney
Subject: Replacement Shipment of Norfolk Pine Trees

Hi, Tim,

I am sorry that you were displeased with our recent shipment of Norfolk pines. I cannot imagine how they could have become infested with aphids, since they were insect free at point of shipment. Because we value your continued business, we are happy to ship a replacement order. The new shipment should arrive in the next 3–5 business days. If I can be of further help, please be sure to call or e-mail.

Jim Watts
Farm Manager
Highland Tree Farms
(123) 555-7596

E-mail Message 2: Salesperson to District Manager

From: Jim Watts [jwatts@pcs.net]
Sent: Wednesday, April 04, 2015 10:13AM
To: Brown, Thomas
Subject: Replacement Shipment to Rodney's Nursery

Tim at Rodney's Nursery claims to have received an aphid-infested shipment of Norfolk pines, but of course we know they were infested after delivery. (The conditions are so bad there that I am amazed any plant survives more than a few weeks.) Because Tim is one of our best customers, I decided to ship a replacement order, even though he's trying to con us on this one. Hope this decision is OK with you.

Jim Watts
Farm Manager
Highland Tree Farms
(123) 555-7596

Both messages are casually written, since e-mail is a less formal method of communication than letters. Notice, however, that the information in each differs, as does the tone. Here are four key questions that will help you address your audience appropriately in the workplace as well as in academic situations:

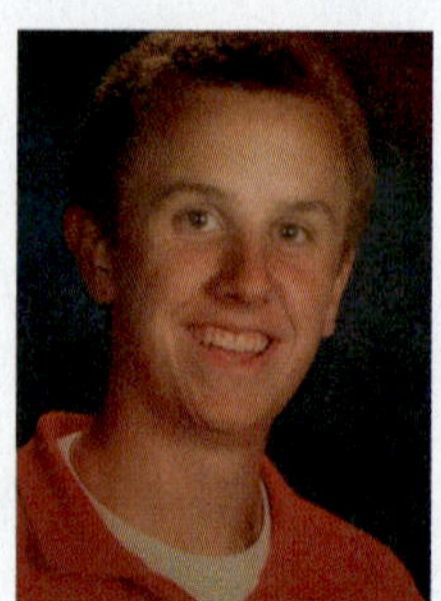

- Who is my audience and what is my relationship with that audience?
- How is the audience likely to react to my message?
- What does the audience already know about the situation?
- What does the audience need to know about the situation?

Jake's audience was his instructor, so he was careful to explain online dating for an older person who might not be familiar with the topic. In later chapters, you will learn more about adapting your writing to your audience and see how professional writers address specific audiences.

Writing for a Purpose

When you call a friend on the phone, you have a reason for calling, even if it is just to stay in touch. When you ask a question in class, you have a purpose for asking. When you describe to a friend an incident you were involved in, you are relating the story to make a point or share an experience. These examples demonstrate that you use spoken communication to achieve specific purposes.

Good writing must also achieve your *intended purpose*. If you write a paragraph on how to change a flat tire, your reader should be able to change a flat tire after reading the paragraph. Likewise, if your purpose is to describe the sun rising over a misty mountaintop, your reader should be able to visualize the scene. If your purpose is to argue that the legal age for drinking alcohol should be 25, your reader should be able to follow your reasoning, even if he or she is not won over to your view. For student writer Jake, his purpose was to explore the relationship between technology and romance, so he focused on showing how technology has changed dating patterns.

Purpose is important in both workplace writing and academic writing. The two e-mail messages just shown reveal two very different purposes. The first message, to the nursery, is intended to keep good relations with a customer who claims that he received infested trees. The second e-mail, to the district manager, is intended to explain why a replacement shipment was sent, even though the claim was not legitimate.

EXERCISE 2-3

WRITING IN PROGRESS

Writing a Paragraph

Directions: Using the topic that you worked on in Exercise 2-1 and Exercise 2-2, complete two of the following activities:

1. Write a paragraph about the topic to a classmate.
2. Write a paragraph about the topic to your English instructor.
3. Write a paragraph about the topic for your campus or local newspaper.

Write a First Draft

■ GOAL 7
Write a first draft

Suppose you are taking a weekend trip and are about to pack your suitcase. You have in mind what you'll be doing and whom you'll see. You look through your entire closet, then narrow your choices to several outfits. You mix and match the outfits, figure out how much will fit in the suitcase, and finally decide what to take.

Writing a draft of a paragraph or an essay is similar to packing for a trip. You have to try out different ideas, see how they work together, express them in different ways, and, after several versions, settle upon what your paper will include. Drafting is a way of trying out ideas to see if and how they work.

A first draft expresses your ideas in sentence form. Work from your list of ideas, and don't be concerned with grammar, spelling, or punctuation at this point. Instead, focus on expressing and developing each idea fully. The following suggestions will help you write effective first drafts:

Tips for Writing an Effective First Draft

1. **After you have thought carefully about the ideas on your list, write one sentence that expresses the main point of your paragraph (working topic sentence) or essay (thesis statement).**
2. **Concentrate on explaining your topic sentence or thesis statement, using ideas from your list.** Focus first on those ideas you like best or that you think express your main point particularly well. Later in the writing process, you may find you need to add other ideas from your list.
3. **Think of a first draft as a chance to experiment with different ideas and ways of organizing them.** While you are writing, if you think of a better way to organize or express your ideas, or if you think of new ideas, make changes. Be flexible. Do not worry about getting your exact wording at this point.
4. **As your draft develops, feel free to change your focus or even your topic, if it has not been assigned.** If your draft is not working out, don't hesitate to start over completely. Go back to generating ideas. It is always all right to go back and forth among the steps in the writing process. Most writers make a number of "false starts" before they produce a draft that satisfies them.
5. **Do not expect immediate success.** When you finish your first draft, you should feel that you have the *beginnings* of a paper you will be happy with. Now, ask yourself if you have a sense of the direction your paper will take. Do you have a main idea? Do you have supporting details? Is the organization logical? If you can answer "yes" to these questions, you have something on paper to work with and revise.

Jake, the student writing about technology and dating, wrote the following first draft of his paper. The highlighting indicates the main point that he developed as he wrote.

First Draft

Technology has boomed and is now an essential in everyone's lives, especially teens. In fact, it has become their lifeline. They don't know how to communicate without it. Technology has even changed the way couples fall in and out of love. Technology and social media have transformed romance and dating.

Everyone knows the couples that incessantly talk, the ones that cannot put their phones down to talk to anyone because they are busy cyber-whispering sweet nothings to each other. Most of their relationship is conducted online; they never really hang out with each other. This is the way it seems that romance and dating in teens has gone since technology hit the scene. The only romance that exists is not romance at all; it is cyber-romance.

Not only has technology taken the meaning out of love it has also expedited the life cycle of a relationship. People can actually begin and end a relationship on the same day. Was this really love at all? Perhaps it was just a pseudo-relationship made easy by technology. The speed at which relationships begin and end is mind-blowing.

Yes, romance seems to blossom more quickly now, thanks to technology, but it also seems that romantic relationships are blossoming in a younger generation. Younger teens and even children have access to social media and technology. Kids learn from older kids and adults, and when they are on the social media they see these pseudo-relationships and think that they need one, too. None of these relationships have any meaning at all.

WRITING IN PROGRESS

Writing a First Draft

Directions: Write the first draft of a paragraph (or two) using the topic for which you put ideas in a logical order in Exercise 2-2.

Think Critically About Incorporating Visuals Into Your Writing

■ GOAL 8
Think critically about incorporating visuals into your writing

Visuals are another way of communicating. They are not a substitute for text, nor are they necessarily the main focus of the text, but a well-chosen visual can serve the following functions:

- Spark interest
- Elicit a reaction
- Provide perspective
- Offer an example
- Help the reader understand a difficult concept

As a writer, you will be the one to choose the visual aids to accompany your text, so be sure you know exactly what you want to accomplish by including them.

Placement is important. If you want to capture the reader's attention, then place the visual in a prominent place, such as at the beginning of an essay or chapter. If you want to support a point you have already made, then insert the visual close to where the point is stated.

There are several ways that you can find visuals to include in your writing. Although the Internet contains a large assortment of visual collections, you must use caution when sourcing from the Web. Use the following guidelines:

Guidelines for Finding Visuals

- **Make sure that you have, at least, a general idea of the type of visual you want to use.** Otherwise, you could waste many hours surfing the Web and never find what you need.
- **Be sure to read the fair use information associated with the particular site that contains the visual you want to use.** Not everything on the Internet is public domain. You may need to seek permission to use a visual, and in some cases, you may even have to pay. For most academic assignments, students may use copyrighted material without permission, but it is always wise to err on the side of caution and check to make sure you can legally use it.
- **Be sure to document the source of the visual in your writing.** See Chapter 11 for documentation sources to consult.

If you cannot find exactly what you want on the Internet, you can always create your own visual. Using computer applications, you can design charts, graphs, or diagrams, and you can even draw your own original creation that perfectly enhances the message of your writing.

Let's take a look at the process Jake used to find and select a visual to include in his final draft. He knew that he wanted it to illustrate the impersonal aspect of a romantic relationship conducted primarily through technology, so he decided to use a photo. He also knew that he wanted the photo to capture the interest of his readers and draw them into the essay. With these purposes in mind, he searched an Internet site using the words *romance and technology* and found the perfect photo. After checking to make sure that he could legally use it, he inserted it into his essay. As you read Jake's final essay on page 61, evaluate the effectiveness of the photo in achieving the purposes Jake had for it.

Finding a Visual

WRITING IN PROGRESS

For the paragraph(s) you wrote in Exercise 2-4, decide whether a visual could be used to illustrate your ideas. If so, decide what type of visual would be appropriate, and conduct an Internet search to locate one. (Types of visuals you might use are discussed in Chapter 1, pp. 19-20.) Insert it in your paragraph.

Revise and Rewrite Drafts

- **GOAL 9**
  Revise and rewrite

Let's think again about the process of packing a suitcase. At first you may think you have included everything you need and are ready to go. Then, a while later, you think of other things that would be good to take. But because your suitcase is full, you have to reorganize everything. When you repack, you take everything out and rethink your selections and their relationships to each other. You might eliminate some items, add others, and switch around still others.

A similar thing often happens as you revise your first draft. When you finish a first draft, you are more or less satisfied with it. Then you reread it later and see you have more work to do. When you revise, you have to rethink your entire paper, reexamining every part and idea. Revising is more than changing a word or rearranging a few sentences, and it is not concerned with correcting punctuation, spelling errors, or grammar. Make these editing changes later when you are satisfied that you have presented your ideas in the optimal way. Revision is your chance to make significant improvements to your draft. It might mean changing, adding, deleting, or rearranging whole sections.

Use the following tips to revise effectively:

Tips for Revising

1. **Reread the sentence that expresses your main point.** It must be clear, direct, and complete. Experiment with ways to improve it.
2. **Reread each of your other sentences or paragraphs.** Does each relate directly to your main point? If not, cross it out or rewrite it to clarify its connection to the main point. If all your sentences or paragraphs suggest a main point that is different from your topic sentence or thesis statement, rewrite it.
3. **Make sure your writing has a beginning and an end.** A paragraph should have a clear topic sentence and concluding statement. An essay should have introductory and concluding portions, their length depending on the length of your essay.
4. **Replace words that are vague or unclear with more specific or descriptive words.**
5. **Seek advice.** If you are unsure about how to revise, visit your writing instructor during office hours and ask for advice, or try peer review. Ask a classmate or friend to read your paper and mark ideas that are unclear or need further explanation.
6. **When you have finished revising, you should feel satisfied with what you have said and with the way you have said it.** You will learn additional strategies for revising in Chapter 9.
7. **Evaluate the writer's use of visuals.** Visuals must provide support for the writer's intended message and be appropriately placed.

Jake's final draft appears on page 61, along with annotations showing the changes he made.

Peer Review

Peer review means asking one or more of your classmates to read and comment on your writing. It is an excellent way to find out what is good in your draft and what needs to be improved. Here are some tips for making peer review as valuable as possible:

When You Are the Writer

1. Prepare your draft in readable form. Double-space your work and print it on standard 8.5″ × 11″ paper. Use only one side of the paper.

2. When you receive your peers' comments, weigh them carefully. Keep an open mind, but do not feel that you must accept every suggestion that is made.
3. If you have questions or are uncertain about your peers' advice, talk with your instructor.

When You Are the Reviewer

1. Read the draft through at least once before making any suggestions.
2. As you read, keep the writer's intended audience in mind (see Chapters 7, 8, and 14). The draft should be appropriate for that audience.
3. Offer positive comments first. Say what the writer did well.
4. Use the Revision Checklist in Chapter 7 (p. 223) to guide your reading and comments. Be specific in your review, and offer suggestions for improvement.

Jake participated in a peer review session with three of his peers. They made the following comments about his draft:

> "Jake, put more of your personality in this essay. It needs some spark!"
>
> "I'm not sure I see a clear conclusion. Your essay just seems to stop."
>
> "Add some real-life details to paragraph #2 and #3."
>
> "Check out sentence #2 in the intro paragraph. It doesn't make sense."

Using Peer Review

Directions: Pair up with a classmate for this exercise. Read and evaluate each other's paragraphs written for Exercise 2-4, using the peer review guidelines above.

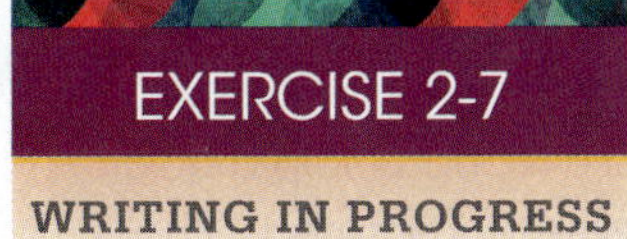

Revising a Draft

Directions: Revise the first draft you wrote for Exercise 2-4, following steps 1 through 6 in the Tips for Revising box.

Proofread Your Final Draft

■ GOAL 10
Proofread for correctness

Proofreading is a final reading of your paper to check for errors. In this final polishing of your work, the focus is on correctness, so don't proofread until you have done all your rethinking of ideas and revision. When you are ready to proofread your writing, you should check for errors in

- sentences (run-ons or fragments).
- grammar.
- spelling.
- punctuation.
- capitalization.

The following tips will ensure that you don't miss any errors.

Tips for Proofreading

1. **Review your paper once for each type of error.** First, read it for run-on sentences and fragments. Take a short break, and then read it four more times, each time paying attention to one of the following: *spelling*, *punctuation*, *grammar*, and *capitalization*.
2. **To find spelling errors, read your paper from last sentence to first sentence and from last word to first word.** Reading in this way, you will not get distracted by the flow of ideas, so you can focus on finding errors. Also use the spell-checker on your computer, but be sure to proofread for the kinds of errors it cannot catch: missing words, errors that are themselves words (such as *of* for *or*), and homonyms (for example, using *it's* for *its*).
3. **Read each sentence aloud, slowly and deliberately.** This technique will help you catch endings that you have left off verbs or missing plurals.
4. **Check for errors one final time after you print out your paper.** Don't do this when you are tired; you might introduce new mistakes. Ask a classmate or friend to read your paper to catch any mistakes you missed.

Here is a paragraph that shows the errors in grammar, punctuation, and spelling that Jake corrected during proofreading.

Not only has technology taken the meaning out of love[,] but it [also] has expedited the life cycle of a relationship. ~~The p~~eople [P] can actually begin and end a relationship on the same day. Love these days seems to take place on a Monday with a quick statement on a social media ~~cite~~ [site] about how life [never] could ~~never~~ be imagined without this one person, and ~~than~~ [then], miraculously by lunchtime, the ~~lover's~~ [lovers] have ~~tweated~~ [tweeted] about ~~too~~ [two] fights and ~~post~~ [posted] mean ~~massages~~ [messages] about each other on ~~they're~~ [their] Facebook pages. By the end of the day, the break-up has been announced to the world. The speed at which relationships begin and end is mind-blowing. Is this really love at all? Perhaps[,] it is just a pseudo-relationship made easy by technology.

Chapter 7, page 224, includes a proofreading checklist.

Proofreading

Directions: Prepare and proofread the final version of the paragraph you have developed throughout this chapter.

READ AND RESPOND: A Student Essay

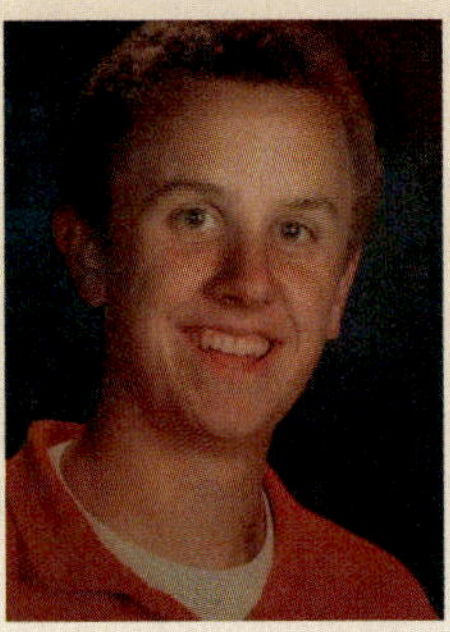

This essay is a later draft of Jake's essay shown on page 55. In this draft, you can see that he expands his ideas (underlined), adds details (underlined), and writes a title and a conclusion. You can see that he added a sentence (highlighted) that states the main point of his essay, his thesis statement. After you have read the essay once, study the annotations. They will help you see the changes Jake made.

Title suggests thesis

The Romance of Technology

Scenario presented to capture reader's attention

1 Consider this scenario. Boy meets girl on Facebook. Boy serenades girl with YouTube video and flirts with her by texting. The couple announces their love to the world on Twitter. Boy decides the relationship just isn't working, and by sending a text, he breaks up with the girl. This scenario may seem far-fetched, but it is all too often the reality. Technological devices have become a lifeline to many people, especially teens and young adults. They don't know how to communicate without these tools. Technology has even changed the way couples fall in and out of love. It has transformed a once sentimental, romantic journey into a meaningless event.

Romance has become a picture of flowers and an electronic message of love.

Thesis

Transition added to guide the reader

Quotation added

More details about romance added

2 One effect of the proliferation of technological tools is the constant talk that is now possible. Everyone knows a couple who talk incessantly. They can't put their phones down to talk to anyone else because they are always busy typing, "You are so cute, and I love you so much." They are pre-occupied, almost 24-7, with cyber whispering sweet nothings to each other. Most of their together time is spent with a technological device that tethers them to each other; they never really hang out with each other in person. Is this what romance looks like? Love used to be conveyed through poems that communicated heartfelt sentiments and flowers that were hand-picked just for that special significant other. Now, romance is a Google search of cute poems and a symbol of a floral bouquet attached to an email or text with a three letter long message, "ily." Really? Is this how true love should be communicated—with a short abbreviated version of the words *I love* you?

3 Not only has technology taken the meaning out of love, but it also has expedited the life cycle of a relationship. People can actually begin and end a

Details about speed of relationship added

relationship on the same day. Love these days seems to take place on a Monday with a quick statement on a social media site about how life never could be imagined without this one person, and then, miraculously by lunchtime, the lovers have tweeted about two fights and posted mean messages about each other on their Facebook pages. By the end of the day, the break-up has been announced to the world. The speed at which relationships begin and end is mind-blowing. Is this really love at all? Perhaps it is just a pseudo-relationship made easy by technology.

New details about children's romances added

4 Yes, romance seems to blossom more quickly now, thanks to technology, but it also seems that romantic relationships are blossoming in a much younger generation. Younger teens and even children have access to social media and technology. Kids learn from older kids and adults, and when they are on social media sites, they see these pseudo-relationships and think that they need one, too. There may still be a few love notes floating around elementary and middle school classrooms, but more common is the love text, love Twitter, love Instagram, or love posting on Facebook. A third grader's greatest concern should be about who will be the captain for kickball at recess. Sadly, it is sometimes about who is "going with" or "In a relationship" with whom on Facebook or Twitter.

Conclusion added: Jake summarizes his major points and reflects on the issue.

5 In conclusion, technology has negatively impacted relationships, especially in the area of romance. Constant chatter has reduced romance to an exchange of quick pseudo-sentiments. The speed of technology has also led to the speed of romantic relationships; they start quickly and end quickly, sometimes all in the same day. Finally, widespread access to technology has enabled even children to declare their affection for boyfriends or girlfriends for all to see. Technology is here to stay, but hopefully, those who have relegated their relationships to the cyber-world will discover the joy and fulfillment of an actual up close and personal relationship that has meaning and longevity.

Examining Writing

1. Evaluate Jake's decision to organize his ideas according to the effects of technology on romance. Do his ideas progress logically from one to another?
2. Evaluate Jake's thesis statement. How could it be revised to be more effective?
3. Evaluate the revisions Jake made to his draft. Which paragraphs could be improved and how?
4. Explain how the visual supports the thesis of Jake's essay.

Writing Assignments MySkillsLab®

1. Think about your own experiences related to relationships and technology. Choose one and write a paragraph or essay describing the experience and how it affected the relationship.

2. Use brainstorming or freewriting to generate ideas for the topic "The Ideal Friend/Girlfriend/Boyfriend." Then write a paragraph or essay describing that ideal person.
3. Jake Frey's essay focuses on the negative effects of technology on dating and romance. Write a paragraph or essay describing what positive effects technology might have on dating and romance.

READ AND RESPOND: A Professional Essay

The Flight from Conversation

Sherry Turkle

Earlier in the chapter on pages 41–44, you read "The Flight from Conversation" and examined the basic structure of the essay. Now it is time to take a closer look at the reading by responding to the questions that follow.

Writing in Response to Reading (See essay on p. 41.)

Checking Your Comprehension MySkillsLab®

Answer each of the following questions using complete sentences.

1. What important new texting skill does the author discuss?
2. What does the author suggest that we value most?
3. To what does the senior partner at a Boston law firm compare the offices of his young associates?
4. Who is Siri, and what function does she serve?
5. Why was the author "haunted" by the elderly woman's reaction to a robot baby seal?

Strengthening Your Vocabulary MySkillsLab®

Using the word's context, word parts, or a dictionary, write a brief definition of each of the following words as it is used in the reading.

1. laments (paragraph 5) ______________________________
2. discrete (paragraph 9) ______________________________
3. illusion (paragraph 14) ______________________________
4. partisan (paragraph 17) ______________________________

Examining the Reading: Using an Idea Map MySkillsLab®

Review the reading by completing the missing parts of the idea map shown below.

VISUALIZE IT!

Title: **The Flight From Conversation**

Thesis: Electronic devices have changed the way we relate to people.

- We are used to being alone together.
  - The one thing we want to control is ________________.
  - At work, a businessman ________________________ ________________________.
  - A 16-year-old ________________________________.
- People avoid real conversations.
  - After a while, we don't even notice the difference in conversation and connection.
  - We actually consider our connections to be __________.
- Online conversation is not the same as face-to-face conversation.
  - We can't really ___ people if we don't have a _________ with them.
  - We actually consider our connections to be __________.
  - Face-to-face conversation takes time.
  - ________________________________.
  - It also helps us learn to ______________________.
  - The more we neglect conversation, the more ____________________.
- Real conversation creates a connection.
  - Some people are willing to talk to a ______ just to have something to __________.
  - An elderly woman ____.
- Online communication creates a false sense of companionship and connection.
  - People don't like to be alone, so they __________________.
  - Instead of calling to share a feeling with someone, ________________.
  - Being connected does not keep us from being lonely.
- Take steps to ______________.
  - Create _____ spaces.
  - Don't use electronic devices in the car.
  - Show children the importance of conversation.
  - Declare a day at work when people actually ____________.
  - Most importantly, __________________________.

Conclusion: ________________________.

Reading and Writing: An Integrated Perspective MySkillsLab®

Get ready to write about the reading by discussing the following.

1. How did the author capture your attention in the opening paragraphs?
2. How would you describe the author's attitude toward or opinion of employees who work with their headphones on?
3. What is the relationship between face-to-face conversations and developing patience?

THINKING VISUALLY

4. The photo shows people alone and in pairs using cell phones. What is the message that author is trying to convey through the photograph?

Thinking and Writing Critically

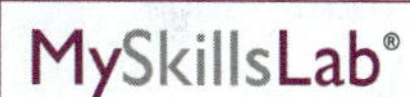

1. Write a sentence that summarizes the author's opinion of communicating through technology.
2. What is the author's purpose in providing the example of people walking on the sand dunes at Cape Cod?
3. What words would you use to describe the author's tone? Does this tone add or detract from the reading? (For an explanation of tone, see p. 256 in Chapter 8.)
4. What other technological devices could the author have used to illustrate her ideas?
5. Do you think the author presents a fair, objective view of the use of technology in communication, or does she express a biased, one-sided view? (For more about bias, see Chapter 13, p. 381.)

Writing Paragraphs MySkillsLab®

1. Write a paragraph summarizing the effects of technology on relationships.
2. Describe your own experiences with using technology to communicate. Have they been positive, negative, or both? How?
3. The author focuses primarily on the negative effects of technology on relationships. Write a paragraph in which you discuss the positive effects that technology has on relationships or the negative effects of technology on relationships.

Writing Essays MySkillsLab®

4. The author states that "the little devices that most of us carry around are so powerful that they change not only what we do, but also who we are." Write an essay in which you discuss how these little devices have changed who you are.
5. Cell phones have presented a challenge to college instructors who are trying to teach while competing with students' use of this device during class. Should cell phones be banned from college classrooms? Write an essay in which you take a stand either for or against this policy. Be sure to support your position with strong examples and details.
6. Cell phones, the Internet, and Facebook have been referred to by some people as time wasters. Add up the time you spend on your phone, the Internet, or your Facebook page in a typical day. Now write an essay exploring the things you could be doing by making different choices with your time. (For example, instead of surfing the Web for an hour, you could have spent that time studying for an upcoming test.)

SELF-TEST SUMMARY

To test yourself, cover the Answer column with a sheet of paper and answer each question in the left column. Evaluate each of your answers as you work by sliding the paper down and comparing your answer with what is printed in the Answer column.

QUESTION	ANSWER
■ GOAL 1 Recognize good writing What does good writing involve?	A good piece of writing ■ requires thinking ■ involves revision ■ expresses ideas clearly ■ is directed toward an audience ■ achieves a purpose ■ uses three basic building blocks: sentence, paragraph, and essay
■ GOAL 2 Compare the reading and writing processes What are the similarities in the two processes?	Both processes focus on ■ generating ideas ■ organizing ideas ■ the presentation of key ideas ■ clear communication/understanding of content ■ thinking critically about content
■ GOAL 3 Use the writing process What are the steps in the writing process?	The six steps are ■ generating ideas ■ organizing ideas ■ considering audience and purpose ■ writing a first draft ■ revising ■ proofreading
■ GOAL 4 Generate ideas What techniques can help you generate ideas?	The techniques are freewriting, brainstorming, branching, and questioning.
■ GOAL 5 Organize ideas How can you organize your ideas?	Look for relationships among ideas, and present ideas logically, building upon one another. Use idea maps to create a visual diagram of the relationships among your ideas.

QUESTION	ANSWER
■ GOAL 6 Consider your audience and purpose What two factors should you consider regardless of what you write?	You should consider the audience for whom you are writing; what is appropriate for one audience may not be appropriate for another. You should also consider your purpose for writing: your reasons for writing will affect the type of information you include and how you present it.
■ GOAL 7 Write a first draft When writing a first draft, what is your goal?	A first draft should express your ideas in sentence and paragraph form. Focus on ideas, not on grammar, spelling, and punctuation.
■ GOAL 8 Think critically about incorporating visuals into your writing What do you need to consider when incorporating visuals into your writing?	Determine the purpose of the visual, the message that you want the visual to convey, and the location of the visual within the text. As you source the visual, be sure to follow fair use requirements and cite the source.
■ GOAL 9 Revise and rewrite What does revision involve?	Revision involves rethinking your ideas and evaluating how effectively you have expressed them. Revise your draft by adding, deleting, changing, and reorganizing your ideas.
■ GOAL 10 Proofread for correctness What proofreading?	Proofreading is checking your paper for errors in sentence structure, grammar, spelling, punctuation, and capitalization.

MySkillsLab®

Visit **Chapter 2, "An Overview of the Writing Process (with Reading),"** in MySkillsLab to test your understanding of chapter goals.

VOCABULARY WORKSHOPS

Vocabulary is important for both readers and writers:

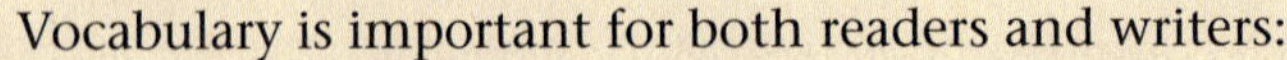

- Readers need a strong vocabulary to grasp what an author means.
- Writers need a strong vocabulary to express their ideas clearly and effectively.

The following set of workshops focuses on vocabulary building strategies. Each workshop offers a technique for increasing your speaking, reading, writing, and listening vocabularies:

- **Vocabulary Workshop 1:** Expanding Your Vocabulary
- **Vocabulary Workshop 2:** Using Context Clues
- **Vocabulary Workshop 3:** Using Word Parts

Each workshop explains a technique and gives you practice using it. Be sure to apply these techniques to everything you read for college, on the job, or for leisure or everyday reading. The more often you use these techniques, the faster your vocabulary will improve.

VOCABULARY WORKSHOP: EXPANDING YOUR VOCABULARY

1

How to Expand Your Vocabulary

Expanding your vocabulary requires motivation, a positive attitude, and skills. Of these, motivation is the most important. To improve your vocabulary, you must be willing to work at it, spending both time and effort to notice and learn new words and meanings.

Expanding your vocabulary is important because

- A strong vocabulary will contribute to both academic and career success.
- Broadening your vocabulary will improve the clarity of your thinking.
- Your reading and writing skills will improve as your vocabulary improves.
- Your vocabulary is a reflection of you, and a strong vocabulary creates a positive image.

This workshop focuses on the skills you need to build your vocabulary.

Reading Widely

One of the best ways to improve your vocabulary is by reading widely and diversely, sampling many different subjects and styles of writing. Through reading, you encounter new words and new uses for familiar words. You also see words used in contexts that you have not previously considered.

Using Words You Already Know

Most people think they have just one level of vocabulary and that this can be characterized as large or small, strong or weak. Actually, everyone has at least four levels of vocabulary, and each varies in strength.

1. Words you use in everyday speech or writing
   Examples: *laptop, leg, lag, lead, leave, lost*
2. Words you know but seldom or never use in your own speech or writing
   Examples: *lethal, legitimate, leverage, locomotion, luscious*
3. Words you've heard or seen before but cannot fully define
   Examples: *logistics, lament, lackadaisical, latent, latitude*
4. Words you've never heard or seen before
   Examples: *lanugo, lagniappe, laconic, lactone, lacustrine*

EXERCISE 1

Levels of Vocabulary

Directions: In the spaces provided below, list five words that fall under each of the four categories listed above. Words for categories 2 through 4 may be taken from the following list.

activate	credible	garbanzo	logic
alien	deletion	gastronome	manual
attentive	delicate	havoc	meditate
congruent	delve	heroic	osmosis
connive	demean	impartial	resistance
continuous	focus	impertinent	voluntary
contort	fraught	liberate	

***Category 1:* Everyday words**	***Category 2:* Known but seldom used words**	***Category 3:* Known words you cannot define well**	***Category 4:* Words never seen before**
__________	__________	__________	__________
__________	__________	__________	__________
__________	__________	__________	__________
__________	__________	__________	__________
__________	__________	__________	__________

To build your vocabulary, try to shift as many words as possible from a less familiar to a more familiar category. This task is not easy. You start by noticing words. Then you question, check, and remember their meanings. Finally, and most important, you use these new words often in your speech and writing.

Looking for Five-Dollar Words to Replace One-Dollar Words

Some words in your vocabulary are general and vague. Try to replace these one-dollar words with five-dollar words that convey your meaning more clearly. The word *good* is an example of a much-overused word that has a general, unclear meaning:

> The movie was so good, it was worth the high admission price.

Try substituting the following words for *good* in the preceding sentence: *exciting, moving, thrilling, scary, inspiring.* Each of these gives more information than the word *good.* Focus on using words that clearly and precisely convey your intended meaning.

Actively Practicing Vocabulary

The *bad news* about vocabulary is that if you don't use it, you will lose it. The *good news* is that you can prevent this from happening.

Here are some suggestions for learning and retaining words. Depending on your learning style, some of the suggestions will work better than others.

- **Learn a word each day.** Find a word a day from a newspaper, magazine, book, TV or radio program and find out its meaning and/or sign up for a word a day from Dictionary.com or Merriam-Webster.com.
- **Write the word immediately, so you remember it.** In fact, write it several times, once in the margin of the text, then again on an index card or in your vocabulary log. Write it again as you test yourself.
- **Write a sentence using the word.** Make the sentence personal: the more meaningful the sentence is, the more likely you are to remember the word.
- **Try to visualize a situation involving the word.** For instance, for the word *restore* (to bring back to its original condition), visualize an antique car restored to its original condition.
- **Draw a picture or diagram that involves the word.** For example, for the word *squander* (to waste), draw a picture of yourself squandering money by throwing dollar bills out of an open car window.
- **Talk about the word.** With a classmate, try to hold a conversation in which each of you uses at least ten new words you have learned. Your conversation may become comical, but you will get practice using new words.
- **Play word games.** Various Web sites offer word games that heighten your word awareness and introduce you to new words. The Merriam-Webster site (http://www.m-w.com) offers a word game that changes daily, and at Freerice.com, every vocabulary quiz item you answer correctly means a donation of 20 grains of rice to the United Nations World Food Program.
- **Try to use the word in your own academic speech or writing as soon as you have learned it.**

- **Give yourself vocabulary tests or, working with a friend, make up tests for each other.**
- **Use the "Strengthening Your Vocabulary"** exercises that accompany each professional reading in this book.

Using Newly Learned Words

Directions: Choose five new words you have recently encountered in your textbooks or class lectures. Use several of the preceding suggestions to learn each of the words.

Develop a System for Learning Unfamiliar Words

You have to make a deliberate effort to remember and use new words, or they will fade from your memory.

The Vocabulary Card System

One of the most practical and easy-to-use systems for expanding your vocabulary is the index card system. It works like this:

1. **Whenever you hear or read a new word that you intend to learn, jot it down in the margin of your notes or mark it in some way.**
2. **Write each new word on the front of an index card, look up the meaning (or meanings) of the word, and write it on the back.** You might also record the word's pronunciation or a sample sentence in which the word is used (see Figure 1).
3. **Whenever you have a few spare minutes, go through your pack of index cards, checking to see if you can remember the meaning of each word.** If you were unable to recall the meaning or if you confused it with another word, retest yourself. Shuffle the cards after each use.

FIGURE 1 SAMPLE VOCABULARY CARDS

4. **After you have gone through your pack of cards several times, separate the words you know from those that you have not learned and concentrate on the words still to be learned.** Shuffle the cards to change their order.
5. **Once you have mastered the entire pack of cards, periodically review them to refresh your memory.**

Some students prefer to use electronic flash cards. A variety of free online services and apps enable you to create flash cards and share them with your classmates. These include Flash Card Machine and StudyBlue.

The Electronic Vocabulary Log

Using a word processing program, create an electronic log for each of your courses. Regularly review both textbook chapters and lecture notes and enter specialized and technical terms that you need to learn, using the three-column format shown in Figure 2. You might subdivide or code your file by textbook chapter so that you can review easily when exams or quizzes on particular chapters are announced. You can also alphabetize the words to create a glossary that will serve as a reference. Keep a print copy handy as you read new chapters and review lecture notes. When studying the words, try scrambling them to avoid learning them in a fixed order.

FIGURE 2 SAMPLE VOCABULARY LOG FOR A PSYCHOLOGY COURSE

Word	Meaning	Page
intraspecific aggression	attack by one animal upon another member of its species	310
orbitofrontal cortex	region of the brain that aids in recognition of situations that produce emotional responses	312
modulation	an attempt to minimize or exaggerate the expression of emotion	317
simulation	an attempt to display an emotion that one does not really feel	319

Using Vocabulary Cards and an Electronic Log

Directions: Select two sets of notes from any course you are taking. Prepare a set of vocabulary cards for the new terms introduced in one set of notes, and create an electronic log for the other set. Review and study both. Which method works best for you?

Learning Specialized Vocabulary

One of the first tasks you will face in a new college course is to learn its specialized language. This is particularly true of introductory courses in which a new discipline or field of study is explained.

Specialized Terminology in Class Lectures

As a part of your note-taking system, develop a consistent way of separating new terms and definitions from other facts and ideas. You might circle or draw a box around each new term; or, as you edit your notes, underline each new term in red; or mark "def." in the margin each time a definition is included. The mark or symbol you use is a matter of preference. Use the suggestions above to organize, learn, and remember the meanings of new terms.

Specialized Terminology in Textbooks

Textbook authors use various means to emphasize new terminology; these include italics, boldfaced type, colored print, marginal definitions, and a new-terms list or vocabulary list at the beginning or end of each chapter.

While you are reading and highlighting important facts and ideas, you should also mark new terminology. Be sure to mark definitions and to separate them from other chapter content.

If you encounter a new term that is not defined or for which the definition is unclear, check the glossary at the back of the book or a subject dictionary for its meaning. Make a note of the meaning in the margin of the page. Use the glossary, or if there is not one, your electronic log or vocabulary cards to test yourself.

Other Unfamiliar Words and Phrases

In addition to adding words to your vocabulary, you can also learn about creative and interesting ways to use language. You may come across uncommon uses for words you already know. As you read, look for the following:

1. **Euphemisms** These are words that hide or disguise the importance, reality, or seriousness of something. ("Ladies' room" is a euphemism for toilet; "victim of friendly fire" is a euphemism for a soldier shot by his or her own comrades.)
2. **Connotative meanings** Words have shades of meaning called connotations. These are the emotional associations that accompany words

for some readers. The word *mother* has many connotative meanings. For some it means a warm, loving caregiver. For others it may suggest a strict disciplinarian.

3. **Jargon** Jargon is specialized terminology used in a particular field of study. Football has its own jargon: *linebackers*, *kickoff*, *touchdown*, and so on. Academic disciplines also have their own language (psychology: *drive*, *motivation*, *stressor*).
4. **Foreign words and phrases** Many Latin, French, and Spanish words have entered our language and are used as if they are part of our language. Here are a few examples:

aficionado	(Spanish)—someone enthusiastic and knowledgeable about something
et cetera	(Latin)—and so forth
faux pas	(French)—embarrassing social blunder
guerrilla	(Spanish)—freedom fighter
status quo	(Latin)—the way things are, an existing state of affairs
tête-à-tête	(French)—a private conversation between two people

5. **Figurative language** Figurative language consists of words and phrases that make sense creatively or imaginatively but not literally. The expression "The exam was a piece of cake" means, creatively, that the exam was easy, as eating cake is easy. But the exam did not literally resemble a cake. Figurative language is a powerful tool that allows writers to create images or paint pictures in the reader's mind.
6. **Neologisms** Neologisms are new words that have recently entered our language. As technology and society change, new words are created. Here are a few examples: podcast (digital episode of a radio, audio, or video series), app (software designed for a specific purpose), and lifecasting (continual broadcasting of events in a person's life via the Internet).

VOCABULARY WORKSHOP: USING CONTEXT CLUES

2

One of the best and fastest ways to figure out meanings of words you don't know is to use the context around the unfamiliar word. **Context** refers to other words and phrases around a given word, either in the same sentence, or in surrounding sentences. Often you can use context to figure out a word you do not know. Try it in the following sentence:

> **Phobias,** such as a fear of heights, water, or confined spaces, are difficult to overcome.

From the clues in the rest of the sentence, you can figure out that *phobias* are fears of specific objects or situations. Such clues are called **context clues.** There are five types of context clues that can help you figure out a word you do not know: *definition*, *synonym*, *example*, *contrast*, and *inference*. These are summarized in the following box:

Five Useful Types of Context Clues

Type of Context Clue	How It Works	Examples
Definition	Writers often define a word after using it. Words and phrases such as *means, refers to*, and *can be defined as* provide an obvious clue that the word's meaning is to follow. Sometimes writers use dashes, parentheses, or commas to separate a definition from the rest of the sentence.	*Corona* refers to the outermost part of the sun's atmosphere. Broad flat noodles that are served covered with sauce or butter are called fettuccine. The judge's candor—his sharp, open frankness—shocked the jury. Audition, the process of hearing, begins when a sound wave reaches the ear.
Synonym	Rather than formally define a word, some writers include a word or brief phrase that is close in meaning to a word you may not know.	The main character in the movie was an amalgam, or combination, of several real people the author met during the war.
Example	Writers often include examples to help explain a word. From the examples, you can often figure out what the unknown word means.	Toxic materials, such as arsenic, asbestos, pesticides, and lead, can cause bodily damage. (You can figure out that *toxic* means "poisonous.") Many pharmaceuticals, including morphine and penicillin, are not readily available in some countries. (You can figure out that *pharmaceuticals* are drugs.)
Contrast	Sometimes a writer gives a word that is opposite in meaning to a word you don't know. From the opposite meaning, you can figure out the unknown word's meaning. (Hint: watch for words such as *but, however, though, whereas*.)	Uncle Sal was quite portly, but his wife was very thin. (The opposite of *thin* is *fat*, so you know that *portly* means "fat.") The professor advocates the testing of cosmetics on animals, but many of her students oppose it. (The opposite of *oppose* is *favor*, so you know that *advocates* means "favors.")
Inference	Often your own logic or reasoning skills can lead you to the meaning of an unknown word.	Bob is quite versatile: he is a good student, a top athlete, an excellent auto mechanic, and a gourmet cook. (Because Bob excels at many activities, you can reason that *versatile* means "capable of doing many things.") On hot, humid afternoons, I often feel languid. (From your experience you may know that you feel drowsy or sluggish on hot afternoons, so you can figure out that *languid* means "lacking energy.")

Context clues do not always appear in the same sentence as the unknown word. They may appear anywhere in the passage, or in an earlier or later sentence. So if you cannot find a clue immediately, look before and after the word. Here is an example:

> Betsy took a *break* from teaching in order to serve in the Peace Corps. Despite the **hiatus**, Betsy's school was delighted to rehire her when she returned.

Notice that the clue for the word *hiatus*, *break*, appears in the sentence before the one containing the word you want to define.

EXERCISE 4 Using Definition and Synonym Clues

Directions: Write a brief definition of each boldfaced word using the definition or synonym clues in each sentence.

1. After taking a course in **genealogy**, Diego was able to create a record of his family's history dating back to the eighteenth century. ________________

2. Louie's **dossier** is a record of his credentials, including college transcripts and letters of recommendation. ________________

3. There was a **consensus**—or unified opinion—among the students that the exam was difficult. ________________

4. After each course heading there was a **synopsis**, or summary, of the content and requirements for the course. ________________

5. When preparing job application letters, Serena develops one standard letter or **prototype**. Then she changes that letter to fit the specific jobs for which she is applying. ________________

EXERCISE 5 Using Example Clues

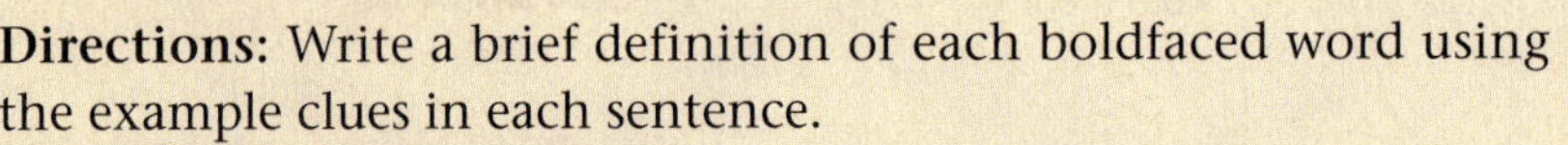

Directions: Write a brief definition of each boldfaced word using the example clues in each sentence.

1. **Histrionics**, such as wild laughter or excessive body movements, are usually inappropriate in business settings. ________________
____

2. Jerry's child was **reticent** in every respect; she would not speak, refused to answer questions, and avoided looking at anyone. ________________

3. Most **condiments**, such as pepper, mustard, and catsup, are used to improve the flavor of foods. ________________

4. Dogs, cats, parakeets, and other **sociable** pets can provide senior citizens with companionship. ________________

5. Paul's grandmother is a **sagacious** businesswoman; once she turned a small ice cream shop into a popular restaurant and sold it for a huge profit. ________________

EXERCISE 6 Using Contrast Clues

Directions: Write a brief definition of each boldfaced word using the contrast clues in each sentence.

1. Freshmen are often **naive** about college at first, but by their second semester they are usually quite sophisticated in the ways of their new school. ________________

2. Although most members of the class agreed with the instructor's evaluation of the film, several strongly **objected**. ________________

3. L'Tanya hid shyly behind her mother when she met new people, yet her brother Matthew was very **gregarious**. ______________________________

4. The child remained **demure** while the teacher scolded, but became loud and assertive afterward. ______________________________

5. Some city dwellers are **affluent**; others live in or near poverty. ___________

EXERCISE 7

Using Logic and Reasoning to Determine Meaning

Directions: Choose the correct definition of each boldfaced word in the following sentences using logic and your own reasoning skills.

______ 1. To **compel** Lin to hand over her wallet, the mugger said he had a gun.

a. discourage c. force
b. entice d. imagine

______ 2. Student journalists are taught how to be **concise** when writing in a limited space.

a. peaceful c. proper
b. clear and brief d. wordy

______ 3. There should be more **drastic** penalties to stop people from littering.

a. extreme c. dirty
b. suitable d. dangerous

______ 4. To **fortify** his diet while weightlifting, Jose took 12 vitamins a day.

a. suggest c. avoid
b. strengthen d. approve of

______ 5. On our wedding anniversary, my husband and I **reminisced** about how we first met.

a. sang c. argued
b. forgot d. remembered

EXERCISE 8

Using Context Clues in Passages

Directions: Working with a classmate, use context clues to determine the meaning of each boldfaced word in the following passages. Write a synonym or brief definition for each. Use a dictionary, if necessary.

1. If you have ever tried to perform heavy manual labor on a hot summer day, you may have become weak and dizzy as a result. If your **exertions** were severe, you may have even collapsed and lost **consciousness** momentarily. If this has happened to you, then you have experienced *heat exhaustion*. Heat exhaustion is a **consequence** of the body's effort to regulate its temperature—in particular, its efforts to get rid of **excess** heat. When the body must get rid of a large quantity of heat, **massive** quantities of sweat can be produced, leading to a significant **reduction** in blood volume. In addition, blood flow to the skin increases markedly, which **diverts** blood from other areas of the body. Together, these changes produce a reduction in blood pressure, which reduces blood flow to the brain and **precipitates** the symptoms just described.

A far more serious condition is *heat stroke*, in which the body's temperature rises out of control due to failure of the **thermoregulatory** system. The skin of individuals experiencing heat stroke has a flushed appearance but will also be dry, in contrast to the **profuse** sweating of heat exhaustion. If someone is experiencing heat stroke, immediate medical attention is of the utmost importance.

—adapted from Germann and Stanfield, *Principles of Human Physiology*, p. 9

1. exertions ______________________
2. consciousness ______________________ ______________________
3. consequence ______________________
4. excess ______________________
5. massive ______________________
6. reduction ______________________
7. diverts ______________________
8. precipitates ______________________
9. thermoregulatory ______________________ ______________________
10. profuse ______________________

2. The homeless are among the extremely poor. They are by definition people who sleep in streets, parks, shelters, and places not intended as **dwellings**, such as bus stations, lobbies, or **abandoned** buildings. Homelessness is not new. There have always been homeless people in the United States. But the homeless today differ in some ways from their **counterparts** of the 1950s and 1960s. More than 30 years ago, most of the homeless were old men, only a **handful** were women, and **virtually** no families were homeless. Today the homeless are younger, and include more women and families with young children. Today's homeless also are more **visible** to the general public because they are much more likely to sleep on the streets or in other public places in great numbers. They also suffer greater **deprivation**. Although in the past homeless men on Skid Row were **undoubtedly** poor, their average income from casual and **intermittent** work was three to four times more than what the current homeless receive. In addition, many of the older homeless had small but **stable** pensions, which today's homeless do not have.

—Thio, *Sociology*, p. 235

1. dwellings ______________________
2. abandoned ______________________
3. counterparts ______________________
4. handful ______________________
5. virtually ______________________
6. visible ______________________
7. deprivation ______________________
8. undoubtedly ______________________
9. intermittent ______________________
10. stable ______________________

3. Some **visionaries** say that we can **transform** nursing homes into warm, inviting places. They started with a clean piece of paper and asked how we could redesign nursing homes so they **enhance** or maintain people's quality of life. The model they came up with doesn't look or even feel like a nursing home. In Green Houses, as they are called, elderly people live in a homelike setting. Instead of a **sterile** hallway lined with rooms, 10 to 12 residents live in a carpeted ranch-style house. They receive medical care suited to their personal needs, share meals at a **communal** dining table, and, if they want to, they can cook together in an open kitchen. They can even play **virtual** sports on plasma televisions. This homelike setting **fosters** a sense of community among residents and staff.

—adapted from Henslin, *Sociology: A Down-To-Earth Approach*, p. 386

1. visionaries ____________________
   ____
2. transform ____________________
3. enhance ____________________
4. sterile ____________________
5. communal ____________________
6. virtual ____________________
7. fosters ____________________

4. Marketers and consumers **coexist** in a complicated, two-way relationship. It's often hard to tell where marketing efforts leave off and "the real world" begins. One result of these **blurred** boundaries is that we are no longer sure (and perhaps we don't care) where the line separating this **fabricated** world from reality begins and ends. Sometimes, we **gleefully** join in the illusion. A story line in a Wonder Woman comic book featured the usual out-of-this-world **exploits** of a **vivacious** superhero. But it also included the real-world proposal of the owner of a chain of comic book stores, who persuaded DC Comics to let him **woo** his beloved in the issue.

—Solomon, *Consumer Behavior*, p. 19

1. coexist ____________________
2. blurred ____________________
3. fabricated ____________________
4. gleefully ____________________
5. exploits ____________________
6. vivacious ____________________
7. woo ____________________

5. Rising tuition; roommates who bug you; social life drama; too much noise; no privacy; long lines at the bookstore; pressure to get good grades; never enough money; worries about the economy, terrorism, and natural disaster all add up to: STRESS! You can't run from it, you can't hide from it, and it can affect you in **insidious** ways that you aren't even aware of. When we try to sleep, it **encroaches** on our **psyche** through outside noise or internal worries over all the things that need to be done. While we work at the computer, stress may interfere in the form of noise from next door, strain on our eyes, and **tension** in our back. Even when we are out socializing with friends, we feel guilty, because there is just not enough time to do what needs to be accomplished. The **precise** toll that stress exacts from us over a lifetime is unknown, but increasingly, stress is recognized as a major threat to our health.

—Donatelle, *Health: The Basics*, p. 57

1. insidious ____________________
   ____
2. encroaches ____________________
3. psyche ____________________
4. tension ____________________
5. precise ____________________

Working with Context Clues

Directions: Bring to class a brief textbook excerpt, editorial, or magazine article that contains difficult vocabulary. Working with another student, each of you locate and underline at least three words in the passage that your partner can define by using context clues. Then work together to reason out each word, checking a dictionary to verify meanings.

A Nonsense Words Activity

Directions: Each student should write five sentences, each containing a nonsense word whose meaning is suggested by the context of the sentence. Here is an example:

> Before I went out to pick up a pizza, I put on my purplut. I buttoned up my purplut and went outside, glad that it was filled with down.
>
> (Can you figure out the meaning of a purplut?)

Form groups of three to five students. Students should take turns reading aloud their sentences as group members guess the meanings of the nonsense words.

VOCABULARY WORKSHOP: USING WORD PARTS

3

Learning word parts—prefixes, roots, and suffixes—is a much more efficient means of building vocabulary than learning single words.

A single prefix can unlock the meaning of 50 or more words. For example, once you learn that the prefix *inter-* means "between," you can define many new words. Here are a few examples:

intercede	interrupt	interstellar
interconnect	interscholastic	intertribal
interracial	intersperse	intervene
interrelate		

Similarly, knowledge of the single root *spec*, which means "to look or see," unlocks numerous word meanings such as the following:

inspect	perspective	spectator
inspector	retrospect	speculate
introspection	retrospection	speculation
introspective		

Learning word parts, then, produces a multiplier effect. The following sections list common prefixes, roots, and suffixes and provide practice in learning them. Before you begin to learn specific word parts, study the following guidelines:

1. **In most cases, a word is built on at least one root.**
2. **Words can have more than one prefix, root, or suffix.**
   a. Words can be made up of two or more roots (*geo-logy*).
   b. Some words have two prefixes (*in-sub-ordination*).
   c. Some words have two suffixes (*beauti-ful-ly*).
3. **Words do not always have both a prefix and a suffix.**
   a. Some words have neither a prefix nor a suffix (*read*).
   b. Others have a suffix but no prefix (*read-ing*).
   c. Others have a prefix but no suffix (*pre-read*).
4. **Roots may change in spelling as they are combined with suffixes (*arid*, *arable*).**
5. **Sometimes, you may identify a group of letters as a prefix or root but find that it does not carry the meaning of the prefix or root.** For example, the letters *m-i-s* in the word *missile* are part of the root and are not the prefix *mis-*, which means "wrong or bad."

Prefixes

Prefixes appear at the beginning of many English words and alter the meaning of the root to which they are connected. Table 1 (p. 82) groups 36 common prefixes according to meaning.

Learning word parts is particularly useful for science courses. Many scientific words are built from a common core of prefixes, roots, and suffixes.

EXERCISE 11

Using Prefixes

Directions: Using the list of common prefixes in Table 1, write the meaning of each of the following boldfaced words. If you are unfamiliar with the root, check its meaning in a dictionary.

1. a **multinational** corporation ______________________
2. **antisocial** behavior ______________________
3. **inefficient** study habits ______________________
4. **postglacial** period ______________________
5. **unspecialized** training ______________________
6. housing **subdivision** ______________________
7. **redefine** one's goals ______________________
8. a **semifinalist** ______________________
9. **retroactive** policies ______________________
10. a sudden **transformation** ______________________

TABLE 1 COMMON PREFIXES

Prefix	Meaning	Example
Amount or Number		
bi-	two	bimonthly
centi-	hundred	centigrade
deci-	ten	decimal
equi-	equal	equidistant
micro-	small	microscope
milli-	thousand	milligram
mono-	one	monocle
multi-	many	multipurpose
poly-	many	polygon
semi-	half	semicircle
tri-	three	triangle
uni-	one	unicycle
Negative		
a-	not	asymmetrical
anti-	against	antiwar
contra-	against, opposite	contradict
dis-	apart, away, not	disagree
in-/il-/ir-/im-	not	illogical
mis-	wrongly	misunderstood
non-	not	nonfiction
pseudo-	false	pseudoscientific
un-	not	unpopular
Direction, Location, or Placement		
circum-	around	circumference
com-/col-/con-	with, together	compile
de-	away, from	depart
ex-/extra-	from, out of, former	ex-wife
hyper-	over, excessive	hyperactive
inter-	between	interpersonal
intro-/intra-	within, into, in	introduction
post-	after	posttest
pre-	before	premarital
re-	back, again	review
retro-	backward	retrospect
sub-	under, below	submarine
super-	above, extra	supercharge
tele-	far	telescope
trans-	across, over	transcontinental

Roots

Roots carry the basic or core meaning of a word. Hundreds of root words are used to build words in the English language. Table 2 lists 30 of the most common and most useful roots.

TABLE 2 COMMON ROOTS

Root	Meaning	Example
aster/astro	star	astronaut
aud/audit	hear	audible
bio	life	biology
cap	take, seize	captive
chron(o)	time	chronology
corp	body	corpse
cred	believe	incredible
dict/dic	tell, say	predict
duc/duct	lead	introduce
fact/fac	make, do	factory
geo	earth	geophysics
graph	write	telegraph
log/logo/logy	study, thought	psychology
mit/miss	send	dismiss
mort/mor	die, death	immortal
path	feeling	sympathy
phono	sound, voice	telephone
photo	light	photosensitive
port	carry	transport
sen/sent	feel	insensitive
scop	see	microscope
scrib/script	write	inscription
spec/spic/spect	look, see	retrospect
tend/tent/tens	stretch or strain	tension
terr/terre	land, earth	territory
theo	god	theology
ven/vent	come	convention
vert/vers	turn	invert
vis/vid	see	invisible
voc	call	vocation

EXERCISE 12

Using Roots

Directions: Use the list of common roots in Table 2 to determine the meanings of the following boldfaced words. Write a brief definition or synonym for each, checking a dictionary if necessary.

1. **bioethical** issues ______________________________
2. **terrestrial** life ______________________________
3. to **desensitize** ______________________________
4. to study **astronomy** ______________________________
5. **synchronize** your watches ______________________________
6. **visualize** the problem ______________________________
7. a religious **missionary** ______________________________
8. **biographical** data ______________________________
9. a **geology** course ______________________________
10. **pathological** behavior ______________________________

Suffixes

Suffixes are word endings that often change the part of speech of a word. For example, adding the suffix *-y* to the noun *cloud* produces the adjective *cloudy*, meaning overcast. Accompanying the change in part of speech is a shift in meaning. Often, several different words can be formed from a single root word with the addition of different suffixes, for example,

Root: class (number of persons or things that share characteristics)

root + suffix = class-ify, class-ification, class-ic

The students were asked to **classify** the rock specimens based on how they were formed. (verb)

In biology, **classification** means systematically grouping organisms into categories. (noun)

The Beatles album *Sergeant Pepper's Lonely Heart's Club Band* is considered a rock **classic**. (adjective)

If you know the meanings of root words and the ways in which different suffixes affect those meanings, you will be able to work out the meanings of unfamiliar words. (A list of common suffixes and their meanings appears in Table 3.) When you find a word you do not know, look for the root. Then, using the sentence the word appears in, its context, work out how the word's meaning changes with the suffix added.

TABLE 3 COMMON SUFFIXES

Suffix	Root	Example	Meaning
State, Condition, or Quality			
-able	touch (v)	touchable (adj)	can be touched
-ance	assist (v)	assistance (n)	act of helping
-ation	confront (v)	confrontation (n)	hostile interaction
-ence	refer (v)	reference (n)	mention of something
-ible	collect (v)	collectible (adj)	able to be collected
-ion	discuss (v)	discussion (n)	informal debate
-ity	superior (adj)	superiority (n)	condition of being superior
-ive	permit (v)	permissive (adj)	allows behavior others would not
-ment	amaze (v)	amazement (n)	total astonishment
-ness	kind (adj)	kindness (n)	being kind
-ous	prestige (n)	prestigious (adj)	esteemed or honored
-ty	loyal (adj)	loyalty (n)	being faithful to commitments
-y	cream (n)	creamy (adj)	smooth and soft
"One Who"			
-ee	pay (v)	payee (n)	one to whom money is payable
-eer	engine (n)	engineer (n)	person skilled in working with machines
-er	teach (v)	teacher (n)	person who instructs
-ist	active (adj)	activist (n)	strong advocate for a cause
-or	advise (v)	advisor (n)	person who gives advice
Pertaining to or Referring to			
-al	autumn (n)	autumnal (adj)	autumn-like
-hood	brother (n)	brotherhood (n)	being like a brother(s)
-ic	hero (n)	heroic (adj)	showing great courage
-ship	friend (n)	friendship (n)	state of being a friend
-ward	home (n)	homeward (adv)	toward home

EXERCISE 13 Using Suffixes

Directions: For each of the words listed, add a suffix so that the word will complete the sentence. Write the new word in the space provided.

1. **behavior**

   __________ therapy attempts to change habits and illnesses by altering people's responses to stimuli.

2. **atom**

   Uranium, when bombarded with neutrons, explodes and produces a heat reaction known as ________ energy.

3. **advertise**

   One important purpose of an ______________ is to inform potential customers about the service or product and familiarize the public with the brand name.

4. **uniform**

   The __________ of a law requires that it must be applied to all relevant groups without bias.

5. **evolution**

   Darwin's theory of natural selection tied the survival of a species to its ____________ fitness—its ability to survive and reproduce.

6. **compete**

   When food sources are not large enough to support all the organisms in a habitat, environmental ____________ occurs.

7. **religion**

   During the Age of Reason in American history, _________ revivals swept the nation.

8. **perform**

   Perhaps an administrator's most important duty is establishing conditions conducive to high employee motivation, which results in better job ____________.

9. **effective**

   A critical factor in evaluating a piece of literature or art is its ____________—how strongly and clearly the artist's message has been conveyed to the audience.

10. **theory**

    __________ have spent decades studying the theory of relativity.

EXERCISE 14

Using Word Parts

Directions: Read each of the following paragraphs and determine the meaning of each boldfaced word. Write a brief definition for each.

1. The values and norms of most **subcultures** blend in with mainstream society. In some cases, however, some of the group's values and norms place it at odds with the dominant culture. **Sociologists** use the term **counterculture** to refer to such groups. To better see this distinction, consider motorcycle enthusiasts and motorcycle gangs. Motorcycle **enthusiasts**—who emphasize personal freedom and speed and **affirm** cultural values of success through work or education—are members of a subculture. In contrast, the Hell's Angels, Pagans, and Bandidos not only stress freedom and speed but also value dirtiness and contempt toward women, work, and education. This makes them a counterculture. Countercultures do not have to be negative, however. Back in the 1800s, the Mormons were a counterculture that challenged the dominant culture's core value of **monogamy**.

—Henslin, *Sociology: A Down-to-Earth Approach*, p. 52

1. subcultures ______________________________
2. sociologists ______________________________
3. counterculture ______________________________
4. enthusiasts ______________________________
5. affirm ______________________________
6. monogamy ______________________________

2. Our **perception** of the richness or quality of the material in clothing, bedding, or upholstery is linked to its "feel," whether rough or smooth, flexible or **inflexible**. We **equate** a smooth fabric, such as silk, with luxury, whereas we consider denim to be practical and **durable**. Fabrics composed of **scarce** materials or that require a high degree of processing to achieve their smoothness or fineness tend to be more expensive and thus we assume they are of a higher class.

—adapted from Solomon, *Consumer Behavior*, pp. 62–63

1. perception ______________________________
2. inflexible ______________________________
3. equate ______________________________
4. durable ______________________________
5. scarce ______________________________

3. The college years mark a critical **transition** period for young adults as they move away from families and establish themselves as **independent** adults. The transition to independence will be easier for those who have successfully accomplished earlier developmental tasks, such as learning how to solve problems, make and evaluate decisions, define and **adhere** to personal values, and establish both casual and **intimate** relationships. People who have not fulfilled these earlier tasks may find their lives interrupted by **recurrent** "crises" left over from earlier stages. For example, if they did not learn to trust others in childhood, they may have difficulty establishing intimate relationships as adults.

—Donatelle, *Health: The Basics*, p. 34

1. transition ______________________________
2. independent ______________________________
3. adhere ______________________________
4. intimate ______________________________
5. recurrent ______________________________

4. In the U.S. legal system, the family has traditionally been defined as a unit consisting of a **heterosexual** married couple and their child or children. Many **scholars** have a more flexible definition of "family" taking into account the **extended** family of grandparents, aunts and uncles, and cousins, and sometimes even people who are not related by blood at all. Class, race, and **ethnicity** are important factors to consider as we define what makes a family.

—adapted from Kunz, *THINK Marriages and Families*, pp. 278–279

1. heterosexual ______________________________
2. scholars ______________________________
3. extended ______________________________
4. ethnicity ______________________________

3 Topics, Main Ideas, and Topic Sentences

LEARNING GOALS

Learn how to . . .

- GOAL 1
  Structure a paragraph
- GOAL 2
  Identify and select topics
- GOAL 3
  Read and write topic sentences
- GOAL 4
  Think critically about topic sentences

THINK About It!

Look at the photograph on this page. What do you see? Create a story or scenario in your mind. Then write a sentence describing what you think has happened.

The sentence you have written states the main point the photograph conveys. It expresses your view of what is happening. When others read the sentence you wrote, they understand your interpretation of the situation. They may agree or disagree with your view, but they will understand it. Both readers and writers, then, communicate and exchange ideas through the effective use of sentences that state a main point, which are called topic sentences.

Reading and Writing Connections

EVERYDAY CONNECTIONS

- **Writing** You are sending an e-mail to the technical support personnel of a computer manufacturer asking for help with a problem. Your **topic sentence** should directly state the problem.
- **Reading** As a support technician, you need to read an e-mail complaint or question and identify the customer's problem before you can provide assistance.

ACADEMIC CONNECTIONS

- **Reading** You are reading a section of a sociology text titled "Communities: Goals and Structures." You try to find a paragraph that defines what a community is.
- **Writing** When answering an essay exam question for the same class, you are asked to briefly define and provide examples of a community. Your **topic sentence** should give a brief definition of *community*.

WORKPLACE CONNECTIONS

- **Writing** You are the manager of a chain restaurant and must write an incident report for corporate headquarters about a theft that occurred on the premises. Your **topic sentence** should state the time, location, date, and item stolen.
- **Reading** As a director at corporate headquarters, you begin reading the report by looking for a sentence in the first paragraph that concisely states what happened.

What Is a Paragraph?

■ GOAL 1
Structure a paragraph

A **paragraph** is a group of related sentences that develop a main thought, or idea, about a single topic. The structure of a paragraph is not complex. There are usually three basic elements: (1) a topic, (2) a topic sentence, and (3) supporting details. The **topic sentence** states the main, or controlling, idea. The sentences that explain this main point are called **supporting details**. These details may be facts, reasons, or examples that provide further information about the topic sentence.

As a writer, these paragraph elements provide you with an easy-to-follow structure for expressing your ideas clearly and effectively. As a reader, these same elements help you know what to look for and ensure that you will understand and remember what you read. This chapter will show you how to identify topics and topic sentences as you read, how to select topics to write about, and how to write clear and concise topic sentences. Chapters 4–6 will show you how to recognize key details as you read and how to provide and organize details as you write.

EXAMINING PROFESSIONAL WRITING

The author of the following article has written several books on the link between diet and health. In the article, he examines a new partnership between a famous fried chicken restaurant chain and a breast cancer advocacy group. This article will be used in this chapter as a model of professional writing and to illustrate the reading techniques discussed.

Thinking Before Reading

Before you read do the following:

1. Preview the reading, using the steps discussed in Chapter 1, page 4.
2. Connect the reading to your own experience by answering the following questions:
   a. How often do you eat fast food? Are you concerned about the effects of fast food on your health?
   b. What do you already know about Susan G. Komen for the Cure?
3. Mark and annotate as you read.

Greed, Cancer, and Pink KFC Buckets

John Robbins

grassroots
involving ordinary people at a local or community level

1 We live in a world of profound contradictions. Some things are just unbelievably strange. At times I feel like I've found a way to adapt to the weirdness of the world, and then along comes something that just boggles my mind. It is ironic that the largest **grassroots** breast cancer advocacy group in the world, a group called "Susan G. Komen for the Cure," has now partnered with the fast food chain KFC, known for its high-fat foods and questionable treatment of its chickens, in a national "Buckets for the Cure" campaign. The program began last month and runs through the end of May.

2 KFC is taking every chance it can manufacture to trumpet the fact that it will donate 50 cents to Komen for every pink bucket of chicken sold. For its part, Komen is announcing on its website that "KFC and Susan G. Komen for the Cure are teaming up . . . to . . . spread educational messaging via a major national campaign which will reach thousands of communities served by nearly 5,000 KFC restaurants."

3 Educational messaging, indeed. How often do you think this "messaging" provides information about the critical importance a healthy diet plays in maintaining a healthy weight and preventing cancer? How often do you think it refers in any way to the many studies that, according to the National Cancer Institute's website, "have shown that an increased risk of developing colorectal, pancreatic, and breast cancer is associated with high intakes of well-done, fried or barbecued meats"? If you guessed zero, you're right.

4 Meanwhile, the American Institute for Cancer Research reports that 60 to 70 percent of all cancers can be prevented with lifestyle changes. Their number one dietary recommendation is to: "Choose predominantly plant-based diets rich in a variety of vegetables and fruits, legumes and minimally processed starchy staple foods." Does that sound like pink buckets of fried chicken?

5 Pardon me for being cynical, but I have to ask, if Komen is going to partner with KFC, why not take it a step further and partner with a cigarette company? They could sell pink packages of cigarettes, donating a few cents from each pack while claiming "each pack you smoke brings us closer to the day cancer is vanquished forever."

6 Whose brilliant idea was it that buying fried chicken by the bucket is an effective way to fight breast cancer? One breast cancer advocacy group, Breast Cancer Action, thinks the Komen/KFC campaign is so **egregious** that they call it "**pinkwashing**," another sad example of commercialism draped in pink ribbons. "Make no mistake," they say, "every pink bucket purchase will do more to benefit KFC's bottom line than it will to cure breast cancer."

egregious
outrageously bad

pinkwashing
using support for breast cancer research to sell products, especially products that can be linked with cancer

7 One thing is hard to dispute. In partnering with KFC, Susan G. Komen for the Cure has shown itself to be numbingly oblivious to the role of diet in cancer prevention. Of course it's not hard to understand KFC's motives. They want to look good. But recent publicity the company has been getting hasn't been helping. For one thing, the company keeps taking hits for the unhealthiness of its food. Just last month, when KFC came out with its new Double Down sandwiches, the products were derided by just about every public health organization for their staggering levels of salt, calories and artery-clogging fat.

8 Then there's the squeamish matter of the treatment of the birds who end up in KFC's buckets, pink or otherwise. People for the Ethical Treatment of Animals (PETA) has an entire website devoted to what it calls Kentucky Fried Cruelty, but you don't have to be an animal activist to be horrified by how the company treats chickens, if you lift the veil of the company's PR and see what actually takes place.

9 When PETA sent investigators with hidden cameras into a KFC "Supplier of the Year" slaughterhouse in Moorefield, West Virginia, what they found was enough to make KFC choke on its own pink publicity stunts. Workers were caught on video stomping on chickens, kicking them and violently slamming them against floors and walls. Workers were also filmed ripping the animals' beaks off, twisting their heads off, spitting tobacco into their eyes and mouths, spray-painting their faces,

and squeezing their bodies so hard that the birds expelled feces—all while the chickens were still alive.

10 KFC, naturally, did everything they could to keep the footage from being aired, but their efforts failed. In fact, the video from the investigation ended up being broadcast by TV stations around the world, as well as on all three national evening news shows, *Good Morning America*, and every one of the major cable news networks. Plus, more than a million people subsequently watched the footage on PETA's website.

11 It wasn't just animal activists who condemned the fast food chain for the level of animal cruelty displayed at KFC's "Supplier of the Year" slaughterhouse. Dr. Temple Grandin, perhaps the meat industry's leading farmed-animal welfare expert, said, "The behavior of the plant employees was atrocious." Dr. Ian Duncan, a University of Guelph professor of applied **ethology** and an original member of KFC's own animal-welfare advisory council, wrote, "This tape depicts scenes of the worst cruelty I have ever witnessed against chickens . . . and it is extremely hard to accept that this is occurring in the United States of America."

ethology
the branch of zoology that studies the behavior of animals in their natural habitats

12 KFC claims, on its website, that its animal-welfare advisory council "has been a key factor in formulating our animal welfare program." But Dr. Duncan, along with five other former members of this advisory council, say otherwise. They all resigned in disgust over the company's refusal to take animal welfare seriously. Adele Douglass, one of those who resigned, said in an SEC filing reported on by the *Chicago Tribune* that KFC "never had any meetings. They never asked any advice, and then they touted to the press that they had this animal-welfare advisory committee. I felt like I was being used."

13 You can see why KFC would be eager to jump on any chance to improve its public image, and why the company would want to capitalize on any opportunity to associate itself in the public mind with the fight against breast cancer. What's far more mystifying is why an organization with as much public trust as Susan G. Komen for the Cure would jeopardize public confidence in its authenticity. As someone once said, it takes a lifetime to build a reputation, but only 15 minutes to lose it.

Examining a Paragraph

Read the following paragraph from "Cancer, Greed, and Pink KFC Buckets," noticing how all the details relate to one point and explain the topic sentence, which is highlighted. The topic sentence identifies the topic as *animal welfare* and states that KFC claims its animal welfare advisory council is key to its animal welfare program.

> KFC claims, on its website, that its animal-welfare advisory council "has been a key factor in formulating our animal welfare program." But Dr. Duncan, along with five other former members of this advisory council, say otherwise. They all resigned in disgust over the company's refusal to take animal welfare seriously. Adele Douglass, one of those who resigned, said in an SEC filing reported on by the *Chicago Tribune* that KFC "never had any meetings. They never asked any advice, and then they touted to the press that they had this animal-welfare advisory committee. I felt like I was being used."

You can think about and visualize paragraph structure as shown on the left and the structure of this particular paragraph as shown on the right,

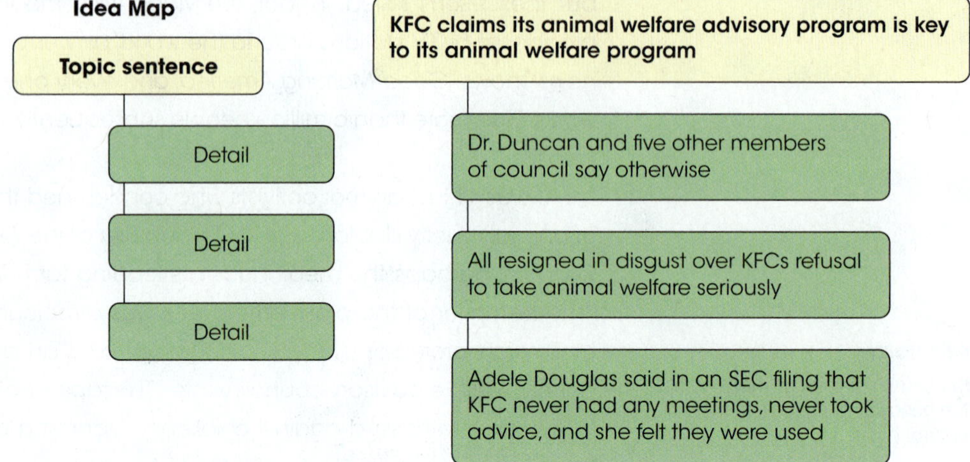

Notice how well the topic sentence and details in the above paragraph work together to develop a main idea. The more general topic sentence is explained by the more specific details. You might ask, "How can I tell what is 'general' and what is 'specific' when I am reading?" Here are a few examples that are drawn from the professional reading. The first two use short topics and details; the last two use topic sentences and detail sentences.

GENERAL	birds
SPECIFIC	chickens, cardinals, robins
GENERAL	fast food restaurants
SPECIFIC	Kentucky Fried Chicken, McDonald's
GENERAL	KFC tried to stop PETA footage of chickens being mistreated from being aired.
SPECIFIC	■ The video was broadcast around the world and on all three national evening shows. ■ More than a million people subsequently watched the footage on PETA's site.
GENERAL	Other people beside animal activists condemned KFC for animal cruelty.
SPECIFIC	■ Dr. Temple Grandin said the workers behavior was atrocious. ■ Dr. Ian Duncan said the tape showed the worst cruelty to chickens that he had ever witnessed.

Notice that in each of these examples, the specific points explain the general by giving examples, reasons, or further information. In the same way, supporting details in a paragraph explain or support a topic sentence.

Now that you have seen how specific details are used to support topic sentences, practice distinguishing between general and specific.

EXERCISE 3-1

Using General and Specific Terms

Directions: For each list of items, select the choice that best describes that grouping.

______ 1. for money, for experience, to meet people
- a. reasons to attend a party
- b. reasons to get a part-time job
- c. reasons to apply for loans
- d. reasons to date

______ 2. U.S. Constitution, Bill of Rights, Federalist Papers, Twenty-Fifth Amendment
- a. policies
- b. historical events
- c. historical documents
- d. party politics

______ 3. Mars, Saturn, Jupiter, Mercury
- a. asteroids
- b. solar systems
- c. galaxies
- d. planets

NEED TO KNOW

Important Terms

Paragraph: a group of sentences that focus on a single idea

Topic: the one thing a paragraph is about

Topic sentence: the sentence that tells what the paragraph is about

Supporting details: those sentences that explain the topic sentence

Identifying and Selecting Topics

■ GOAL 2
Identify and select topics

Topics are important to both readers and writers. Identifying the topic of a paragraph helps readers to understand what it is about. Choosing focused topics helps writers focus their thoughts and organize their ideas.

Reading: Locating the Topic of a Paragraph

You already know that the topic is the general subject of an entire paragraph. Every sentence in a paragraph in some way discusses or explains this topic. To find the topic of a paragraph, ask yourself: What is the one idea the author is discussing throughout the paragraph? Read the following paragraph with that question in mind:

When PETA sent investigators with hidden cameras into a KFC "Supplier of the Year" slaughterhouse in Moorefield, West Virginia, what they found was enough to make KFC choke on its own pink publicity stunts. Workers were caught on video stomping on chickens, kicking them and violently slamming them against floors and walls. Workers were also filmed ripping the animals' beaks off, twisting their heads off, spitting tobacco into their eyes and mouths, spray-painting their faces, and squeezing their bodies so hard that the birds expelled feces—all while the chickens were still alive.

In this example, the writer is discussing one topic—the mistreatment of chickens in KFC slaughterhouses—throughout the paragraph. Notice that words related to mistreatment—*stomping, kicking, slamming, twisting, spitting,* and *squeezing*—provide clues to the topic. Writers often repeat key words or use related words to discuss and emphasize their main point.

EXERCISE 3-2 Reading: Locating Topics

Directions: After reading each of the following paragraphs, select the choice that best represents the topic of the paragraph.

_____ **1.** You've probably heard that older men die before older women virtually everywhere in the world. In the United States, women are expected to live an average of 80.4 years, while men live only 75.2 years. Sociologists attribute many factors to this trend. For example, men have higher testosterone levels than women, which may make men more likely to abuse alcohol and tobacco, drive aggressively, and engage in other life-threatening behaviors. Men also choose riskier types of work and become involved in wartime aggression, which are connected to men's decreased life expectancy. Studies also show that women are less likely to experience life-threatening illnesses and health problems than men are.

—Carl, *Think Sociology*, p. 211

a. women's health
b. men and risky behaviors
c. testosterone and age
d. men's life expectancy

_____ **2.** Many people look back to the 1950s as the golden age of the traditional family, but was it really? Teenage pregnancy rates were higher in the 1950s than they are today, although a higher proportion of teenage mothers were married (primarily due to "shotgun weddings," a colloquialism that developed from the idea that many fathers of pregnant girls had to force, possibly with a weapon, a man to marry his daughter once she became pregnant). Many families were unable to survive the traumas of war and its aftermath, and the divorce rate rose from one in six in 1940 to one in four marriages in 1946. Although many families prospered in the years following World War II, many others suffered from economic hardship. In 1948, *Newsweek* reported that most of the 27 million schoolchildren in the United States were badly in need of medical or dental care, while more than 900 thousand children were malnourished.

—Kunz, *THINK Marriages & Families*, p. 8

a. teenage pregnancy rates
b. the effect of war on divorce
c. family problems in the 1950s
d. golden age

_____ **3.** In the past few years, social networking sites such as MySpace, Facebook, and Twitter have become hugely popular across all ages. Despite the opinions of some that young people are in danger of turning into crouching androids glued to their computers, research shows that the majority of friendships are still maintained offline. Offline friendships are characterized by more interdependence, depth, understanding, and commitment, but online friendships can gain some of these qualities with time. Most online friends tend to be rather cautious about disclosing personal information. However, this does not apply to people with a negative view of themselves and others; they instead seem to share more information, possibly in an attempt to become more self-confident in their interactions. Interestingly, even in online friendships people seem to gain more satisfaction when befriending people of a similar age and place of residence.

—Kunz, *THINK Marriages & Families,* p. 82

a. offline vs. online friendships
b. technology and self-image
c. personal information sharing online
d. satisfaction in online friendships

_____ **4.** A century ago politicians used to say, "Vote early and often." Cases such as West Virginia's 159,000 votes being cast by 147,000 eligible voters in 1888 were not that unusual. Largely to prevent corruption associated with stuffing ballot boxes, states adopted voter registration laws around the turn of the century, which require individuals to first place their name on an electoral roll in order to be allowed to vote. Although these laws have made it more difficult to vote more than once, they have also discouraged some people from voting at all. Voter registration requirements in the United States are, in part, to blame for why Americans are significantly less likely to go to the polls than citizens of other democratic nations.

—Edwards et al., *Government in America,* p. 313

a. voter turnout
b. voter registration
c. voter eligibility
d. voter fraud

_____ **5.** Compared with the technical resources of a theater of today, those of a London public theater in the time of Queen Elizabeth I seem hopelessly limited. Plays had to be performed by daylight, and scenery had to be kept simple: a table, a chair, a throne, perhaps an artificial tree or two to suggest a forest. But these limitations were, in a sense, advantages. What the theater of today can spell out for us realistically, with massive scenery and electric lighting, Elizabethan playgoers had to imagine and the playwright had to make vivid for them by means of language. Not having a lighting technician to work a panel, Shakespeare had to indicate the dawn by having Horatio, in *Hamlet,* say in a speech rich in metaphor and descriptive detail:

> But look, the morn in russet mantle clad
> Walks o'er the dew of yon high eastward hill.

—Kennedy and Gioia, *Literature,* p. 1243

a. impact of technological limitations on Elizabethan theater
b. benefits of modern technology in theater performances
c. effects of Shakespeare's writing style
d. the use of language to make ideas vivid

Writing: Selecting a Topic

The first step in writing an effective paragraph is to select a topic that you are knowledgeable and comfortable writing about. It is worth spending time to think of possible topics and to discover what you know about each before making a selection and beginning to write. Chapter 2, pages 47–49 describes four techniques—freewriting, brainstorming, branching , and questioning—for generating ideas about a topic.

The student writer we will follow in this chapter, Kate Atkinson, was given an assignment to write an essay in response to an article about the US and Russian education systems. Once she had determined the main point of her essay, she worked on developing topics—main ideas—for each of her supporting paragraphs.

EXAMINING STUDENT WRITING

A good way to learn to read and write essays is to study a model. By examining the student essay below by Kate Atkinson, you will learn how to narrow a topic and write clear and effective topic sentences. Throughout the rest of the chapter, we will refer to Kate's essay to illustrate techniques and strategies.

Kate Atkinson is a student at Beloit College in Wisconsin, where she is studying sociology and Russian. Kate wrote this essay in response to an article in the Moscow News. *Kate studied Russian during high school and used her study abroad experience in Russia in responding to the article.*

Title announces subject of essay

The Russian and U.S. School Systems

Kate Atkinson

Introduction draws reader in by discussing ways Russia and U.S. view each other

Thesis statement

1 Russia and the U.S. share a complex history riddled with conflict and mutual mistrust. In the years since the Cold War and collapse of the Soviet Union, the two countries have worked to set aside their differences but tension still simmers beneath the surface. Russia is still viewed by many Americans as remote, mysterious, and even dangerous. Similarly, Russians harbor both admiration and contempt for America's economic prowess and superpower status. One thing both countries have in common, however, is an excellent system of education and impressive literacy rates (both above ninety-nine percent). Writes Mark H. Teeter for the *Moscow News*, "Russians and Americans share a long tradition of dimly perceiving each other's societies, and recent developments on both countries' school fronts neatly illustrate this through-a-glass-darkly effect." Though both systems are highly acclaimed, they are each as different as the countries they belong to.

First subject introduced: Russia and education

Topic sentence: school attendance in Russia

2 In Russia, primary and secondary school education is compulsory from around age seven to age fifteen, after which students either go on to vocational school, join the work force, or remain in secondary school for two more years in order to graduate and go on to higher education. This decision is usually not made by the student, but by a combination of factors including family standards and expectations, class,

and location. Students who come from a family of industrial workers, for example, will usually go on to become one themselves. Russian students specialize early on in school, and as a result they know from a young age what type of career they are headed for. In recent years, specialized schools called "gymnasia" have become increasingly common in which students can focus on subjects such as music and foreign languages.

Topic sentence: curriculum in Russia

3 The Russian Ministry of Education determines the curriculum, and as a result, all schools meet a certain national standard of education (Teeter). Along with the usual requirements, the Russian curriculum emphasizes oral communication, memorization, and recitation. Russian school children are well-versed in the poetry of the beloved poet Pushkin and can recite famous lines without hesitation.

Topic sentence: classroom conduct in Russia

4 In the Russian classroom, the code of conduct between students and teachers is formal and respectful. When a teacher enters the room at the beginning of class, all students hastily rise and wait for the teacher's greeting. Personal relationships are discouraged and the teacher's sole responsibility is to relay information to be memorized by the students.

Author switches to second topic: US and education

Topic sentence: attendance in US

5 In the U.S., students must attend school between the ages of six and seventeen, and after passing all required courses they graduate and either go on to higher education or join the military or work force. The number of students who go on to higher education has increased dramatically in the past decade as job opportunities have become more competitive and college degrees more accessible to people of all ages and backgrounds. U.S. students have a vast network of private and public universities, liberal arts colleges, and community colleges at their fingertips and therefore, a great deal of choice in the course of their education.

Topic sentence: US curriculum

6 Unlike Russia, the United States does not have a country-level curriculum. Instead, independent city, state, and community boards determine curriculums, and each state has its own Department of Education (Teeter). The boards work closely with the schools they monitor and can work to tackle problems such as bullying more effectively than a national ministry. However, the flexibility in curriculum from state to state has led to some schools' not meeting the national literacy standard, and issues such as what is an appropriate approach to sex education and whether to teach creation science versus evolution are widely debated (Teeter).

Topic sentence: classroom conduct in US

7 In general, American students have more freedom in the classroom and the student-teacher relationship is less rigid. Teachers are generally more tolerant of laid back behavior in class but often do not get the respect they deserve.

Conclusion: a final discussion of the two different systems

8 The similarities and differences in these two systems of education closely mirror the history and values of the countries themselves. Russia still clings to rigid national control and standards while the U.S. allows for more freedom in the learning exchange. Both countries could learn from the other and work to smooth out the wrinkles in their acclaimed systems. In order for this to happen however, the two super powers would have to put the past aside and work to perceive each other through less biased lenses.

Works Cited

Teeter, Mark H. "Schools of Hard Knocks." *The Moscow News*, 29 Mar. 2010, www.themoscownews.com/5th_columnist/20100329/55425914.html. Accessed 26 Feb. 2011.

Writing: Refining Your Topic

To write a good paragraph, you need a manageable topic, one that is the right size. Your topic must be general enough to allow you to add interesting details that will engage your reader. It must also be specific or narrow enough that you can cover it adequately in a few sentences. If your topic is too general, you will end up with a few unrelated details that do not add up to a specific point. If your topic is too narrow, you will not have enough to say.

Suppose you have decided to write a paragraph about sports. Here is your topic.

sports as a favorite activity for many people

This topic is much *too broad* to cover in one paragraph. Think of all the different aspects you could write about. Which sports would you consider? Would you write about both playing sports and watching them? Would you write about both professional and amateur sports? Would you write about the reasons people enjoy sports? The topic must be more specific:

watching professional football on Sunday afternoons with my family

Here you have limited your topic to a specific sport (football), a specific time (Sunday afternoon), and some specific fans (your family).

Here are other examples of topics that are too general. Each has been revised to be more specific.

TOO GENERAL	Influence of my parents
REVISED	Influence of my parents on my choice of college
TOO GENERAL	Sex education
REVISED	How sex education in high school helps students talk more openly

If your topic is *too specific* (narrow), you will not have enough details to use in a paragraph, or you may end up including details that do not relate directly to the topic. Suppose you decide to write a paragraph about the Internet and come up with this topic:

the role of the Internet in keeping me in touch with friends and family

What else would your paragraph say? You might name some specific friends and where they are, but this list would not be very interesting. This topic is too specific. It might work as a detail, but not as the main point of the paragraph. To correct the problem, ask, "What else does the Internet allow me to do?" You might say that it allows you to stay in touch with friends by e-mail, that it makes doing research for college papers easier, and that the World Wide Web has information on careers and even specific job openings. Here is a possible revised topic:

the Internet as an important part of my personal, college, and work life

Here are a few other examples of topics that are too narrow, along with revisions for each one:

TOO NARROW	voter participation
REVISED	Americans who do not exercise their right to vote
TOO NARROW	child-care leave
REVISED	flexible child-care leave policy at Markel Carpet Company

How can you tell if your topic is too general or too specific? Try brainstorming or branching to generate ideas. If you find you can develop the topic in many different directions, or if you have trouble choosing details from a wide range of choices, your topic is probably too general. If you cannot think of anything to explain or support it, your topic sentence is too specific.

After reading the assigned article on the Russian and US school systems and brainstorming for ideas, Kate decided to write about the similarities and differences between the two systems based on her experiences as a student in both (she attended Gymnasia #17 in Petrozavodsk as an exchange student in 10th grade).

Once she had determined the overall topic for her paper, she started working on the body paragraphs, brainstorming ideas to support her main point. Here are some of the paragraph topics she initially listed and her revisions to them:

TOO NARROW:	education compulsory from age seven to fifteen in Russia
REVISED:	educational paths for Russian students
TOO BROAD:	educational curriculum in US
REVISED:	US curriculum in contrast with Russian curriculum

EXERCISE 3-3 Writing: Narrowing Topics

Directions: Narrow or broaden each of the following topics it so that it can be developed in a single paragraph.

1. Behavior of sports fans
2. Number of used cell phones discarded each year
3. Minority group discrimination on campus
4. Acreage destroyed by wildfires each year
5. procrastination

Reading and Writing Topic Sentences

■ GOAL 3
Read and write topic sentences

Once you know how to locate and develop a topic, you can easily locate and write topic sentences.

Reading: Locating Topic Sentences

You learned earlier that the *topic sentence* of a paragraph is its most important point. It is also the most *general* statement the writer makes about the topic. Pick out the most general statement among the following sentences.

1. Animals differ according to when they sleep.
2. Some animals sleep during daylight while others sleep during darkness.
3. Animals' sleeping habits differ in a number of ways.
4. Hibernation is another kind of sleep for some animals.

Did you choose sentence 3 as the most general statement? Now we will change this list into a paragraph by rearranging the sentences and adding a few facts.

> [1]Animals' sleeping habits differ in a number of ways. [2]They differ according to what time of day they sleep. [3]Some animals sleep during daylight hours while others sleep during darkness. [4]They also differ in the length of time they sleep. [5]Other animals sleep for weeks or months at a time when they hibernate.

In this brief paragraph, the topic sentence appears first in the paragraph. Notice that it is the most general statement in the paragraph. All the other sentences are specific details that explain it.

Reading: Tips for Locating Topic Sentences

Here are some tips that will help you find topic sentences.

1. **Identify the topic.** As you did earlier, figure out the general subject of the entire paragraph. In the preceding sample paragraph, "animals' sleeping habits" is the topic.
2. **Locate the most general sentence (the topic sentence).** This sentence must be broad enough to include all of the other ideas in the paragraph. The topic sentence in the sample paragraph ("Animals' sleeping habits differ in a number of ways.") covers all of the other details in that paragraph.
3. **Study the rest of the paragraph.** The topic sentence must make the rest of the paragraph meaningful. It is the one idea that ties all of the other details together. In the sample paragraph, sentences 2, 3, 4, and 5 all give specific details about how animals' sleeping habits differ.

Reading: Placement of Topic Sentences

Writers often place their topic sentence first in the paragraph—a position that enables the writer to state his or her main idea and then move on to explain it. The topic sentence can also be placed last or in the middle. On occasion a writer may choose to state the main idea once at the beginning of the paragraph and restate it at the end or use both sentences to fully explain his or her main idea. Although a topic sentence can be located anywhere in a paragraph, it is usually *first* or *last*.

Visual	Placement	Example
General: **Topic Sentence** Detail Specific: Detail Detail	**Topic Sentence First** Here the writer defines the term "focus group" and then provides details about focus groups.	**A focus group** is a small group, usually consisting of about seven to ten people who are brought together to discuss a subject of interest to the researcher. Focus groups are commonly used today in business and politics; that flashy slogan you heard for a political campaign or a new toothpaste was almost certainly tested in a focus group to gauge people's reactions. Social researchers may use a focus group to help design questions or instruments for quantitative research or to study the interactions among group members on a particular subject. In most cases, researchers ask predetermined questions, but the discussion is unstructured. Focus groups are a relatively cheap method of research and can be completed quickly. They also allow for the flexible discussions and answers that are desirable in qualitative research —Kunz, *THINK Marriages & Families*, p.36
Detail Specific: Detail Detail General: **Topic Sentence**	**Topic Sentence Last** Here the author discusses water as a limiting resource and concludes that water will become more limited throughout the 21st century.	In the developing world 1.1 billion people still lack access to safe drinking water, 2.6 billion do not have access to adequate sanitation services, and more than 1.6 million deaths each year are traced to waterborne diseases (mostly in children under five). All too often in developing countries, water is costly or inaccessible to the poorest in society, while the wealthy have it piped into their homes. In addition, because of the infrastructure that is used to control water, whole seas are being lost, rivers are running dry, millions of people have been displaced to make room for reservoirs, groundwater aquifers are being pumped down, and disputes over water have raised tensions from local to international levels. Fresh water is a limiting resource in many parts of the world and is certain to become even more so as the 21st century unfolds. —Wright and Boorse, *Environmental Science*, p. 247
Specific: Detail Detail General: **Topic Sentence** Detail Specific: Detail	**Topic Sentence in Middle** Here the author discusses how one species nearly became extinct and concludes that government regulations are necessary to prevent this from happening again.	In colonial days, huge flocks of snowy egrets inhabited the coastal wetlands and marshes of the southeastern United States. In the 1800s, when fashion dictated fancy hats adorned with feathers, egrets and other birds were hunted for their plumage. By the late 1800s, egrets were almost extinct. In 1886, the newly formed National Audubon Society began a press campaign to shame "feather wearers" and end the practice. The campaign caught on, and gradually, attitudes changed; new laws followed. Government policies that protect animals from overharvesting are essential to keep species from the brink of extinction. Even when cultural standards change due to the efforts of individual groups (such as the National Audubon Society), laws and policy measures must follow to ensure that endangered populations remain protected. Since the 1800s, several important laws have been passed to protect a wide variety of species. —Wright and Boorse, *Environmental Science: Toward a Sustainable Future*, p. 150
General: **Topic Sentence** Specific: Detail Detail Specific: Detail Detail General: **Topic Sentence**	**Topic Sentence First and Last** The first and last sentences together explain that the NCI takes an aggressive strategy to finding and testing samples for cancer suppression.	The National Cancer Institute (NCI) has taken a brute-force approach to screening species for cancer-suppressing chemicals. NCI scientists receive frozen samples of organisms from around the world, chop them up, and separate them into a number of extracts, each probably containing hundreds of components. These extracts are tested against up to 60 different types of cancer cells for their efficacy in stopping or slowing growth of the cancer. Promising extracts are then further analyzed to determine their chemical nature, and chemicals in the extract are tested singly to find the effective compound. This approach is often referred to as the "grind 'em and find 'em" strategy. —Belk and Maier, *Biology*, p. 334

EXERCISE 3-4 Reading: Locating Topic Sentences

Directions: Underline the topic sentence in each of the following paragraphs.

1. The United States has a severe fire problem that if not addressed, will continue to worsen drastically. Fire statistics show that our nation, one of the richest and most technologically sophisticated countries in the world, lags behind its peer nations in fire security. Nationally, there are millions of fires, thousands of deaths, tens of thousands of injuries, and billions of dollars lost each year—figures which far exceed comparable statistics for other industrialized countries. In 2001, for example, the direct value of property destroyed in fires was $11 billion ($44 billion if the World Trade Center loss is included). More recently in 2004, direct property losses from fires were estimated at over $9.8 billion.

   —Loyd and Richardson, *Fundamentals of Fire and Emergency Services*, p. 12

2. The star system has been the backbone of the American film industry since the mid 1910s. Stars are the creation of the public, its reigning favorites. Their influence in the fields of fashion, values, and public behavior has been enormous. "The social history of a nation can be written in terms of its film stars," Raymond Durgnat has observed. Stars confer instant consequence to any film they appear in. Their fees have staggered the public. In the 1920s, Mary Pickford and Charles Chaplin were the two highest paid employees in the world. Contemporary stars such as Julia Roberts and Tom Cruise command salaries of many millions per film, so popular are these box-office giants. Some stars had careers that spanned five decades: Bette Davis and John Wayne, to name just two.

   — Giannetti, *Understanding Movies*, p. 251

3. For decades, we have looked at our steadily increasing life expectancy rates and proudly proclaimed that Americans' health has never been better. Recently, however, health organizations and international groups have attempted to quantify the number of years a person lives with a disability or illness, compared with the number of healthy years. The World Health Organization summarizes this concept as **healthy life expectancy**. Simply stated, healthy life expectancy refers to the number of years a newborn can expect to live in full health, based on current rates of illness and mortality and also on the quality of their lives. For example, if we could delay the onset of diabetes so that a person didn't develop the disease until he or she was 60 years old, rather than developing it at 30, there would be a dramatic increase in this individual's healthy life expectancy.

   —Donatelle, *Health: The Basics*, p. 6

4. Are you "twittered out"? Is all that texting causing your thumbs to seize up in protest? If so, you're not alone. Like millions of others, you may find that all of the pressure for contact is more than enough stress for you! Known as technostress, the bombardment is defined as stress created by a dependence on technology and the constant state of being plugged in or wirelessly connected, which can include a perceived obligation to respond, chat, or tweet.

   —Donatelle, *Health: The Basics*, p.66

5. In the past, exposure to liability made many doctors, nurses, and other medical professionals reluctant to stop and render aid to victims in emergency situations, such as highway accidents. Almost all states have enacted a **Good**

Samaritan law that relieves medical professionals from liability for injury caused by their ordinary negligence in such circumstances. Good Samaritan laws protect medical professionals only from liability for their *ordinary negligence*, not for injuries caused by their gross negligence or reckless or intentional conduct. Most Good Samaritan laws protect licensed doctors and nurses and laypersons who have been certified in CPR. Good Samaritan statutes generally do not protect laypersons who are not trained in CPR—that is, they are liable for injuries caused by their ordinary negligence in rendering aid.

— Goldman and Cheeseman, *Paralegal Professional*, p. 459

Writing: Developing Effective Topic Sentences

As a writer, it is important to develop clear and concise topic sentences that help your readers understand your ideas and guide them through your paragraphs. A good topic sentence does two things:

- It makes clear what the paragraph is about—the topic.
- It expresses a viewpoint about the topic.

An effective topic sentence always expresses a viewpoint about the topic. A viewpoint is an attitude or focus about a topic. If the topic is wild game hunting, there are several viewpoints that you could express about it:

- Wild game hunting helps control overpopulation of wildlife.
- Wild game hunting involves killing animals for pleasure.
- Wild game hunting allows hunters to experience and appreciate nature.

Each of the above examples offers a different attitude toward the topic. In contrast, notice how the following sentences do *not* express a viewpoint.

- There are 2 million wild game hunters in the United States.
- Wild game hunting season often begins in the fall.

If you write a topic sentence without a viewpoint, you will find you have very little to write about in the remainder of the paragraph.

If you look at Kate's essay, you will see that she started each paragraph with a clear topic sentence that indicated her topic and her viewpoint about it. Now complete the following exercise to look more closely at her topic sentences.

EXERCISE 3-5

Reading: Identifying Viewpoint

Directions: For each of the following topic sentences, underline the viewpoint expressed toward the topic.

1. Russia and the United States share a complex history riddled with conflict and mutual mistrust.
2. The Russian Ministry of Education determines the curriculum and as a result all schools meet certain national standards of education.
3. Unlike Russia, the United States does not have a county-level curriculum.
4. In the classroom, the code of conduct between students and teachers is formal and respectful.

EXERCISE 3-6

Writing: Expressing a Viewpoint About a Topic

Directions: For each of the following topic sentences, write a topic sentence that expresses a different viewpoint about the topic.

1. It is better to live in a city than in the country because the city offers many more activities and opportunities to its residents.

____

____

2. Because tobacco products harm people's health, all tobacco products should be banned.

____

3. Social networking sites like Facebook and MySpace create communities of close-knit friends.

____

____

4. *Dancing with the Stars* entertains us by allowing celebrities to exhibit their unknown dance talents.

____

____

Now that you know how to develop a manageable topic and determine your point of view, you are ready to put the two together and write topic sentences.

Writing: Broad Versus Narrow Topic Sentences

A topic sentence should be neither too broad nor too narrow. Either produces an ineffective paragraph.

Topic Sentences That Are Too Narrow

If your topic sentence is too narrow, you will not have enough to write about to complete a paragraph. Topics that are too narrow often lack a viewpoint.

TOO NARROW: Almost 90% of Americans own cell phones.

REVISED: Americans own and use a wide variety of cell phones, depending on their work and personal needs.

Below is an example of a topic sentence Kate revised after realizing it was too narrow and would be hard to write about or find details to support.

TOO NARROW: In Russia, primary and secondary education is compulsory from around age seven to age fifteen.

REVISED: In Russia, primary and secondary education is compulsory from around age seven to age fifteen, after which students either go on to vocational school, join the work force, or remain in secondary school for two more years in order to graduate and go on to higher education.

To revise a topic sentence that is too narrow, use the following tips:

- State a clear viewpoint about your topic.
- Broaden your topic to include a wider group or range of items.
- Expand your topic to include causes and effects or comparisons or contrasts.

Topic Sentences That Are Too Broad

If your topic sentence is too broad, you will have trouble covering all aspects of it in a single paragraph. Topics that are too broad often lead to rambling or disorganized writing. You will find that you have too many general statements and not enough specifics to support them.

TOO BROAD:	Internet crime in the world today is increasing dramatically.
REVISED:	Phishing scams are responsible for increases in identify theft among senior citizens in our town.

In the example below, Kate first wrote a very broad topic sentence that she revised after finding she could only make very general statements to support it. The revised topic sentence indicates she is contrasting the US and Russian systems and allows her to focus on the main differences in curriculum between the two countries.

TOO BROAD:	There are many types of educational curriculum in the US.
REVISED:	Unlike Russia, the United States does not have a country-level curriculum.

To revise a topic sentence that is too broad, use the following tips:

- Narrow your topic by subdividing it.
- Rewrite your topic sentence to focus on one aspect or part of the topic.
- Apply the topic sentence to a specific time and place.
- Consider using one of your details as a topic sentence.

As you write your topic sentences, keep the following tips in mind:

Tips for Writing Effective Topic Sentences

Use the following suggestions to write clear topic sentences:

1. **Your topic sentence should state the main point of your paragraph.** It should identify your topic and express a view toward it.
2. **Be sure to choose a manageable topic**—one that is neither too general nor too specific. Topic sentences that are too general often promise more than they can deliver in a single paragraph. They lead to writing that is vague and rambling. Topic sentences that are too specific produce weak paragraphs because there is not enough to say about them.
3. **Make sure your topic sentence is a complete thought.** Be sure your topic sentence is not a fragment or run-on sentence (see pp. 535 and 540).

(continued)

4. **Place your topic sentence first in the paragraph.** Topic sentences often appear in other places in paragraphs, as described earlier, or their controlling idea is implied, not stated. For now, it will be easiest for you to put yours at the beginning. That way, as you write, you can make sure you stick to your point, and your readers will immediately be alerted to that point.
5. **Avoid announcing your topic.** Sentences that sound like announcements are usually unnecessary. Avoid such sentences as "This paragraph will discuss how to change a flat tire," or "I will explain why I object to legalized abortion." Instead, directly state your main point: "Changing a flat tire involves many steps," or "I object to abortion on religious grounds."

Not all expert or professional writers follow all of these suggestions. Sometimes, a writer may use one-sentence paragraphs or include topic sentences that are fragments to achieve a special effect. You will find these paragraphs in news and magazine articles and other sources. Although professional writers can use these variations effectively, you probably should not experiment with them too early. It is best while you are polishing your skills to use a more standard style of writing, as you can see Kate did in her essay.

EXERCISE 3-7 Writing: Evaluating Topic Sentences

Directions: Evaluate each of the following topic sentences and mark them as follows:

E = effective
A = announcement
S = too specific
G = too general
N = not complete thought

_____ 1. This paper will discuss the life and politics of Simón Bolívar.

_____ 2. Japanese culture is fascinating to study because its family traditions are so different from American traditions.

_____ 3. The admission test for the police academy includes vocabulary questions.

_____ 4. The discovery of penicillin was a great step in the advancement of modern medicine.

_____ 5. I will talk about the reasons for the popularity of reality television shows.

_____ 6. A habit leading to weight gain.

_____ 7. Each year Americans are the victims of more than 1 million auto thefts.

_____ 8. The White House has many famous rooms and an exciting history.

_____ 9. There are three factors to consider when buying a flat-screen TV.

_____ 10. Iraq has a long and interesting history.

EXERCISE 3-8

Writing: Revising Topic Sentences

Directions: Analyze the following topic sentences. If a sentence is too general or too specific, or if it makes a direct announcement or is not a complete thought, revise it to make it more effective.

1. World hunger is a crime.

   REVISED ______________________________

2. E-mail is used by a great many people.

   REVISED ______________________________

3. I will point out the many ways energy can be saved in the home.

   REVISED ______________________________

4. Because Congress is very important in the United States.

   REVISED ______________________________

5. In 2010, over 10,000 people died in alcohol-impaired driving crashes.

   REVISED ______________________________

Think Critically About Topic Sentences

■ GOAL 4
Think critically about topic sentences

Often, topic sentences are simple statements of fact that cannot be disputed. However, not all topic sentences are completely factual. Sometimes a topic sentence presents an opinion about a topic, and that statement may not offer all sides of the story. (To learn more about distinguishing fact and opinion, refer to Chapter 12.) Look at the following passage:

> No doubt about it, lobbying is a growth industry. Every state has hundreds of public relations practitioners whose specialty is representing their clients to legislative bodies and government agencies. In North Dakota, hardly a populous state, more than 300 people are registered as lobbyists in the capital city of Bismarck. The number of registered lobbyists in Washington, D.C., exceeds 10,000 today. In addition, there are an estimated 20,000 other people who have slipped through registration requirements but who nonetheless ply the halls of government to plead their clients' interests.
>
> In one sense, lobbyists are expediters. They know local traditions and customs, and they know who is in a position to affect policy. Lobbyists advise their clients, which include trade associations, corporations, public interest groups and regulated utilities and industries, on how to achieve their goals by working with legislators and government regulators. Many lobbyists call themselves "government relations specialists."
>
> —Vivian, *The Media of Mass Communication*, pp. 278–279

The topic sentence of the first paragraph is a statement of fact; the author can prove without a doubt that "lobbying is a growth industry." The topic sentence of the second paragraph is: "Lobbyists are expediters." That is, lobbyists help their clients influence the government in their favor. But this topic sentence presents *only* "one sense" of the topic. What is the other sense or view? Lobbying is actually a controversial activity, and many people believe that lobbyists spend large amounts of money influencing government employees in unethical or illegal ways. However, that belief is not reflected in the topic sentence of this passage.

EXERCISE 3-9 Reading: Analyzing Topics

Directions: For each of the following sets of topic sentences, specify the topic that is being discussed. Note that each topic sentence presents a different facet of (or opinion about) the topic.

1. - "The continued flow of immigrants into the United States has created a rich, diverse society that has been beneficial to the country."
   - "The presence of guest workers from South America in states like Arizona and California has a positive effect on the U.S. economy."
   - "Because the country is suffering from high unemployment, we must reduce the number of people who come here looking for jobs."

   Topic: ______________________________

2. - "Most scientists agree that temperatures now are warmer than they were 20 years ago."
   - "It is hard to draw any definite conclusions from the hundreds of studies that have considered whether climate change is occurring or not."
   - "People who claim that the Earth is now hotter miss the point that the Earth has been getting warmer over the last several thousand years, not just the last 50 years."

   Topic: ______________________________

READ AND RESPOND: A Student Essay

The Russian and U.S. School Systems

Kate Atkinson

The questions and activities below refer to Kate's essay "The Russian and U.S. School Systems" on page 98 that we have used as a model throughout the chapter. Now you are ready to examine her writing and write in response to her essay.

Examining Writing (See essay on p. 98.)

1. How does Kate indicate to her readers that she will be addressing two topics in her essay?
2. Does each paragraph in Kate's essay address a narrow and specific topic?
3. Evaluate the effectiveness of her topic sentences.
4. In each paragraph, does Kate provide enough details to explain and support the topic sentence?
5. What overall attitude toward education in the two countries does Kate reveal throughout the essay?

Writing Assignments

1. In her essay Kate compares and contrasts two different but highly successful systems of education. Create a summary of the main points of comparison she addresses in the essay.
2. Write a paragraph about an aspect of American education (or that of another country, if you have experienced it) that you think makes the system valuable and important.

READ AND RESPOND: A Professional Essay

Greed, Cancer, and Pink KFC Buckets

John Robbins

You read the professional essay "Greed, Cancer, and Pink KFC Buckets" earlier in the chapter, where it was used to demonstrate reading techniques. Now it is time to examine it more closely by answering the following questions.

Writing in Response to Reading (See essay on p. 91.)

Checking Your Comprehension MySkillsLab®

Answer each of the following questions using complete sentences.

1. Describe the "Buckets for the Cure" campaign.
2. According to the American Institute for Cancer Research, what percentage of all cancers can be prevented with lifestyle changes?
3. What is the number one dietary recommendation of the American Institute for Cancer Research?

4. What is "pinkwashing" and what does it have to do with the Komen/KFC campaign?

5. Write a brief summary of what PETA investigators found at the KFC "Supplier of the Year" slaughterhouse in West Virginia. How did KFC's animal-welfare advisory council react?

Strengthening Your Vocabulary MySkillsLab®

Using the word's context, word parts, or a dictionary, write a brief definition of each of the following words as it is used in the reading.

1. profound (paragraph 1) ______
2. advocacy (paragraph 1) ______
3. cynical (paragraph 5) ______
4. vanquished (paragraph 5) ______
5. derided (paragraph 7) ______
6. atrocious (paragraph 11) ______
7. jeopardize (paragraph 13) ______
8. authenticity (paragraph 13) ______

Examining the Reading: Drawing an Idea Map

Create an idea map of the reading that starts with the title and thesis and then lists the author's main points. Use the guidelines on page 15.

Reading and Writing: An Integrated Perspective MySkillsLab®

Get ready to write about the reading by discussing the following:

1. Discuss why Komen chose to partner with KFC. Do you think the "Buckets for the Cure" campaign will be considered successful?

2. Write a journal entry that summarizes the author's opinion regarding the partnership between Komen and KFC. Do you agree or disagree with his opinion?

3. Evaluate the introduction of the essay. What does it add to the piece of writing? How successful is it in capturing your interest?

THINKING VISUALLY

4. How does the photo accompanying this essay add to or detract from the material? Do you think a different photo would be more effective? What would it show?

Thinking and Writing Critically MySkillsLab®

1. Did the description of animal abuse at KFC's supplier affect your opinion of fast food in general and KFC in particular? Why or why not?

2. The author included both facts and opinions to support his thesis in this essay. Find examples of both and evaluate their effectiveness.

3. What is the author's purpose for writing this essay? Who is his intended audience?

Writing Paragraphs MySkillsLab®

1. How would this essay be different if it were written as a strictly factual report? Write a paragraph in which you summarize the facts of the essay in objective language.

2. Write a paragraph explaining whether you agree or disagree that Susan G. Komen for the Cure has "jeopardize[d] public confidence in its authenticity" by partnering with KFC.

3. The author points to the importance of a healthy diet in preventing cancer. Do you think most people (including yourself) make that connection? Write a paragraph explaining your answer.

Writing Essays MySkillsLab®

4. Is it appropriate for advocacy organizations such as Komen to promote their causes using commercial means? Write an essay explaining why or why not. Try to think of other advocacy groups that have formed such partnerships, on either a national or a local level.

5. What responsibility do restaurants and other commercial enterprises have toward consumer health? Write an essay exploring this question. In your own experience, what effect does "educational messaging" from advertising campaigns have on your lifestyle choices?

6. Imagine that you are a member of an animal-welfare advisory council for a large company. What guidelines would you promote for the company to follow regarding animal welfare? Write an essay describing your ideas for animal welfare in a commercial setting.

SELF-TEST SUMMARY

To test yourself, cover the Answer column with a sheet of paper and answer each question in the left column. Evaluate each of your answers as you work by sliding the paper down and comparing your answer with what is printed in the Answer column.

QUESTION	ANSWER
■ GOAL 1 Structure a paragraph What is a paragraph and what are its three key elements?	A paragraph is a group of related sentences that develop one thought or idea. The three key elements are the *topic*, *topic sentence*, and *supporting details*.
■ GOAL 2 Identify and select topics How do I identify and select the topic of a paragraph?	To locate the topic, look for the one thing the author is discussing throughout the paragraph. To select a topic, use freewriting, brainstorming, branching, and questioning to generate ideas.

(continued)

(continued)

QUESTION	ANSWER
■ GOAL 3 Read and write topic sentences How can I identify topic sentences and write effective topic sentences?	To locate a topic sentence, choose the most general sentence that includes all the other ideas in the paragraph. To write a topic sentence, identify your topic and express a viewpoint about it. Be sure your topic sentence is neither too broad nor too narrow.
■ GOAL 4 Think critically about topic sentences How can I think critically about topic sentences?	Be alert for topic sentences that express opinions. Consider whether there are other views that can be held about the topic.

MySkillsLab®

Visit **Chapter 3, "Topics, Main Ideas, and Topic Sentences,"** in MySkillsLab to test your understanding of chapter goals.

4

Details, Transitions, and Implied Main Ideas

THINK About It!

The photograph above shows a flight departure screen in an airport. It's purpose is to assist travelers in locating information on departing flights. The main point of the screen is that flights depart according to a schedule. In creating the screen the airlines had to gather flight numbers, destinations, and departure times.

To avoid confusion and to make the information easily accessible to travelers, the screen is organized by departure time, from earliest to latest. It also includes destination and flight number information. Not shown is information on which gates flights are leaving from and how close they are to departure.

Because the airlines' operations depend on travelers getting to departure gates promptly, the information on the screen is clear and accurate. As you will see in this chapter, details are important to both readers and writers—those presenting the information and those receiving and using it.

LEARNING GOALS

Learn how to . . .

- **GOAL 1** Understand details, transitions, and implied main ideas
- **GOAL 2** Identify supporting details
- **GOAL 3** Select and organize details to support your topic sentence
- **GOAL 4** Use transitions to guide your reading and writing
- **GOAL 5** Find implied main ideas

Reading and Writing Connections

EVERYDAY CONNECTIONS

- **Reading** You read your auto insurance policy for coverage information and instructions on how to file a claim for an auto accident in which you were involved.
- **Writing** You write the accident claim report, including clear and accurate details that are essential to proving you were not at fault.

ACADEMIC CONNECTIONS

- **Reading** You read a section of a psychology text titled, "What Happens When We Sleep?"
- **Writing** For an exam in psychology, you answer an essay question that asks you to explain the stages of sleep. By giving clear, accurate details about each stage, you will earn full credit.

WORKPLACE CONNECTIONS

- **Reading** As a sales rep for a mechanical supply company, you read e-mails from several customers saying that a valve you sell has been malfunctioning.
- **Writing** You write a report about the faulty valve for the manufacturing department of your company, including full details describing the problem.

What Are Details, Transitions, and Implied Main Ideas?

■ GOAL 1
Understand details, transitions, and implied main ideas

Supporting details are those facts and ideas that prove or explain the main idea of a paragraph as expressed in the topic sentence. **Transitions** are linking words and phrases that connect the details and pull the paragraph together. **Implied main ideas** are thoughts suggested, but not directly stated in a topic sentence.

As a reader, your task is to examine how details support and explain a topic sentence. You can use transitions to guide you through a paragraph and help you recognize when a writer is moving from one important detail to the next. When you find a paragraph without a topic sentence, use the details to reason out the implied main idea.

As a writer, your task is to select appropriate details to fully explain and support your topic sentence. Use transitions to guide your readers and help them identify your important details. Unless you have a specific reason for writing a paragraph with an implied main idea, it is usually better to write paragraphs that have clear topic sentences.

EXAMINING PROFESSIONAL WRITING

The following article first appeared in *The Atlantic* magazine. This article will be used in this chapter as a model of professional writing and to illustrate the reading techniques discussed. As you read, notice how the author uses various types of detail to convey the main ideas of the essay.

Thinking Before Reading

1. Preview the reading, using the steps discussed in Chapter 1, page 4.
2. Connect the reading to your own experience by answering the following questions:
   a. Have you ever been to a food bank in your community, either as a volunteer or as a client? What was the experience like?
   b. Do you think student hunger is a problem at your school? Does your school offer programs to assist hungry students?
3. Mark and annotate as you read.

Among Dorms and Dining Halls, Hidden Hunger

Kate Robbins

1 Cherie Bromley-Taylor has an open door policy with the students she works with at San Diego City College. So when one catches her in the middle of lunch, needing help to navigate the CalWORKs welfare-to-work program she helps facilitate, she doesn't hesitate to invite him or her to have a seat. What does make her hesitate, however, is a trend that she began to notice. "The student would come in and they would be so hungry that they would ask me for the apple I just took a bite of," she says. "The student's stomach is growling and head is aching, and they're telling me they're hungry. So I would feed them."

2 Asking around, Bromley-Taylor realized she was not alone. Many of her colleagues were regularly giving hungry students five dollars here and there to buy lunch or dinner. When the staff had potluck meetings, they often found students lurking by the door, eying the spread. While college students are known for their **insatiable** appetites, this went beyond the eternal collegiate quest for free snacks—these students were hungry because they couldn't afford food. Bromley-Taylor wanted to do something, so last November she helped launch a free bag lunch program for City students.

insatiable
not able to be satisfied

3 Programs like this one are popping up at campuses from Florida to Oregon, responding to the problem of low food security among college and university students. While the question of how to stretch minimal financial aid dollars or wages from part-time work to pay for a wide range of expenses has long been an issue for students, it's only gotten worse with the recent recession, say program administrators. Parents have fewer resources to help out, there is greater competition for work-study jobs, and many schools have increased tuition to cover their expenses. On-campus meal plans are often cost-prohibitive.

4 At City, the nonperishable sack lunches contain some sort of protein, fruit, a bottle of water, and a couple of snacks, and are available to any of the community college's students. Since beginning in November, Bromley-Taylor says the school has handed out an average of about 10 lunches a day. Because of limited resources, students can take advantage of the lunch service only once a week, meaning that about 50 students use the program each week.

5 Bromley-Taylor came up with this model of food assistance after doing a needs assessment of City's students. She learned that the community college's students—most of whom are older re-entry students and many of whom are recent immigrants or refugees—were going without food to get by on limited budgets. "Much of our population is below poverty level," she says, "so when they get a thousand-dollar financial aid check, it goes toward a backpack, class materials. Not food." "Food is food," says Jessica Pannell, a second-year City student who not only partakes in the program but also helps facilitate it. "It's a priority, but it's not as much a priority as a **car note** or transportation or a bill."

car note
slang for car payment

6 The survey also found that although students knew about resources like community food banks and church soup kitchens, they often had little access to transportation, leaving them on campus for long hours with little to eat. "You're at school all day and it's difficult to pay attention," Pannell says. "You want to go to sleep, especially on test days. You're stressed out. There's anxiety just because you're hungry."

Pannell says the advent of the bag lunch program is helping to change that. "It's a good hands-on program," she says, describing students who come running in for **sustenance** before class or tests. "This way they don't go to school starving."

sustenance
nourishment

7 Two hours north of City College's campus, at one of the nation's most elite public universities, UCLA students are also experiencing food insecurity. Last fall's announcement of a 32-percent tuition hike exacerbated the problem, according to senior engineering major Abdallah Jadallah. Even before the increase, he noticed that many of his classmates were struggling to feed themselves, trying to get by on one meal a day—cheap but filling Taco Bell bean burritos are a particularly popular choice for the day's nourishment. He also noticed that many of the school's campus organizations regularly offered refreshments at their meetings and events, the leftovers from which were then thrown away. He found the **discrepancy** disturbing, so he went to the university's community programs office and requested a space to set aside leftovers for hungry students. The UCLA Food Closet was born.

discrepancy
a difference or conflict between things that should be the same

8 The closet, really a small converted office, houses a donated refrigerator, an office cabinet that stands in as a pantry, and a table. Students can use the microwave in the building's kitchen to heat their meals, such as ramen or cans from a recent gift of ten Costco-sized cases of pork and beans. The Food Closet is kept open throughout the day so that students can come and go with relative anonymity.

Living on Ramen noodles.

9 "It's hard for them to admit they're going through this," says Thuy Huynh, an advisor who helps administer the student-run food closet. So in her requests for donations, she asks specifically for compact, transportable food items that can easily be concealed in a backpack. "Students are embarrassed to be caught in the closet, so having something that they can grab and go [is essential]. They take a couple of things and then leave for the day."

This sensitivity to privacy makes it difficult to track precisely how many students use the pantry, but Huynh estimates that between 30 and 50 students visit each day. The hidden nature of student hunger also made it difficult to gain support at first, she says. "People don't realize it's an issue. This is a middle-class campus."

10 Even when the problem is revealed, a tension often persists between helping these students and serving populations perceived as being in greater need. At the pioneering college food pantry founded in 1993 at Michigan State University, the staff was criticized initially for taking away donations from more traditional food banks. But that perception has gradually changed, says Kristin Moretto, director of the MSU Student Food Bank, which now operates with an annual budget of around $40,000. "We are not taking resources away from the rest of the community. The Lansing food bank has more resources because we exist. If we didn't, our students would be going over there."

11 That university students are a needy population may take some getting used to, but the idea of helping them access food on campus is spreading. Both Moretto and UCLA's Jadallah have been receiving calls from universities around the nation seeking advice on starting similar programs. "The old 'I didn't go to college because my parents couldn't afford it' is gone," Moretto says. "More people are funding themselves to go to college and are trying to figure it out." And as they do, some may need help along the way.

Reading: Identify Supporting Details

■ GOAL 2
Identify supporting details

Supporting details are those facts and ideas that prove or explain the main idea of a paragraph. While all the details in a paragraph support the main idea, not all details are equally important. As you read, try to identify and pay attention to the most important details. Pay less attention to details of lesser importance. The **major details** directly explain the main idea. The **minor details** may provide additional information, offer an example, or further explain one of the major details.

The diagram in Figure 4-1 shows how details relate to the main idea and how details vary in degree of importance. In the diagram, less important details appear below the important details they explain.

FIGURE 4-1

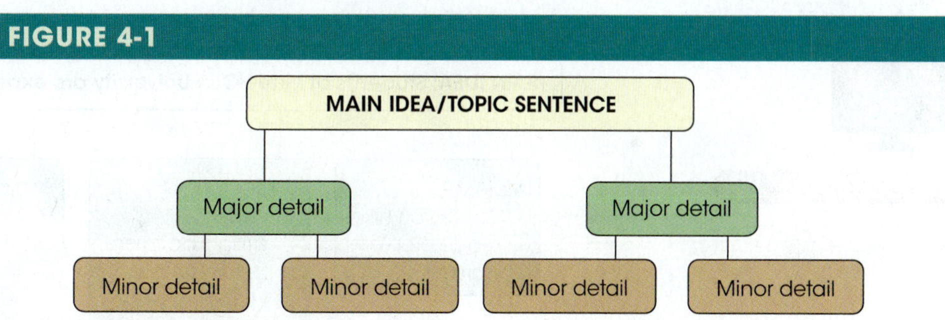

Read the following paragraph and study the diagram that follows.

The skin of the human body has several functions. First, it serves as a protective covering. In doing so, it accounts for 17 percent of the body weight. Skin also protects the organs within the body from damage or harm. The skin serves as a regulator of body functions. It controls body temperature and water loss. Finally, the skin serves as a receiver. It is sensitive to touch and temperature.

FIGURE 4-2

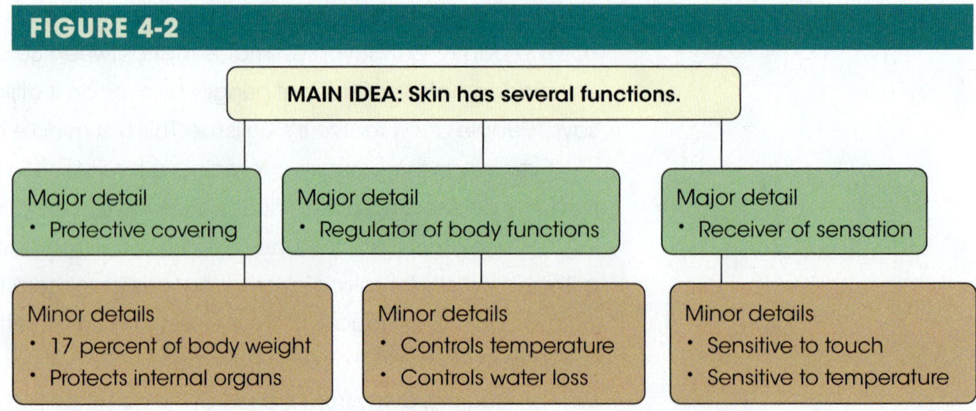

From the diagram in Figure 4-2 you can see that the details that state the three functions of skin are the major details. Other details, such as "protects internal organs," provide further information and are at a lower level of importance.

Read the following paragraph from the professional essay you just read (para. 7), and try to pick out the more important details.

> Two hours north of City College's campus, at one of the nation's most elite public universities, UCLA students are also experiencing food insecurity. Last fall's announcement of a 32-percent tuition hike exacerbated the problem, according to senior engineering major Abdallah Jadallah. Even before the increase, he noticed that many of his classmates were struggling to feed themselves, trying to get by on one meal a day—cheap but filling Taco Bell bean burritos are a particularly popular choice for the day's nourishment. He also noticed that many of the school's campus organizations regularly offered refreshments at their meetings and events, the leftovers from which were then thrown away. He found the discrepancy disturbing, so he went to the university's community programs office and requested a space to set aside leftovers for hungry students. The UCLA Food Closet was born.

This paragraph could be diagrammed as follows:

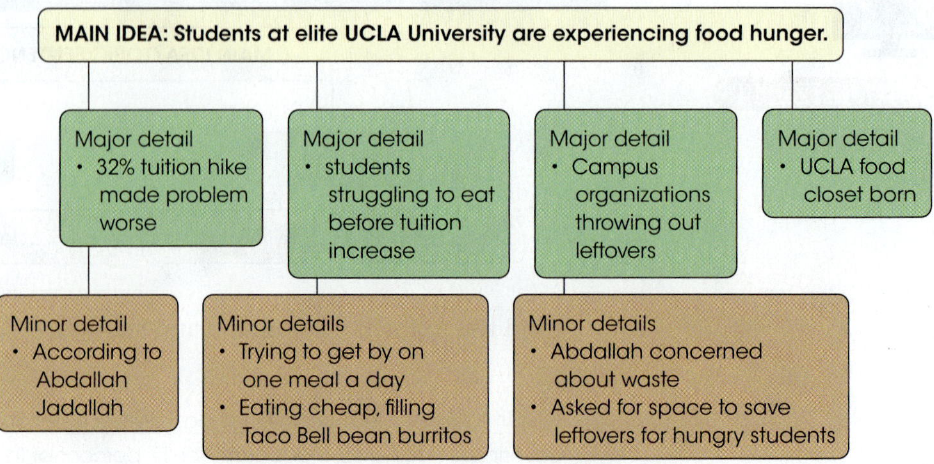

EXERCISE 4-1 Reading: Identifying Major Details

Directions: Read each of the following paragraphs and write the numbers of the sentences that contain only the most important major details.

Paragraph 1

[1]There are four main characteristics of a tourism product. [2]The first is service, which is intangible because it cannot be inspected physically. [3]For example, a tourist cannot sample a Caribbean cruise or a European tour before purchasing one. [4]The second characteristic is that the tourism product is largely psychological in its attraction. [5]It is more than airline seats or car rentals; it is the temporary use of a different environment, its culture, heritage, and experiences. [6]A third characteristic is that the product frequently varies in quality and standards. [7]A tourist's hotel experience may be excellent one time and not so good at the next visit. [8]A fourth characteristic of the tourism product is that the supply of the product is fixed. [9]For example, more hotel rooms cannot be instantly created to meet increased demand.

—adapted from Walker and Walker, *Tourism: Concepts and Practices*, p. 11

Major details: ____

Paragraph 2

[1]To be patented, an invention must be novel, useful, and nonobvious. [2]An invention is *novel* if it is new and has not been invented and used in the past. [3]If the invention has been used before, it is not novel and cannot be patented. [4]An invention is *useful* if it has some practical purpose. [5]For example, an inventor received a patent for "forkchops," which are a set of chopsticks with a spoon at one handle-end and a fork on the other handle-end. [6]This invention is useful. [7]If the invention is *nonobvious*, it qualifies for a patent; if the invention is obvious, then it does not qualify for a patent. [8]For example, inventors received a patent for a cardboard sleeve that can be placed over a paper coffee cup so that the cup will not be as hot as if there were no sleeve. [9]This invention is novel, useful, and nonobvious.

—adapted from Goldman and Cheeseman, *The Paralegal Professional*, pp. 736–737

Major details: ____

Paragraph 3

[1]People who exercise their mental abilities have been found to be far less likely to develop memory problems and even senile dementias such as Alzheimer's in old age. [2]"Use it or lose it" is the phrase to remember. [3]Working challenging crossword puzzles, for example, can be a major factor in maintaining a healthy level of cognitive functioning. [4]Reading, having an active social life, going to plays, taking classes, and staying physically active can all have a positive impact on the continued well-being of the brain.

—adapted from Ciccarelli and White, *Psychology: An Exploration*, p. 249

Major details: ____

Reading: Identifying Major and Minor Details

Directions: Read each of the following paragraphs, and then answer the multiple-choice questions about the diagram that follows.

Paragraph 1

Don't be fooled by words that sound impressive but mean little. Doublespeak is language that fails to communicate; it comes in four basic forms. **Euphemisms** make the negative and unpleasant appear positive and appealing, for example, calling the firing of 200 workers "downsizing" or "reallocation of resources." **Jargon** is the specialized language of a professional class (for example, the computer language of the hacker); it becomes doublespeak when used to communicate with people who aren't members of the group and who don't know this specialized language. **Gobbledygook** is overly complex language that overwhelms the listener instead of communicating meaning. **Inflated language** makes the mundane seem extraordinary, the common exotic ("take the vacation of a lifetime; explore unsurpassed vistas"). All four forms can be useful in some situations, but, when spoken or listened to mindlessly, they may obscure meaning and distort perceptions.

—DeVito, *Messages: Building Interpersonal Communication Skills*, p. 130

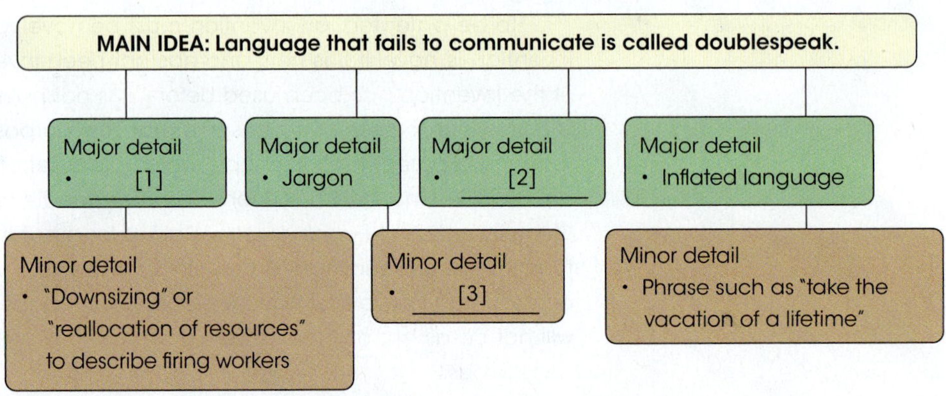

_____ 1. The correct word to fill in the blank labeled [1] is
   a. Doublespeak.
   b. Euphemisms.
   c. Negative.
   d. Positive.

_____ 2. The correct word or phrase to fill in the blank labeled [2] is
   a. Complex language.
   b. Specialized language.
   c. Gobbledygook.
   d. Mundane.

_____ 3. The correct phrase to fill in the blank labeled [3] is
   a. Obscure meanings.
   b. Distort perceptions.
   c. A professional class.
   d. The computer language of the hacker.

Paragraph 2

The risks associated with the consumption of alcohol are determined in part by how much an individual drinks. An **occasional drinker** is a person who drinks an alcoholic beverage once in a while. The occasional drinker seldom becomes intoxicated, and such drinking presents little or no threat to the health of the individual. A **social drinker** is someone who drinks regularly in social settings but seldom consumes enough alcohol to become intoxicated. Social drinking, like occasional drinking, does not necessarily increase health risks. **Binge drinking** is defined as having five drinks in a row for men or four in a row for women. Binge drinking can cause significant health and social problems. In comparison to nonbinge drinkers, binge drinkers are much more likely to have unprotected sex, to drive after drinking, and to fall behind in school.

—Pruitt and Stein, *Health Styles*, pp. 108, 110

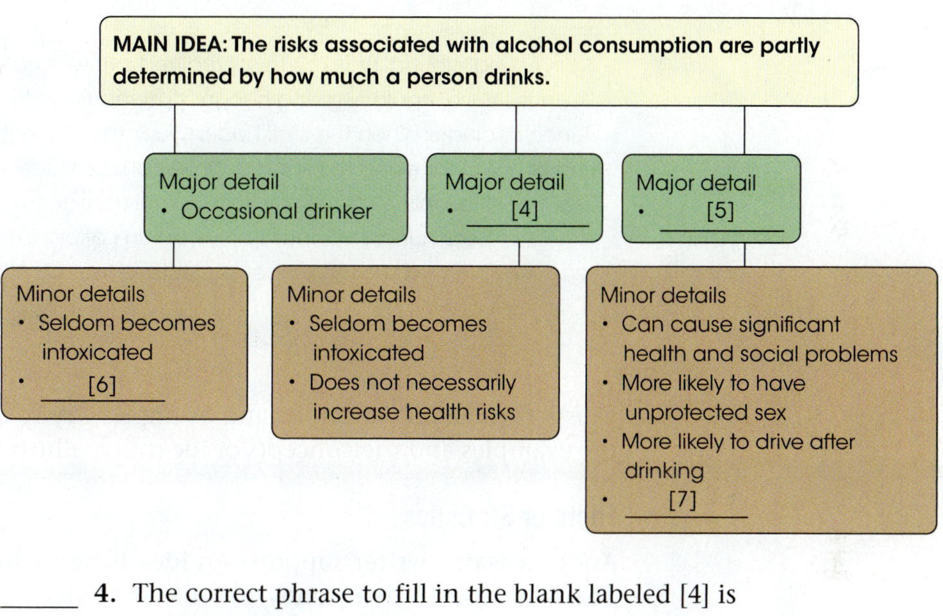

_____ **4.** The correct phrase to fill in the blank labeled [4] is
- **a.** Binge drinking.
- **b.** Alcohol consumption.
- **c.** Health risks.
- **d.** Social drinker.

_____ **5.** The correct phrase to fill in the blank labeled [5] is
- **a.** Social drinker.
- **b.** Binge drinking.
- **c.** Health problems.
- **d.** Social problems.

_____ **6.** The correct phrase to fill in the blank labeled [6] is
- **a.** Occasional drinker.
- **b.** Social drinker.
- **c.** Little or no health threat.
- **d.** Drinks regularly in social settings.

_____ **7.** The correct phrase to fill in the blank labeled [7] is
- **a.** More likely to fall behind in school.
- **b.** More likely to have health problems.
- **c.** Little or no health threat.
- **d.** Four or five drinks in a row.

Types of Supporting Details

There are many types of details a writer can use to explain or support a main idea, and the way a writer explains and supports an idea may influence how readily you accept or agree with it. The most common types of supporting details are (1) examples, (2) facts or statistics, (3) reasons, (4) descriptions, and (5) steps or procedures. Each will be briefly discussed here.

Examples

One way a writer may support an idea is by using examples. Examples make ideas and concepts real and understandable. In the following paragraph from the professional essay on hidden hunger (para. 2), the writer uses examples to illustrate how common it is for students to be hungry.

> Asking around, Bromley-Taylor realized she was not alone. Many of her colleagues were regularly giving hungry students five dollars here and there to buy lunch or dinner. When the staff had potluck meetings, they often found students lurking by the door, eying the spread. While college students are known for their insatiable appetites, this went beyond the eternal collegiate quest for free snacks—these students were hungry because they couldn't afford food. Bromley-Taylor wanted to do something, so last November she helped launch a free bag lunch program for City students.

As you read illustrations and examples, try to see the relationship between the examples and the concepts or ideas they illustrate.

Facts or Statistics

Another way a writer supports an idea is by including facts and/or statistics. The facts and statistics may provide evidence that the main idea is correct. Or the facts may further explain the main idea. For example, to prove that the divorce rate is high, the author may give statistics about the divorce rate and the percentage of the population that is divorced. Notice how, in the following paragraph from the professional essay (para. 4), the main idea stated in the first sentence—that sack lunches are made available to all City College students—is supported with specific facts about the program and its operation.

> At City, the nonperishable sack lunches contain some sort of protein, fruit, a bottle of water, and a couple of snacks, and are available to any of the community college's students. Since beginning in November, Bromley-Taylor says the school has handed out an average of about 10 lunches a day. Because of limited resources, students can take advantage of the lunch service only once a week, meaning that about 50 students use the program each week.

Reasons

A writer may support an idea by giving reasons *why* a main idea is correct. A writer might explain *why* nuclear power is dangerous or give reasons *why* a new speed limit law should be passed by Congress. In the following paragraph (para. 3), the author of the hidden hunger essay explains why free bag lunch programs for students are "popping up at campuses from Florida to Oregon."

> Programs like this one are popping up at campuses from Florida to Oregon, responding to the problem of low food security among college and university students. While the question of how to stretch minimal financial aid dollars or wages from part-time work to pay for a wide range of expenses has long been an issue for students, it's only gotten worse with the recent recession, say program administrators. Parents have fewer resources to help out, there is greater competition for work-study jobs, and many schools have increased tuition to cover their expenses. On-campus meal plans are often cost-prohibitive.

Descriptions

When the topic of a paragraph is a person, object, place, or process, the writer may develop the paragraph by describing it. Descriptions are details that help you create a mental picture of the object. In the following paragraph (para. 8), the author of the professional reading describes the space that houses the UCLA Food Closet and how it is used.

> The closet, really a small converted office, houses a donated refrigerator, an office cabinet that stands in as a pantry, and a table. Students can use the microwave in the building's kitchen to heat their meals, such as ramen or cans from a recent gift of ten Costco-sized cases of pork and beans. The Food Closet is kept open throughout the day so that students can come and go with relative anonymity.

Steps or Procedures

When a paragraph explains how to do something, the paragraph details are often lists of steps or procedures to be followed. For example, if the main idea of a paragraph is how to prepare an outline for a speech, then the details would list or explain the steps in preparing an outline. There is no one paragraph in the professional essay that lists steps or procedures, although paragraphs 5 and 6 describe how Bromley-Taylor came up with a model for a food assistance program based on a needs assessment, a process that includes several steps .The following paragraph is a good example of a description of a process—how fog is produced.

> Warm breezes blow over the ocean. When the moist air moves from warmer to cooler waters or from warm water to cool land, it chills. As it chills, water vapor molecules begin coalescing rather than bouncing off one another upon glancing collisions. Condensation takes place, and we have fog.
>
> —Hewitt, *Conceptual Physics*, p. 259

EXERCISE 4-3 Reading: Identifying Types of Details

Directions: Each topic sentence is followed by a list of details that could be used to support it. Label each detail as *example, fact or statistic, reason, description*, or *step or procedure*.

1. *Topic sentence:* Every April 15th, millions of Americans make their way to the post office to mail their income tax forms.

______________ Corporate taxes account for about 10 cents of every federal revenue dollar, compared with 47 cents from individual income taxes.

______________ This year, the Burnette family filed a return that entitles them to a substantial refund on their state income taxes.

______________ In order to submit an income tax return, you must first obtain the proper forms.

—Edwards et al., *Government in America*, pp. 458–459

2. *Topic sentence:* Historical and cultural attractions can be found in a variety of shapes, sizes, and locations throughout the world.

______________ In Europe, for every museum that existed in 1950, there are now more than four.

______________ Living History Farms, located near Des Moines, Iowa, is an attraction that offers a "hands-on" experience for visitors.

______________ More and more communities and countries are taking action to preserve historical sites because they attract visitors and generate income for local residents.

—Cook et al., *Tourism*, p. 209

3. *Topic sentence:* Many Americans are obsessed with losing weight.

______________ Weight loss obsession is often triggered by major events looming in the near future, such as a high school reunion or a "milestone" birthday.

______________ The two ways to lose weight are to lower caloric intake (through improved eating habits) and to increase exercise (expending more calories).

______________ Studies show that on any given day in America, nearly 40 percent of women and 24 percent of men over the age of 20 are trying to lose weight.

______________ Juan, a college freshman from Raleigh, admits that he has been struggling with a weight problem since he reached puberty.

—Donatelle and Davis, *Access to Health*, pp. 358, 371

4. *Topic sentence:* In the 1920s, many young American writers and artists left their country behind and became expatriates.

_______________ One of the most talented of the expatriates was Ernest Hemingway.

_______________ The expatriates flocked to Rome, Berlin, and Paris, in order to live cheaply and escape what seemed to them the "conspiracy against the individual" in America.

_______________ Some earned a living as journalists, translators, and editors, or made a few dollars by selling a poem to an American magazine or a painting to a tourist.

—Garraty and Carnes, *The American Nation*, p. 706

5. *Topic sentence:* The Anasazi Indians are best known for their artistic, architectural, and technological achievements.

_______________ The Anasazi used all of the available materials to build their settlements; with wood, mud, and stone, they erected cliff dwellings and the equivalent of terraced apartment houses.

_______________ The Anasazi built one structure with 500 living units; it was the largest residential building in North America until the completion of an apartment house in New York in 1772.

_______________ One example of their technological genius was their use of irrigation: they constructed sand dunes at the base of hills to hold the runoff from the sometimes torrential rains.

_______________ The Anasazi produced pottery that could rank in beauty with any in the world.

—Brummet et al., *Civilization*, p. 348

EXERCISE 4-4 Reading: Identifying Types of Details

Directions: For each of the first five paragraphs in the professional essay on pages 117–119, identify the type or types of details used by the author. Write your answers below.

1. Type(s) of details: _______________
2. Type(s) of details: _______________
3. Type(s) of details: _______________
4. Type(s) of details: _______________
5. Type(s) of details: _______________

Thinking Critically About Details

Writers choose the details they provide to support a main idea. They rarely have the time, or the space, to list every available supporting detail. Consider the following paragraph from the professional essay (para. 5):

> Bromley-Taylor came up with this model of food assistance after doing a needs assessment of City's students. She learned that the community college's students—most of whom are older re-entry students and many of whom are recent immigrants or refugees—were going without food to get by on limited budgets. Pannell says the advent of the bag lunch program is helping to change that. "It's a good hands-on program," she says, describing students who come running in for sustenance before class or tests. "This way they don't go to school starving."

The author provides two details to support the topic sentence "Bromley-Taylor came up with this model of food assistance after doing a needs assessment of City's students." These are: (1) many older and immigrant students were going without food to save money, and (2) the bag lunch program is helping decrease student hunger, as students can pick up a sack lunch before classes or tests. But the author could also have chosen other details. For example, she could have discussed how the survey was set up or other models that were considered.

As you read, be aware of the details that the writer has chosen to include. Has the writer omitted any important details to make a stronger case? Has he or she used any specific words to influence you? For example, suppose you are looking to rent an apartment, and you see an ad that reads as follows:

> 1 bedroom, 1 bath apartment. Cozy and cute, very conveniently located. Monthly rent includes water and gas. Most appliances also included. On-street parking is available.

This apartment may seem appealing, but look carefully at the details. What exactly does "cozy" mean? Often, the word *cozy* really means "small." And "conveniently located" might mean the apartment is located at a busy intersection (which might be very noisy). The rent includes water and gas . . . but what about electricity? "Most" appliances are included—which ones aren't? (Maybe you'd have to buy a stove or a refrigerator.) And the fact that on-street parking is "available" doesn't guarantee that you'll always get a parking spot in front of the building.

EXERCISE 4-5 Reading: Thinking Critically About Details

Directions: Read each paragraph and answer the questions that follow.

A. A lot of people are looking for a "magic pill" that will help them maintain weight loss, reduce their risk of diseases, make them feel better, and improve their quality of sleep. Although many people are not aware of it, regular physical activity is this "magic pill." That's because it promotes physical fitness: the ability to carry out daily tasks with vigor and alertness, without undue fatigue, and with ample energy to enjoy leisure-time pursuits and meet unforeseen emergencies.

—Thompson and Manore, *Nutrition for Life*, p. 302

1. What essential ingredient of good health/physical fitness is missing from this paragraph? ______________________________

B. The world's most livable cities are not those with "perfect" auto access between all points. Instead, they are cities that have taken measures to reduce outward sprawl, diminish automobile traffic, and improve access by foot and bicycle in conjunction with mass transit. For example, Geneva, Switzerland, prohibits automobile parking at workplaces in the city's center, forcing commuters to use the excellent public transportation system. Copenhagen bans all on-street parking in the downtown core. Paris has removed 200,000 parking places in the downtown area. Curitiba, Brazil, is cited as the most livable city in all of Latin America. The achievement of Curitiba is due almost entirely to the efforts of Jaime Lerner, who, serving as mayor for many decades, guided development with an emphasis on mass transit rather than cars. The space saved by not building highways and parking lots has been put into parks and shady walkways, causing the amount of green area per inhabitant to increase from 4.5 square feet in 1970 to 450 square feet today.

—Wright and Boorse, *Environmental Science: Toward a Sustainable Future*, p. 604

2. What is the main idea of the paragraph?

____

____

3. Which four cities are offered as examples (supporting details) of livable cities?

____

4. By not listing any U.S. examples of "livable cities," what might the author be implying (but not stating directly)?

____

____

5. What other cities might have been mentioned as having good systems of mass transit? (Hint: Think of U.S. cities that have reliable train and bus service.)

____

____

EXAMINING STUDENT WRITING

A good way to learn to read essays and write essays is to study a model. By examining the student essay below by Yesenia De Jesus you will learn how to identify topics and topic sentences as you read and how to create clear and effective topic sentences as you write. Throughout the rest of chapter, we will use parts of Yesenia's essay to illustrate techniques and strategies for using details and transitions in an essay.

Yesenia De Jesus is in her junior year at Palm Beach State College. Her essay is a true story. She was hesitant to write about her experience initially, but her teacher persuaded her to do so, and Yesenia felt that if telling her story influenced or inspired even one student to take chances and be successful, it was worth sharing such a personal story. Yesenia submitted this essay to Writing Rewards, a Pearson-sponsored essay contest open to students in college writing classes. Her essay was selected for use in this book because it is a strong example of a narrative essay.

Title: Suggests positive outcome of the essay

From Bullet to Blue Sky

Yesenia De Jesus

Introduction

Background information about the neighborhood

Descriptive details about the victim

A dramatic and interest-catching thesis

1 The sun was in the process of its morning stretch. While the residents of gated communities came alive to be greeted by the tropical heat of south Florida, the stragglers of the universe awoke to the sounds of a 9 mm dispersing its gun powder to the blue sky. The ghetto houses that sheltered these citizens were painted different colors; some exposed faded paint, and others told stories in graffiti, inspired by gang artists marking their territories. Roll bars protected the windows covered with filthy bed sheets that not even dogs would lie on. Broken toy pieces scattered over the dead grass in the yard outside. The lanky, dark-haired girl lay in her bed twisting and turning, trying to catch a cool wave from the ceiling fan that spun and thumped overhead all night. She always heard the same dogs barking; her ears still rang from the sound of that gun. She still felt the warm, thin blood that stained her hands. She still felt a sharp, pounding pain along her left side; for every breath she took, the pain reminded her she was human. She had witnessed many shootings before; she had seen more blood in her days. Why was this shooting any different? It was because for the first time she was the victim. I understood her pain, for I was that girl.

Topic sentence

Transitional words and phrases organize ideas and guide the reader through the paragraph

Details about the school and the writer's math class

Dialogue adds interest and detail to the story

2 It all started with Mr. Tangye in the fall of 2004, an inspiring math teacher, who convinced me that I had more to offer this world than I had thought. As the bell rang at Conniston Middle School, we marched like zombies to our classes. I passed through dark hallways of vandalized lockers with torn papers and ripped books scattered over the ground like a dump. I made my way past the miserable teachers and devilish students. The administrators surrounded the hallways like a S.W.A.T. team, commanding everyone to go to class. I walked into Mr. Tangye's math class; he had a bright, white smile that hurt my eyes every time I looked at him. Before I could make it to my seat, Mr. Tangye handed me a paper that itched my fingers; it was a math test. I stared at that test, and I begged my brain to wake up! The other kids shuffled the paper back and forth on top of their desks or used it as a pillow on which to lay their heads. I secretly tried my best at every problem and flippantly turned it in. As the bell rang, I dashed for the exit. I swiftly dropped off my homework, but Mr. Tangye caught me and pulled me aside to show me my test. He said, "You are the only one who has passed the test." Then as Mr. Tangye showed my grade to me, he said, "You are on the borderline of failing or passing this class, I'd like to see you pass!" I listened to every word he said because I was tired of being perceived as an idiot.

Topic sentence

3 As I finished out the rest of that day, all I could think about was whether to study or not to study. I hated being stuck between a world that offered happiness and stability, whose proverb was "anything is possible" and a world that followed the theory of Charles Darwin's "survival of the fittest." People in my world struggled for everything—money, power, respect, even the last piece of fried chicken. My world had an underground feudal system to follow with rules to be respected, lines not to be crossed. Although this world was violent, senseless, crazy, it was my world. This unmerciful, savage world . . . I was comfortable in it. I felt super-glued to this world; I felt guilty leaving it behind, like a crack head quitting dope. I silenced that inner voice that begged me to stay. I was going to make it out of my world of hardship and struggle and bullets.

Topic sentence

4 When I got home, I was greeted by a warm aroma from the kitchen, where I always found my mother. We greeted each other in our usual exchange. After I gave my mother a brief overview of how school went, I rushed to my room to study. I was tired of the struggles, fights, problems, which by birth, I did not deserve. I was going to be somebody; I was going to do something with my life. I was not going to be another Al Capone or Bonnie with a Clyde. I was going to be somebody the way God intended. I was going to earn a living the right, clean way, but in order to be somebody, I needed an education. I would have to get an "A" on my chapter test in Mr. Tangye's math class. I had to do it. I would!

Topic sentence

5 Four gruesome weeks passed. I slept, ate, and studied. The morning of the test, I woke up early. I studied some more, for I wanted to be alert in case an unusual math problem was on the test. I left early that day to ask a few questions. Usually, I took a longer route to school to avoid crossing enemy lines, but I rushed through a shortcut. The shortcut led me to the back of the school, where boys played basketball and girls double-dutched after school, but the recess court was empty. No one stood in the courtyard but me. My eyes locked on the formula sheet I memorized. Suddenly, I heard a familiar sound as gunshots sliced the morning air; tires screeched. As I walked toward the school building, I felt something drizzle down the side of my torso. I grabbed my shirt; something slightly tickled me. It was wet. It was not sweat; it was blood. Three small holes pierced my skin, leaving bloody trails racing down my hip. I had been shot. It happened so quickly. I threw my paper and books, bloody from my handprint, on the ground. I screamed at top of my lungs, not because I had been shot, but because I knew I could not take my math test, the test I had studied so damn hard for. My memory faded before I collapsed. A former fire rescuer spotted me on the ground and got help.

Topic sentence

6 As I lay in my bed at home, I tried to crawl around my brain; I wanted a reason why God led me to this path. I was not connected to these savages, who shot me. These thugs just wandered around the neighborhood trying to find an ordinary person to become a victim, whose fate would carry a dark message.

Topic sentence

7 When I was shot, it did not overpower my life; it empowered my spirit. As I got out of bed, I tried to convince myself I should stay there, but I could not find any good reason. My injuries were three-days fresh, but I was determined to take that math test. I reached to find the strength from deep within my soul to move. The pain gripped my side like 500 needles repeatedly stabbing my ribs. I grabbed a chair so deeply that I bent my nails backwards. My arms and legs shook. I screamed with every movement I made, yet the agonizing pain only intensified. I gripped my book

as I walked out the door. Slow steps minimized the pain. I gave my mother a kiss as the bus approached the curb. She touched my arm and reassured me that I could make up the test after I healed completely. I objected because I was ready for this test now. I told my mom that morning that I tried to better myself. This neighborhood, this ghetto, hardship-world I lived in tried to bring me down; it tried to kill me. I refused to allow it.

Conclusion: The story ends on a positive, self-affirming note

8 On a sunny day with blue sky above, I dropped my coins into the bus depositor, found a seat, and quietly, painfully moaned along the ride. My mother waved to me as the bus drove off. She was staring at me with a satisfied expression upon her face, for she knew she was raising a fighter, a winner, and a believer. She was raising a somebody.

Writing: Select and Organize Details to Support Your Topic Sentence

■ GOAL 3
Select and organize details to support your topic sentence

The details you choose to support your topic sentence must be both relevant and sufficient. **Relevant** means that the details directly explain and support your topic sentence. For example, if you were to write a paragraph for your employer explaining why you deserve a raise, it would not be relevant to mention that you plan to use the money to go to Florida next spring. A vacation has nothing to do with—is not relevant to—your job performance.

Sufficient means that you must provide enough information to make your topic sentence understandable and convincing. In your paragraph explaining why you deserve a raise, it would probably not be sufficient to say that you are always on time. You would need to provide more information about your job performance: for example, that you always volunteer to work holidays, that you've offered good suggestions for displaying new products, and that several customers have written letters praising your work.

In addition to choosing relevant and sufficient details, be sure to select a variety of details, use specific words, and organize your paragraph effectively.

Selecting Relevant Details

Relevant details directly support your topic sentence. They help clarify and strengthen your ideas, whereas irrelevant details make your ideas unclear and confusing. Here is the first draft of paragraph 6 from Yesenia's essay. Can you locate the detail that is not relevant?

[1]As I lay in my bed at home, I tried to crawl around my brain. [2]I looked at the clock and saw how slowly time was passing. [3]I wanted a reason why God led me to this path. [4]I was not connected to these savages, who shot me. [5]These thugs just wandered around the neighborhood trying to find an ordinary person to become a victim, whose fate would carry a dark message.

Sentence 2 does not belong in the paragraph. Yesenia is explaining her thoughts after she was shot and the reference to the clock does not relate to her topic.

Use the following simple test to be sure each detail you include belongs in your paragraph:

Test for Relevant Details

1. Read your topic sentence in combination with each of the other sentences in your paragraph. For example,
   - read topic sentence + last sentence.
   - read topic sentence + second-to-last sentence.
   - read topic sentence + third-to-last sentence.
2. For each pair of sentences, ask yourself, "Do these two ideas fit together?" If your answer is "No," then you have found a detail that is not relevant to your topic. Delete it from your paragraph.

Another student wrote the following paragraph on the subject of the legal drinking age. As you read it, cross out the details that are not relevant.

> [1]The legal drinking age should be raised to 25. [2]Anyone who drinks should be old enough to determine whether or not it is safe to drive after drinking. [3]Bartenders and others who serve drinks should also have to be 25. [4]In general, teenagers and young adults are not responsible enough to limit how much they drink. [5]The party atmosphere enjoyed by so many young people encourages crazy acts, so we should limit who can drink. [6]Younger people think drinking is a game, but it is a dangerous game that affects the lives of others.

Which sentence did you delete? Why did you delete it? The third sentence does not belong in the paragraph because the age of those who bartend or serve drinks is not relevant to the topic. Sentence 5, about partying, should also be eliminated or explained because the connection between partying and drinking is not clear.

EXERCISE 4-6

Writing: Identifying Relevant Details

Directions: Place a check mark by those statements that provide relevant supporting details.

1. Sales representatives need good interpersonal skills.

   ______ **a.** They need to be good listeners.

   ______ **b.** They should like helping people.

   ______ **c.** They should know their products well.

2. Water can exist in three forms, which vary with temperature.

   ______ **a.** At a high temperature, water becomes steam; it is a gas.

   ______ **b.** Drinking water often contains mineral traces.

   ______ **c.** At cold temperatures, water becomes ice, a solid state.

3. Outlining is one of the easiest ways to organize facts.

_____ a. Formal outlines use Roman numerals and letters and Arabic numerals to show different levels of importance.

_____ b. Outlining emphasizes the relationships among facts.

_____ c. Outlines make it easier to focus on important points.

WRITING IN PROGRESS

Writing: Drafting a Paragraph

Directions: Write a paragraph answering one of the following questions that relate to Yesenia's essay. When you've finished, use the test on page 133 to make certain each detail is relevant.

1. Who has inspired you to change your life?
2. Describe a frightening situation or life-threatening event you have experienced that has impacted the way you think or act.
3. Tell about a challenging academic situation you have experienced and how you dealt with it.
4. Tell about a workplace challenge you have overcome.
5. When have you struggled with the decision to stay in college, and what motivated you to keep going?

Including Sufficient Details

Including **sufficient detail** means that your paragraph contains an adequate amount of specific information for your readers to understand your main idea. Your supporting details must thoroughly and clearly explain why you believe your topic sentence is true. Be sure that your details are specific; do not provide summaries or unsupported statements of opinion.

Let's look at a first draft of a paragraph Yesenia wrote about the topic of whether to study or not study.

I came home from school and talked to my mother. Then I went to my room to study. I was tired but I really needed to study. I had to do well on my math test.

This paragraph is filled with general statements. It does not explain what Yesenia talked to her mother about or why she was tired. No detail is given about why it was important for her to do well on her test and her motivation for studying is not described. There is not sufficient support for the topic sentence. Here is the revised version:

When I got home, I was greeted by a warm aroma from the kitchen, where I always found my mother. We greeted each other in our usual exchange. After I gave my mother a brief overview of how school went, I rushed to my room to study. I was tired of the struggles, fights, problems, which by birth, I did not deserve. I was going to be somebody; I was going to do something with my life. I was not going to be another Al Capone or Bonnie with a Clyde. I was going to be somebody the way God intended. I was going to earn a living the right, clean way, but in order to be somebody, I needed an education. I would have to get an "A" on my chapter test in Mr. Tangye's math class. I had to do it. I would!

If you have trouble thinking of enough details to include in a paragraph, try brainstorming or one of the other techniques for generating ideas described in Chapter 2. Write your topic sentence at the top of a sheet of paper. Then list everything that comes to mind about that topic. Include examples, events, incidents, facts, and reasons. You will be surprised at how many useful details you think of.

When you finish, read over your list and cross out details that are not relevant. (If you still do not have enough, your topic may be too specific. See pp. 103–104.) The section "Organizing Details Effectively" below will help you decide in what order you will write about the details on your list.

Writing: Evaluating and Revising a Paragraph

Directions: Reread the paragraph you wrote for Exercise 4-7 to see if it includes sufficient detail. If necessary, revise your paragraph to include more detail, always making sure the details you add are relevant. Use a prewriting technique, if necessary, to generate additional details.

Types of Supporting Details

There are many types of details that you can use to explain or support a topic sentence. As discussed earlier in this chapter (pp. 124–125), the most common types of supporting details are (1) examples, (2) facts or statistics, (3) reasons, (4) descriptions, and (5) steps or procedures. It is advisable to vary the types of details you use, and to choose those appropriate to your topic.

Writing: Using a Variety of Supporting Details

Directions: Working with a classmate, for each topic sentence, write at least three different types of details that could be used to support it. Label each detail as *example, fact or statistic, reason, description,* or *steps or procedure.*

1. People make inferences about you based on the way you dress.
2. Many retailers with traditional stores have decided to market their products through Web sites as well.
3. Many Americans are obsessed with losing weight.
4. Historical and cultural attractions can be found in a variety of shapes, sizes, and locations throughout the world.
5. Using a search engine is an effective, though not perfect, method of searching the Internet.

Organizing Details Effectively

Yesenia concluded her essay with a paragraph describing her bus ride to take her math test. She drafted the paragraph and then revised it. As you read each version, pay particular attention to the order in which she arranged the details.

FIRST DRAFT

It was a sunny day with a blue sky above. My mother waved at me as the bus drove off. She knew she was raising a fighter, a winner, a believer, a somebody. I dropped my coins into the bus depositor and found a seat. I quietly, painfully moaned along the ride. My mother was staring at me with a satisfied expression upon her face.

REVISION

On a sunny day with blue sky above, I dropped my coins into the bus depositor, found a seat, and quietly, painfully moaned along the ride. My mother waved to me as the bus drove off. She was staring at me with a satisfied expression upon her face, for she knew she was raising a fighter, a winner, and a believer. She was raising a somebody.

Did you find the revision easier to read? In the first draft, Yesenia recorded details as she thought of them. There is no logical arrangement to them. In the second version, she arranged the details in the order in which they happened. Yesenia chose this arrangement because it fit her details logically. The three common methods for arranging details are as follows:

1. Time sequence
2. Spatial arrangement
3. Least/most arrangement

Time Sequence

Time sequence means the order in which something happens. For example, if you were to write about a particularly bad day, you could describe the day in the order in which everything went wrong. You might begin with waking up in the morning and end with going to bed that night. If you were describing a busy or an exciting weekend, you might begin with what you did on Friday night and end with the last activity on Sunday. In the following paragraph (para. 5), Yesenia uses time sequence to describe the events that led up to the shooting and how she reacted to it.

Four gruesome weeks passed. I slept, ate, and studied. The morning of the test, I woke up early. I studied some more, for I wanted to be alert in case an unusual math problem was on the test. I left early that day to ask a few questions. Usually, I took a longer route to school to avoid crossing enemy lines, but I rushed through a shortcut. The shortcut led me to the back of the school, where boys played basketball and girls double-dutched after school, but the recess court was empty. No one stood in the courtyard but me. My eyes locked on the formula sheet I memorized. Suddenly, I heard a familiar sound as gunshots sliced the morning air; tires screeched. As I walked toward the school building, I felt something drizzle down the side of my torso. I grabbed my shirt; something slightly tickled me. It was wet. It was not sweat; it was blood. Three small holes pierced my skin, leaving bloody trails racing down my hip. I had been shot. It happened so quickly. I threw my paper and books, bloody from my handprint, on the ground. I screamed at top of my lungs, not because I had been shot, but because I knew I could not take my math test, the test I had studied so damn hard for. My memory faded before I collapsed. A former fire rescuer spotted me on the ground and got help.

Spatial Arrangement

Suppose you are asked to describe the room in which you are sitting. You want your reader, who has never been in the room, to visualize it, so you need to describe, in an orderly way, where items are positioned. You could describe the room from left to right, from ceiling to floor, or from door to window. In other situations, your choices might include front to back, inside to outside, near to far, east to west, and so on. This method of presentation is called **spatial arrangement**. How are the details arranged in the following excerpt from Yesenia's introductory paragraph?

> The sun was in the process of its morning stretch. While the residents of gated communities came alive to be greeted by the tropical heat of south Florida, the stragglers of the universe awoke to the sounds of a 9 mm dispersing its gun powder to the blue sky. The ghetto houses that sheltered these citizens were painted different colors; some exposed faded paint, and others told stories in graffiti, inspired by gang artists marking their territories. Roll bars protected the windows covered with filthy bed sheets that not even dogs would lie on. Broken toy pieces scattered over the dead grass in the yard outside.

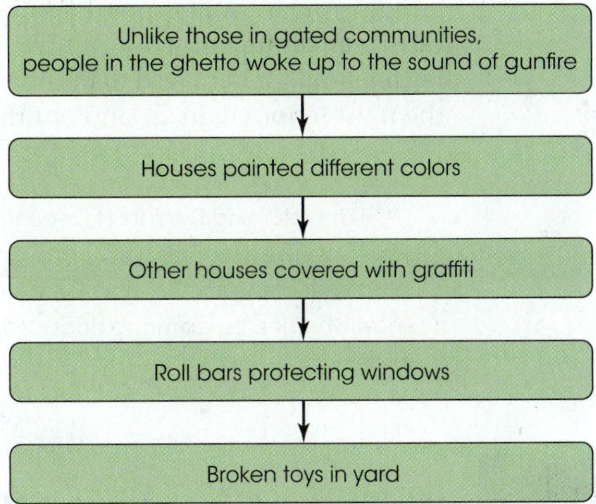

The topic you are writing about will often determine the arrangement you choose. In writing about a town, you might choose to begin with the center and then move to each surrounding area. In describing a building, you might go from bottom to top.

Writing: Using Spatial Arrangement

Directions: Indicate which spatial arrangement you would use to describe the following topics. Then write a paragraph on one of the topics.

1. A local market or favorite store
2. A photograph you value
3. A prized possession
4. A building in which you work
5. Your campus cafeteria, bookstore, or lounge

The Least/Most Arrangement

Another method of arranging details is to present them in order from least to most or most to least, according to some quality or characteristic. For example, you might arrange details from least to most *expensive*, least to most *serious*, or least to most *important*. In her essay, Yesenia uses the least/most arrangement in paragraph 6, where she moves from the less important details of the morning she was shot—getting up early, having breakfast, studying, and leaving early—to the most important ones—taking a short cut through enemy lines, where she was shot, and the injuries she sustained.

VISUALIZE IT!

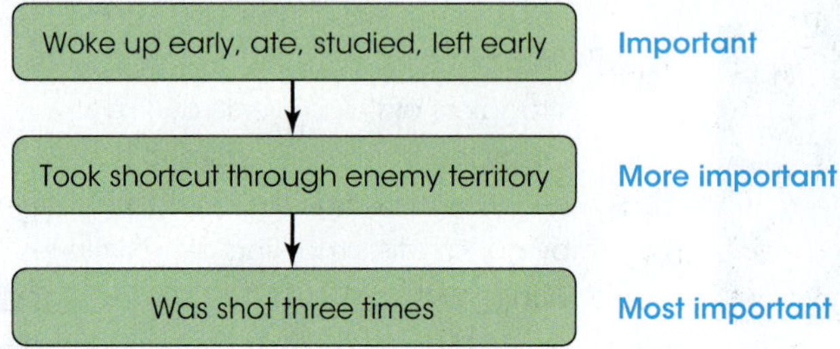

You can also arrange details from most to least. This structure allows you to present your strongest point first. Many writers use this method to construct a case or an argument. For example, if you were writing a business letter requesting a refund for damaged mail-order merchandise, you would want to begin with the most serious damage and put the minor complaints at the end, as follows:

> I am returning the tablet I recently received from you in the mail. It will not switch on, even though I have charged it for a full day. There is a crack in the top left corner of the screen, and there are two deep scratches on the back. I do not know whether the damage occurred in transit or before mailing, but I do expect a full refund.

EXERCISE 4-11

Writing: Using Least/Most Arrangement

Directions: Write a paragraph supporting one of the following topics. Organize your details using the most-to-least or least-to-most arrangement.

1. Reasons why you enjoy a particular sport or hobby
2. Five special items in your closet
3. Three favorite musicians or musical groups
4. Things to remember when renting an apartment
5. Why you like city (or small-town or country) living

Using Specific Words

When you write a paragraph, use specific words to give your reader as much information as possible. You can think of words the way an artist thinks of colors on a palette. Vague words are brown and muddy; specific words are brightly colored and lively. Try to paint pictures for your reader with specific, vivid words. Here are a few examples of vague words along with more specific words or phrases for the same idea:

VAGUE	fun
SPECIFIC	thrilling, relaxing, enjoyable, pleasurable
VAGUE	dark
SPECIFIC	hidden in gray-green shadows
VAGUE	experienced
SPECIFIC	five years in the job
VAGUE	tree
SPECIFIC	red maple

The following suggestions will help you develop your details. Study each example from Yesenia's essay.

1. **Use specific verbs.** Choose verbs (action words) that help your reader picture the action.

VAGUE	There was a sound of gunshots and a car driving away.
SPECIFIC	Suddenly, I heard a familiar sound as gunshots sliced the morning air; tires screeched.

2. **Give exact names.** Include the names of people, places, objects, and brands.

VAGUE	My math teacher always had a big smile.
SPECIFIC	I walked into Mr. Tangye's math class; he had a bright, white smile that hurt my eyes every time I looked at him.

3. **Use adjectives before nouns to convey details.**

VAGUE	The school was a mess.
SPECIFIC	I passed through dark hallways of vandalized lockers with torn papers and ripped books scattered over the ground like a dump.

4. **Use words that appeal to the senses.** Choose words that suggest touch, taste, smell, sound, and sight.

VAGUE	People in south Florida woke up to warm weather and guns being fired.
SPECIFIC	While the residents of gated communities came alive to be greeted by the tropical heat of south Florida, the stragglers of the universe awoke to the sounds of a 9 mm dispersing its gun powder to the blue sky.

To summarize, use words that help your readers create mental pictures.

VAGUE	The houses in this neighborhood were rough.
SPECIFIC	The ghetto houses that sheltered these citizens were painted different colors; some exposed faded paint, and others told stories in graffiti, inspired by gang artists marking their territories.

EXERCISE 4-12

Writing: Using Specific Words

Directions: Rewrite these vague sentences, using specific words.

1. The concert was really good.

   ____

2. The birthday cake was nice.

   ____

3. I found an interesting Web site on the Internet.

   ____

4. I read a good book.

   ____

5. The meeting was long.

   ____

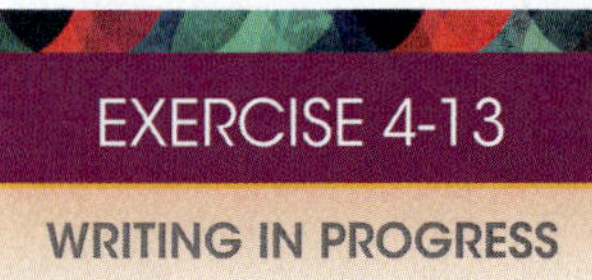

EXERCISE 4-13

WRITING IN PROGRESS

Writing: Revising a Paragraph

Directions: Reread the paragraph you revised in Exercise 4-8. As you read, underline any vague or general words. Then replace the underlined words with more specific ones.

NEED TO KNOW

Important Terms

Relevant details: Details that directly explain the topic sentence

Sufficient details: Details that provide adequate support of the topic sentence

Time sequence: Arranging ideas in the order in which they happen

Spatial arrangement: Arranging ideas according to their position in space

Least/most arrangement: Presenting ideas from least to most or most to least according to some quality or characteristic

Specific words: Words that provide a great deal of information

Transitional words and phrases: Words that lead the reader from one detail to another

Use Transitions to Guide Your Reading and Writing

■ GOAL 4
Use transitions to guide your reading and writing

Transitions are linking words or phrases used to lead the reader from one idea to another. If you get in the habit of recognizing transitions, you will see that they often guide you through a paragraph, helping you to read it more easily.

When writing, be sure to provide transitions to connect your ideas and show how your ideas are related. Use them to guide your readers through your paragraph. Think of them as signposts to tell your reader where your paragraph is going or what is coming next.

In the following excerpt from the professional reading, notice how the circled transitions lead you from one important detail to the next.

While college students are known for their insatiable appetites, this went beyond the eternal collegiate quest for free snacks—these students were hungry because they couldn't afford food. Bromley-Taylor wanted to do something, so last November she helped launch a free bag lunch program for City students.

Also, review paragraph 2 of Yesenia's essay (p. 130), where transitional words and phrases have been highlighted, to see how she used transitions to organize her writing and guide her reader.

Not all paragraphs contain such obvious transitions, and not all transitions serve as such clear markers of major details. Transitions may be used to alert you to what will come next in the paragraph. If you see the phrase *for instance* at the beginning of a sentence, then you know that an example will follow. When you see the phrase *on the other hand*, you can predict that a different, opposing idea will follow. Table 4-1 lists some of the most common transitions used within a paragraph and indicates what they tell you.

TABLE 4-1 COMMON TRANSITIONS

Type of Transition	Example	What It Tells the Reader
Time Sequence	*first, later, next, finally*	The author is arranging ideas in the order in which they happened.
Example	*for example, for instance, to illustrate, such as*	An example will follow.
Enumeration	*first, second, third, last, one, another, next*	The author is marking or identifying each major point. (Sometimes these may be used to suggest order of importance.)
Continuation	*also, in addition, and, further, another*	The author is continuing with the same idea and is going to provide additional information.
Contrast	*on the other hand, in contrast, however*	The author is switching to a different, opposite, or contrasting idea from that previously discussed.
Comparison	*like, likewise, similarly*	The writer will show how the previous idea is similar to what follows.
Cause/Effect	*because, thus, therefore, since, consequently*	The writer will show a connection between two or more things, how one thing caused another, or how something happened as a result of something else.
Summation	*to sum up, in conclusion*	The writer will draw his or her ideas together.

Reading: Making Predictions

Directions: Each of the following beginnings of paragraphs uses a transitional word or phrase to tell the reader what will follow in the paragraph. Working in pairs, read each, paying particular attention to the underlined word or phrase. Then discuss what you would expect to find next in the paragraph. Summarize your findings in the space provided.

1. Price is not the only factor to consider in choosing a pharmacy. Many provide valuable services that should be considered. For instance, . . .

   ____

2. There are a number of things you can do to prevent a home burglary. First, . . .

   ____

3. Most mail order businesses are reliable and honest. However, . . .

____

4. One advantage of a compact stereo system is that all the components are built into the unit. Another, . . .

____

5. Taking medication can have an effect on your hormonal balance. Therefore, . . .

____

6. To select the presidential candidate you will vote for, you should examine his or her philosophy of government. Next . . .

____

7. Eating solely vegetables drastically reduces caloric and fat intake, two things on which most people overindulge. On the other hand, . . .

____

8. Asbestos, a common material found in many older buildings in which people have worked for decades, has been shown to cause cancer. Consequently, . . .

____

9. Cars and trucks are not designed randomly. They are designed individually for specific purposes. For instance, . . .

____

10. Jupiter is a planet surrounded by several moons. Likewise, . . .

____

EXERCISE 4-15 Writing: Choosing Transitional Words

Directions: Read each of the following sentences. In each blank, write a transitional word or phrase from the box below that makes sense in the sentence.

next	however	for example	another	consequently
because	similarly	such as	to sum up	in addition

1. After a heart attack, the heart muscle is permanently weakened; ________________ its ability to pump blood throughout the body may be reduced.
2. Some metals, ________________ gold and silver, are represented by symbols derived from their Latin names.
3. In order to sight-read music, you should begin by scanning it. ________________ you should identify the key and tempo.
4. The *Oxford English Dictionary*, by giving all present and past definitions of words, shows how word definitions have changed with time. ________________, it gives the date and written source where each word appears to have first been used.

5. Some scientists believe intelligence to be determined equally by heredity and environment. ________________, other scientists believe heredity to account for about 60 percent of intelligence and environment for the other 40 percent.

6. Tigers tend to grow listless and unhappy in captivity. ________________, pandas grow listless and have a difficult time reproducing in captivity.

7. ________________, the most important ways to prevent heat stress are to (1) allow yourself time to get used to the heat, (2) wear the proper clothing, and (3) drink plenty of water.

8. Many people who are dissatisfied with the public school system send their children to private schools. ________________ option that is gaining in popularity is homeschooling.

9. Studies have shown that it is important to "exercise" our brains as we age. ________________, crossword puzzles are a good way to keep mentally fit.

10. Buying smaller-sized clothing generally will not give an overweight person the incentive to lose weight. People with weight problems tend to eat when they are upset or disturbed, and ________________ wearing smaller clothing is frustrating and upsetting, overweight people will generally gain weight by doing so.

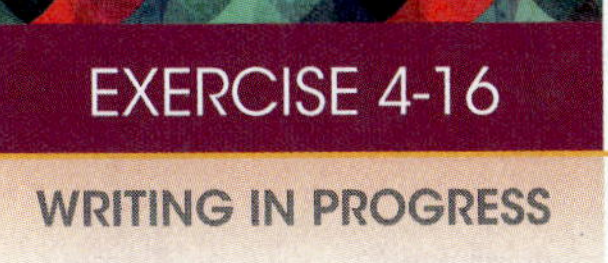

Writing: Revising a Paragraph

Directions: Review the paragraph you wrote for Exercise 4-11. Underline any transitions you used. Revise the paragraph by adding transitional words or phrases to clarify your details.

Reading: Identify Implied Main Ideas

■ GOAL 5
Find implied main ideas

As you know, when a writer leaves his or her main idea unstated, it is up to you, the reader, to look at the details in the paragraph and figure out the writer's main point. The details, when taken together, will all point to a general and more important idea. You might want to think of such a paragraph as the pieces of a puzzle. You must put together the pieces or details to determine the meaning of the paragraph as a whole. Use the following steps as a guide to find implied main ideas.

Tips for Identifying Implied Main Ideas

1. **Find the topic.** As you know, the *topic* is the general subject of the entire paragraph. Ask yourself: "What is the one thing the author is discussing throughout the paragraph?"
2. **Figure out what is the most important idea the writer wants you to know about that topic.** Look at each detail and decide what larger idea is being explained.
3. **Express this main idea in your own words.** Make sure that the main idea is a reasonable one. Ask yourself: "Does it apply to all of the details in the paragraph?"

Men's friendships are often built around shared activities—attending a ball game, playing cards, working on a project at the office. Women's friendships, on the other hand, are built more around a sharing of feelings, support, and "personalism." One study found that similarity in status, in willingness to protect one's friend in uncomfortable situations, in academic major, and even in proficiency in playing Password were significantly related to the relationship closeness of male-male friends but not of female-female or female-male friends.

—DeVito, *Messages: Building Interpersonal Communication Skills*, p. 290

The general topic of this paragraph is friendships. More specifically, the paragraph is about the differences between male and female friendships. Three details are given: (1) men's friendships are based on shared activities, (2) women's friendships are based on shared feelings, and (3) similarity is important in men's friendships but not in women's. Each of the three details is a difference between male and female friendships. The main point the writer is trying to make, then, is that men and women have different criteria for building friendships. You can figure out this writer's main idea even though no single sentence states this directly. You might visualize this paragraph as follows:

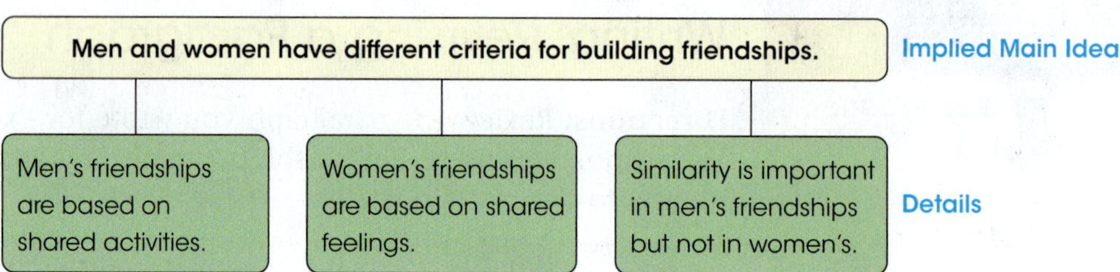

Here is another paragraph. Read it and then fill in the diagram that follows:

By now most people know that the herb Echinacea may help conquer the common cold. Herbal remedies that are less well known include flaxseed, for treating constipation, and fennel, for soothing an upset stomach. In addition, the herb chamomile may be brewed into a hot cup of tea for a good night's sleep.

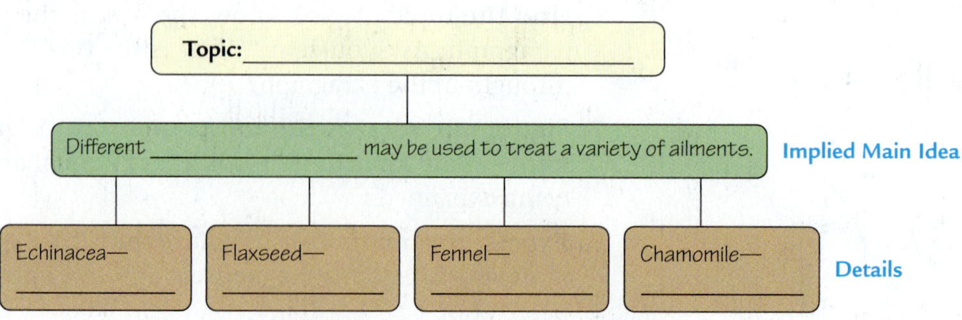

EXERCISE 4-17 Reading: Locating Implied Meaning

Directions: For each of the following paragraphs, write a sentence that states its implied main idea.

1. As recently as 20 years ago, textbooks on child psychology seldom devoted more than a few paragraphs to the behaviors of the neonate—the newborn through the first 2 weeks of life. It seemed as if the neonate did not do much worth writing about. Today, most child psychology texts devote substantially more space to discussing the abilities of newborns. It is unlikely that over the past 20 years neonates have gotten smarter or more able. Rather, psychologists have. They have devised new and clever ways of measuring the abilities and capacities of neonates.

   —Gerow, *Psychology: An Introduction*, p. 319

   Implied main idea: ______________________________

   ____

2. Severe punishment may generate such anxiety in children that they do not learn the lesson the punishment was designed to teach. Moreover, as a reaction to punishment that they regard as unfair, children may avoid punitive parents, who therefore will have fewer opportunities to teach and guide the child. In addition, parents who use physical punishment provide aggressive models. A child who is regularly slapped, spanked, shaken, or shouted at may learn to use these forms of aggression in interactions with peers.

   —Newcombe, *Child Development*, p. 354

   Implied main idea: ______________________________

   ____

3. Most sporting goods manufacturers have long sold products for women, but this often meant simply creating an inferior version of the male product and slapping a pink label on it. Then the companies discovered that many women were buying products intended for boys because they wanted better quality, so some of them figured out that they needed to take this market segment seriously. Burton Snowboard Company was one of the early learners. When the company started to offer high-quality clothing and gear made specifically for women, female boarders snapped them up. Burton also changed the way it promotes these products and redesigned its Web site after getting feedback from female riders.

   —adapted from Solomon, *Consumer Behavior*, p. 189

   Implied main idea: ______________________________

   ____

EXERCISE 4-18 Reading: Analyzing Paragraphs

Directions: Read each paragraph and answer the questions that follow.

Paragraph 1

Thanks to the Internet, you can shop 24 hours a day without leaving home, you can read today's newspaper without getting drenched picking up a hard copy in a rainstorm, and you don't have to wait for the 6:00 news to find out what the weather will be like tomorrow—at home or around the globe. And, with the increasing use of handheld devices and wireless communications, you can get that same information—from stock quotes to the weather—even when you're away from your computer.

—Solomon and Stuart, *The Brave New World of E-Commerce*, p. 13

1. What is the topic? ______________________________

2. What is the implied main idea? ______________________________

____

Paragraph 2

Research suggests that women who are considered attractive are more effective in changing attitudes than are women thought to be less attractive. In addition, more attractive individuals are often considered to be more credible than less attractive people. They are also perceived to be happier, more popular, more sociable, and more successful than are those rated as being less attractive. With respect to shape and body size, people with fat, round silhouettes are consistently rated as older, more old-fashioned, less good-looking, more talkative, and more good-natured. Athletic, muscular people are rated as more mature, better looking, taller, and more adventurous. Tall and thin people are rated as more ambitious, more suspicious of others, more tense and nervous, more pessimistic, and quieter.

—Beebe and Masterson, *Communicating in Small Groups*, p. 150

3. What is the topic? ______________________________

4. What is the implied main idea? ______________________________

____

Paragraph 3

Any zookeeper will tell you that the primate house is their most popular exhibit. People love apes and monkeys. It is easy to see why—primates are curious, playful, and agile. In short, they are fun to watch. But something else drives our fascination with these wonderful animals: We see ourselves reflected in them. The placement of their eyes and their small noses appear humanlike. They have hands with fingernails instead of paws with claws. Some can stand and walk on two legs for short periods. They can finely manipulate objects with their fingers and opposable thumbs. They show extensive parental care, and even their social relations are similar to ours—they tickle, caress, kiss, and pout.

—adapted from Belk and Maier, *Biology: Science for Life with Physiology*, p. 236

5. What is the topic? ______________________________

6. What is the implied main idea? ______________________________

____

Paragraph 4

The Web has enabled people to work, "talk" to friends across town and across the ocean, and buy goods from online retailers without leaving their houses. It has also made some criminal enterprises and unethical behavior easier to accomplish and harder to trace—for example, people can scam others out of large sums of money, buy college term papers, and learn how to build a bomb.

—adapted from Divine et al., *America Past and Present*, p. 449

7. What is the topic? ______________________________

8. What is the implied main idea? ______________________________

Paragraph 5

Sleep conserves body energy so that we are rested and ready to perform during high-performance daylight hours. Sleep also restores the neurotransmitters that have been depleted during the waking hours. This process clears the brain of unimportant details as a means of preparing for a new day. Getting enough sleep to feel ready to meet daily challenges is a key factor in maintaining optimal physical and psychological status.

—Donatelle and Davis, *Access to Health*, p. 42

9. What is the topic? ______________________

10. What is the implied main idea? ______________________

____

READ AND RESPOND: A Student Essay

From Bullet to Blue Sky

Yesenia De Jesus

The questions and activities below refer to Yesenia's essay "From Bullet to Blue Sky" on page 130 that we have used as a model throughout the chapter. Now you are ready to examine her writing and write in response to her essay.

Examining Writing

1. Draw an idea map of Yesenia's essay, placing the events she describes in chronological order.
2. Was the essay interesting and engaging? Why or why not?
3. Evaluate the level and type of detail included in this essay. Was there too much or too little detail, or a sufficient amount?
4. Did Yesenia include sufficient introductory and background information? If not, what further information was needed?
5. Did Yesenia use details related to all five senses? Circle examples of each sense she used.

Writing Assignments

1. Yesenia made a decision to study hard and pass the math test. Write a paragraph describing your response to a difficult academic or workplace challenge.
2. Write a narrative essay describing a frightening or life-threatening event you experienced. Explain how it happened and describe its effect on you.
3. Yesenia was inspired by her math instructor, Mr. Tangye. Write an essay describing someone who has inspired you. Explain how and why he or she inspired you, and give examples showing how that person has changed your life.

READ AND RESPOND: A Professional Essay

Among Dorms and Dining Halls, Hidden Hunger

Kate Robbins

Writing in Response to Reading (See essay on p. 117.)

Checking Your Comprehension MySkillsLab®

Answer each of the following questions using complete sentences.

1. What do students receive through the food assistance program at San Diego City College?
2. Cherie Bromley-Taylor created City's program after doing a survey of the community college's students. What did the survey reveal about City's students?
3. What did Abdallah Jadallah notice that prompted him to start a food pantry at UCLA?
4. Why was the food pantry at Michigan State University criticized initially?

Strengthening Your Vocabulary MySkillsLab®

Identify at least five words used in the reading that are unfamiliar to you. Using context, word parts, or a dictionary, write a brief definition of each word.

Examining the Reading: Drawing an Idea Map

Create an idea map of the reading that starts with the title and thesis and then lists the author's main points. Use the guidelines on page 15.

Reading and Writing: An Integrated Perspective MySkillsLab®

Get ready to write about the reading by discussing the following:

1. What does the title "Hidden Hunger" mean? What other titles might be appropriate for this selection?
2. Evaluate the introduction. Why does the author begin by telling about Cherie Bromley-Taylor?
3. Identify at least three different types of details that the author uses to support her ideas. Which details were most effective or compelling? What other details might she have used to support her ideas?
4. What transitions can you identify that lead the reader from one detail to another? Highlight transitions in the selection.
5. Discuss the statistics about how many students use the food program at City College and the food pantry at UCLA. Did these numbers surprise you?
6. Identify the topic of paragraph 11 and express the implied main idea in your own words.
7. Find and highlight examples of specific, vivid words and phrases in the selection, especially those that help you create a mental picture.

8. Why does the author include such a detailed description of the food pantry at UCLA? What does this description add to your understanding of the subject?
9. Have you ever helped feed someone who was hungry? Write a journal entry describing what you did and why you did it.

THINKING VISUALLY

10. Describe the photograph that accompanies the reading. How effectively does the photograph illustrate the subject? What other photos or visuals could accompany the reading that would contribute to its meaning?

Thinking and Writing Critically MySkillsLab®

1. Why is relative anonymity important at the UCLA food closet? Explain what is meant by the "hidden nature of student hunger" (paragraph 13).
2. Discuss San Diego City College's student population, as described in paragraphs 6 and 7. How is it different from UCLA? Why does the author include both these schools?
3. How accurate and reliable are the author's sources? How do you know the people quoted in the reading know what they are talking about? (For more about evaluating a source, see Chapter 12, pp. 349–354.)
4. Express the author's conclusion in your own words. How would you describe her attitude toward her subject? What impression does she leave the reader with at the end of the reading?

Writing Paragraphs MySkillsLab®

1. Write a paragraph describing the author's purpose in writing about this subject. Who is her audience? (For more about purpose and audience, see Chapter 2, pp. 52–54.)
2. The author describes the food assistance programs at three different schools. Write a paragraph summarizing the major details of each school's program, including how each program started.
3. Do you agree with the City student who says food is not as much a priority as a car note or transportation or a bill? How do you prioritize expenses on a limited budget? Write a paragraph explaining your answers.

Writing Essays MySkillsLab®

4. Recall a situation during college when you have needed assistance, perhaps with a difficult class or with housing, tuition, or even food. Who helped you? Why did this person offer you assistance? How did the experience affect your own willingness to help someone else? Write an essay describing the situation and exploring the answers to these questions.
5. Write an essay in the form of a letter to the editor of your school newspaper describing the problem of student hunger. Include a description of the successful programs discussed in this selection and any other food assistance programs you know about.
6. If you think student hunger exists at your school, what would you be willing to do to address the problem? Which of the programs described in the article do you think would work best at your school? Why? Write an essay explaining the steps you could take to respond to the problem of low food security among students at your school.

SELF-TEST SUMMARY

To test yourself, cover the Answer column with a sheet of paper and answer each question in the left column. Evaluate each of your answers as you work by sliding the paper down and comparing your answer with what is printed in the Answer column.

QUESTION	ANSWER
■ GOAL 1 Understand details, transitions, and implied main ideas What are details, transitions, and implied main ideas?	*Supporting details* are facts and ideas that prove or explain a paragraph's main idea. *Transitions* are linking words and phrases that pull the paragraph together by connecting the details. *Implied main ideas* are thoughts suggested but not directly stated in a topic sentence.
■ GOAL 2 Identify supporting details What is the difference between major and minor details?	Major details directly explain a paragraph's main idea. Minor details provide additional information, offer an example, or further explain a major detail.
What are the most common types of supporting details?	The most common types of supporting details are examples, facts or statistics, reasons, descriptions, and steps or procedures.
■ GOAL 3 Select and organize details to support your topic sentence How do you select and organize details?	■ Use relevant details that directly explain and support the topic sentence. ■ Use sufficient (enough) details to make your topic sentence understandable and convincing. ■ Use a variety of details to develop your topic sentence. ■ Organize your details logically, using *time sequence, spatial,* or *least-to-most arrangements*. ■ Use specific words and phrases to help your readers create a mental picture of the place, person, or event you are describing. Choose action words, give exact names, include adjectives, and choose words that appeal to the senses.
■ GOAL 4 Use transitions to guide your reading and writing How do transitions guide your reading and writing?	Transitions lead readers from one idea to another. See Table 4-1 for a list of common transitions used within a paragraph and what they tell readers. Transitions enable writers to connect ideas and show how they are related.
■ GOAL 5 Find implied main ideas How do you find an implied main idea?	To find an implied main idea, first find the topic. Next, figure out what is the most important idea the writer wants you to know about that topic. Finally, express this main idea in your own words.

Visit **Chapter 4, "Details, Transitions, and Implied Main Ideas,"** in MySkillsLab to test your understanding of chapter goals.

Organization: Basic Patterns

5

LEARNING
GOALS

Learn how to . . .

- GOAL 1
  Identify patterns of organization
- GOAL 2
  Read and write using time sequence: chronological order, process, and narration
- GOAL 3
  Read and write using description
- GOAL 4
  Read and write using example

THINK About It!

Study the photograph above. Assume it appeared on an animal rights activism Web site. Write a sentence explaining what impression or feeling the photograph creates.

Suppose you volunteer for an activist group that opposes keeping wild animals in captivity solely for human entertainment. You have been asked to help draft an article to submit to the local newspaper explaining the group's mission. In order to write an effective article, you might first read about animals in captivity, learning how they are treated and the problems they face.

Next, you would plan how to write the article, considering various effective ways to develop it. One way you might develop the article would be to narrate—or tell the story—of a particular animal, following it from capture through captivity. Another method would be to describe animals in captivity, focusing on their living conditions, behavioral problems, and health issues. A third approach might be to make a statement that wild animals have a poor quality of life in captivity and support this statement with examples of particular animals. These three methods, *narration*, *description*, and *example*, are effective ways to develop your ideas.

These methods could also be used to write an essay from the opposing viewpoint—that keeping animals in captivity preserves species, saves lives, and builds public awareness and appreciation. You will learn how to read and write each of these methods in this chapter.

Reading and Writing Connections

EVERYDAY CONNECTIONS

- **Reading** You read a review of a new restaurant in which the reviewer vividly describes the restaurant's warm and inviting atmosphere and recommends several delicious-sounding items on the menu.
- **Writing** You write an e-mail to a friend explaining that the new restaurant is pricey by giving examples of the costs of specific menu items such as fried shrimp and Caesar salad.

ACADEMIC CONNECTIONS

- **Reading** You read a section of an American government text called "The Presidency" that describes the process of impeachment as written in the Constitution.
- **Writing** For an assignment in American government, you write a summary of the series of events leading up to the impeachment and acquittal of President Bill Clinton.

WORKPLACE CONNECTIONS

- **Writing** As an EMT (emergency medical technician), you write a report detailing your response to a 911 call involving a gas leak at a home near an elementary school.
- **Reading** Your supervisor reads the memo and suggests alternative measures you could have taken to evacuate students more quickly.

What Are Patterns of Organization?

GOAL 1 Identify patterns of organization

There are several commonly used ways to organize a paragraph or essay—known as **patterns of organization**—that writers use to present their ideas. Depending on what they want to accomplish, they choose the pattern that will most effectively convey their message. As a reader, if you can see how a paragraph or essay is organized, it is easier to understand and remember the information in it. In this chapter you will learn how to read and write three common patterns: (1) time sequence (chronological order, process, and narration), (2) description, and (3) example.

METHOD OF DEVELOPMENT	WHAT IT DOES	AN EXAMPLE OF ITS USE
Chronological order	Explains events in the order in which they occurred	Telling the history of cake making since ancient times
Process	Explains how something is done or how something works	Explaining how to make a cake
Narration	Tells a story that makes a point	Telling a story that involves cake
Description	Uses sensory details to help the reader visualize a topic	Describing the look, taste, texture, or flavor of cake
Example	Explains a concept by giving concrete instances that demonstrate what it is	Giving examples of celebrations in which cake is served

Additional patterns of organization will be covered in Chapter 6. By learning to identify and use each pattern, you will develop a variety of new approaches to reading and writing paragraphs.

EXAMINING PROFESSIONAL WRITING

In the following essay, the author describes her experience as an American women taking the subway to work in a foreign country. This article will be used in this chapter as a model of professional writing and to illustrate the reading and writing techniques discussed. As you read, pay particular attention to the author's descriptive details.

Thinking Before Reading

1. Preview the reading using the steps discussed in Chapter 1, page 4.
2. Connect the reading to your own experience by answering the following questions:
   a. If you have ever traveled to another country, how comfortable were you as a foreigner in a strange land? How did the locals react to you?
   b. What qualities do you think people around the world share or have in common?
3. Mark and annotate as you read.

Cairo Tunnel

Amanda Fields

1 I nudge through the turnstile, putting the stiff yellow ticket in my pocket and crossing a footbridge to the other side of the tracks, where I head toward the cluster of women on the platform. It's rush hour. Morning salutations compete with beehive intensity. I scoot forward and back. Soon, the Metro barrels up, and the women's car, painted with a red stick-lady in a triangle skirt, sighs open.

2 I shove and fold in with a throng of women heading to low-paying public-sector jobs, or to clean expatriates' houses such as mine, or to public school. Once inside, there is no need to hold onto the metal bars, already bombarded with curled hands, wrapped over and bullying each other. We are like books on a shelf, supporting each other's weight.

3 A short woman, eyes looming behind a black mask, presses her gloved hands flat against my chest. I only see the eyes, dark and liquid—she is without a mouth or nose or ears or cheekbones or eyebrows. I look down the length of my buttoned blouse, to her fingertips, to my skin. Still, I can smell her sour breath, and she can probably smell mine. I find my hands and legs in immovable positions. Someone tentatively touches my hair, probably a little girl.

4 It is April, and hot. A single fan rotates. I can see the dust on its blades, and the windows are dingy and cracked, and through them the slums of Cairo whip by, the crumbling grey buildings, the jumbled sand and trash. The back of my shirt grows slick. At each stop, more women force themselves in, and I begin to feel the pressure on my ribs, the itchy cloth of the woman in **niqab** against my bare arms. Even schoolgirls, writhing with giggles, are a burden to the rest of us. All is gravity and physicality. The Metro rattles into a dark tunnel, one weak bulb lighting the car. We might squeeze each other to death.

niqab
a veil that covers a woman's head and face

5 I was warned about taking the Metro in Cairo. My upper-class students had warned that there would be staring, pushing, insults. And that was just in the women's car. I had heard stories of women taunting each other for the tint of their skin, of women in niqab shouting about Allah and bared flesh. Desperate women would sneak on the Metro without a ticket and peddle tissues and crumbling cosmetics for a few **pounds**. Cover your arms, said my students. Deny the American University, they advised.

pounds
unit of currency in Egypt, equivalent to about 17 U.S. cents

6 I try to breathe deeply, my chest barely moving beneath the woman's hands. I once heard a rumor about a study of Cairo's traffic patterns. The Japanese scientists couldn't figure out how it worked, how there weren't multiple car accidents every second. I have learned to put faith in this inscrutability.

7 Some of the women look at me with frankness, but I cannot sense what they see. They cling to each other in something more than physical necessity. Most of them look tired. Behind me, a fleeting space opens. I grapple for a handhold, clenching a breast, then a stomach. "Sorry," I mutter.

8 Then a woman in lime-colored **hijab** says, "Welcome." Her makeup is minimal, like mine. She wears a pantsuit, an oversized purse against her hip. She smiles. When I respond in stilted Arabic, other women smile, eyes crinkling. The woman in niqab looks up. As we near Sadat station, a schoolgirl taps my shoulder to let me know it is time to start shoving toward the door, assuming, rightly, that I'm going to the university.

hijab
a headscarf that covers a woman's hair but leaves her face bare

9 The car slows to the blur of hundreds of faces, hundreds of clamoring women. I try to stick with the schoolgirl as we push through women staying, women going, women trying to get on before others can depart. The woman with the lime-colored hijab prods me forward. As we pass, a Sudanese girl gets spun in a circle as easily as a rack of clothes, her braids flying.

10 A sea of women—we crest, then topple out, gripping each other, pressing, patting in a womanly empathy so familiar in Cairo. I can't understand how I'm not falling, how I'm not getting trampled. I can't understand how we carry each other in such smooth uncertainty. And all the while, women are laughing, I am laughing. We have this in common.

READING AND WRITING TIME SEQUENCE: CHRONOLOGICAL ORDER, PROCESS, AND NARRATION

What Is Time Sequence?

■ GOAL 2
Read and write using time sequence: chronological order, process, and narration

Time sequence refers to writing that uses time as the organizing principle. When writers tell a story, they usually present events in **chronological order**, starting with the first event, continuing with the second, and so on. Writers use the **process pattern** to explain how something is done, like changing a flat tire, or how something works, such as how a tornado is formed. **Narration** is another pattern that uses time sequence to tell a story, but writers use it to provide a specific viewpoint rather than just list the order in which events occurred.

You can visualize and draw the chronological order and process patterns as follows:

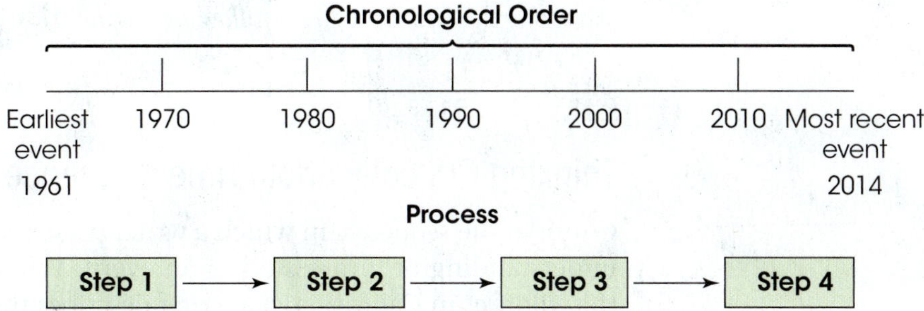

Reading Chronological Order and Process

When you read stories for an English class or material in a history or political science text, you will often encounter chronological order. When writers use this pattern, they often include time transitions, such as *first*, *next*, and *finally* (see box on p. 156) and dates to help readers keep track of the sequence of events. Notice how the authors of the following paragraph from a history text use chronological order and time sequence transitions (highlighted) to discuss the evolution of organized baseball. Identifying these types of transitions when you read will help you recognize chronological order and process.

> Organized baseball teams first emerged in the 1840s, but the game only became truly popular during the Civil War, when it was a major form of camp recreation for the troops. After the war professional teams began to appear, and in 1876 teams in eight cities formed the National League. The American League followed in 1901. After a brief period of rivalry, the two leagues made peace in 1903, the year of the first World Series.
>
> —adapted from Garraty and Carnes, *The American Nation*, p. 518

In the professional essay on page 153, the author uses time sequence throughout, telling the story, in chronological order, of a morning when she took the Cairo Metro train from where she lived to her job at the American University. She starts by describing how she pushed through the turnstile, crossed the footbridge, and entered the carriage. Then she describes her experiences on the train as she travelled to her destination and ends with a paragraph about leaving the train.

Writers also follow a time sequence when they use the **process pattern**—when they explain how something is done or made. In the following paragraph, the author explains how to make a basic white sauce. Notice the time transitions (highlighted) and the use of the word *steps* in the topic sentence, which provides a clue to the kind of pattern that will be used.

> To make a basic white sauce, follow a few easy steps. First, melt two tablespoons of butter over low heat. Next, add two tablespoons of flour and stir until the flour and butter are combined. Then add one cup of milk and continue stirring over low heat. Finally, when the mixture has thickened, add salt and pepper, or other seasonings, to taste.

Common Time Sequence Transitions

after	*as soon as*	*finally*	*in addition*	*meanwhile*	*then*
also	*before*	*first*	*last*	*next*	*until*
another	*during*	*following*	*later*	*second*	*when*

Thinking Critically About Time Sequence

Consider the sequence in which a writer presents details, as they shape a reader's understanding or impression of an event. When recounting an event such as the wildfires in California, if a writer describes the emergency responses in a disorderly fashion, switching back and forth between teams and responses without regard to sequence, the reader may get the impression that the response effort was not well managed. However, if a writer describes the response efforts team by team, in time sequence, the reader will get the impression that the response effort was orderly and systematic. Be sure to check other sources to determine whether you are getting a fair and objective view of an event.

Also, check that you are receiving complete information about the steps in a process. One writer may choose to include a caution about pitfalls or problems, such as "be sure not to overbake the cookies or they will be dry and hard." However, other writers may not be as helpful or as forthcoming, making a process seem easy and simple when it is actually quite complex.

EXERCISE 5-1

Understanding Chronological Order and Process

Directions: Using either chronological order or process, put each of the following groups of sentences in the correct order. For each sentence, write a number from 1 to 4 in the space provided, beginning with the topic sentence.

1. ______ Rail travel originated in Europe in 1825, and four years later, North America welcomed the advent of passenger rail service.

   ______ Transcontinental service began in the United States in 1869 and in Canada in 1885.

   ______ Passenger rail service has been an important form of domestic transportation for more than 175 years.

   ______ In 1875 Fred Harvey introduced the golden age of passenger railroad service in the U.S., with the addition of dining cars and lodging facilities.

   —adapted from Cook, Yale, and Marqua, *Tourism: The Business of Travel*, p. 102

2. ______ Next, chemicals are released that attract even more platelets to the site.

   ______ Basically, once damage has occurred, blood elements called platelets immediately begin to cling to the injured site.

______ This rapidly growing pile-up of platelets initiates the sequence of events that finally forms a clot.

______ Blood clotting is a normal response to a break in the lining of a blood vessel.

—adapted from Marieb, *Human Anatomy & Physiology*, p. 13

3. ______ In the final stage, disorientation is often complete, and the person becomes completely dependent on others for eating, dressing, and other activities.

______ These symptoms accelerate in the second stage, which also includes agitation and restlessness, loss of sensory perceptions, muscle twitching, and repetitive actions.

______ During the first stage, symptoms include forgetfulness, memory loss, impaired judgment, increasing inability to handle routine tasks, disorientation, and depression.

______ Alzheimer's disease is characteristically diagnosed in three stages.

—adapted from Donatelle and Davis, *Access to Health*, p. 533

EXAMINING STUDENT WRITING

A good way to learn to read and write essays is to study a model. By examining the student essay below by Leila Kaji, you will learn how to write clear process paragraphs and essays. Leila's essay will be used to illustrate some of the writing techniques and strategies discussed in this chapter.

Leila Kaji is a senior at the University of North Carolina in Chapel Hill, North Carolina, where she is double majoring in linguistics and dramatic art. In a composition class, she was asked to write an essay on a process that would appeal to her college peers. Using her own experience as well as those of her friends, she wrote this essay to help others successfully navigate the rough waters of ending a relationship. Leila's essay was selected for use in this book because it is a strong example of a process essay. As you read, study the annotations to note her use of time sequence and transitions.

Title suggests a "how-to" essay.

The End of the Road: A Guide to Break Ups

Leila Kaji

Introduction

1 College is a very exciting time, filled with loads of new people, new experiences, and the opportunity for new romantic endeavors! But unless the first person you're romantically interested in is your soul mate and you end up getting married and living happily ever after, you're going to have to deal with a break up. Contrary to popular belief, break ups are not the end of the world. They might be a bit taxing emotionally, but with a few simple pointers, you will become a break-up expert, equipped with all the necessary skills to successfully deal with the end of a relationship.

Thesis identifies the process and what can be accomplished by using the process

Topic sentence

Background information

Writer uses second-person point of view.

2 There are plenty of reasons to break up with your significant other. They can be very serious and noteworthy, or they can be incredibly simple, even petty reasons. You can break up with someone because your lives have gone in two different directions, or because the spark in the relationship is gone. You can end it because the person no longer makes you feel special and wanted. If he or she cheated on you, it's definitely time to call it quits. Maybe you just really hate the way this person eats, or you don't like his or her friends, or you have simply found someone else. No matter what your reason, remember that this is your choice. You are allowed to feel what you feel, and if being with this person doesn't make you happy anymore, find someone who does! You are in no way required to stay with someone if you don't want to be with him. Period.

Transition

Topic sentence identifies step #1. Steps are presented sequentially.

3 So the time has come to break up with your romantic partner. Congratulations! You're overdue for some quality "me time," and this whole boyfriend/girlfriend situation is really cramping your style. Time to move on! The first question is how do you do the actual breaking up? While some immature individuals may disagree, there is only one answer; you do the deed in person. You may *not*, under any circumstance, break up with your partner via text. Again, to make sure you understand: No text break ups! Only the lowest of the low resort to ending a relationship with someone through a pathetic text, and you're no coward! You want to do it right! Therefore, the first step of breaking up with someone is to find a time to meet with him or her *in person*. It's up to you to decide the location. Maybe you want to do it in a public area so your partner won't cause a scene. Or maybe you feel like giving your partner the courtesy of meeting in private, so he or she can hide the tears of utter loss and despair after losing the best thing to ever happen to him or her. That part is completely up to you.

Transition

Topic sentence identifies step #2.

Writer identifies pitfall.

Further information about step #2.

4 Now that you're face-to-face with your current partner, it's time for the second and hardest part of the process, when you need to lay everything out on the table. Break ups are difficult situations, but you want to make sure you're saying all that you need to say. Now is not the time to hold anything in. Most likely, your partner will be a bit confused, and you do owe him or her an explanation. A lesser person would end things without another word, but you're better than that. Get out everything you feel, and allow your partner to do the same. The more communication at this point in the process, the better chance that you and your partner will remain friends after this is all over, if you so choose.

Transition

Background information about step #3

Topic sentence identifies step #3

Writer identifies pitfall.

5 This leads us to the aftermath of the break up: the relationship after the relationship. Now this is something that will really depend on your specific situation. Maybe you never want to see this person again. Maybe you really just want to go back to being friends. Maybe you just want some time apart, but you don't want to completely disregard the thought of you two getting back together at some point later on down the road. No matter what you want in the future, it might be best to set some clear boundaries now, when the break up process is actually happening. If you don't, it will be much too easy to fall back into the relationship because it's what you're used to, even if it's not what you want. To avoid confusion and possible heartache, set very clear boundaries now. If you decide to re-evaluate things after

a bit of time has passed, that's fine, but be sure you are both on the same page of where you stand with each other.

Conclusion emphasizes the importance of the process.

6 The end of a relationship can be a very difficult time. Chances are, you will be feeling many different and possibly conflicting emotions, and that's okay. But now, you no longer have to worry about the *process* of breaking up with someone. That should now come naturally to you, and if it doesn't, it's nothing a little practice won't fix! The main thing you have to remember, however, is that your happiness comes above all else. If being with someone doesn't put the biggest smile on your face and bounce in your step, it's not worth it. Now is not the time to be wasting your life with someone who doesn't give you all that you deserve. You are a beautiful, radiant, unique human being, and you deserve the best. If you're not getting the best, it's time to go out and practice those new breaking-up skills!

Writing Process Paragraphs

A **process** is a series of steps or actions that one follows in a particular order to accomplish something. When you assemble a toy, bake a cake, rebuild an engine, or put up a tent, you do things in a specific order. A **process paragraph** explains the steps to follow in completing a process. The steps are given in the order in which they are done. Here is a paragraph describing the process of jury selection.

> Jury selection is a systematic process. The pool of potential jurors is selected from voter or automobile registration lists. Potential jurors are asked to fill out a questionnaire. Lawyers for each party and the judge can ask questions of prospective jurors to determine if they would be biased in their decision. Jurors can be "stricken for cause" if the court believes that the potential juror is too biased to render a fair verdict. Lawyers may also exclude a juror from sitting on a particular case without giving any reason for the dismissal. Once the appropriate number of jurors is selected (usually six to twelve jurors) they are impaneled to hear the case and are sworn in. The trial is ready to begin.
>
> —Goldman and Cheeseman, *The Paralegal Professional*, p. 266

In this paragraph the writer identifies four steps. Notice that they are presented in the order in which they happen. You can visualize a process paragraph as follows. Study the model and the map that are given below for the paragraph above.

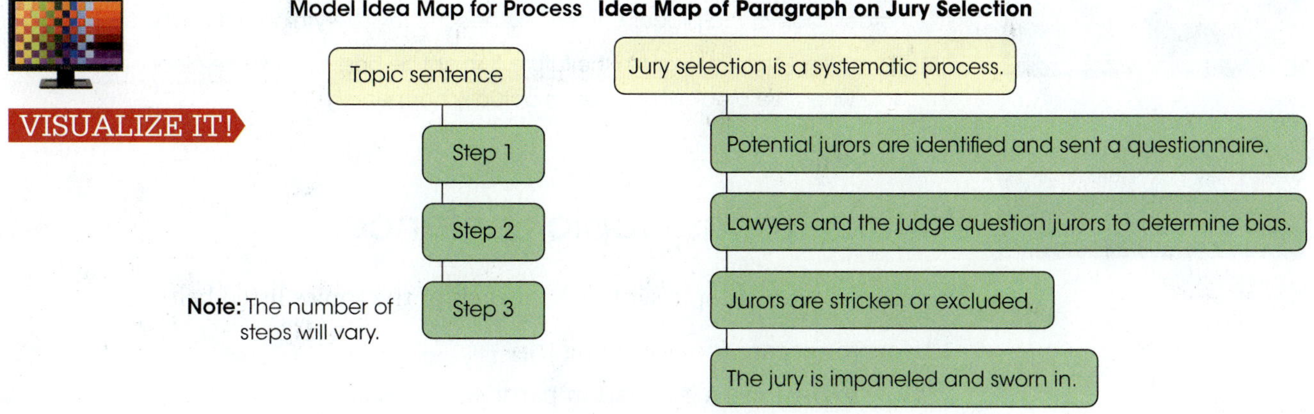

Types of Process Paragraphs

There are two types of process paragraphs—a "how-to" paragraph and a "how-it-works" paragraph:

- **A "how-to" paragraph explains how something is done.** For example, it may explain how to change a flat tire, aid a choking victim, or locate a reference source in the library. Leila's essay is a good model of a "how-to" essay, and contains three paragraphs—3, 4, and 5—that each describe one step in the process of breaking up with a boyfriend or girlfriend.
- **A "how-it-works" paragraph explains how something operates or happens.** For example, it may explain the operation of a pump, how the human body regulates temperature, or how children acquire speech.

Developing a process paragraph involves writing a topic sentence and explaining each step clearly and thoroughly.

Writing a Topic Sentence for a Process Paragraph

For a process paragraph, your topic sentence should accomplish two things:

1. **It should identify the process or procedure.**
2. **It should explain to your reader why familiarity with it is useful, interesting, or important (*why* he or she should learn about the process).** Your topic sentence should state a goal, offer a reason, or indicate what can be accomplished by using the process.

Here are two examples of topic sentences that contain both of these important elements:

- Reading maps, a vital skill if you are taking vacations by car, is a simple process, except for the final refolding.
- Because reading is an essential skill, all parents should know how to interest their children in recreational reading.

Here are the topic sentences from Leila's body paragraphs that lay out the three major steps she discusses in the breakup process:

- Therefore, the first step of breaking up with someone is to find a time to meet with him or her *in person*.
- Now that you're face-to-face with your current partner, it's time for the second and hardest part of the process, when you need to lay everything out on the table.
- No matter what you want in the future, it might be best to set some clear boundaries now, when the break up process is actually happening.

EXERCISE 5-2 Writing Process Topic Sentences

Directions: Write a topic sentence for each of the topics listed below.

1. How to prepare for a camping trip
2. How to organize a graduation party

3. How to find specific items on the Internet
4. How to build or repair _______________
5. How _______________ works

Explaining the Steps in a Process

Use the following tips when explaining each step in a process:

1. **Include only essential, necessary steps.** Avoid comments, opinions, and unnecessary information because they may confuse your reader.
2. **Assume that your reader is unfamiliar with your topic** (unless you know otherwise). Be sure to define unfamiliar terms and describe clearly any technical or specialized tools, procedures, or objects.
3. **Use a consistent point of view.** Use either the first person (*I*) or the second person (*you*) throughout. Don't switch between them.
4. **List needed equipment.** For how-to paragraphs, tell your readers what they will need to complete the process. For a how-to paragraph on making chili, list the ingredients, for example.
5. **Identify pitfalls and problems.** Alert your readers about potential problems and places where confusion or error may occur. For instance, warn your chili-making readers to add chili peppers gradually and to taste the chili frequently along the way.

Organizing a Process Paragraph

Process paragraphs should be organized sequentially according to the order in which the steps are done or occur. It is usually a good idea to place your topic sentence first. Placing it in this position provides your reader with a purpose for reading. Be sure to use transitional words and phrases to signal your readers that you are moving from one step to another. Common transitions are listed in the box on page 156.

EXERCISE 5-3

Writing a Process Paragraph

Directions: Using one of the topic sentences you created in Exercise 5-2, write a paragraph using the tips listed above. Be sure to use appropriate transition words throughout your paragraph.

Reading Narration

Narration is similar to chronological order and process but it differs in one respect—it shapes events to make a point. Chronological order and process are often used in textbooks and other types of writing intended to explain, but narration is more often used in essays, like "Cairo Tunnel," where the purpose is to present a viewpoint or tell a story to make a point. In "Cairo Tunnel," the author uses narration to show that despite all the bad things she had heard could happen to an American riding in the women's carriage of the Metro, and her fear that they might happen, when she responds to an overture of friendship, everything changes for the better.

Although narration is not frequently used in textbook writing, there are times when it can be effective, as illustrated in this paragraph from a criminal justice text in which the writer tells a story to explain how the plea of insanity became a legal defense.

> It was Daniel M'Naghten, a woodworker from Glasgow, Scotland, who became the first person to be found not guilty of a crime by reason of insanity in 1844. M'Naghten had tried to assassinate Sir Robert Peel, the British prime minister. He mistook Edward Drummond, Peel's secretary, for Peel himself and killed Drummond instead. At his trial, defense attorneys argued that M'Naghten suffered from vague delusions centered on the idea that the Tories, a British political party, were persecuting him. Medical testimony at the trial supported the defense's assertion that he didn't know what he was doing at the time of the shooting. The jury accepted M'Naghten's claim, and the insanity defense was born. Later, the House of Lords defined the criteria necessary for a finding of insanity.
>
> —adapted from Schmalleger, *Criminal Justice*, p. 84

You can visualize a narrative paragraph as follows. Study the model (shown left) and the map for this paragraph.

Model Idea Map for Narration

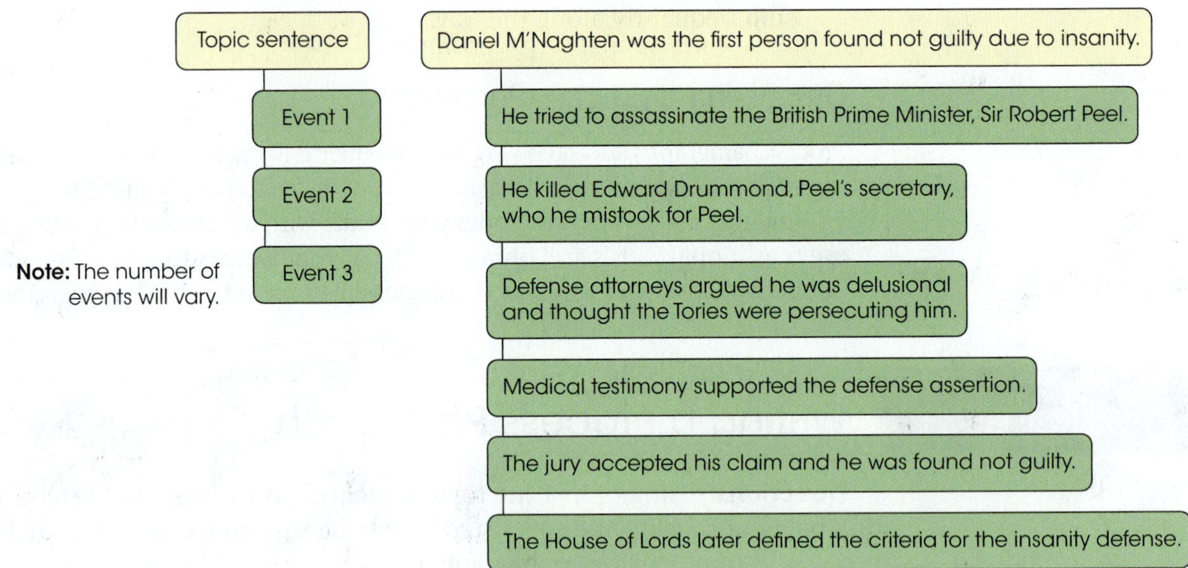

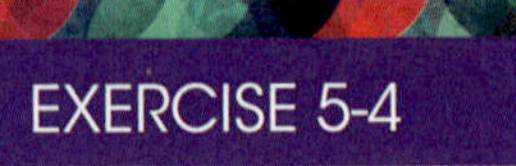

EXERCISE 5-4 Understanding Narration

Directions: For each paragraph below, identify the main point of the writer's narrative and write it in the space provided.

1. At one time, passenger pigeons were the most numerous species of birds in North America and perhaps in the world. They nested and migrated in huge flocks and probably numbered in the billions. When flocks passed overhead, the sky would be dark with pigeons for days at a time. Although the

Native Americans had long hunted these birds, the demise of the passenger pigeon is usually tied to the arrival of the Europeans, who increased the demand for pigeons as a source of food and sport. The birds were shot and netted in vast numbers; by the end of the nineteenth century, an animal species that had been looked on as almost indestructible because of its enormous numbers had almost completely disappeared. The last known passenger pigeon died in the Cincinnati Zoo in 1914.

—Miller et al., *The Economics of Public Issues*, pp. 163–164

Main point: ______________________________

2. After Arun Bharat Ram returned to India with a degree from the University of Michigan, his mother announced that she wanted to find him a wife. Arun would be a good catch anywhere: 27 years old, educated, well mannered, intelligent, handsome—and, not incidentally, heir to a huge fortune. Arun's mother already had someone in mind. Manju came from a middle-class family and was a college graduate. Arun and Manju met in a coffee shop at a luxury hotel—along with both sets of parents. He found her pretty and quiet. He liked that. She was impressed that he didn't boast about his background. After four more meetings, including one at which the two young people met by themselves, the parents asked their children whether they were willing to marry. Neither had any major objections.

—Henslin, *Essentials of Sociology*, p. 337

Main point: ______________________________

3. Coffee is one drink that people enjoy the world over. Coffee was first used by nomads in Ethiopia, where, according to legend, it was discovered by a goatherd who noticed that goats exhibited unusual energy after eating the red berries. The goatherd, named Kaldi, tried the berries himself and experienced an energy surge. A monk from a nearby monastery boiled the berries to make a drink, the ancestor of coffee as we know it today. Sometime between 1000 and 1300, coffee was made into a beverage. And although some authorities date coffee's earliest cultivation to late-sixth-century Yemen, coffee isn't mentioned in literature until the end of the first millennium.

—Benton and DiYanni, *Arts and Culture*, p. 576

Main point: ______________________________

Writing Narration Paragraphs

The technique of making a point by telling a story is called **narration**. Narration is *not* simply listing a series of events—"this happened, then that happened." Narration shapes and interprets events to make a point. Notice the difference between the two paragraphs below.

Paragraph 1: Series of Events from Paragraph 8 of "Cairo Tunnel"

A woman says hello and smiles. I respond in stilted Arabic. Other women smile. A girl taps me on the shoulder to let me know I should get off the train.

Paragraph 2: Narrative Paragraph from "Cairo Tunnel"

Then a woman in lime-colored hijab says, "Welcome." Her makeup is minimal, like mine. She wears a pantsuit, an oversized purse against her hip. She smiles. When I respond in stilted Arabic, other women smile, eyes crinkling. The woman in niqab looks up. As we near Sadat station, a schoolgirl taps my shoulder to let me know it is time to start shoving toward the door, assuming, rightly, that I'm going to the university.

—Amanda Fields, "Cairo Tunnel"

The first paragraph retells events in the order in which they happened, but with no shaping of the story. The second paragraph, a narrative, also presents events in the order in which they happened, but uses these events to make a point: the author's attempt to reply in Arabic to the women who speaks to her causes other women in the train to relax and to accept and help her. Thus, all details and events work together to support that point.

Writing a Topic Sentence for a Narrative Paragraph

Developing a narrative paragraph involves writing a topic sentence and presenting sufficient details to support it. Your topic sentence should accomplish two things:

1. **It should identify your topic.**
2. **It should reveal your attitude toward your topic.**

For example, suppose you are writing about visiting a zoo. Your topic sentence could take your narrative in a variety of directions, each of which would reveal a very different attitude toward the experience.

- During my recent visit to the zoo, I was saddened by the animals' behavior in captivity.
- A recent visit to the zoo gave my children a lesson in geography.
- My recent visit to the zoo taught me more about human nature than about animals.

EXERCISE 5-5

Writing Narrative Topic Sentences

Directions: Complete three of the following topic sentences by adding information that describes an experience you have had related to the topic.

Example **My first job** *was an experience I would rather forget.*

1. Holidays ______________________
2. A frightening event ______________________
3. My first day on campus ______________________
4. Online sites ______________________
5. My advisor/instructor ______________________

Including Sufficient Details

A narrative paragraph should include enough detail to support your topic sentence and allow your reader to understand fully the experience you are writing about. Be sure you have answered most of the following questions:

- *What* events occurred?
- *Where* did they happen?
- *When* did they happen?
- *Who* was involved?
- *Why* did they happen?
- *How* did they happen?

Organizing a Narrative Paragraph

The events in a narrative are usually arranged in the order in which they happened. Transitions are especially important in narrative paragraphs because they identify and separate events from one another. Useful transitions are shown below.

Common Narration Transitions

after	*during*	*following*	*next*	*therefore*
after that	*finally*	*in the beginning*	*second*	*third*
at last	*first*	*later*	*then*	*while*

EXERCISE 5-6

Writing a Narration Paragraph

Directions: Using one of the topic sentences you wrote in Exercise 5-5, brainstorm a list of relevant and sufficient details to support it, and write a narrative paragraph using time sequence order and transitions as needed.

READING AND WRITING DESCRIPTION

What Is Description?

- GOAL 3
Read and write using description

Descriptive writing involves using words and phrases that appeal to the senses—taste, touch, smell, sight, and hearing. As a writer, your task is to use language to help your readers visualize or imagine an object, person, place, or experience. As a reader, your task is to pay attention to these descriptive details, examine what they reveal, and take away an impression or overall feeling of the item being described. Below is a descriptive paragraph (para. 3) from the professional reading "Cairo Tunnel."

> A short woman, eyes looming behind a black mask, presses her gloved hands flat against my chest. I only see the eyes, dark and liquid—she is without a mouth or nose or ears or cheekbones or eyebrows. I look down the length of my buttoned blouse, to her fingertips, to my skin. Still, I can smell her sour breath, and she can probably smell mine. I find my hands and legs in immovable positions. Someone tentatively touches my hair, probably a little girl.
>
> —Amanda Fields, "Cairo Tunnel"

Study the model of a descriptive paragraph and the map for this paragraph shown below.

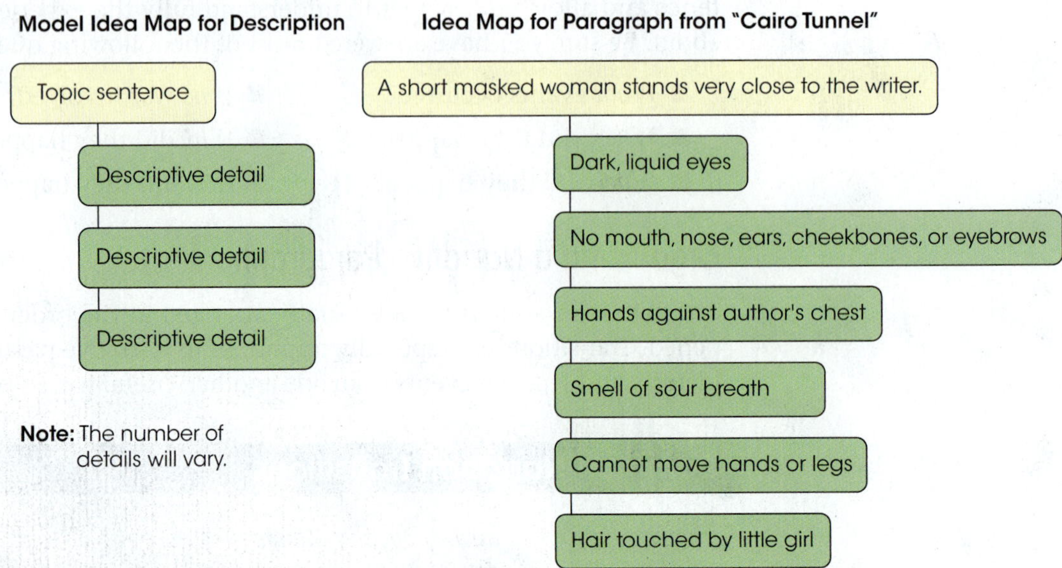

The writer of this paragraph described the sights, sounds, smells, and physical sensations she experienced when riding the metro in Cairo. As you read the paragraph what did you sense and feel? Could you almost see, smell, and feel what she was describing? And did it leave you with an impression of how crowded the trains are in the morning rush hour?

Reading Description

A descriptive paragraph has three key features—a *dominant impression*, *sensory details*, and *descriptive language*. As you read descriptive writing, pay attention to each of these features.

1. The **dominant impression** is the single, main point that all of the details in the paragraph prove or support. To find the dominant impression, ask yourself, "What do all these details and descriptions, taken together, mean or suggest?" Often, this dominant impression is unstated; it is left for you to infer.
2. **Sensory details** are those that relate to what you see, hear, touch, taste, and smell. Each detail is important, but the details, when added together, create the overall impression. Be careful not to skip details, and for each, consider what it contributes to the overall meaning. For example, in the description of a man, the detail that his hair was uncombed by itself does not mean much. However, when added together with details that his nails were dirty, his shirt unevenly buttoned, and his shoes untied, the writer creates the impression of the person as careless and unkempt.
3. **Descriptive language** uses words that create a visual or imaginary picture of the topic. As you read, be sure to read slowly enough to allow the language to "sink in." Mark and annotate particularly striking or unusual words and phrases, too. Stop and reflect, as well, about why a particularly descriptive phrase was chosen.

When writing a descriptive paragraph, writers use transitions to orient their readers. Some common transitions are shown on the next page.

Common Description Transitions

Spatial	**Least/Most**
above, below, beside, inside, outside	*first, primarily, second, secondarily*
across, facing, in front of, nearby, next to, to the left, to the right	*also important, most important*

Thinking Critically About Description

Evaluate the descriptive details that a writer chooses to include, as these shape your attitude toward the subject. For example, a writer can create different impressions of a restaurant by giving details that make it seem pleasant and enjoyable or by selecting details that make it seem unappealing and undesirable, so it is important to do some research to get an accurate picture of your subject.

Consider what descriptive details or facts the writer omitted, if any. Does the writer give you a complete picture of the subject, or has he or she selected details that will sway you in one direction or another? For example, a newspaper ad from a local animal shelter may describe a cat that is up for adoption as fun-loving, cuddly, and playful. But did the writer mention that it cannot get along with other cats and is terrified of other small pets?

EXERCISE 5-7

Reading Descriptive Paragraphs

Directions: Underline the topic sentence in the following paragraph and highlight particularly descriptive details.

Michelangelo's restless, unceasing quest for perfection helps explain why he was not content to stay only with the art of sculpture. He also aspired to be the greatest painter the world had ever known. His biggest challenge—even greater than that of the seventeen-foot block of marble that became *David*—was a task given him by Pope Julius II: to paint the ceiling of the Sistine Chapel inside the Vatican. Michelangelo's imagination was immediately stirred. There was the height itself, as close to heaven as his art was ever likely to take him. There was the huge expanse of the ceiling, allowing for a series of paintings on religious themes that would at the same time present to the viewer a totally unified effect. And there was the challenge that fresco posed, for the plaster had to be applied to the ceiling and painted before it was completely dry. Legend has it that the artist worked almost single-handedly for four long years, lying on his back for hours at a time while plaster continually dripped down on his face. But Michelangelo was both passionate and businesslike in his work. He had assistants, and the project was carefully planned—and kept secret even from the pope until the gasp-filled unveiling.

—Janaro and Altshuler, *The Art of Being Human*, p. 136

Writing Descriptive Paragraphs

As discussed above, a descriptive paragraph has three key features: a dominant impression, sensory details, and descriptive language. Be clear before writing what single main point you want to make. Then try to imagine your topic—the person, place, thing, or experience. Depending on what your topic is, brainstorm what it makes you see, hear, smell, taste, or feel, and use these details to support your topic sentence. As you write, use descriptive language, words that help your readers imagine your topic and make it exciting and vivid to them. Consider the following sentences. The first is dull and lifeless; the second describes what the writer sees and feels.

NONDESCRIPTIVE	A short woman stood close to me.
DESCRIPTIVE	A short woman, eyes looming behind a black mask, presses her gloved hands flat against my chest.

Making your details more descriptive is not difficult. Use the guidelines below.

NEED TO KNOW

Using Descriptive Details

1. **Use verbs that help your reader picture the action.**

NONDESCRIPTIVE	The boy walked down the beach.
DESCRIPTIVE	The boy ambled down the beach.

2. **Use exact names.** Include the names of people, places, brands, animals, flowers, stores, streets, products—whatever will make your description more precise.

NONDESCRIPTIVE	Kevin parked his car near the deserted beach.
DESCRIPTIVE	Kevin parked his maroon Saturn convertible at Burke's Garage next to the deserted beach.

3. **Use adjectives to describe.** Adjectives are words that describe nouns. Place them before or after nouns to add detail.

NONDESCRIPTIVE	The beach was deserted.
DESCRIPTIVE	The remote, rocky, windswept beach was deserted.

4. **Use words that appeal to the senses.** Use words that convey touch, taste, smell, sound, and sight.

NONDESCRIPTIVE	The tide was going out.
DESCRIPTIVE	The fiery setting sun burned back from the fine sheet of water left by the retreating tide.

Writing a Topic Sentence for a Descriptive Paragraph

Your dominant impression should be expressed in your topic sentence, usually at the beginning of the paragraph. Notice that each of the following topic sentences expresses a different dominant impression of Niagara Falls:

- Niagara Falls is stunningly beautiful and majestic.
- The beauty of Niagara Falls is hidden by its tourist-oriented, commercial surroundings.
- Niagara Falls would be beautiful to visit if I could be there alone, without the crowds of tourists.

Your overall impression is often your first reaction to a topic. Suppose you are writing about your college snack bar. Think of a word or two that sums up how you feel about it. Is it noisy? Smelly? Relaxing? Messy? You could develop any one of these descriptive words into a paragraph. For example, your topic sentence might be,

The snack bar is a noisy place that I try to avoid.

The details that follow would then describe the noise—the clatter of plates, loud conversations, chairs scraping the floor, and music blaring.

EXERCISE 5-8

Writing Descriptive Topic Sentences

Directions: Brainstorm a list of words that sum up your reaction to each of the following topics. Then develop each list of words into a topic sentence that expresses a dominant impression and could lead to a descriptive paragraph.

Example

TOPIC A parent or guardian

REACTION Dad: loving, accepting, smart, helpful, calm, generous

TOPIC SENTENCE My whole life, my father has been generous and helpful in the way he let me be myself.

1. TOPIC A library, gym, or other public place that you have used

REACTION ______________________________

TOPIC SENTENCE ______________________________

____

____

2. TOPIC A music video, movie, or song

REACTION ______________________________

TOPIC SENTENCE ______________________________

____

____

3. TOPIC A person in the news

REACTION ______________________________

TOPIC SENTENCE ______________________________

____

____

Organizing a Descriptive Paragraph

Among the common methods of ordering details in descriptive writing are the following:

- **Spatial arrangement.** You organize details according to their physical location. (See Chapter 4, p. 137, for a discussion of this method.) For example, you could describe a favorite newsstand by arranging your details from right to left or from front to back.
- **Least/most arrangement.** You organize details in increasing or decreasing order, according to some quality or characteristic, such as importance. (See Chapter 4, p. 138, for a discussion of this method.) Suppose your overall impression of a person is that she is disorganized. You might start with some minor traits (she can never find a pen) and move to more serious and important characteristics of disorganization (she misses classes and forgets appointments).

Whatever method you choose to arrange your details, you will want to use good transitional words and phrases between details. Useful transitions are shown in the box on page 167.

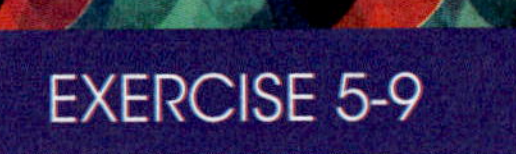

EXERCISE 5-9

Writing a Descriptive Paragraph

Directions: Using one of the topic sentences you wrote in Exercise 5-8, brainstorm details that support the dominant impression it conveys. Use these details to develop and write a paragraph. Assume that your reader is unfamiliar with what you are describing. Use descriptive language and organize your paragraph using a spatial or least/most arrangement, and use transitions as needed.

READING AND WRITING EXAMPLE

What Is an Example?

■ GOAL 4
Read and write using example

An **example** is a specific instance or situation that explains a general idea or statement. Apples and grapes (specific) are examples of fruit (general). Martin Luther King Day and Thanksgiving Day are specific examples of national holidays (general). Here is a paragraph (para. 5) from the professional essay "Cairo Tunnel," which offers four examples people used to warn the writer against using the Metro.

> I was warned about taking the Metro in Cairo. My upper-class students had warned that there would be staring, pushing, insults. And that was just in the women's car. I had heard stories of women taunting each other for the tint of their skin, of women in niqab shouting about Allah and bared flesh. Desperate women would sneak on the Metro without a ticket and peddle tissues and crumbling cosmetics for a few pounds. Cover your arms, said my students. Deny the American University, they advised.
>
> —Amanda Fields, "Cairo Tunnel"

Notice that the paragraph gives four examples of why she should not travel on the train. You can visualize an example paragraph as follows. Study the model and the map for the Metro paragraph.

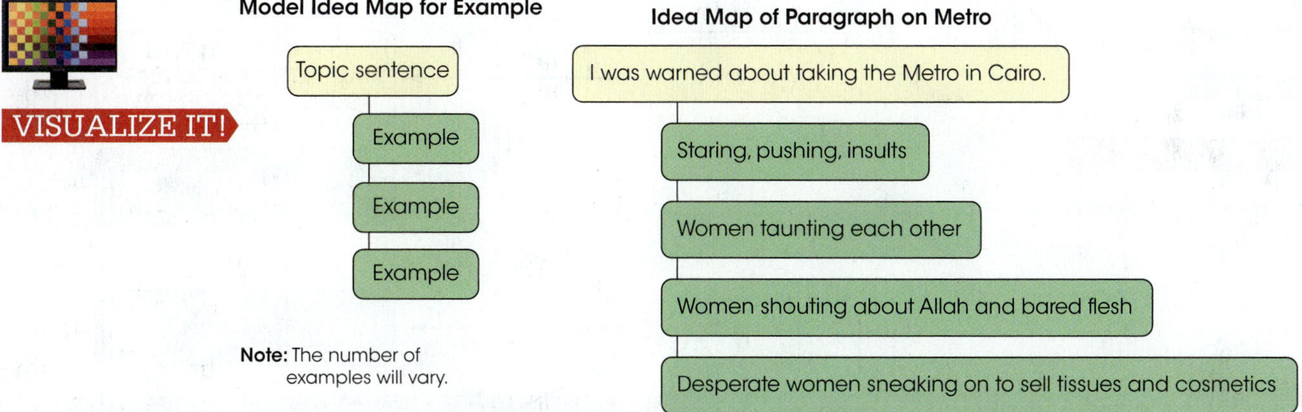

As a writer you can use examples to make unfamiliar, difficult, or complicated ideas clear or make abstract ideas more concrete and understandable for your reader. Depending on the knowledge and sophistication of your audience, you may include more or fewer examples, depending on what is needed to be sure the message is understood.

As a reader, you can use examples to make what you are reading come alive and seem more real. You can also use them to see how the topic connects to real-world situations. Examples often help you realize the use or importance of the idea being illustrated. To test your understanding of the idea being illustrated, try to think of additional examples that illustrate it. If you cannot, it is possible that you may not yet fully understand the idea. If so, rereading may be helpful.

Reading Example

When organizing a paragraph, a writer often states the main idea in a topic sentence first and then follows it with one extended example or several shorter ones. In a longer piece of writing, a separate paragraph may be used for each example.

Notice how this example pattern is developed in the following paragraph where the writers signal the reader that examples are to follow by using the transitions *for example*, *such as*, and *for instance*.

New technologies are helping to make alternative sources of energy cost-effective. In Pennsylvania and Connecticut, for example, the waste from landfills is loaded into furnaces and burned to generate electricity for thousands of homes. Natural sources of energy, such as the sun and the wind, are also becoming more attractive. The electricity produced by 300 wind turbines in northern California, for instance, has resulted in a savings of approximately 60,000 barrels of oil per year. Solar energy also has many applications, from pocket calculators to public telephones to entire homes, and is even used in spacecraft, where conventional power is unavailable.

—adapted from Bergman and Renwick, *Introduction to Geography*, p. 356 and Carnes and Garraty, *The American Nation*, p. 916

You could visualize the paragraph as follows:

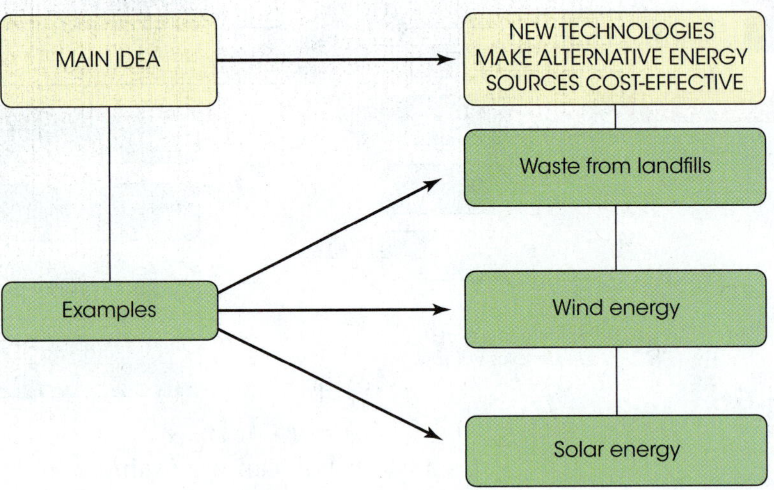

By using examples and transitions, the writer describes alternative sources of energy. Although writers do not always use transitions with examples, be on the lookout for them as you read.

Common Example Transitions

also	*to illustrate*	*one example*
another example	*for instance*	*such as*
for example		

Thinking Critically About Example

Study the nature and types of examples a writer chooses. Pay particular attention to what feature or features of the topic he or she decides to show. If all the examples in an essay about the use of video games by teenagers demonstrate negative effects, then the writer may have an intentional or unintentional bias against video games. Also consider whether the examples are typical and representative of what the writer is trying to explain. For instance, are the examples typical of how most teenagers play and use the games?

Consider whether the examples create an emotional response. If so, the writer may be using the example to sway you to accept a particular viewpoint toward the topic. For instance, a detailed example of a greyhound dog suffering from neglect, locked in a tiny kennel, may be included in an essay intended to persuade you to oppose greyhound racing.

EXERCISE 5-10 Understanding the Example Pattern

Directions: The following paragraphs, both of which are about animal habitats, use the example pattern. Read each paragraph and answer the questions that follow.

Paragraph 1

HABITAT AND NICHE

Habitat refers to the kind of place—defined by the plant community and the physical environment—where a species is biologically adapted to live. For example, a deciduous forest, a swamp, and a grassy field are types of habitats. Different types of forests (for instance, coniferous versus tropical) provide markedly different habitats and support different species of wildlife. Because some organisms operate on very small scales, we use the term *microhabitat* for things like puddles, sheltered spaces by rocks, and holes in tree trunks that might house their own small community.

—Wright, *Environmental Science*, pp. 56–57

1. What transition does the author use to introduce the examples of types of habitats?

____

2. List three examples of habitats.

____

3. Does the topic sentence occur first, second, or last?

____

4. What transition does the author use to introduce an example of a type of forest?

____

5. What transition does the author use to introduce examples of microhabitats?

____

6. List the three examples of microhabitats.

   a. _______________

   b. _______________

   c. _______________

Paragraph 2

Even when different species occupy the same habitat, competition may be slight or nonexistent because each species has its own niche. An animal's ecological **niche** refers to what the animal feeds on, where it feeds, when it feeds, where it finds shelter, how it responds to abiotic factors, and where it nests. Basically, the niche is the sum of all of the conditions and resources under which a species can live. Similar species can coexist in the same habitat, but have separate niches. Competition is minimized because potential competitors are using different resources. For example, woodpeckers, which feed on insects in deadwood, do not compete with birds that feed on seeds. Bats and swallows both feed on flying insects, but they do not compete because bats feed on night-flying insects and swallows feed during the day.

—Wright, *Environmental Science*, p. 57

7. Does the topic sentence of this paragraph occur first, second, or last?

____

8. What transition does the author use to introduce species that are not competing within a habitat?

____

9. Why is competition minimized between species that have different niches?

____

10. The author gives two examples of pairs of species that do not compete in the same habitat. List the pairs.

a. _______________

b. _______________

Writing Example Paragraphs

One of the clearest ways to explain something is to give an example. This is especially true when a subject is unfamiliar. Suppose, for instance, you are taking a course in child psychology and your sister asks you to explain what aggressive behavior is in children. You might explain by giving examples of aggressive behavior, such as biting other children, striking playmates, and throwing objects at others. Through examples, your sister would get a fairly good idea of what aggressive behavior is.

Writing an example paragraph involves writing a topic sentence and selecting appropriate examples to support it.

Writing a Topic Sentence

Your topic sentence should accomplish two things:

1. **It should identify your topic.**
2. **It should make a general statement that the examples support.**

Here are a few examples of topic sentences. Can you predict the types of examples each paragraph would contain?

- Consumers often purchase brand names they have seen advertised in the media.
- Advertisers use attention-getting devices to make a lasting impression in the minds of their consumers.
- Some teenagers are obsessed with instant messaging, using it to the extreme and forsaking other forms of communication.

EXERCISE 5-11

Writing a Topic Sentence for an Example Paragraph

Directions: Select one of the topics listed below, narrow it, and write a topic sentence for it.

1. The behavior of professional athletes
2. The value of saving money
3. People's eating habits
4. Local food movements
5. Computer and Internet monitoring

Choosing Appropriate Examples

Make sure the examples you choose directly support your topic sentence. Use the following guidelines in choosing examples:

1. **Choose clear examples.** Do not choose an example that is complicated or has too many parts; your readers may not be able to see the connection to your topic sentence clearly.
2. **Use a sufficient number of examples to make your point understandable.** The number you need depends on the complexity of the topic and your readers' familiarity with it. One example is sufficient only if it is well developed. The more difficult and unfamiliar the topic, the more examples you will need. For instance, if you are writing about how purchasing books at the college bookstore can be viewed as an exercise in patience, two examples may be sufficient. However, if you are writing about religious intolerance, you probably will need more.
3. **Include examples that your readers are familiar with and understand.** If you choose an example that is out of the realm of your readers' experience, the example will not help them understand your main point.
4. **Vary your examples.** If you are giving several examples, choose a wide range from different times, places, people, and so on.
5. **Choose typical examples.** Avoid outrageous or exaggerated examples that do not accurately represent the situation you are discussing.

6. **Each example should be as specific and vivid as possible, accurately describing an incident or situation.** Include as much detail as is necessary for your readers to understand how the situation illustrates your topic sentence.
7. **Make sure the connection between your example and your main point is clear to your readers.** If the connection is not obvious, include an explanation. For instance, if it is not clear that poor time management is an example of poor study habits, explain how the two relate.

Organizing an Example Paragraph

Be sure to arrange your examples logically. You might arrange them from most to least important or least to most important. (See Chapter 4, p. 138.) You might also arrange them chronologically if the examples are events in the past. For example, if you are reporting on how early educational experiences influenced you, you might begin with the earliest situation and progress to the most recent.

Regardless of the order you use, be sure to connect your examples with transitional words and phrases like those shown in the box on page 172.

EXERCISE 5-12 Writing an Example Paragraph

Directions: Using the topic sentence you generated in Exercise 5-11, generate examples to support it, and write an example paragraph. Present your details in a logical order, using transitions as needed.

READ AND RESPOND: A Student Essay

The End of the Road: A Guide to Break Ups

Leila Kaji

Examining Writing (Leila's essay is on p. 157.)

1. Evaluate Leila's thesis statement. Is it effective? Why or why not?
2. Was the essay interesting and engaging? Why or why not?
3. Evaluate the level of detail included in this essay. Was there too much or too little detail, or a sufficient amount of detail?
4. Did Leila include sufficient introductory and background information? If not, what further information was needed?
5. Did Leila present the major steps that one should follow in breaking up with a significant other? If not, what other steps are needed, and where should they appear in the sequence?
6. What is your first overall impression of the visual included with this essay? What point is the author making about breaking up by including this visual?

Writing Assignments

1. Leila explains the process of breaking up with a boyfriend or girlfriend, but there are also other types of relationships that have to be ended for one reason or another. Write a paragraph explaining how you have ended a relationship with someone. Be sure to include the steps you followed and the success or lack of success that the process yielded.

2. Leila writes that "the main thing you have to remember, however, is that your happiness comes above all else." Write a paragraph in which you describe the things that make you happy.

3. Leila wrote on a process that would be helpful to her college peers. Now you get to do the same. Write an essay in which you explain a process that would be of interest and help to your peers. Be sure to review the structure of Leila's essay and the annotations.

READ AND RESPOND: A Professional Essay

Cairo Tunnel

Amanda Fields

Writing in Response to Reading (See essay on p. 153.)

Checking Your Comprehension MySkillsLab®

Answer each of the following questions using complete sentences.

1. Where is the author going and how is she getting there?
2. Why did the author's students advise her to "deny the American University" (para. 6)?
3. Explain what the author means when she says, "All is gravity and physicality" in paragraph 4?
4. What does the author say she has in common with the women on the Metro?

Strengthening Your Vocabulary MySkillsLab®

Identify at least five words used in the reading that are unfamiliar to you. Using context, word parts, or a dictionary, write a brief definition of each word.

Examining the Reading: Drawing An Idea Map

Create an idea map of the reading that starts with the title and thesis and then lists the author's main points. Use the guidelines on page 15.

Reading and Writing: An Integrated Perspective

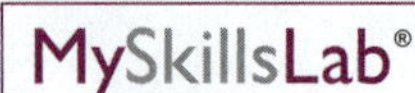

Get ready to write about the reading by discussing the following:

1. Why do you think the author chooses to ride the subway despite the warnings? Do you think she is ultimately glad she did?
2. What does the author say about the other women riding the subway with her? What part of Cairo does she observe through the subway windows? Explain how her observations and descriptions help create a dominant impression.
3. Compare the author's tone in the first paragraph with that in the last paragraph. (For more about tone, see Chapter 12, p. 358). Write a journal entry describing how the last paragraph leaves you feeling about the author's experience.
4. Evaluate the title. How effectively does it capture your interest? What other title would be effective and appropriate?
5. How does the writer organize her details? Does her pattern of organization suit the subject? Consider the types of details she uses as well as what she might be leaving out.

THINKING VISUALLY

6. How does the photograph reflect what the author has described in the reading? What other photographs might be used to illustrate this essay?

Thinking and Writing Critically

1. What do you think the author's purpose is for writing this article? Who is her intended audience?
2. Interestingly, "Cairo Tunnel" does not have a clearly expressed thesis statement. Write one as part of an introductory paragraph to add to the start of the selection.
3. What dominant impression does the author, Amanda Fields, create regarding the women's car of the Cairo Metro?
4. Find and highlight words, phrases, descriptions, or bits of conversation that reveal the writer's attitude toward the subject. For example, in paragraph 4 the writer uses vivid and specific language to reveal how she feels about being on the crowded subway: "The back of my shirt grows slick . . . I begin to feel the pressure on my ribs, the itchy cloth of the woman in niqab against my bare arms . . . We might squeeze each other to death."
5. Identify words in the selection that have positive and negative connotations. How do these words help create an impression? (For more about connotative language, see Chapter 13, pp. 373–374.)

Writing Paragraphs MySkillsLab®

1. How does the author help the reader to visualize what she has seen? Identify examples of vivid language in the reading that help the reader see what the author is describing.

2. In this essay, the author takes the reader along on her journey to work. Think about a journey you take each day, either to class or your job, and write a "how-to" paragraph explaining the steps you take to get from Point A (your home or dorm) to Point B (your class or job).

3. The author clearly stands out as a foreigner among her fellow passengers. Write a paragraph about an experience in which you were clearly different from the people around you. How did you feel about being different? How did people respond to you?

Writing Essays MySkillsLab®

4. A kind word and a smile from a stranger dramatically changed the author's unpleasant subway ride to a memorable, cross-cultural experience. When has a seemingly small gesture from someone made a dramatic difference in your day (or your life)? Write an essay describing your experience.

5. How might one of the other people on the subway have described the same subway ride? Rewrite the essay from another person's point of view. You may choose the woman in niqab, the woman in lime-colored hijab, or the schoolgirl who tapped the author on the shoulder, or you may imagine another person not mentioned in the original essay.

6. Write an essay describing your own experience in an unfamiliar place. Begin with a topic sentence such as "My experience in _______ was memorable in many ways." Support your topic sentence with specific examples, and include sensory details and descriptive language to make your experience vivid for readers.

SELF-TEST SUMMARY

To test yourself, cover the Answer column with a sheet of paper and answer each question in the left column. Evaluate each of your answers as you work by sliding the paper down and comparing your answer with what is printed in the Answer column.

QUESTION	ANSWER
■ GOAL 1 Identify patterns of organization What are patterns of organization, and how do they help readers and writers?	Patterns of organization are methods of organizing information. Common patterns include *chronological order, process, narration, description,* and *example.* Patterns help writers present ideas in a clear and logical manner and help readers see how information is related.

(continued)

(*continued*)

QUESTION	ANSWER
■ GOAL 2 Read and write using time sequence Which patterns use time sequence and how?	*Chronological order* presents events in the order in which they happened. *Process* explains how something is done or how something works, in a particular order. *Narration* uses time sequence to tell a story or make a point.
■ GOAL 3 Read and write using description What is description?	*Description* uses words and phrases that appeal to the senses—taste, touch, smell, sight, hearing—to create a dominant impression that helps readers imagine an object, person, place, or experience.
■ GOAL 4 Read and write using example What is an example, and how do you develop an example paragraph?	An *example* is a specific instance or situation that explains a general idea or statement. Developing an example paragraph involves writing a topic sentence and choosing appropriate examples to illustrate it.

MySkillsLab®

Visit **Chapter 5, "Organization: Basic Patterns,"** in MySkillsLab to test your understanding of chapter goals.

Organization: Additional Patterns

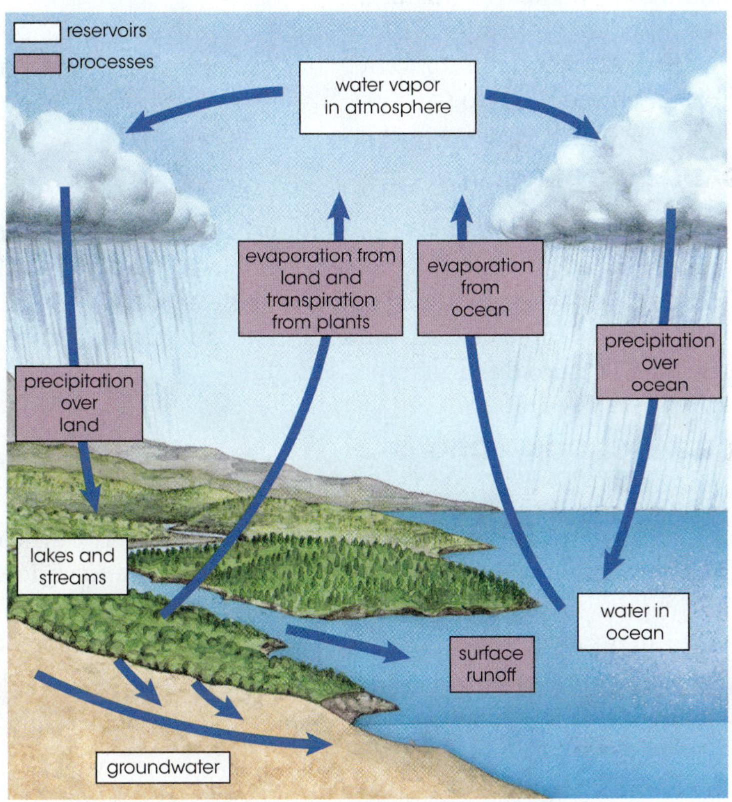

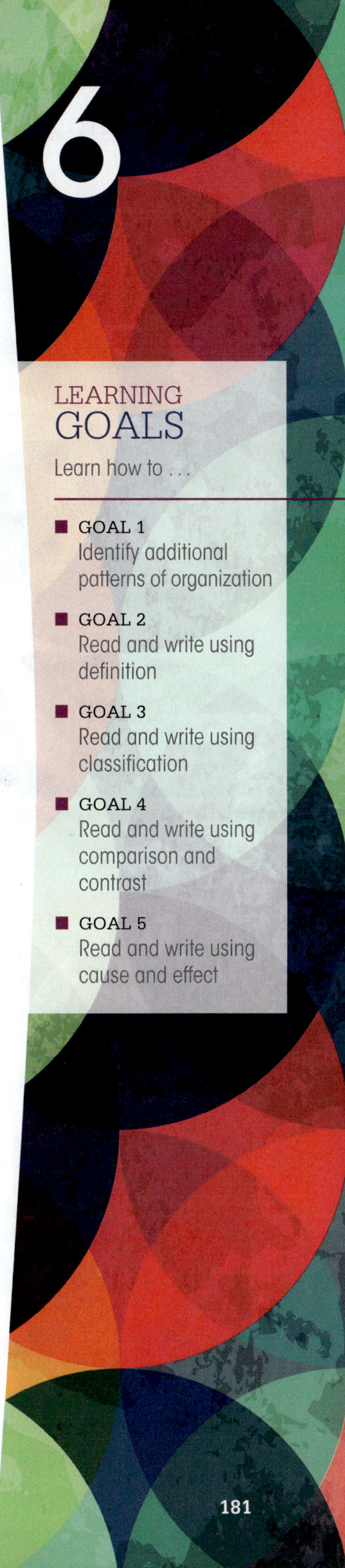

LEARNING GOALS

Learn how to . . .

- GOAL 1 Identify additional patterns of organization
- GOAL 2 Read and write using definition
- GOAL 3 Read and write using classification
- GOAL 4 Read and write using comparison and contrast
- GOAL 5 Read and write using cause and effect

THINK About It!

Suppose you are taking a biology course and the chapter you are studying this week contains the diagram on this page. Write a sentence describing what it shows or explains.

To figure out the diagram, you used a number of different thought patterns. You had to focus on cause and effect relationships; you could see that water vapor in the atmosphere passes through clouds and creates precipitation over land, for instance. Definitions were also useful and important; you had to pay attention to terminology—*transpiration, surface runoff,* and *evaporation*, for example. Perhaps you compared how evaporation occurs over land with how it occurs over ocean water, thus using the comparison and contrast pattern. You might also have classified the types of water—groundwater, ocean water, and surface runoff.

You can see that regardless of whether you are reading the diagram, drawing your own diagram to test your recall for study and review purposes, or writing about evaporation for an in-class paper or exam, these patterns are very useful in helping you organize information. In this chapter you will learn to both read and write using these four patterns.

Reading and Writing Connections

EVERYDAY CONNECTIONS

- **Reading** You read an online movie review comparing and contrasting two films: the original, which was released in 1970, and a 2014 remake of the film.
- **Writing** You write an e-mail to a friend summarizing the plot of the recently released film to help her decide whether it is suitable for her ten-year-old to see.

ACADEMIC CONNECTIONS

- **Reading** You read an assignment for geology in which you must learn the twelve broad categories for classifying types of soil.
- **Writing** For an exam in geology, you write an answer explaining the effects of three factors—time, climate, and topography—on the formation of different types of soil.

WORKPLACE CONNECTIONS

- **Reading** You read an article in a veterinary journal about the causes and effects of laryngeal trauma in dogs. The article includes a brief description of where the larynx is situated relative to the pharynx, the trachea, and the esophagus in a dog's throat.
- **Writing** As a veterinary technician, you write a report for a dog owner explaining the definition of the term *laryngeal trauma* based on the article you read.

What Are Additional Patterns of Organization?

■ GOAL 1
Identify additional patterns of organization

In addition to the patterns discussed in Chapter 5, there are several other patterns that help readers grasp ideas and help writers develop and organize their writing, which you will learn about in this chapter: *definition, classification, comparison and contrast*, and *cause and effect* (see Table 6-1).

TABLE 6-1

Pattern of Organization	What It Does	An Example of Its Use
Definition	Explains a topic by discussing its characteristics	Defining wind power as a form of renewable energy and including some of its important characteristics
Classification	Explains a topic by organizing it into categories or parts	Discussing the use of wind power in different countries
Comparison and Contrast	Shows how things are similar and/or different	Comparing and contrasting wind power with other forms of renewable energy
Cause and Effect	Explains why things happen or what happens as a result of an event or action	Explaining the positive and negative effects of wind power

You will also become familiar with the transitions that will help you read and write using each of these patterns.

EXAMINING PROFESSIONAL WRITING

In this reading, from a textbook titled *Environment: The Science Behind the Stories*, the authors examine the consequences of the growing amount of electronic waste in our world. This reading will be used to illustrate some of the reading and writing techniques discussed in this chapter. As you read it, identify the effects of e-waste and of e-waste recycling.

Thinking Before Reading

1. Preview the reading, using the steps discussed in Chapter 1, page 4.
2. Connect the reading to your own experience by answering the following questions:
   a. What kinds of things do you recycle on a regular basis?
   b. What new electronic devices—cell phone, laptop, MP3 player, and so forth—have you bought in the past year? What happened to the old electronic devices you replaced?
3. Mark and annotate as you read.

E-Waste and E-Waste Recycling

Jay Withgott and Scott Brennan

1 Today's proliferation of computers, printers, cell phones, handheld devices, TVs, DVD players, fax machines, MP3 players, and other electronic technology has created a substantial new source of waste (see **ENVISION IT**, below). These products have short lifetimes before people judge them obsolete, and most are discarded after only a few years. The amount of this **electronic waste**—often called **e-waste**—is growing rapidly, and now comprises 2% of the U.S. solid waste stream. Over 3 billion electronic devices have been sold in the United States since 1980. Of these, half have been disposed of, about 40% are still being used (or reused), and 10% are in storage. American households discard close to 400 million electronic devices per year—two-thirds of them still in working order.

2 Of the electronic items we discard, roughly four of five go to landfills and **incinerators**, where they have traditionally been treated as conventional solid waste. However, most electronic products contain heavy metals and toxic flame retardants, and recent research suggests that e-waste should instead be treated as hazardous waste. The **EPA** and a number of states are now taking steps to keep e-waste out of conventional sanitary landfills and incinerators and instead treat it as hazardous waste.

incinerators
furnaces designed to burn waste completely

EPA
Environmental Protection Agency

3 More and more e-waste today is being recycled. The devices are taken apart, and parts and materials are refurbished and reused in new products. According to

ENVISION IT

EPA estimates, Americans were recycling 15% of e-waste in 1999, and this rose to 18% by 2007. However, so many more items have been manufactured each year that the amount of e-waste we sent to landfills and incinerators in that time period increased by a greater amount. Disposal has risen faster than recycling: In 2007 we recycled 45 million more tons of e-waste than in 1999, but we also disposed of 169 million more tons of e-waste in landfills and incinerators.

4 Besides keeping toxic substances out of our environment, e-waste recycling is beneficial because a number of trace metals used in electronics are globally rare, so they can be lucrative to recover. A typical cell phone contains close to a dollar's worth of precious metals. Every bit of metal we can recycle from a manufactured item is a bit of metal we don't need to mine from the ground, so "mining" e-waste for precious metals helps reduce the environmental impacts that mining exerts. By one estimate, 1 ton of computer scrap contains more gold than 16 tons of mined ore from a gold mine. In one of the more intriguing efforts to promote sustainability through such recycling, the 2010 Winter Olympic Games in Vancouver produced its stylish gold, silver, and bronze medals from metals recovered from recycled and processed e-waste!

5 There are serious concerns, however, about the health risks that recycling may pose to workers doing the disassembly. Wealthy nations ship much of their e-waste to developing countries, where low-income workers disassemble the devices and handle toxic materials with minimal safety regulations. These environmental justice concerns need to be resolved, but if electronics recycling can be done responsibly, it seems likely to be the way of the future.

leach
leak or seep out

6 In many North American cities, used electronics are collected by businesses, nonprofit organizations, or municipal services, and are processed for reuse or recycling. So next time you upgrade to a new computer, TV, DVD player, cell phone, or handheld device, find out what opportunities exist in your area to recycle your old ones.

READING AND WRITING DEFINITION

What Is Definition?

■ GOAL 2
Read and write using definition

A **definition** is an explanation of what something is. It has three essential parts:

1. The term being defined
2. The group, or category, to which the term belongs
3. Its distinguishing characteristics

Suppose you had to define the term *cheetah*. If you said it was a cat, then you would be stating the group to which it belongs. **Group** means the general category of which something is a part. If you said a cheetah lives in Africa and southwest Asia, has black-spotted fur, is long-legged, and is the fastest animal on land, you would be giving some of its distinguishing characteristics. **Distinguishing characteristics** are those details that allow you to tell an item apart from others in its same group. The details about the cheetah's fur, long legs, and speed enable a reader to distinguish it from other large cats in Africa and southwest Asia. Here are a few more examples:

TERM	GROUP	DISTINGUISHING CHARACTERISTICS
opal	gemstone	greenish blue colors
comedian	entertainer	makes people laugh
fear	emotion	occurs when a person feels threatened or in danger

Here is a sample definition paragraph from a geography text.

> **Humid subtropical climates** have several defining characteristics. They occur in latitudes between about 25 and 40 degrees on the eastern sides of continents and between about 35 and 50 degrees on the western sides. These climates are relatively warm most of the year but have at least occasional freezing temperatures during the winter. Most humid subtropical climates have deciduous species of vegetation that lose their leaves in autumn and become dormant in winter. Eastern China, the southeastern U.S., and parts of Brazil and Argentina are the largest areas of humid subtropical climates.
>
> —adapted from Bergman and Renwick, *Introduction to Geography*, p. 280

In the paragraph above, the term being defined is *humid subtropical climates*. Its group is *types of climate*, and its distinguishing characteristics are detailed. You can visualize a definition paragraph by studying the following model (shown left) and the map for the paragraph (shown right).

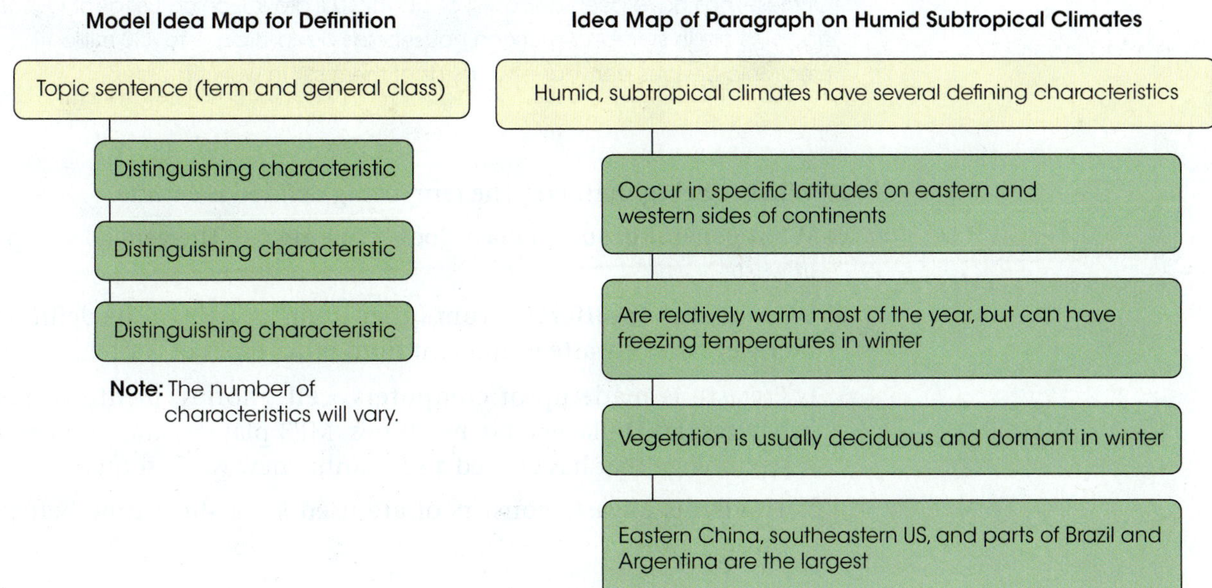

EXERCISE 6-1

Defining Terms by Group and Distinguishing Characteristics

Directions: For each term listed below, give the group it belongs to and at least two of its distinguishing characteristics.

Term	Group	Distinguishing Characteristics
1. baseball	______	______
2. a role model	______	______
3. blogging	______	______
4. terrorism	______	______
5. facial expressions	______	______

Reading Definition

As you read passages that use the definition pattern, keep these questions in mind:

1. What is being defined?
2. What general group or class does it belong to?
3. What distinguishes it—makes it different—from other items or ideas?

Apply these questions to the paragraph 1 from "E-Waste and E-Waste Recycling":

> Today's proliferation of computers, printers, cell phones, handheld devices, TVs,\DVD players, fax machines, MP3 players, and other electronic technology has created a substantial new source of waste (see **ENVISION IT**, below). These products have short lifetimes before people judge them obsolete, and most are discarded after only a few years. The amount of this **electronic waste**—often called e-waste—is growing rapidly, and now comprises 2% of the U.S. solid waste stream. Over 3 billion electronic devices have been sold in the United States since 1980. Of these, half have been disposed of, about 40% are still being used (or reused), and 10% are in storage. American households discard close to 400 million electronic devices per year—two-thirds of them still in working order.

- **What is being defined?** The term being defined is *e-waste*.
- **What general group or class does it belong to?** The general group is *types of waste*.
- **What makes it different from other items or ideas?** The definition lists four ways that e-waste is different from other types of waste:
  1. E-waste is made up of computers, cell phones, printers, handheld devices, DVD players, fax machines, MP3 players, and other electronic technology that has created a substantial new waste source.
  2. The items e-waste consists of are used for a short time before being thrown away.

3. The amount of e-waste is growing rapidly and makes up 2% of the U. S. solid waste stream.
4. U. S. households throw out close to 400,000,000 devices per year, two thirds of which still work.

Combining Definition and Example

It is important to note that definitions are often combined with examples. For instance, if someone asks you to define the term *fiction writer*, you might begin by saying that a fiction writer is someone who creates novels and stories that describe imaginary people or events. You might also give some examples of well-known fiction writers, such as Ernest Hemingway or Stephen King. When definition and example are used together in this way, you can visualize the pattern as follows:

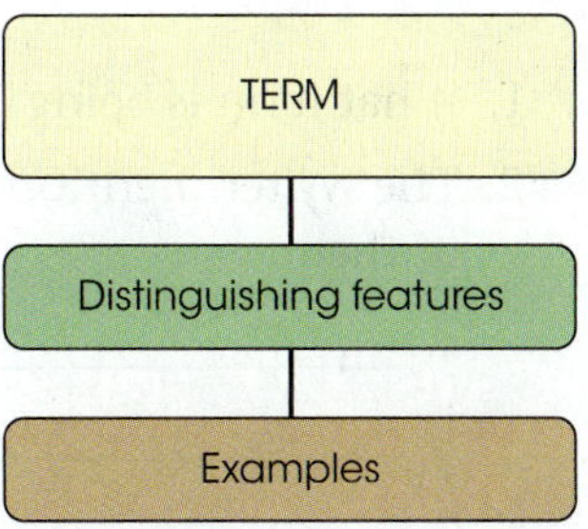

You will often encounter the definition and example pattern in your textbooks. An author will define a term and then use examples to explain it further, as shown in the previous passage from the professional reading. First the authors defined *e-waste*, and then they provided several examples to make the definition more understandable. You have probably already noticed that textbook authors often put an important term in **boldfaced** type when they define it. This makes it easier for students to find definitions as they read or study for tests. They also use transitional words and phrases to signal that a definition is being presented (see box below).

Common Definition Transitions

are those that	*involves*	*is literally*
can be defined as	*is*	*means*
consists of	*is a term that*	*occurs when*
corresponds to	*is called*	*refers to*
entails	*is characterized by*	

Thinking Critically About Definition

Depending on the topic, some definitions are objective and straightforward (e.g., a definition of the term *photosynthesis* in a biology textbook). Others tend to be more subjective, involving interpretation, bias, and opinion (e.g., a writer defining what constitutes racism or discrimination), so be sure to ask yourself whether you agree or disagree with the author's stance, and determine whether the author provides sufficient evidence to support his or her opinion.

EXERCISE 6-2 Understanding the Definition Pattern

Directions: Read each paragraph and answer the questions that follow.

Paragraph 1

No time to socialize? Surely you can spare six minutes. That's how long potential couples usually spend getting acquainted while **speed dating**—an accelerated form of dating in which men and women choose whether to see each other again based on a very short interaction. Originally created for young Jewish singles in 1999, speed dating now provides homosexuals, heterosexuals, and a number of religious and ethnic groups with an opportunity to participate in quick, one-on-one dates with like-minded singles. Individuals spend six minutes talking to each date. If both individuals are interested, they are provided with each other's e-mail addresses.

—Kunz, *THINK Marriages & Families*, p. 119

1. What term is being defined? ____________________
2. The writer mentions several distinguishing features of this term. List three of them.
   a. ____________________
   ____
   b. ____________________
   c. ____________________

Paragraph 2

The **nervous system**, the master controlling and communicating system of the body, has three overlapping functions: (1) It uses millions of sensory receptors to monitor changes occurring both inside and outside the body. These changes are called stimuli and the gathered information is called *sensory input*. (2) It processes and interprets the sensory input and decides what should be done at each moment—a process called *integration*. (3) It causes a response by activating our muscles or glands; the response is called *motor output*. An example will illustrate how these functions work together. When you are driving and see a red light ahead (sensory input), your nervous system integrates this information (red light means "stop"), and your foot goes for the brake (motor output).

—Marieb, *Human Anatomy & Physiology*, p. 387

3. What term is being defined? ____________________
4. In defining this term, the writer mentions three distinguishing features. List them below.
   a. ____________________
   b. ____________________
   c. ____________________

Writing Definition Paragraphs

Developing a definition paragraph involves writing a topic sentence and adding explanatory details.

Writing a Topic Sentence

The topic sentence of a definition paragraph should accomplish two things:

1. **It should identify the term you are explaining.**
2. **It should place the term in a general group.** It may also provide one or more distinguishing characteristics.

In the topic sentence below, the term being defined is *psychiatry*, the general group is "a branch of medicine," and its distinguishing feature is that it "deals with mental and emotional disorders."

> Psychiatry is a branch of medicine that deals with mental and emotional disorders.

Writing a Topic Sentence

Directions: Write a topic sentence that includes a group and a distinguishing characteristic for each of the following items.

1. Instagram
2. horror movies
3. hip-hop
4. car
5. contra dancing

Adding Explanatory Details

Your topic sentence will usually *not* be sufficient to give your reader a complete understanding of the term you are defining. You will need to explain it further in one or more of the following ways:

1. **Give examples.** Examples can make a definition more vivid and interesting to your reader. (To learn more about using examples, see Chapter 5, p. 170.)
2. **Break the term into subcategories.** Breaking your subject down into subcategories helps to organize your definition. For example, you might explain the term *discrimination* by listing some of its types: *racial*, *gender*, and *age*.
3. **Explain what the term is not.** To bring the meaning of a term into focus for your reader, it is sometimes helpful to give counterexamples, or to discuss in what ways the term means something different from what one might expect.
4. **Trace the term's meaning over time.** If the term has changed or expanded in meaning over time, it may be useful to trace this development as a way of explaining the term's current meaning.
5. **Compare an unfamiliar term to one that is familiar to your readers.** If you are writing about rugby, you might compare it to football, a more familiar sport. Be sure to make the connection clear to your readers by pointing out characteristics that the two sports share.

Organizing a Definition Paragraph

You should logically arrange the distinguishing characteristics of a term. You might arrange them from most to least familiar or from more to less obvious, for example. Be sure to use strong transitional words and phrases to help your readers follow your presentation of ideas, guiding them from one distinguishing characteristic to another. Useful transitional words and phrases are shown in the box on page 187.

Writing a Definition Paragraph

Directions: Select one of the topic sentences you wrote for Exercise 6-3. Write a paragraph defining that topic, using transitions as needed.

READING AND WRITING CLASSIFICATION

What Is Classification?

■ GOAL 3
Read and write using classification

Classification is a process of sorting people, things, or ideas into groups or categories to make them more understandable. Your dresser drawers are probably organized by categories, with T-shirts and socks in different drawers. Convenience stores, phone directories, and restaurant menus arrange items in groups according to similar or shared characteristics. In reading and writing, the classification pattern is used to explain a topic by describing its types or parts. It is often used when a topic is difficult or complex.

Textbook writers often use the classification pattern to explain an unfamiliar or complicated topic by dividing it into more easily understood parts. These parts are selected on the basis of common characteristics. For example, a psychology textbook writer might explain human needs by classifying them into two categories, primary and secondary. Or in a chemistry textbook, various compounds may be grouped or classified according to common characteristics, such as the presence of hydrogen or oxygen.

Here is a sample classification paragraph:

> Horticulture, the study and cultivation of garden plants, is a large industry. Recently it has become a popular area of study. The horticulture field consists of four major divisions. First, there is pomology, the science and practice of growing and handling fruit trees. Then there is olericulture, which is concerned with growing and storing vegetables. A third field, floriculture, is the science of growing, storing, and designing flowering plants. The last category, ornamental and landscape horticulture, is concerned with using grasses, plants, and shrubs in landscaping.

This paragraph approaches the topic of horticulture by describing its four areas or fields of study. You could diagram the paragraph as follows:

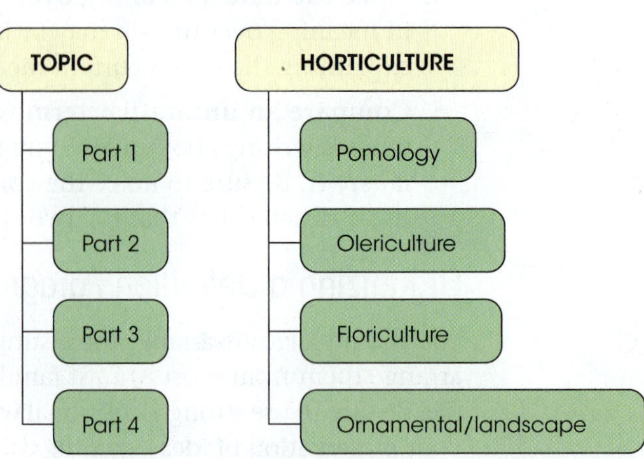

Reading Classification

When reading textbook material that uses the classification pattern, be sure you understand *how* and *why* the topic was divided as it was. This technique will help you remember the most important parts of the topic. In the following paragraph, the topic, staffing of large city newspapers, is divided according to responsibilities. In a paragraph written for a different purpose, it would be possible to classify the staff by age, ethnicity, or salary, for example.

> A newspaper is published primarily to present current news and information. For large city newspapers, more than 2,000 people may be involved in the distribution of this information. The staff of large city papers, headed by a publisher, is organized into departments: editorial, business, and mechanical. The editorial department, headed by an editor-in-chief, is responsible for the collection of news and preparation of written copy. The business department, headed by a business manager, handles circulation, sales, and advertising. The mechanical department is run by a production manager. This department deals with the actual production of the paper, including typesetting, layout, and printing.

You could diagram this paragraph as follows:

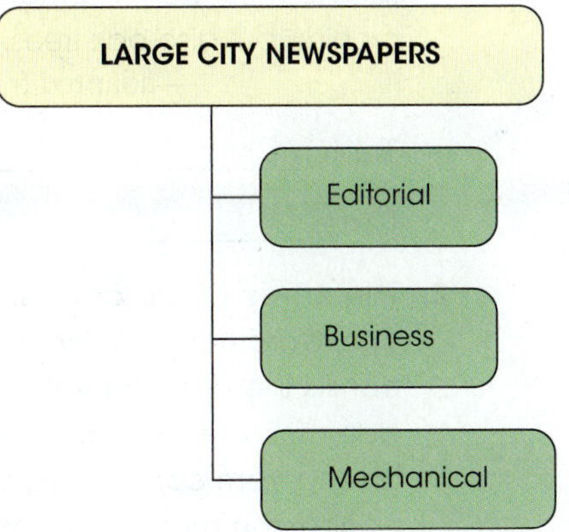

Paragraphs and passages that are organized using classification frequently use transitional words and phrases to guide the reader. These include the following:

Common Classification Transitions

another	*different stages of*	*last*
another kind	*finally*	*one*
classified as	*first*	*second*
comprises	*include*	*types of*
different groups that	*is composed of*	*varieties of*

Thinking Critically About Classification

When reading classification paragraphs and essays, be sure to examine the categories the writer has chosen to see if they cover most or all of the subject. For example, if you are reading an essay about the types of Facebook users, does the article cover most types of users, or are some left out? Consider whether each category is treated in equal and sufficient detail. If some categories are treated in depth and others are not fully explained, you might wonder if the author has a bias against or special interest toward some of the categories.

Also examine whether the principle of classification is appropriate and reasonable and suited to the author's purpose. For instance, if you are reading about unhealthy fast-food restaurants, it would be appropriate to classify the restaurants by the amounts of high-calorie food they serve, but it would not be useful to categorize them according the type of clientele they serve.

EXERCISE 6-5 Reading: Analyzing Classification Paragraphs

Directions: Read each of the following passages. Then identify the topic and the parts into which each topic is divided.

1. We can separate the members of the plant kingdom into a mere four types. These are the *bryophytes*, which include mosses; the *seedless vascular plants*, which include ferns; the *gymnosperms*, which include coniferous ("cone-bearing") trees; and the *angiosperms*, a vast division of flowering plants—by far the most dominant on Earth today—that includes not only flowers such as orchids, but also oak trees, rice, and cactus.

   —adapted from Krogh, *Biology: A Guide to the Natural World*, p. 429

   Topic: ____________________

   Parts: ____________________

2. The name of the cancer is derived from the type of tissue in which it develops. Carcinoma (carc = cancer; omo = tumor) refers to a malignant tumor consisting of epithelial cells. A tumor that develops from a gland is called an adenosarcoma (adeno = gland). Sarcoma is a general term for any cancer arising from connective tissue. Osteogenic sarcomas (osteo = bone; genic = origin), the most frequent type of childhood cancer, destroy normal bone tissue and eventually spread to other areas of the body. Myelomas (myelos = marrow) are malignant tumors, occurring in middle-aged and older people, that interfere with the blood-cell-producing function of bone marrow and cause anemia. Chondrosarcomas (chondro = cartilage) are cancerous growths of cartilage.

   —Tortora, *Introduction to the Human Body*, p. 56

   Topic: ____________________

   Parts: ____________________

   The amount of space that people prefer varies from one culture to another. North Americans use four different "distance zones." *Intimate distance* extends to about 18 inches from our bodies. We reserve this space for comforting, protecting, hugging, intimate touching, and love-making. *Personal distance* extends from 18 inches to 4 feet. We reserve it for friends and acquaintances and ordinary conversations. *Social distance*, extending out from us about 4 to 12 feet, marks impersonal or formal relationships. We use this zone for such things as job interviews. *Public distance*, extending beyond 12 feet, marks even more formal relationships. It is used to separate dignitaries and public speakers from the general public.

—adapted from Henslin, *Sociology: A Down-to-Earth Approach*, pp. 109, 111

Topic: ______________________________

Parts: ______________________________

Writing Classification Paragraphs

Developing a **classification paragraph** involves deciding on a basis of classification for the subject you are discussing, writing a topic sentence, and explaining each subgroup.

Deciding on What Basis to Classify Information

To write a paper using classification, you must first decide on a basis for breaking your subject into subgroups. Suppose you are given an assignment to write about some aspect of campus life, and decide to classify the campus services into groups. You could classify them by benefit, location, or type of facility, depending on what you wanted the focus of your writing to be.

The best way to plan your classification paragraph is to find a good general topic and then brainstorm different ways to break it into subgroups or categories.

EXERCISE 6-6

WORKING TOGETHER

Writing: Brainstorming to Classify Topics

Directions: For each of the following topics, brainstorm to discover different ways you might classify them. Compare your work with that of a classmate and select the two most effective classifications.

1. **Topic** Crimes

   WAYS TO CLASSIFY ______________________________

   ____

   ____

2. **Topic** Movies

   WAYS TO CLASSIFY ______________________________

   ____

   ____

3. **Topic** Web sites ______________________________

   WAYS TO CLASSIFY ______________________________

   ____

   ____

Most topics can be classified in a number of different ways. Stores can be classified by types of merchandise, prices, size, or customer service provided, for example. Use the following tips for choosing an appropriate basis of classification:

Tips for Choosing a Basis for Classification

- **Consider your audience.** Choose a basis of classification that will interest them. Classifying stores by size may not be as interesting as classifying them by merchandise, for example.
- **Choose a basis that is uncomplicated.** If you choose a basis that is complicated or lengthy, your topic may be difficult to write about. Categorizing stores by prices may be unwieldy, since there are thousands of products sold at various prices.
- **Choose a basis with which you are familiar.** While it is possible to classify stores by the types of customer service they provide, you may have to do some research or learn more about available services in order to write about them.

Writing a Topic Sentence

Once you have chosen a way to classify a topic and have identified the subgroups you will use, you are ready to write a topic sentence. Your topic sentence should accomplish two things:

1. **It should identify your topic.**
2. **It should indicate how you will classify items within your topic.**

The topic sentence may also mention the number of subgroups you will use. Here are a couple of examples:

- Three relatively new types of family structures are single-parent families, blended families, and families without children.
- Since working as a waiter, I've discovered that there are three main types of customer complaints.

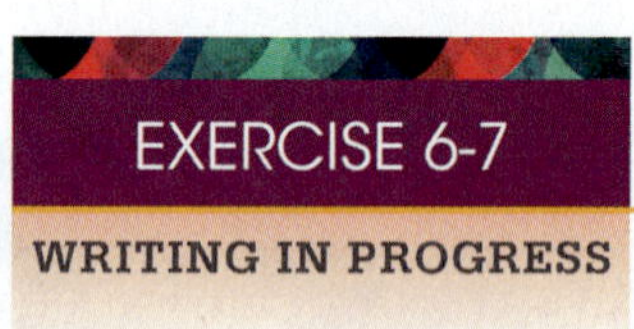

WRITING IN PROGRESS

Writing a Topic Sentence

Directions: Choose one of the following topics, and brainstorm a list of possible ways to classify it. Then write a topic sentence that identifies the topic and explains your method of classification.

1. professional athletes or their fans
2. bad drivers
3. diets
4. cell phone users
5. friends

Explaining Each Subgroup

The details in your paragraph should explain and provide further information about each subgroup. Depending on your topic and/or your audience, it may be necessary to define each subgroup. If possible, provide an equal amount of detail for each subgroup. If you define or offer an example for one subgroup, you should do the same for each of the others.

Organizing a Classification Paragraph

The order in which you present your categories depends on your topic. Possible ways to organize the categories include from familiar to unfamiliar, from oldest to newest, or from simpler to more complex. Be sure to use transitions to signal your readers that you are moving from one category to another. Useful transitions are shown in the box on page 191.

Writing a Classification Paragraph

Directions: For the topic sentence you wrote in Exercise 6-7, write a classification paragraph. Be sure to identify and explain each group. Use transitions as needed.

READING AND WRITING COMPARISON AND CONTRAST

What Are Comparison and Contrast?

■ GOAL 4
Read and write using comparison and contrast

You use comparison and contrast every day. For example, when you decide which pair of shoes to buy, where to apply for a part-time job, or what topic to choose for a research paper, you are thinking about similarities and differences.

Writers use comparison or contrast to explain how something is similar to or different from something else. **Comparison** treats similarities, whereas **contrast** emphasizes differences. For example, a writer who is *comparing* two U.S. presidents would focus on their shared features: experience in politics, leadership characteristics, and commitment to fulfill the duties of the office. But a writer who is *contrasting* the two presidents would discuss how they differ in foreign policy, education, family background, and so forth.

As you read, you will find passages that only compare, some that only contrast, and some that do both. Below are model maps for the two basic patterns.

Model Idea Map for Comparison

Topic sentence
Similarity 1
Similarity 2
Similarity 3

Note: The number of similarities will vary.

Model Idea Map for Contrast

Topic sentence
Difference 1
Difference 2
Difference 3

Note: The number of differences will vary.

Reading Comparison and Contrast

When you read, look for both similarities and differences. First, establish what is being compared or contrasted to what. Next determine whether similarities, differences, or both are being presented. Usually the topic sentence will express the basic relationship between the ideas or items being discussed. For example, a topic sentence that states "It is important to make a distinction between amnesia and forgetting" indicates the paragraph is primarily about differences. On the other hand, a topic sentence that says "The president made two compatible proposals on economic development" emphasizes similarities. Finally, decide whether the comparison or contrast is the author's central purpose or whether it is used only as a means of support for the main idea.

When writers use comparison or contrast, sometimes they also include transitions to introduce each important point they are making.

Common Comparison and Contrast Transitions

To show similarities		To show differences	
alike	*just as*	*although*	*in spite of*
also	*like*	*as opposed to*	*instead*
as well as	*likewise*	*despite*	*nevertheless*
both	*resembles*	*differs from*	*on the other hand*
correspondingly	*share*	*however*	*unlike*
in common	*similarly*	*in contrast*	*whereas*
in comparison	*to compare*		
in the same way	*too*		

Comparison

A writer who is concerned only with similarities may identify the items to be compared and then list the ways they are alike. The following paragraph describes apparent similarities between two planets, Earth and Mars.

> Early telescopic observations of Mars revealed several uncanny resemblances to Earth. The Martian rotation axis is tilted about the same amount as Earth's, and on both planets a day lasts about 24 hours. In addition, Mars has polar caps, which we now know to be composed primarily of frozen carbon dioxide, with smaller amounts of water ice. Telescopic observations also showed seasonal variations in surface coloration over the course of the Martian year (about 1.9 Earth years). All these discoveries led to the perception that Mars and Earth were at least cousins, if not twins. By the early 1900s, many astronomers—as well as the public—envisioned Mars as nearly Earth-like, possessing water, vegetation that changed with the seasons, and possibly intelligent life.
>
> —adapted from Bennett, *The Cosmic Perspective*, p. 249

Such a pattern can be diagrammed as follows:

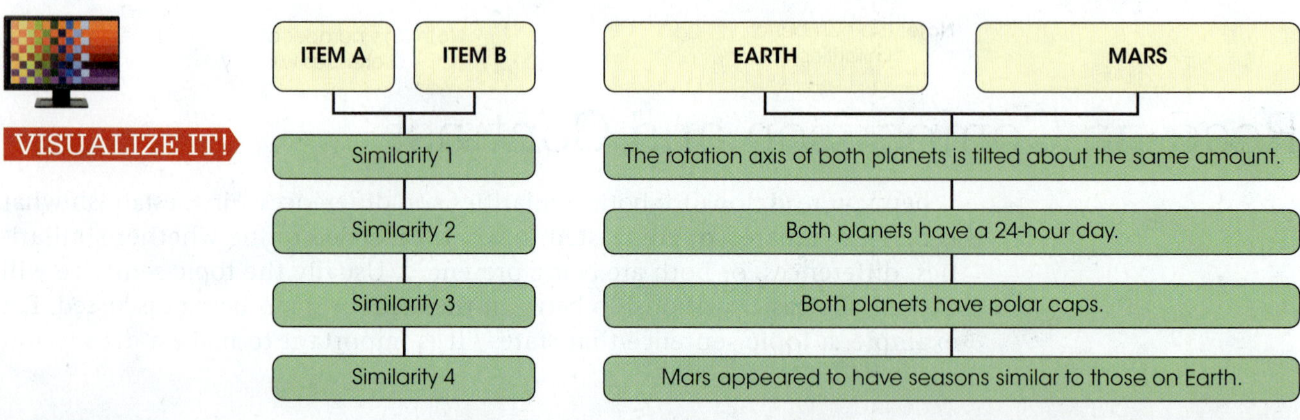

Look at the paragraph again, and notice the clues the writers provide about what kind of pattern they are following. In the first sentence—the topic sentence—the phrase *several uncanny resemblances* tells you that the paragraph will be about the similarities between Earth and Mars. The writers also use the words *same* and *both*, which signal that a comparison is being made, and use the transitions *in addition* and *also* to help the reader follow the main points of the comparison. As you read, be on the lookout for words that indicate comparison or contrast.

Contrast

The following paragraph was written to point out only the differences between two types of tumors:

> Not all tumors are **malignant** (cancerous); in fact, most are **benign** (noncancerous). Benign and malignant tumors differ in several key ways. Benign tumors are generally composed of ordinary-looking cells enclosed in a fibrous shell or capsule that prevents their spreading to other body areas. Malignant tumors, in contrast, are usually not enclosed in a protective capsule and can therefore spread to other organs. Unlike benign tumors, which merely expand to take over a given space, malignant cells invade surrounding tissue, emitting clawlike protrusions that disrupt chemical processes within healthy cells.
>
> —adapted from Donatelle, *Health: The Basics*, p. 324

Such a pattern can be diagrammed as follows:

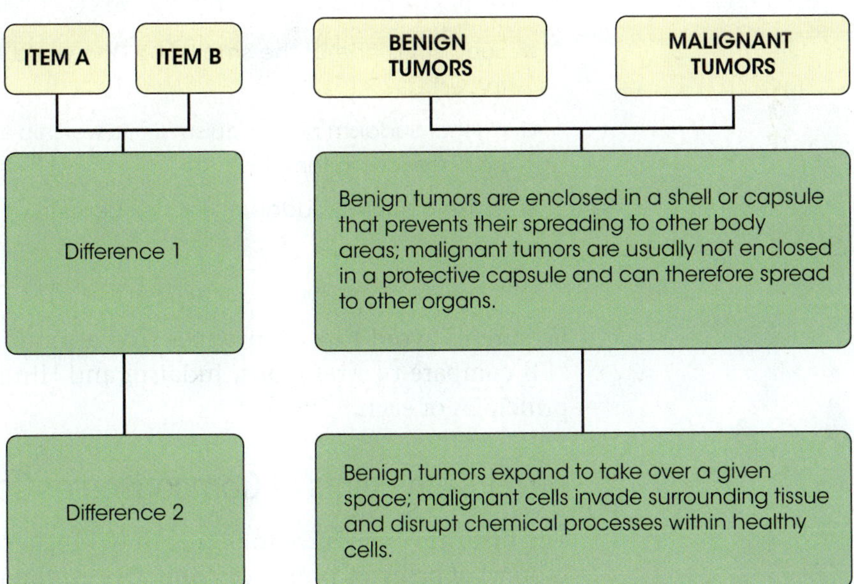

Look at the preceding paragraph again, and circle the contrast clues you can find (use the box on page 196 to help you).

Thinking Critically About Comparison and Contrast

Evaluate whether the author treated all the topics equally and fairly. Comparison and contrast always involves two or more topics, and the amount of coverage and level of objectivity or subjectivity should be approximately the same for each.

Check that the same points of comparison are covered for each topic. For example, a writer comparing two- and four-year colleges should cover the same points of comparison for each, such as degrees offered, class size, faculty accessibility, and so forth. It would be unfair to use points of comparison that reveal all the advantages of two-year colleges and only the disadvantages of four-year schools.

Writing Comparison or Contrast Paragraphs

When writing paragraphs, it is often best to focus either on similarities or on differences, instead of trying to cover both. Essay-length pieces can focus on both similarities and differences, but it is often easier to concentrate on one or the other. Developing a comparison or contrast paragraph involves writing a topic sentence and developing points of comparison or contrast.

Writing a Topic Sentence

Your topic sentence should do two things:

1. **It should identify the two subjects that you will compare or contrast.**
2. **It should state whether you will focus on similarities, differences, or both.**

Here are a few sample topic sentences that meet the requirements above:

- Judaism is one of the smallest of the world's religions; Hinduism is one of the largest.
- Neither Judaism nor Hinduism limits worship to a single location, although both hold services in temples.
- Unlike Hinduism, Judaism teaches belief in only one God.

Be sure to avoid topic sentences that announce what you plan to do such as "I'll compare two religions, Judaism and Hinduism, and discuss the founding principles of each."

Developing Points of Comparison or Contrast

The first thing you have to decide in writing a comparison or contrast paragraph is on what bases, or **points of comparison**, you will compare or contrast your two subjects. Suppose you are comparing two different jobs that you have held. Points of comparison could be your salary, work schedule, required tasks, responsibilities, relationships with other employees, relationship with your boss, and so forth. If your purpose is to show what you learned from the jobs, then you might compare the tasks you completed and your responsibilities. If you want to make a case that working conditions in entry level jobs are poor, then you might use responsibilities, work schedule, and relationship with your boss as points of comparison.

EXERCISE 6-9

WRITING IN PROGRESS

Developing Points of Comparison and Contrast and Writing Topic Sentences

Directions: For three of the topics below, brainstorm lists of similarities or differences. Review your lists and choose points of comparison or contrast. Then write topic sentences for them.

Example

Subject: two restaurants

Items A and B: Blue Mesa and Chico's

Similarities	Differences
1. Both specialize in Mexican food.	1. Blue Mesa is much more expensive than Chico's.
2. Both serve lunch and dinner.	2. Chico's is a chain, while Blue Mesa is a single restaurant.
3. Both are located on the east side of town.	3. Only Chico's offers takeout.
4. Both employ college students.	4. Blue Mesa is closed on Mondays, while Chico's is open every day.
5. Both have a special menu for children.	5. Only Blue Mesa accepts reservations.

Comparison topic sentence: Blue Mesa and Chico's restaurants are so similar it is hard to choose which to eat at.

Contrast topic sentence: The differences between Blue Mesa and Chico's restaurants go far beyond the quality of the food.

1. two special places
2. two favorite pastimes
3. two styles of dress
4. two motorbikes
5. two public figures
6. two sports
7. two college classes
8. two relatives

Organizing a Comparison or Contrast Paragraph

Once you have identified similarities or differences between two items and drafted a topic sentence, you are ready to organize your paragraph. There are two ways you can organize a comparison or contrast paragraph:

- subject by subject
- point by point

Subject-by-Subject Organization

In the **subject-by-subject method**, you write first about one of your subjects, covering it completely, and then about the other, covering it completely. To develop each subject, for instance your first and second jobs, focus on the same kinds of details and discuss the same points of comparison in the same order. Organize your points within each topic, using a most-to-least or least-to-most arrangement.

VISUALIZE IT!

Model Idea Map for Subject-by-Subject Organization

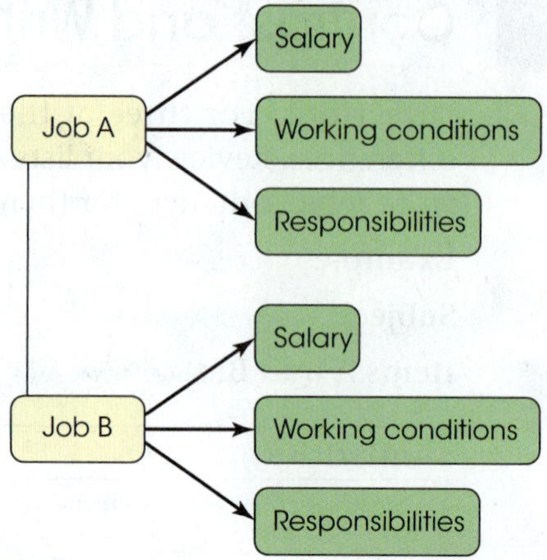

EXERCISE 6-10

WRITING IN PROGRESS

Writing a Paragraph Using Subject-by-Subject Organization

Directions: Using the subject-by-subject method of organization, write a comparison or contrast paragraph on one of the topics you worked with in Exercise 6-9.

Point-by-Point Organization

In the **point-by-point method of organization**, you discuss both of your subjects together for each point of comparison or contrast. For a paragraph on jobs, for example, you would write about the salary for Job A and Job B, and then you would write about working conditions for Job A and Job B, and so on, always discussing the same subject first for each point. If your paragraph focuses only on similarities or only on differences, arrange your points in a least-to-most or most-to-least pattern.

VISUALIZE IT!

Model Idea Map for Point-by-Point Organization

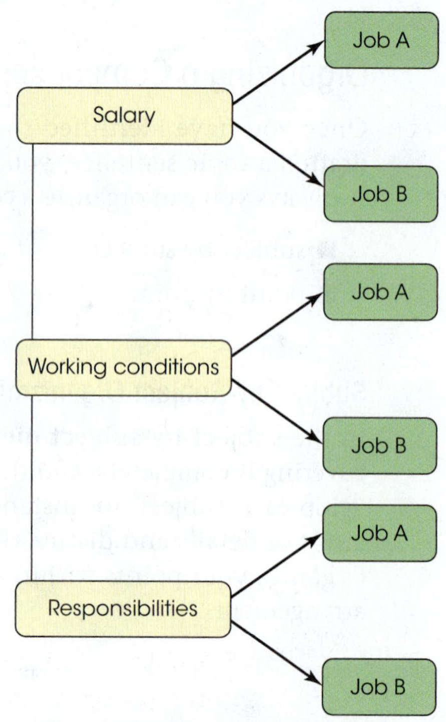

Transitions are particularly important in comparison and contrast writing. Because you are discussing two subjects and covering similar points for each, your readers can easily become confused. Useful transitions are shown in the box on page 196.

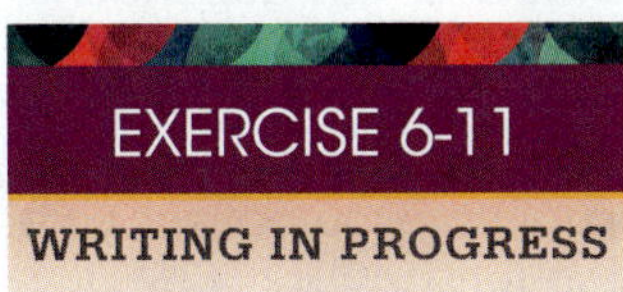

EXERCISE 6-11

WRITING IN PROGRESS

Writing a Paragraph Using Point-by-Point Organization

Directions: Using the point-by-point method of organization, write a comparison or contrast paragraph on one of the topics you worked with in Exercise 6-9.

EXAMINING STUDENT WRITING

A good way to learn to read and write essays is to study a model. By examining the student essay below by Jessica Nantka, you will learn how to write cause and effect paragraphs and essays.

Jessica Nantka is a student at the State University College at Buffalo, where she is majoring in elementary education. For her writing class, Jessica was asked to write a cause and effect essay; she chose to write about the benefits of joining the military. As you read, notice that she devotes one paragraph to each benefit.

Straightforward title

Benefits of Joining the Military

Jessica Nantka

1 The military has been around for many centuries in one form or another. It has been the basis for many societies, but today joining the military is a controversial issue. Throughout the many wars our world has seen, people have begun to realize the negative outcomes war and military service can have. Despite these negative effects, there are many reasons why joining the military is appealing and beneficial.

Thesis statement

Effect 1: travel opportunities

2 Joining the military is a great way to see the world. Through various assignments and deployments, people can travel all around the world at the government's expense. They may not have a great deal of free time while in another country, as they would if they were on vacation; however, just being there and experiencing life is gratifying enough. For example, my father traveled a lot when he was in the Navy; he traveled to Europe, Asia, and the Middle East and in the limited time he had, he briefly visited many of the worlds' most scenic and historical areas.

Effect 2: educational benefits

3 Educational benefits are another reason for joining the military. Schooling is offered, and the military may even pay for a large portion of the tuition bill, depending on a number of factors such as length of service, active duty or reserve status, and so forth ("Benefits"). Enlistees can often get loans from the military for the rest, too. The military is very supportive of soldiers who are obtaining degrees, and it encourages enlisted men and women to begin their studies while enlisted.

Effect 3: job training

4 Military enlistment offers great job training and many career options. Many enlistees are encouraged to select jobs in categories they are interested in, and they receive valuable job training and experience. When they leave the military, they find themselves ready to step into a job in the real world. Having served in the military is a great thing to have on a resume, too.

Effect 4: health care coverage

5 Soldiers can obtain excellent health care for themselves and their dependents. Active duty soldiers receive free medical and dental care. Other services, such as counseling, are available depending on need. As veterans, retired soldiers and their families may be eligible for benefits which include hospital care, outpatient care, and medical supplies, again depending on the length of their service and other factors. Enlistees have to stay in for many years, though, to qualify for lifetime health-care (Clayton).

Effect 5: financial benefits

6 Enlisting in the military also makes financial sense in a lot of ways; there are many benefits. Military personnel can shop at the commissary and save a lot of money because things are sold there at a discount to military members and their families. The military pays a salary as well as offering free accommodation on base or providing a housing allowance, depending on factors such as a person's rank, location, and number of dependents. It may pay for food, too. If you serve for 20 years, you get a pension for life ("Military").

Effect 6: character building

7 Another reason many people, including myself, think about joining the armed forces is to build strength: strength for now, strength for later. Due to the fact that I am a female, many people treat me as though I am weak—but I am not. I want to prove to myself and others that I can do whatever I set my mind to do. The military offers training that will help me become a stronger person.

Effect 7: personal pride and public recognition

8 Honor and respect is obtained by serving in the military: pride for one's country is another reason why people join the military. Military personnel are respected and looked up to because they love their country so much that they will do anything for it. They fight to keep the rights that were set in place many years ago, to protect their country, and seek revenge on those that threaten it. President John F. Kennedy once said, "Ask not what your country can do for you, ask what you can do for your country." I remember that quote every time I think of joining the military. There are many things one can do to serve one's country such as volunteering with the Red Cross or Habitat for Humanity, but there is only one place in which one can actually protect one's country—the military.

Conclusion: refers back to the idea of joining the military being controversial

9 Most parents fear their children's joining the armed forces; they do not want them to die in times of war. However, what they have to understand is the strength and pride that their children have. Every time I look at a soldier, I see respect and honor. To me, soldiers are the best; they are my heroes.

Works Cited

"Benefits: The G.I. Bill." U.S. Army, www.goarmy.com/benefits/education-benefits/plan-for-your-future/the-gi-bill.html. Accessed 19 Apr. 2016.

Clayton, Romeo. "10 Reasons to Join the Military." *The Military Wallet*, 23 Mar. 2012, themilitarywallet.com/reasons-to-join-the-military.

"The Military Retirement System." *Military.com*, www.military.com/benefits/military-pay/the-military-retirement-system.html. Accessed 15 Mar. 2016.

READING AND WRITING CAUSE AND EFFECT

What Are Cause and Effect?

■ GOAL 5
Read and write using cause and effect

Causes are explanations of why things happen. **Effects** are explanations of what happens as a result of an action or event. Each day we face situations that require cause and effect analysis. Why will my car not start? Why did I not get my student loan check? How will my family react if I decide to get married? Here is a cause and effect paragraph from the professional essay on e-waste (para. 4). In it, the writers discuss the positive effects of recycling e-waste.

> Besides keeping toxic substances out of our environment, e-waste recycling is beneficial because a number of trace metals used in electronics are globally rare, so they can be lucrative to recover. A typical cell phone contains close to a dollar's worth of precious metals. Every bit of metal we can recycle from a manufactured item is a bit of metal we don't need to mine from the ground, so "mining" e-waste for precious metals helps reduce the environmental impacts that mining exerts. By one estimate, 1 ton of computer scrap contains more gold than 16 tons of mined ore from a gold mine. In one of the more intriguing efforts to promote sustainability through such recycling, the 2010 Winter Olympic Games in Vancouver produced its stylish gold, silver, and bronze medals from metals recovered from recycled and processed e-waste!

In this paragraph, the writers identify one cause (recycling e-waste) and three effects (keeping toxic substances out of the environment, recovery of rare trace metals, and reducing the environmental impacts of mining for those rare metals). Note that they also use examples to make their points.

You can visualize a cause and effect paragraph as follows. Study the model (shown left) and the map for the paragraph (shown right).

VISUALIZE IT!

Model Idea Map for Cause and Effect

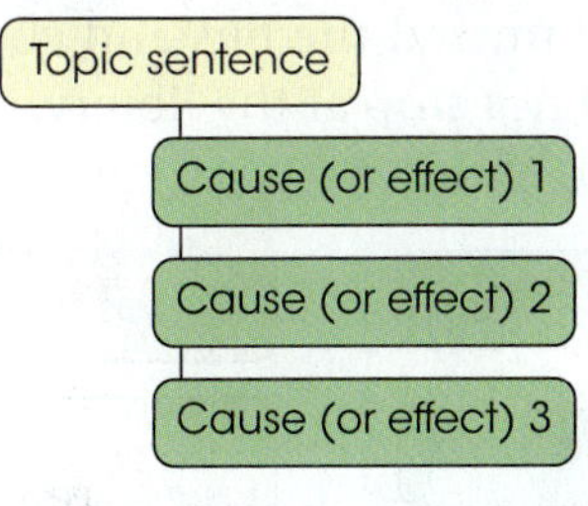

Note: The number of causes or effects will vary.

Idea Map of Paragraph 4 from Benefits of Recycling E-Waste

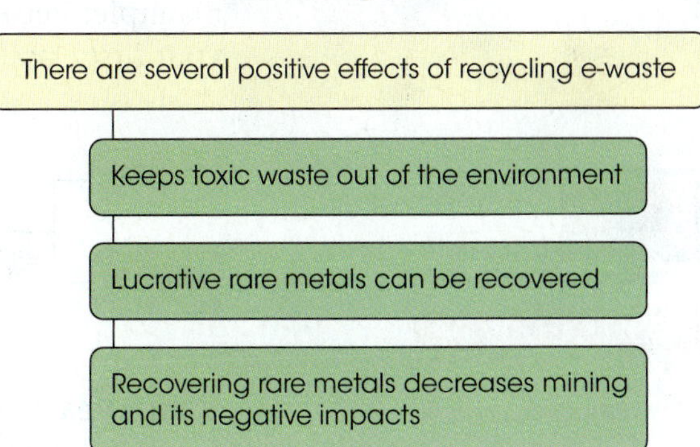

Reading Cause and Effect

When reading material is organized in the cause and effect pattern, pay close attention to the topic sentence. It usually states the cause and effect relationship that is detailed throughout the paragraph. As you read, look for specific causes and effects and determine the connection(s) between them.

Several possible relationships are described by the cause and effect pattern:

1. **Single Cause–Single Effect.** One cause produces one effect.

   Example: Omitting a key command will cause a computer program to fail.

2. **Single Cause–Multiple Effects.** One event produces several effects.

   Example: The effects of inflation include shrinking real income, increasing prices, and higher interest rates.

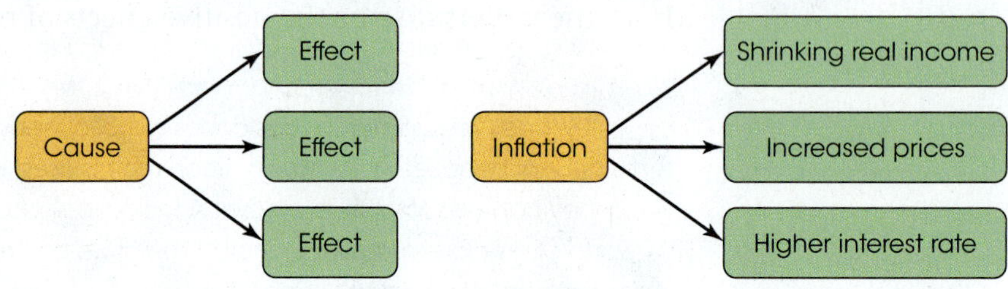

3. **Multiple Causes–Single Effect.** Several events work together to produce a single effect.

   Example: Attending class regularly, reading assignments carefully, and taking good lecture notes produce good exam grades.

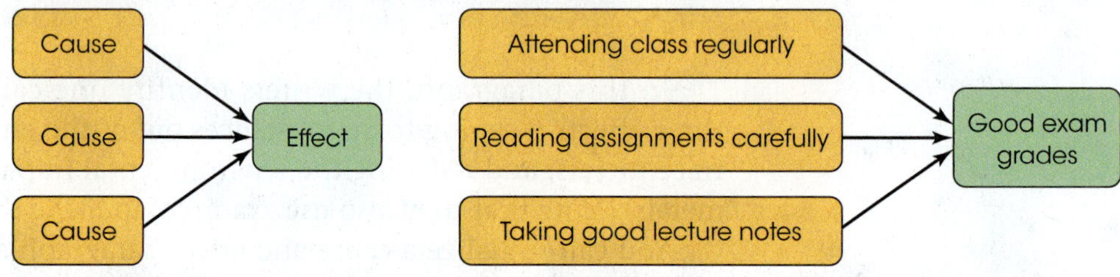

4. **Multiple Causes–Multiple Effects.** Several events work together to produce several effects.

   Example: Because you missed the bus and couldn't get a ride, you missed your first class and did not stop at the library.

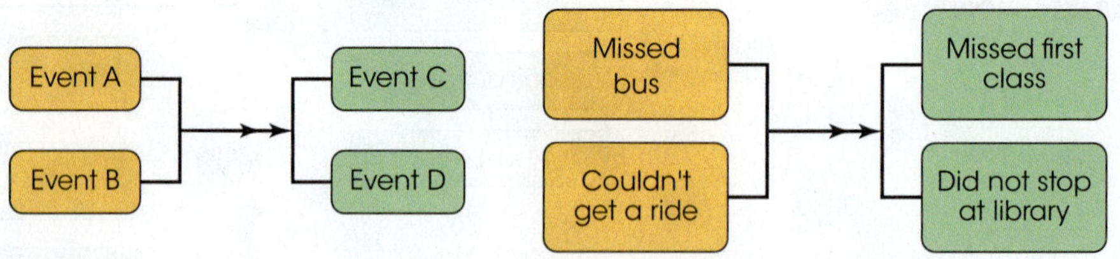

5. **Chain Reaction of Causes and Effects.** In a chain reaction, each event in a series influences the next.

   Example: Your backpack was stolen, so you lost your keys, which meant you were locked out of your apartment, so you missed a phone call about a job, which led to you not being hired.

Also, watch for words that show cause and effect. Writers often use specific words to show why or how an event is caused by another (some common ones are listed in the box below). Read the following sentences from paragraph 3 of the professional essay:

> According to EPA estimates, Americans were recycling 15% of e-waste in 1999, and this rose to 18% by 2007. However, so many more items have been manufactured each year that the amount of e-waste we sent to landfills and incinerators in that time period increased by a greater amount.

The word *however* ties the cause— more electronic devices being produced—to the effect— despite increased recycling, more e-waste is being sent to landfills and incinerators. Here is another example from Jessica's essay:

> Educational benefits are another reason for joining the military.

Here the words *another reason* tie the cause—joining the military—to the effect—educational benefits.

Common Cause and Effect Transitions

For causes	For effects
because	*as a result*
because of	*consequently*
cause is	*hence*
due to	*one result is*
for	*results in*
for this reason	*therefore*
one cause is	*thus*
one reason is	
since	
stems from	

Thinking Critically About Cause and Effect

Check for errors in logic. One of the most common reasoning errors is to assume that a cause and effect relationship exists between two events that occurred at the same time. If you take an aspirin and then feel dizzy, you might reason that the aspirin caused the dizziness. But, if you took the aspirin because you have the flu, the dizziness may be unrelated to the aspirin, although both occurred at the same time. As you read cause and effect writing, then, be sure to evaluate whether the author has provided sufficient evidence to support one event causing another.

Evaluate whether the author's description of the cause and effect relationship is complete and objective. Has the author identified all relevant causes and/or effects? For example, a writer may argue that the death penalty causes undue pain and suffering to the prisoner and his or her family. To be objective, however, the writer should consider other effects of the death penalty as well, such as retribution for crimes committed, and so forth. Certainly writers are free to be subjective and present only reasons supporting their opinions, but they should do so openly. It is the reader's responsibility to recognize and evaluate the opposing viewpoints.

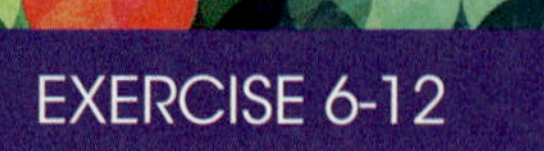
EXERCISE 6-12

Reading: Understanding Cause and Effect Patterns

Directions: Read the following paragraph, which discusses the multiple causes of a single effect (pattern 3 on p. 204), and answer each of the following questions.

Although ulcers are commonly associated with stress, they can be caused by other risk factors. Chronic use of aspirin and other nonsteroidal anti-inflammatory drugs can result in an increased risk of ulcer because these agents suppress the secretion of both mucus and bicarbonate, which normally protect the lining of the GI tract from the effects of acid and pepsin. The risk of ulcer is also increased by chronic alcohol use or the leakage of bile from the duodenum into the stomach, both of which can disrupt the mucus barrier. Surprisingly, ulcers are usually not associated with abnormally high rates of stomach-acid secretion; more often than not, acid secretion is normal or even below normal in most people with ulcers.

—adapted from Germann and Stanfield, *Principles of Human Physiology*, p. 622

1. What effect is the writer discussing? ______________________________

2. List four causes described by the authors.

   a. ______________________________

   b. ______________________________

   c. ______________________________

   d. ______________________________

3. Underline the transitional words and phrases that indicate the cause and effect pattern.

As you worked on Exercise 6-12, did you notice that the topic sentence tells the reader that the paragraph will be about causes, referred to as *risk factors*? As noted earlier, topic sentences often provide this important clue in a cause and effect paragraph, so pay close attention to them.

EXERCISE 6-13

Reading: Using Cause and Effect Transitions

Directions: Read the following paragraph, and answer the questions that follow.

Although it was a frightening experience, Bill's heart attack last year has had several positive effects. First, Bill realized that his diet had to change. He has eliminated the high-fat, high-sodium foods that were a major cause of his health problems, replacing them with healthy, low-fat foods that he can prepare at home. Another aspect of Bill's life that has changed because of his heart attack is his attitude toward exercise. He used to drive everywhere; now he walks whenever possible. In addition, he has started an exercise program approved by his doctor. As a result, he looks and feels better than he has in years. Finally, Bill's heart attack served as a powerful reminder of the importance of his family. Consequently, he has adjusted his work schedule so that he is able to spend more time with the people he loves.

1. What cause is being discussed? ______________________________

2. What three effects does the writer mention?

   a. ______________________________

   b. ______________________________

   c. ______________________________

3. Does the topic sentence tell you that this will be a cause and effect paragraph?

   ____

4. Underline the cause and effect words.

5. List four transitions that the writer uses to lead the reader through the information.

   a. __________ b. __________ c. __________ d. __________

Writing Cause and Effect Paragraphs

Writers use the **cause and effect** pattern to explain why an event or action caused another event or action. For example, if you were describing a skiing accident to a friend, you would probably follow a cause and effect pattern. You would tell what caused the accident and what happened as a result. Developing a **cause and effect paragraph** involves distinguishing between causes and effects, writing a topic sentence, and providing relevant and sufficient details.

Distinguishing Between Cause(s) and Effect(s)

How can you distinguish between causes and effects?

- To determine the *causes* of actions or events, ask the question: "Why did this event or action happen?"
- To identify *effects* of actions or events, ask the question: "What happened because of this event or action?"

Let's consider an everyday situation: you lost your set of keys, so you are locked out of your apartment. Why are you locked out of the apartment? What is the cause? You are locked out because you lost your keys. This is a simple case in which one cause produces one effect. You can diagram this situation as follows:

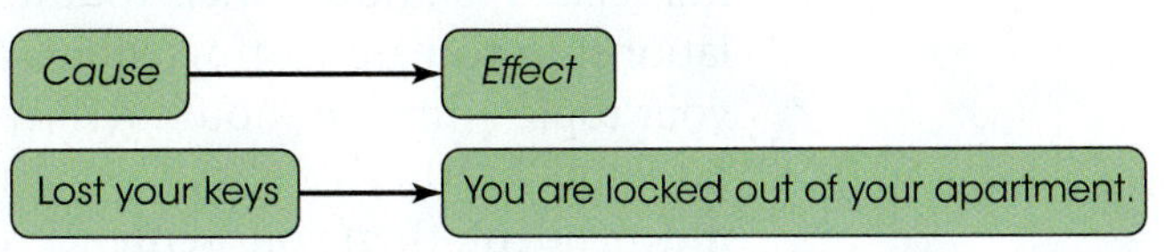

Another way to look at this situation would be to consider the fact that you have lost your keys. What happened because you lost them? What is the effect? You were locked out of your apartment. Most situations, of course, are much more complicated than this one, and, as shown on page 204, there are a number of possible cause and effect relationships. When analyzing a cause and effect situation that you plan to write about, ask yourself the following questions:

1. What are the causes? What are the effects? (To help answer these questions, draw a diagram of the situation.)
2. Which should be emphasized—cause or effect?
3. Are there single or multiple causes? Single or multiple effects?
4. Is a chain reaction involved?

Jessica was asked to write a cause and effect essay. She was aware that some people focus only on the negative outcomes of military service, so she wanted to point out the advantages of joining the military. To get started, she asked herself the question "What benefits occur as a result of joining the military?" and brainstormed a list of possibilities.

EXERCISE 6-14 Identifying Causes and Effects

Directions: Identify possible causes and effects for three of the following topics.

1. Spending too much time surfing the Internet
2. Academic cheating or dishonesty
3. An important decision you made
4. The popularity of YouTube
5. Earning good grades

Writing a Topic Sentence

To write effective topic sentences for cause and effect paragraphs, do the following:

1. **Clarify the cause and effect relationship.** Before you write, carefully identify the causes and the effects. If you are uncertain, divide a sheet of paper into two columns. Label one column "Causes" and the other "Effects." Brainstorm about your topic, placing your ideas in the appropriate column.
2. **Decide whether to emphasize causes or effects.** In a single paragraph, it is best to focus on either causes or effects—not both. For example, suppose you are writing about students who work two part-time jobs. You need to decide whether to discuss why they work two jobs (causes) or what happens to students who work two jobs (effects). Your topic sentence should indicate whether you are going to emphasize causes or effects. (In essays, you may consider both causes and effects.)
3. **Determine whether the events are related or independent.** Analyze the causes or effects to discover if they occurred as part of a chain reaction or are not related to one another. Your topic sentence should suggest the type of relationship you are writing about. If you are writing about a chain of events, your topic sentence should reflect this—for example, "A series of events led up to my brother's decision to join the military." If the causes or effects are independent, then your sentence should indicate that—for example, "Young men and women join the military for a number of different reasons."

Once Jessica had a list of ideas, she decided to focus on one cause (joining the military) and multiple beneficial effects. She made an outline for her essay and wrote a topic sentence for each of her main points, as shown below. Each of her topic sentences clearly draws a connection between joining the military and a specific benefit of doing so,

1. Joining the military is a great way to see the world.
2. Educational benefits are another reason for joining the military.
3. Military enlistment offers great job training and many career options.
4. Enlisting in the military also makes financial sense in a lot of ways; there are many benefits.
5. Soldiers can obtain excellent health care for themselves and their dependents.
6. Another reason many people, including myself, think about joining the armed forces is to build strength: strength for now, strength for later.
7. Honor and respect is obtained by serving in the military: pride for one's country is another reason why people join the military.

EXERCISE 6-15

WRITING IN PROGRESS

Writing a Topic Sentence

Directions: For one of the topics you chose in Exercise 6-14, decide whether you will focus on causes or effects. Then write a topic sentence for a paragraph that will explain either causes *or* effects.

Providing Relevant and Sufficient Details

Each cause or effect you describe must be relevant to the situation introduced in your topic sentence. Each cause or reason requires explanation, particularly if it is *not* obvious. Jot down a list of the causes or reasons you plan to include. This process may help you think of additional ones and will give you a chance to consider how to explain or support each cause or reason. You might decide to eliminate one or to combine several.

Once Jessica had drafted her topic sentences, she did some research, including talking to friends in the military and checking out the U. S. army site, as well as additional brainstorming to come up with details, including examples, that would support her topic sentences. She found useful information on the army website about financial, health, and other benefits and talked to her father about his travel experiences when he was in the navy.

Organizing a Cause and Effect Paragraph

There are several ways to arrange the details in a cause and effect paragraph. The method you choose depends on your purpose in writing, as well as on your topic. Suppose you are writing a paragraph about the effects of a hurricane on a coastal town. Several different arrangements of details are possible:

1. **Chronological.** A chronological organization arranges your details in the order in which situations or events happened. For example, the order in which damage

occurs during the course of a hurricane would become the order in which you present your details about the event. A chronological arrangement works for situations and events that occurred in a specific order.

2. **Order of importance.** In an order-of-importance organization, the details are arranged from least to most important or from most to least important. In describing the effects of a hurricane, you could discuss the most severe damage first and then describe lesser damage. Alternatively, you could build up to the most important damage for dramatic effect.
3. **Spatial.** Spatial arrangement of details uses physical or geographical position as a means of organization. In recounting the hurricane damage, you could start by describing damage to the beach and then work toward the center of town.
4. **Categorical.** This method of arrangement divides the topic into parts or categories. Using this arrangement to describe hurricane damage, you could recount what the storm did to businesses, roads, city services, and homes.

Because cause and effect relationships can be complicated, be sure to use transitional words and phrases to signal your reader which are causes and which are effects. Useful transitions are shown in the box on page 205.

Jessica decided to devote one paragraph to each of her points and organized each paragraph based on what worked best for its topic. She used transitional words in her topic sentences and paragraphs to make her points and flow of ideas clear to her readers.

NEED TO KNOW

A Review of Patterns and Transitional Words

Pattern	Characteristics	Transitional Words
Definition	Explains the meaning of a word or phrase	*are those that, can be defined as, consists of, corresponds to, entails, involves, is, is a term that, is called, is characterized by, is literally, means, occurs when, refers to*
Classification	Divides a topic into parts based on shared characteristics	*another, another kind, classified as, comprises, different groups that, different stages of, finally, first, include, is composed of, last, one, second, types of, varieties of*
Comparison and Contrast	Discusses similarities and/or differences among ideas, theories, concepts, objects, or persons	Similarities: *alike, also, as well as, both, correspondingly, in common, in comparison, in the same way, just as, like, likewise, resembles, share, similarly, to compare, too* Differences: *although, as opposed to, despite, differs from, however, in contrast, in spite of, instead, nevertheless, on the other hand, unlike, whereas*
Cause and Effect	Describes how one or more things cause or are related to another	Causes: *because, because of, cause is, due to, for, for this reason, one cause is, one reason is, since, stems from* Effects: *as a result, consequently, hence, one result is, results in, therefore, thus*

READ AND RESPOND: A Student Essay

Benefits of Joining the Military

Jessica Nantka

Examining Writing

1. How does Jessica introduce the subject?
2. Jessica refers to the negative effects of joining the military, but does not enumerate them. Should she have? How would this have affected the essay?
3. Suggest ways Jessica could make the introduction more lively and engaging.
4. What parts of the essay did you find the most persuasive?

Writing Assignments

1. You are taking a course in computer basics. Your instructor has asked the class to write a paragraph explaining why spamming—the process of sending advertisements to a large number of e-mail addresses—is a wasteful practice. Write a paragraph giving reasons why spamming is wasteful.
2. In your criminal justice class you are studying white-collar crimes—nonviolent crimes that are carried out in one's place of employment. Write a paragraph exploring reasons why an employee might commit a crime against his or her company.
3. For a health and wellness class, you have been asked to choose an unhealthy practice or habit and to write an essay defining it and explaining why it is unhealthy. (You might choose smoking, binge drinking, or overeating, for example.)

READ AND RESPOND: A Professional Essay

E-Waste and E-Waste Recycling

Jay Withgott and Scott Brennan

Writing in Response to Reading

Checking Your Comprehension MySkillsLab®

Answer each of the following questions using complete sentences.

1. Of the more than 3 billion electronic devices sold in the United States since 1980, list the percentages of those that have been disposed of, are still being used, and are in storage.
2. How many electronic devices do American households discard per year?
3. What are the environmental justice concerns associated with e-waste recycling?

Strengthening Your Vocabulary MySkillsLab®

Identify at least five words used in the reading that are unfamiliar to you. Using context, word parts, or a dictionary, write a brief definition of each word.

Examining the Reading: Drawing an Idea Map

Create an idea map of the reading that starts with the title and thesis and then lists the author's main points. Use the guidelines on page 15.

Reading and Writing: An Integrated Perspective MySkillsLab®

Get ready to write about the reading by discussing the following:

1. Evaluate the title, "E-Waste and E-Waste Recycling." What other titles would be interesting and effective?
2. Discuss the e-waste statistics cited in this selection. Which statistics were most surprising to you and why?
3. Discuss the benefits of e-waste recycling. In your opinion, which benefit described in the selection was most compelling? Why?
4. What does *environmental justice* mean to you? Write a journal entry giving your definition of the term.
5. In this selection, the authors describe positive and negative effects of e-waste recycling. Create an idea map that starts with the title and thesis of the essay and then lists the positive and negative effects of e-waste recycling.
6. List at least three sets of causes and effects that are discussed in this reading, carefully separating the causes from the effects.
7. Which method have the authors used to organize details: chronological, order of importance, spatial, or categorical?

THINKING VISUALLY

8. What is the purpose of the photograph that accompanies the reading? How does it reflect the content of the reading?

Thinking and Writing Critically MySkillsLab®

1. Three suggestions are listed within the photograph for how to make a difference. Evaluate each suggestion. Are they realistic and practical? Can you think of other ways to make a difference?
2. Express the authors' thesis in your own words. What is their purpose for writing this article? Who is their intended audience?
3. What is the authors' tone throughout the selection? What words and phrases reveal the authors' attitude toward the subject of e-waste? (For more about tone, see Chapter 12, p. 358.)

4. Why do the authors call Vancouver's Olympic medals "one of the more intriguing efforts" (paragraph 4)?

5. Evaluate the types of details the authors use to support their ideas. What other facts or information might they have included? Do they show any bias in their choice of details? (For more about bias, see Chapter 13, p. 381.)

Writing Paragraphs MySkillsLab®

1. Did this article influence your opinion about donating or recycling your old electronics? Will it make you "think twice" before buying a new electronic gadget? Write a paragraph explaining your answers.

2. Write a paragraph describing how you can reduce the amount of waste that you generate in your own life. Include electronic waste as well as other types of waste, such as plastic, paper, glass, and so forth.

3. Think about the recyclable items you use on a regular basis. What items do you always recycle? Sometimes recycle? Never recycle? Write a paragraph classifying the recyclable items you use into these three categories and explaining why.

4. Write a paragraph describing the last time you bought an electronic gadget such as a cell phone or MP3 player. Did you comparison shop among two or more items that met the same basic requirements? Explain how you chose between the different ones you considered purchasing. After reading this article, would you have been willing to pay more if the price included the cost of recycling?

Writing Essays MySkillsLab®

5. Imagine that you must convince your college administration, your dorm, or a campus group to begin an e-waste recycling program. Write a persuasive essay in which you discuss the consequences of electronic waste and the importance of an e-waste recycling program.

6. Write an essay addressing the environmental justice concerns mentioned in this selection. How might such concerns be resolved? What responsibility do the manufacturers of electronic devices have to the environment and to the workers handling e-waste?

7. The use of recycled metals to create Olympic medals is cited as one effort to promote sustainability through e-waste recycling. Can you think of other uses or applications for recycled metals? Write an essay exploring the possibilities.

SELF-TEST SUMMARY

To test yourself, cover the Answer column with a sheet of paper and answer each question in the left column. Evaluate each of your answers as you work by sliding the paper down and comparing your answers with what is printed in the Answer column.

QUESTION	ANSWER
■ GOAL 1 Identify additional patterns of organization What are some additional patterns of organization?	Additional patterns of organization are *definition, classification, comparison and contrast,* and *cause and effect.* See Table 6-1 (p. 182) for a review of characteristics and transitions for each of these patterns.
■ GOAL 2 Read and write using definition What are the three essential parts of a definition?	The three essential parts are **1.** The term being defined **2.** The group or category to which the term belongs **3.** Its distinguishing characteristics
■ GOAL 3 Read and write using classification How does classification explain a subject?	Classification explains a subject by identifying and describing its types or categories.
■ GOAL 4 Read and write using comparison and contrast What are comparison and contrast?	Comparison treats similarities, whereas contrast emphasizes differences.
What are two ways to organize a comparison or contrast paragraph?	You may organize a comparison or contrast paragraph either subject by subject or point by point.
■ GOAL 5 Read and write using cause and effect What are causes and effects?	Causes are explanations of why things happen, whereas effects are explanations of what happens as a result of an action or event.
What are four ways to organize cause and effect paragraphs?	Cause and effect paragraphs may be organized chronologically, in order of importance, spatially, or in categories.

Strategies for Revising Paragraphs

7

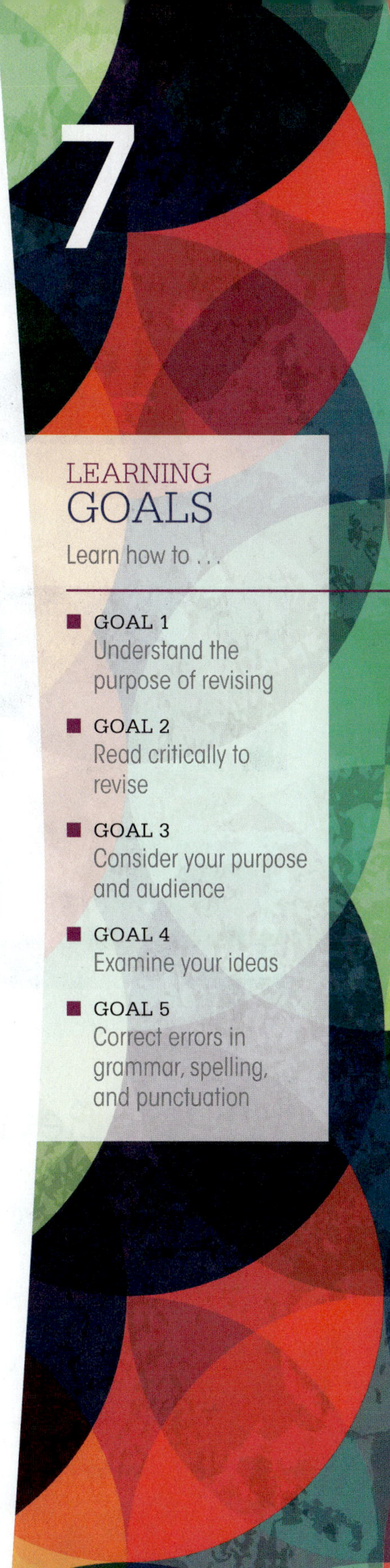

LEARNING GOALS

Learn how to . . .

- GOAL 1 Understand the purpose of revising
- GOAL 2 Read critically to revise
- GOAL 3 Consider your purpose and audience
- GOAL 4 Examine your ideas
- GOAL 5 Correct errors in grammar, spelling, and punctuation

THINK About It!

The two photographs above show the same room in two different conditions. Write a sentence describing what was done in order to make the room more livable.

The person who lived there obviously looked around the room, assessed what needed to be done, and then made a plan for reorganizing and cleaning up the room. The same process occurs in writing. First, the writer looks over a draft, perhaps reading it three or four times, assessing what needs to be done and creating a plan to improve it. Next, the writer makes revisions that may involve reorganization, adding material to strengthen the paragraph, and deleting material that is not useful. Finally the writer edits or cleans up the paragraph, clarifying any confusions, choosing more effective wording, and checking grammar, spelling, punctuation, and mechanics.

All of the changes a writer makes are made with his or her readers in mind. Changes are made to make the message clear, easy to understand, and free of distracting errors. In this chapter, you will learn how to assess a draft and effectively revise and edit it.

Reading and Writing Connections

EVERYDAY CONNECTIONS

- **Reading** After repeatedly rereading the user's manual that accompanies new software you purchased, you draw an idea map to help you understand and organize the information so you can figure out why the software will not install properly.
- **Writing** You write a complaint letter to the company that sold you the defective software, and then revise it when your friend says you should explain more about how the problem has inconvenienced you and why you should receive your money back.

ACADEMIC CONNECTIONS

- **Writing** You reread and revise an outline for a speech because you realize the speech needs to appeal more directly to your audience.
- **Reading** You read the draft of a classmate's speech and decide to revise your own speech to include more details.

WORKPLACE CONNECTIONS

- **Writing** You revise a memo you are sending to your boss after you reread it and realize it only focuses on your complaints about a situation and does not include your suggestions for how to remedy it.
- **Reading** You read about a job opening for applicants bilingual in Spanish and English, and you revise your cover letter to tailor it to the job and to reflect changes you have made to your résumé.

What Is Revision?

■ GOAL 1
Understand the purpose of revising

Revising a paragraph involves examining your ideas by reading, most likely several times, every idea and sentence you have written and often making major changes to them. You might add ideas, delete details, or rearrange parts. **Editing** is a part of the revision process that focuses on clarity and correctness. It involves reading to identify words and phrases to add or delete, as well as to correct your grammar, spelling, punctuation, and mechanics. Before you go on, you may want to review the material in "Revise and Rewrite Drafts" in Chapter 2 (p. 57), and "Edit and Proofread Your Final Draft" (p. 59) including the paragraph on peer review.

In this chapter you will learn a variety of helpful techniques for revising paragraphs. You may wonder why many of the examples you will see in this chapter, including the sample student writing, show essays, not individual paragraphs. This is because, in addition to looking within a single paragraph to examine how ideas connect and relate, it is also important to examine how ideas flow from paragraph to paragraph. Revision involves seeing how ideas fit together within and between paragraphs, so it is important to show paragraphs within the context of a full essay. This chapter, along with Chapter 9 will equip you with all the skills you need to read, evaluate, and revise both paragraphs and essays.

Read Critically to Revise

■ GOAL 2
Read critically to revise

The first step in preparing to revise a paragraph is to read it critically with the purpose of finding out what works and what does not. Use the following suggestions, in addition to those listed in Chapter 2.

It is easy to like your own work and feel you have done a great job, so mentally prepare yourself to look at your writing from afar, as if someone else wrote it. Right after you finish a paragraph, it is especially difficult to see how to improve it. Whenever possible, let your draft sit a day or two before returning to it to revise.

Allow enough time to read your paragraph several times, each for a different purpose. It is difficult to check for all aspects of writing at the same time. Instead, use the following strategy:

- **Read the paragraph once, examining content.** Does it say what you want it to say? If it doesn't, make the necessary changes, and then read it again. If you aren't sure if your meaning is clear, ask a friend or classmate to review your draft.
- **Read the paragraph again, evaluating how effectively you have expressed your ideas,** again making changes to improve the draft. Reread to make sure your changes work.
- **Read the paragraph a third time, checking for correctness.** You might want to read the draft several times, looking for one common error at a time.

EXAMINING STUDENT WRITING

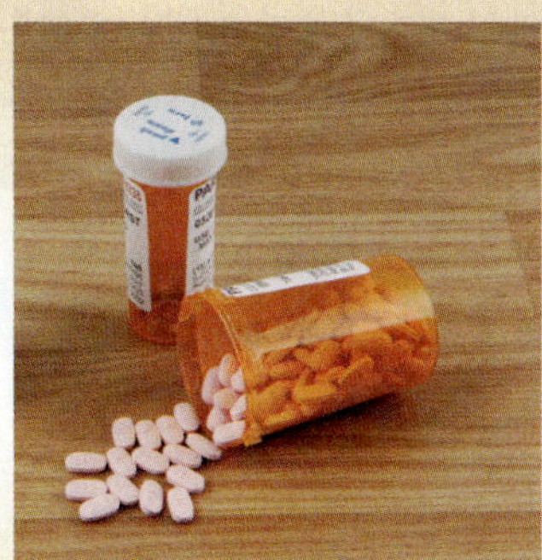

A good way to learn to read your work critically and revise your paragraphs effectively is to study a model. We will follow student Elizabeth Lawson's writing throughout the chapter, from first draft to final essay, examining individual paragraphs as we work on different revision strategies. Shown below is her first draft. Elizabeth asked a classmate to review it and make suggestions as a peer reviewer, and those comments are included.

Elizabeth Lawson (she requested that we change her name to protect her privacy) is a student at an Illinois college. She is working on her bachelor's degree in psychology and hopes to become a high school guidance counselor. In her writing class, Elizabeth was given the following assignment: Write an essay describing a difficult or challenging situation that you faced.

FIRST DRAFT

1 It seems that everyday on the news you hear about some Hollywood celebrity or sports star having an addiction problem whether it's steroids or alcohol or painkillers or something even worse like crystal meth. You think it can never happen to you because your life is fine and you can deal with your issues, no problem. But now I understand it more. For example who can blame a baseball player for juicing up on steroids? They make a boatload of money to hit home runs and steroids make them stronger. If they don't hit homeruns, they get knocked off the team and who wants to lose all that money?

This is an interesting introduction, but I don't understand why you go into detail on steroids. They're not part of the experience you are describing in your essay.

2 But the main reason I understand it more is because I went through an addiction myself. It wasn't steroids, as a woman who is 5 feet tall I would look pretty silly being all muscular like that, but it was tranquilizers.

I don't see a clear thesis statement anywhere in the first two paragraphs.

3 I can't really complain about my life because I know how good I had it. I was raised by a single mom and she did a great job. She was the youngest of six children who were all born in different cities, and she was the only girl with five brothers. Her mother and father moved around a lot because her father was a traveling salesman. We were always so close, I remember when my father died (I was 8) we made a deal that we were going to be a team and stick together. It was just the two of us and she worked super hard to put food on the table and buy me things I wanted but she couldn't really afford (which makes me feel selfish now, but that's another story). Of course we had our fights especially when I was a teenager but she was always like a mixture of a good friend that I liked to talk to, plus a parent who tried to teach me the right things to do. I made mistakes, everyone does, but at the end of the day we watched out for each other. One time I heard some neighbor women gossiping about her, I marched right up to them and told them to knock it off because they had no idea what she went through. She actually punished me for being rude to the neighbors but when she was dying several years later she told me how proud of me she was when I did that.

4 Because that's what happened, she died. I couldn't get over it. I couldn't study, I couldn't eat, and worst of all I couldn't sleep. I just kept thinking about what a great person she was and how much I missed her, and luckily I didn't feel guilty about mistreating her because I was with her till the end (she died of cancer), so as we promised each other, we were a team. I was exhausted and having panic attacks, I even hallucinated once or twice. I was 22 years old and in college and you would think a grown woman would be able to handle it. I fell apart. I was crying all the time. I was a total mess. I refused to go to a counselor because I thought I could deal with it on my own. Well I was wrong about that.

5 Then my uncle, my mother's brother, came to visit me and he took one look at me and said how awful I looked. He had a prescription for tranquilizers and he gave some to me because I felt like if I didn't get some sleep I was going to die. So I took one and it worked so incredibly well, it relaxed me and I fell asleep and I woke up the next day after sleeping about 15 hours. I also felt super relaxed and much, much less upset so I went to the doctor and asked for a prescription and he gave it to me but said he would do it only if I went to a grief counselor also so I took those pills twice a day for 3 months and they helped me sleep and get over all my upset. The problem was they also took away my energy. And talking about everything with the counselor (Jane) was a huge load off my mind, so at the end of the 3 months I thought, OK, I don't need these pills anymore, so I stopped taking them.

The essay does not have a concluding paragraph that summarizes what you learned from your experience.

6 And that is when it started. My heart sped up after a couple of days without the pills. My vision got bad and I had cramps. I could not sleep at all for a couple days. I would just lay there with my heart going too fast. Then something happened that really scared me. I started feeling like my brain wasn't working right. That really scared me, I was terrified and thought I was having a stroke. So I went to the emergency room and

they figured out what was happening, I was having withdrawal symptoms from going off the meds too fast. It turns out that the type of medication I was on, you have to stop taking it gradually otherwise you get these terrible effects. They gave me one of the tranquilizers I was taking and the problems stopped almost immediately. And then this is the part you would not believe. It took me almost six months to stop taking those pills. I had to reduce the dose by a tiny amount, take that dose for a week, then reduce the dose a little more, take that for a week, then reduce it again and again and so on until I could stop taking it. Finally I got off it and I feel better. I still miss my Mom though.

Peer Review Comments

Elizabeth,

Your essay really made me understand what you went through and how addictions can happen without a person realizing it. I was also touched by how you describe your relationship with your mother. Here are a few changes you could make:

1. What point are you trying to make in the whole essay? You describe what you went through, but I would like to know how the experience changed your life or how you feel different as a result of it.
2. Did your friends know what you were going through, or did you hide it from them? Why were you afraid to ask for help?
3. It is hard to find topic sentences in some of the paragraphs. Some of the paragraphs seem long and unfocused. Can you split them up and deal with just one main idea at a time, and maybe eliminate some of the unnecessary details?

You didn't mention which tranquilizer you were taking. I think it would be a good idea to name it, so that people who read your essay will know the dangers of it when they see it.

Writing: Consider Your Purpose and Audience

■ GOAL 3
Consider your purpose and audience

As was mentioned in Chapter 2, good writing should achieve your purpose and be directed toward a specific audience. When you are ready to revise, read your draft through once or twice to get an overall impression of it. Then decide whether the paragraph accomplishes what you want it to. If it doesn't, try to identify what went wrong, using the Revision Checklist on page 223. If it is difficult to identify the reasons a draft does not achieve its purpose, ask a friend or classmate to read your writing and summarize what it does accomplish. This information will often give you clues about how to improve the piece.

To evaluate whether your writing is suited to your audience, read it from the audience's viewpoint. Try to anticipate what ideas your audience might find unclear, what additional information might be needed, and whether the overall reaction will be positive or negative. Imagine that someone else wrote the piece and you are reading it for the first time. Does it keep your interest and make some fresh and original points? Could you treat your subject in a more engaging way?

Reading and Writing: Examine Your Ideas

■ GOAL 4
Examine your ideas

The most important part of revision is reevaluating your ideas. Think of revision as an opportunity to reassess your ideas in order to make what you are writing as effective as possible.

Often simply reading and rereading your writing does not help you to recognize what to change or improve. One of the best ways to discover what to revise is to use an idea map, a visual display of the ideas you have written about in a paragraph or essay that allows you to see how ideas relate and connect to one another. An idea map can help you check two important features of your writing:

- your use of relevant and sufficient detail.
- the logical organization of your ideas.

To draw a paragraph revision idea map, follow these steps:

1. Write a shortened topic sentence at the top of your paper.
2. Then go through your paragraph sentence by sentence and list each detail that directly supports the topic sentence.
3. If you spot an example of one of the details already listed, or a further explanation of a detail, write it underneath the detail it relates to and indent it.
4. If you spot a detail that does not support or is not related to anything else, write it to the right of your list, as in the sample below.

VISUALIZE IT!

Sample Revision Map

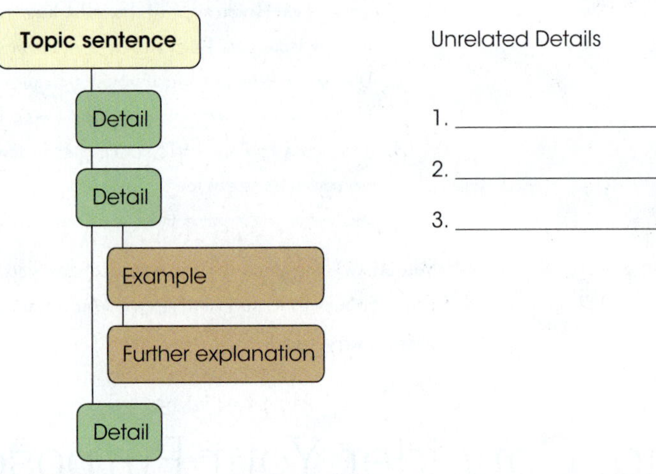

Relevant and Sufficient Detail

As you revise, you want to be sure you have provided enough information about your subject and that all your details directly support your topic sentence. Drawing an idea map allows you to see if you have explained each detail adequately. You will also see immediately any details that are not relevant.

Here is the first draft of a paragraph 5 written by Elizabeth for her assignment. Her idea map follows.

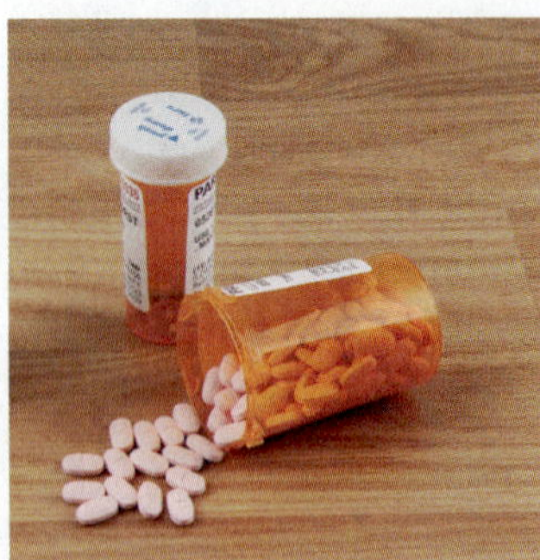

First Draft

My uncle came to visit me and said how awful I looked. He gave me some prescription tranquilizers because if I didn't get some sleep I was going to die. So I took one and woke up the next day after sleeping about 15 hours. I also felt super relaxed and much, much less upset so I went to the doctor. His office was fairly close to where I live. I asked for a prescription and he gave it to me but said he would do it only if I went to a grief counselor also. I had really thought I could deal with my grief without help. I took those pills twice a day for 3 months and they helped me sleep and get over all my upset. The problem was they also took away my energy. I wondered what my mother would have said about the pills and the grief counselor. And it seemed to help talking about everything with the counselor, so at the end of the 3 months I thought, OK, I don't need these pills anymore, so I stopped taking them.

Sample Revision Map

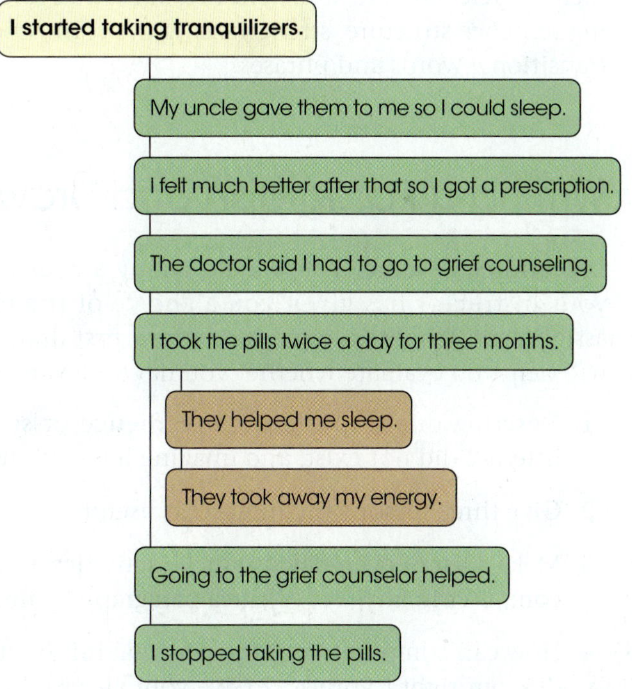

Elizabeth's map showed her how she had structured her paragraph, how her ideas connected, and whether there were enough details to support her main ideas. By studying this map, she could spot details that did not fit and ideas that needed further development or explanation. Elizabeth found three details (see right side of map) that did not support her original topic sentence. She realized that two of these details related instead to why the grief counselor was helpful. Elizabeth rewrote her paragraph to include this idea, added more explanation in her revised paragraph, and focused her topic sentence.

First Revision

Then my uncle, my mother's brother, came to visit me, and after seeing how awful I looked, he gave me some medication. He had a prescription for a tranquilizer called Ativan (also called lorazepam) and he gave some to me because I felt like if I didn't get some sleep I was going to die. So I took one and it worked so incredibly well, it relaxed me and I fell asleep and I woke up the next day after sleeping about 15 hours. I also felt super relaxed and much, much less upset so I went to the doctor and asked for a prescription and he gave it to me but said he would do it only if I went to a grief counselor also so I took those pills twice a day for 3 months and they really helped me. The problem was they also took away my energy. And talking about everything with the counselor at my college (Jane) was a really big help. She helped me see something I didn't see on my own: that I would feel like I was betraying my mother if I went to someone other than her for help and advice. Jane also asked, Wouldn't my mother want me to be happy instead of crying all the time? Of course it made complete sense! So at the end of the 3 months I thought, OK, I don't need these pills anymore, so I stopped taking them.

This second draft focuses more directly on the newly sharpened topic and includes relevant and sufficient detail. Further revisions might focus on improving sentence structure, strengthening the connection among details, and adding transitional words and phrases.

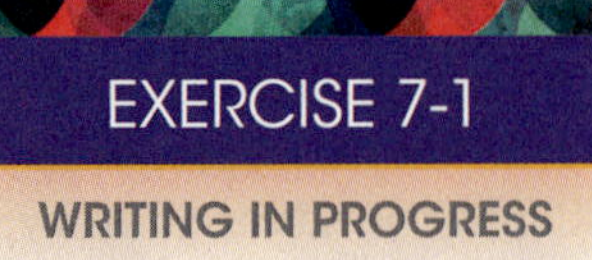

Writing a Paragraph and Drawing an Idea Map

Directions: Assume that you are taking a course in communication and that your instructor has given you a choice of the following topics as your first assignment. Choose a topic and write a first draft. Then draw an idea map that will help you evaluate whether you have relevant and sufficient detail.

1. Describe one important convenience or service you would miss if the Internet did not exist, and imagine life without it.
2. Give three reasons the Internet is useful.
3. Make a list of everyday products, activities, or services that do not require a computer in any way. Write a paragraph summarizing your findings.
4. How can computers and the personal information stored in them jeopardize our right to privacy? Give your views.
5. A computer-controlled robot has been developed to perform specialized types of surgery. Discuss the advantages and disadvantages of this innovation.

Logical Organization of Ideas

Another major issue to consider as you revise is whether you have arranged your ideas in a way your readers can follow. As we saw in Chapter 4, even if you have plenty of detail, the wrong organization can throw your readers off track. In addition, you need to make sure you use transitional words and phrases to help readers follow your thoughts.

Revision maps are also useful for checking your organization. By listing the ideas in the order in which they appear in your paragraph, you can see if they are arranged logically. Study the following paragraph (para. 4) from Elizabeth's first draft and then her revision map.

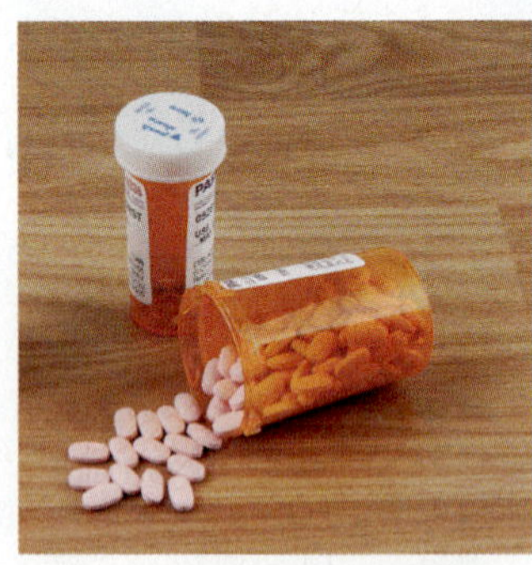

First Draft

Because that's what happened, she died. I couldn't get over it. I couldn't study, I couldn't eat, and worst of all I couldn't sleep. I just kept thinking about what a great person she was and how much I missed her, and luckily I didn't feel guilty about mistreating her because I was with her till the end (she died of cancer), so as we promised each other, we were a team. I was exhausted and having panic attacks, I even hallucinated once or twice. I was 22 years old and in college and you would think a grown woman would be able to handle it. I fell apart. I was crying all the time. I was a total mess. I refused to go to a counselor because I thought I could deal with it on my own. Well I was wrong about that.

Sample Revision Map

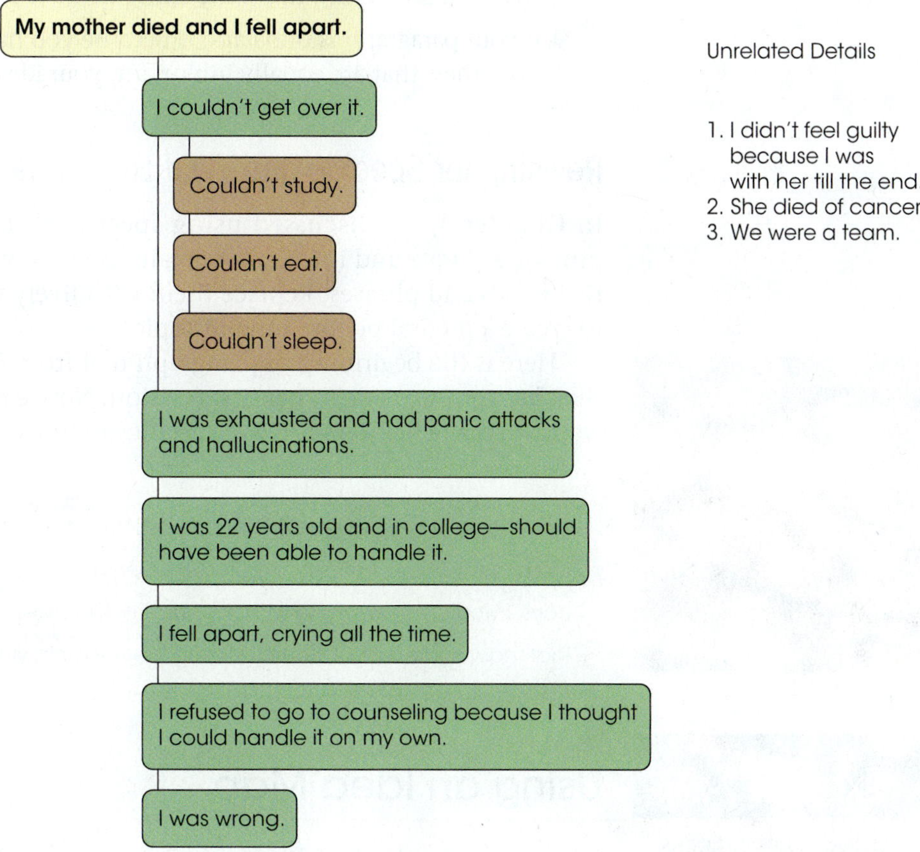

The map shows that the details are not arranged in any specific order. Since most of them relate to what happened to Elizabeth after her mother died, these details could be arranged from past to present. Elizabeth arranged the details in chronological order in her second draft.

First Revision

It was when she died that I fell apart and started having all sorts of problems I never had before. I was 22 years old and in college and you would think a grown woman would be able to handle it. But I fell apart, I was crying all the time. I just kept thinking about what a great person she was and how much I missed her. But the weeks went by and I couldn't get over it. I couldn't study, I couldn't eat, and worst of all I couldn't sleep. I was exhausted and having panic attacks, I even hallucinated once or twice. I was a total mess and I refused to go to a counselor because I thought I could deal with it on my own. Well I was wrong about that.

Notice she revised her topic sentence, added transitional words and phrases, and included the phrase "But the weeks went by" to signal the reader that she was describing events in the order in which they occurred.

Idea maps are also useful for identifying several other common writing problems.

- If you strayed from your topic, you will see it happening on your idea map.

- If your paragraph is repetitious, you will realize as you study your idea map that you are saying the same thing more than once.
- If your paragraph is unbalanced because you have emphasized some ideas and not others that are equally important, your idea map will show it.

Revising for Specific and Vivid Language

In Chapter 4, we discussed using specific and vivid words and phrases to provide accurate and interesting detail. As you revise, look for drab, nondescriptive words and phrases. Replace them with lively words that enable your reader to create a mental picture of your topic.

Here is the beginning of paragraph 6 of from Elizabeth's first draft, showing the changes she made in her first revision. Notice how she changed and replaced words to make her details more specific and vivid.

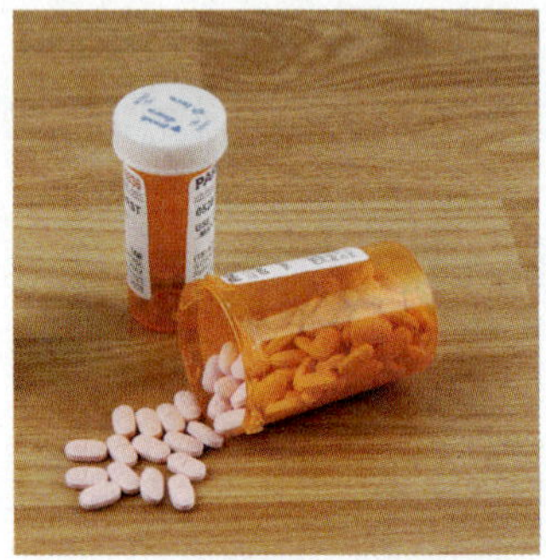

the trouble *started racing like crazy*
And that is when ~~it~~ started. My heart ~~sped up~~ after a couple of days without
blurry *started getting weird cramps* *a wink and went 72 hours*
the pills. My vision got ~~bad~~ and I ~~had cramps~~. I could not sleep ~~at all for a couple~~
without sleep *racing a mile a minute*
~~days~~. I would just lay there with my heart ~~going too fast~~. Then something happened
zaps of electricity in my *like my brain was short-circuiting.*
that really scared me. I started feeling ~~like my~~ brain ~~wasn't working right~~,

EXERCISE 7-2

WRITING IN PROGRESS

Using an Idea Map

Directions: Study the idea map of the paragraph you wrote for Exercise 7-1. Evaluate your arrangement of details. If they are not arranged logically, number them on your map and revise your paragraph. After you have examined your ideas, you should make sure that you have expressed them effectively and appropriately. That is, you should determine whether the language you have chosen is specific and vivid, whether it is suited to your audience, and whether it achieves your purpose for writing.

During revision, there is a lot to think about. This Revision Checklist will help you keep in mind important questions to ask about your writing.

Revision Checklist

1. Who is your audience? How interested are they in your subject and how much do they know about it? Is your paragraph suited to your audience?
2. What is your purpose? Does your paragraph accomplish your purpose?
3. Is your main point clearly expressed in your topic sentence?
4. Is each detail relevant? Does each explain or support the topic sentence directly?
5. Have you supported your topic sentence with sufficient detail to make it understandable and believable?
6. Do you use specific and vivid words to explain each detail?
7. Do you connect your ideas with transitional words and phrases?

FIRST REVISION—SHOWING CHANGES IN IDEAS

Added title and her name

My Unexpected Addiction

Elizabeth Lawson

1 It seems that everyday on the news you hear about some Hollywood celebrity or sports star having an addiction problem whether it's steroids or alcohol or painkillers or something even worse like crystal meth. You think it can never happen to you because your life is fine and you can deal with your issues, no problem. But now I understand it more because I developed an addiction of my own, and I had to struggle to free myself from it. In the process I learned a few things about myself and what makes me tick. It all happened so fast that I didn't know what was happening at the time, but looking back now I understand it better.

Added thesis statement, which is actually two sentences here

2 There's no reason I should have developed an addiction, because I had a basically good life with a stable, loving mother. I was raised by a single mom and she did a great job. We were always so close I remember when my father died (I was 8) we made a deal that we were going to be a team and stick together. It was just the two of us and she worked super hard to put food on the table and buy me things I wanted but she couldn't really afford. Of course we had our fights especially when I was a teenager but she was always like a mixture of a good friend that I liked to talk to, plus a parent who tried to teach me the right things to do. I made mistakes, everyone does, but at the end of the day we watched out for each other. One time I heard some neighbor women gossiping about her, I marched right up to them and told them to knock it off because they had no idea what she went through. She actually punished me for being rude to the neighbors but when she was dying several years later she told me how proud of me she was when I did that.

Combined paragraphs 2 and 3, cut irrelevant details, and wrote strong new topic sentence

3 It was when she died that I fell apart and started having all sorts of problems I never had before. I was 22 years old and in college and you would think a grown woman would be able to handle it. But I fell apart, I was crying all the time. I just kept thinking about what a great person she was and how much I missed her. But the weeks went by and I couldn't get over it. I couldn't study, I couldn't eat, and worst of all I couldn't sleep. I was exhausted and having panic attacks, I even hallucinated once or twice. I was a total mess and I refused to go to a counselor because I thought I could deal with it on my own. Well I was wrong about that.

Reorganized paragraph and wrote stronger topic sentence

4 Then my uncle, my mother's brother, came to visit me , and after seeing how awful I looked, he gave me some medication. He had a prescription for a tranquilizer called Ativan (also called lorazepam) and he gave some to me because I felt like if I didn't get some sleep I was going to die. So I took one and it worked so incredibly well, it relaxed me and I fell asleep and I woke up the next day after sleeping about 15 hours. I also felt super relaxed and much, much less upset so I went to the doctor and asked for a prescription and he gave it to me but said he would do it only if I went to a grief counselor also so I took those pills twice a day for 3 months and they really helped me. The problem was they also took away my energy. And talking about everything with the counselor at my college (Jane) was a really

Wrote stronger topic sentence and added details, like name of medication and information about her counselor

big help. She helped me see something I didn't see on my own: that I would feel like I was betraying my mother if I went to someone other than her for help and advice. Jane also asked, Wouldn't my mother want me to be happy instead of crying all the time? Of course it made complete sense! So at the end of the 3 months I thought, OK, I don't need these pills anymore, so I stopped taking them.

5 And that is when the trouble started. My heart started racing like crazy after a couple of days without the pills. My vision got blurry and I started getting weird cramps. I went 72 hours without sleep. I would just lay there with my heart racing a mile a minute. Then something happened that really scared me, I started feeling zaps of electricity in my brain, like my brain was short-circuiting. I was terrified and thought I was having a stroke. So I went to the emergency room and they figured out what was happening, I was having withdrawal symptoms from going off the meds too fast. It turns out that the type of medication (called a benzodiazepine, or benzo for short) I was on, you have to stop taking it gradually otherwise you get these terrible effects. They gave me an Ativan and the problems stopped almost immediately. And then this is the part you would not believe. I had to reduce the dose by a tiny amount, take that dose for a month, then reduce the dose a little more, take that for a month, then reduce it again and again and so on until I could stop taking it.

Added concluding paragraph that summarizes experiences and lessons learned

6 It took me almost six months to reduce my dose to zero. And I learned a few things about myself and the world through the experience. First, maybe all the celebrities you read about with their addiction problems actually deserve a little sympathy instead of scorn. Maybe they, like me, had a problem they were trying to deal with, and things got out of control without them ever realizing it. Second, people with addictions are not bad people or even low class people. They are trying to cope with their problems but don't know the right way to do it. Third, and probably most important, I realized that it is OK to ask for help when you need it. If I had gone to grief counseling early, or even if I went to a support group while Mom was sick, I would have had more support and more understanding of what people go through and how to cope with it. I still miss Mom, but I know she's up there, proud that I overcame my addiction and smiling proudly the way she did when she reminded me about the time I told off those stupid neighbors.

Edit for Correctness

■ GOAL 5
Correct errors in grammar, spelling, and punctuation

Errors (mistakes) in grammar, spelling, and punctuation make your writing less effective. A writer who seems careless loses the reader's confidence. **Editing** is a process of making corrections. It is an important *final step* to writing a good paragraph. Of course, if you notice an error while you are drafting or revising, you should correct it. In general, however, focus on looking for errors only after you are satisfied with the content and organization of your paragraph.

What Errors to Look For

Many students wonder how they will ever learn enough to spot all the errors in their writing. The job is easier than you think! Most students make certain types of errors. The Handbook (p. 497) addresses the most common errors students make:

- sentence fragments (p. 534)
- run-on sentences (p. 539)
- subject-verb agreement (p. 550)
- pronoun-antecedent agreement (p. 553)
- pronoun reference (p. 555)
- shifts and mixed constructions (p. 565)
- when to use commas (p. 581)
- dangling modifiers (p. 564)
- misplaced modifiers (p. 563)
- verb tense (p. 543)
- coordinate sentences (p. 567)
- subordinate clauses (p. 569)
- parallelism (p. 571)
- using colons and semicolons (p. 584)

The following Proofreading Checklist will remind you to check for spelling, punctuation, and other mechanical errors.

Proofreading Checklist

1. Does each sentence end with an appropriate punctuation mark (period, question mark, exclamation point, or quotation mark)?
2. Is all punctuation within each sentence correct (commas, colons, semicolons, apostrophes, dashes, and quotation marks)?
3. Is each word spelled correctly?
4. Have you used capital letters where needed?
5. Are numbers and abbreviations used correctly?
6. Are any words left out?
7. Have you corrected all typographical errors?
8. Are your pages in the correct order and numbered?

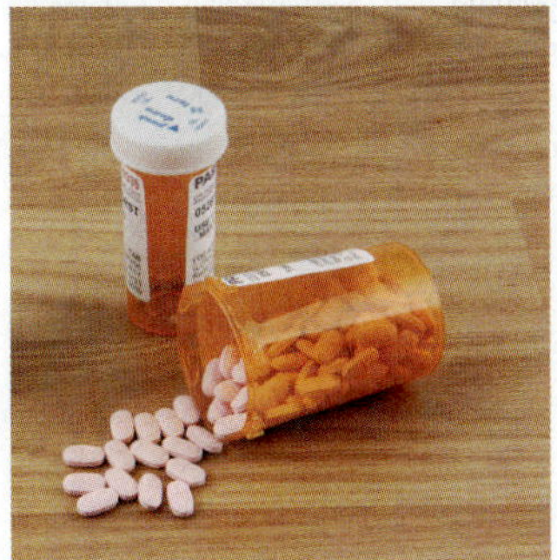

Elizabeth used the proofreading checklist when she edited and proofread her essay. Here is a paragraph 2 showing her corrections:

1. Fixed fused sentence
2. Added commas to set off parenthetical phrase
3. Eliminated unnecessary word to make essay sound more formal
4. Added parentheses
5. Eliminated sexist language

There's no reason I should have developed an addiction, because I had a basically good life with a stable, loving mother. I was raised by a single mom and she did a great job. We were always so close[.] ① I remember when my father died (I was ~~8~~ eight years old) we made a deal that we were going to be a team and stick together. It was just the two of us and she worked ~~super~~ very hard to put food on the table and buy me things I wanted but she couldn't ~~really~~ afford. Of course we had our fights[,] ② especially when I was a teenager[,] but she was always ③ ~~like~~ a mixture of a good friend that I liked to talk to, plus a parent who ~~tried to teach~~ taught me the right things to do. I made mistakes[(] ④ everyone does[)], but at the end of the day we watched out for each other. One time I heard some neighbor[s] ⑤ ~~women~~ gossiping about her[, and] I marched up to them and told them to ~~knock it off~~ stop because they had no idea what she went through. She actually punished me for being rude to the neighbors[,] but when she was dying ~~several~~ years later she told me ~~how~~ proud of me ~~she was when I did~~ for doing that.

Keeping an Error Log

Many students consistently make certain types of errors and not others. You can identify and learn to avoid yours by keeping a record of your mistakes. Use an error log like the sample shown below. Each time your instructor returns a paper, count how many errors you made of each type, and enter that number in the log. Soon you will see a pattern. You can then review your final drafts to locate these specific errors.

If you make frequent spelling errors, be sure to use the spell-checker on your computer. Also, keep a separate list of the words you misspell. Study them and practice writing them correctly.

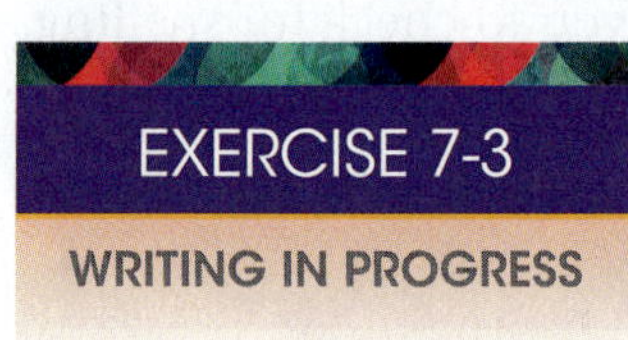

Using an Error Log

Directions: Check the paragraph you wrote for Exercise 7-1 for errors, and correct any you find. Enter them in an error log (see sample).

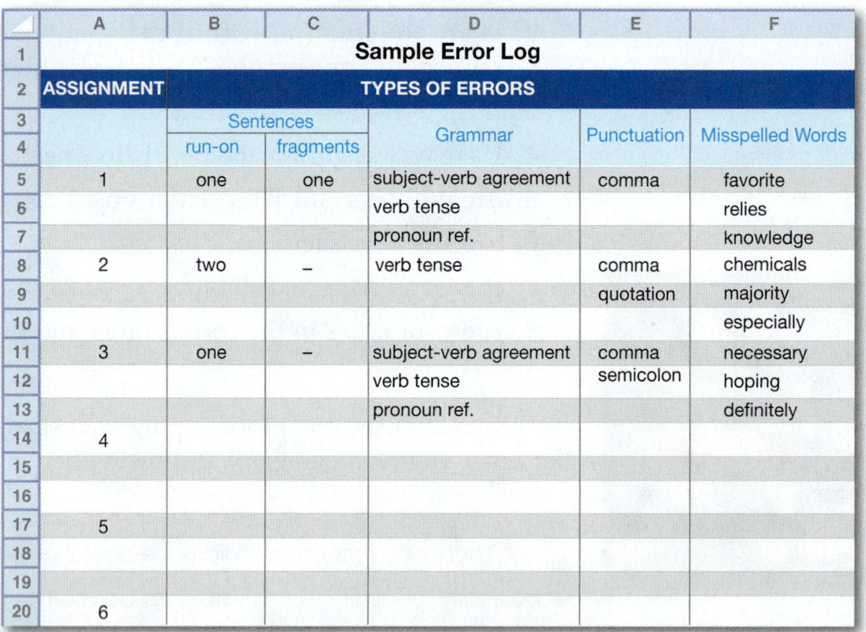

	A	B	C	D	E	F
1	Sample Error Log					
2	ASSIGNMENT	TYPES OF ERRORS				
3		Sentences		Grammar	Punctuation	Misspelled Words
4		run-on	fragments			
5	1	one	one	subject-verb agreement	comma	favorite
6				verb tense		relies
7				pronoun ref.		knowledge
8	2	two	–	verb tense	comma	chemicals
9					quotation	majority
10						especially
11	3	one	–	subject-verb agreement	comma	necessary
12				verb tense	semicolon	hoping
13				pronoun ref.		definitely
14	4					
15						
16						
17	5					
18						
19						
20	6					

READ AND RESPOND: A Student Essay

You have already read and studied Elizabeth's first draft (p. 217) and first revision (p. 225) of her essay about a difficult or challenging situation she had faced. The third draft shows the editing corrections Elizabeth made in sentence structure, grammar, punctuation, and spelling. Study each draft carefully to learn how the revision process works.

SECOND REVISION—SHOWING EDITING AND PROOFREADING

An Unexpected Addiction

Elizabeth Lawson

¶ It seems that every day on the news you hear about some Hollywood celebrity or ~~sports star~~ athlete having an addiction problem, whether ~~it's~~ steroids, ~~or~~ alcohol, or painkillers ~~or something even worse like crystal meth~~. You think it can never happen to you because your life is fine and you can deal with your own issues. ① ~~no problem.~~ But now I understand ~~it~~ addiction more because I developed ~~an addiction~~ one of my own, and I had to struggle to free myself from it. In the process I learned a few things about myself. ~~and what makes me tick. It all happened so fast that I didn't know what was happening at the time, but looking back now I understand it better.~~

1. Eliminated comma splice

There's no reason I should have developed an addiction, because I had a basically good life with a stable, loving mother. I was raised by a single mom and she did a great job. We were always so close. ② I remember when my father died (I was ~~8~~ eight years old) we made a deal that we were going to be a team and stick together. It was just the two of us and she worked ~~super~~ very hard to put food on the table and buy me things I wanted but she couldn't ~~really~~ afford. Of course we had our fights, ③ especially when I was a teenager, but she was always ④ ~~like~~ a mixture of a good friend that I liked to talk to, plus a parent who ~~tried to teach~~ taught me the right things to do. I made mistakes, ⑤ (everyone does) but at the end of the day we watched out for each other. One time I heard some neighbors ⑥ ~~women~~ gossiping about her, and I marched ~~right~~ up to them and told them to ~~knock it off~~ stop because they had no idea what she went through. She actually punished me for being rude to the neighbors but when she was dying ~~several~~ ten years later she told me ~~how~~ she was proud of me ~~she was when I did~~ for doing that.

2. Fixed fused sentence
3. Added commas to set off parenthetical phrase
4. Eliminated unnecessary word to make essay sound more formal
5. Added parentheses
6. Eliminated sexist language

It was when she died that I fell apart and started having ~~all sorts of~~ problems I had never had before. I was 22 years old and in college, ⑦ and ~~you would think a grown woman would be able to~~ I thought I could handle ~~it~~ my mother's death ⑧. But I fell apart; I was crying all the time. I ~~just~~ kept thinking about what a great person she was and how much I missed her. ~~But the weeks went by and I couldn't get over it.~~ I couldn't study, I couldn't eat, and worst of all I couldn't sleep. I was exhausted and having panic attacks. I even hallucinated once or twice. I was a total mess, ~~and~~ but I refused to go to a counselor because I thought I could deal with ~~it~~ my problems on my own. Well, I was wrong about that.

7. Made change to keep narrative voice consistent (I instead of you)
8. Fixed unclear pronoun reference

Then my uncle, my mother's brother, came to visit me. ~~and~~ He took one look at me and said how awful I looked. He had a prescription for a tranquilizer called Ativan (also called lorazepam) and he gave me some pills to help me sleep. ~~to me because I felt like if I didn't get some sleep I was going to die. So~~ I took one and it worked ~~so~~ incredibly

well, it relaxed me and I fell asleep and I woke up the next day after sleeping about
9. Eliminated redundancy 15 hours. I also felt super relaxed and much, much less upset so I went to the doc-
10. Fixed run-on sentence tor and asked for a prescription and he gave it to me but said he would do it only if I went to a grief counselor also so I took those pills twice a day for 3 months and they really helped me. The problem was they also took away my energy. And talking about everything with the counselor at my college (Jane) was a really big help. She helped me see something I didn't see on my own: that I would feel like I was betraying my mother if I went to someone other than her for help and advice. Jane also asked, Wouldn't my mother want me to be happy instead of crying all the time? Of course, it made complete sense! So at the end of the 3 months I thought, OK, I don't need these pills anymore, so I stopped taking them.

And that is when the trouble started. My heart started racing like crazy after a couple of days without the pills. My vision got blurry and I started getting weird cramps. I went 72 hours without sleep. I would just lay there with my heart racing
11. Eliminated cliché a mile a minute. Then something happened that really scared me, I started feeling zaps of electricity in my brain, like my brain was short circuiting. I was terrified and thought I was having a stroke. So I went to the emergency room and they figured out what was happening, I was having withdrawal symptoms from going off the meds too fast. It turns out that the type of medication I was on, (called a benzodiazepine, or benzo for short) you have to stop taking it gradually otherwise you get these terrible effects. They gave me an Ativan and the problems stopped almost immediately. And then this is the part you would not believe I had to reduce the dose by a tiny amount, take that dose for a week, then reduce the dose a little more, take that for a week, then reduce it again and again and so on until I could stop taking it.

It took me almost six months to reduce my dose to zero. And I learned a few things about myself and the world through the experience. First, maybe all the celebrities you read about with their addiction problems actually deserve a little sympathy instead of scorn. Maybe they, like me, had a problem they were trying to deal with, and things got out of control without them ever realizing it. Second, people with addictions are not bad people or even low class people. They are trying to cope with their problems but don't know the right way to do it. Third, and probably most important, I realized that it is OK to ask for help when you need it. If I had gone to grief counseling early, or even if I went to a support group while Mom was sick, I would have had more support and more understanding of what people go through and how to cope with it. I still miss Mom, but I know she's up there, proud that I overcame my addiction and smiling proudly the way she did
12. Eliminated slang when she reminded me about the time I told off those stupid neighbors.

Examining Writing

1. Highlight the topic sentences in Elizabeth's second revision and evaluate their use. Does each announce the main point of the paragraph? Do any need further revision?
2. Evaluate Elizabeth's use of detail. Did she provide sufficient detail? In what paragraphs could greater detail have been provided?
3. What did you learn about the revision process from Elizabeth's second and third drafts?

Writing Assignments

1. Did this essay change your attitude toward people with addictions? Write a paragraph explaining whether you agree or disagree with Elizabeth that celebrities and other people with addictions deserve sympathy rather than scorn.
2. Have you ever confronted a nosy or gossipy person? Write a paragraph describing your experience, including why you decided to confront the person, how the person reacted, and what you learned from the experience.
3. Complete the same assignment that Elizabeth did by writing an essay about a difficult or challenging event or experience.

READ AND RESPOND: A Professional Reading

Thinking Before Reading

The following essay was published anonymously in *Inside Higher Ed* to protect the privacy of the author's son. As you read, notice the types of details used to support the author's thesis.

1. Preview the reading, using the steps discussed in Chapter 1, page 4.
2. Connect the reading to your own experience by answering the following questions:
   a. Do you play games online or on your phone? Have you ever been hooked on a particular game?
   b. What types of games seem to be marketed toward your age group? What makes the marketing effective or appealing?
3. Mark and annotate as you read.

Students Vulnerable to Computer Gaming Addiction

1 Until the academic warning letter from my son's college arrived home last December 23rd following his fall freshman term, he assured us that he was getting Bs in his classes. Confronted with this letter, he broke down in tears, admitted that he spent most of the last half of the semester playing an online computer game, and didn't attend the final weeks of classes nor even sit for his exams.

2 An activity that started out in high school for fun and as a coping strategy for stress had hijacked his brain, and he lost control. He was addicted—as are nearly 2 million other U.S. college students. And if the computer game industry continues to succeed in its marketing strategy to hook youth on their products, its market success will trigger bigger avalanches of academic warning letters every December—unless college leaders take action to address this worsening epidemic.

3 For the past six years as an administrator at a large community college, I've focused on developing workforce education programs that have helped hundreds of at-risk students succeed in college programs. However, as a parent of a game-addicted college student living away from home on a college campus, I felt powerless to help my son succeed in his own college launch. As a young adult, he's responsible for his choices, and he chose games over college success. At the same time, the heart of addiction is a loss of control, and still-developing teenagers like my son are especially vulnerable to the instant gratification of games that can entrap them into addiction before they know what has hit them. My hope is that our family's story can help the higher education family grapple with this epidemic, so that other parents' sons and daughters don't experience the calamitous crash that my son did at college.

Excessive Gaming Linked to Lower Academic Performance

4 Because computer game-playing is legal, hidden away in dorm rooms, and doesn't result in obvious impairments like drug or alcohol addiction, the problem has stayed under the radar. However, many studies have linked excessive computer game-playing to lower academic performance, as well as a variety of disorders often treated at campus health centers, such as depression, anxiety, ADHD, and social phobias.

5 In one of the most authoritative studies, a longitudinal study of 3,000 third- through eighth-graders in Singapore, researchers from Iowa State University and elsewhere found 9 percent of gamers to be "pathological," meaning that their gaming damaged multiple parts of their lives, including school performance. Just like my son, they didn't grow out of it on their own, either. Two years later, 84 percent of the pathological gamers in this study were still experiencing similar impacts, a finding that suggests that nearly 10 percent of first-year college students bring these pathologies to college with them. Students who reported pathological impacts played an average of 31 hours

every week. Gaming within this subculture of students is so prevalent that my son convinced himself that 5–8 hours of daily gaming when he started college was normal.

6 Once these students arrive on campus, freed from the constraints of high school attendance monitors and parental oversight, students are more likely to binge on gaming, with results that can be as traumatic as my son's. In the 2011 National Survey of Student Engagement, completed by 27,000 first-year students, over one-third of incoming males and nearly one-fourth of females reported playing computer games more than 16 hours per week. These students had lower SAT scores and lower high school grades, and completed fewer AP courses. So, they come to college less prepared to succeed, and are likely to fall further behind if their addiction takes root more deeply.

7 An older 2003 study of college students by The Pew Internet and American Life Project confirmed this crowding out effect, with nearly half (48 percent) of college student gamers reporting that gaming keeps them from studying. Perhaps the former Federal Communications Commissioner Deborah Taylor was ahead of her time in 2008, when she created a brief media firestorm with a speech in which she claimed that "one of the top reasons for college dropouts in the U.S. is online gaming addiction—such as World of Warcraft."

Emulating the Tobacco Industry's Marketing Strategy

8 This problem is poised to get much worse. More and more online computer games are designed to profit by hooking addicts—starting at a young age—on their products, just as cigarette makers profited for decades by hooking young nicotine addicts for a lifetime. This Christmas, children being groomed by game-makers will find "Halo" and "World of Warcraft"-themed Lego sets under the tree. At a 2010 conference, one industry executive admitted that "we have to bring them in and keep them addicted and make them keep playing." After the computer game industry succeeded in getting and keeping my son addicted at college, he was hardly recognizable as the high school senior with a 3.7 GPA, 2100 SAT, and active participation as a high school athlete and trombonist in five bands. In a 2010 magazine article, an anonymous game designer described the creepy science of addiction that designers are engineering into their products.

9 Game-makers' profits increasingly rely on addiction. Consider the meteoric rise of the game that became an addiction as strong as crack for my son: Riot Games' "League of Legends." In 2009, Riot Games released "League of Legends" as one of the first free-to-play online massive multiplayer games, which require no upfront subscription payment. They extract money from players later, after they get hooked. By the fall of 2012, Riot Games reported that "League of Legends" had 70 million registered player names and 12 million "daily active users" (likely addicts) worldwide. The company's business model was attractive enough to score a massive $400 million payoff for the company's founders when they sold the company in 2011. Its phenomenal success has included a Pavlovian response within the industry to design even more intense free-to-play games that seek to ensnare and addict its customers—with youth and college students directly in their crosshairs. This prospect should motivate every dean of student services into action to warn students, starting with the first day of freshman orientation.

Campus Strategies to Address Computer Addiction

10 Such warnings are rare, however. "Given that college students are at the epicenter of America's computer addiction epidemic, I'm shocked at how few colleges and universities are addressing this problem aggressively," says Hilarie Cash, executive director of ReStart Internet Addiction Recovery Center, and author of Video Games and Your Kids. One reason is that the problem of compulsive or pathological computer gaming is often hidden from college officials by addicted students. For example, when the dean of student services asked my son why he was withdrawing from college, he said "because of depression"—without mentioning that he had spent nearly every waking hour in the last month of the semester compulsively playing a computer game while isolated in his dorm room. This kind of response is typical of many addicts, who feel a deep sense of shame about their out-of-control compulsion for gaming and engage in elaborate self-deceptions and lies to protect their addiction and their self-image. My son thought he was the only student with this problem.

11 Tracy Markle, Founder of Collegiate Coaching Services, has directly observed a chilling rise in pathological computer gaming among her young adult clients. "When we conduct our initial assessments on new male clients, 75% have some level of computer gaming and/or Internet abuse issue that contributes to the original presenting problems such as poor academic performance, difficulty concentrating, and social anxieties." In addition to these reported problems, Markle points to other indicators of potential gaming addiction problems with college students, such as frequent absences from classes, roommate complaints, social isolation, and calls or e-mails from concerned parents.

12 Cash and Markle both encourage college and university leaders to provide in-service training to build awareness among staff—especially front-line leaders such as resident assistants, teaching assistants, and student health clinicians—on how to recognize the warning signs of computer gaming. Colleges can also launch students awareness campaigns to warn students of these problems, and encourage affected students to seek help rather than to retreat into dangerous isolation. If my son's college had trained its resident advisers to recognize that holing up in your dorm room all day, not emerging for classes, ordering delivery pizzas alone every night, and turning away friends at his doorway are all signs of a potential problem, he might have been steered to get help before he crashed so completely. Cash also encourages campus leaders to develop new campus resources, such as offering a 12-step group to address computer gaming, and building a referral network of local therapists who have experience with this unique form of addiction.

13 Computer game companies already have their grip on nearly 10 percent of college students. They are coming after more of them, with more potent products. You can't stop them. But college and university officials can begin to address this issue by doing what we do best—education—starting with ourselves to learn more about growing epidemic of pathological computer gaming. Without action, we need to be prepared to mail even more academic warning letters each semester.

Writing in Response to Reading

Checking Your Comprehension MySkillsLab®

Answer each of the following questions using complete sentences.

1. What is the author's son addicted to?
2. According to the National Survey of Student Engagement, what are three results of playing games more than 16 hours per week?
3. Explain how the gaming industry emulates the marketing strategy of the tobacco industry.
4. What reason did the author's son give for withdrawing from college?
5. What reason(s) does the author give for why more campuses haven't addressed the problem of computer gaming?

Strengthening Your Vocabulary 

Identify at least five words used in the reading that are unfamiliar to you. Using context, word parts, or a dictionary, write a brief definition of each word.

Examining the Reading: Drawing an Idea Map

Create an idea map of the reading that starts with the title and thesis and then lists the author's main points. Use the guidelines on page 15.

Reading and Writing: An Integrated Perspective MySkillsLab®

Get ready to write about the reading by discussing the following:

1. Discuss the opening paragraph of the reading. Why did the author begin this way? Evaluate the effectiveness of this introduction.
2. Evaluate the types of details the author uses to support his thesis. Which details were most effective? Did any of the statistics shock or surprise you?
3. Why does the author explain what he does for a living? What is ironic about his profession, in light of his son's problem?
4. The author describes an extensive study of students in Singapore (paragraph 5). Do you think the study is representative of American students? Why or why not?
5. What was the author's purpose in writing this essay? Do you think he was successful? Why or why not? Write a journal entry explaining your answers.
6. Why does the author say Deborah Taylor was ahead of her time in 2008 (paragraph 7)? Do you agree that she was?

THINKING VISUALLY

7. What is the purpose of the photograph that accompanies the reading? What details in the photograph correspond to the author's message?
8. Why does the author compare the computer gaming industry to the tobacco industry? How accurate is this comparison?
9. What does the author mean by the phrase "Pavlovian response" (paragraph 9)? Discuss this phrase and how it applies to computer gaming.

Thinking and Writing Critically MySkillsLab®

1. How did the author organize the ideas and details in this reading? Find a paragraph that is organized using cause and effect or another pattern, and create an idea map for that paragraph.
2. Express the author's thesis in your own words.
3. What is the author's tone throughout the reading? How do you know what the author's attitude is toward this subject? (For more about tone, see Chapter 12, p. 358.)
4. Who is the author's intended audience? Discuss how this essay might be different if it had been written for a different audience such as students or parents.
5. Is this reading mostly fact or opinion? Find examples of both and evaluate their effectiveness. (For more about fact and opinion, see Chapter 12, p. 354.)
6. Who is the author talking about when he says "You can't stop them" (paragraph 13)? Explain what he means and whether or not you agree.
7. Both the student essay and the professional reading in this chapter are concerned with forms of addiction. Compare the two readings. How are they similar? How are they different? What is most or least effective about each?

Writing Paragraphs MySkillsLab®

1. Write a paragraph summarizing the marketing strategy used by computer gaming companies. What is your opinion of a strategy that targets children?
2. How is the word *pathological* defined in paragraph 5? Reflect on some of your own habits and activities. Write a paragraph about one of your behaviors that could be described as pathological in some way.
3. The author uses words such as *creepy* and *chilling* to describe gaming and its effects. What other examples of connotative language does the author use? Write a paragraph giving several examples.

Writing Essays MySkillsLab®

4. According to the author, computer gaming companies "already have their grip on nearly 10 percent of college students." What would you say to warn students about gaming? What details from the selection would you cite? What other arguments would you make to help students avoid this form of addiction? Write an essay directed toward college students explaining the negative effects of gaming and exploring the answers to these questions.
5. The author concludes by calling the reader to action. What does he want the reader to do? Summarize the actions he believes need to happen to address pathological computer gaming. What actions seem most useful or effective to you? Why? Write an essay explaining your answers.
6. Have you ever had to deal with an addiction, either your own or that of someone close to you? Did the author's description of his son's experience, including the sense of shame and self-deception, seem accurate? Write an essay describing your experience.

SELF-TEST SUMMARY

To test yourself, cover the Answer column with a sheet of paper and answer each question in the left column. Evaluate each of your answers as you work by sliding the paper down and comparing your answer with what is printed in the Answer column.

QUESTION	ANSWER
■ GOAL 1 Understand the purpose of revising What is involved in revising and editing?	Revising involves rereading every idea and sentence in a paragraph you have written and making changes to them as needed. Editing involves adding or deleting words and sentences, as well as correcting errors in grammar, spelling, and punctuation.
■ GOAL 2 Read critically to revise Why and how do you read a paragraph critically to revise?	Read your paragraph critically in order to find out what works and what doesn't. Read it several times, examining content, evaluating how effectively you have expressed your ideas, and checking for correctness. Use the Revision Checklist on page 223.
■ GOAL 3 Consider your purpose and audience How do you evaluate your purpose and audience?	To evaluate purpose, reread your draft and decide whether it accomplishes what you want it to. Ask a peer to read your writing and summarize what it accomplishes. To evaluate audience, read your paragraph from the audience's viewpoint, or imagine that someone else wrote it and you are reading it for the first time.
■ GOAL 4 Examine your ideas How can an idea map help you examine your ideas?	An idea map can help you check your use of relevant and sufficient detail as well as the logical organization of your ideas.
■ GOAL 5 Correct errors in grammar, spelling, and punctuation Why is it important to edit for correctness, and what tools can you use to do so?	Errors in grammar, spelling, and punctuation make your writing less effective and decrease the reader's confidence in what you write. Use an error log to help you avoid errors you make consistently, and refer to the Proofreading Checklist on page 224 for a list of questions to help you spot errors.

MySkillsLab®

Visit **Chapter 7, "Strategies for Revising Paragraphs,"** in MySkillsLab to test your understanding of chapter goals.

PART THREE READING AND WRITING ESSAYS

8 Reading, Planning, and Organizing Essays

LEARNING GOALS

Learn how to . . .

- GOAL 1 Understand the purpose of an essay
- GOAL 2 Read essays effectively
- GOAL 3 Express your ideas in essay form
- GOAL 4 Choose a topic
- GOAL 5 Generate ideas about your topic
- GOAL 6 Consider audience, purpose, and tone
- GOAL 7 Write a thesis statement
- GOAL 8 Plan and organize your essay

THINK About It!

The above photograph shows the Tibet Railway, a $4.2 billion investment, passing through rural countryside. It was included in an essay discussing changes occurring within the country. Suppose you were asked to write an essay in response to the essay and photograph. Before beginning to write, what would you do?

First you would have to read the essay and understand the point it makes. Then, you would study, analyze, and interpret the photograph. You would study the scene and think about the value and impact of the railway in the rural countryside. You would also read and reread the essay, searching for clues from the writer as to why this particular photograph is included and what it is intended to illustrate. If you felt you needed more information, you might Google the Tibet Railway to read and learn more about it. Once you felt you had adequate information, you might make notes or use brainstorming to generate ideas to write about. Once you had ideas to work with, you would begin to think about how to organize and fit them together. Reading, planning, and organization are important in most writing that you do, and this chapter will guide you through the process.

Reading and Writing Connections

EVERYDAY CONNECTIONS

- **Reading** You read a newspaper article about a group of cycling enthusiasts who want to improve and expand the bike trail system in your state. The group is hoping to gain funding through a transportation bill in Congress.
- **Writing** In response to the newspaper article, you write a letter to your state senators and ask for their support in developing and funding the bike trail system.

ACADEMIC CONNECTIONS

- **Reading** In your Introduction to Literature class, you read an essay by Alice Walker on what it is like to be a black female writer in America.
- **Writing** You write an essay for a literature exam in which you refer to Alice Walker's essay in discussing her novel *The Color Purple*.

WORKPLACE CONNECTIONS

- **Reading** You read an article online in *Fortune* magazine about small businesses that have started using cell phones and credit card swipers to process credit card transactions at locations outside of the business office.
- **Writing** As the owner of a lawn care business, you write a proposal to obtain a small business loan to buy the credit card software and equipment you read about in the online article.

Why Read and Write Essays?

■ GOAL 1
Understand the purpose of an essay

An **essay** is a group of paragraphs that examine a single topic and focus on a single idea about that topic. If you know how essays are structured, you will be able to read them more easily and write them more effectively.

Reading essays enables you to learn about a topic and discover an author's perspective, viewpoint, or approach toward the topic. When you read good writing you can assume that the writer has worked through the writing process, doing a lot of work before you see the piece. He or she has brainstormed to generate ideas, narrowed a topic, considered his or her audience and purpose, and planned, drafted, revised, and edited the article or essay.

Writing an essay allows you the opportunity to present your ideas on a topic and explain and support those ideas. In this chapter, we will focus on the structure of essays, using the professional readings, and planning essays, using the work of student writer Ted Sawchuck.

EXAMINING PROFESSIONAL WRITING

The following reading, "Mind Your Own Browser," appeared in *Technology Review* in March–April 2011. As you read, notice how the author presents and develops his thesis statement, how he organizes his essay, and how he introduces and concludes his essay. You will be asked to apply what you learn about the elements of an essay in this chapter to this reading.

Thinking Before Reading

1. Preview the reading, using the steps discussed in Chapter 1, page 4.
2. Connect the reading to your own experience by answering the following questions:
   a. How important is it to you to protect your privacy online? What precautions do you take?
   b. Should companies be allowed to collect information about you?
3. Mark and annotate as you read.

Mind Your Own Browser

Simson L. Garfinkel

1 Most of us depend on free web services, from Google to Facebook, but unless you're careful, using them has a price: your privacy. Web advertisers, who keep these sites in business, track what you do online in order to deliver targeted, attention-grabbing ads. Your web browser reveals a surprising amount about you, and advertisers are keen to find out even more.

2 A new draft report from the Federal Trade Commission (FTC) recommends the creation of a "Do Not Track" mechanism that would let Internet users choose, with the click of a button, whether to allow advertisers to track them. While this would offer better privacy controls than exist currently, the FTC's approach falls short, because tracking technology is interwoven into our most popular websites and mobile services (without tracking, they simply don't work) and businesses are opposed to reform.

3 Few people realize that many web ads are tailored using huge amounts of personal data collected, combined, and cross-referenced from multiple sources—an approach known as "behavioral advertising." Advertisers ferret out clues to where you live, where you work, what you buy, and which TV shows you watch, then refine their ads accordingly.

4 Behavioral advertising works. A study conducted by Microsoft Research Asia found that users were up to seven times likelier to click on targeted ads than on nontargeted ones. Targeted ads earn much more for websites—an average of $4.12 per

thousand views versus $1.98 per thousand for regular ads, according to a study commissioned by the Network Advertising Initiative, a trade group that promotes self-regulation.

5 While many people are simply opposed on principle to unrestricted tracking, there are real risks involved. Without safeguards, tracking techniques could be exploited to steal identities or to hack into computers. And the big databases that advertisers are building could be misused by unscrupulous employers or malicious governments.

6 Over the past 15 years the United States has developed a peculiar approach to protecting consumer privacy. Companies publish detailed "privacy policies" that are supposed to explain what information they collect and what they plan to do with it. Consumers can then choose whether they want to participate.

7 The FTC report says that this model no longer works (if it ever did). "Many companies are not disclosing their practices," FTC chairman Jon Leibowitz says. "And even if companies do disclose them, they do so in long, incomprehensible privacy policies and user agreements that consumers don't read, let alone understand."

8 The FTC is trying to rein this in. It recommends, for example, that companies collect information only when there is a legitimate business need to do so, and asks them to destroy that information when they no longer need it. It also wants companies to do a better job of explaining their policies to consumers.

9 Of course, real choice requires more than clear information—it requires options. At the moment, that means activating the "private browsing" mode built into modern web browsers (which prevents sites from accessing cookies) or using browser plug-ins that automatically block ads and certain tracking technologies.

10 But there is no rule prohibiting advertisers from circumventing private-browsing modes, and many are doing so. The FTC's solution to this problem is "Do Not Track," loosely modeled on the agency's popular "Do Not Call" list. Instead of a centralized list of consumers who don't want to be tracked, however, they envision a browser setting that would transmit an anonymity request to web advertisers. If behaviorally targeted ads really are beneficial to consumers, most people will leave the feature switched off. Otherwise, websites better get used to $1.98 per thousand ads viewed.

11 Browser makers have started building tracking controls for their software. Google recently released an add-on for Chrome called Keep My Opt-Outs, and Microsoft has announced a similar feature for Internet Explorer 9 called Tracking Protection. These features tell websites when someone doesn't want to be tracked. But it's still up to companies to honor this request. And, unsurprisingly, the advertising industry fiercely opposes tracking restrictions, especially if they are enabled in browsers by default.

12 The real problem with "Do Not Track" is that it derives from an earlier understanding of web advertising—that ads are distributed to news sites, search engines, and other destinations that don't necessarily need to know

who you are. Nowadays many popular websites are unusable unless you let them track you.

13 Take Facebook: The website has seen explosive ad-revenue growth precisely because it tracks users' interests in great detail. There's no way to turn off tracking and still use the site. Thanks to Facebook Connect, which lets you log on to other websites with your Facebook credentials, and the "Like" button, which sends links from external pages back to your profile, Facebook now tracks you across the web. Or, more accurately, you tell Facebook where you are.

14 Smartphones will accelerate this trend. Already, many phones deliver ads based on your GPS-determined position. Future ads might depend on the applications you've installed, whom you've called, even the contents of your address book.

15 There is a way to resolve this conundrum: Create simple and enforceable policies that limit companies' retention and use of consumer data. These could be dictated by the government or, conceivably, built into browsers and customized by users. For example, you could tell Google to archive your searches forever, but make them anonymous after six months. You could tell Facebook to keep your posts indefinitely, but use them for advertising purposes only for a year.

vested interests
the groups who benefit most from an existing system or activity

16 Unfortunately, any kind of reform will face stiff opposition from **vested interests**. But if the government wants to defend us from privacy-trampling advertising, it needs more than "Do Not Track."

Read Essays to Build Comprehension and Recall

■ GOAL 2
Read essays effectively

Reading an essay involves understanding what the writer says and remembering what you read so you can discuss and write about it. To understand the writer's ideas, it is helpful to analyze the essay's essential parts. Understanding how essays are organized will help you read them more effectively and efficiently.

Reading: Understanding the Structure of an Essay

Essays may be encountered in anthologies, newspapers, and magazines of all types. Essays follow a standard organization and usually have the following parts:

- title
- introduction
- thesis statement
- supporting information in body paragraphs
- conclusion

The structure of an essay is similar to that of a paragraph in that it explores a single idea about a topic; in an essay this is called the **thesis statement**. Like a paragraph, in which details support a topic sentence, an essay provides ideas and details that support the thesis statement, each main idea discussed in a body paragraph. However, unlike a paragraph, an essay deals with a broader topic and the idea that it explores is often more complex. You can visualize the structure of an essay as follows:

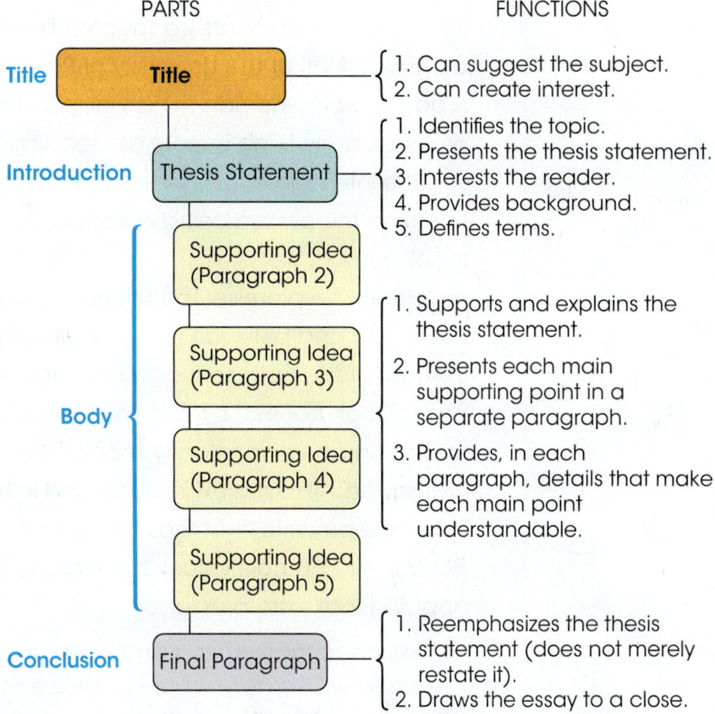

Note: There is no set number of paragraphs that an essay should contain. This model shows six paragraphs, but in actual essays, the number will vary greatly.

Let's examine the function of each of these parts of an essay in greater detail by referring to an essay titled "To Catch a Liar." It was written by Sandra Parshall and first appeared in a blog titled *Poe's Deadly Daughters*.

Title — **TO CATCH A LIAR**

Author — Sandra Parshall

Source Information —
From *Poe's Deadly Daughters*, A Blog for Mystery Lovers
The author of this article is a journalist and author of four mystery novels. You can find more information about her at her Web page http://www.sandraparshall.com/.

Introduction: interest-catching question

1 Do you think you're pretty good at spotting when somebody's lying? Sorry, but I'll bet you're not as sharp as you think you are.

2 Researchers have found that most people have a dismally low success rate, even in a lab setting where they know for certain that some of those they're studying are lying. If we're especially vigilant, we might spot half of all lies—which means we'll miss half. Police officers aren't much better than the rest of us, although they improve with experience. Those super-cops who can always detect a lie, like the fictional Special Agent Gibbs on the TV show *NCIS*, do exist in reality, but they're extremely rare and psychologists have yet to

determine how they do it. Since the detective's ability to spot lies is crucial to crime-solving, some scientists are finding ways to teach the skill to cops.

Thesis Statement

Body

3 *Scientific American Mind* magazine's September/October issue reports on experiments conducted by one of them, social psychologist Aldert Vrij of the University of Portsmouth in England. Vrij's work is based on the human mind's inability to think along multiple tracks simultaneously. Lying is more demanding than simply telling the truth, so if the interrogator gives the suspect's mind too much to process at one time, the person being questioned is likely to slip up if he's trying to sell a phony story.

Details about Vrig's research study

4 Here's the premise: The liar has to worry about keeping his story consistent and believable, first of all—which means suppressing all thought of the truth so it doesn't inadvertently slip out—but he also has to "look honest" by controlling his expression and body movements. And he's constantly monitoring the cop's reaction to what he's saying. All that is exhausting, and if the interrogator adds even a little more pressure, that may be enough to trip up a liar.

5 Vrij and his colleagues have found several useful strategies for applying that extra pressure.

- First, discount sweating and general nervousness. Even an honest person will be nervous under police scrutiny.
- One way to trip up a liar is to ask the suspect to tell his or her story backward, beginning at the end. Devising a false story and keeping it straight is hard enough without the burden of having to recount phony events in reverse. In lab tests, this greatly increased mistakes and the likelihood of catching a liar.
- Interrogators can also rattle a suspect by insisting that he maintain eye contact. Liars have trouble concentrating on their stories if they're looking directly into the eyes of the people they're lying to.
- Asking suspects to draw pictures of what they're describing can also reveal the liars. Their pictures will show fewer details than those drawn by truth-tellers, and often the pictures won't be consistent with verbal descriptions.

Conclusion

6 These easy techniques have proven highly effective in the lab and should help police in the real world do their work more efficiently. Best of all, they're simple enough to be used by fictional cops who aren't endowed with the special mental powers of Special Agent Gibbs.

Final comment on the usefulness of the strategies

The Title

The title usually suggests the subject of the essay and is intended to capture the reader's interest. Some titles are highly descriptive and announce exactly what the essay will be about as the title "To Catch a Liar" does. Other titles are less directly informative. Some essays also include a subtitle that provides additional information. In an essay titled "Citizenship or Slavery?" the title is mainly intended to capture your interest while the subtitle, "How Schools Take the Volunteer Out of Volunteering," focuses you more clearly on what the essay will be about.

Reading: Analyzing Titles

Directions: Working with a classmate, decide what you expect to be discussed in essays with each of the following titles.

1. Animal Rights: Right or Wrong

   ___

2. Firearms, Violence, and Public Policy

   ___

3. The Price of Power: Living in the Nuclear Age

   ___

   ___

4. The Nature and Significance of Play

   ___

5. Uncivil Rights—The Cultural Rules of Anger

   ___

   ___

6. Mind Your Own Browser

   ___

   ___

The Introduction

The **introduction**, usually one or two paragraphs long, sets the scene for the essay and places the subject within a framework or context. The introduction may

- present the thesis statement of the essay.
- offer background information (explain television addiction as an issue, for example).
- define technical or unfamiliar terms (define *addiction*, for example).
- build your interest (give an instance of an extreme case of television addiction).

Notice how in the essay "To Catch a Liar" these goals are accomplished in the first two paragraphs.

EXERCISE 8-2

Reading: Analyzing an Introduction

Directions: Read only the first two paragraphs of the essay "Mind Your Own Browser" by Simson L. Garfinkel on page 240. What types of information do they provide?

___

___

The Thesis Statement

The **thesis statement** of an essay is its main point. All the other ideas and paragraphs in the essay support this point. Once you identify an essay's thesis, you have discovered the key to its meaning. The thesis is usually stated in a single sentence (although it can be expressed in two or three sentences) that appears in the introductory paragraphs. It often follows the background information and the attention-getter. In "To Catch a Liar" the thesis is stated at the end of the second paragraph. Occasionally, an author will first present evidence in support of the thesis and then state the thesis at the end of the essay. This organization is most common in argumentative essays (see Chapter 14).

You may also find, on occasion, that an author implies rather than directly states the thesis; the thesis is revealed through the supporting paragraphs. When you cannot find a clear statement of the thesis, ask yourself this question: "What is the one main point the author is making?" Your answer is the implied thesis statement.

Here are a few sample thesis statements.

- Due to its negative health effects, cigarette smoking is once again being regarded as a form of deviant behavior.
- Career choice is influenced by numerous factors including skills and abilities, attitudes, and life goals.
- Year-round school will provide children with a better education that is more cost-effective.

EXERCISE 8-3

Reading: Identifying a Thesis Statement

Directions: Read the entire essay "Mind Your Own Browser" (p. 240), and write its thesis statement below.

____

____

____

____

The Body

The **body** of the essay contains sentences and paragraphs that explain or support the thesis statement. This support may be in the form of

- examples.
- descriptions.
- facts.
- statistics.
- reasons.
- anecdotes (stories that illustrate a point).
- personal experiences and observations.
- quotations from or references to authorities and experts.
- comparisons.

Most writers use various types of supporting information. In the essay "To Catch a Liar (p. 243), the author uses several types of information in her supporting paragraphs. Notice how she gives an example of a super-cop in paragraph 2 and offers reasons why lying is complex in paragraph 4. Paragraph 5 presents facts and description.

EXERCISE 8-4

Reading: Analyzing Supporting Information

Directions: Review the essay "Mind Your Own Browser" (p. 240), and mark where the body begins and ends. Then, in the margin beside each supporting paragraph, label the type(s) of supporting information the author used.

The Conclusion

An essay is brought to a close with a brief conclusion, not a summary. (A summary provides a review of the key ideas presented in an article. Think of a summary as an outline in paragraph form. The order in which the information appears in the summary reflects the order in which it appears in the article itself.) A **conclusion** is a final statement about the subject of the essay. A conclusion does not review content as a summary does. Instead, a conclusion often refers back to, but does not repeat, the thesis statement. It may also suggest a direction for further thought or introduce a new way of looking at what has already been said. The essay "To Catch a Liar" ends with a conclusion that comments on the usefulness of the strategies presented.

EXERCISE 8-5

Reading: Analyzing a Conclusion

Directions: Explain how the conclusion of "Mind Your Own Browser" draws the essay to a close.

____

____

Reading for Retention, Recall, and Response

Once you understand what the author of an essay is saying, your task is to remember what you read so you can react and respond to it. Use the following strategies to build your retention and response skills.

Strategies to Build Retention and Response Skills

- **Highlight as you read.** Sorting ideas that are important to remember from those that are not will strengthen your recall and identify ideas to which to respond. (See Chapter 2 for highlighting techniques.)
- **Annotate as you read.** It is helpful to record your thinking as you read, so you do not lose track of your reactions as you encounter other new ideas. Writing

your ideas will help cement them in your mind, and your annotations will be a good starting point for review. (See Chapter 2 for annotating techniques.)

- **Connect ideas to your background experience.** By connecting what you have read to your own experiences, you create memory links that will help you recall the information. These connections are also useful when finding ideas to write about in response to the essay.
- **Identify the organization pattern(s) used.** Patterns help guide your reading and help you see how ideas fit together. Once you see how ideas fit together, you will be able to remember them more easily. (See Chapters 5 and 6 for more about patterns.)
- **Review and write after reading.** When you have finished reading an essay, quickly review its major points by rereading your highlighting and annotations. Review will give you the big picture: it will help you see the essay as a whole, rather than as single paragraphs, which is an important step for both retention and response.

EXERCISE 8-6 Reading: Strengthening Recall

Directions: Highlight, annotate, and identify the pattern(s) used in the essay "Mind Your Own Browser" (p. 240). Then write a sentence or two connecting the reading to your own experience. How well did these strategies work to strengthen your recall? Write a few sentences evaluating each as a method of helping you remember what you read.

Thinking Critically About Essays

Essays require close examination. In order to be able to discuss and write about an essay you have read, be sure to evaluate and analyze it using all the critical reading skills presented in Chapters 12–14, and the "Thinking Critically About . . . " sections in previous chapters. Important critical thinking questions to ask about essays include

- **Who is the author and is he or she qualified to write about the topic of the essay?** For professional essays, check to see if you recognize the author's name, and try to learn something about his or her qualifications to write about the topic. For "To Catch a Liar," there is information about the author at the beginning of the essay that suggests she would be knowledgeable about lying.
- **What is the author's purpose?** Is the writer trying to present information, convince you of something, entertain you, or express an attitude or opinion? For "To Catch a Liar," the author's purpose is to inform.
- **Does the author provide adequate support for his or her ideas?** Is a variety of supporting information provided? An essay that relies entirely upon the author's personal experiences, for example, to support a thesis, may be of limited use for research purposes. In "To Catch a Liar," the author provides research evidence, reasons, and strategies.
- **Did the author supply sources, references, and citations for ideas not his or her own?** You should be able to verify the information presented and turn to those sources should you wish to read more about the topic. As is common

practice for essays published in popular sources, full citation and source information is not included for "To Catch a Liar."

- **Analyze any visuals that accompany the essay.** Determine their purpose and how they relate to the essay.

Write Essays to Express Ideas

■ GOAL 3
Express your ideas in essay form

Why write an essay? Writing an essay gives you the opportunity to present your ideas to an audience Writing an essay is a process similar to writing a paragraph. If you can do one, you can do the other. The structure is similar, and they have similar parts. Think of the organization of a paragraph as modeling the organization of an essay, with one idea being explained by supporting details. Because an essay is at least five paragraphs long, and usually longer, it needs an opening paragraph that focuses the reader's attention and gives needed background information. It also needs a conclusion to draw the ideas discussed together and bring it to a close.

In the rest of this chapter, you will practice how to select a topic and generate ideas about it; consider audience, purpose, and tone; write a thesis statement; and plan and organize an essay. Then in Chapter 9 you will practice how to write a draft—including an introduction, conclusion, and title—and evaluate, revise, and proofread it.

EXAMINING STUDENT WRITING

A good way to learn to read essays and write essays is to study a model. In this chapter and in Chapter 9, you will follow Ted Sawchuck, a student writer, as he brainstorms, drafts, and revises an essay on dating in the Internet age.

Ted was a student at the University of Maryland majoring in journalism when he wrote this essay. Ted was the editor of the college newspaper and decided to write an essay about social networking sites and narrowed his topic to online dating relationships. The final version of his essay is shown below.

Descriptive title: identifies the essay's subject

Relationships 2.0: Dating and Relating in the Internet Age

Ted Sawchuck

Introduction: background on Facebook

1 Facebook is a social networking Internet site. It allows a user to conveniently connect online with people, make friends, and join interest groups via his or her computer. It also allows a user to learn more about his or her friends, as well as post text, photos, video links, and information. Facebook has become widely popular. Much has been written about it in my student newspaper, but no one has yet dug into how the site affects relationships on our campus, and specifically the dating process. Each stage of the dating process is influenced by Facebook; on our campus, not all the changes have been positive.

Thesis statement

Topic sentence: identifies first stage of online dating

2 At the University of Maryland, the dating process begins like this: get someone's name; look him or her up on Facebook; then use that information to decide how to

proceed. When I meet someone and she sets off those neurons that make me hum "Maybe it's love," I do a Facebook search. A profile page will tell me her age, indicate whether or not she is taken, and give me a decent idea (if the profile is not privacy protected) of what image she is trying to present. Note that I do not trust Facebook to tell me who people are—merely who they want to show other people they are. I look through photos and see what the person values enough to show me. I check posted links because what someone thinks is worth sharing is another window into who she is.

Transitional sentence

Topic sentence: identifies second stage of online dating

3 After using Facebook to check out someone, I have a decent idea of whether she is a probable friend or possible romantic interest. Next I hit Google—searching first with her e-mail address, then with her name, and next with her nickname. This search turns up message boards, possibly her blog, and maybe even a Flickr site, all worth plumbing for details about my new fascination.

Topic sentence: states first drawback of online dating

4 I have serious doubts as to whether being able to download someone's self with a little searching on Facebook and Google is actually a good thing for beginning a relationship. For one thing, online searches result in tons of information with absolutely no context. Judging what you learn without cross-referencing it with the person is a recipe for misinterpretative disaster, yet checking means admitting you have been snooping. I snoop anyway.

Topic sentence: starts with transitional word identifies second drawback of online dating

5 Also, on Facebook, everyone seems reduced to a set of bullet points—"goth, tall, cat person"—that you rely on before even meeting the person. In real life, careful observation can reveal truths about people they will not discuss online, especially things they do not want generally known. However, a fidgety, nervous guy who sweats when he sees a pretty girl may have a better chance sending a Facebook message, which can be drafted and redrafted and edited and rewritten and shown to friends before sending, than approaching her in real life, so it does have its benefits.

Topic sentence: identifies third drawback of online dating

6 The dating process works well online initially, but real connections are only formed by spending substantial time together in person. Online talks, even via Skype or webcam, are still only a fraction of the real experience and convey only a fraction of the information one can glean during an in-person encounter. Time spent online communicating with someone can build connections that lead to a relationship or strengthen a current one. However, tone, pauses, nuance, and volume are all stripped from instant messages. Human laughter beats "LOL" any day, and holding her while she tells you about her day wins whenever possible.

Topic sentence: identifies fourth drawback of online dating

7 Facebook can also provide new avenues for infidelity. One way is through chatting online. It is very poor form to chat up someone else's girlfriend in a bar, but when chatting online there is no boyfriend looming over you to enforce boundaries. Combine that freedom with the very personal qualities of online relationships and the large amount of time most people spend online and you have a situation that anyone who's dating anyone who goes online a lot should worry about. The poke feature—a virtual way to let someone know you are thinking about him or her without actually saying anything—is another way Facebook can promote infidelity. One of my friends who has a boyfriend uses them to let me know when she is thinking about me. It amounts to several pokes a day, and she receives ones from me whenever she crosses my mind. She does it to let me know she is thinking about me frequently, which is great for me and not so hot for her boyfriend.

Topic sentence: introduces discussion of how to break up online

8 Breaking up is hard to do but the Internet makes it easier. Once a relationship ends, you do not want to get a continually updated feed of information about the other person from any source. Knowing someone is getting over you and trying to date is one thing; knowing she is doing it at seven-thirty at Club Kozmo with someone she met last

weekend is another. So now my list for after leaving someone includes blocking her on instant messaging, taking her e-mail address out of my quick contacts list and out of my e-mail's auto-complete list, avoiding her blog and defriending her on Facebook. Forget one step and the "getting over her" process becomes that much harder. There is a measure of comfort to be found in thinking someone has fallen off the face of the earth romantically, especially if your return to dating has not been as successful as hers.

Conclusion: Ted offers advice on online dating breakups

9 Cutting someone off requires effort. Any bit of forgotten information is another barb, another pang, another realization of what you have lost. Invariably, you will miss something and see a status update or a text message or a voice mail. It helps at times, when missing someone so badly means wishing she were dead. Once you get over it yourself, refriend the person if you can do it without going crazy. Sometimes a little bit of ignorance can be blissful indeed, but most connections are worth preserving.

Choose a Topic

■ GOAL 4
Choose a topic

In some situations, your instructor will assign a topic; other times you will be free to choose your own. Below you will find suggestions for handling either situation. In both situations, however, be sure to do the following:

- **Find out the expected length of the paper.** If your instructor does not give a page or word count, be sure to ask. Knowing his or her expectations will help you know how much information to include.
- **Pay attention to due dates and specific requirements.** Keep track of when your essay is due. Some instructors may also require that a preliminary draft or a working thesis statement be submitted before the final deadline. Many instructors penalize late papers or may even refuse to accept them.
- **Find out what format you should follow in submitting your paper.** You need to know what is expected in terms of a cover sheet, margins, double or single spacing, documentation style, and so forth. Some instructors may prefer essays submitted electronically, while others may require a paper copy.

Working with Assigned Topics

In many situations, your instructor will either assign a topic or give you a choice of several topics. Be sure to read and study the assignment carefully before you begin. (If your instructor gives the assignment orally, record as much as you can of what he or she says so you can review it later.) Usually your instructor will offer clues as to what is expected, and you can use these to guide you as you plan and draft your essay. Use the following tips:

Tips for Planning and Drafting an Essay

- **Determine the purpose of the assignment.** Identify, as precisely as you can, what your instructor wants you to do. Is the purpose of the essay to inform (present information), express your feelings, explore an issue, or persuade?
- **Watch for clue words that suggest how to write and organize your essay.** Instructors often use words that suggest what you should write about and how to organize the information. Here is a sample assignment:

Assignment: Define what a bully is, and explain how to deal with one.

The two important clue words here are *define* and *explain*. This is a two-part assignment: first you should define, or explain, what a bully is, and then you should offer advice on how to cope with bullying behavior using examples. Refer to Table 8-1 (p. 250) for a list of clue words and how to use them as you respond to assigned topics.

- **Connect the assignment to classroom instruction.** What skills taught recently in class does your instructor want you to apply as you write? For the above assignment, for example, you might have been learning how to define terms or exploring how to use examples to support a thesis (for instance, you could give examples of situations in which a bully was handled).

TABLE 8-1 CLUE WORDS AND HOW TO USE THEM

Clue Word	Example	Information to Include
Describe	Describe the process of tattooing or another form of body art.	Tell how something happened, including how, who, where, and why.
Compare	Compare the levels of violence in two forms of public entertainment.	Show how items are similar; include details or examples.
Contrast (differentiate)	Contrast the health care system in the United States with that in England.	Show how the items are different; include details or examples.
Argue	Argue that pets are valuable for human therapy.	Give reasons or evidence, or establish that a concept or theory is correct, logical, or valid.
Justify	Justify the decision to keep the names of rape victims private.	Give reasons that support an action, event, or policy.
Criticize	Criticize the campus policy on Internet usage.	Make judgments about quality or worth; include both positive and negative aspects, explaining or giving reasons for your judgments.
Evaluate	Evaluate the strategies our society has used to control drunk driving.	React to the topic in a logical way. Discuss the merit, strengths, weaknesses, advantages, or limitations of the topic, explaining your reasons.
Discuss	Discuss the effectiveness of gun control laws.	Consider important characteristics and main points.
Summarize	Summarize the arguments for and against offering sex education courses in public schools.	Cover the major points in brief form.
Define	Define *sexist language* and include several examples.	Give an accurate meaning of the term with enough detail to show that you really understand it.

EXERCISE 8-7

Analyzing Writing Assignments

Directions: For each of the following writing assignments, underline key words that suggest the purpose of the assignment.

1. Discuss the issue of sex education in public schools.
2. Evaluate the level of violence on two or more popular television shows.
3. Explore the problems of living at home with parents.

4. Write an essay arguing for or against the testing of cosmetic beauty products on animals.
5. Compare two television commercials, examining their purpose and the persuasive devices that they use.

Choosing Your Own Topic

When your instructor gives you an assignment, you may not like the topic, but at least a good part of the preliminary work has been done for you. When your instructor allows you to choose your own topic, you have to brainstorm for ideas and explore possible topics using the prewriting techniques described in Chapter 2 (pp. 47–48). Use the following suggestions to help you choose an appropriate, effective, and workable topic:

Suggestions for Finding an Effective Topic

- **Take time to think about your choice.** Do not grab the first topic you come across. Instead think it through, and weigh its pros and cons. It is often helpful to think of several topics and then choose the one you feel you are best prepared to write about.
- **Choose a topic that interests you.** You will feel more like writing about it and will find you have more to say.
- **Write about something familiar.** Select a topic you know a fair amount about. Otherwise, you will have to research your topic in the library or online. Your experience and knowledge of a familiar topic will provide the content of your essay.
- **Use a writing journal as a source for ideas.** Use it to record your feelings, reactions, and impressions.
- **Discuss possible topics with a friend or classmate.** These conversations may help you discover worthwhile topics.

Table 8-2 lists additional sources of ideas for essay topics.

TABLE 8-2 SOURCES OF IDEAS FOR ESSAY TOPICS

Sources of Ideas	Examples
Your daily life. Pay attention to events you attend, activities you participate in, and routines you follow.	Attending a sporting event may suggest topics about professional athletes' salaries, sports injuries, or violence in sports.
Your college classes. Both class lectures and discussions as well as reading assignments may give you ideas for topics.	A class discussion in sociology about prejudice and discrimination may suggest you write about racial or ethnic identities, stereotypes, or types of discrimination (age, gender, weight, etc.).
Your job. Your responsibilities, your boss, your co-workers, and your customers are all sources of ideas.	Watching a family with wild, misbehaving children throwing food and annoying other customers in a restaurant may prompt you to write about restaurant policies, child rearing, or rude and annoying behavior.
The media. Radio, television, movies, newspapers, magazines, and online sources all contain hundreds of ideas for a topic each day.	A commercial for a weight-loss product may suggest an essay on society's emphasis on thinness or the unrealistic expectations for body image presented in commercials.

Writing: Brainstorming Topics

Directions: Using the suggestions listed in Table 8-2, make a list of five possible topics you could use to write a two- to three-page, double-spaced essay.

Generate Ideas About Your Topic

■ GOAL 5
Generate ideas about your topic

Once you have chosen a working topic, the next step is to generate ideas about it. This step will help you determine whether the topic you have selected is usable. It will also provide you with a list of ideas you can use in planning and developing your essay. If you have trouble generating ideas about a topic, consider changing topics. Here are four methods for generating ideas. (See pp. 47–48 in Chapter 2 for a detailed review of each.)

1. **Freewriting.** Write nonstop for a specified time, recording all the ideas that come to mind on the topic.
2. **Brainstorming.** Write a list of all ideas that come to mind about a specific topic.
3. **Questioning.** Write a list of questions about a given topic.
4. **Branching.** Draw a diagram showing possible subtopics into which your topic could be divided.

When Ted was assigned a two-page paper on a topic of his choice, he decided to write about online social networking sites. To generate ideas, Ted used brainstorming and wrote the following list of ideas:

SOCIAL NETWORKING SITES

Keep tabs on and connect with friends

Create your own profile—describe yourself as you like

Profiles aren't necessarily true or accurate

Receive requests from people who want to friend you

People date online

People cheat on spouses through online relationships

Employers check applicants' Facebook sites

Unless blocked, private information can be seen by strangers

High school students use them too

Facebook and MySpace are popular ones

What did people do before these sites were available?

EXERCISE 8-9

WRITING IN PROGRESS

Writing: Generating Ideas

Directions: Select one of the topics you listed in Exercise 8-8. Use freewriting, brainstorming, questioning, or branching to generate ideas about the topic.

Narrowing Your Topic Further

Avoid working with a topic that is either too broad or too narrow. If your topic is too narrow, you will find you don't have enough to write about. If it is too broad, you will have too much to say, which will create several related problems:

- You will tend to write in generalities.
- You will not be able to explore each idea in detail.
- You will probably wander from topic to topic.
- You will become unfocused.

It is difficult to know if your topic is too broad, but here are a few warning signals:

- You feel overwhelmed when you try to think about the topic.
- You don't know where to start.
- You feel as if you are going in circles with ideas.
- You don't know where to stop.

You can use the ideas you generate during brainstorming, freewriting, questioning, or branching to help narrow your topic. One or more of those ideas may be a more manageable topic.

Often, more than one round of narrowing is necessary. You may need to reduce a topic several times by dividing it into smaller and smaller subtopics. You can do this by using one of the prewriting techniques again, or you can use a simple diagram to help you. After studying his brainstorming, Ted decided to write about online relationships. The following diagram shows how Ted further narrowed the topic of online relationships.

In this way, he wound up with several manageable topics related to online relationships to choose from. Finally, he decided to write about online dating relationships.

A question many students ask is, "How do I know when to stop narrowing?" For an essay, you will need at least three or four main points to support your thesis. Make sure that you have at least this number and that you can support each one with adequate detail. If you cannot do this, you'll know you have narrowed too far.

Writing: Narrowing Topics

Directions: Working with a classmate, narrow three of the following topics. Continue narrowing each one until you find a topic about which you could write a five- to seven-paragraph essay. Circle your final topic choice for each.

1. advertisements
2. spam
3. colleges
4. news reporting
5. politicians
6. wildlife preservation
7. parenting

WRITING IN PROGRESS

Writing: Narrowing a Topic

Directions: Use the topic you generated ideas about in Exercise 8-9 and narrow it to a workable topic about which you could write a five- to seven-paragraph essay.

Consider Audience, Purpose, and Tone

■ GOAL 6 Consider audience, purpose, and tone

It is important to consider your audience, purpose, and tone when planning your essay.

Considering Your Audience

A student wrote the following paragraph on preparing a dessert as part of an essay for a class assignment. His audience was his classmates.

> Of course, every meal must come to an end, which brings us to dessert. Crème brûlée makes an elegant ending to a special meal. Although crème brûlée often has a vanilla flavor, it can be infused with lavender, anise, or even cardamom. Or you may prefer chocolate instead; in that case, be sure to use couverture quality if you can find it. Once you have whisked together the ingredients, pour the mixture through a chinois. Then divide the custard among ramekins and place them in a bain-marie to bake. After the custards cool, you are ready to carmelize the tops. The brûlée should be made with turbinado sugar for best results; carmelizing the turbinado can be done easily with a butane torch or a salamander.

His classmates found the paragraph confusing. Why? This writer made a serious error: he failed to analyze his audience. He assumed they knew as much about cooking and food as he did. Readers who are not familiar with cooking techniques would need more background information. Terms specific to creating this dessert should have been defined.

Analyzing your audience is always the first step when writing any essay. It will help you decide what to say and what type of detail to include. Here are some key questions to begin your analysis:

- Is my reader familiar with the topic?
- How much background or history does my reader need to understand the information?

- Do I need to define any unfamiliar terms?
- Do I need to explain any unfamiliar people, places, events, parts, or processes?

Ted answered these questions in the following way:

- **Is my reader familiar with the topic?** Most people are familiar with Facebook and other social networking sites, although they may not know how Facebook affects the dating process.
- **How much background or history does my reader need to understand the information?** My readers need to know what Facebook allows users to do online.
- **Do I need to define any unfamiliar terms?** I might need to explain what a Flickr site is.
- **Do I need to explain any unfamiliar people, places, events, parts, or processes?** I should explain the steps I take when breaking up with someone online.

You will follow the same process that Ted did, asking and answering these questions. Suppose you are writing an essay on how to find an apartment to rent. As you plan your essay, you need to decide how much information to present. This decision involves analyzing both your audience and your purpose. First, consider how much your audience already knows about the topic. If you think your readers know a lot about renting apartments, briefly review in your essay what they already know and then move on to a more detailed explanation of new information.

On the other hand, if your topic is probably brand new to your readers, capture their interest without intimidating them. Try to relate the topic to their own experiences. Show them how renting an apartment resembles something they already know how to do. For example, you might compare renting an apartment to other types of shopping for something with certain desired features and an established price range.

If you are uncertain about your audience's background, it is safer to include information they may already know rather than to assume that they know it. Readers can skim or skip over information they know, but they cannot fill in gaps in their understanding without your help.

Considering Your Purpose

Once you have made decisions about your audience, you will want to identify your purpose. The three main purposes for writing are

- **To express yourself.** In expressive essays, you focus on your feelings and experiences. You might, for example, write an expressive essay about the value of friendship.

- **To inform.** Informative essays are written to present information. An essay on how to save money is an informative essay.
- **To persuade.** Persuasive essays attempt to convince readers to accept a particular viewpoint or take a particular action. A persuasive essay might attempt to convince you that zoos are inhumane.

When planning your essay, keep your essay focused on its purpose. Decide what you want your essay to accomplish, and focus on how to meet that goal.

EXERCISE 8-12 Defining Audience and Purpose

Directions: For each of the following topics, define at least two different audiences and purposes. Explain how your essays would differ.

1. The lack of privacy in our society
2. The value of sports
3. Balancing job and school
4. Choosing a career
5. How to make new friends

EXERCISE 8-13 Evaluating the Purpose of Ted's Essay

Directions: Identify Ted's purpose for writing his essay. How did you determine your answer?

____

____

Deciding on an Appropriate Tone

Tone means how you sound to your readers and how you feel about your topic. An essay can have a serious, argumentative, or informative tone, for example. A humorous, sarcastic, flip, or very informal tone can detract from your essay and suggest that what you say should not be taken seriously. As a general rule, your tone should reflect your relationship to your audience. The less familiar you are with your audience, the more formal your tone should be.

Here are a few examples of sentences in which the tone is inappropriate for most academic and career writing and how they could be revised to be appropriate for an academic audience.

INAPPROPRIATE	I think Taylor would be so amazing for the assistant manager job. She works really hard, she is super nice to customers, and she always shows up when she says she will.
REVISED	I highly recommend Taylor for the assistant manager job. She is reliable and hardworking, and she has excellent customer service skills.

INAPPROPRIATE	It would be great if you'd let me know about the work-study program. I'm mainly wanting to know how I'd go about working as a tutor at the community outreach center.
REVISED	Please advise me about the requirements for the work-study program. I am especially interested in becoming a tutor at the community outreach center.
INAPPROPRIATE	I freaked out when I found out my brother blew off class to go shoot hoops.
REVISED	I was upset to learn that my brother missed class to play basketball.

Follow these suggestions to help keep your tone appropriate:

1. Avoid slang expressions.
2. Use first-person pronouns (*I, me*) sparingly.
3. Make your writing sound more formal than casual conversation or a letter to a close friend.
4. To achieve a more formal tone, avoid informal or everyday words. For example:

   Use *met* instead of *ran into*.

   Use *children* instead of *kids*.

   Use *annoying* instead of *bugging*.

EXERCISE 8-14 Revising Tone

Directions: Revise each of the following statements to give it a more formal tone.

1. The new cafeteria manager changed up the menu so it's way better than it was last year.
2. The guy who runs the gym I go to is old school; he is all about weights, push-ups, and jump ropes.
3. For spring break this year, I mostly just hung out with my bros.
4. Lots of people were hating on the band at first, but by the third song everyone was out there dancing.
5. Emily Dickinson is an awesome poet; her poems are dope.

EXERCISE 8-15 Determining the Tone of Ted's Essay

Directions: What tone does Ted use in his essay? Write a list of five words or phrases that illustrate his tone. Do you think his tone is appropriate? Why, or why not?

____

____

____

Write a Thesis Statement

■ GOAL 7
Write a thesis statement

A thesis statement very rarely just springs into a writer's mind: it evolves and, in fact, may change during the process of prewriting, grouping ideas, drafting, and even revising.

Grouping Your Ideas to Discover a Thesis Statement

Once you have narrowed your topic and you know what you want to write about, the next step is to group or connect your ideas to form a thesis. Let's see how Ted produced a thesis following these steps.

First, Ted chose to freewrite on his computer about his topic of online dating to discover more ideas about it. Read his freewriting now before you continue with this section.

I use Facebook, to keep tabs on what my friends do, buy, and feel. It showed me when my friend crusaded to get his girlfriend back, that my sociology of gender prof was up at 3 a.m., and the journalism student I'm still crushing on is also a fan of Green Day. I upload videos and post links. It's an essential part of my life and relationships. Facebook owned the college crowd from its launch. Dating at U of M goes like this:

1. Get someone's name.
2. Look the person up on Facebook.
3. Use that information to decide how to proceed.

A Facebook search is the first thing I do when I meet someone. I don't trust Facebook to tell me who people are. I look through photos, check links, because what someone thinks is worth sharing is another window into who she is. I Facebook poke a friend (with boyfriend) when she crosses my mind. She does it to me too. Every relationship after my first was carried out at least partially over email and instant messaging. I met Sunshine in a public chat room and we talked via instant messaging for five years and fell in love. The relationship didn't work out, but technology made it possible. I met Maggie at a campus newspaper meeting and it was nice updating and confirming our relationship together. When we broke up, I defriended her on Facebook, blocked her on instant messenger, and took her e-mail address out of my contacts list. Breaking up was hard to do before the Internet!

Once he completed his freewriting, he highlighted usable ideas and tried to group or organize them logically. In his freewriting Ted saw three main groups of ideas: finding someone to date, dating, and breaking up, so he sorted his ideas into those categories. Once Ted had grouped his ideas into these three categories, he wrote a working thesis statement.

Working Thesis Statement: The dating process using Facebook involves screening, dating, and breaking up.

This working thesis statement identifies his topic—dating online using Facebook—and suggests that he will examine how the dating process works. You can see that this thesis statement grew out of his idea groupings.

Furthermore, this thesis statement gives readers clues as to how the essay will be organized. A reader knows from this preview the order in which steps in the dating process will be discussed.

Tips for Grouping Ideas

How do you know which ideas to group? Look for connections and relationships among the ideas that you generate during prewriting. Here are some suggestions:

Tips for Grouping Ideas

1. **Look for categories.** Think of categories as titles or slots in which ideas can be placed. Look for a general term that is broad enough to cover several of your ideas. For example, suppose you are writing a paper on where sexual discrimination occurs. You could break down the topic by location.

SAMPLE THESIS STATEMENT	Sexual discrimination exists in the workplace, in social situations, and in politics.

2. **Try organizing your ideas chronologically.** Group your ideas according to the clock or calendar. Ted organized the dating process in the order in which it happens, from start to finish.

SAMPLE THESIS STATEMENT	Tracing metal working from its early beginnings in history to modern times reveals certain social and economic patterns.

3. **Look for similarities and differences.** When working with two or more topics, see if they can be approached by looking at how similar or different they are.

SAMPLE THESIS STATEMENT	Two early biologists, Darwin and Mendel, held similar views about evolution.

4. **Separate your ideas into causes and effects or problems and solutions.** Events and issues can often be analyzed in this way.

SAMPLE THESIS STATEMENT	Both employer and employees must work together to improve low morale in an office.

5. **Divide your ideas into advantages and disadvantages or pros and cons.** When you are evaluating a proposal, product, or service, this approach may work.

SAMPLE THESIS STATEMENT	Playing on a college sports team has many advantages but also several serious drawbacks.

6. **Consider several different ways to approach your topic or organize and develop your ideas.** As you consider what your thesis statement is going to be, push yourself to see your topic from a number of different angles or a fresh perspective. For example, Ted could have considered how online dating differs from traditional dating, or he could have examined his freewriting and decided to focus on his personal history using Facebook to date.

Writing an Effective Thesis Statement

Think of your thesis statement as a promise; it promises your reader what your paper will deliver. Here are some guidelines to follow for writing an effective thesis statement:

Guidelines for Writing an Effective Thesis Statement

1. **It should state the main point of your essay.** It should not focus on details; it should give an overview of your approach to your topic.

TOO DETAILED	A well-written business letter has no errors in spelling.
REVISED	To write a grammatically correct business letter, follow three simple rules.

2. **It should assert an idea about your topic.** Your thesis should express a viewpoint or state an approach to the topic.

LACKS AN ASSERTION	Advertising contains images of both men and women.
REVISED	In general, advertising presents men more favorably than women.

3. **It should be as specific and detailed as possible.** For this reason, it is important to review and rework your thesis *after* you have written and revised drafts.

TOO GENERAL	Advertisers can influence readers' attitudes toward competing products.
REVISED	Athletic-shoe advertisers focus more on attitude and image than on the actual physical differences between their product and those of their competitors.

4. **It may suggest the organization of your essay.** Mentioning key points that will be discussed in the essay is one way to do this. The order in which you mention them should be the order in which you discuss them in your essay.

DOES NOT SUGGEST ORGANIZATION	Public-school budget cuts will negatively affect education.
REVISED	Public-school budget cuts will negatively affect academic achievement, student motivation, and the drop-out rate.

5. **It should not be a direct announcement.** Do not begin with phrases such as "In this paper I will" or "My assignment was to discuss."

DIRECT ANNOUNCEMENT	The purpose of my paper is to show that businesses lose money due to inefficiency, competition, and inflated labor costs.
REVISED	Businesses lose money due to inefficiency, competition, and inflated labor costs.

6. **It should offer a fresh, interesting, and original perspective on the topic.** A thesis statement can follow the guidelines above, but if it seems dull or predictable, it needs more work.

PREDICTABLE	Circus acts fall into three categories: animal, clown, and acrobatic.
REVISED	Each of the three categories of circus acts—animal, clown, and acrobatic—is exciting because of the risks it involves.

WRITING IN PROGRESS

Writing: Writing a Thesis, Defining Purpose and Audience, and Generating Ideas

Directions: For the topic you chose in Exercise 8-11, write a working thesis statement, define your purpose and audience, and generate additional ideas to include in your essay.

Plan and Organize Your Essay

■ GOAL 8
Plan and organize your essay

Planning pays off when it comes to essay writing. The more you think through your essay before you write it, the easier the actual writing will be. You have defined your audience and purpose and created a working thesis statement. This section will show you how to use your thesis statement to guide the rest of your planning.

Using Outlining and Idea Mapping

Outlining is one good way to organize your ideas, discover the relationships and connections between them, and show their relative importance. As you learned in Chapter 1, an outline generally follows a format that begins with your first major idea, followed by supporting details, your second major idea followed by supporting details, and so on. Here is a working outline of Ted's essay.

Working Thesis Statement: The dating process using Facebook involves screening, dating, and breaking up.

A. First stage of online dating
   1. Get someone's name.
   2. Look up the person on Facebook.
   3. Use that information to decide how to proceed.

4. Drawback of screening someone online
   a. Tons of information is given with no context
   b. Checking information with the person means you have been snooping

B. Dating online versus dating in person
   1. online communication not the same as in person
   2. Facebook can promote infidelity

C. Breaking up is hard but easier on Internet
   1. block instant messenger
   2. delete email address from quick contacts
   3. defriend on Facebook

Another way to write a solid, effective essay is to plan its development using an idea map, a list of the ideas you will discuss in the order you will present them. Here is a partial idea map for Ted's essay on online dating.

VISUALIZE IT!

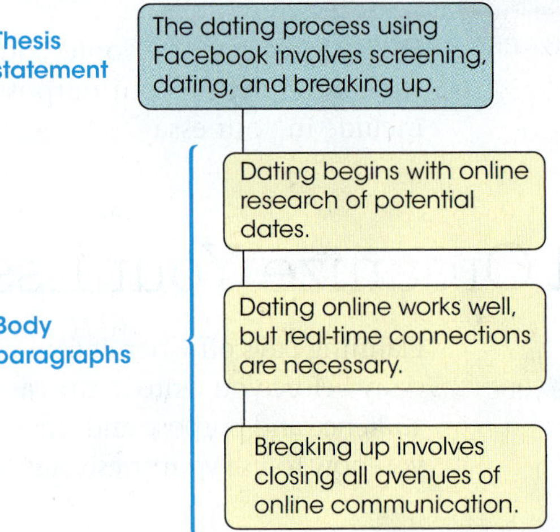

EXERCISE 8-17

WRITING IN PROGRESS

Writing: Drawing a Map or Outline

Directions: For the ideas you generated in Exercise 8-16, draw a map or outline connecting your ideas.

Obtaining Complete and Correct Information

At times, you know enough about your topic to explain it clearly and completely. At other times, however, you need additional information. For ideas on how to locate, use, and document sources, consult Chapter 11, "Writing Essays Using Sources."

Organizing Your Essay

Analyzing your audience and purpose will also help you choose which pattern or patterns of organization to use. Essays use the patterns of organization that you learned about in Chapters 5 and Chapter 6: *chronological order*, *process*, *narration*, *description, example, definition, classification, comparison and contrast,* and *cause and effect.* You can select the one that suits your audience and purpose best.

Ted's essay on online dating uses the chronological order pattern. Your pattern of organization depends on your purpose. See Table 8-3 for examples. You may also use more than one of these patterns of organization. You might define a behavior and then offer examples to explain it. Or you might explain how a group of people are classified and then discuss similarities and differences between the classifications.

TABLE 8-3 CHOOSING A PATTERN OF ORGANIZATION

If Your Purpose Is to . . .	Use . . .
Explain events in the order they occurred	Chronological order (see Chapter 5)
Tell a story that makes a point	Narration (see Chapter 5)
Present a visual or sensory image	Description (see Chapter 5)
Explain how something works or how to perform a specific task	Process (see Chapter 5)
Explain a topic, using specific examples	Example (see Chapter 5)
Explain what something is	Definition (see Chapter 6)
Explain a topic by showing the parts into which it can be divided or the group to which it belongs	Classification (see Chapter 6)
Emphasize similarities or differences between two topics or explain something by comparing it to something already familiar	Comparison and Contrast (see Chapter 6)
Explain why something happened	Cause and Effect (see Chapter 6)

READ AND RESPOND: A Student Essay

Relationships 2.0: Dating and Relating in the Internet Age

Ted Sawchuck

The questions and activities below refer to Ted's freewriting on page 258.

Examining Writing

1. What other ideas do you see in Ted's freewriting that might be used to write an essay with a different focus?
2. What pattern of organization could Ted use to organize his essay?

Writing Assignments

Assume you are taking the course "Interpersonal Communication Skills." In addition to tests and quizzes, your instructor requires two papers. For your first paper, choose one of the assignments below, and use one method of prewriting to generate ideas about it. Then review your prewriting, try to group your ideas, and write a working thesis statement.

1. Watch a portion of a television program with the sound turned off. If you could understand what was happening, write a paper explaining how you knew.
2. Suppose you are applying for a full-time job today and your prospective employer asks you to describe your "people skills." Write an essay answering the employer's question.
3. We encounter conflict in our daily lives. Write a paper describing a recent conflict you had and how you and the other person handled the situation.
4. Describe a communication breakdown between you and another person. Why did it happen? Could it possibly have been prevented? How?
5. Describe a situation in which a person's body language (gestures, posture, facial expressions) allowed you to understand what he or she was really saying. Describe the body language and what it told you.

READ AND RESPOND: A Professional Essay

Mind Your Own Browser

Simson L. Garfinkel

Writing in Response to Reading

Checking your Comprehension MySkillsLab®

Answer each of the following questions using complete sentences.

1. Describe the FTC's recommendation and explain why the author believes this approach does not do enough to protect consumer privacy.
2. What is behavioral advertising?
3. What are two risks to unrestricted tracking?
4. What are privacy policies supposed to do? According to the FTC, why don't privacy policies work?
5. What are the two options currently available to consumers who want to limit or prevent tracking?
6. How does the author say the problem can be resolved?

Strengthening Your Vocabulary MySkillsLab®

Identify at least five words used in the reading that are unfamiliar to you. Using context, word parts, or a dictionary, write a brief definition of each word.

Examining the Reading: Drawing an Idea Map

Create an idea map of the reading that starts with the title and thesis and then lists the author's main points. Use the guidelines on page 15.

Reading and Writing: An Integrated Perspective MySkillsLab®

Get ready to write about the reading by discussing the following:

1. How effective is the title? What other title might work for this subject?
2. Evaluate the opening paragraph of the reading. How does it reveal both what the essay is about and how the author feels about the subject?
3. What is the author's purpose in writing this essay? In your opinion, does he achieve his purpose? Write a journal entry explaining your answers.
4. What is the author's thesis? Express it in your own words.
5. Evaluate the types of evidence the author uses to support his thesis. Which evidence is most effective or convincing? What other evidence might he have included?
6. Discuss the author's tone and how he reveals his feelings about his subject. For example, why does he describe the government's approach to protecting consumer privacy as "peculiar" (paragraph 6)?

THINKING VISUALLY

7. Explain the purpose of the illustration that accompanies the reading. How does it reinforce the essay's thesis?
8. Do you agree that privacy policies and user agreements are long and incomprehensible? Discuss whether you typically read and are able to understand the information. Why or why not?

Thinking and Writing Critically MySkillsLab®

1. In the list of suggestions for choosing your own topic for an essay (p. 253), "Choose a topic that interests you" and "Write about something familiar" are listed. How can you tell that the topic of this essay—the ineffectiveness of consumer privacy protections—interests the author? How is the author familiar with his topic?
2. Who is the author's intended audience? What background information might the audience need to understand this essay?
3. How would you go about verifying the information presented in this essay? What sources would you consult to read more about the topic?
4. Do you think there is bias in this reading? Why or why not? Find examples if you believe there is. (For more about bias, see Chapter 13, p. 381.)
5. What inferences can you make based on this selection? For example, what types of privacy controls do you think advertisers want? (For more about making inferences, see Chapter 12, p. 346.)

Writing Paragraphs MySkillsLab®

1. Do you think behaviorally targeted ads are beneficial to consumers? Write a paragraph explaining why or why not.

2. Were you aware that your online interests and activities were being tracked on sites such as Facebook? Write a paragraph describing your response to this information.

3. How important is it to you to protect your privacy online? Write a paragraph answering that question and describing what actions you take to protect your privacy.

Writing Essays MySkillsLab®

4. Write an essay evaluating the author's suggestions for resolving the problem of tracking. Do you believe his ideas would work? Why or why not? What actions would you be willing to take to limit companies' access to your information?

5. What responsibility does the government have toward consumer protection online? What responsibility do businesses have toward their consumers? What is your own personal responsibility regarding your online privacy? Write an essay addressing each of these questions.

6. The author says that "the advertising industry fiercely opposes tracking restrictions" and any reform will be resisted. Imagine that you must convince the advertising industry to accept tracking restrictions and write a persuasive essay detailing why industry should do so.

SELF-TEST SUMMARY

To test yourself, cover the Answer column with a sheet of paper and answer each question listed in the left column, Evaluate each of your answers as you work by sliding the paper down and comparing your answer with what is printed in the Answer column.

QUESTION	ANSWER
■ GOAL 1 Understand the purpose of an essay What do essays do, and how are essays organized?	An essay introduces an idea, states it, explains it, and draws a conclusion about it. Essays include an introductory paragraph and thesis statement, supporting paragraphs, and a conclusion.
■ GOAL 2 Read essays effectively How can you read essays effectively?	Examine each part of the essay closely, assess the author's credentials, consider any background information that is provided, express the thesis in your own words, and identify the organizational pattern.
■ GOAL 3 Express your ideas in essay form Why do you write essays?	Essays allow you to express your ideas in an organized structure aimed at a specific audience. The structure of an essay is similar to that of a paragraph except that an essay requires an introduction and conclusion.

(continued)

(*continued*)

QUESTION	ANSWER
■ GOAL 4 Choose a topic How do you develop an assigned topic?	For an assigned topic, determine the purpose of the assignment, connect it to classroom instruction, and watch for clue words suggesting how to write and organize your essay.
How do you choose your own topic?	For your own topic, take your time choosing a topic that interests you and is familiar, and use sources of ideas listed in Table 8-2 on page 251.
■ GOAL 5 Generate ideas about your topic How do you generate ideas and narrow your topic?	Generate ideas by freewriting, brainstorming, questioning, and branching. Narrow your topic into subtopics until you find one that is manageable. A diagram can help you reduce a topic as well.
■ GOAL 6 Consider audience, purpose, and tone How do you analyze your audience?	Analyze your audience by considering how much readers know about the topic; try to relate the topic to readers' own experiences.
What are the three main purposes for writing?	The three main purposes for writing are to express yourself, to inform, and to persuade.
What does *tone* mean?	**Tone** means how you sound to your readers and how you feel about your topic; your tone should reflect your relationship to your audience.
■ GOAL 7 Write a thesis statement What makes a thesis statement effective?	An effective thesis statement ■ states the main point of your essay. ■ expresses an idea about your topic. ■ is specific and detailed. ■ may suggest the organization of the essay. ■ is not a direct announcement. ■ offers a fresh perspective on your topic.
■ GOAL 8 Plan and organize your essay What is involved in planning and organizing your essay?	Planning your essay involves ■ using outlining and mapping to organize your ideas. ■ obtaining complete and correct information about your topic. Organizing your essay involves analyzing your audience and purpose to help you choose the most appropriate pattern of organization for your essay. See Table 8-3 on page 263 for a list of patterns of organization.

MySkillsLab®

Visit **Chapter 8, "Reading, Planning, and Organizing Essays,"** in MySkillsLab to test your understanding of chapter goals.

9 Drafting and Revising Essays

LEARNING GOALS

Learn how to . . .

- **GOAL 1** Draft an essay
- **GOAL 2** Read while drafting an essay
- **GOAL 3** Write and revise the body of an essay
- **GOAL 4** Write introductions, conclusions, and titles
- **GOAL 5** Think critically as you revise your draft
- **GOAL 6** Edit and proofread

THINK About It!

Study the photograph above, showing wind turbines in operation. Write a sentence that states your view on whether wind turbines are worthwhile and efficient energy sources.

The sentence you have written could be the thesis statement for an essay on wind turbines. You might have written that wind turbines are an important alternative energy source and more turbines should be built. Or you might have stated that wind turbines are unreliable and inefficient and should be phased out. Or perhaps you felt you did not know enough about wind turbines, their problems or benefits, and decided you needed to research the topic.

After reading about the issue, maybe you decided that wind turbines are a viable alternative energy sources and drafted a thesis statement saying that wind turbines, despite variable energy production rates, have benefits that far outweigh their disadvantages and should be a further developed as an alternative energy source. Regardless of the thesis you wrote you would need to reread and reevaluate it as your essay developed. Likewise, the evidence you offer in support of your thesis needs to be drafted, evaluated and revised. This chapter will focus on skills for drafting, revising, editing, and proofreading an essay.

Reading and Writing Connections

EVERYDAY CONNECTIONS

- **Reading** You read a letter from your insurance agent suggesting adding coverage to your homeowner's insurance policy.
- **Writing** You write a letter requesting reconsideration of an insurance claim that was denied.

ACADEMIC CONNECTIONS

- **Reading** You read a section of your art history textbook describing American folk art, craft, and design.
- **Writing** You write an essay for your art history course describing your visit to a folk art exhibit at a local gallery.

WORKPLACE CONNECTIONS

- **Reading** You read the prospectus, or business plan, of a company you are planning to visit as part of a sales trip.
- **Writing** You write a report summarizing activities and outcomes of a recent sales trip.

What Is a Draft?

■ GOAL 1
Draft an essay

A **draft** is a tentative or preliminary version of an essay. You should plan to write several drafts and to read and evaluate them carefully before you end up with an essay you are satisfied with. Use the following general suggestions for getting started (also refer to the tips for drafting in Chapter 2 on page 55); then work on drafting each paragraph as described on the following pages.

Tips for Drafting Essays

- **Leave time between your drafts.** If you try to write too many drafts in one sitting, you may find it difficult to sort them all out and see the strengths and weaknesses of each one.
- **Think of drafting as a chance to experiment.** Find out what works and what does not. You might want to write your essay several different ways, trying out different approaches, different content, and different ways of organizing the information.
- **Focus on ideas, not correctness.** Especially for the first few drafts, concentrate on recording your ideas. Do not worry yet about grammatical errors or sentence structure, for example.
- **Be prepared to make major changes.** Often as your essay develops, you may realize that you want to change direction or that you should further limit your topic. Do not hesitate to do so.

Read While Drafting

■ GOAL 2
Read while drafting an essay

Reading, rereading, analyzing, and evaluating are all important parts of drafting an essay and preparing to revise it. To be an effective writer, you have to read and think critically about your draft, considering whether your draft says what you want it to say and whether it does so clearly and effectively. Rereading will help you

- stay focused on the topic.
- realize where you need to add further explanation or support.
- decide when to start a new paragraph.
- know when transitions are needed to connect your ideas.
- recognize when you repeat yourself.
- recognize that you need to think more about organization.

Write and Revise the Body of an Essay

■ GOAL 3
Write and revise the body of an essay

Drafting involves expressing your thesis statement and supporting it with evidence. At various stages in the drafting process, you may decide to rewrite, revise, or completely change your thesis statement. Remember, a thesis statement should explain what your essay is about and also give your readers clues about its organization. You may not know, for example, how your essay will be organized until you have written one or more drafts. (See Chapter 8, pp. 258–261 for more details on thesis statements.)

Drafting Body Paragraphs

Once you have a working thesis statement, you are ready to start planning and writing the individual paragraphs of your essay. It is often best to start with the body of the essay, those paragraphs that provide the support for your thesis statement. There are a number of different ways you can begin drafting the body of your essay. Some students write an outline; others draw a graphic organizer; still others write a list of topic sentences that support the thesis. Don't worry too much about the order of the items in your draft. At this point it is more important to get your ideas down in writing. In later drafts you can rearrange your ideas.

Once you have identified topics or topic sentences that support your thesis, you are ready to write first-draft paragraphs. These, too, may change, so concentrate primarily on making sure that each topic sentence supports the thesis and that each paragraph has a clear topic sentence (see Chapter 3), supporting details (see Chapter 4), and transitions (see Chapter 4).

EXAMINING STUDENT WRITING

In Chapter 8, we followed student writer Ted Sawchuck in planning and organizing an essay on online dating. In this chapter we will observe how Ted drafted, revised, and proofread his essay. Here is the initial list of topic sentences Ted wrote for the first draft of his online dating essay.

Facebook owns the college crowd and is widely popular for dating.
Here's how the dating process works at the U. of Maryland.
I use Facebook to check someone out.
Dating works well online initially, but cannot compare with face-to-face contact.
Facebook can encourage infidelity.
Breaking up was hard to do before the Internet.

You will see that he changed, added, and expanded these topic sentences as he wrote his first draft, which appears on page 274.

Supporting Your Thesis with Substantial Evidence

Every essay you write should offer substantial evidence in support of your thesis statement. This evidence makes up the body of your essay. **Evidence** can consist of personal experience, anecdotes (stories that illustrate a point), examples, reasons, descriptions, facts, statistics, and quotations (taken from sources).

Many students have trouble locating concrete, specific evidence to support their thesis. Though prewriting yields plenty of good ideas and helps you focus your thesis, prewriting ideas may not always provide sufficient evidence. Often you need to brainstorm again for additional ideas. At other times, you may need to consult one or more sources to obtain further information on your topic (see Chapter 11, p. 326).

Ted realized that he did not have enough evidence to support his thesis on online dating. Table 9-1 lists ways to support a thesis statement and gives an example of how Ted could use each in his essay.

TABLE 9-1 WAYS TO ADD EVIDENCE

Topic: Online Dating	
Explain Your Thesis by . . .	**Example**
Telling a story (narration)	Relate a story about an online dating experience.
Adding descriptive detail (description)	Add a description of a social network profile.
Explaining how something works (process)	Explain how a person can change his or her relationship status on Facebook.
Giving an example	Discuss specific instances of prescreening a potential date using Google.
Discussing types or kinds (classification)	Discuss types of profiles people create of themselves.
Giving a definition	Explain the meaning of terms such as *profile, poking,* or *defriending.*
Making distinctions	Contrast prescreening a date online and without the use of a computer.
Making comparisons	Compare two social networking sites.
Giving reasons	Explain why breaking up is difficult when so many online connections exist.
Analyzing effects	Explain how online profiles can be misleading.

Each example in this table is a way for Ted to add evidence to his essay. But he does not need to use all of them; instead, he should choose the ones that are most appropriate for his audience and purpose. Ted could also use different types of evidence in combination. For example, he could *tell a story* that illustrates the *effects* of misleading online profiles.

Use the following guidelines in selecting evidence to support your thesis:

Guidelines for Selecting Evidence to Support Your Thesis

1. **Be sure your evidence is relevant.** That is, it must directly support or explain your thesis.
2. **Make your evidence as specific as possible.** Help your readers see the point you are making by offering detailed, concrete information. For example, if you are explaining the effects of right-to-privacy violations on an individual, include details that make the situation come alive: names of people and places, types of violations, and so forth.
3. **Be sure your information is accurate.** It may be necessary to check facts, verify stories you have heard, and ask questions of individuals who have provided information.
4. **Locate sources that provide evidence.** Because you may not know enough about your topic and lack personal experience, you may be unable to provide strong evidence. When this happens, locate several sources on your topic. Consult Chapter 11, page 331, for information on synthesizing sources.
5. **Be sure to document any information that you borrow from other sources.** See Chapter 11, page 334, for further information on crediting sources.

Now let's take a look at how Ted developed his essay on online dating. As you read, notice, in particular, the types of evidence he uses and how his thesis statement promises what his essay should deliver. In this first draft he uses his freewriting from page 258 and his list of topic sentences on page 273.

Ted's First Draft

Facebook is a social networking Internet site. It allows a user to connect with people, make friends, and join interest groups using the convenience of their own computer. It also allows a user to learn more information about said friends, as well as post text, photos, video, links, and information.

Facebook has become widely popular. Much has been written about it in my student newspaper, but no one has yet dug into what the site has done to change our relationships, and specifically the dating process. The dating process has changed dramatically since Facebook came on the scene. *The dating process using Facebook involves screening, dating, and breaking up.*

I know when Facebook friends break up, fail tests, and hate their parents, but I don't really know them as people, just infobits on an LCD. The dating process works well initially over this medium, but real connections are only formed with substantial time-spending, preferably in person. Online talks, even via Skype or webcam, are still only a fraction of the experience and do not convey as high a percentage of the information one can glean during an in-person encounter.

At the University of Maryland, the dating process begins like this: get someone's name; look him or her up on Facebook; use that information to decide how to proceed. When I meet someone and she sets off those neurons that make me hum "Maybe it's love," I do a Facebook search. A profile page will tell me her age, indicate whether or not she's taken, and give me a decent idea (if the profile is not privacy protected) of what image she's trying to present. Note that I don't trust Facebook to tell me who people are—merely who they want to show people they are. I look through photos and see what they value enough to show me. I check posted links because what someone thinks is worth sharing is another window into who she is. On Facebook, everyone seems reduced to a set of bullet points—"goth, tall, cat person"—that we rely on before even meeting someone. In real life, careful observation can reveal truths about people they won't discuss, especially things they don't want known.

After using Facebook to research the person, I have a decent idea of whether she's a probable friend or romantic interest. Next I hit Google—first searching with her e-mail address, then with her name, then with her nickname if I have reason to believe the person I'm into uses the Internet for more than e-mail. This turns up message boards, possibly her blog, and maybe even a Flickr site, all worth plumbing for details about my new fascination.

I have serious doubts as to whether being able to download someone's self with a little searching on Facebook and Google is actually a good thing for beginning relationships. For one, online searches result in tons of information with absolutely no context. Judging what you learn without cross-referencing it with the person him- or herself is a recipe for misinterpretative disaster, yet checking means admitting you've been snooping. I snoop anyway.

Internet access means access to your romantic interest, even during work in many cases. E-mail replaces IM for quick messages because many jobs require e-mail use. The Internet lets you do couples things like play Scrabble or check up on each other regardless of distance.

Time spent communicating with someone, especially just one person, can build connections that lead to relationships or strengthen current ones. Although Skyping someone is about as emotionally satisfying as being courteously deferential, you still get to hear his or her voice. Tone, pauses, nuance, and volume are all stripped from instant messages—at least Skype gives you those back. Human laughter beats "LOL" in pixels any day, but holding her while she tells you about her day wins whenever possible.

Facebook can also provoke new frontiers of infidelity. One way is through chatting online. It's very poor form to chat up someone else's girlfriend in a bar, but when chatting online there's no boyfriend looming over you to enforce her morality. Combine that freedom with the very personal qualities of online relationships and the large amount of time most people spend online and you've got a formula anyone who's dating anyone who gets online should worry about.

The poke feature is another way Facebook can promote infidelity. One of my friends who has a boyfriend uses it to let me know when she's thinking about me. It amounts to several pokes a day, and she receives one when she crosses my mind. She does it to let me know she's thinking about me frequently, which is great for me and not so hot for her boyfriend.

(*continued*)

(*continued*)

Breaking up is hard to do, but the Internet makes it easier. You don't want to get a continually updated feed of information about that person. Knowing someone's getting over you and trying to date is one thing; knowing they're doing it at seven-thirty at Club Kozmo with someone they met last weekend is another.

After I leave someone, he or she disappears from instant messaging, my e-mail contacts, Facebook friends, and my web bookmarks. Forget one step and the "getting over her" process becomes that much harder. There's a measure of comfort to be found in thinking someone's fallen off the face of the earth romantically, especially if your return to dating hasn't been as successful. After the relationship ends, I like the flood of data the Internet provides much less than in my prescreening stage.

That level of cutting someone off requires an amount of effort commonly reserved for reporters on deadline or college students who fell asleep before they got to the all-nighter. You become like a recovering alcoholic, not just avoiding them in person. Certain sites take on new meaning. Any bit of forgotten information is another barb, another pang, another realization. Invariably, you'll miss something and see a status update or a text message or a voice mail. It helps at times, when missing someone so badly means wishing the person were dead. Once you get over it, refriend the person if you can do it without going crazy. Sometimes a little bit of ignorance can be blissful indeed, but most connections are worth preserving.

Evaluating a Draft

Directions: Working with a classmate, evaluate Ted's first draft. What problems do you see? What revisions does he need to make? Assume you are working together as peer reviewers (see Chapter 2, p. 58). Write a response to Ted, explaining both the strengths and weaknesses of his first draft.

Writing a First Draft

Directions: Using your working thesis statement from Chapter 8, Exercise 8-16 as a guide, draft at least three body paragraphs of an essay. Support your thesis statement with at least three types of evidence.

Using Transitions to Make Connections

To produce a well-written essay, be sure to make it clear how your ideas relate to one another. There are several ways to do this:

1. **Use transitional words and phrase to make your essay flow smoothly and to communicate clearly.** Table 9-2 lists useful transitions for each method of organization. Notice the use of these transitional words and phrases in Ted's first draft: *next, for one, although, another, after.*
2. **Write a transitional sentence.** This sentence is usually the first or last sentence in a paragraph. It might come before the topic sentence or it might *be*

the topic sentence. Its purpose is to link the paragraph in which it appears with the paragraph before or after it.

3. **Repeat key words.** Repeating key words also enables your reader to stay on track. Key words often appear in your thesis statement, and, by repeating some of them, you remind your reader of your thesis and how each new idea is connected to it.

You need not repeat the word or phrase exactly as long as the meaning stays the same. You could substitute "keeps your audience on target" for "enables your reader to stay on track," for example. The following excerpt from Ted's essay on online dating illustrates the use of key-word repetition.

Facebook can also provoke new frontiers of infidelity. One way is through chatting online. It's very poor form to chat up someone else's girlfriend in a bar, but when chatting online there's no boyfriend looming over you to enforce her morality. Combine that freedom with the very personal qualities of online relationships and the large amount of time most people spend online and you've got a formula anyone who's dating anyone who gets online should worry about.

TABLE 9-2 USEFUL TRANSITIONAL WORDS AND PHRASES

Type of Connection	Transitional Words and Phrases
Importance	*most important, above all, especially, particularly important*
Spatial relationships	*above, below, behind, beside, next to, inside, outside, to the west (north, etc.), beneath, near, nearby, under, over*
Time sequences	*first, next, now, before, during, eventually, finally, at last, later, meanwhile, soon, then, suddenly, currently, after, afterward, after a while, as soon as, until*
Recounting events or steps	*first, second, then, later, in the beginning, when, while, after, following, next, during, again, after that, at last, finally*
Examples	*for example, for instance, to illustrate, in one case*
Types	*one, another, second, third*
Definitions	*means, can be defined as, refers to, is*
Similarities	*likewise, similarly, in the same way, too, also*
Differences	*however, on the contrary, unlike, on the other hand, although, even though, but, in contrast, yet*
Causes or results	*because, consequently, since, as a result, for this reason, therefore, thus*
Restatement	*in other words, that is*
Summary or conclusion	*finally, to sum up, all in all, evidently, in conclusion*

EXERCISE 9-3

WRITING IN PROGRESS

Analyzing a Draft

Directions: Review the draft you wrote for Exercise 9-2. Analyze how effectively you have connected your ideas. Add key words or transitional words, phrases, or sentences, as needed.

Write the Introduction, Conclusion, and Title

■ GOAL 4
Write introductions, conclusions, and titles

The introduction, conclusion, and title of an essay each serve a specific function. Each strengthens your essay and helps your reader understand your ideas.

Writing the Introduction

Although your introductory paragraph appears first in your essay, it does *not* need to be written first. In fact, it is sometimes best to write it last, after you have developed your ideas, written your thesis statement, and drafted your essay. An **introductory paragraph** has three main purposes:

- to capture your reader's interest.
- to provide any necessary background information.
- to present your thesis statement.

Here are some suggestions on how to interest your readers in your topic.

Techniques for Writing Introductions

TECHNIQUE	EXAMPLE
Ask a provocative or controversial question.	*What would you do if you were sound asleep and woke to find a burglar in your bedroom?*
State a startling fact or statistic.	*Did you know that the federal government recently spent $$687,000 on a research project that studied the effect of Valium on monkeys?*
Begin with a story or an anecdote.	*Mark Brown, a social worker, has spent several evenings riding in a police cruiser to learn about neighborhood problems.*
Use a quotation.	*Oscar Wilde once said, "Always forgive your enemies—nothing annoys them so much."*
State a little-known fact, a myth, or a misconception.	*It's hard to lose weight and even harder to keep it off. Right? Wrong! A sensible eating program will help you lose weight.*

Note: A straightforward, dramatic thesis statement can also capture your reader's interest, as in the following example:

My new Facebook friend rapidly became my new Facebook nightmare.

An introduction should also provide the reader with any necessary background information. Consider what information your reader needs to understand your essay. You may, for example, need to define the term *genetic engineering* for a paper on that topic. At other times, you might need to provide a brief history or give an overview of a controversial issue. Ted provided a definition of what

Facebook is and how it works in the introduction to the final version of his essay (see p. 247).

Writing thesis statements was discussed in Chapter 8 (see p. 258); most instructors prefer them to appear near or at the end of your introductory paragraph.

EXERCISE 9-4
WRITING IN PROGRESS

Writing an Introduction

Directions: Write, or revise, an introduction to the essay you wrote for Exercise 9-2.

Writing the Conclusion

The **concluding paragraph** of your essay has two functions: It should reemphasize your thesis statement by reminding the reader of it and its main points. It should also draw the essay to a close. It should not be a direct announcement, such as "This essay has been about" or "In this paper I hoped to show that." Ted ended the final draft of his essay with a conclusion that acknowledged how painful breaking up can be but with the suggestion that is worth trying to stay friends with ex-partners (see p. 248).

It's usually best to revise your essay at least once *before* working on the conclusion. During your first or second revision, you often make numerous changes in both content and organization, which may, in turn, affect your conclusion. Here are a few effective ways to write a conclusion. Choose one that will work for your essay:

Effective Ways to Write a Conclusion

1. **Suggest a new direction for further thought.** Raise a related issue that you did not address in your essay, or ask a series of questions.
2. **Look ahead.** Project into the future. Consider outcomes or effects.
3. **Return to your thesis.** If your essay is written to prove a point or convince your reader of the need for action, it may be effective to end with a sentence that recalls your main point or calls for action. If you choose this way to conclude, don't merely repeat your first paragraph. Be sure to reflect on the thoughts you developed in the body of your essay.
4. **Summarize key points.** Especially for longer essays, briefly review your key supporting ideas. In shorter essays, this tends to be unnecessary.

If you have trouble writing your conclusion, you may need to work further on your thesis or organization.

EXERCISE 9-5
WRITING IN PROGRESS

Writing a Conclusion

Directions: Write or revise a conclusion for the essay you wrote for Exercise 9-2.

Selecting a Title

Although the title appears first in your essay, it is often the last thing you should write. The **title** should identify the topic in an interesting way, and it may also suggest the focus, and capture the reader's attention. To select a title, reread your final draft, paying particular attention to your thesis statement and your overall method of development. Here are a few examples of effective titles:

- "Surprise in the Vegetable Bin" (for an essay on vegetables and their effects on cholesterol and cancer)
- "Denim Goes High Fashion" (for an essay describing the uses of denim for clothing other than jeans)
- "Babies Go to Work" (for an essay on corporate-sponsored day-care centers)

Tips for Writing Accurate and Interesting Titles

1. **Write a question that your essay answers.** For example: "Why Change the Minimum Wage?"
2. **Use key words that appear in your thesis statement.** If your thesis statement is "The new international trade ruling threatens the safety of the dolphin, one of our most intelligent mammals," your title could be "New Threat to Dolphins."
3. **Use brainstorming techniques to generate options.** Don't necessarily use the first title that pops into your mind. If in doubt, try out some options on friends to see which is most effective.

WRITING IN PROGRESS

Selecting a Title

Directions: Come up with a good title for the essay you wrote for Exercise 9-2.

Think Critically About and Revise Your Draft

■ GOAL 5
Think critically as you revise your draft

The first step in preparing to revise a draft is to read it critically to find out what works and what does not. Thinking critically about your draft involves examining, evaluating, and revising your ideas as well as the content and structure of your draft.

Examining Your Ideas

Revising is a process of closely evaluating your draft to determine whether it accomplishes what you want it to. This is the time to be sure the essay says what you want it to say and that it does so in a clear and effective way. Later, once you are confident that your ideas are expressed clearly, you can move to editing, in which you make sure your essay is error free.

General Essay Revision Strategies

Here are some general suggestions for revising your final essay draft. Also refer to the Tips for Revising box in Chapter 2, page 58, and the strategies for revising paragraphs presented in Chapter 7.

- **Allow time between finishing your last draft and revising, if possible.** When you return to the draft, you will have a clear mind and a new perspective.

- **Look for common problems.** If you usually have trouble, for example, with writing thesis statements or with using transitions, then evaluate these features closely each time you revise.
- **Read the draft aloud.** You may hear ideas that are unclear or realize they are not fully explained.
- **Ask a friend to read your paper aloud to you.** If the person hesitates or seems confused or misreads, he or she may be having trouble grasping your ideas. Reread and revise any trouble spots.
- **Read a print copy.** Although you may be used to writing on a computer, your essay may read differently when you see a paper copy.

Using Revision Maps to Revise

In Chapter 7, you learned to draw revision maps to evaluate paragraphs. The same strategy works well for essays, too. A revision map will help you evaluate the overall flow of ideas as well as the effectiveness of individual paragraphs.

To draw an essay revision map, work through each paragraph, recording your ideas in abbreviated form, as shown below. Then write the key words of your conclusion. If you find details that do not support the topic sentence, record those details to the right of the map.

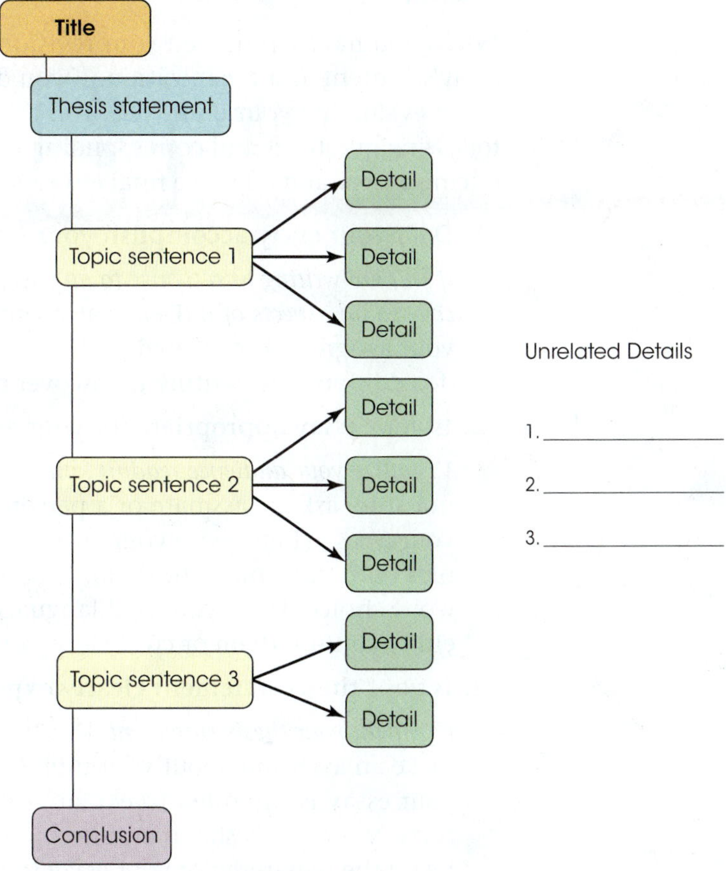

When you've completed your revision map, conduct the following tests:

1. **Read your thesis statement along with your first topic sentence.** Does the topic sentence clearly support your thesis? If not, revise to make the relationship clearer. Repeat this step for each topic sentence.

2. **Read your topic sentences, one after the other, without corresponding details.** Is there a logical connection between them? Are they arranged in the most effective way? If not, revise to make the connection clearer or to improve your organization.
3. **Examine each individual paragraph.** Are there enough relevant, specific details to support the topic sentence?
4. **Read your introduction and then look at your topic sentences.** Does the essay deliver what the introduction promises?
5. **Read your thesis statement and then your conclusion.** Are they compatible and consistent? Does the conclusion agree with and support the thesis statement?

EXERCISE 9-7

WRITING IN PROGRESS

Drawing a Revision Map

Directions: Draw a revision map of the essay you wrote for Exercise 9-2 and make necessary revisions.

Examining Content and Structure

When you have completed your revision map, you are ready to evaluate your essay's content and organization. If you do not ask yourself the right questions when evaluating your draft, you won't discover how to improve it. Each of the following questions and corresponding revision strategies will guide you in producing a clear and effective final essay.

1. **Does your essay accomplish your purpose?**

   If you are writing in response to an assignment, reread it and make sure you have covered all aspects of it. Delete any sentences or paragraphs that do not fulfill your assignment or stated purpose. Do you have enough ideas left? If not, do additional freewriting to discover new ideas.

2. **Is your essay appropriate for your audience?**

   Visualize your audience reading your essay. How will they respond? If you are not sure, ask a classmate or a person who is part of your audience to read your essay. Then revise your essay with your audience in mind. Add examples that may appeal to them; delete those that would not. Examine your word choice. Have you used language that is understandable and will not either confuse them or create a negative impression?

3. **Is your thesis statement clearly expressed?**

   Highlight your thesis statement. Does it state the main point of your essay and make an assertion about your topic? If not, write one sentence stating what your essay is intended to explain or show. Use this sentence to help you revise your thesis statement. If you revise your thesis statement, be sure to revise the remainder of your essay to reflect your changes.

4. **Does each paragraph support your thesis?**

   Reread each topic sentence. Does each clearly and specifically explain some aspect of your thesis statement? If not, revise or drop the paragraph. Does the essay contain enough information to fully explain your thesis and make it understandable to your reader? If not, do additional prewriting to help you discover more ideas. If you are stuck, your thesis statement may be too narrow or you may need to read more about your topic. Be sure to give credit for any ideas you borrow from print or online sources. (Refer to Chapter 11 for information on how to give credit to sources you use.)

5. **Is your essay logically organized?**

   Examine your revision map to be sure your paragraphs are in the right order. If not, rearrange them. Be sure to add sentences or transitions to connect your ideas and show your new organization. Use Table 8-3, "Choosing a Pattern of Organization," on page 263 to consider different ways you might rearrange your ideas.

6. **Have you used transitions to connect your ideas?**

   Circle all transitional words, phrases, and sentences. Do you use transitions to move from each main point to another? If not, add transitions, referring to Table 9-2, page 277, as needed.

7. **Are your introduction, conclusion, and title effective?**

   Reread your introduction. If it does not lead your reader into the essay and/or does not offer needed background information, it needs revision. Revise by assuming your reader knows little about the topic and has shown little interest. Decide what to add to help this uninterested reader get involved with your essay. *Next, reread your conclusion.* Does it draw the essay to a close and remind the reader of your thesis statement? If not, revise it using the suggestions on page 279. *Finally, reconsider your title.* Is it an appropriate label for your essay? If it does not draw your reader into the essay, try to think of a snappier, more interesting title.

Ted used the revision strategies outlined above, and after examining his idea map made a number of changes to his initial draft including combining and moving paragraphs, deleting repetitive and irrelevant content, and organizing his paper to better support his thesis.

Revising Thesis Statements

The best time to evaluate and, if necessary, revise your thesis statement is after you have written a first draft. When evaluating your thesis statement, ask the following questions:

1. **Does my essay develop and explain my thesis statement?** As you write an essay, its focus and direction may change. Revise your thesis statement to reflect any changes. If you discover that you drifted away from your original thesis and want to maintain it, work on revising so that your paper delivers what your thesis promises.
2. **Is my thesis statement broad enough to cover all the points made in the essay?** As you develop your first draft, you may find that one idea leads naturally to another. Both must be covered by the thesis statement. For example, suppose your thesis statement is "Media coverage of national political events shapes public attitudes toward politicians." If, in your essay, you discuss media coverage of international events as well as national ones, then you need to broaden your thesis statement.
3. **Does my thesis statement use vague or unclear words that do not clearly focus the topic?** For example, in the thesis statement "The possibility of

animal-organ transplants for humans is interesting," the word *interesting* is vague and does not suggest how your essay will approach the topic. Instead, if your paper discusses both the risks and benefits of these transplants, this approach should be reflected in your thesis: "Animal-organ transplants for humans offer both risks and potential benefits."

Evaluating and Revising Thesis Statements

Directions: Working with a classmate, identify what is wrong with the following thesis statements, and revise each one to make it more effective:

1. Jogging has a lot of benefits.
2. Getting involved in campus activities has really helped me.
3. Budgeting your time is important.
4. Commuting to college presents problems.
5. The movie is about parenting.
6. Counseling can help people with problems.
7. Violence on television must be brought to an end.
8. Divorce laws are unfair and favor women.
9. Fad diets are losing their appeal.
10. Automobile air bags save lives.

Revising Your Working Thesis Statement

Directions: Revisit your working thesis statement from Exercise 8-16 and revise it based on the suggestions above.

Revising Paragraphs

Once you are satisfied with the overall content and structure of your essay, next evaluate each paragraph. Ask yourself each of the following questions about each paragraph. For any items for which you answer no, refer to the pages listed for revision help.

- Is the topic of the paragraph specific enough so that it can be adequately covered in a single paragraph? (Chapter 3, p. 103)
- Does the topic sentence clearly identify the topic and express a point of view about it? (Chapter 3, p. 106)
- Are there enough relevant details to support the topic sentence? (Chapter 4, pp. 132–135)
- Are the details arranged in a logical order? (Chapter 4, pp. 135–138)
- Are transitional words and phrases used to connect my ideas? (Chapter 4, p. 140)

Revising Sentences and Words

Once you are satisfied with your paragraphs, examine each sentence by asking the following questions:

- **Are your sentences wordy?** Do they express your meaning in as few words as possible? Here is an example of a wordy sentence, along with a possible revision. Notice that the first sentence contains empty words that do not contribute to its meaning.

WORDY	In light of the fact that cell phone technology changes, every year or so, upgrading your cell phone is what everybody has to do.
REVISED	Cell phone technology changes yearly, so regular upgrades are necessary.

- **Do your sentences repeat the same idea in slightly different words?** Here is an example of a sentence that is redundant.

REDUNDANT	My decision to choose to attend college was the best decision I have made in a long time
REVISED	Choosing to attend college was one of my best decisions.

- **Do all of your sentences follow the same pattern?** That is, are they all short, or do they all start the same way? Do they seem choppy or monotonous? Sentences that are too similar make your writing seem mechanical and uninteresting. Also try to expand or combine several short sentences.
- **Do you use strong active verbs?** These make your writing seem lively and interesting. Which of the following sentences is more interesting?

  - The puppy was afraid of a laundry basket.
  - The puppy whimpered, quivered, and scampered away when my sister carried a laundry basket into the room.

  The second sentence helps you visualize the situation, while the first is simply factual. Reread your essay looking for verbs that seem dull or convey very little meaning. Replace them, using a dictionary or thesaurus as needed.
- **Have you used concrete, specific language?** Your words should convey as much meaning as possible. Which phrase in each of the following pairs provides more meaning?

a fun vacation	or	a white-water rafting trip
many flowers	or	lavender, petunias, and white begonias

  Reread your essay and highlight words that seem dull and ordinary. Use a dictionary or thesaurus to help you find more concrete and specific replacements.
- **Have you used words with appropriate connotations?** A word's connotative meaning is the collection of feelings and attitudes that come along with the word. The words *strolled*, *swaggered*, and *lumbered* all mean walking in a forward

direction, but only *swaggered* would be appropriate when describing someone walking in a bold and arrogant manner. To be sure you have used words with appropriate connotations, check any you are unsure of in a dictionary.

- **Have you avoided clichés?** A cliché is a tired, overused expression that carries little meaning. Here are a few examples.

better later than never	shoulder to cry on
light as a feather	hard as a rock
green with envy	bite the bullet

Reread your essay and replace clichés with more exact and descriptive information. You could, for example, replace *shoulder to cry on* with *sympathetic and understanding best friend* or *bite the bullet* with *accept responsibility*.

- **Have you avoided sexist language?** Sexist language expresses narrow or unfair assumptions about men's and women's roles, positions, or value. Here are a few examples of sexist language:

SEXIST	A compassionate **nurse** reassures **her** patients before surgery.
REVISED	Compassionate **nurses** reassure **their** patients before surgery.
SEXIST	Many **policeman** hold college degrees.
REVISED	Many **police officers** hold college degrees.

- **Have you used standard American English and avoided using nonstandard dialect?** While dialects such as Black English, Spanglish, and Creole are acceptable in many situations, they are not acceptable when writing essays for college classes. If you speak a dialect of English in addition to standard American English, be sure to reread your essay and replace any dialect words or expressions.

Evaluating and Revising a Draft

Directions: Evaluate your draft of the essay you revised in Exercise 9-7, using the questions in the preceding section. Make revisions as needed.

Edit and Proofread

- GOAL 6
  Edit and proofread

Once you are satisfied that your essay expresses your ideas as you intended and is organized in a logical way, you are ready to make sure your essay is clear, error free, and presented in acceptable manuscript form. At this stage, you should try to correct errors in spelling, punctuation, and grammar, as well as typographical errors. Use the following tips.

Tips for How to Edit and Proofread Effectively

- **Work with a double-spaced print copy of your essay.** You are likely to see more errors when working with a print copy than you do with an electronic version.
- **Use your Error Log** (see p. 228). Read your paper once looking for the errors you make the most often.

- **Read your essay backward, starting with the last sentence and working toward the first.** Reading this way will help you focus on errors without the distraction of the flow of ideas.
- **Read your essay aloud.** You may catch errors in agreement, use of dialect, or punctuation.
- **Ask a classmate to proofread your paper.**

Common Errors to Avoid

Here is a list of the most common errors students make in their writing: sentence fragments, run-on sentences, subject-verb agreement, pronoun-antecedent agreement, pronoun reference, shifts and mixed constructions, dangling or misplaced modifiers, verb tense, coordinate sentences, subordinate clauses, parallelism, comma usage, and colon and semicolon usage. Use the Brief Grammar Handbook (p. 497) to learn how to identify and correct these common errors in your writing.

Using Spell-Checkers and Grammar Checkers

While a spell-checker can help you spot some spelling and keyboarding errors, you cannot trust the program to catch all of your errors. Although it can detect misspelled words, it cannot detect when a word is used inappropriately. For example, it cannot distinguish whether you should use *there* or *their* in a particular sentence. When the spell-checker finds a misspelled word, it may suggest a list of alternatives and highlight the one it considers most likely to be correct. Be sure to verify the suggested spelling with a dictionary, since some of the suggestions may be wrong.

Grammar- and style-checkers may identify some incorrect grammar and awkward or incomplete sentences. However, you cannot count on them to find all the problems. They may also identify sentences that are correct and need no editing. Therefore use these checkers cautiously.

Using a Proofreading Checklist

Use the proofreading checklist on page 288 to remind you of the types of errors to look for when proofreading.

Presenting Your Essay

Before your instructor even begins to read your essay, he or she forms a first impression of it. A paper that is carelessly assembled, rumpled, or has handwritten corrections creates a negative first impression. Use the following suggestions to present your paper positively. Always follow carefully any guidelines or requests that your instructor makes on format, method of submission, and so forth.

- Make sure your name, course and section number, and date appear at the top of your essay (unless otherwise specified by your instructor).
- Type and double-space your essay.
- Number the pages and staple or paperclip them together.
- Present a neat, clean copy. (Carry it in a manila folder or envelope until you turn it in so it does not get rumpled or dirty.)
- If you need to make last-minute corrections, reprint your essay; do not make hand corrections.
- Avoid adjusting the margins to meet a page-length limit.
- If submitting your paper online, be sure to use an appropriate subject line identifying the submission.

Revision and Proofreading Checklists

Revision Checklist for PARAGRAPHS

1. Who is your audience? How interested are they in your subject, and how much do they know about it? Is your paragraph suited to your audience?
2. What is your purpose? Does your paragraph accomplish your purpose?
3. Is your main point clearly expressed in your topic sentence?
4. Is each detail relevant? Does each explain or support the topic sentence effectively?
5. Have you supported your topic sentence with sufficient detail to make it understandable and believable?
6. Do you use specific and vivid words to explain each detail?
7. Do you connect your ideas with transitional words and phrases?

Revision Checklist for ESSAYS

1. Is your essay appropriate for your audience?
2. Does your essay accomplish your purpose?
3. Is your thesis statement clearly expressed?
4. Does each paragraph support your thesis?
5. Is your essay logically organized?
6. Have you used transitions to connect your ideas?
7. Are your introduction, conclusion, and title effective?

Proofreading Checklist

1. Does each sentence end with an appropriate punctuation mark (period, question mark, exclamation point, or quotation marks)?
2. Is all punctuation within each sentence correct (commas, colons, semicolons, apostrophes, dashes, and quotation marks)?
3. Is each word spelled correctly?
4. Have you used capital letters where needed?
5. Are numbers and abbreviations used correctly?
6. Are any words left out?
7. Have you corrected all typographical errors?
8. Are your pages in the correct order and numbered?

Editing and Proofreading Your Essay

Directions: Using the suggestions in this section and the revision and proofreading checklists, proofread and edit your essay.

READ AND RESPOND: A Student Essay

Relationships 2.0: Dating and Relating in the Internet Age

Ted Sawchuck

Examining Writing (Ted's final essay is on p. 249)

1. Compare Ted's working thesis *"The dating process using Facebook involves screening, dating, and breaking up"* with his final thesis on page 249. How did he change it?
2. Compare his first draft on page 274 with his final draft on page 249. What content did he delete? What did he add? Why do you think he made these decisions?
3. How did his organization change?
4. Evaluate his title, introduction, and conclusion.
5. What other changes would you recommend to further improve the essay?

Writing Assignments

1. For an education class, write an essay examining the trend toward online college courses. Do research to discover what is offered at your college and other nearby colleges. Summarize your findings in a short essay.
2. For a health class, you are asked to write an essay comparing two popular diets. Choose two diets, such as the Fast Diet and the Mediterranean Diet research what is involved in each, and report your findings in an essay.
3. For a business management class, your instructor has given the following assignment: Choose two local business franchises that sell the same products. You might choose two fast-food restaurants, two shoe stores, or two drugstores, for example. Visit both businesses and research each on the Internet. Write an essay comparing the two businesses. Indicate which you feel is likely to be more profitable over the course of the next year.

READ AND RESPOND: A Professional Essay

This essay is an excerpt from the book *Dragnet Nation: A Quest for Privacy, Security, and Freedom in a World of Relentless Surveillance* by Julia Angwin. As you read, identify the author's topic, her thesis, and the types of details she includes to support her point.

Thinking Before Reading

1. Preview the reading, using the steps discussed in Chapter 1, page 4.
2. Connect the reading to your own experience by answering the following questions:
   a. Do you think the benefits of technology are worth the sacrifice of some of your privacy?
   b. Have you ever experienced a violation of your privacy? How did the experience change how you protect your privacy?
3. Mark and annotate as you read.

You're Under Surveillance

In 'private' online forums, at malls, and even at home, said Julia Angwin, someone is tracking you.

1 SHARON AND BILAL couldn't be more different. Sharon Gill is a 42-year-old single mother who lives in a small town in southern Arkansas. She ekes out a living trolling for treasures at yard sales and selling them at a flea market. Bilal Ahmed, 36, is a single, Rutgers-educated man who lives in a penthouse in Sydney, Australia. He runs a chain of convenience stores.

2 Although they have never met in person, they became close friends on a password-protected online forum for patients struggling with mental health issues. Sharon was trying to wean herself from anti-depressant medications. Bilal had just lost his mother and was suffering from anxiety and depression.

3 From their far comers of the world, they were able to cheer each other up in their darkest hours. Sharon turned to Bilal because she felt she couldn't confide in her closest relatives and neighbors. "I live in a small town," Sharon told me, "I don't want to be judged on this mental illness."

4 But in 2010, Sharon and Bilal were horrified to discover they were being watched on their private social network.

5 It started with a break-in. On May 7, 2010, PatientsLikeMe noticed unusual activity on the "Mood" forum where Sharon and Bilal hung out. A new member of the site, using sophisticated software, was attempting to "scrape," or copy, every single message off PatientsLikeMe's private "Mood" and "Multiple Sclerosis" forums.

6 PatientsLikeMe managed to block and identify the intruder: It was the Nielsen Co., the media-research firm. Nielsen monitors online "buzz" for its clients, including drug-makers. On May 18, PatientsLikeMe sent a cease-and-desist letter to Nielsen and notified its member of the break-in.

7 But there was a twist. PatientsLikeMe used the opportunity to inform members of the fine print they may not have noticed when they signed up. The website was also selling data about its members to pharmaceutical and other companies.

8 The news was a double betrayal for Sharon and Bilal. Not only had an intruder been monitoring them, but so was very place that they considered to be a safe space.

9 Even worse, none of it was necessarily illegal. Nielsen was operating in a gray area of the law even as it violated the terms of service at PatientsLikeMe. And it was entirely legal for PatientsLikeMe to disclose to its members in its fine print that it would sweep up all their information and sell it.

Google servers: The company tracks its users, but 'the largest of the dragnets' are the NSA's.

10 WE ARE LIVING in a Dragnet Nation—a world of indiscriminate tracking where institutions are stockpiling data about individuals at an unprecedented pace. The rise of indiscriminate tracking is powered by the same forces that have brought us the technology we love so much—powerful computing on our desktops, laptops, tablets, and smartphones,

11 Before computers were commonplace, it was expensive and difficult to track individuals. Governments kept records only of occasions, such as birth, marriage, property ownership, and death. Companies kept records when a customer bought something and filled out a warranty card or joined a loyalty club. But technology has made it cheap and easy for institutions of all kinds to keep records about almost every moment of our lives.

12 The combination of massive computing power, smaller and smaller devices, and cheap storage has enabled a huge increase in indiscriminate tracking of personal data. The trackers include many of the institutions that are supposed to be on our side, such as the government and the companies with which we do business.

13 Of course, the largest of the dragnets appear to be those operated by the U.S. government. In addition to its scooping up vast amounts of foreign communications, the National Security Agency is also scooping up Americans' phone calling records and Internet traffic, according to documents revealed in 2013 by the former NSA contractor Edward Snowden.

14 Meanwhile, commercial dragnets are blossoming. AT&T and Verizon are selling information about the location of their cellphone customers, albeit without identifying them by name. Mall owners have started using technology to track shoppers based on the signals emitted by the cellphones in their pockets. Retailers such as Whole Foods have used digital signs that are actually facial recognition scanners.

15 Online, hundreds of advertisers and data brokers are watching as you browse the Web. Looking up "blood sugar" could tag you as a possible diabetic by companies that profile people based on their medical condition and then provide drug companies and insurers access to that information. Searching for a bra could trigger an instant bidding war among lingerie advertisers at one of the many online auction houses.

16 IN 2009, 15-YEAR-OLD high school student Blake Robbins was confronted by an assistant principal who claimed she had evidence that he was engaging in "improper behavior in his home." It turned out that his school had installed spying software on the laptops that it issued to the school's 2,300 students. The school's technicians had activated software on some of the laptops that could snap photos using the webcam. Blake's webcam captured him holding pill-shaped objects. Blake and his family said they were Mike and Ike candies. The assistant principal believed they were drugs.

17 Blake's family sued the district for violating their son's privacy. The school said the software had been installed to allow technicians to locate the computers in

case of theft. However, the school did not notify students of the software's existence, nor did it set up guidelines for when the technical staff could operate the cameras.

18 An internal investigation revealed that the cameras had been activated on more than 40 laptops and captured more than 65,000 images. Some students were photographed thousands of times, including when they were partially undressed and sleeping. The school board later banned the school's use of cameras to surveil students.

19 On April 5, 2011, John Gass picked up his mail in Needham, Mass., and was surprised to find a letter stating that his driver's license had been revoked. "I was just blindsided," John said.

20 John is a municipal worker—he repairs boilers for the town of Needham. Without a driver's license, he could not do his job. He called the Massachusetts Registry of Motor Vehicles and was instructed to appear at a hearing and bring documentation of his identity. They wouldn't tell him why his license was revoked.

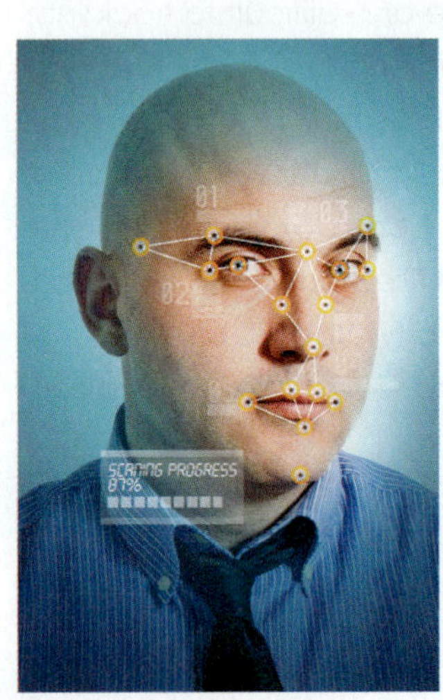

Facial recognition software.

21 When John showed up for his hearing, he learned that the RMV had begun using facial recognition software to search for identity fraud. The software compared license photos to identify people who might have applied for multiple licenses under aliases. The software had flagged him and another man as having similar photos and had required them to prove their identities.

22 John was a victim of what I call the "police lineup"—dragnets that allow the police to treat everyone as a suspect. This overturns our traditional view that our legal system treats us as "innocent until proven guilty."

23 The most obvious example of this is airport body scanners. The scanners conduct the most intrusive of searches—allowing the viewer to peer beneath a person's clothes—without any suspicion that the person being scanned is a criminal. In fact, the burden is on the individual to "prove" his or her innocence, by passing through the scanner without displaying any suspicious items.

24 John Gass luckily was given a chance to plead his case. But it was an absurd case. He was presented with a photo of himself from 13 years ago.

25 "It doesn't look like you," the officer said.

26 "Of course it doesn't," John said. "It's 13 years later. I was a hundred pounds lighter."

27 John presented his passport and his birth certificate, and his license was reinstated. But the officers wouldn't give him any paperwork to prove that it was reinstated. He wanted a piece of paper to show his boss that he was okay to drive again.

28 John filed a lawsuit against the RMV, claiming that he had been denied his constitutionally protected right to due process. The RMV argued that he had been given a window of opportunity to dispute the revocation because the letter had been mailed on March 24 and the license wasn't revoked until April 1. John didn't pick up his mail until April 5. The Suffolk County Superior Court granted the RMV's motion to dismiss. Gass appealed, but the appellate court also ruled against him.

29 John felt betrayed by the whole process. He now is very careful around state police because he worries that he won't be treated fairly. "There are no checks and balances," he said. "It is only natural humans are going to make mistakes. But there is absolutely no oversight."

30 THESE STORIES ILLUSTRATE a simple truth: Information is power. Anyone who holds a vast amount of information about us has power over us.

31 At first, the information age promised to empower individuals with access to previously hidden information. We could comparison shop across the word for the best price, for the best bit of knowledge, for people who shared our views.

32 But now the balance of power is shifting, and large institutions—both governments and corporations—are gaining the upper hand in the information wars, by tracking vast quantities of information about mundane aspects of our lives.

33 Now we are learning that people who hold our data can subject us to embarrassment, or drain our pocketbooks, or accuse us of criminal behavior. This knowledge could, in turn, create a culture of fear.

34 Consider Sharon and Bilal. Once they learned they were being monitored on PatientsLikeMe, Sharon and Bilal retreated from the Internet. Bilal deleted his posts from the forum. He took down the drug dosage history that he had uploaded onto the site. Sharon stopped using the Internet altogether and doesn't allow her son to use it without supervision.

35 They started talking by phone but missed the online connections they had forged on PatientsLikeMe. "I haven't found a replacement," Sharon said. Bilal agreed: "The people on PLM really know how it feels."

36 But neither of them could tolerate the fear of surveillance. Sharon said she just couldn't live with the uncertainty of "not knowing if every keystroke I'm making is going to some other company," she said. Bilal added, "I just feel that the trust was broken."

37 Sharon and Bilal's experience is a reminder that for all its technological pyrotechnics, the glory of the digital age has always been profoundly human. Technology allows us to find people who share our inner thoughts, to realize we're not alone. But technology also allows others to spy on us, causing us to pull back from digital intimacy.

38 When people ask me why I care about privacy, I always return to the simple thought that I want there to be safe, private spaces in the word for Sharon and Bilal, for myself, for my children, for everybody. I want there to be room in the digital world for letters sealed with hot wax. Must we always be writing postcards that can—and will—be read by anyone along the way?

Excerpted from Dragnet Nation: A Quest for Privacy, Security, and Freedom in a World of Relentless Surveillance *by Julia Angwin, Published in February 2014 by Times Books, an imprint of Henry Holt and Company, LLC.*

Writing in Response to Reading

Checking Your Comprehension MySkillsLab®

Answer each of the following questions using complete sentences.

1. How did Sharon Gill and Bilal Ahmed become friends?
2. Who was the intruder on the PatientsLikeMe Web site? What was the intruder trying to do when it was blocked?
3. According to the author, what three factors have combined to enable a huge increase in tracking of personal data?
4. What group does the author say operates the largest dragnet?
5. Why did Blake Robbins's family sue the school district?
6. Explain why John Gass's license was revoked.

Strengthening Your Vocabulary MySkillsLab®

Identify at least five words used in the reading that are unfamiliar to you. Using context, word parts, or a dictionary, write a brief definition of each word.

Examining the Reading: Using an Idea Map

Create an idea map of "You're Under Surveillance." Start with the title and thesis and include the main ideas and conclusion.

Reading and Writing: An Integrated Perspective MySkillsLab®

Get ready to write about the reading by discussing the following:

1. Evaluate the title, "You're Under Surveillance." What does the title suggest about the author's attitude toward her subject? What other titles would be appropriate and effective for this reading?
2. Evaluate the introduction and conclusion. Does the introduction lead you into the essay? Does the conclusion draw the essay to a close and remind you of the author's thesis statement?
3. Write a journal entry expressing the author's thesis in your own words. Has the author provided sufficient evidence to support her thesis?
4. Discuss the three stories the author uses to illustrate her point (Sharon and Bilal, Blake Robbins, and John Gass). Whose story did you find most compelling? Why?
5. How does the author organize and connect her ideas throughout the reading? Find and underline transitions that lead the reader from one idea to another.
6. Choose a word or phrase that describes the author's tone. Is it appropriate for her subject?

THINKING VISUALLY

7. What is shown in the first photograph on page 291? Explain the purpose of the photograph.
8. Describe the second photograph, on page 292. What aspect of the reading does this photograph illustrate or correspond to? How effective is the photograph?

Thinking and Writing Critically MySkillsLab®

1. What is the author's purpose in writing this essay? Did she accomplish her purpose?
2. Who is the intended audience for this essay? What reaction do you think the intended audience had to this essay?
3. How does the author try to influence your opinions in this selection? Is she successful?
4. What impression does the author create with her choice of words? Find examples of emotional or connotative language throughout the essay.
5. Does the author present a balanced argument? Is there bias in this essay? Consider what information the author has omitted. What would be the opposing argument to hers? (For more about bias and argument, see Chapter 13, pp. 381–385 and Chapter 14.)
6. Why does the author include quotes from Sharon and Bilal and John Gass? What effect do these quotes have on your impression of their stories?

Writing Paragraphs MySkillsLab®

1. Write a paragraph explaining what the author means when she says, "We are living in a Dragnet Nation" (paragraph 8). Do you agree? Why or why not?
2. Examine the author's statement that "Information is power" (paragraph 26). Do people who hold information about us have power over us? Write a paragraph explaining your answer and giving examples from your own life.
3. What information in the essay did you find most surprising or shocking? Will anything you read or learned in the essay change how you act online or in other situations such as shopping or traveling? Write a paragraph explaining your answers.

Writing Essays MySkillsLab®

4. Examine the author's claim that the traditional view of our legal system—"innocent until proven guilty"—has been overturned, as illustrated by her examples of police lineups and airport body scanners. Do you find airport body scanners intrusive? Do you accept the author's claim that the burden has shifted to the individual to prove his or her innocence in such situations? Is the value of increased security worth a loss of privacy to you? Write an essay exploring the answers to these questions.
5. In your opinion, what are the most significant benefits of technology? What are technology's biggest pitfalls? Consider the ways that technology has enhanced and complicated your life, and write an essay exploring how you feel about the Information Age.

SELF-TEST SUMMARY

To test yourself, cover the Answer column with a sheet of paper and answer each question in the left column. Evaluate each of your answers as you work by sliding the paper down and comparing your answer with what is printed in the Answer column.

QUESTION	ANSWER
■ GOAL 1 Draft an essay What are four suggestions for drafting an essay?	(1) Leave time between drafts. (2) Experiment with different approaches, content, and ways of organizing information. (3) Focus on ideas, not correctness. (4) Be prepared to make major changes.
■ GOAL 2 Read while drafting an essay Why is it important to read while you are drafting an essay?	Reading your draft helps you stay focused on the topic, decide where to add information or transitions or start a new paragraph, think more about organization, and realize when you are repeating information.

(continued)

(*continued*)

QUESTION	ANSWER
■ GOAL 3 Write and revise the body of an essay Why is it best to begin with the body paragraphs, and how do you start to draft them?	Body paragraphs provide the support for your thesis statement. You can begin drafting by writing an outline; drawing a graphic organizer, or writing a list of topic sentences that support the thesis. Concentrate on making sure each topic sentence supports the thesis, is supported with evidence, and includes transitions.
What is involved in using evidence to support your thesis? How do you use transitions to make connections among your ideas?	Evidence can consist of personal experience, anecdotes, examples, reasons, descriptions, facts, statistics, and quotations. Evidence should be relevant, specific, and accurate, and sources should be documented. For a list of ways to add evidence, see Table 9-1 on page 273. Make connections among your ideas by using transitional words and phrases, writing transitional sentences, and repeating key words. See Table 9-2 on page 277 for useful transitional words and phrases.
■ GOAL 4 Write introductions, conclusions, and titles What should an introduction, conclusion, and title do?	An introduction should present your thesis, interest your reader, and provide background information. A conclusion should reemphasize your thesis statement and draw the essay to a close. A title should identify the topic in an interesting way.
■ GOAL 5 Think critically as you revise your draft How do you think critically about your draft?	Think critically by examining your ideas and by considering your essay's content and structure. Use the Revision Checklists on page 288.
■ GOAL 6 Proofreading What does proofreading involve?	Proofreading involves making sure your essay is clear, error free, and presented in an acceptable form. Use the Proofreading Checklist on page 288 to remind you of what to look for when proofreading.

MySkillsLab®

Visit **Chapter 9, "Drafting and Revising Essays,"** in MySkillsLab to test your understanding of chapter goals.

Reading and Writing Essays with Multiple Patterns

10

LEARNING GOALS

Learn how to . . .

- GOAL 1 Define a multi-pattern essay
- GOAL 2 Recognize multiple patterns of organization in readings
- GOAL 3 Write a multi-pattern essay

THINK About It!

Pictured above is one of the world's most famous paintings, the *Mona Lisa*. How much do you know about this masterpiece, which was painted by Leonardo da Vinci in the 1500s? To learn more about the image, you might consult an art appreciation textbook or a biography about the artist. Each reading would provide different types of information. For example, the art appreciation textbook would likely provide a good deal of description about the *Mona Lisa*, while a biography would provide a narrative of Leonardo's life. Other sources might contain more than one pattern of organization. For instance, an article in the art journal *ArtForum* might compare and contrast Leonardo with another famous Italian artist, Michelangelo, and argue that Leonardo was the more accomplished painter. As you read various sources, you will use the techniques you've learned earlier in this text, including previewing, writing guide questions, highlighting, annotating, and summarizing.

In Chapters 5 and 6 you learned to recognize the pattern of organization used in a reading. Many sources, including textbooks and other college-oriented materials, use more than one pattern of organization. Multiple patterns permit richer, deeper analysis of a topic. This chapter focuses on reading and writing essays that use more than one pattern. You will learn how to recognize the use of multiple patterns in an essay. You will also learn how to use multiple patterns when writing your own essays.

Reading and Writing Connections

EVERYDAY CONNECTIONS

- **Reading** You are having trouble sleeping, so you search the Internet for insomnia cures. You read an article that *defines* the term insomnia, *describes* the symptoms, and offers a list of suggestions to help you fall asleep (*definition, example, process*).
- **Writing** On the comments section of the Web page, you post a note about your own experiences with insomnia (*narration*) and how a lack of sleep is affecting your life (*cause and effect*).

ACADEMIC CONNECTIONS

- **Reading** You read a chapter titled "Personal Communication" in a communications textbook. The reading not only *classifies* the different types of communication, it also teaches you how to be a more effective communicator (*process*).
- **Writing** On an essay exam for your communications class, your instructor asks you to define the three types of personal distance (*definition, classification*) and to explore the similarities and differences among them (*comparison and contrast*).

WORKPLACE CONNECTIONS

- **Reading** You work in a hospital. Your co-workers want to unionize in order to receive better pay and working conditions. You read the union pamphlet, which *describes* and provides *examples* of good working conditions at other hospitals and lists the benefits of joining a union (*cause and effect*).
- **Writing** The hospital's managers ask you to write a report on problems with employee motivation and morale. Your report will identify the *causes* of the problem and propose a step-by-step solution (*process, argument*). The report may describe the experiences of several workers (*narrative*).

What Is a Multi-Pattern Essay?

■ GOAL 1
Define a multi-pattern essay

Readings and essays that combine patterns of organization are often called **multi-pattern**, or **multimodal**. Think back to the image that opens this chapter, the *Mona Lisa*. If you were asked to write an essay about it, you might find yourself thinking, "This painting is so famous and so complicated, using just one pattern of organization won't do justice to the topic." As a result, you may choose to write an essay that combines *definition*—by explaining who the real Mona Lisa was (the wife of Francesco del Giocondo, an Italian nobleman)—along with a *description* of Mona Lisa's famous smile or the scenery behind her and *analysis* of the painter's techniques.

EXAMINING PROFESSIONAL WRITING

The following reading first appeared in *The Atlantic* in June 2014. As you read, notice how the author answers the question in the title using multiple patterns of organization throughout the essay.

Thinking Before Reading

1. Preview the reading, using the steps discussed in Chapter 1, page 4.
2. Connect the reading to your own experiences by answering the following questions:
   a. Have you ever seen—or participated in—an eating competition?
   b. What makes an activity into a competition or sport?
3. Mark and annotate as you read.

What Is the High Art of Competitive Eating?

Gabriel Muller

Major League Eating.

1 Sweat stinging his eyes, George Shea, wearing a straw hat and blue blazer, stood on an outdoor stage in Salisbury, Maryland, on a recent Sunday afternoon and yelled at a crowd of 200 spectators. "Are you ready, people?" Shea howled,

and the crowd cheered back at him. "It's go time. It's go time-time. It's see you on the other side time-time!" Behind Shea on stage, more than a dozen men and women in orange Major League Eating t-shirts stood over metal bowls containing 24 pounds of chicken wings. The audience cheered louder. Here were the world's most decorated competitive eaters, and they had come to Winterplace Park on the Eastern Shore to see who would go home as the nation's most prolific consumer of poultry. These participants and spectators help define a new community called competitive eating that is growing in popularity and is, by some, considered a sport.

2 "There is something about the notion of eating performatively under a short period of time that brought a community together," said Vivian Nun Halloran, a professor of food studies at Indiana University. "It's a very strange concept."

3 That community, as we know it today, emerged in 1972, when two public relations agents, Morty Matz and Max Rosen, organized the first iteration of the Nathan's Hot Dog Eating Contest on Coney Island. After graduating from college, Shea got a job with Matz and Rosen who tasked him with expanding the Nathan's competition from a local public relations novelty to a national sports spectacle. Today, the contest is a multi-million dollar media extravaganza and has spun off into a standalone league, with international competitions centered around everything from mayonnaise to pepperoni rolls.

4 "When I started, there was no phrase 'competitive eating.' There was no anything," Shea, who chairs Major League Eating, the sport's governing body, told me. "There was no Joey Chestnut, there was no Kobayashi, there was no nobody."

5 The hot dog rivalry between Joey Chestnut and Takeru Kobayashi, the leading Japanese eater, is the best known scandal in competitive eating, and hurled the sport to international fame in the mid-2000s. For spectators, Chestnut and Kobayashi's feud, which lasted until the league terminated Kobayashi for breach of contract, represented a narrative of global proportions—our country versus theirs. It also garnered Shea lucrative television contracts—exclusivity with ESPN until 2017—a rapidly growing audience, and hundreds of thousands of dollars in annual prize money, though Shea declined to provide numbers around the company's revenue. Shea's venture is profitable, and even spin-off events, like the chicken wing contest I attended in Maryland, draw the nation's top competitors and a dedicated base of watchers and amateur eaters.

6 Staring at a vat of chicken wings backstage before the Eastern Shore competition was Crazy Legs Conti—who, when I asked for his real name, produced a driver's license with the name Crazy Legs Conti—and two female colleagues preparing for the afternoon's binge. "With the chicken wings, you figure out a strategy. You take a look at the paddles, the drumsticks," Conti said when I asked what he was looking at. His eyes moved along the line of chicken bowls. "Which has more meat," Conti, who ranks 17th in the world, asked me. "The drumstick or the paddle?"

7 "The drumstick," I said, deciding the wings looked a good deal scrawnier.

8 "You would think that. But the meat-to-bone ratio is .49 for the drumstick, and the paddle is .66," he said. Conti took 100 wings, wore a lab coat and safety goggles, and measured out across five trials the specific meat measurements of the chicken wings.

9 Conti's pre-contest preparation is remarkably scientific and not uncommon in its rigor—especially among top-ranked eaters who take seriously the cerebral and high-endurance elements of their sport. Some eaters have been known to undergo hypnosis, practice daily hand-eye coordination exercises, and fast for days to maximize their body's potential for efficient and massive food intake.

10 Many eaters, like "Wild" Bill Myers, who came to the Maryland contest with his fiancée of 15 years, were quick to remind me that competitive eating demands much more from the eater than the ability to guzzle huge quantities of food—it's also about precision. Stuffing your face is a helpful but not sufficient victory plan when you've got only 12 minutes to win. A good eater, according to Myers, needs to be strategic about which bites to take, how often to chew, and when to maneuver between swallowing and eating more food. This is especially tricky with chicken wings, which are irregularly shaped and have bones. The winner is determined by weighing the bowl before and after the competition, in order to establish the total weight eaten.

11 With this kind of focus from participants, it might seem reasonable to place competitive eating among the ranks of other legitimate sports; a strong audience base, highly organized league structure, and meticulous training regimen add an element of validity, and Major League Eating considers competitive eating a demanding athletic undertaking. But what kind of well-founded sport calls attention to such brazen gluttony and the revolting digestive processes of the human body? Instead of zeroing in on an athlete's physiological vigor and agility, competitive eating plays an antithetical role—a sort of sport in reverse.

12 The Nathan's Hot Dog eating competition, Shea's showpiece summer contest, debuted on live television a decade ago and will draw more than 35,000 people to Coney Island this Fourth of July, but the sport—and this term is debatable—lacks any semblance of physical grace or athletic form. Its winners take in very little cash and their celebrity is limited to a niche group of competitive eating fanatics. Why, then, would anyone risk public humiliation, potential damage to long-term health, and a grueling training routine to perform an activity which, to some, serves a gimmicky marketing need and, even worse, a conspicuous display of American gluttony?

13 "Go, go, go!" Shea yelled over blaring techno music as the competitors rushed to gulp down more meat. "Two minutes and thirty seconds left!"

14 Juliet Lee, a 48-year-old Chinese immigrant who owns a hair salon near College Park, Maryland, was struggling to keep her mouth closed as she stuffed handfuls of chicken scraps into her cheeks. Because there isn't much time to chew, Lee downs tennis ball-sized clumps of food with water before digging back into her bowl. The audience's response alternated between cheering her on and grunting with disgust as they wondered if, just maybe, she might puke it all out.

15 As Lee's 100-pound body heaved, I couldn't help wondering whether my fascination with her public eating was oddly sadistic. Here was a woman—a small-business owner, a mother of two teenage girls, someone with no evident or outward antisocial behavior—voluntarily compromising her body and exhibiting her physical vulnerabilities in front of hundreds of screaming watchers. The voracity and determination with which she devoured her chicken made me

Juliet Lee, center (Major League Eating).

uncomfortable: How much humiliation will one go through for competition? But for Lee, the exercise of competitive eating is cathartic and has, over the past seven years, freed her of a range of body image issues that she'd suffered from since childhood.

16 Lee, who grew up in Nanjing, remembered needing to curb her appetite in order to appear more ladylike to a conservative Chinese family. "'Oh you eat so much,' my family would say. It was not elegant and kind of embarrassing. People made fun of me," she said. "Since I started eating contests, I've started to be proud of myself, and I've stopped feeling ashamed of my appetite," she said. "I think the most important thing is that I feel better about myself. Emotionally, I didn't feel good about eating so much. That was kind of a dark side of my life. Now it's a bright spot."

17 Although Lee has arrived at a new level of freedom around the competitive lifestyle of eating contests, athletics enthusiasts and experts remain skeptical about the activity's status as an actual sport. "Real sports," writes British philosopher Colin McGinn in his book-length study on disgust, "accentuate the potential for coordinated movement in the human body, while bracketing the disgust elements most evident in stasis." He continues: "No longer laden and squelchy, the body is now light and steely, a source of pure kinetic energy, like the body of a god."

18 I wonder if "Wild" Bill Myers, a self-proclaimed athlete, whose 360-pound body, shuddering and sludgy with sweat, broke down fistfuls of grease-dunked bird meat in front of hundreds of onlookers, would agree with McGinn's commendatory description. But for McGinn, competitive eating is "not really a sport at all, grotesque to watch, and of merely minority interest." Say that to the 1.95 million people who tuned into ESPN to watch the Nathan's contest in 2009. And when I called McGinn to tell him about a major professional league that supports those exact athletes he dismisses as gluttonous goons, his opinion didn't budge.

19 "It seems almost like a parody of a sport," McGinn told me. "Here is a person exercising some skill—I suppose in some sense—but at the same time, doing it in the service of something that's just drawing attention to the organic body." By divorcing the eating from its physiological purpose—or "by decoupling the act of eating from its most basic raison d'etre: hunger"—we create a spectacle that, in a uniquely absurdist way, has no grounding in our normal reality, Halloran, the food studies professor, argues in a 2004 article. This extreme decontextualization—something akin to seeing the Eiffel Tower in Las Vegas, or even a rigged wrestling match—leaves us with a "simultaneous experience of sensual revulsion and pleasure."

20 Halloran also suggests we enjoy a special type of pleasure from watching somebody else struggle to keep their body under control. To illustrate, take the weightlifter who appeared to defecate in her jumpsuit in the 2000 Olympics and

quickly became a YouTube phenomenon, not for her latent athletic prowess, but for the suddenness—and cringe-wreaking awkwardness—in which her bowels apparently gave out. For another example go back to 1984, when Gabriela Andersen-Schiess, an otherwise accomplished Swiss long-distance runner, stumbled in 37th place in the first-ever Olympic women's marathon in Los Angeles. Andersen-Schiess staggered like a Mary Shelley character toward the finish line, completely dehydrated, with buckled knees and a hunched back. The audience gasped as Andersen-Schiess stubbornly pushed through her inevitable physiological shutdown. After 2 hours and 48 minutes, she hobbled across the finish line, collapsing instantly, face-first, into a group of medics. "It's almost as if the person is committing suicide in front of you," McGinn said. "You try to marvel at their masochism."

21 "Any sportsman can decide to make a competition out of anything," he added. "Talk about crapping contests. You could do that—a very avant-garde person could do that. And a very avant-garde artist can make a pile of shit and put it in a museum."

22 But risk of public humiliation and self harm haven't deterred a new generation of competitive eaters who grew up on the ESPN broadcasts to find something accomplishable in the activity. Take Ric Best, a 22-year-old senior at Yale, who chugged a gallon of Poland Spring water every morning to stretch out his stomach until he—usually without exception—vomited. Best, who goes by the Tudor-inspired moniker King Hungry VIII in eating contests, is what the major leaguers call a "newb"—but an inspired one. After watching his first eating competition in 2009—it was all-you-can-eat spinach—in Boston, Best's friends bet each other that they could probably do the same and even come out on top. For Best and his friends, a win seemed within reach.

23 "We all eat. We all eat more than we should sometimes," Jason Bernstein, a senior programming and acquisitions director at ESPN, said. "I'm not necessarily certain as to what it takes to shoot over a 6-foot-8 power forward coming at me for a three-pointer, while 16,000 fans are watching me in the stadium and perhaps 40 million worldwide. But I can certainly get my arms around eating a hot dog fairly quickly."

Recognize Multiple Patterns When Reading

■ **GOAL 2**
Recognize multiple patterns of organization in readings

Recognizing multiple patterns in a reading has several benefits for you as a reader:

- It helps you better understand the reading's overall organization and its key points.
- It helps you develop a fuller understanding of the topic.
- It helps you prepare for essay examinations, which often require the use of these patterns in your answers.

Most multi-pattern readings have one dominant, or **primary**, pattern. The primary pattern is the reading's key organizing principle. It provides the framework on which the writer builds support for the thesis statement or central thought. Additional, or **secondary**, patterns provide further explanation, details, clarification, and information.

Identifying the Primary Pattern of Organization in a Multi-Pattern Essay

Table 10-1 provides a summary of the key organizational patterns, as well as an example of how each pattern might be used with the topic of skateboarding. (For more detail on each pattern, see Chapters 5 and 6.)

Here are some suggestions for how to determine a multi-pattern reading's primary pattern of organization, using examples from Table 10-1:

- **Look for the thesis statement or central thought.** Examine it closely to identify which pattern it signals. For example, the following thesis statement signals a comparison and contrast pattern: "Even though skiing and skateboarding both pose great risks, each sport is unique in several ways."
- **Look for transition words that signal the primary pattern.** In the skiing/skateboarding thesis statement, the transitions *even though* and *both* signal the comparison and contrast pattern.
- **If you cannot determine the primary pattern from the thesis statement or central thought, examine the supporting details.** Ask yourself what the reading does (its overall purpose) and refer to the second column of Table 10-1 to help you determine the primary pattern.
- **In an essay, check the concluding paragraph.** Often, the closing paragraph summarizes the essay, reviewing the writer's key point and primary organizational pattern.

TABLE 10-1 PATTERNS OF ORGANIZATION

Pattern	What It Does	An Example of Its Use
Chronological Order/Process	Chronological order presents details in the order in which they occur. Process explains how something is done or how it works, usually step by step.	An explanation of the steps to follow in preparing for a skateboarding competition. If the reading is arranged chronologically, the reader would follow these steps in sequence.
Narration	Tells a story that makes a point	A story of how a particular skateboarder became interested in skateboarding
Description	Uses sensory details to help readers visualize a topic	A description of a particular skateboard or skateboarder
Example	Explains a concept by providing concrete instances or illustrations	A discussion of several ways skateboarding can increase physical fitness and build stamina
Definition	Explains a topic by discussing its characteristics	Defining skateboarding as a boarding sport, including some of its unique characteristics
Classification	Explains a topic by organizing it into categories or parts	A discussion of the types of people who typically enjoy skateboarding
Comparison and Contrast	Shows how things are similar and/or different	Comparing or contrasting two sports: skateboarding and snow skiing
Cause and Effect	Explains why things happen or what happens as a result of them	Explaining why skateboarding is an enjoyable and popular sport and the sport's effects on the lives of skateboarders
Argument	Presents a line of reasoning intended to persuade readers to accept a viewpoint or take a specific action	Arguing for or against a ban prohibiting skateboarding in busy, populated public places

EXERCISE 10-1

Reading: Identifying Primary Patterns of Organization

Directions: Identify the primary pattern of organization signaled by each of the following thesis statements.

1. The life of Marilyn Monroe was glamorous, shocking, and ultimately tragic.

____

2. As a developed nation and world leader, the United States must ban the death penalty, which is both unjust and inhuman.

____

3. To get a novel published, you must first write the manuscript. You must then find an agent, make the changes he or she requests, and then wait while the agent submits your work to various editors.

____

EXERCISE 10-2

Reading: Identifying the Primary Pattern in the Professional Essay

Directions: Identify the primary pattern of organization used in the professional reading "What Is the High Art of Competitive Eating?" on page 299. Explain how you determined the primary pattern.

____

____

Identifying Secondary Patterns of Organization in a Multi-Pattern Essay

Within a reading, **secondary patterns** provide additional support, explanation, details, and information. While understanding the primary pattern will give you a good overall sense of the reading, recognizing the information in the secondary patterns will provide you with a greater understanding of the topic.

After you have analyzed the thesis statement or central thought and identified the primary pattern, use these tips to identify the reading's secondary patterns:

- **Keep the length of the reading in mind.** The longer the reading, the more likely it uses multiple patterns.
- **In an essay, examine the topic sentences of the body paragraphs.** These may point to secondary patterns.
- **Throughout the reading, look for transition words that signal secondary patterns.** Annotate the reading, making notes about the patterns in the margins.
- **Watch for single sentences that use secondary patterns.** In many readings, it's common to find a definition, description, and example within a single sentence.

EXERCISE 10-3

Reading: Identifying Secondary Patterns of Organization in the Professional Reading

Directions: Use the questions below to identify secondary patterns of organization in "What Is the High Art of Competitive Eating?" (p. 299).

1. Which pattern is used in paragraph 3? What transitions signal this pattern?

 ____

 ____

2. The author uses cause and effect in paragraph 9. What are the causes and what is the effect?

 ____

 ____

3. Which paragraphs use the description pattern? How do you know?

 ____

 ____

4. Which pattern is used in paragraph 20? What transitions signal this pattern?

 ____

 ____

EXERCISE 10-4

Reading: Identifying Secondary Patterns of Organization

Directions: In addition to the primary pattern you identified for each of the thesis statements in Exercise 10-1, choose a secondary pattern that would provide you with a greater understanding of the topic.

EXAMINING STUDENT WRITING

A good way to learn to read and write essays is to study a model. By examining the student essay below by Dejohn Harris you will learn how to plan, organize, and write essays using multiple patterns. Throughout the rest of the chapter, we will use parts of Dejohn's essay to illustrate techniques and strategies.

Dejohn was arrested for crimes he committed when he belonged to an infamous Los Angeles street gang, the Crips. In prison, he converted to Islam and decided to pursue an education on his release. As a student in an LA community college, he was asked to write a multi-pattern essay for the following assignment:

> A *subculture* is a group within a larger, more mainstream culture, often with its own set of rules, beliefs, and expected behaviors. Often, members of the subculture reject larger society and choose to live in their own world.

For example, fans of the Japanese art called *anime* or *manga* compose a subculture, as do punk rockers, bikers, and Goths. Write an essay about a subculture to which you belong or have belonged. If you do not belong to a subculture, identify a subculture that you have observed, encountered, or experienced. Be sure to illustrate and explain your ideas in the context of a multi-pattern essay.

Gang Life: Better from the Outside

Dejohn Harris

1 When I was 12 years old, my favorite cousin, Sean, who was 16 at the time, was shot and killed in a drive-by shooting. He was a good student and a fantastic basketball player. His high school coach was talking to several colleges about getting a scholarship for him. Sean was not a gang member, but his girlfriend's brother belonged to the Crips, one of L.A.'s biggest and most dangerous gangs. Sean was hanging out with his girlfriend and her brother, and someone from the Bloods, a rival gang, drove past and took a shot at the brother. He missed the brother and killed my cousin instead. I can still remember how angry I felt when I got the news. Two days later, a Crip stopped me when I was walking home from school. He asked me if I wanted to let the Bloods get away with what they did. I said no, I wanted them to pay. And that is how I became a gang member at the age of 12. A lot of people are shocked when someone tells them that gangs recruit kids who are not even teenagers yet, but there is a lot more to being in a gang than any outsider realizes or hears about. For example, many people don't understand the difference between a "street family" and a "decent family," and the fact that coming from a street family makes you much more likely to join a gang.

2 Though most people do not realize it, most gangs have plenty of female members. Looking back to my days as a Crip, I would guess that about one out of every ten Crips was female. Like the guys, the girls who join gangs are looking for support and a family, because their mothers are junkies and their fathers are gone. Sometimes they are the girlfriends of Crips, and they end up joining the gang because they want to be a part of their boyfriend's life and also part of a group. Something these girls never talk about is the way they were sexually molested when they were younger, but I know this is true about a lot of them. Two of the female Crips I was closest to, Tamika and Jocelyn, both confided in me that their mothers' boyfriends had taken advantage of them and mistreated them. But even though many gang members are female, they are never in charge. In other words, they are never the gang leader.

3 Because the media focuses on the "ghetto" and the "hood" and all the negative stereotypes that go with them, many people don't realize how family life leads young people to join a gang. If you come from a decent family, you probably will not join a gang, but if you come from a street family, you probably will. What do these terms mean? A "decent family" is a family that tries to support itself honestly. Usually they go to church and work their social lives around church activities. So the church becomes their extended family, and they do not have to look to gangs for support. In contrast, a "street family" is one that is focused on public respect and

an emphasis on physical strength, the idea being that a man should do whatever it takes to protect his family. Coming from a street family leads to thug life, and thug life leads to joining a gang, which is just one big street family. Maybe if the media showed more positive role models for inner-city kids, and told stories of all the hard-working mothers and fathers who try to protect their kids from crime and drugs, street life would not seem so glamorous to 12-year-olds.

4 Another little-known piece of information is the fact that many, many gang members try to leave the gang. They look around at the drugs, and the violence, and the murders, and the fact they may end up dead, and they decide gang life isn't right for them. But by that point it is too late. Once you are in, the leaders usually will not let you out. Some gangs have a practice called "jumping out," where people who want to leave get beaten mercilessly. If they live through it, they can leave the gang. If they die, well, they also get their wish to leave the gang.

5 I could write many more pages providing additional examples of little-known facts about life in a gang. I could talk about the weekly meetings we had to attend, the monetary dues we had to pay, the crimes we had to commit, the way we got our nicknames, and the types of graffiti we used to tag our territory. I could talk about the price I paid to leave the gang. All of it would be interesting to people who do not know anything about gangs, and a lot of it would be shocking. But let me tell you: I can write this essay because I lived as a gang member. And it is not as glamorous or fun as rap music makes it sound. It drains your individuality, your soul, and your morality. It is much better for your life, your happiness, your friends, and your family if you read about gangs instead of joining one.

Write a Multi-Pattern Essay

■ **GOAL 3**
Write a multi-pattern essay

As you begin your brainstorming and prewriting activities, develop your multi-pattern essay using the following steps:

- Generate ideas, narrow your topic, and plan your essay.
- Select primary and secondary patterns.
- Write a thesis statement that reflects your primary pattern.
- Draft your introduction, body paragraphs, and conclusion. Ensure your topic sentences reflect the secondary patterns you have chosen to use.
- Throughout the essay, use transitions to help readers follow your thought patterns.
- Check to make sure your conclusion revisits your thesis statement and primary pattern.

Generating and Organizing Ideas About Your Topic

As you learned in Chapter 2, you can use freewriting, brainstorming, branching, and questioning to generate ideas for your writing (see p. 47). Dejohn, who had lived deeply within the street gang subculture for many years, decided to write about gangs in response to the assignment from his instructor (p. 306) and to use the technique of brainstorming to generate and organize his ideas. Dejohn used the list he brainstormed to focus his topic and determine the best content and organization for his essay.

1. Crips' intense rivalry with another gang, the Bloods
2. how I got involved in the gang
3. why people join gangs
4. what I had to do to prove myself
5. the hierarchy and types of gang members
6. the crimes I committed: theft, vandalism, turf wars, drug dealing (other crimes I didn't commit: murder, drive-by shootings)
7. my time in prison
8. things most people don't know about gangs
9. how we're different from motorcycle gangs like the Hell's Angels
10. the code of the street, "respect," and "street cred"
11. gang leaders
12. "decent families" (less likely to join a gang) vs. "street families" (more likely to join a gang)
13. how a gang is like a big family
14. the "rules"
15. gangs' love of guns

Selecting Primary and Secondary Patterns

As you think about combining patterns, remember that your essay should always have one primary pattern. The main pattern provides the framework on which you build support for your thesis statement. Additional patterns provide further details and information but should not distract your reader from the main pattern.

Combining primary and secondary patterns of organization is often effective (1) when writing a longer essay or term paper, as it can be difficult to sustain one pattern for several pages; (2) when you want to explore multiple facets of a topic from a variety of perspectives; or (3) in essay exams that require you to demonstrate your analytical abilities. For example, a history exam may ask the following question: "How did the American Civil War differ from the American Revolution? How were the two wars similar? Describe the effects of each war on the structure of the U.S. government." This question is asking you to combine two patterns: comparison and contrast and cause and effect.

What to Consider When Choosing a Primary Pattern of Organization

Consider these five main factors when choosing a primary pattern of organization:

1. **The Assignment** Sometimes you can choose a topic to write about, but instructors often provide specific writing assignments or writing prompts. Analyzing the assignment will help you determine the primary pattern of organization for your essay. Look in the assignment for key words and phrases that offer clues.

Dejohn's sociology instructor gave his class the writing assignment on page 306. The assignment makes it clear that Dejohn should select a subculture and write an essay about it. The key word *illustrate* in the assignment is a clue that the primary pattern of organization should be example.

2. **Your Purpose** When an instructor gives you a specific writing assignment, your purpose for writing is quite clear: to answer the question that has been raised. However, when you must choose your own topic, you need to determine your purpose for writing. You can clarify your purpose by asking yourself these questions:
   - What am I trying to accomplish?
   - What do I want my readers to understand after they've read my essay?'

To fulfill the assignment to write about a subculture to which he belonged, Dejohn decided to write about street gangs. His purpose was to explain the subculture of gang life by describing how he became involved in it and how gangs operate. He wanted his readers to understand the factors that lead teenagers to become involved with gangs.

3. **Your Audience** All good writing takes the audience into account. To help determine the primary pattern of organization for your essay, ask yourself these questions:
   - How much do my readers know about the topic?
   - What can I assume about my readers' backgrounds and experiences?
   - Who is most likely to read what I've written?

In writing his essay about street gangs, Dejohn assumed his readers had little or no knowledge about gangs, but knew a little about the negative stereotypes the media portrays of the "ghetto" and the "hood." Dejohn knew his audience was his sociology instructor, so he was careful to include plenty of details about the subculture and to define terms such as "decent family" and "street family."

4. **The Complexity of Your Topic** Some topics are simply more complex or more multifaceted than others. For a simple essay about why you like a specific place, you could write effectively using one of the less complicated patterns, such as description or narration. However, for an essay on a much more complicated topic like street gang subculture, you will want to choose a pattern that allows for greater depth of analysis, such as example, comparison and contrast, cause and effect, or definition.

After thinking about the best way to organize his essay, Dejohn decided to focus on point #8 on his list: *things most people don't know about gangs*. He believed that many of the other points on his list would fit within that category and would provide vivid examples that would meet the requirements of his assignment.

5. **The Course for Which You Are Writing** Each college discipline makes heavy use of specific types of analysis and writing patterns. For instance, literature classes often focus on narrative because stories and novels are generally written with the narrative pattern. When you receive a writing assignment, consider which pattern would work best as your primary pattern. Doing so will usually fulfill your instructor's expectations and help you get the best grade.

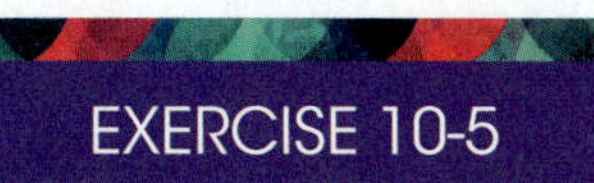

EXERCISE 10-5

Writing: Choosing Primary Patterns of Organization

Directions: Choose a primary pattern of organization for each of the following writing assignments.

1. Lovers of mystery novels often separate them into different categories: hard-boiled, cozy, caper, private detective, and police procedural. Define and provide examples of each category.

2. Those who do not often travel on airplanes are often unprepared for the demands of air travel. What steps can an inexperienced traveler take to ensure a comfortable airline flight?

3. Two of the most famous American poets are Emily Dickinson and T.S. Eliot. How did each poet approach the writing of poetry? In what ways are the poems of Dickinson and Eliot similar? In what ways are they different?

EXERCISE 10-6

Writing: Considering Audience and Purpose When Choosing a Primary Pattern

Directions: Analyze the following writing assignment and answer the questions that follow.

> **Writing assignment:** You are a volunteer for a charitable foundation that "rescues" golden retrievers. People who can no longer take care of their pets contact your foundation, and volunteers provide foster homes for the animals until a permanent home can be found. The president of the foundation has asked you to prepare a letter asking people to donate $10 to the organization.

1. Describe your intended audience.
2. What is your purpose for writing?
3. Brainstorm a list of ideas your readers might find helpful or illuminating.
4. Determine a primary pattern of organization for the assignment.

What to Consider When Choosing Secondary Patterns of Organization

Secondary patterns are used to explain and support your primary pattern of organization. The patterns you choose depend on the types of supporting information that best suit your purpose and appeal to your audience. You can use one secondary pattern or several. Be sure the supporting information you use directly supports your thesis statement. (See Chapters 5 and 6 for details on types of patterns.)

Because he wanted to emphasize his personal experience with the topic, Dejohn decided to use narrative about how he got involved in gangs in his introduction as a secondary pattern. He also realized he would need to define terms, explain why things happened, and describe similarities and differences between gang and non-gang members, so he decided to use definition, cause and effect, and comparison and contrast as secondary patterns.

Table 10-2 shows how Dejohn used the patterns he chose. If he were writing for a different audience or had a different purpose in mind, he could have used other patterns, and examples of how he could have used them are shown in the second part of the table.

TABLE 10-2 DEJOHN'S USE OF PATTERNS OF ORGANIZATION

Secondary Patterns	How Dejohn Used Them
Narration	Dejohn recounts the story of the shooting of his cousin Sean.
Example	Dejohn lists examples of specific aspects of gang life.
Cause and Effect	Dejohn explains why both guys and girls join gangs.
Definition and Comparison and Contrast	Dejohn defines the terms "decent family" and "street family" and explains how they differ.
Secondary Patterns that Dejohn Did Not Use	**How Dejohn Could Have Used Them**
Description	Dejohn could have described gang rules, initiations, actions, and wars.
Classification	Dejohn could have divided gang members into types based on their role or function in the gang.
Chronological Order/Process	Dejohn could have provided an explanation, in sequence, of the steps that lead up to a gang war.
Argument	Dejohn could have argued that gangs should be controlled by community leadership groups.

EXERCISE 10-7

Writing: Using Multiple Patterns of Organization

Directions: Analyze the following writing assignment and answer the questions that follow.

Writing assignment: Compare and contrast the high school experience with the college experience. Some topics you might consider: social life, interaction with instructors, costs, and demands on your time.

1. According to the assignment, which primary pattern of organization should you use?
2. What secondary patterns would you choose to support your thesis statement?

Writing a Thesis Statement that Reflects Your Primary Pattern

Once you have narrowed your topic, write a thesis statement that will serve as the organizing principle for your essay. The thesis statement should reflect your primary pattern. For example, Dejohn's thesis statement signals that his primary pattern of organization will be example:

A lot of people are shocked when someone tells them that gangs recruit kids who are not even teenagers yet, but there is a lot more to being in a gang than any outsider realizes or hears about.

Writing: Narrowing a Topic and Writing a Thesis Statement

Directions: Choose one of the following topics and use freewriting, brainstorming, branching, or questioning (or any combination of these techniques) to generate ideas about it. Narrow your topic, select the primary and secondary patterns you will use, and write a working thesis statement.

1. comfort food
2. hope
3. friendship
4. sport
5. death
6. a treasured memento
7. single parenthood
8. strange addictions
9. gay marriage
10. white lies

Drafting an Introduction

In a typical essay, the introductory paragraph accomplishes three goals:

- It introduces the topic and provides any necessary background information.
- It stimulates the reader's interest.
- It provides a thesis statement as the essay's main point and key organizing principle.

Using multiple patterns in your essay's introduction can help you accomplish all these goals, allowing you to specify your primary method and hint at your secondary methods. Your thesis statement should indicate the primary pattern of organization you plan to use. Dejohn's final version of his introductory paragraph, annotated to show how he achieved the three goals listed above, is shown below. Although he drafted it first, he significantly revised it after completing his body paragraphs.

Paragraph opens with narrative that introduces the topic, provides background information, and stimulates reader interest →

Definitions of the Crips and Bloods included →

Thesis statement signals the primary pattern of organization (example) →

Closing sentence of paragraph suggests that comparison and contrast will also be used in the essay →

When I was 12 years old, my favorite cousin, Sean, who was 16 at the time, was shot and killed in a drive-by shooting. He was a good student and a fantastic basketball player. His high school coach was talking to a bunch of colleges about getting a scholarship for him. Sean wasn't a gang member, but his girl-friend's brother belonged to the Crips, one of L.A.'s biggest and most dangerous gangs. Sean was hanging out with his girlfriend and her brother, and someone from the Bloods, a rival gang, drove past and took a shot at the brother. He missed the brother and killed my cousin instead. I can still remember how angry I felt when I got the news. Two days later, a Crip stopped me when I was walking home from school. He asked me if I wanted to let the Bloods get away with what they did. I said no, I wanted them to pay. And that's how I became a gang member at the age of 12. A lot of people are shocked when someone tells them that gangs recruit kids who aren't even teenagers yet, but there's a lot more to being in a gang than any outsider realizes or hears about. For example, many people don't understand the difference between a "street family" and a "decent family," and the fact that coming from a street family makes you much more likely to join a gang.

EXERCISE 10-9

WRITING IN PROGRESS

Writing: Drafting an Introduction

Directions: Write an introductory paragraph for an essay on the topic you developed a thesis statement for in Exercise 10-8. Be sure to introduce your topic in a way that stimulates reader interest, include any necessary background information, and provide your thesis statement.

Drafting Body Paragraphs

Draft your body paragraphs to support your thesis statement. Make sure everything in your essay, regardless of the pattern you use, supports your thesis. When using secondary patterns in the body of your essay, make sure each paragraph has a topic sentence that signals the secondary pattern. Each sentence in the paragraph should then provide support for the topic sentence.

Once Dejohn made the decision to use example as his primary pattern of organization, he organized his thoughts and decided to focus on three key examples. The following list summarizes Dejohn's ideas for topic sentences and explains his strategy for supporting them.

1. Most gangs have female members. I'm going to tell the story of Tamika and Jocelyn, who were tougher than many of the guys I knew. (narration, description)
2. People think all city kids come from street families, because the media never report on decent families. I have to explain the difference between a "street family" and a "decent family." I also want to point out that most people never hear about all the honest, hard-working people who live in the inner city. (comparison and contrast, argument)
3. Most gang members want to get out of the gang and/or have tried to get out of the gang. I need to explain why people join gangs and then why they want to leave. (cause and effect)

Once he had a first draft of his topic sentences and introductory paragraph, Dejohn wrote the body of his essay, which is shown below. The annotations indicate how he used secondary patterns to support and explain his thesis statement.

Example #1 Topic Sentence →

Comparison: Guys and girls →

Cause and Effect: Why people join gangs →

Narrative →

Though most people don't realize it, most gangs have plenty of female members. Looking back to my days as a Crip, I would guess that about one out of every ten Crips was female. Like the guys, the girls who join gangs are looking for support and a family, because their mothers are junkies and their fathers are gone. Sometimes they are the girlfriends of Crips, and they end up joining the gang because they want to be a part of their boyfriend's life and also part of a group. Something these girls never talk about is the way they were sexually molested when they were younger, but I know this is true about a lot of them. Two of the female Crips I was closest to, Tamika and Jocelyn, both told me that their mothers'

Transitional phrase →

Example #2 Topic Sentence (includes Cause and Effect) →

Definitions of *decent family* and *street family* →

Comparison and Contrast →

Cause and Effect →

Argument →

Transitional word →

Example #3 →

Definition →

Cause and Effect →

boyfriends had taken advantage of them and mistreated them. But even though many gang members are female, they are never in charge. In other words, they are never the gang leader.

Because the media focuses on the "ghetto" and the "hood" and all the negative stereotypes that go with them, many people don't realize how family life leads young people to join a gang. If you come from a decent family, you probably won't join a gang, but if you come from a street family, you probably will. What do these terms mean? A "decent family" is a family that tries to support itself honestly. Usually they go to church and work their social lives around church activities. So the church becomes their extended family, and they don't have to look to gangs for support. In contrast, a "street family" is one that is focused on public respect and an emphasis on physical strength, the idea being that a man should do whatever it takes to protect his family. Coming from a street family leads to thug life, and thug life leads to joining a gang, which is just one big street family. Maybe if the media showed more positive role models for inner-city kids, and told stories of all the hard-working mothers and fathers who try to protect their kids from crime and drugs, street life wouldn't seem so glamorous to 12-year-olds.

Another little-known piece of information is the fact that many, many gang members try to leave the gang. They look around at the drugs, and the violence, and the murders, and the fact they may end up dead, and they decide gang life isn't right for them. But by that point it is too late. Once you're in, the leaders usually won't let you out. Some gangs have a practice called "jumping out," where people who want to leave get beaten mercilessly. If they live through it, they can leave the gang. If they die, well, they also get their wish to leave the gang.

Using Transitions to Help Readers Follow Your Thought Patterns

Use the transitional words and phrases you learned in Chapters 5 and 6 to help readers follow your thought patterns throughout your essay. Refer to the tables of transitional words and phrases often used with each pattern of development in those chapters.

EXERCISE 10-10

WRITING IN PROGRESS

Writing: Drafting Body Paragraphs

Directions: Outline your essay, and draft body paragraphs using the secondary patterns of organization you chose to explain and support your thesis.

Drafting a Conclusion

A good concluding paragraph both summarizes the essay and reminds readers of its key organizing principles. Be sure you have restated your thesis and primary pattern of organization. Doing so will ensure that your readers understand your purpose and main points.

As a former gang member, Dejohn thought the best way to close his essay would be to discourage young people from joining a gang. To accomplish that goal, he revisited his thesis statement, once again pointing to the essay's primary pattern of organization, and he closed his essay with a strong cause and effect statement and a strong argument.

Closing paragraph refers to essay's primary method of organization (example) →

The effects of gang membership on the individual →

Closing argument based on the author's experiences →

I could write many more pages providing additional examples of little-known facts about life in a gang. I could talk about the weekly meetings we had to attend, the monetary dues we had to pay, the crimes we had to commit, the way we got our nicknames, and the types of graffiti we used to tag our territory. I could talk about the price I paid to leave the gang. All of it would be interesting to people who do not know anything about gangs, and a lot of it would be shocking. But let me tell you: I can write this essay because I lived as a gang member. And it is not as glamorous or fun as rap music makes it sound. It drains your individuality, your soul, and your morality. It is much better for your life, your happiness, your friends, and your family if you read about gangs instead of joining one.

EXERCISE 10-11

WRITING IN PROGRESS

Writing: Drafting a Conclusion

Directions: Write a concluding paragraph for your essay that draws your essay to a close and reminds the reader of your thesis and main points.

EXERCISE 10-12

WRITING IN PROGRESS

Writing: Revising, Editing, and Proofreading

Directions: Read and evaluate your essay to determine whether it accomplishes your goals. Revise your essay using the essay revision strategies in Chapter 9 and checklists on page 288, and use transitions to ensure that it flows smoothly.

READ AND RESPOND: A Student Essay

Gang Life: Better from the Outside

Dejohn Harris

1. What are the negative stereotypes that Dejohn refers to in the third paragraph? Should he have provided more detailed information about these?
2. Can you suggest an alternative title for the essay?
3. Summarize the reasons why females join gangs. How are these reasons different from those of males?
4. Suppose Dejohn wants to turn his essay into a five-page term paper for his sociology class. What advice would you give him? Which topics from his brainstorming list or from his concluding paragraph would you find most interesting?
5. How could Dejohn's essay be improved?

Writing Assignments

For one of the following assignments, use the process described in this chapter to narrow your topic and outline a multi-pattern essay, specifying your primary pattern as well as the secondary patterns you will use. Then draft, revise, and proofread your paper.

1. For a business class, you are asked to write an essay about advertising. You can choose to write about any aspect of the topic. For example, you might write about one brand's specific advertising strategy (Coca-Cola, Levi's, or any other company you find interesting) or about the advertisements you have found most entertaining or annoying.
2. For a communications class, you are assigned an essay on the topic of social media. In the assignment, your instructor specifies that you can explore any aspect of the topic that you find interesting. So, for example, you might compare and contrast two popular forms of social media (such as Facebook and Twitter), or you might talk about the effects of social media on your life or on the lives of today's teenagers.
3. You are taking a biology class, and your instructor assigns an essay on the general topic of the common cold. He provides no further details. How would you go about narrowing the topic to one you find interesting? Which patterns of organization would you use? How would you get your reader interested in the topic in the opening paragraph? Draft your essay and share it with two classmates. Then incorporate their feedback into your revised, final, proofread essay.

READ AND RESPOND: A Professional Essay

What Is the High Art of Competitive Eating?

Gabriel Muller

Thinking Before Reading (See essay on p. 299)

You read this essay earlier in this chapter and have determined its primary pattern of organization and identified some of the secondary patterns used by the author. Now it is time to examine the reading more closely.

Writing in Response to Reading

Checking Your Comprehension MySkillsLab®

Answer each of the following questions using complete sentences.

1. What is George Shea's job?
2. Who are Joey Chestnut and Takeru Kobayashi, and what is their relationship?
3. According to "Wild" Bill Myers, what three aspects of competitive eating does a good eater need to be strategic about?

4. What happened to Juliet Lee as a result of competing in eating contests?
5. Give one example of Halloran's suggestion that we enjoy seeing people struggle to keep their body under control.
6. What did Rick Best do to stretch his stomach for competition?

Strengthening Your Vocabulary MySkillsLab®

Identify at least five words used in the reading that are unfamiliar to you. Using context, word parts, or a dictionary, write a brief definition of each word.

Examining the Reading: Drawing an Idea Map

Create an idea map of "What is the High Art of Competitive Eating?" Start with the title and thesis and list the main points of the essay and the conclusion.

Reading and Writing: An Integrated Perspective MySkillsLab®

Get ready to write about the reading by discussing the following:

1. Why does the author begin the essay by describing George Shea? What does this introductory paragraph suggest about how the author will approach the subject?
2. Discuss why the author includes quotes from various people throughout the essay. What do these quotes add to your understanding of and response to the subject? How accurate and reliable are these sources?
3. Discuss the description of Crazy Legs Conti's pre-contest preparations (paragraphs 6–9). What impression does the author create by including these details?
4. What does the author mean by describing competitive eating as "a sort of sport in reverse" (paragraph 11)?
5. Are you, like Colin McGinn, skeptical about the status of eating contests as an actual sport? Why do you think such competitions are so popular? Write a journal entry answering these questions and giving your definition of "real sports."
6. Why does the author include the description of Juliet Lee in paragraphs 14–16? Discuss what her story adds to the essay.
7. What is the effect of beginning this essay with a photograph? What can you predict about the subject and tone of the essay by looking at the photograph?
8. What is the purpose of the second photograph (p. 302)? How does the photograph reflect or correspond to details in the essay?

Thinking and Writing Critically MySkillsLab®

1. How does the author's choice of words reveal his attitude toward the subject? How does the use of connotative language affect your response to the subject? Find and underline examples of connotative language throughout the essay.
2. Express the author's thesis in your own words.

3. What does "high art" in the title mean? Evaluate the effectiveness of the title.

4. Evaluate the types of details the author uses to support his ideas. Which details are most effective? What other details might he have included?

5. Who is the author's intended audience? What do you think the audience's reaction to this essay is?

6. Define the author's purpose in writing this essay. Is he trying to convince his readers to take an action or agree with his viewpoint? Does he succeed in achieving his purpose?

7. Evaluate the conclusion. Why did the author end the essay this way?

Writing Paragraphs MySkillsLab®

1. Would you ever compete in an eating contest? Why or why not? What food would you choose to consume if you were in such a contest? Write a paragraph explaining your answer.

2. Write a paragraph answering the author's question at the end of paragraph 12: "Why, then, would anyone risk public humiliation, potential damage to long-term health, and a grueling training routine to perform an activity which, to some, serves a gimmicky marketing need and, even worse, a conspicuous display of American gluttony?"

3. How would you go about convincing someone like Colin McGinn that competitive eating is really a sport? How would you try to persuade a competitive eater like "Wild" Bill Myers that competitive eating is *not* a sport? Choose one of these questions and write a persuasive paragraph from that viewpoint.

Writing Essays MySkillsLab®

4. What types of competitions (sports or otherwise) do you find most interesting? Why? In your opinion, what are the best and worst aspects of any kind of competition? Write an essay explaining your answers and exploring both the positive and negative aspects of competition.

5. The author refers to elements of competitive eating as "cerebral and high-endurance" (paragraph 9). What endeavors have you undertaken that could be described in these terms? Write an essay describing something in your own life that required you to put forth an effort similar to the top-ranked eaters described in the essay.

6. Do you think that we enjoy a special type of pleasure from watching someone struggle to keep their body under control, as suggested by Halloran (paragraph 20)? What was your response to the examples of such struggles? Would you "try to marvel at their masochism," as suggested by McGinn? Write an essay answering these questions and responding to Halloran and McGinn.

SELF-TEST SUMMARY

To test yourself, cover the Answer column with a sheet of paper and answer each question in the left column. Evaluate each of your answers as you work by sliding the paper down and comparing your answer with what is printed in the Answer column.

QUESTION	ANSWER
■ GOAL 1 Define a multi-pattern essay What is a multi-pattern essay?	A multi-pattern essay is one that uses more than one pattern of organization.
■ GOAL 2 Recognize multiple patterns of organization in readings Why is it important to recognize multiple patterns within a reading?	Recognizing multiple patterns helps you understand the reading's overall organization and key points, develop a deeper understanding of the topic, and prepare for essay exams.
How do you recognize primary and secondary patterns?	The primary pattern is the reading's key organizing principle and provides the framework on which the writer builds support for the thesis statement. Secondary patterns provide further explanation, details, clarification, and information.
■ GOAL 3 Write a multi-pattern essay What factors should you consider when choosing a primary pattern of organization?	When choosing a primary pattern, consider the assignment, your purpose, your audience, the complexity of your topic, and the course for which you are writing.
What process should you follow to write a multi-pattern essay?	To write a multi-pattern essay, begin by generating ideas about your topic, then narrow the topic and select primary and secondary patterns. Next, write a thesis statement that reflects your primary pattern. Draft your introduction, body paragraphs, and conclusion. Include topic sentences that reflect secondary patterns and use transitions to help readers follow your thought patterns. Make sure your conclusion revisits your thesis statement and primary pattern.

MySkillsLab®

Visit **Chapter 10, "Reading and Writing Essays with Multiple Patterns,"** in MySkillsLab to test your understanding of chapter goals.

Writing Essays Using Sources

11

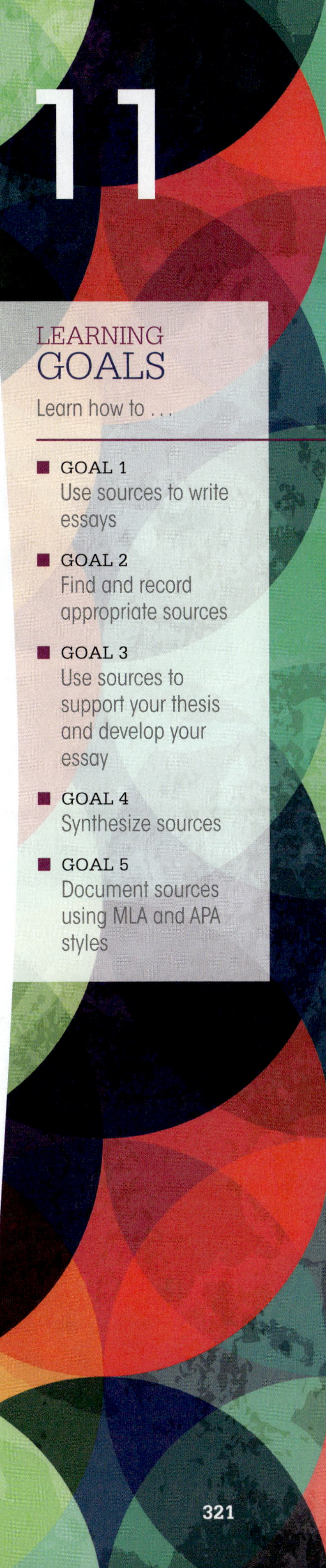

LEARNING GOALS

Learn how to . . .

- GOAL 1
  Use sources to write essays
- GOAL 2
  Find and record appropriate sources
- GOAL 3
  Use sources to support your thesis and develop your essay
- GOAL 4
  Synthesize sources
- GOAL 5
  Document sources using MLA and APA styles

THINK About It!

The sky divers shown in the above photograph are participating in an extreme sport—group skydiving. This sport requires careful preparation, extensive training, and exact execution. Write a sentence explaining how writing an essay is like learning a sport, either an extreme sport or a more traditional one. You might write about the sport shown in the photograph or another sport of your choice.

Although both learning a sport and writing an essay take effort, each can be broken down into manageable parts. Both require a systematic approach as well. In order to become a good athlete, you learn and practice skills; you listen to your coach, read books about your sport, and talk with peers; and you synthesize (combine) everything you hear and read and decide what steps you need to take in order to improve your performance. To write an essay, you begin by reading about the topic, systematically choosing and evaluating sources, selecting appropriate parts to read carefully, making notes, and pulling together the information from various sources. Then, as you begin writing, you also follow a process. You plan and organize your ideas, draft, revise, and edit. In this chapter you will learn the steps in writing essays using sources and how to correctly credit your sources.

Reading and Writing Connections

EVERYDAY CONNECTIONS

- **Reading** As part of your vacation planning, you read reviews of several hotels in the city that you are going to visit. You also consult the hotels' Web sites to find out about their vacation packages, room options, and proximity to local attractions.
- **Writing** After your vacation, you write a letter to the editor of a local travel magazine telling readers about your trip, explaining the process you went through in order to have a successful vacation, and the different sources they could access to plan their own trip.

ACADEMIC CONNECTIONS

- **Reading** You read a chapter in your American history textbook discussing the responsibilities of the president as commander in chief of the U.S. armed forces as well as several articles about how recent presidents have acted in this role.
- **Writing** You write an essay in which you compare and contrast the actions of two presidents as commanders in chief during times of war, citing the sources you read.

WORKPLACE CONNECTIONS

- **Reading** You read about expanding populations in three cities so you can conduct a market analysis to determine which city would be best for a new branch of your company.
- **Writing** You write a summary of your research and provide detailed support for your recommendation for the city to be considered for a new company branch.

What Is an Essay That Uses Sources?

■ GOAL 1
Use sources to write essays

Many assignments in college require you to integrate your reading and writing skills by locating and reading several sources of information on a topic and then using them to support your ideas in an essay or report. At other times you may be asked to integrate your skills by examining print and online sources and coming up with a new idea or thesis about them in the form of a research paper. In this chapter you will integrate your reading and writing skills by selecting and narrowing a topic, developing a thesis, using sources to find information on your topic, pulling together (synthesizing) ideas from the sources to support your thesis, writing an essay, and documenting your sources.

EXAMINING STUDENT WRITING

By examining the following documented student essay by Adam Simmons, you will learn how to research a topic, synthesize information, avoid plagiarism, and write a correctly documented and formatted paper using sources. Throughout

the rest of the chapter, we will use parts of Adam's essay to illustrate techniques and strategies.

Adam Simmons is a first-year student at a state university, where he is majoring in criminal justice. For his sociology class, Adam was asked to write an essay that examined the pros and cons of a social problem or issue, using MLA format. We will follow Adam's progress as he selects his sources, develops a thesis statement, and writes his essay.

Student's last name and page number appear flush right on every page

Simmons 1

Student name, instructor's name, course number, and date are placed flush left

Adam Simmons

Professor Martin

Sociology 101

12 November 2014

Title is centered and is not in capitals, underlined, or in quotation marks

Weighing the Consequences of Censorship in Media

Thesis statement

Should music lyrics be censored if they contain violent or objectionable references? Should pornography be censored? Should media be prevented from reporting on the private lives of celebrities and politicians? Should news media report events that might endanger national security? These are examples of controversial questions about which people hold different opinions. Each side has good intentions. Those who favor censorship say it protects people or the country, while those who oppose censorship believe that censorship limits the Constitutional right to freedom of speech, but there should be a middle ground.

Topic sentence states reason in support of censorship

People in favor of censorship of the media often talk about the morality of the content. A common argument is that some media contain inappropriate material that could unintentionally be seen by young children. In this case, inappropriate material is defined as pornographic, violent, vulgar, or sexual in any way. This could lead to the loss of their innocence or even to danger. The argument is that it could lead kids to try and repeat what they are seeing on the television or what they are hearing about in music (Robinson 42). Censoring such materials children would

Simmons 2

not expose children to things that might not be appropriate for their age, so censorship would protect children. They would also be protected from potentially harmful people.

Topic sentence states second reason supporting censorship

Some people also believe that censorship is important when it is used to protect military information since, as President Obama was quoted as saying, "Leaks related to national security can put people at risk" (Warren). With the government monitoring what information the media offer, it is less likely that information the government does not want leaked out will be made public. This could mean keeping troops safe and protecting domestic and foreign policy, especially in wartime when enemies can track news sources to find out about U.S. strategy. It can also help keep dangerous information, such as details about weaponry, from getting into the wrong hands.

Topic sentence notes censorship can be dangerous

Censorship has some dangers, though. It can be viewed as directly violating the First Amendment of the Constitution and taking away freedom of speech. The amendment states "Congress shall make no law . . . abridging the freedom of speech, or of the press. . . ." There are some who say the First Amendment acts as a "complete barrier to government censorship" (Pember and Calvert 43); since the Constitution creates this ban, censorship is in effect unlawful. However, the 76th Congress enacted the Smith Act that modified the interpretation of this amendment, making it "a crime to advocate the violent overthrow of the government" (Pember and Calvert 52).

Topic sentence indicates there are further reasons for concern

There are other reasons that people object to censorship. Some people argue that censorship can also be abused by the government, and in the wrong hands it can lead to a loss of freedom of speech and halt a flow of ideas in a society, as

Simmons 3

seen under various dictatorships (Karaim 307). It can also be said that censorship stifles creativity. Saying that some works are immoral or unsuitable is making a legal statement that some art is good and some art is bad ("What Is Censorship?"). Art, in itself, is subjective and cannot really be labeled that way. If art has to be made to meet the requirements of the censors, then it will never be able to be completely creative and free.

Conclusion compares the two approaches to censorship

Both viewpoints about censorship approach the topic with the hope of doing what is best for society, but they come at it from completely different angles. One hopes to make things better by removing immoral or dangerous speech, and the other seeks to let every person have the ability to say what he or she wants regardless of whether it is seen moral by others. Both viewpoints have merits and risks. Many cases hinge on judgment, interpretation, and opinion. What types of song lyrics are objectionable? What constitutes pornography? Who decides what events might endanger national security? What aspects of private lives of celebrities or politicians might be considered off-limits for the media? The issue of censorship is one about which many people feel strongly, but there is not an easy answer, nor is the solution clear-cut. Instead it is a matter of degree, interpretation, and definition. Let's consider situations on a case-by-case basis, and in all cases, let reason, logic, and good will prevail.

Adam lists questions that the two approaches raise

Writer finishes with appeal for a common sense approach

Works Cited page appears at the end of the paper and starts on a new page.

Title is centered.

Entries are listed alphabetically by last name or by title if there is no author. Entries start flush left and are double-spaced. Second and subsequent lines are indented half an inch.

Simmons 4

Works Cited

Karaim, Reed. "China Today." *CQ Researcher*, vol. 24, no. 13, 4 Apr. 2014, pp. 289-312, library.cqpress.com/cqresearcher/document.php?id=cqresrre2014040400.

Pember, Don R., and Clay Calvert. *Mass Media Law*. 17th ed., McGraw Hill, 2011.

Robinson, Kerry H. *Innocence, Knowledge and the Construction of Childhood: The Contradictory Nature of Sexuality and Censorship in Children's Contemporary Lives*. Taylor and Francis, 2013.

Warren, James. "President Obama Defends Aggressive Actions to Investigate National Security Leaks, But Says Press Must Be Safeguarded Too." *Daily News* [New York], 16 May 2013, www.nydailynews.com/news/national/president-promises-balance-protect-national-security-free-press-article-1.1346017.

"What Is Censorship?" *American Civil Liberties Union*, www.aclu.org/what-censorship. Accessed 27 May 2014.

Reading: Find and Record Appropriate Sources

■ GOAL 2
Find and record appropriate sources

Libraries are filled with sources—print, electronic, and more. They house thousands of books, journals, videos, DVDs, pamphlets, tapes, and newspapers, as well as computers that enable you to access the World Wide Web. Yet this very abundance of sources means that one of the hardest parts of doing research is locating the sources that will be the most help to you.

Many books have been written on how to do research and how to use and document print and electronic sources. Therefore, this section gives only a brief overview of the research process and offers advice on how to get started.

For his essay, Adam found information in a variety of sources, both electronic and print. His Works Cited list includes a news magazine, a law textbook, a newspaper, and an article from the American Civil Liberties Union Web site.

Tips for Finding Appropriate Sources

Suppose you are writing an essay about differences in men's and women's communication styles. Although you will find many sources on your topic, not all will be appropriate for your particular assignment. Some sources may be too technical; others may be too sketchy. Some may be outdated, others too opinionated. Your task is to find sources that will give you good, solid, current information or points of view. Use the following tips:

1. **Consult a reference librarian.** If you are unsure of where to begin, ask a reference librarian for advice.
2. **Use a systematic approach.** Start by using general sources, either print or electronic, such as general reference books. Then, as needed, move to more specific sources such as periodicals and journals.
3. **Use current sources.** For many topics, such as controversial issues or scientific or medical advances, only the most up-to-date sources are useful. For other topics, such as the moral issues involved in abortion or euthanasia, older sources can be used. Before you begin, decide on a cutoff date before which you feel information will be outdated and therefore not useful to you.
4. **Sample a variety of viewpoints.** Try to find sources that present different viewpoints on the same subject rather than counting on one source to contain everything you need. Various authors take different approaches and have different opinions on the same topic, all of which can increase your understanding of the topic.
5. **Preview articles by reading abstracts or summaries.** Many sources begin with an abstract or end with a summary, so read them to determine whether the source is going to be helpful.
6. **Read sources selectively.** Do not waste time reading an entire book or article; skim to avoid parts that are not on the subject and to locate portions that relate directly to the topic. To read selectively,
   - use indexes and tables of contents to locate the portions of books that are useful and appropriate. In articles, use abstracts or summaries as a guide to the material's organization: the order in which ideas appear in the summary or abstract is the order in which they appear in the source itself.
   - after you have identified useful sections, preview to get an overview of the material.
   - use headings to select sections to read thoroughly.
7. **Choose reliable, trustworthy sources.** The Internet contains a great deal of valuable information, but it also contains rumor, gossip, hoaxes, and misinformation. Before using a source, evaluate it by checking the author's credentials, considering the sponsor or publisher of the site, checking the date of posting, and verifying links. If you are uncertain about the information presented on a site, verify the information by cross-checking it with another source.
8. **Look for sources that lead to other sources.** Some sources include a bibliography, which could provide leads to other works related to your topic. Follow links included in electronic sources.

Recording Sources to Avoid Plagiarism

Keep track of all the sources you use. There are important reasons for doing this:

- **You are more likely to avoid plagiarism if you keep accurate records of your sources. Plagiarism** is using an author's words or ideas without acknowledging that you have done so. It is a serious ethical error and legal violation. In some colleges, plagiarism is sufficient cause for failing a course or even being dismissed from the college. You can easily avoid plagiarism by properly acknowledging your sources within your paper.

- **All sources you use must be cited.** When you use sources in an essay, you must acknowledge them all at the end of your paper in a bibliography, or "Works Cited" or "References" list. Providing your reader with information on your sources is called **documentation.**
- **You may want to refer to the source again.**

Be sure to record all publication information about each print and electronic source you decide to use.

- **For print sources,** record the title, author(s), volume, edition, date of publication, publisher, and page number(s).
- **For online sites,** record the author, title of the work, title of the Web site, version or edition used, the publisher of the site, the date of publication, and the URL or DOI.

You may want to use index cards or a small bound notebook to record source information, using a separate card or page for each source. Other options are photocopying pages from print sources, downloading and/or printing information from Web site sources, cutting and pasting links and information into a Word document, and bookmarking sites that might be useful for future reference. Adam used a combination of these strategies: he started a Word file for listing sources and copying links into, as well as downloading and printing some of the articles he found. (You will learn how to document sources you use later in this chapter.)

Also, keep in mind that a good essay does not just consist of a series of quotations strung together. Instead, you should combine information you find in sources to come up with new ideas, perspectives, and responses to your topic. Annotating, outlining, paraphrasing, and summarizing are all important skills for doing this and are covered in Chapter 1:

- annotating (p. 13)
- outlining (p. 16)
- paraphrasing (p. 24)
- summarizing (p. 26)

Writing: Use Sources to Support Your Thesis and Develop Your Essay

- GOAL 3
Use sources to support your thesis and develop your essay

Adam chose to write his assigned essay on the pros and cons of censorship. After brainstorming to generate ideas, he created a working thesis statement: "There are different viewpoints about censorship in the media." In order to present a convincing argument, he needed to find facts, statistics, and evidence to support his opinions. He realized he would need some or all of the following evidence to support his main ideas:

- definitions of terms such as *morality* and *inappropriate material.*
- facts about the effects of leaks related to national security.

- evidence from experts in the field of Constitutional law.
- examples of the stifling effects of censorship in dictatorships.

To gather this information, he went to his college library and consulted both print and online sources.

Once you decide what major idea to work with, you are ready to develop an essay. Use your newly discovered idea as your working thesis statement. Then use details, documented properly, from each source to develop and support your thesis statement. Follow these guidelines to properly use sources you find:

Guidelines for Proper Use of Sources

1. **Write a first draft of your essay.** Before consulting sources to support your ideas, work through the first three steps of the writing process: *prewriting*, *organizing*, and *drafting*. Decide on a working thesis statement and write your own ideas about the topic down on paper. Once you have drafted your essay, you will be able to see what types of supporting information are necessary. If you research first, you might get flooded with facts and with other writers' voices and viewpoints, and lose your own.
2. **Analyze your draft to identify where you need additional information.** Read your draft looking for unsupported statements, underlining them as you find them. Then make a list of needed information, and form questions that need to be answered. Some students find it effective to write each question on a separate index card. For example, Adam underlined the following sentence in his second paragraph:

Some media contain inappropriate material that could unintentionally be seen by young children.

To support this statement, he needed to provide a definition of the term "inappropriate material" and then explain the potential effects of such material on young children, information he found in a book by Kerry Robinson.

The following types of statements benefit from supporting information:

- **Opinions**

EXAMPLE	Censorship has some dangers though.
NEEDED INFORMATION	What evidence supports that opinion? What are the dangers?

- **Broad, general ideas**

EXAMPLE	Censorship stifles creativity.
NEEDED INFORMATION	In what ways? Can creative works, such as art, be labeled as immoral or unsuitable?

- **Cause and effect statements**

EXAMPLE	Censorship can lead to a loss of freedom of speech and halt a flow of ideas in a society.
NEEDED INFORMATION	In what societies has this happened?

- **Statements that assert what should be done**

EXAMPLE	Censorship is important when it is used to protect military information.
NEEDED INFORMATION	What happens when information related to national security is leaked? What are the risks of the government's monitoring what information the media offers?

3. **Record information and note sources.** As you locate needed information, make a decision about the best way to record it, using one of the methods discussed on page 327, and be sure to include complete bibliographic information for each source.

   As you consult sources, you will probably discover new ideas and perhaps even a new approach to your topic. For example, as Adam read through his sources, he learned that although the Constitution establishes the right to freedom of speech, Supreme Court cases have modified the interpretation of the First Amendment; certain types of speech are subject to censorship. He recorded this new idea, along with its source, in his Word file.

4. **Revise your paper.** Begin by reevaluating your thesis based on your research. You may need to fine-tune or revise it as a result of what you have learned. Add new supporting information (the next section of this chapter discusses how to synthesize information from other sources), and then reevaluate your draft, eliminating statements for which you could not locate supporting information, statements you found to be inaccurate, and statements for which you found contradictory evidence.

WRITING IN PROGRESS

Developing a Thesis Statement for a Documented Paper

Directions: Choose one of the following broad topics. Use a prewriting strategy to narrow the topic and develop a working thesis statement (see p. 47). Locate at least three reference sources that are useful and appropriate for writing an essay of two to three pages on the topic you have developed. Be sure to record all the bibliographic information for each source.

1. Privacy on social media sites
2. Date rape
3. Gay marriage
4. The evolution of rock and roll
5. The spread, control, or treatment of bird flu
6. Internet dating
7. Controversy over college athletic scholarships
8. Legalized gambling (or lotteries)

Critical Thinking: Synthesize Sources

■ GOAL 4
Synthesize sources

Synthesis is a process of using information from two or more sources in order to develop new ideas about a topic or to draw conclusions about it. Many college assignments require you to synthesize material—that is, to locate and read several sources on a topic and use them to write an essay. For example, in a sociology course, you may be asked to consult several sources on the topic of organized crime and then write an essay describing the relationship between organized crime and illegal-drug sales. In a marketing class, your instructor may direct you to consult several sources on advertising strategies and on the gullibility of young children, and to write an essay weighing the effects of television commercials on young children.

Did you notice that, in each of the above examples, you were asked to come up with a new idea, one that did not appear in any of the sources but was *based on* all the sources? Creating something new from what you read is one of the most basic, important, and satisfying skills you will learn in college. Synthesis is also often required in the workplace:

- As a sales executive for an Internet service provider company, you may be asked to synthesize what you have learned about customer hardware problems.
- As a medical office assistant, you may have extensive problems with a new computer system. The office manager asks you to write a memo to the company that installed the system, categorizing the types of problems you have experienced.
- As an environmental engineer, you must synthesize years of research in order to make a proposal for local river and stream cleanup.

How to Compare Sources to Synthesize

Comparing sources is part of synthesizing. Comparing involves placing sources side by side and examining how they are the same and how they are different. However, before you begin to compare two or more sources, be sure you understand each fully. Depending on how detailed and difficult each source is, use annotating, paraphrasing, and summarizing or underline, outline, or draw idea maps (see Chapter 1 for more details on each) to make sure that you have a good grasp of your source material.

Let's assume you are taking a speech course in which you are studying nonverbal communication, or body language. You have chosen to study one aspect of body language: eye contact. Among your sources are the following excerpts:

SOURCE A

Eye contact, or *gaze*, is also a common form of nonverbal communication. Eyes have been called the "windows of the soul." In many cultures, people tend to assume that someone who avoids eye contact is evasive, cold, fearful, shy, or indifferent; that frequent gazing signals intimacy, sincerity, self-confidence, and respect; and that the person who stares is tense, angry, and unfriendly. Typically, however, eye contact is interpreted in light of a pre-existing relationship. If a relationship is friendly, frequent eye contact elicits a positive impression. If a relationship is not friendly, eye contact is seen in negative terms. It has been said that if two people lock eyes for more than a few seconds, they are either going to make love or kill each other (Kleinke, 1986; Patterson, 1983).

—Brehm and Kassin, *Social Psychology*, p. 149

SOURCE B

Eye contact often indicates the nature of the relationship between two people. One research study showed that eye contact is moderate when one is addressing a very high-status person, maximized when addressing a moderately high-status person, and only minimal when talking to a low-status person. There are also predictable differences in eye contact when one person likes another or when there may be rewards involved.

Increased eye contact is also associated with increased liking between the people who are communicating. In an interview, for example, you are likely to make judgments about the interviewer's friendliness according to the amount of eye contact shown. The less eye contact, the less friendliness. In a courtship relationship, more eye contact can be observed among those seeking to develop a more intimate relationship. One research study (Saperston, 2003) suggests that the intimacy is a function of the amount of eye gazing, physical proximity, intimacy of topic, and amount of smiling. This model best relates to established relationships.

—Weaver, *Understanding Interpersonal Communication*, p. 321

To compare these sources, ask the following questions:

1. **On what do the sources agree?** Sources A and B recognize eye contact as an important communication tool. Both agree that there is a connection between eye contact and the relationship between the people involved. Both also agree that more frequent eye contact occurs among people who are friendly or intimate.
2. **On what do the sources disagree?** Sources A and B do not disagree, though they do present different information about eye contact (see the next item).
3. **How do they differ?** Sources A and B differ in the information they present. Source A states that in some cultures the frequency of eye contact suggests certain personality traits (someone who avoids eye contact is considered to be cold, for example), but Source B does not discuss cultural interpretations. Source B discusses how eye contact is related to status—the level of importance of the person being addressed—while Source A does not.
4. **Are the viewpoints toward the subject similar or different?** Sources A and B both take a serious approach to the subject of eye contact.
5. **Does each source provide supporting evidence for major points?** Source A cites two references. Source B cites a research study.

After comparing your sources, the next step is to form your own ideas based on what you have discovered.

How to Develop Ideas About Sources

Developing your own ideas is a process of drawing conclusions. Your goal is to decide what both sources, taken together, suggest. Together, Sources A and B recognize that eye contact is an important part of body language. However, they focus on different aspects of how eye contact can be interpreted. You can conclude that studying eye contact can be useful in understanding the relationship between two individuals: you can judge the relative status, the degree of friendship, and the level of intimacy between the people. After reading and thinking about his sources, Adam realized that there were quite different, even opposite, points of view on the topic of censorship. He decided to outline the pros and cons in his essay and then provide

his opinion on the topic, based on a synthesis of what he had learned. Based on this decision, he revised his thesis statement to more accurately reflect his point:

> Those who favor censorship say it protects people or the country, while those who oppose censorship believe that censorship limits the Constitutional right to freedom of speech, but there should be a middle ground.

EXERCISE 11-2

Synthesizing Sources

Directions: Read each of the following excerpts from sources on the topic of lost and endangered species. Synthesize these two sources, using the steps listed above, and develop a thesis statement about the causes of the decline and loss of plant and animal species.

SOURCE A

What Causes Extinction?

Every living organism must eventually die, and the same is true of species. Just like individuals, species are "born" (through the process of speciation), persist for some period of time, and then perish. The ultimate fate of any species is **extinction**, the death of the last of its members. In fact, at least 99.9% of all the species that have ever existed are now extinct. The natural course of evolution, as revealed by fossils, is continual turnover of species as new ones arise and old ones become extinct.

The immediate cause of extinction is probably always environmental change, in either the living or the nonliving parts of the environment. Two major environmental factors that may drive a species to extinction are competition among species and habitat destruction.

Interactions with Other Species May Drive a Species to Extinction

Interactions such as competition and predation serve as agents of natural selection. In some cases, these same interactions can lead to extinction rather than to adaptation. Organisms compete for limited resources in all environments. If a species' competitors evolve superior adaptations and the species doesn't evolve fast enough to keep up, it may become extinct.

Habitat Change and Destruction Are the Leading Causes of Extinction

Habitat change, both contemporary and prehistoric, is the single greatest cause of extinctions. Present-day habitat destruction due to human activities is proceeding at a rapid pace. Many biologists believe that we are presently in the midst of the fastest-paced and most widespread episode of species extinction in the history of life on Earth. Loss of tropical forests is especially devastating to species diversity. As many as half the species presently on Earth may be lost during the next 50 years as the tropical forests that contain them are cut for timber and to clear land for cattle and crops.

SOURCE B

Reasons for the Decline of Species

Extinctions of the distant past were caused largely by processes of climate change, plate tectonics, and even asteroid impacts. Current threats to biodiversity include: habitat destruction, pollution, invasive species, population, and overexploitation. The losses in the future will be greatest in the developing world, where biodiversity is greatest and human population growth is highest. Africa and Asia have lost almost two-thirds of their original natural habitat.

Habitat Change

By far the greatest source of biodiversity loss is the physical alteration of habitats through the processes of conversion, fragmentation, simplification, and intrusion. Habitat destruction has already been responsible for 36% of the known extinctions and is the key factor in the currently observed population declines. Natural species are adapted to specific habitats, so if the habitat changes or is eliminated, the species go with it.

Pollution

Another factor that decreases biodiversity is pollution, which can directly kill many kinds of plants and animals, seriously reducing their populations. For example, nutrients (such as phosphorus and nitrogen) that travel down the Mississippi River from the agricultural heartland of the United States have created a "dead zone" in the Gulf of Mexico, an area of more than 10,000 square miles (as of 2008) where oxygen completely disappears from depths below 20 meters every summer. Shrimp, fish, crabs, and other commercially valuable sea life are either killed or forced to migrate away from this huge area along the Mississippi and Louisiana coastline. Pollution destroys or alters habitats, with consequences just as severe as those caused by deliberate conversions. Every oil spill kills seabirds and often sea mammals, sometimes by the thousands.

—adapted from Wright and Boorse, *Environmental Science*, pp. 140 and 144

WRITING IN PROGRESS

Synthesizing Sources and Writing a First Draft

Directions: Using the steps listed on page 332, synthesize the three reference sources you gathered for Exercise 11-1. Then write a first draft of the essay on the topic you chose. If any of these sources are dated or not focused enough for your thesis, you may need to locate additional ones.

WRITING IN PROGRESS

Recording Sources

Directions: List source information for the essay you drafted in Exercise 11-3 to use in your Works Cited or References list. See page 327 for tips on what information to include.

Document Sources Using MLA or APA Styles

■ GOAL 5
Document sources using MLA and APA styles

You can incorporate researched information into your paper in one of two ways: (1) summarize or paraphrase the information or (2) quote directly from it. In both cases, you must give credit to the authors from whom you borrowed the information by documenting your sources in a list of references so your reader can locate it easily. Failure to provide documentation of a source is called plagiarism: using an author's words or ideas without acknowledging that you have done so (see p. 327 for how to avoid plagiarism).

Documentation

Both the Modern Language Association (MLA) and the American Psychological Association (APA) use a system of in-text citation: a brief note in the body of the text that refers to a source that is fully described in the alphabetized Works Cited list (MLA) or References list (APA) at the end of the paper. The MLA format is typically used in English and humanities papers (see student essay on p. 323), while the APA format is commonly used in social science papers.

An Overview of the MLA Style

MLA guidelines now focus on citing sources based on a series of simple principles and elements that can be applied to a wide variety of source types and formats. For a comprehensive review of the new system, consult the *MLA Handbook*, 8th edition, or access the MLA Web site (www.style.mla.org).

When you refer to, summarize, paraphrase, quote, or in any way use an author's words or ideas, you must indicate their original source by inserting an in-text citation that refers your reader to the "Works Cited" list. If you name the author in your sentence, only include the page number in the citation; if you do not name the author, include both the author's name and page number in the citation. When you include a quotation, use an introductory phrase to signal that the quotation is to follow, as in the examples below.

> Miller poses the idea that if a good story is supposed to be a condensed version of life, then life should be lived like a good story in the first place (39).
>
> If a good story is supposed to be a condensed version of life, then life should be lived like a good story in the first place (Miller 39).
>
> According to Miller, "[quotation]." As Miller notes, "[quotation]." In the words of Miller, "[quotation]."

When citing a source, use the Elements Diagram below to select and organize relevant information. MLA uses the term *container* when a source (like an article) appears in a larger source (such as a magazine or newspaper). Note that Container 1 provides primary source information for the author and/or title in elements 1 or 2, so include all relevant information for elements 3-9 in the order shown. As the primary source may also appear within a second container (e.g., an article is in a journal, and the journal is found in a database), you also need to document information for elements 3-9 that is relevant to this second container.

Elements Diagram	Core Elements	Description of Elements	Examples
1. Author. 2. Title of source. **Container 1 (primary source information)**	1. Author.	• Last name, first name • Second author's name written first name, last name • Three or more authors, reverse first name and follow with comma and "et al." • For non-author creators, add labels and spell them out • Treat pseudonyms as author names	• Carr, James I. • Carr, James I., and Martha Hopkins. • Fuentes, José, et al. • García, Emma, editor. • Cook, Douglas, translator. • @Cmdr_Hadfield.

(continued)

3. Title of container,
4. Other contributors,
5. Version,
6. Number,
7. Publisher,
8. Publication date,
9. Location.

Container 2 (where you found the primary source, e.g., database, Web site, online archive)

3. Title of container,
4. Other contributors,
5. Version,
6. Number,

2. Title of source.	• Place title in quotation marks if it is part of larger source (e.g., a poem, essay, TV episode, blog post, or tweet), followed by a period.	• "The Bee" (poem); "Everybody Dies" (TV episode); "On Noise" (essay); "Inside the Collapse of The New Republic" (blog post)
	• Place title in italics if it is self-contained (e.g., a book, play, TV series, Web site, or album), followed by a period.	• *Florence Gordon* (novel); *King Lear* (play); *House* (TV series); *The New Yorker* (Web site); *Cool It* (album)
3. Title of container,	• If the source is part of a larger whole, that whole is considered a container; it is italicized and followed by a comma.	• Ronnie Corbett, performer. "We Love British Comedy." *Facebook,*
	• If the title of the source is the whole source, it appears as element 2, and there may be no entry for element 3.	• Maugham, W. Somerset. *Of Human Bondage.* Viking Penguin, 1963.
	• A container can be nested in a second container (see diagram on left).	• Barnard, Neal D., et al. "Vegetarian and Vegan Diets in Type 2 Diabetes Management." *Nutrition Reviews*, vol. 67, no. 5, pp. 255–263. *NCBI,* doi:10.1111/ j.1753-4887.2009.00198.x.
4. Other contributors,	• Place other important contributors to a work after the title of the container, preceded by a descriptor: *adapted by, performed by, directed by* or *general editor* or *guest editors,* and followed by a comma.	• Dickinson, Emily. "Griefs." *Emily Dickinson: Selected Poems,* edited by Stanley Applebaum, Dover Thrift Editions, 1990, p. 25.
5. Version,	• Indicate if there is more than one version of the source: *Updated ed., Expanded ed., 13th ed., director's cut,*	• McWhorter, Kathleen. *In Concert: Reading and Writing.* 2nd ed., Pearson, 2016.
6. Number,	• Use abbreviations "vol." and "no." for volume and issue number, separated by a comma.	• Bivins, Corey. "A Soy-free, Nut-free Vegan Meal Plan." *Vegetarian Journal,* vol. 30, no. 1, pp. 14-17.
7. Publisher,	• Name of organization primarily responsible for producing source, followed by a comma.	• Pearson, Penguin, Netflix, Twentieth Century Fox
	• If two or more organizations are equally responsible, cite both with forward slash between them.	• Lee, Malcolm D., director. *Barbershop: The Next Cut.* Performance by Ice Cube, MGM / New Line Cinema, 2016.
	• Use "U" for university and "P" for Press.	• Oxford UP (abbreviation for Oxford University Press)

(continued)

7. Publisher,	8. Publication date,	• Cite the most relevant date, followed by a comma. If you are citing a print work found online, use the date of the online posting.	• Lilla, Mark. "The President and the Passions." *The New York Times Magazine*, 19 Dec. 2010, p. MM 13.
8. Publication date,	9. Location.	• For print sources, provide page numbers preceded by p. or pp. and followed by a period.	• Maugham, W. Somerset. *Of Human Bondage*. Viking Penguin, 1963, p. 211.
9. Location.		• For online sites, MLA recommends providing a URL (check with your professor) or DOI (preferred), followed by a period. Drop "http://" if it appears in URL.	• Woolf, Virginia. "A Haunted House." *Monday or Tuesday*, Harcourt Brace, 1921. *Bartleby.com*, www.bartleby.com/85/.

An Overview of the APA Style

The table below presents representative samples of APA in-text citation, References documentation, and Internet source citation. For a comprehensive overview of APA style, refer to the *Publication Manual of the American Psychological Association* (6th ed.), access the APA site at http://www.apastyle.org, or visit the Purdue University Online Writing Lab (OWL) at http://owl.english.purdue.edu.

You can also use an online site like http://easy.bib.com to generate citations. **HOWEVER**, these sites are only as good as the information you type into them; if you do not include all the required information, the citation will not be correct.

APA In-Text Citations

When you refer to, summarize, paraphrase, quote, or in any way use another author's words or ideas, you must indicate the source from which you took them by inserting an **in-text citation** that refers your reader to your source list, called "**References**," which is a complete alphabetized list of all the sources you have used. The examples below are representative of some common in-text citation uses.

1. **When the author is named in the sentence or phrase, insert the publication date in parentheses after the author's name.**

> In his book *A Million Miles in a Thousand Years: What I Learned While Editing My Life*, Donald Miller (2009) poses the idea that if a good story is supposed to be a condensed version of life, then life should be lived like a good story in the first place (p. 39).

2. **If the author is not named in the sentence, then include both the author's name and the publication date in the citation.**

> If a good story is supposed to be a condensed version of life, then life should be lived like a good story in the first place (Miller, 2009, p. 39).

(*continued*)

3. When you include a quotation in your paper, you should use an introductory phrase that includes the author's last name followed by the date of publication in parentheses.

Miller (2009) comments that he "wondered whether a person could plan a story for his life and live it intentionally" (p. 39).

APA References List

Your list of works cited should include all the sources you referred to, summarized, paraphrased, or quoted in your paper. Start the list on a separate page at the end of your paper and title it "References." Arrange the entries alphabetically by each author's last name. If an author is not named (as in an editorial), then alphabetize the item by title. Double-space between and within entries. Start entries flush left, and if they run more than one line, indent subsequent lines half an inch.

1. The basic format for a book

Author | Year | Title | Place of Publication | Publisher

Lin, M. (2011). *Kid a.* New York: Continuum.

2. The basic format for a periodical

Author | Date | Title | Publication | Volume number | Page

Harvey, G. (2010). Bob Dylan in America. *The New York Review of Books, 57*(18), 34.

Internet Sources

Most electronic references are formatted the same as print ones, starting with the author name, date, and title. These are followed by either a Digital Object identifier (DOI) or URL. (Always include the DOI if it is available; otherwise, include the URL.) In addition, APA does not require an access date if there is a publication date or edition or version number or if the source is stable. If you have to break a URL or DOI, do so before a period or slash and do not use a hyphen.

1. The basic format for an article from an online periodical

Authors | Date | Title

Cunningham, J. A., & Selby, P. (2007). Relighting cigarettes: How common is it? *Nicotine and Tobacco Research,*. 9, 621-623. doi: 10.1080/14622200701239688

Publication | Vol. | Page # | Digital object identifier (DOI)

2. The basic format for a government publication found on the Internet

Government Agency | Date | Publication

U.S. Financial Crisis Inquiry Commission. (2010). *The financial crisis inquiry report: Final report of the National Commission on the Causes of the Financial and Economic Crisis in the United States.* Retrieved from http://www.fdlp.gov

URL

Revising a Draft

WRITING IN PROGRESS

Directions: Using the checklist below, revise the first draft of the essay you wrote in Exercise 11-3.

Revision Checklist

1. Does your paragraph or essay accomplish your purpose?
2. Does your paragraph or essay provide your audience with the background information they need?
3. Is your main point clearly expressed?
4. Have you supported your main point with sufficient detail from sources to make it understandable and believable?
5. Is each detail relevant? Does each one explain or support your main point?
6. Is your paragraph or essay logically arranged?
7. Have you used transitions to connect your ideas within and between paragraphs?
8. Have you credited each source from which you paraphrased, summarized, or directly quoted?
9. Have you used an appropriate documentation style?
10. Does your concluding sentence or paragraph reemphasize your topic sentence or thesis statement?

Writing a Works Cited/References List

Directions: Using either MLA style or APA style, add in-text citations and write a Works Cited/References list for the essay that you revised in Exercise 11-5. Be sure to include entries for all your sources.

READ AND RESPOND: A Student Essay

Weighing the Consequences of Censorship in Media

Adam Simmons

The questions and writing assignments below refer to the student essay "Weighing the Consequences of Censorship in Media." Throughout the chapter, you followed Adam as he selected his sources, developed his thesis statement, and wrote his essay. Now you are ready to examine Adam's essay more closely and write in response to reading it.

Examining Writing (See essay on pp. 323–326)

1. How is this essay organized?
2. Examine Adam's use of sources. What does each reference to a source contribute to this essay?
3. Suggest an introduction that could be more interesting.

4. For what audience does Adam seem to be writing?
5. Are there any details that do not seem relevant to the thesis?
6. Does the author provide adequate support for the two sides of the argument that he presents? If not, what additional details could he have included (facts, statistics, informed opinion, etc.)?

Writing Assignments

1. For a criminal justice class, you are asked to write an essay about a technological innovation that has impacted the US criminal justice system. After researching several innovations, narrow your focus to one specific technological innovation and explore its development and use in the field of criminal justice. Report your findings in a short essay.
2. In your business marketing class, your instructor has asked you to write an essay about one facet of consumer behavior. After brainstorming, you decide to write on how consumers make decisions about what to purchase. Do further research to limit your topic, and then report your findings in an essay using at least three sources.
3. For a business management class, your instructor has given the following assignment: Choose two local business franchises that sell the same products (e.g., two fast-food restaurants, two shoe stores, or two restaurants). Visit both businesses and research each on the Internet. Write an essay comparing the two businesses. Indicate which you feel is likely to be more profitable over the course of the next year.

SELF-TEST SUMMARY

To test yourself, cover the Answer column with a sheet of paper and answer each question in the left column. Evaluate each of your answers as you work by sliding the paper down and comparing your answer with what is printed in the Answer column.

QUESTION	ANSWER
■ GOAL 1 Use sources to write essays What is involved when you write essays using sources?	Using sources for essays involves finding appropriate sources, accurately recording information from them, and organizing and synthesizing the information to support your thesis.
■ GOAL 2 Find and record appropriate sources How do you find appropriate sources?	To find sources, consult a reference librarian; use a systematic approach, starting with general sources; use current and reliable sources; sample different viewpoints; preview by reading abstracts or summaries; read selectively; and follow leads to additional sources.

QUESTION	ANSWER
How do you record sources?	Use note cards or a small notebook to record critical source information; photocopy print sources, and download and/or print and bookmark online sources.
■ GOAL 3 Use sources to support your thesis and develop your essay How do you use sources to support your thesis and develop your essay?	Use sources to find facts, statistics, and other evidence that support your thesis. Write a first draft, analyze where you need support, revise your thesis if necessary based on new information, research sources to find relevant facts, opinions, and other evidence, and record the sources you use.
■ GOAL 4 Synthesize sources What does it mean to synthesize sources?	Synthesizing means locating several sources on a topic and putting together the ideas you discover to create new ideas and insights about the topic.
■ GOAL 5 Document sources using MLA and APA Styles Why is it important to document your sources?	When you quote, paraphrase, or summarize a source, you must credit the author in order to avoid plagiarism.
How do you document sources?	Two common methods for citing and documenting sources are the MLA and APA styles.
What is MLA style, and when is it used?	The Modern Language Association (MLA) style is typically used for documenting sources in English and the humanities and consists of in-text citations that refer readers to a Works Cited list of all sources used organized alphabetically by authors' last names.
What is APA style, and when is it used?	The American Psychological Association (APA) style is used for documenting sources in psychology and other social sciences and consists of in-text citations that refer readers to a References list of all sources used organized alphabetically by authors' last names.

Visit **Chapter 11, "Writing Essays Using Sources,"** in MySkillsLab to test your understanding of chapter goals.

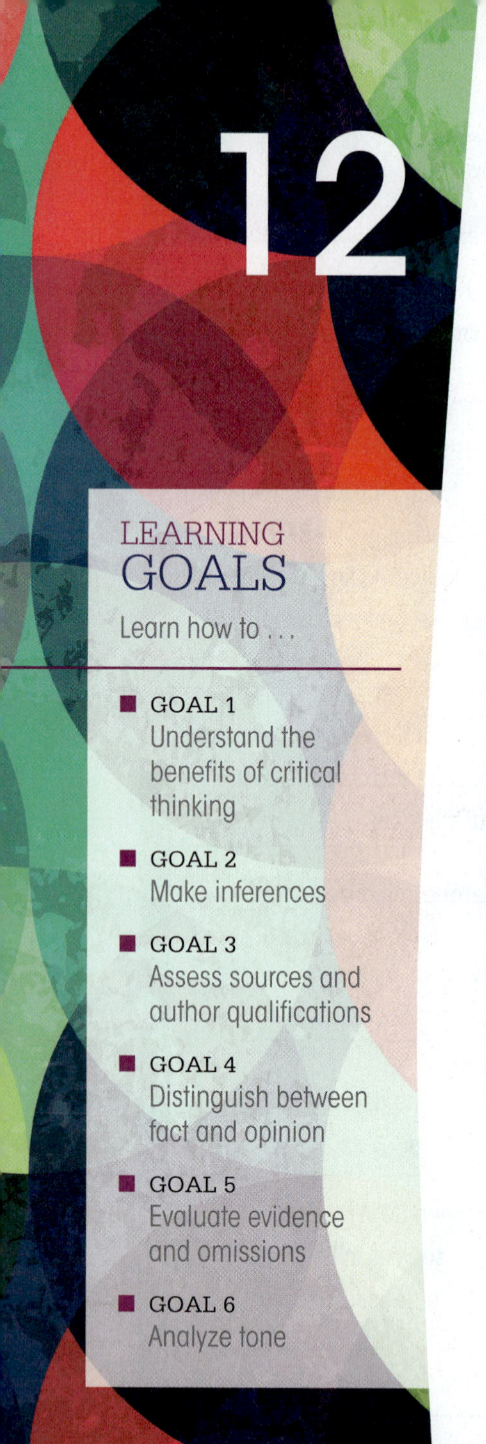

12 Critical Thinking: Making Inferences and Analyzing the Author's Message

LEARNING GOALS

Learn how to . . .

- **GOAL 1** Understand the benefits of critical thinking
- **GOAL 2** Make inferences
- **GOAL 3** Assess sources and author qualifications
- **GOAL 4** Distinguish between fact and opinion
- **GOAL 5** Evaluate evidence and omissions
- **GOAL 6** Analyze tone

THINK About It!

The newspapers and tabloids shown in this photograph contain a wide variety of information. Some of these sources make sensational claims and report implausible events, while others report factual information in a clear and straightforward manner. How can you know which stories report factual information and which offer opinions and misleading information? How would you know which sources are trustworthy and able to be used as sources when writing essays? Write a few sentences summarizing what factors you would consider in evaluating a source.

This chapter will teach you a number of critical thinking skills that are important for both reading and writing. Topics include making inferences, evaluating evidence, and analyzing tone.

Reading and Writing Connections

EVERYDAY CONNECTIONS

- **Reading** You read an opinion piece in your newspaper about the importance of technology in elementary schools. To support this viewpoint, the writer cites a survey of more than 1,000 teachers and school administrators in the United States.
- **Writing** As a volunteer at your child's school, you are asked to draft a letter for the school's fund-raising campaign to buy new computers. In your letter, you refer to the survey cited in the newspaper article, keeping the tone of your letter informative as well as positive and energetic.

ACADEMIC CONNECTIONS

- **Reading** You read an article assigned in your political science class that criticizes candidates for accepting money from political action committees (PACs). You notice that the writer uses negative words such as *destructive* and *outrageous*.
- **Writing** In response to the article, you write an essay arguing for campaign finance reform. You support your argument with facts, reasons, and examples, and you use in-text citations to give credit to your sources.

WORKPLACE CONNECTIONS

- **Reading** You read an e-mail from a co-worker asking you to serve as a reference in her application for a job in another city. You know that she recently became a grandmother and you make an inference that she will be relocating to be closer to her new grandchild.
- **Writing** You write a reference for your co-worker, sincerely recommending her for the job and including examples of her professionalism and strong work ethic.

How Does Critical Thinking Apply to Reading and Writing?

■ GOAL 1
Understand the benefits of critical thinking

Critical thinking should take place at all times, no matter what you read or write. For example:

- **When reading a college textbook**, you might ask yourself whether the author is trying to influence your opinions.
- **When reading a newspaper**, you might ask yourself if the journalist is telling the full story or if she is leaving something out.
- **When writing an essay**, you might consider whether you have fully explained your ideas or omitted important points or essential information.

- **When writing a research paper,** you should be certain that you use reliable sources and that you support your ideas with strong factual evidence.

The ability to think and read critically offers many benefits to writers. Specifically, critical thinking allows you to

- distinguish good information from incomplete, inaccurate, or misleading information.
- write paragraphs, essays, term papers, and essay exams that exhibit a strong understanding of what you've read.

EXAMINING PROFESSIONAL WRITING

This article first appeared in *Salon* magazine in July 2010. In it, the author describes how her perception of homelessness changed after her own brother became homeless. This excerpt will be used throughout this chapter to give you practice in analyzing a writer's message.

Thinking Critically

1. Preview the reading, using the steps discussed in Chapter 1, page 4.
2. Connect the reading to your own experience by answering the following questions:
   a. How would you describe the homeless people you have seen in your city?
   b. Have you ever tried to help someone who did not want your help?
3. Mark and annotate as you read.

A Brother Lost

Ashley Womble

1 Like any New Yorker, I was no stranger to homeless people. I passed by them on my way to the shiny glass tower where I worked for a glossy women's magazine: the older lady perched atop a milk crate in the subway station, the man curled up in a dirty sleeping bag and clutching a stuffed animal. They were unfortunate ornaments of the city, unlucky in ways I never really considered.

2 Until one hot summer day in 2009 when my little brother Jay left his key on the coffee table and walked out of his house in West Texas to live on the streets. In the days that followed I spent hours on the phone with detectives, social workers, and even the FBI, frantically trying to track him down. A friend designed a "Missing" poster using the most recent picture I had of him; he was wearing a hoodie and a Modest Mouse T-shirt, a can of beer in his hand and a deer-in-headlights expression on his face. I created a Facebook group and contacted old acquaintances still living in our hometown of Lubbock, begging everyone I even remotely knew to help me find him. No luck. If it had been me, a pretty young white woman, chances are my face would have been all over

the news—but the sudden disappearance of a 20-year-old guy with paranoid schizophrenia didn't exactly warrant an **Amber Alert**.

Amber Alert
a child abduction alert system

3 In the year and a half that mental illness had ravaged my brother's mind, I'd learned to lower my expectations of what his life would be like. The smart kid who followed politics in elementary school probably wouldn't become a lawyer after all. Instead of going to college after high school, Jay became obsessed with 9/11 conspiracy theories. What began as merely eccentric curdled into something manic and disturbing: He believed the planners of 9/11 were a group of people called "the Cahoots" who had created a 24-hour television network to monitor his actions and control his thoughts. Eventually, his story expanded until the Cahoots became one branch of the New World Order, a government whose purpose was to overturn Christianity, and he had been appointed by God to stop it.

4 This made it hard for him to act normal, even in public. He'd lost his job busing tables after yelling "Stop the filming and hand over the tapes" to everyone dining in the restaurant. Having friends or even a coherent conversation wouldn't be possible unless he took the antipsychotic medication he'd been prescribed while he was in the mental hospital. A legal adult, he was allowed to refuse treatment, and he did. Otherwise the Cahoots would win.

5 I counted each day he'd been missing until they became weeks, until the number was so high I wondered if he was even still alive. That number was about the only thing I continued to keep track of. Dirty clothes and dishes piled up at home, I missed deadlines at work, and I got out of bed only if it was absolutely necessary. I cried often, but especially during thunderstorms, a reminder that wherever my brother was, he was unprotected. Eventually it became clear that I was losing it, too. So I did what my brother wouldn't allow himself to do: I started taking a pill that helped usher away my anxiety and depression.

6 Weeks after Jay disappeared, police in Maryland found him talking to a spider and had him hospitalized. He stayed for 72 hours. Then he went missing again.

7 September 11, 2009, was one of those drizzling mornings when I thought of my brother. There was the usual undertone of reverent sadness in the city, but for me, the date was a reminder of all that had gone wrong inside Jay's mind. And on that day my phone finally rang.

8 "Hello." Jay's Southern drawl was unmistakable. I sat straight up in my desk chair at work wondering what I should do. Record the call? Take notes?

9 "Where are you?" I asked, as images of him sitting in a jail cell or stranded alone in an alley flashed in my head.

10 "Manhattan," he said.

11 My heart filled with hope. Then he asked me if I'd gone to the witchcraft celebration at the World Trade Center, where the Sorcerers had ordered the wind and the rain to destroy the ceremony. Once again, I just felt like a helpless stranger.

12 I asked nervously if I could buy him dinner. To my surprise, he agreed. Twenty minutes later I met him near Penn Station; he was hunched under an

awning next to a big blue tarp that covered his backpack and the paisley duffel he'd once borrowed. His pale skin had tanned and hair covered his face. He was staring at people as they walked by, but he didn't see me until I said his name. Standing face-to-face with him, I could see that he had lost a lot of weight. His cheekbones jutted out from his once-full face. If I had seen his picture I would have gasped. Instead, I just held out my arms.

Zagat
a guide that publishes ratings of restaurants

13 **Zagat** has no recommendations for where to take your homeless brother to dinner. We settled on the Mexican chain Chevys and sat in a booth near the back. He told me about hitchhiking to New York and sleeping in Central Park until the cops kicked him out. He grinned as he talked about sleeping on the steps of a downtown school, his smile still as charming as it had been when he was 7.

14 "Do you consider yourself homeless?" I asked.

15 "Oh, yes!" he answered proudly.

16 I wondered if the constant motion of wandering from town to town helped quiet the voices he heard. If it was his own kind of medication and, if so, could I really tell him that was the wrong way to live?

17 Earlier in the year I'd bribed him with a trip to visit me on the condition that he took his meds. Now he was sitting in front of me, and as much as I wanted to let him stay in my apartment, I knew I couldn't let him (my therapist discouraged it and my roommate rightly put her foot down). I approached the topic cautiously, my voice shaking as I asked, "Do you know why you can't stay with me?" His voice small and shamed, he answered, "Because I won't take my medication." He had always denied that he had schizophrenia, but his admission gave me hope that maybe some day that would change.

18 I tried to quiet my own inner voice, which told me Jay needed to be in the hospital where a team of psychiatrists could experiment with medications that would fix his mind. I could do some things for my brother: I could give him a little money for cigarettes. I could buy him a new backpack, a sleeping bag, good walking shoes. But the more I pushed him to get help, the more my own sanity escaped me.

19 So I let him go. He went to New Jersey. Florida. Louisiana. To a place where he told me from a pay phone he wouldn't call anymore because he didn't want me to know his whereabouts. I can only imagine what he looks like after a year on the streets: His hair must be long, skin tan and hardened, and his rail-thin body caked in dirt. He probably doesn't look much different from the homeless people I pass by on the streets of New York City. Seeing them makes my heart ache, makes me think about those they may have left behind, people who long to dust them off and put them on the right path but who know, in the end, it's not their choice.

Make Inferences

■ GOAL 2
Make inferences

Reading involves much more than just understanding what an author says. You also have to figure out what an author is suggesting or implying. An **inference** is an educated guess or prediction about something unknown based on available facts and information. It is the logical connection that you draw between what you observe or know and what you do not know.

Here are a few everyday situations. Make an inference for each.

- A well-dressed man walks toward the front of your lecture hall on the first day of class.
- You see a young woman in a shopping mall wearing a wedding ring pushing a baby in a stroller with two young children following her.

In the first situation, a good inference might be that the man is the instructor because he is not dressed like the average student. However, it is possible that the man is a student who has an important appointment right after class. In the second situation, one inference is that the woman was married very young and had three children in a row; another possibility is that she is married but is just babysitting the children.

When you make inferences about what you read, you go beyond what a writer says and consider what he or she *means*. Writers may directly state some ideas but hint at others. It is left to the reader, then, to pick up on the clues or suggestions and to figure out the writer's unstated message. This chapter will show you how to do so.

Reading: How to Make Inferences

Making an inference is a thinking process. As you read, you are following the writer's thoughts. You are also alert for ideas that are suggested but not directly stated. Because each inference depends on the situation, the facts provided, and the reader's knowledge and experience, there is no simple, step-by-step procedure to follow.

However, here are a few guidelines to keep in mind as you read. These will help you get in the habit of looking beyond the factual level.

Guidelines for Making Inferences

1. **Be sure you understand the literal meaning of what you read.** Before you can make inferences, you need a clear grasp of the facts, the writer's main ideas, and the supporting details.
2. **Notice details.** Often a particular detail provides a clue that will help you make an inference. When you spot a striking or unusual detail, ask yourself: Why did the writer include this piece of information? Remember that there are many kinds of details, such as descriptions, actions, and conversations.
3. **Add up the facts.** Consider all the facts taken together. Ask yourself: What is the writer trying to suggest with this set of facts? What do all these facts and ideas point toward?
4. **Look at the writer's choice of words.** A writer's word choice often suggests his or her attitude toward the subject. Notice, in particular, descriptive words, emotionally charged words, and words that are very positive or negative.
5. **Understand the writer's purpose.** An author's purpose, which is discussed later in this chapter (p. 352), affects many aspects of a piece of writing. Ask yourself: Why did the author write this?
6. **Be sure your inference is supportable.** An inference must be based on fact. Make sure there is sufficient evidence to justify any inference you make.

EXERCISE 12-1

Understanding Inferences

Directions: Read each of the following passages. Based on the information contained in each, use inference to determine whether the statements that follow it are likely to be true (T) or false (F). Write your answers in the space provided.

A. Targeting Inner-City Consumers

Cigarette, beer, and fast-food marketers have generated controversy in recent years by their attempts to target inner-city minority consumers. For example, McDonald's and other chains have drawn criticism for pitching their high-fat, salt-laden fare to low-income, urban residents. Similarly, R.J. Reynolds took heavy flak in the early 1990s when it announced plans to market Uptown, a menthol cigarette targeted toward low-income blacks. It quickly dropped the brand in the face of a loud public outcry and heavy pressure from African-American leaders.

—adapted from Armstrong and Kotler, *Marketing: An Introduction*, p. 192

_____ 1. R.J. Reynolds withdrew its ads because it was concerned about the risk of lung cancer among low-income blacks.

_____ 2. Low-income urban consumers are fast-food consumers.

_____ 3. McDonald's salt-laden foods include burgers and fries.

_____ 4. These companies have never in the past targeted any specialized groups.

_____ 5. Due to the outcry, McDonald's began offering healthier choices.

B. Is Laughter the Best Medicine?

Lucy went to the hospital to visit Emma, a neighbor who had broken her hip. The first thing Lucy saw when the elevator door opened at the third floor was a clown, with an enormous orange nose, dancing down the hall, pushing a colorfully decorated cart. The clown stopped in front of Lucy, bowed, and then somersaulted to the nurses' station. A cluster of patients cheered. Most of them were in wheelchairs or on crutches. Upon asking for directions, Lucy learned that Emma was in the "humor room," where the film *Blazing Saddles* was about to start.

Since writer Norman Cousins's widely publicized recovery from a debilitating and usually incurable disease of the connective tissue, humor has gained new respectability in hospital wards around the country. Cousins, the long-time editor of the *Saturday Review*, with the cooperation of his physician, supplemented his regular medical therapy with a steady diet of Marx brothers' movies and *Candid Camera* film clips. Although he never claimed that laughter alone effected his cure, Cousins is best remembered for his passionate support of the notion that, if negative emotions can cause distress, then humor and positive emotions can enhance the healing process.

—Zimbardo and Gerrig, *Psychology and Life*, p. 501

_____ 6. The clown was at the hospital to celebrate a patient's birthday.

_____ 7. *Blazing Saddles* and Marx brothers' movies would be classified as comedy films.

_____ 8. Cousins believed that humor should be only a part of a person's health-care plan.

_____ 9. Lucy watched the movie with Emma.

_____ 10. Emma probably used a wheelchair or crutches to reach the humor room.

EXERCISE 12-2 Using Inferences

Directions: Based on your reading of "A Brother Lost" on page 344, answer the following questions:

1. What might the author be implying about her brother's condition when she describes him as "wearing a hoodie and a Modest Mouse T-shirt, a can of beer in his hand and a deer-in-headlights expression on his face?"
2. What does working in a "shiny glass tower . . . for a glossy women's magazine" suggest about the author's status in life?
3. The author writes, "dirty clothes and dishes piled up at home, I missed deadlines at work, and I got out of bed only if it was absolutely necessary." From this statement, what can you infer about her emotional condition?
4. When the author took her brother to dinner, they "sat in a booth near the back." What might the location of the booth suggest about the author's feelings about her brother?
5. Does the title of this piece, "A Brother Lost," have more than one meaning? Make inferences about what the title means and what it suggests about the author's attitude toward her subject.

Writing: Thinking Critically About Inferences

If you want to be completely sure that your readers understand your message, state it directly. If you only imply an idea and do not directly state it, there is a chance your reader may miss your point. Worse yet, there is a possibility that less than careful readers may infer an idea you had not intended, creating a misunderstanding or miscommunication.

There are occasions in which you may deliberately leave an idea unstated. You may want to lead your readers to an idea, but let them figure it out for themselves, thinking it was their idea. Especially in argument, you may want to lead your readers to take action or accept a particular viewpoint, but you may prefer not to make a direct plea. When following this strategy, be sure to supply enough detail and evidence so your readers make the desired inference.

Assess the Source and Author Qualifications

■ GOAL 3
Assess sources and author qualifications

Two very important considerations in evaluating any written material are the source in which it was printed and the authority, or qualifications, of the author.

Reading: Considering the Source

Your reaction to and evaluation of printed material should take into account its source. Often the source of a piece of writing can indicate how accurate, detailed, and well documented an article is. Consider this example: Suppose you are in the library trying to find information on sleepwalking for a term paper. You locate the following sources, each of which contains an article on sleepwalking. Which would you expect to be the most factual, detailed, and scientific?

- an encyclopedia entry on sleepwalking
- an article titled "Strange Things Happen While You Are Sleeping" in *Woman's Day*
- an article titled "An Examination of Research on Sleepwalking" in *Psychological Review*

You would expect the encyclopedia entry to provide only a general overview of the topic. You might expect the article in *Woman's Day* to discuss various abnormalities that occur during sleep, as well as to relate several unusual or extreme cases of sleepwalking, rather than to present a factual analysis of the topic. The article in *Psychological Review*, a journal that reports research in psychology, is the one that would contain a factual, authoritative discussion of sleepwalking. You can see from this example that from the source alone you can make predictions about the content and approach used.

Ask the questions in the following Need to Know box to evaluate a source:

NEED TO KNOW

How to Evaluate a Source

1. What reputation does the source have?
2. Who is the audience for whom the source is intended?
3. Are references or documentation provided?

Reading: Considering the Author's Credentials

To evaluate printed material, you must also consider the competency of the author. Use the following guidelines to assess a writer's expertise.

Checking and Evaluating Author Credentials in . . .

- **Textbooks.** In textbooks, the author's college or university affiliation, and possibly his or her title, may appear on the title page beneath the author's name, in the preface, or on the back cover. Based on his or her education and teaching experience, you can infer whether the author is knowledgeable about the topic.
- **Nonfiction books and general market paperbacks.** A synopsis of the author's credentials and experiences may be included on the book jacket or the back cover. There is also often additional material available on the publisher's and/or author's Web site.
- **Newspapers, magazines, and reference books.** In these sources, you are given little or no information about the writer. You can rely on the

judgment of the editors or publishers to assess an author's authority and/or check the Web site for the publication, where you may find more biographical information about columnists and reporters. You could also Google a writer to find out more about his or her background and experience.

Evaluating Sources

Directions: Working with a classmate, predict and discuss how useful and appropriate each of the following sources would be for the situation described.

1. Using an article from *Working Mother* on family aggression for a term paper for your sociology class

   ____

2. Quoting an article in *The New York Times* on recent events in China for a speech titled "Innovation and Change in China"

   ____

3. Reading an article titled "Bilingual Education in the Twenty-First Century" printed in the *Educational Research Quarterly* for a paper arguing for increased federal aid for bilingual education

   ____

   ____

4. Using an article in *TV Guide* on television's coverage of crime and violence for a term paper on the effects of television on society

   ____

5. Using information from a book written by former First Lady Laura Bush in a class discussion on use and abuse of presidential power

   ____

   ____

Evaluating the Professional Article

Directions: Read the note that precedes "A Brother Lost" on page 344, and search the Web for information on Ashley Womble. Based on the article and what you have read and researched, assess her credentials for writing about homelessness and how reliable a source she is. Be prepared to share your answer.

Reading: Evaluating Internet Sources

Although the Internet contains a great deal of valuable information and resources, it also contains rumor, gossip, hoaxes, and misinformation. In other words, not all Internet sources are trustworthy. You must evaluate a source before accepting it. Here are some guidelines to follow when evaluating Internet sources.

Evaluating the Content of a Web Site

When evaluating the content of a Web site, evaluate its appropriateness, its source, its level of technical detail, its presentation, its completeness, and its links.

- **Evaluate appropriateness.** To be worthwhile, a site should contain the information you need. If it does not address your questions in sufficient detail, check the links on the site to see if they lead you to more detailed information, or search for a more useful site.
- **Evaluate the source.** Ask yourself "Who is the sponsor?" and "Why was this site put up on the Web?" The sponsor is the person or organization who paid for the creation and placement of the site on the Web; who they are will often suggest the purpose of a site. For example, a site sponsored by Nike has a commercial purpose, while a site sponsored by a university library is educational or informational. If you are uncertain who sponsors a Web site, check its URL, its copyright, and the links it offers, or try to locate the site's home page.
- **Evaluate the level of technical detail.** A site's level of technical detail should be suited to your purpose. Some sites may provide information that is too sketchy for your search purposes; others assume a level of background knowledge or technical sophistication that you lack.
- **Evaluate the presentation.** Information should be well written and presented. If it is not, you should be suspicious. An author who did not take time to present ideas clearly and correctly may not have taken time to collect accurate information either.
- **Evaluate completeness.** Does the site address all aspects of the topic that you feel it should? If you discover that a site is incomplete, search for sites that provide a more thorough treatment of the topic.
- **Evaluate the links.** Many reputable sites supply links to other related sites. Make sure that the links are current and the sites they link to are reliable sources of information. If the links do not work or the sources appear unreliable, you should question the reliability of the site itself. Also determine whether the links provided are comprehensive or only present a representative sample. Either is acceptable, but the site should make clear the nature of the links it is providing.

Evaluating Content

Directions: Evaluate the content of the following sites. Explain why you would either trust or distrust each site as a source of reliable content.

1. http://legacy.earlham.edu/~peters/knotlink.htm
2. http://www.age-of-the-sage.org/psychology/
3. http://www.habitat.org

Evaluating the Accuracy and Timeliness of a Web Site

When using information on a Web site for an academic paper, it is important to be sure that you have found accurate and up-to-date information. One way to determine the accuracy of a Web site is to compare it with print sources (periodicals and books) on the same topic. If you find a wide discrepancy between the Web site and the printed sources, do not trust the Web site. Another way to determine a site's accuracy is to compare it with other Web sites that address the same topic. If discrepancies exist, further research is needed to determine which site is more accurate.

Tips for Evaluating Accuracy

The site itself will also provide clues about the accuracy of its information. Ask yourself the following questions:

- **Are the author's name and credentials provided?** A well-known writer with established credentials is likely to author reliable, accurate information. If no author name is given, you should question whether the information is accurate.
- **Is contact information for the author included on the site?** Sites often provide an e-mail address where the author may be contacted.
- **Is the information complete or in summary form?** If it is a summary, use the site to find the original source. Original information has less chance of error and is usually preferred in academic papers.
- **If opinions are offered, are they presented clearly as opinions?** Authors who disguise their opinions as facts are not trustworthy.
- **Does the writer make unsubstantiated assumptions or base his or her ideas on misconceptions?** If so, the information presented may not be accurate.
- **Does the site provide a list of works cited?** As with any form of research, sources used to put information up on a Web site must be documented. If sources are not credited, you should question the accuracy of the Web site.

Although the Web is well known for providing up-to-the-minute information, not all Web sites are current.

Tips for Evaluating Timeliness

Evaluate a site's timeliness by checking the following dates:

- the date on which the Web site was published (put up on the Web)
- the date when the document you are using was added
- the date when the site was last revised
- the date when the links were last checked

This information is usually provided at the end of the site's home page or at the end of the document you are using.

EXERCISE 12-6 Evaluating Accuracy and Timeliness

Directions: Evaluate the accuracy and timeliness of two of the sites you evaluated for Exercise 12-5.

Writing: Thinking Critically About Source and Authority

As critical thinkers, your readers will assess your qualifications and knowledge of the subject you are writing about. Many factors can create an image of you as a serious, competent writer, qualified to write on your topic. These include the following:

- **A correct, error-free essay that is neatly presented.** Readers may assume that if you have not taken the time to present your paper carefully, you may not have taken the time to research or think through your ideas, either.
- **A well-documented paper.** If you use sources, be sure to give your sources credit using in-text citations and a Works Cited list (see Chapter 11 for more detailed information on how to do this). Failure to credit sources is dishonest, and your readers may realize it.
- **An honest approach to the topic.** If you are not an expert on your topic, do not present yourself as one. If you do have expertise on your topic, you might build mention of your expertise into the essay for the purpose of establishing your credibility. For example, if you are a first responder for your community volunteer fire company and are writing about accidents that occur when drivers are texting, you might acknowledge your experience responding to accidents.

Distinguish Between Fact and Opinion

■ GOAL 4
Distinguish between fact and opinion

Facts are statements that can be verified—that is, proven to be true. **Opinions** are statements that express feelings, attitudes, or beliefs and are neither true nor false. Opinions are sometimes signaled by the use of such key words or phrases as *apparently, this suggests, some believe, it is likely that, seemingly, in my view*, and *one explanation is*.

Facts

Martin Luther King, Jr., was assassinated in 1968.

The main source of food for Native Americans was the buffalo.

Opinions

Americans should give up their cars and take public transportation instead.

By the year 2025, food shortages will be a major problem in most Asian countries.

Opinions can be divided into two categories. **Informed opinions** are made by people whose learning and experience qualify them to offer expert opinions. **Uninformed opinions** are made by those who have few qualifications. To determine whether an opinion is informed or not, ask these questions:

- What experience does this person have regarding the subject matter?
- What do other respected authorities think of this person?
- Is the opinion expressed in a respectful way? Or is it expressed in a manner that is disrespectful or intolerant?
- Does the opinion appear in a respected publication, or is it found on a Web site where people can say whatever they want?

Be sure to read the directions to your writing assignments carefully. If the assignment calls for strictly factual reporting, do not offer your opinion.

EXERCISE 12-7 Distinguishing Between Fact and Opinion

Directions: Each of the following paragraphs contains both fact and opinion. Read each paragraph and label each sentence as fact or opinion.

A. [1]Flowering plants that are native to the South include purple coneflower and rose verbena. [2]In the view of many longtime gardeners, these two plants are an essential part of the Southern landscape. [3]Trees that are native to the South include a variety of oaks, as well as flowering dogwoods and redbuds. [4]Dogwoods are especially lovely, with their white, pink, or coral blossoms announcing the arrival of spring. [5]For fall color, the deep red of the Virginia willow makes a spectacular show in the native Southern garden.

1. ______________ **4.** ______________

2. ______________ **5.** ______________

3. ______________

B. [1]Today, many companies provide child-care assistance, either on- or off-site, for their employees. [2]This suggests that employers are becoming aware that their workers' family concerns can affect the company's bottom line. [3]The Eli Lilly pharmaceutical company, for example, has built two child-development centers with a total capacity of more than 400 children. [4]In addition to assistance with daily child care, Bank of America reimburses employees for child-care expenses related to business travel. [5]It seems clear that other, less progressive employers will have to follow these companies' leads in order to attract and retain the best employees.

1. ______________ **4.** ______________

2. ______________ **5.** ______________

3. ______________

C. [1]Preparing a will is an important task that people ignore because they prefer not to think about their own death. [2]However, if you die without a will, the courts will determine how your assets should be distributed, as directed by state law. [3]Even more important than establishing a will, in my opinion, is expressing your willingness to be an organ donor upon your death. [4]Each year, twenty-five thousand new patients are added to the waiting list for organ transplants. [5]The legacy of an organ donor is far more valuable than any material assets put in a will.

1. ______________ **4.** ______________

2. ______________ **5.** ______________

3. ______________

EXERCISE 12-8 Identifying Facts and Opinions in the Professional Article

Directions: List three facts and three opinions from "A Brother Lost" on page 344. Are the opinions you identified informed or uninformed opinions? How can you tell?

Writing: Thinking Critically About Fact and Opinion

Facts are the building blocks of many paragraphs and are essential to good writing. Opinions, however, may or may not be appropriate, depending on your purpose and the nature of the writing task or assignment. If you are writing a summary, for instance, your opinion of the material does not belong in it, unless you have been asked to analyze or comment on the source text. If you are writing a research paper, your personal opinions are not useful or appropriate.

In some other types of assignments, the use of personal opinion may be appropriate, as long as you substantiate or provide evidence to support it. In writing a response to a poem for a literature class, for example, it is certainly appropriate to express your reactions and feelings about it, as long as you support your opinions with references to the poem. Or in writing an essay about Super Bowl advertising, you may express a viewpoint that the commercials are the best part of the show or that they are extravagant wastes of money. Again, you should give reasons, examples, and so forth to support your viewpoint. Never just offer opinions without explanation and justification.

Evaluate Evidence and Omissions

■ GOAL 5
Evaluate evidence and omissions

Many writers who express their opinions, state viewpoints, or make generalizations provide evidence to support their ideas, as discussed in Chapter 11. Your task as a critical reader is to examine this evidence and assess its quality and its adequacy. In addition to evaluating the evidence the author has provided, you must also consider what the author has chosen to leave out. Writers may mislead their readers by omitting important information.

Reading: What Evidence Has the Author Provided?

You should be concerned with two factors: the type of evidence being presented and the relevance of that evidence. Types of evidence include the following:

- personal experience or observation.
- statistical data.
- examples, descriptions of particular events, or illustrative situations.
- analogies (comparisons with similar situations).
- historical documentation.
- experimental evidence.
- reasons.

Each type of evidence must be weighed in relation to the statement it supports. Acceptable evidence should directly, clearly, and indisputably support the case or issue in question.

EXERCISE 12-9

Identifying Evidence

Directions: For each of the following statements, discuss the type or types of evidence that you would need in order to support and evaluate the statement with a classmate.

1. Individuals must accept primary responsibility for the health and safety of their babies.

____

2. Apologizing is often seen as a sign of weakness, especially among men.

____

3. There has been a steady increase in illegal immigration over the past fifty years.

____

4. More college women than college men agree that abortions should be legal.

____

5. Car advertisements sell fantasy experiences, not means of transportation.

____

Reading: What Information Has the Author Omitted?

Writers can mislead their readers by omission. Here are five common ways writers mislead their readers:

1. **Omitting essential details.** The writer may deliberately leave out details that are relevant and important to understanding the topic. Consider whether the writer presents a complete picture of the topic.
2. **Ignoring contradictory evidence or selectively reporting details.** To be fair, a writer should report all of the evidence, not just evidence that he or she wants the reader to know. Does the writer leave out certain details or evidence that contradicts his or her conclusions?
3. **Making an incomplete comparison.** A writer may claim that something is "better" without explaining what it is better *than*. Consider whether the writer has completed the comparison.
4. **Using passive voice.** Writers may avoid revealing information by using a sentence structure that does not identify who performed a specified action.
5. **Using unspecified nouns and pronouns.** Writers may also avoid revealing information by using nouns and pronouns (such as *they* or *it*) that do not refer to a specific person or thing.

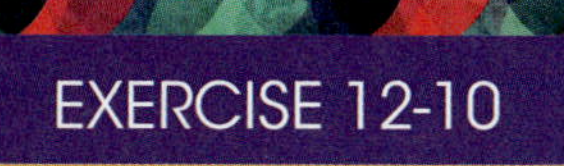

Analyzing Omissions

Directions: For each of the following statements, indicate what information is missing.

1. They raised test scores in that state.

____

2. Some animal testing has been banned in other countries.

____

3. They say the Columbia River has too many dams.

____

4. Anyone can get on the Internet.

____

5. The check was probably forged.

____

EXERCISE 12-11

Identifying Evidence and Analyzing Omissions

Directions: Reread "A Brother Lost" on page 344, and annotate it to identify the types of evidence the author provides to support her point about homeless people. Look for any omissions. Does the author appear to omit essential details or ignore contradictory evidence, for instance? If, so, what information is missing?

Writing: Thinking Critically About Evidence

As you draft essays, one of your main tasks is to provide adequate, reliable, and appropriate data and evidence to support your thesis statement. (For more on using evidence to support your thesis, see Chapter 9, p. 273, and Chapter 11, p. 328.) Good writers try to vary the data they choose to suit their audience and their purpose. Examples may be appropriate for one audience, but facts and statistics may be more appealing to another. To achieve your purpose, select your evidence carefully. If your purpose is to persuade your readers to take action, such as to vote for a particular political candidate, reasons are needed. But you may also want to include descriptions of the candidate's achievements or draw comparisons to other successful political figures.

Be sure not to omit details that are relevant and important to the topic. Doing so will make your readers distrust you and question your ideas.

Analyze Tone

■ GOAL 6
Analyze tone

The tone of a speaker's voice helps you interpret what he or she is saying. If a friend says to you "Would you mind closing the door?" you can tell by his tone of voice whether he is being polite, insistent, or angry. If your partner says "Where did you get that coat?" She may really want to know where you got it or being sarcastic and indicating how much she dislikes it. So **tone** refers to the attitude or feeling a writer expresses about his or her subject and reveals his or her intended meaning.

Writers can express a variety of different tones. In the following example, notice how each writer reveals a different attitude toward the same subject:

- We cannot trust our police chief; he is corrupt and completely ignorant of our community's problems.
- Our feelings of disappointment over the police chief's actions are overwhelming; we truly believed he would be the one to turn our community around, but he has betrayed us just like his predecessor.
- Is anyone really surprised by the scandal surrounding our police chief? Trusting a city official is like trusting a fox in a hen house.

In the first example, the writer is angry, in the second the writer is sad and disappointed, and in the third the writer is cynical. There are a wide range of tones:

- **An instructive tone.** The writer values his or her subject and thinks it is important for the reader to know about it. Information about the subject is presented in a straightforward, helpful manner.

  When purchasing a piece of clothing, one must be concerned with quality as well as with price. Be certain to check for the following: double-stitched seams, matched patterns, and ample linings.

- **A sympathetic tone.** The writer reveals sympathy or sorrow toward the subject.

  The forlorn, frightened-looking child wandered through the streets alone, searching for someone who would show an interest in helping her find her parents.

- **A convincing tone.** The writer feels his or her ideas are correct and urges readers to accept them.

  Child abuse is a tragic occurrence in our society. Strong legislation is needed to control the abuse of innocent victims and to punish those who are insensitive to the rights and feelings of others. Write to your congressional representative today.

- **An entertaining tone.** The writer finds the subject light and amusing and wishes to share this with his or her readers.

  Gas prices are climbing again, which means some super-hard driving decisions in our family. Driving to the gym is definitely out—besides, walking builds character as well as muscle. And when Cousin Stanley comes to town, I hope he does not expect to be chauffeured around; walking may help him lose a couple of pounds that need to go. Of course, the 50-mile trek to Edgar's Easter Egg Extravaganza is a no-go this spring. Tough times = tough choices!

- **A nostalgic tone.** The writer is thinking about past times or events. The writer is often sentimental, recalling the past with happiness, sadness, or longing.

  It was a quieter, less-pressured world before the advent of the cell phone. People made appointments to meet and kept them. People spent time talking together, not lost in their individual cyber-worlds. And best of all, your mother, brother, partner, or boss could not contact you 24/7.

- **An outraged tone.** The writer expresses anger and indignation toward something he or she finds offensive.

  It is appalling that people sit on bus seats talking loudly on their cell phones and expecting me to listen to their ignorant conversations. I'd like to grab their cell phones and throw them out the window.

A writer's tone is intended to rub off on you, so to speak. Tone is also directly tied to the author's purpose (see Chapter 2). A writer whose tone is humorous hopes you will be amused. A writer whose tone is convincing hopes you will accept his or her viewpoint.

EXERCISE 12-12 Recognizing Tone

Directions: Select the word from the box that best describes the tone of each of the following statements. Not all of the words will be used.

optimistic hopeful, positive
angry extremely annoyed, mad
admiring approving, holding a high opinion
cynical distrustful, doubting
excited feeling enjoyment and pleasure
humorous amusing, making people laugh
disapproving disliking, condemning
formal serious, official
informative factual
sarcastic saying the opposite of what is meant
apathetic lacking enthusiasm, energy, or interest

1. Taking a young child to a PG-13 movie is inappropriate and shows poor judgment on the part of the parents. ________________
2. The brown recluse spider has a dark, violin-shaped marking on the upper section of its body. ________________
3. The dedication and determination of the young men and women participating in the Special Olympics were an inspiration to everyone there. ________________
4. It does not matter to me which mayoral candidate wins the election, so I won't bother to vote. ________________
5. Nobody is ever a complete failure; he or she can always serve as a bad example. ________________
6. The councilman once again demonstrated his sensitivity toward the environment when he voted to allow commercial development in an area set aside as a nature preserve. ________________
7. The success of the company's youth mentoring program will inspire other business groups to establish similar programs. ________________
8. Professional athletes have no loyalty toward their teams or their fans anymore, just their own wallets. ________________
9. We were thrilled to learn that next year's convention will be held in San Antonio—we've always wanted to see the Alamo! ________________
10. To be considered for the president's student-of-the-year award, an individual must demonstrate academic excellence as well as outstanding community service, and the individual must furnish no fewer than four letters of reference from faculty members. ________________

EXERCISE 12-13

Recognizing the Tone of the Professional Article

Directions: Underline words in "A Brother Lost" on page 344 that indicate the author's tone. It may change from one paragraph to the next. Choose one word that best describes the author's overall tone. What other words could you use to describe her tone in specific paragraphs?

Writing: Thinking Critically About Tone

The tone you use contributes to or detracts from meaning. Be sure to use a tone that is appropriate for your readers. Consider the following factors about your readers.

- **Knowledge of the topic.** If your readers are not knowledgeable about the topic, you might use a supportive, helpful tone. If they are familiar with the topic, the same helpful, supportive tone may be insulting.
- **Background and experience of your readers.** Consider the education level, training, professional position, and factors such as the age and gender of your audience when adopting a tone. A letter written to a panel of community leaders might use a deferential tone because they expect to be treated with respect, while a letter to the editor might use a less formal, but informative tone.
- **Attitudes and beliefs of your readers.** If your readers are likely to agree with your ideas, using a strongly emotional tone may seem inappropriate and unnecessary. If your readers are likely to disagree with your ideas, an energetic, positive, convincing tone may help sway your readers.

EXERCISE 12-14

Preparing to Write Critically

Directions: Assume that you have been assigned to write an essay on one of the topics below. On a separate sheet of paper, describe how you would approach the assignment, including what sources you would use, whether your essay would include opinion as well as fact, what data and evidence you would use to support your thesis, and what tone you would use.

1. the health benefits of coffee (or another drink or food of your choice)
2. the qualities of a good teacher or coach
3. the value of bartering for items and services
4. the advantages of Zipcar or other car sharing programs
5. the downsides of being connected to social media

READ AND RESPOND: A Student Essay

At the time he wrote this essay, Chase Beauclair was a senior at the University of Washington, where he was pursuing a double major in Political Science and Law, Societies, and Justice. After graduating, he planned to take a year off from school to gain professional experience and then apply to law school.

Title suggests thesis

The Role of Sports in Life

Chase Beauclair

Opening sentence attracts readers by focusing on a shared interest

Introduction provides background information about the topic

Thesis statement

1 There is very little in life that people love more than watching and participating in sports and athletics. In fact, people of all cultures, religions, and races share this interest and are drawn to the competitiveness of sports and the excitement that they experience as spectators. Sports gives people an opportunity to interact socially and bond with each other. As a form of entertainment, people have a wide variety of preferences on what type of sporting events they like to watch and what level of personal involvement they are willing to invest in being a fan of a particular sport, team, or athlete. Regardless of the level of personal involvement, almost every individual is captivated by certain sporting events and dedicates time to watching and discussing the competition and its results. There are many reasons people enjoy sports, but there are four key elements that sports enthusiasts share: people identify with and respect athletic talent; there is so much variety there is something for everyone; social groups, like schools, cities, and countries, are represented by specific teams; and people can use sports as an outlet for competitiveness.

Topic sentence

Transition words here, and at the beginning of paragraphs 3 and 4, lead the reader to each of the author's points.

Examples support the topic sentence.

2 The first reason that people are attracted to sports is that, to some degree, everyone has engaged in athletic, physical activity so that they have a respect for the accomplishments of exceptionally talented athletes. Everyone has been exhausted by running a short distance or lost their balance walking down the street. Everyone has gone bowling, driven a car, or tried to jump and touch the rim of a basketball hoop. People are fascinated with sports because they know the physical demands of the competition and are immediately in awe of the skill that the athletes demonstrate. Along with the appreciation of the talents of the athletes, people also recognize and respect the level of dedication that sports and athletic training require. People respect others who dedicate themselves wholly to a goal and sacrifice for the sake of achievement, and athletes perfectly represent a level of devotion that everyone finds admirable. The combination of ability and dedication are fascinating to spectators and represents the most basic level of attraction to sports.

Topic sentence

3 The second factor that attracts people to sports is the unbelievably wide range of athletic competition available to watch. In the United States, baseball, football, basketball, hockey, soccer, and NASCAR make up the most televised sporting events, but there are also many other events available to fans. While most people enjoy following at least one of the major sports, there are so many other sporting events that there is truly something for everyone. The Olympics consist mostly of sports outside of the American mainstream, yet every four years the entire country is captivated by the various events. People who avoid more traditional sports all year, flock to major events like the tour de France or the Masters golf tournament. People may not have the same preferences, but they all enjoy watching some form of athletic sporting competition.

Topic sentence

4 The third reason that sports are an essential part of all cultures is the fact that sports teams represent social groups, such as schools, cities, and countries.

Sports teams help to build a sense of social community within groups so that there is a greater sense of unity and pride. In many cases, people are automatically tied to a particular team because of where they live or where they go to school. Even if people are not particularly fans of a certain sport, they can usually share comments on the condition of their sports teams at any given time. People build social identities based on where they are from and where they went to school, and the sports teams become a part of those identities. Becoming an avid follower of the local or collegiate sports team provides instant access to a large community of fans and creates a greater sense of belonging in those communities.

Transition indicates that this is the last major point

Topic sentence

Descriptive language

5 The final reason that people devote themselves to being a sports fan is the fact that devotion to a particular team can provide a sense of personal accomplishment and act as a healthy way to express their competitiveness. The joyous feeling of victory and shared disappointment of defeat unites the fans with each other and with the team. The personal investment that people have in a team often results in the release of strong emotions. The outcome of the game carries emotional weight and the ups and downs throughout the competition are moments of relief and anxiety. The emotional experience of being a spectator is a healthy way to participate in the competition without having any real stake in the outcome.

The conclusion restates the thesis

Sentence summarizes the four reasons

Chase reflects on the value of sports to society

6 While there is wide variety of sports that people enjoy following and various levels of personal involvement, the reasons they first became interested in the sport probably had something to do with one of the four attractions to athletic competition. The understanding and respect for athletes combined with the variety of athletic events, the social nature of sports, and the emotional expression makes sports one of the most beloved aspects of all cultures. The natural attraction to sports is what makes them so widely accepted among very diverse groups of people, and without them a sense of community and emotional balance would be missing from society.

Examining Writing

1. Has the author presented himself as a serious, competent writer? What evidence do you base your answer on?
2. List the types of evidence the author uses in his essay.
3. Underline any statement of opinion. Has the author provided reasons, examples, or other evidence for any opinions he offers?
4. Evaluate whether the author has provided sufficient evidence to support his thesis.
5. Choose a word or phrase that describes the author's tone. Is it suitable for his purpose or audience?
6. Highlight any paragraphs that require you to make inferences. Has the author supplied sufficient detail and evidence for any inferences he expects his readers to make?
7. How would you describe the author's tone in this essay? Identify words and sentences that reveal his attitude toward the subject.
8. Evaluate the effectiveness of the title. Suggest a title that might be more effective.

Writing Assignments

1. The author writes that "people have a wide variety of preferences on what type of sporting events they like to watch." Write a paragraph in which you describe your favorite sport and explain why you like it.
2. The author states that people "have a respect for the accomplishments of exceptionally talented athletes." Write a paragraph in which you describe your favorite athlete and give examples of his or her accomplishments.
3. Although college athletics plays an important role in building community, it also can be a source of great controversy. One controversy surrounding college athletics is the issue of paying student athletes. Write an essay in which you take a stand on this issue. You should support your thesis by providing reasons either for or against paying student athletes.

READ AND RESPOND: A Professional Essay

A Brother Lost

Ashley Womble

The questions and activities below refer to article "A Brother Lost" on page 344. You have been working with this article throughout the chapter and have mastered much of its content. Now you are ready to examine it, integrate and apply ideas and write in response to reading it.

Writing in Response to Reading

Checking Your Comprehension

Answer each of the following questions using complete sentences.

1. Explain who Jay is. How old was he when he disappeared, and what mental illness does he have?
2. What does Jay believe about 9/11? Explain the term "the Cahoots."
3. What caused Jay to lose his job?
4. How did the author eventually handle her anxiety and depression?
5. When does Jay finally contact the author? Why can't he stay with her?
6. What does the author do for Jay? What is she unable to do?

Strengthening Your Vocabulary

MySkillsLab®

Identify at least five words used in the reading that are unfamiliar to you. Using context, word parts, or a dictionary, write a brief definition of each word.

Examining the Reading: Drawing an Idea Map

Create an idea map of the reading that starts with the title and thesis and then lists the author's main points. Use the guidelines on page 15.

Reading and Writing: An Integrated Perspective

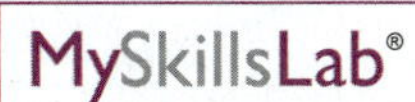

Get ready to write about the reading by discussing the following:

1. How do you typically react when you see a homeless person? Will the author's story change how you react next time? Write a journal entry explaining your answers and describing how this reading makes you feel about homelessness and homeless people.
2. How does the author organize the details in this essay? What makes this pattern of organization effective for her material?
3. How does the author conclude this essay? How would you describe her feelings in the last paragraph?
4. What is the purpose of the illustration that accompanies the reading (p. 363)? What details do you notice about it that reflect the author's story? Suggest other illustrations that would be appropriate and effective.

THINKING VISUALLY

Thinking and Writing Critically

1. The author describes the homeless as the "unfortunate ornaments of the city" (para. 1). What does she mean by this figurative expression?
2. Do you think the author believes that mentally ill people should be institutionalized and forced to take medication? Why or why not?
3. How would you express the author's thesis? Evaluate the details the author uses to support her thesis. Which details are most effective?
4. Consider the author's choice of descriptive words such as *ravaged* and *curdled*. How do these words help make her story more effective? How does

this language affect your response to the subject? Underline examples of descriptive words and emotionally charged language.

5. Why does the writer include her conversations with her brother? What aspect of her subject do these conversations illustrate?

Writing Paragraph MySkillsLab®

1. Think of a situation in which you tried to help someone who was unwilling or unable to be helped, and describe that experience.

2. Try to put yourself in the author's shoes and imagine what you would have done. Do you think you would have been able to let your brother (or sister, or other loved one) go? Explain your answer.

3. Do you agree with the author that the news media would have been more interested in her disappearance than that of her mentally ill brother? Explain your answer.

Writing Essay MySkillsLab®

4. The writer's experience shows that each homeless person is someone's brother, sister, daughter, son—in other words, a real person. Explain how you viewed homeless people before reading this article, and how you view them now, after reading this article.

5. We sometimes make assumptions or generalizations about a certain group until we meet a member of that group who changes our opinion. Think of an individual who changed your viewpoint toward a group, perhaps an elderly person or someone with a disability, a person from another culture or political party, or even a homeless or mentally ill person, and write an essay about your experience.

6. In this article, the author must come to terms with letting her brother make his own choice about what is the "right path" for him. Write an essay about freedom of choice. You may focus on a difficult choice you made for yourself, or one that you believed represented the right path for another person. How did the choice work out in the end?

SELF-TEST SUMMARY

To test yourself, cover the Answer column with a sheet of paper and answer each question in the left column. Evaluate each of your answers as you work by sliding the paper down and comparing your answer with what is printed in the Answer column.

QUESTION	ANSWER
■ GOAL 1 Understand the benefits of thinking critically What are the benefits of critical thinking?	Critical thinking allows you to distinguish good information from inaccurate or incomplete information and to show in your writing a strong understanding of what you've read.

QUESTION	ANSWER
■ GOAL 2 Make inferences What is an inference and how do you make inferences?	An inference is an educated guess about something unknown based on available information. To make an inference, understand the literal meaning first, notice details, add up the facts, notice the writer's choice of words, understand the writer's purpose, and be sure your inference is supportable.
■ GOAL 3 Assess sources and author qualifications How do you evaluate the source of material and the qualifications of the author?	To evaluate a source, consider the source's reputation, the audience for whom the source is intended, and whether documentation or references are provided. Look for a textbook author's credentials on the title page; for nonfiction books and general market paperbacks, look on the book jacket or back cover.
What factors should be considered when evaluating Internet sources?	Evaluate Internet sources by considering appropriateness, source, level of technical detail, and presentation. Also evaluate the completeness, accuracy and timeliness of the site.
■ GOAL 4 Distinguish between fact and opinion What is the difference between facts and opinions?	Facts are statements that can be verified, or proven to be true. Opinions are statements that express feelings, attitudes, or beliefs and are neither true nor false.
■ GOAL 5 Evaluate evidence and omissions How do you evaluate evidence?	Consider the type of evidence being presented and the relevance of that evidence.
How do writers mislead by omission?	Writers mislead by omitting essential details, ignoring contradictory evidence, making incomplete comparisons, using the passive voice, and using unspecified nouns and pronouns.
■ GOAL 6 Analyze tone What is tone, and what are some examples of tone?	Tone refers to the attitude or feeling a writer expresses about his or her subject. Examples of words commonly used to describe tone are *instructive*, *sympathetic*, *convincing*, *entertaining*, *nostalgic*, and *outraged*.

MySkillsLab®

Visit **Chapter 12, "Critical Thinking: Making Inferences and Analyzing the Author's Message,"** in MySkillsLab to test your understanding of chapter goals.

13 Critical Thinking: Evaluating the Author's Techniques

LEARNING GOALS

Learn how to . . .

- **GOAL 1** Evaluate the author's techniques
- **GOAL 2** Understand connotative and figurative language
- **GOAL 3** Analyze assumptions
- **GOAL 4** Evaluate generalizations
- **GOAL 5** Identify bias

THINK About It!

How would you describe the person in the photo? Words like *modern*, *individualistic*, and *unique* may come to mind. However, no matter how you would describe her, one thing is clear: she expresses herself very clearly through her sense of style. The same way that people express individual style through hair, clothing, and jewelry choices, authors express themselves with a variety of techniques that move beyond simple words on a page. In this chapter you will see how writers can persuade using colorful language, make assumptions and generalizations that may or may not be based on facts, and reveal their biases. Thinking critically about an author's techniques will improve your reading skills and help you write more effectively.

Reading and Writing Connections

EVERYDAY CONNECTIONS

- **Reading** You read a parenting blog that addresses the question of when children are old enough to be left at home alone. One writer makes a generalization that all children over 12 are old enough, while another makes an assumption that the parents of "latch-key kids" don't want to pay for child care.
- **Writing** You write a response based on your experience as a elementary school teacher (and as a parent), suggesting ways to determine when a child is ready to be left at home alone. You make it clear that you are expressing a bias by beginning your comments with the phrase, "In my opinion."

ACADEMIC CONNECTIONS

- **Reading** You read an article assigned in your economics class in which the writer compares the U.S. housing market to a roller coaster on which many "riders" started out excited and thrilled but were sick to their stomachs by the time the ride ended.
- **Writing** For an exam in economics, you write an essay discussing the factors that led to the mortgage crisis. You are careful to provide adequate and sufficient evidence, and you decide to revise your word choice for describing mortgage brokers from "greedy con artists" to "unscrupulous lenders."

WORKPLACE CONNECTIONS

- **Reading** In your part-time job at a discount retail store, you read an inventory bulletin indicating that toy trucks and foam dart guns are to be stocked under "Boys' Activities" and arts-and-crafts items are to be stocked under "Girls' Interests."
- **Writing** You write an e-mail to your manager proposing that the inventory categories be revised so that toys are stocked in aisles according to age or type of activity rather than according to assumptions based on gender.

Why Evaluate the Author's Techniques?

■ GOAL 1
Evaluate the author's techniques

Critical thinking, reading, and writing involve examining not only *what* is said but *how* it is said. Readers need to consider what an author is trying to accomplish and what techniques he or she uses to do so. Writers need to carefully choose techniques that will help them achieve their purpose, convey their message, and reach their audience.

In this chapter you will learn to look at language and discover how word choice affects meaning. You will learn to be alert for assumptions and generalizations—beliefs held by writers that are not necessarily stated but underlie their assertions—which have an impact on the strength or validity of their stated ideas. You will also be asked to consider your assumptions and to use them appropriately as you write. Finally, you will learn to look for bias in what you read and become aware of bias in your own thinking and writing.

EXAMINING PROFESSIONAL WRITING

Thinking Before Reading

In the following article, the author discusses the difficult working conditions faced by workers in the seafood industry in Santa Rosalia, Mexico. This excerpt will be used throughout this chapter to demonstrate and provide practice with evaluating an author's techniques.

Before you read:

1. Preview the reading, using the steps discussed in Chapter 1, page 4.
2. Connect the reading to your own experience by answering the following questions:
   a. What were working conditions like at your most recent job?
   b. How important is it for you to know the source of the food that you eat?
3. Mark and annotate as you read.

Sweatshops at Sea

Virginia Sole-Smith

1 It was a little after eight in the evening, and the sun was just beginning to set over the Gulf of California. Our small motorboat, known here in Santa Rosalia, Mexico, as a *panga*, sped out over the shimmering water. The breezy sea air felt good and clean after the heat of the day, and soon Delmar, the 26-year-old squid fisherman who had agreed to take us out for his night's work, was cracking open cans of **Tecate**. When we reached Delmar's fishing spot, he cut the engine and flipped on a tiny lightbulb duct-taped to a pole on the middle bench of the *panga*. Floating all around us were dozens of other *pangas*, and as night fell, the dots of light twinkled like a hundred fallen stars. It was beautiful and peaceful. Then we began to fish.

Tecate
a brand of Mexican beer

2 Delmar unraveled a glow-in-the-dark plastic tube fitted with sharp metal hooks that was attached to a thousand feet of clear fishing line. He tossed it overboard, wrapping the other end around a piece of scrap wood. When the line went tight after a few minutes, he began to pull, bare hand over bare hand, hauling the line back up through hundreds of feet of water. Seconds later, a 40-pound Humboldt squid splashed up from the depths with an enormous spray of salt water and sticky black ink. From tentacles to tail, it was almost as long as the *panga* was wide.

Machete
a large, heavy knife

3 In one fluid movement, Delmar yanked the squid out of the water, slapped it down, grabbed a rusty **machete**, and chopped off its head. Four hours later, the piles of red squid bodies and heads had grown so large that we had to balance with our feet braced awkwardly against the slick benches. When we had to move around the boat, we'd slip on spare eyeballs and black slime, and occasionally a spastic tentacle would wrap itself around the odd ankle. To make matters even worse, there were no life vests, radios, or emergency lights on board Delmar's *panga*.

4 It's no wonder that, every season, at least two or three fishermen like Delmar die at sea. The unsafe, grotesque working conditions on the water are just one of the many problems facing the working people of Santa Rosalia, a town of around 10,000 that is located in Baja California Sur. There are no spring break parties here. The dirty waterfront is devoted to three squid factories and the *panga* docks, because fishing the millions of Humboldt squid swimming in 25 square miles of Santa Rosalia's waters is the only game in town.

5 The squid processing plants—Korean-owned Brumar de San Bruno, Korean-owned Hanjin Mexico, and Chinese-owned Pesquera de Longing, SA—buy each day's catch from middlemen who have frozen the price the fishermen receive for their squid at just two pesos per kilo. That means most consider a $50 paycheck for a 10-hour fishing trip to be a good night. And it is, at least when you compare those wages to what the fishermen's wives, mothers, and daughters make working in the plants themselves, which—far from the federal labor offices in Mexico City—operate Wild West style.

6 Rosa Ceseña Ramirez began working in the Hanjin Mexico factory in 1994. She never knew when a shift was going to start or how long it would last. "You can either drink coffee for hours to stay awake, or sleep on the factory floor like an animal," Rosa explains. "Once the squid arrives, we have to work until it's all

Tightening U.S. seafood regulations could improve human rights in Mexico.

processed, even if it takes until the next afternoon. Then we go home for a few hours to sleep and see our kids, and have to come right back that evening."

7 The breaking point for Rosa came in November 2002, when Hanjin Mexico allegedly failed to pay its workers a federally mandated annual bonus and shortchanged their weekly paychecks. Rosa gathered signatures and filed a complaint with the Santa Rosalia labor office. Rosa says Hanjin Mexico responded by firing her and more than 90 workers. Eight years later, the former Hanjin Mexico workers are still waiting for the labor office to resolve their dispute, and conditions at all three Santa Rosalia factories have worsened.

8 At the neighboring Pesquera de Longing, workers report that only two toilets are available for more than 80 workers. Conditions at Brumar de San Bruno are no better. Most of the workers are migrant laborers who come from other Mexican states and live at the plant in a long, barracks-style dorm. "There are six of us sleeping in one room and whenever it's time to go back to work, the Koreans just open the door and yell, 'Let's go,'" worker Sonia Sanchez says. "They don't care if you're undressed or sleeping. We're treated like slaves."

9 The owners of the Santa Rosalia factories vehemently deny all of their workers' complaints, which is why Enlace International, a coalition of unions and worker centers in Mexico and the United States, is now approaching year eight of a campaign to create better working conditions for Santa Rosalia's labor force. "There will never be any enforcement of the labor laws in Mexico because this is a country with $212 billion in foreign debts," says Garrett Brown, coordinator of the Maquiladora Health and Safety Support Network. "If Americans want to help these workers, getting our government and banks to forgive Mexico's debt would be a big first step."

10 Another big step would be to tighten U.S. regulation of imported seafood. According to U.S. Department of Agriculture data, imports of processed squid from China totaled more than 1.1 million pounds in 2009 (along with 120 million pounds of unprocessed squid). But figuring out which U.S. retailers to hold accountable for the dire conditions in Santa Rosalia is all but impossible. "Seafood is often shipped from port to port before it reaches the United States, and it can be relabeled upon entry and exit, so we have no way of telling where it originally came from," explains Patrick Woodall of Food and Water Watch, a nonprofit consumer advocacy organization in Washington, D.C. "Companies can catch squid in Mexico, then ship it back to China for processing so they can take advantage of even cheaper labor markets and lower food safety regulations, then send it back to the United States. . . . There's just no way to trace it all."

11 Meanwhile Rosa balances her day job at a local supermarket with raising funds for the local union. She holds meetings for interested workers in the playground of the local school and writes letters to government officials. The process is slow, and more workers suffer every day. But Rosa is not deterred. "We know that one day it will be our daughters working in those factories," she says. "One part of my heart is sad for all the bad things that have happened. But the other part of my heart is happy because I know we are supporting one another."

Understand Connotative and Figurative Language

■ GOAL 2
Understand connotative and figurative language

Writers know that words influence a reader greatly, and they choose their words carefully. For this reason, reading critically involves understanding the connotative meanings of words and how they affect the reader, as well as understanding and evaluating figurative language.

Reading Connotative Language

All words have one or more standard meanings. These meanings are called **denotative meanings**. Think of them as dictionary meanings. They tell us what the words name. Many words also have connotative meanings. **Connotative meanings** include the feelings and associations that may accompany a word. For example, the denotative meaning for the word *flag* is a piece of cloth used as a national emblem. To many, the American flag is a symbol of patriotism and love of one's country. To others, though, it may be a symbol of oppression or merely a decorative item used on national holidays.

Connotative meanings, then, are powerful tools of language. Writers use words with specific connotative meanings to stir your emotions or to bring to mind positive or negative associations. Would you rather your jacket made of manmade fibers was called *fake* or *synthetic*? Would you rather be part of a *crowd* or a *mob*? While each pair of words has similar meanings, *fake* and *mob* have negative connotations. So it is important when you read to be alert for meanings suggested by the author's word choice.

In "Sweatshops at Sea," the author writes

> But figuring out which U.S. retailers to hold accountable for the **dire** conditions in Santa Rosalia is all but impossible. (paragraph 10)

The word *dire* means *desperate* or *extreme* and indicates that the author believes the working conditions in Santa Rosalia are very bad and need to be changed. If she had chosen to use other words here like *poor* or *unsatisfactory*, she would have conveyed less sense of outrage or urgency.

EXERCISE 13-1 Reading: Recognizing Connotative Meanings

Directions: For each of the following pairs of words, underline the word with the more positive connotation.

1. dent	dimple	**6.** expose	reveal
2. bold	brash	**7.** untidy	grubby
3. cheap	frugal	**8.** haughty	proud
4. displease	repel	**9.** deckhand	sailor
5. tipsy	drunk	**10.** job	chore

EXERCISE 13-2

Writing: Using Connotative Meanings

Directions: For each word listed, write a word that has a similar denotative meaning but a negative connotation. Then write a word that has a positive or neutral connotation.

Word	Negative Connotation	Positive or Neutral Connotation
Example: costly	extravagant	expensive
1. small	______	______
2. take	______	______
3. talk	______	______
4. desire	______	______
5. famous	______	______

EXERCISE 13-3

Reading: Analyzing Connotative Meanings in "Sweatshops at Sea"

Directions: Highlight five words in the essay and indicate whether they have positive or negative connotations. What is the author's purpose in using each of these words?

Writing: Using Connotative Language Carefully

Word meanings are very powerful. You can shape your readers' attitudes and responses to your topic in part by the connotative meanings of words you choose. Use the following strategies to evaluate your word choice:

- **Reread drafts.** Once you have written a draft and revised so that you are satisfied with the overall content and organization, reread it once looking only at your choice of words and phrases.
- **Circle any words with emotional impact.**
- **Examine the connotative meaning of the words you circled.** Ask yourself, "What emotion does this word or phrase suggest?" and "Is this the meaning I really want to convey?"
- **Revise, if necessary.**

Reading Figurative Language

Figurative language makes a comparison between two unlike things that share one common characteristic; it makes sense creatively or imaginatively, but not literally. If you say that your apartment looks as if it has been struck by a tornado, you are comparing two unlike things—your apartment and the effects of a tornado—and you mean that the apartment is a mess, not that it was actually hit by a tornado.

Here is an example of figurative language from "Sweatshops at Sea":

> Floating all around us were dozens of other *pangas*, and as night fell, the dots of light twinkled like a hundred fallen stars. (paragraph 1)

By comparing the lights of the fishing boats at night to fallen stars, the author conveys the image of how the lights from many boats flickered as they rose and fell on the water.

Figurative language is a powerful tool that allows writers to create images or paint pictures in the reader's mind. Figurative language also allows writers to suggest an idea without directly stating it. If you say the councilman bellowed like a bear, you are suggesting that the councilman was animal-like, loud, and forceful, but you have not said so directly. By planting the image of bear-like behavior, you have communicated your message to your reader.

There are three primary types of figurative language—*similes*, *metaphors*, and *personification*.

1. A **simile** uses the words *like* or *as* to make the comparison:

> The computer hums like a beehive.
>
> After 5:00 P.M. our downtown is as quiet as a ghost town.

2. A **metaphor** states or implies the relationship between the two unlike items. Metaphors often use the word *is*.

> The computer lab is a beehive.
>
> After 5:00 P.M. our downtown is a ghost town.

3. **Personification** compares humans and nonhumans according to one characteristic, attributing human characteristics to ideas or objects. If you say "the wind screamed its angry message," you are giving the wind the humanlike characteristics of screaming, being angry, and communicating a message. Here are two more examples:

> The sun mocked us with its relentless stare.
>
> After two days of writer's block, her pen started dancing across the page.

Be sure to analyze the author's motive for using figurative language. Often, a writer uses it as a way of describing rather than telling. A writer could say "The woman blushed" (telling) or "The woman's cheeks were as red as the setting sun" (describing).

NEED TO KNOW

How to Evaluate Figurative Language

When evaluating figurative language, ask the following questions:

1. Why did the writer make the comparison?
2. What is the basis of the comparison, that is, the shared characteristic?
3. Is the comparison accurate?
4. What images do you have in your mind? How do these images make you feel?
5. Is the comparison positive or negative?
6. Are several different interpretations possible?

Reading: Analyzing Figurative Language

Directions: With a classmate, discuss how the writer of each of the following passages uses figurative language to create a specific impression. Then compare your analysis with those of your classmates.

1. As a vacation port of call, Southern California has got it all. It's like a giant geographic theme park. Want to lap up glistening waves and bury your feet in the sand? The beach beckons. How about thick forests with fir- and pine-covered mountains? The majestic Angeles National Forest is a quick drive from Los Angeles. I prefer to use Dante's "Inferno" as my Baedeker [a guidebook for travelers]. Every summer, whenever I get the itch for a little rest and relaxation, I venture deep into the inner circle of hell—otherwise known as Palm Springs.

   —Mark Weingarten, "Palm Springs in August: The Ducks Use Sunblock," *The New York Times*, August 9, 2002

2. Thick as a truck at its base, the Brazil-nut tree rises 10 stories to an opulent crown, lord of the Amazon jungle. It takes the tree a century to grow to maturity; it takes a man with a chain saw an hour to cut it down. "It's a beautiful thing," nods Acelino Cardoso da Silva, a 57-year-old farmer. "But I have six hungry people at home. If the lumberman turns up, I'll sell."

   —Margolis, "A Plot of Their Own," *Newsweek*

3. If parenting is like an endurance race, senior year should be the section where parents triumphantly glide toward the finish line with a smiling graduate-to-be alongside. Instead, it's often more like heartbreak hill at the 20-mile mark of the Boston marathon, the bump that leaves parents exhausted and wondering what they were thinking 17 years ago.

   —Dunnewind, "Launching Kids to Independence," *Seattle Times*

Reading: Analyzing Figurative Language in "Sweatshops at Sea"

Directions: Below are two examples of figurative language from "Sweatshops at Sea." For each one, indicate whether it is a simile, metaphor, or example of personification, and explain how the author uses it to create a mood or an impression. Then create two new metaphors or similes that could be used in the reading to further explain a situation or action.

1. "'You can either drink coffee for hours to stay awake, or sleep on the factory floor like an animal.'" (paragraph 6) ______________________

   ____

   ____

2. "'They don't care if you're undressed or sleeping. We're treated like slaves.'" (paragraph 8) ______________________

   ____

3. ______________________

   ____

Writing: Using Figurative Language Effectively

Figurative language can make your writing lively, interesting, and engaging. It is also a creative way to describe and explain. To use it effectively, use the following suggestions:

- **Use fresh, interesting figures of speech.** Avoid using tired, overused expressions that have become clichés.
- **Make clear comparisons.** Because figurative language makes a comparison between two unlike things, be sure that you create figurative expressions that compare items for which the likeness is obvious and that do not suggest similarities you do not intend. For example, if you say, "Michael eats like a horse," it is clear that you are comparing only eating qualities and not suggesting that Michael is horselike in other respects. However, if you say, "Michael is a horse, and everyone in the restaurant recognized it," it is unclear what characteristics Michael and the horse share.
- **Avoid figurative expressions when you want to be precise, exact, and direct.** Figurative expressions leave room for interpretation and can lead to misinterpretation.

EXERCISE 13-6

Writing Figurative Expressions

Directions: Convert each of the following statements into a sentence using figurative language.

Example: I Am Nervous. I Feel As If I Have A Thousand Butterflies Fluttering In My Stomach.

1. He was hungry. ______
2. The clouds were beautiful. ______
3. Everyone argued. ______
4. The test was hard. ______
5. My friend laughed. ______

Analyze Assumptions

- GOAL 3
  Analyze assumptions

Here are some examples of assumptions:

- You're going to make that mistake again, are you? (The assumption is that you have already made the mistake at least once.)
- When you're mature, you'll realize you made a mistake. (The assumption is that you are not mature now.)
- You are as arrogant as your sister. (The assumption is that your sister is arrogant.)

An **assumption** is an idea or principle a person accepts as true and makes no effort to prove or substantiate. He or she then develops ideas based on that assumption. For example, an author may believe the legal system is biased against poor defendants, and beginning with that assumption, develop an argument for how to provide better legal support to people without financial resources. However, if you believe the legal system is working well, you might not support any changes in defense funding for the poor, and unless the writer provided clear evidence for his point, you would not accept his argument.

Read the following paragraph. What is the writer assuming?

> Speaking from developments in my own family, there are way too many young students out there whose focus centers on partying, dress competition, music, souped-up cars and sex. Goal-setting and accomplishment in their studies as they prepare themselves for what is a highly competitive world do not figure too prominently in their day-to-day lives.
>
> —Editorial, "School's First Week Provides a Few Bright Exceptions," *Toronto Star*

This writer is assuming, based only on the evidence of his or her own family, that far too many students are focused on having fun rather than on studying and preparing for a career. Without further evidence to support this assumption, the reader cannot trust this writer's conclusion. Writers often make assumptions and make no effort to prove or support them. If a writer's assumption is wrong or unsubstantiated, then the statements that follow from the assumption should be questioned.

EXERCISE 13-7 Writing: Identifying Assumptions

Directions: For each statement listed below, write at least one underlying assumption.

1. Grocery stores should reduce the number of weekly sale items and lower overall prices.

____

2. Eliminating essay exams in psychology courses would diminish students' writing abilities.

____

3. More public transit should be added to our cities to reduce traffic and pollution.

____

4. Endangered species should be bred in captivity to ensure their survival.

____

5. Artists do not need grants from the government because they sell their works for such high prices.

____

Reading: Identifying and Evaluating Assumptions

Directions: Working in pairs, identify the assumption(s) in each of the following passages. Then discuss whether the authors have provided valid support for their assumptions.

1. Most kids, of course, listen barely if at all to what adults say. Instead they watch what adults do. And, for better or worse, there may be no lesson we impart to them so efficiently as how we adults react to events that upset us, from a fender-bender to a threatening new era of conflict.

   —Editorial, "Raising the Sept. 11 Generation," *Chicago Tribune*

2. Most products—from cigarette lighters to medicine bottles—have to be designed to protect against foreseeable misuse. But there is no regulator to help the plaintiffs: guns and tobacco are the only products that the Consumer Product Safety Commission does not oversee. And even though lawsuits have often helped push up safety standards elsewhere, there are plenty of conservative judges who do not think it is the courts' job to create gun laws.

   —Editorial, "From the Hip; Gun Control," *The Economist* (U.S.)

3. In the meantime, a disturbing message is being sent to the guys and girls in the little leagues. Practice hard, work out, eat nutritiously—and sneak illegal steroids because, after all, winning and setting records are everything. And besides, if you make it big, you'll have enough money to care for your broken body.

   —Editorial, "Steroids Should Be Tagged Out," *San Jose Mercury News*

4. Britain on Wednesday marked the 150th anniversary of its public toilets. This reminds us of the barbaric lack of such facilities in the United States. Along with an increasingly chaotic and unfair health system, sparse public transportation and a paucity of neighborhood parks, the absence of public loos here evokes America's depressing distance from the perfect place that pathological patriots assert that it is.

   —Editorial, "Sign of Civilization," *Providence Journal*

Reading: Identifying Assumptions in the Professional Article

Directions: Reread "Sweatshops at Sea" on page 370. Does the author make assumptions? If so, what are they? Are they supported with evidence? If so, what kind?

Writing: Making Reasonable Assumptions

First and foremost, try to identify and evaluate your own assumptions about a topic to ensure your ideas are logical and well-founded. Also be aware that your readers may agree or disagree with your assumptions. If you think they are likely to disagree, then you may need to explain your assumptions in detail and demonstrate why they are valid.

Evaluate Generalizations

■ GOAL 4
Evaluate generalizations

What do the following statements have in common?

> Dogs are vicious and nasty.
>
> Politicians never tell the truth.
>
> Parents want their children to grow up to be just like them.

Although the subjects are different, each is a generalization. Each makes a broad statement about an entire group—dogs, politicians, and parents—based on the writer's experience with some members of that group. It necessarily involves the writer's judgment. The first statement says that dogs are vicious and nasty. Yet the writer could not be certain that this statement is true unless he or she had seen *every* existing dog.

The question that must be asked about all generalizations is whether they are accurate. How many dogs did the writer observe and how much research did he or she do to justify the generalization? When you read, try to think of exceptions to generalizations—in this instance, a dog that is neither vicious nor nasty—and look beyond the general statement for details, proof, and evidence.

NEED TO KNOW

How to Evaluate Generalizations

A critical reader should do the following:

1. **Evaluate the type and quality of evidence provided as support.** If there is no evidence to support a generalization, you cannot assume it is true. The more detailed and researched the evidence provided, the more likely the generalization is accurate.
2. **Evaluate the specifics.** For the statement "Pets are always troublesome," ask what kind of pets the author is referring to—a pet potbellied pig, an iguana, or a cat? Then ask what is meant by troublesome—does it mean the animal is time-consuming, requires special care, or behaves poorly?
3. **Think of exceptions.** For the generalization "Medical doctors are aloof and inaccessible," can you think of a doctor you have met or heard about who was caring and available to his or her patients? If so, the generalization is not accurate in all cases.

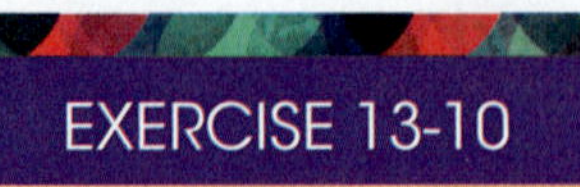

EXERCISE 13-10

Reading: Identifying Generalizations

Directions: Read each of the following items and underline each generalization.

1. Child care workers are undereducated in relation to the importance of their jobs. A whole generation of children is being left day after day in the hands of women with little more than high-school-level education.

These children will suffer in the future for our inattention to the child care employment pool.

2. Americans have had enough of libraries providing Internet pornography to children. They want filtering on all computers or computers used in libraries. When will librarians listen to their customers (who also pay their salaries)?

3. For the past few years, drivers have been getting worse. Especially guilty of poor driving are the oldest and youngest drivers. There should be stricter tests and more classes for new drivers and yearly eye exams and road tests for drivers once they hit age 60. This is the only way to ensure the safety of our roads.

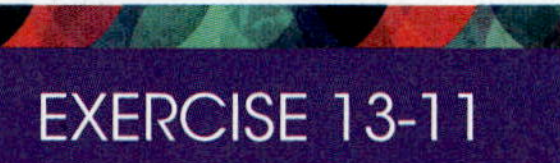

Reading: Evaluating Generalizations

Directions: Working with a classmate, indicate what questions you would ask and what types of information you would need to evaluate each of the following generalizations.

1. Vegetarians are pacifists, and they do not own guns.
2. Most crimes are committed by high school dropouts.
3. It always rains in Seattle.
4. Private school students get a better education than public school students.
5. Scientists don't believe in any kind of higher power.

Writing: Making Generalizations Based on Sufficient Evidence

A topic sentence is a generalization that you support in the remainder of your paragraph. Likewise, a thesis statement is a generalization that you explain throughout the remainder of your essay. Always be sure to provide adequate and sufficient evidence in support of these kinds of statements. (For more on adequate and sufficient evidence, see Chapter 4, p. 132, and Chapter 9, p. 273.)

Identify Bias

■ GOAL 5
Identify bias

Think of a television commercial you have seen recently, perhaps for a particular model of car. The ad tells you the car's advantages—why you want to buy it—but does it tell you its disadvantages? Does it describe ways in which the model compares unfavorably with competitors? Certainly not. Do you feel the ad writer is being unfair? Probably not. We expect advertisers to present a one-sided, or biased, view of their products. We do not expect them to tell us about potential problems like low gas mileage, inferior engine parts, or a limited warranty because we know they want us to buy what they are selling.

In contrast, we expect other forms of writing to be fair and balanced; otherwise they are presenting a biased point of view. You can think of **bias** as a writer's prejudice; if an author is biased, then he or she is partial to one point of view rather than another on a controversial issue.

In the following excerpt from "Sweatshops at Sea," (paragraphs 4 and 5) the author's choice of words (see highlighting) reveal her attitude toward the owners of the squid factories.

> It's no wonder that, every season, at least two or three fishermen like Delmar die at sea. The unsafe, grotesque working conditions on the water are just one of the many problems facing the working people of Santa Rosalia, a town of around 10,000 that is located in Baja California Sur. There are no spring break parties here. The dirty waterfront is devoted to three squid factories and the *panga* docks, because fishing the millions of Humboldt squid swimming in 25 square miles of Santa Rosalia's waters is the only game in town.
>
> The squid processing plants—Korean-owned Brumar de San Bruno, Korean-owned Hanjin Mexico, and Chinese-owned Pesquera de Longing, SA—buy each day's catch from middlemen who have frozen the price the fishermen receive for their squid at just two pesos per kilo. That means most consider a $50 paycheck for a 10-hour fishing trip to be a good night. And it is, at least when you compare those wages to what the fishermen's wives, mothers, and daughters make working in the plants themselves
>
> —Sole-Smith, "Sweatshops at Sea"

NEED TO KNOW

Identifying Bias

To identify bias, ask the following questions:

1. Is the author acting as a reporter—presenting facts—or as salesperson—providing only favorable information?
2. Does the author feel strongly about or favor one side of the issue?
3. Does the author use connotative or figurative language to create a positive or negative image?
4. Does the author seem emotional about the issue?
5. Are there other views toward the subject that the writer does not recognize or discuss?

EXERCISE 13-12 Reading: Identifying Bias

Directions: Read each of the following statements, and place a check mark in front of the ones that reveal bias.

_____ 1. Cities should be designed for the pedestrian, not the automobile.

_____ 2. There are more channels than ever before on cable television.

_____ 3. The current system of voter registration is a sham.

_____ 4. Professional sports have become elitist.

_____ 5. Space exploration costs millions of dollars each year.

EXERCISE 13-13 Reading: Identifying Bias

Directions: After reading each passage, select the choice that best answers each of the questions that follow.

A. The fact that different climate studies reach widely different conclusions is not surprising. Much of the global warming debate centers on the output of highly questionable computer models that conjure figures from scarcely understood variables, dubious raw data and gaping holes filled with assumptions that usually confirm the researchers' biases. No wonder that even as reliable temperature measurements show global temperatures have flatlined or been falling for the past decade, claims of imminent catastrophe have grown more shrill. Garbage in, warming out.

—Editorial, "A Climate of Fraud," *The Washington Times,* November 30, 2011, p. 2

______ **1.** The author seems biased against
- **a.** all computer models.
- **b.** global warming advocates.
- **c.** global warming measurement.
- **d.** climate study.

______ **2.** Which of the following phrases best reveals the author's bias?
- **a.** "widely different conclusions"
- **b.** "temperatures have flatlined"
- **c.** "gaping holes filled with assumptions"
- **d.** "global warming debate centers on"

B. Is it any surprise that Americans can't save any money for their retirement? The system is stacked against the average American, who goes to work, pays taxes, supports a family, and barely scrapes together enough to send the kids to college. Out-of-control property taxes and the high costs of health care only add to the burden. Throw in an unexpected car repair, a malfunctioning furnace, or a company that decides to give your job to someone overseas, and you have a real recipe for financial disaster. Meanwhile, CEO's earn hundreds of millions of dollars a year, sail on yachts, own mansions on the waterfront, and send their children to the finest schools, where they'll meet other children of the wealthy and network their way to success. Yes, my friends, the time has come to pass legislation that puts a cap on CEO salaries and forces companies to share their profits with the people who make it possible. You know, the unsung men and women whose sole purpose right now is to put money in the CEO's pocket.

______ **3.** The author seems biased against
- **a.** college graduates
- **b.** CEO's
- **c.** banks and other financial institutions
- **d.** politicians

______ **4.** Which of the following phrases reveals the author's basis in favor of workers?
- **a.** "average American"
- **b.** "network their way to financial success"
- **c.** "a cap on CEO salaries"
- **d.** "unsung men and women"

C. Some readers say, "Give me a nice book to hold in my hands. I want to turn the pages, feel the weight, mark my place with my favorite bookmark." I am not one of those readers. I'm not saying that printed books are bad. But I just don't have the room for them. I live in a small, one-bedroom apartment, and printed books take up a lot of space—and every square inch counts when you live in a studio apartment. With my tablet, all of my books are available to me at any time. I can own hundreds, thousands, even millions of books—and still have room in my apartment for my clothes, my furniture, and my plants. If I'm stuck on an airplane with a book I don't like, I simply click over to another book. I don't have to lug heavy books with me any more, and my tablet lets me adjust the type size of my favorite books to accommodate my aging eyes. So, yes, long live the printed book, and all that—but grant me the right to love my amazing little electronic device.

_____ 5. The author is biased in favor of
- **a.** reading
- **b.** hardcover books
- **c.** softcover books
- **d.** e-books

_____ 6. Which phrase reveals the author's bias in favor of a particular way of reading?
- **a.** "I'm not saying that printed books are bad"
- **b.** "every square inch counts"
- **c.** "my amazing little electronic device"
- **d.** "long live the printed book"

EXERCISE 13-14

Reading: Analyzing Bias

Directions: Working with a classmate, identify the author's bias in each of the following statements. Then discuss how you determined the author's biases.

1. Now that Americans are vulnerable to attack in the United States by terrorists, gun control should no longer be an issue for our politicians to waste time debating. Law-abiding, innocent citizens need the means to protect themselves from foreign enemies right here in their homeland. We must reduce the risk of losing more lives to extremists by allowing our people to carry weapons for defense.

2. I have expressed in the past that police officers should refrain from enforcing immigration laws so that police departments can maintain good relations with Hispanics. If Latinos fear that police will report them or their family members to the immigration service, they might fear coming forward to help solve crimes.

—Salinas, "Will All Hispanic Men Be Suspect?" *Seattle Post-Intelligencer*

3. Parents trust their children less and less these days. Convinced beyond a doubt that violent video games will turn their sons and daughters into criminals, parents go to the extreme by banning all forms of electronic entertainment from their homes. Instead of seizing the opportunity to teach a child about limits, self-regulation, and good taste, moms and dads all over America are unwittingly increasing the desire for taboo entertainment. Today's kids are not being allowed to experiment and test themselves while under their parents' supervision. This parental disservice can only lead to a backlash in the future when young men and women experiment with risky behaviors as soon as they leave their parents' tight hold.

4. Those clamoring to shut down the farmers, however, should look hard at the prospect of a prairie full of subdivisions and suburban pollution: car exhaust, lawn and garden fertilizers, wood stoves, sewage. Certainly, the smoke from field burning is an annoyance, particularly to the hard-hit Sandpoint area, and to some it's a health hazard. But the benefits the sturdy farmers produce 50 weeks of the year shouldn't be dismissed casually.

—Oliveria, "Burning Will Go; That's Not All Good," *Spokesman Review*

5. Money doesn't grow on trees, but some trees might as well be pure gold. The world's voracious (and growing) appetite for wood, paper, and other forest products is driving a stampede to mow down forests. Much of this logging is illegal.

—Haugen, "Logging Illogic," *World Watch*

Writing: Handling Bias Openly

Readers appreciate the open and straightforward expression of ideas and mistrust writers who pretend to be objective while actually presenting a one-sided viewpoint. There are writing situations in which you will want to express your opinions and reveal your bias. When these occur, be sure to do so openly. One way to make it clear that you are expressing a bias is to include phrases such as "in my opinion," "one viewpoint is," or "one way of looking at." It is also helpful to mention opposing viewpoints by referring to or summarizing them, and by refuting them, if you choose.

READ AND RESPOND: A Student Essay

Aurora Gilbert is a student at Columbia University, studying Business Management and Hispanic Studies. She hopes to attend graduate school for public health and go on to work for global health in Latin America.

Aurora wrote this essay as an assignment in her psychology class. The assignment required that she write an essay explaining an obsession or fascination with a strange phenomenon existing in society today. As you read, pay special attention to how Aurora uses connotative and figurative language to communicate her attitude toward the topic and make the writing more appealing and engaging for her readers.

Title suggests thesis

TV's Bloody Obsession: *Why Vampire Television is Dangerously Appealing*

Aurora Gilbert

Introduction: Gilbert describes an engaging scene to capture the interest of her readers

1 A peculiar creature has infiltrated popular culture and seduced audiences around the globe. He is haunting bookstores, starring in movies, and dominating television channels; he is the vampire. Audiences worldwide have been fascinated with vampires for over a century, beginning most famously with Bram Stoker's novel, *Dracula*. In recent years, vampire fiction has surged in popularity with books and movies such as *Twilight*, and television shows such as *Buffy the Vampire Slayer*, *Vampire Diaries*, and *True Blood*. What makes audiences so attracted to this strange genre? It is the intriguing nature of the vampire, the tragically beautiful human-vampire romance, and the added excitement of other supernatural beings. Vampire television dramas in particular bring childhood superpower fantasies to life and up the ante of regular, human-centered TV dramas.

Thesis statement

Topic sentence

2 The greatest appeal of vampire TV drama comes from the mesmerizing nature of the vampire himself. He is a being who was once human, but at one point was bitten by a vampire and became one himself. Vampires are "undead" creatures that survive on human blood and can only walk the earth at night, forced to sleep in the ground during the day. The vampire does not age or die, and a human can only fully destroy him by driving a stake through his heart. Vampires are particularly mysterious and wise, as they have been alive far longer than the average human can live; they have seen the passing of time, coming and going of humans, and waves of history. They feed on humans, drinking their blood for sustenance. Vampires are by nature evil, yet they are also tragic and sympathy-inducing characters. Each vampire was "turned" by another vampire before him, so all vampires are actually victims of a gruesome crime. They were made vampire, usually unwillingly, cut off forever from human life and their loved ones. The vampire still clings to remnants of the past though he is a slave to his evil urges. He remembers his family, the sunlight, and his beating heart, but he is condemned to walk the night forever.

Background information on vampires

Topic sentence

3 In recent vampire TV dramas, a component that audiences find increasingly compelling is the romance between vampire and human being. This relationship is the ultimate tragic romance, the ultimate spin on a heart wrenching *Romeo and Juliet*–type story. The vampire, usually a male, is dark, handsome, and incredibly intelligent. The human is attracted to the vampire's mysterious qualities, and the vampire sees in the human a certain innocence, tenderness, and beauty that he lost from himself a long time ago. The vampire is strong and without fear, protecting the human from all danger. The human gives the vampire the joy that he lost when he became undead. However, this darkly beautiful relationship cannot last. The vampire is repulsed by the daylight, and his instinct drives him to gruesomely feed on the blood of humans, putting the human herself in danger at times. The human will eventually grow old, and the vampire will have to watch her get sick and die, losing her forever while he lives on, watching the passing of history.

Topic sentence

4 Audiences of vampire TV drama have learned that where there are vampires, there are usually other supernatural creatures to be found; these creatures keep the audience on its toes with a diversity of new and surprising fantastical powers. Werewolves always seem to crop up in vampire dramas, usually as an opposing force to vampires. The contention between vampires and werewolves make for epic, Homeric-type battles but with the added factor of super-human strength and powers. Other supernatural creatures that surface in vampire TV dramas, such as HBO's *True Blood*, are werepanthers, shape shifters, fairies, and witches. Each supernatural creature has its own unique set of powers, which compete and interact with the powers of others.

Gilbert uses a question as a topic sentence

5 Why are these supernatural creatures so fascinating to watch? Perhaps it is because most people have wished, at least at one point in their lives, that they had a supernatural power of their own. As children, most people played the game "what superhuman power would you have?" to dream up their wildest and most impressive supernatural desires. Vampire TV dramas bring these childhood wishes to life. Have a dream of being able to read minds? Fairies can do that. Wish to be able to turn into any kind of animal? Shape shifters can. Dreamt of having the power to cure people of disease? Witches can. Wish to heal wounds, have superhuman strength, and stay youthful forever? Vampires can do so.

Topic sentence

6 Vampire TV dramas offer the high dramatic quality of any other popular TV drama, but they add a spark of magic into the mix. Just like regular TV dramas, there are romances and rivalries, family feuds and political conflicts, but these plot twists are

enhanced by the fantastical. When the main character meets a handsome man in the local diner, he turns out to be a vampire who only leaves his home after sundown. When a new woman comes to town claiming to be a social worker, she turns out to be a witch with not-so-charitable intentions. A character is seriously injured and on the verge of death, but is saved by a vampire whose blood can cure wounds. These shows make reality more exciting and magical, tweaking the rules of everyday life and catering to the audience's daydreaming minds.

Conclusion: Gilbert issues a warning and summarizes her main points.

7 Before leaping into the realm of vampire TV drama, prospective viewers should beware of two caveats. The first is that these shows can be gory. Vampire TV dramas are not typically violent with regard to explosions and firearms, but there is a lot of bloodshed. Watching vampires sucking the blood of human prey can be jarring at first, but after some getting used to, it becomes strangely normal. The second caveat to keep in mind when watching such shows is that they are extremely addicting. Starting to watch a vampire show should not be taken lightly. It is highly likely that after the first episode, a new viewer will be sucked into this new mysterious world, unable to pull her eyes from the screen. If one has the stomach to endure the gore and time to devote to a television show, she will not be disappointed by the vampire TV drama; one click of the remote can bring on a new world of fascinating vampires, tragically beautiful romance, and a plethora of dazzling supernatural creatures and magical powers.

Examining Writing

1. What does the title suggest about the thesis of this essay? Evaluate the effectiveness of the title, introduction, and conclusion.
2. Highlight words with strong connotative meanings. Examine each and determine whether the word conveys the writer's meaning accurately. If not, jot down alternatives.
3. Upon what assumptions is the essay based? Write out the assumptions, and evaluate each one to determine whether it is reasonable.
4. Evaluate any figurative expressions. Do they make fair comparisons? Could the essay be improved by the use of figurative expressions? If so, add them.
5. What is the author's attitude toward her topic? Does she openly express bias? Cite evidence from the essay to support your answer.
6. What type of visual could Aurora have chosen to enhance her essay? Describe the visual and explain how it could support her thesis.

Writing Assignments

1. Aurora refers to vampire television as a "bloody obsession." Perhaps vampire television does not interest you, but chances are that you may be "hooked" on another television show or series. In a paragraph, describe your TV obsession and explain why you like it.
2. Fantasy and science fiction have always been popular genres for people of all ages. In a paragraph, explain why you like or dislike reading fantasy literature or viewing fantasy movies and/or television shows.
3. According to Aurora, we all have wished at some point in our life to have a supernatural power. What supernatural power would you like to have? Write a short essay explaining the supernatural power, why you would like to have it, and how you would use it.

READ AND RESPOND: A Professional Essay

Sweatshops at Sea

Virginia Sole-Smith

The questions and activities below refer to the article "Sweatshops at Sea," that we have used as a model throughout the chapter. Now you are ready to more closely examine the article and write in response to it.

Writing in Response to Reading (See essay on pp. 370–372.)

Checking Your Comprehension MySkillsLab®

Answer each of the following questions using complete sentences.

1. Explain what a *panga* is and briefly describe the work that occurs on it. What makes this work dangerous?
2. Who owns the squid processing plants described in this essay?
3. Describe conditions at the Hanjin Mexico factory. What caused Rosa Ceseña Ramirez to reach her breaking point, and how did her employer respond?
4. What is Enlace International and what is it trying to accomplish?
5. According to the essay, what are two big steps that would help the Mexican workers?

Strengthening Your Vocabulary MySkillsLab®

Identify at least five words used in the reading that are unfamiliar to you. Using context, word parts, or a dictionary, write a brief definition of each word.

Examining the Reading: Drawing an Idea Map

Create an idea map of the reading that starts with the title and thesis and then lists the author's main points. Use the guidelines on page 15.

Reading and Writing: An Integrated Perspective MySkillsLab®

Get ready to write about the reading by discussing the following:

1. Evaluate the introductory paragraphs of the essay. How does the initial description of the fishing trip contrast with the work that takes place on the boat and in the factories?
2. Discuss why this essay is called "Sweatshops at Sea." Can you think of other titles that would be as effective?
3. What impression does the author create in paragraph 3? Why does she include these details? In a journal entry, write about your reaction to the description of the scene on the fishing boat.

4. Why does the author include quotes from Rosa Ceseña Ramirez and Sonia Sanchez? Evaluate the accuracy and reliability of these two sources as well as the other two sources quoted in the selection.

THINKING VISUALLY

5. Why does the author end the essay with Rosa? Evaluate the effectiveness of this conclusion.

6. What aspects of the essay are illustrated by the photograph? Discuss details in the photograph that correspond to descriptions in the essay.

Thinking and Writing Critically MySkillsLab®

1. What is the author's purpose for writing this article? Who is her intended audience?

2. Can you identify any bias in this piece? Consider whether facts or opposing viewpoints were omitted that might have presented a different story.

3. Does the author make generalizations? Try to think of exceptions to any generalizations you find in the essay.

4. Evaluate the evidence the author uses to support her thesis. What evidence was most effective or compelling? Why? What other types of evidence might she have used to support her thesis?

5. Describe the author's tone. How do you know how she feels about her subject?

6. Evaluate the effectiveness of the photograph that accompanies the reading. What other illustrations or photographs would be effective in helping the author achieve her purpose?

Writing Paragraph MySkillsLab®

1. What is the most difficult work you have ever done? Write a paragraph describing your experience and what made it difficult.

2. Did this essay make you sympathetic to the plight of these workers? Why or why not? Write a paragraph explaining your answer.

3. Were you surprised to learn about the business practices surrounding imported seafood? Write a paragraph explaining your answer and whether this information will affect your consumption of seafood or other imported foods.

Writing Essays MySkillsLab®

4. What can you tell from this reading about the author's attitude toward the workers and the owners of the factories? Write an essay examining the ways in which the author reveals her feelings toward each.

5. Why do you think Rosa Ceseña Ramirez is undeterred after eight years? Write an essay from her point of view explaining her motivations and her commitment to this cause.

6. Consider the two steps that are suggested as ways to improve conditions for the labor force. Do you agree or disagree that these actions should be taken? Can you think of other steps that might be effective? Write an essay explaining your answers.

SELF-TEST SUMMARY

To test yourself, cover the Answer column with a sheet of paper and answer each question in the left column. Evaluate each of your answers as you work by sliding the paper down and comparing your answer with what is printed in the Answer column.

QUESTION	ANSWER
■ GOAL 1 Evaluate the author's techniques What is involved in evaluating an author's techniques?	Evaluating an author's techniques involves examining the author's word choice, assumptions, generalizations, and bias.
■ GOAL 2 Understand connotative and figurative language What are denotative and connotative meanings?	Denotative meanings are the standard, dictionary meanings of words; connotative meanings include the feelings and associations that accompany a word.
What does figurative language do, and what are the three primary types of figurative language?	Figurative language makes a comparison between two unlike things that share a common characteristic. The three primary types of figurative language are similes, metaphors, and personification.
■ GOAL 3 Analyze assumptions What is an assumption?	An assumption is an idea or principle the writer accepts as true and makes no effort to prove or substantiate.
■ GOAL 4 Evaluate generalizations What is a generalization?	A generalization is a statement made about a large group based on the writer's experience with some members of that group.
How do you think critically about generalizations?	To think critically about generalizations, evaluate types of evidence, the quality of evidence, and the specifics, and try to think of exceptions.
■ GOAL 5 Identify bias What is bias and how do you identify it?	Bias is a preference for or prejudice against a person, object, or idea; biased material is one-sided. To identify bias, ask yourself what facts were omitted and what impression you would have if different words were used.

MySkillsLab®

Visit **Chapter 13 "Critical Thinking: Evaluating the Author's Techniques,"** in MySkillsLab to test your understanding of chapter goals.

Critical Thinking: Reading and Writing Arguments

14

LEARNING GOALS

Learn how to . . .

- **GOAL 1** Understand the use of argument
- **GOAL 2** Recognize the parts of an argument
- **GOAL 3** Read an argument effectively
- **GOAL 4** Think critically about arguments
- **GOAL 5** Write argument essays

THINK About It!

Study the above photograph. What issue is addressed by the signs that the protester is carrying and wearing? Write a paragraph that answers the following questions: What position (pro or con) does the protester take on the issue? What are some of the possible reasons for agreeing with this position?

The paragraph you have just written is a brief argument. An argument presents logical reasons and evidence to support a point of view on an issue. In this chapter you will learn how to read arguments effectively, think critically about arguments, and write arguments that persuade readers to support your point of view.

Reading and Writing Connections

EVERYDAY CONNECTIONS

- **Reading** You read an essay in the student newspaper calling on students to boycott the campus cafeteria because of a lack of appetizing and nutritional foods. The writer offers several examples and quotes other students in support of his claim.
- **Writing** As a student council member, you write a letter to school administrators and the cafeteria manager, urging them to revise the menu. You argue that more students will use the cafeteria while benefiting from healthier, more appealing options.

ACADEMIC CONNECTIONS

- **Reading** For a business management class, you read an article that argues against the "open office" concept, in which managers work alongside employees rather than in private offices.
- **Writing** You write an essay for business management arguing in favor of the "open office" concept. You include facts and statistics that indicate higher levels of efficiency, productivity, and morale in open offices as compared with traditional office arrangements.

WORKPLACE CONNECTIONS

- **Reading** In your job at a grocery store, you read a memo from your manager defending the store's decision to stop giving free samples to customers.
- **Writing** You write an e-mail to your manager arguing that the free sample policy be continued. You acknowledge your manager's claim that it is expensive, but you argue that the expense is offset by the number of customers who purchase a product after receiving a free sample.

What Is an Argument?

■ GOAL 1
Understand the use of argument

An **argument** is a line of reasoning intended to persuade the reader or listener to agree with a particular viewpoint or take a particular action. If you turn on the television or radio, or open a magazine or newspaper, you are sure to encounter the most common form of argument—advertising. Commercials and ads are attempts to persuade you to buy a particular product or service. For example,

- Use Tooth Cleanser Paste with Extra Whitening for a knockout smile!
- Drive the new EBZ for an out of this world experience.
- Marty's Catsup turns a hot dog into a taste explosion.

Many arguments, however, are presented more formally with reasons and evidence to support them. Here are two examples of these types of arguments:

- Many students have part-time jobs that require them to work late afternoons and evenings during the week. These students are unable to use the library during the week. Therefore, library hours should be extended to weekends.
- Because parents have the right to determine their children's sexual attitudes, sex education should take place in the home, not at school.

The Parts of an Argument

■ GOAL 2
Recognize the parts of an argument

An **argument** presents reasons for accepting a belief or position or for taking a specific action. It has three essential parts:

- **An issue** is the problem or controversy that the argument addresses. It is also the topic of an argument paragraph or essay.
- **A claim** is the particular point of view a writer has on an issue. There are always at least two points of view on an issue; often there are several. For example, you may advocate for strict gun control (with no one but the police and military carrying weapons), moderate gun control (where those with permits may carry, but not conceal, weapons) or no gun control (believing that everyone has a second amendment right to bear arms).
- **Support** consists of the details that demonstrate a claim is correct and should be accepted. There are three types of support: *reasons*, *evidence*, and *emotional appeals*.

Good arguments also often contain a **refutation** that considers opposing viewpoints and attempts to disprove them. For example, a claim could be made that baseball players' use of steroids is unhealthy and unfair. An opposing viewpoint may be that steroid use enhances performance, making games more fun for fans. This opposing viewpoint could be refuted by providing evidence that fans would prefer to see games played without the use of performance-enhancing drugs or by providing facts about the serious side effects of steroid use.

Issue	Claim	Support	Refutation
Fracking	Fracking is dangerous, so we should pursue alternative energy sources.	Fracking pollutes groundwater, triggers earthquakes, and degrades air quality.	The many risks outweigh the benefits of cheap energy and economic growth.
Plus-minus grading system at Blank U	The plus-minus grading system is confusing and unnecessary.	It costs instructors extra time, employers do not understand it, and it complicates the computation of GPA.	Although it brings Blank U in line with other schools, there is no evidence they have benefited from using it.

Here is a sample argument written by a student. Note how he presents reasons and evidence for taking a specific action.

Buckle Up

As a paramedic, I am the first to arrive at the scene of many grim and tragic accidents. One awful accident last month involved four women in one car. The front-seat passenger died instantly, another died during a mercy flight to the nearest hospital, one lost both legs, and one walked away from the accident without serious injury. Only one woman was wearing a seat belt. Guess which one. Though many people protest and offer excuses, seat belts do save lives.

Many people avoid wearing seat belts and say they'd rather be thrown free from an accident. Yet they seldom realize that the rate at which they will be thrown is the same rate at which the car is moving. Others fear being trapped inside by their seat belt in case of a fire. However, if not ejected, those without a belt are likely to be stunned or knocked unconscious on impact and will not be alert enough to escape uninjured.

Seat belts save lives by protecting passengers from impact. During a crash, a body slams against the windshield or steering wheel with tremendous force if unbelted. The seat belt secures the passenger in place and protects vital organs from injury.

Recent statistics demonstrate that a passenger is five times more likely to survive a crash if a seat belt is worn. Life is a gamble, but those are good odds. Buckle up!

This writer introduces the topic with a startling example from his personal experience. The thesis statement occurs at the end of the first paragraph. The second paragraph offers evidence that supports the writer's thesis, and the third considers and rejects opposing points of view. The last paragraph concludes the essay by offering a convincing statistic and reminding the reader of the thesis "Buckle up." You can visualize this short argument as follows:

VISUALIZE IT!

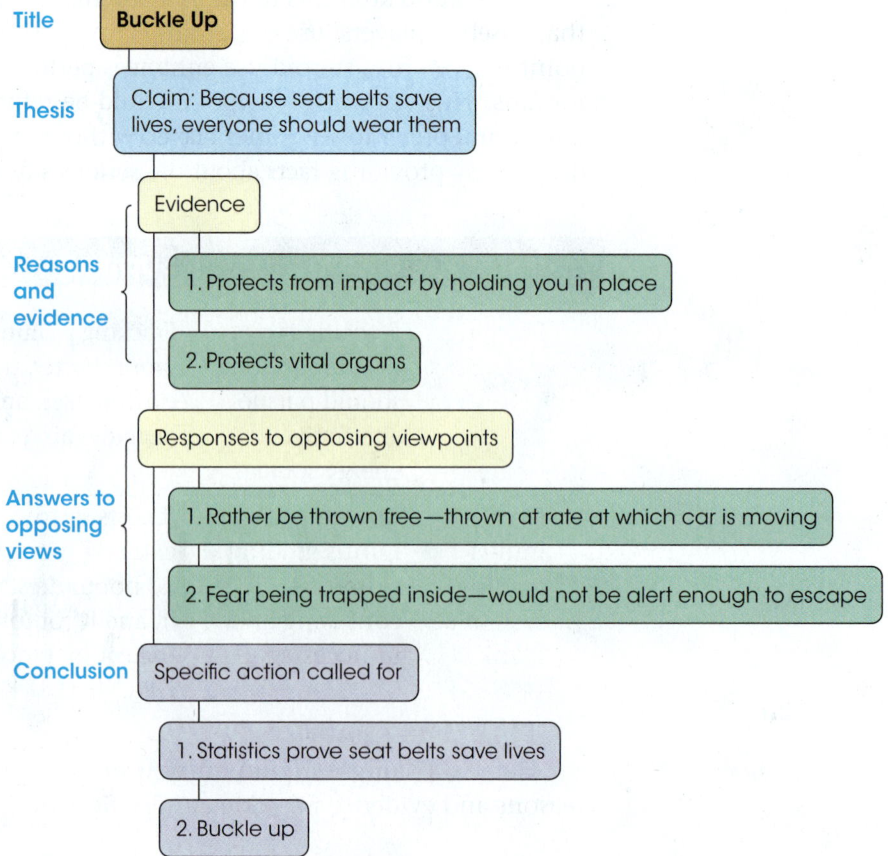

EXERCISE 14-1 Reading: Understanding Issues

Directions: For each of the following issues, place a check mark in front of the statement that makes a claim about the issue.

1. Issue: Community service

_____ **a.** Twenty hours of community service is required at Dodgeville High School.

_____ **b.** Community service should be required of all high school students.

_____ **c.** Some students voluntarily perform many hours of community service yearly.

2. Issue: State-required vaccinations

_____ **a.** Parents who wish to opt out of vaccine requirements for their children should be given that right.

_____ **b.** Vaccinations prevent children dying from many communicable diseases.

_____ **c.** States issue lists of vaccines that are required in order for children to attend public school.

3. Issue: Public libraries and the Internet

_____ **a.** People should be able to view whatever sites they choose at the public library.

_____ **b.** Filtering software cannot block all offensive Web sites.

_____ **c.** Many public libraries filter their Internet access.

4. Issue: Sports fan behavior

_____ **a.** Many football stadiums now have alcohol-free seating areas.

_____ **b.** Tickets to athletic events are expensive, so fans should be free to act however they choose.

_____ **c.** Sports arena security forces eject unruly fans.

5. Issue: Wikipedia as a research source

_____ **a.** Faculty at some colleges ban the use of Wikipedia in academic papers.

_____ **b.** Anyone can write entries or correct those written by others.

_____ **c.** Because Wikipedia lacks quality control, it should be used with caution.

6. Issue: The spread of infectious diseases

_____ **a.** Because infectious diseases are becoming more antibiotic resistant, they are difficult to treat.

_____ **b.** Due to international travel, infectious diseases can spread from continent to continent within days.

_____ **c.** Because infectious diseases spread quickly and are often life-threatening, those exposed to infectious diseases should voluntarily quarantine themselves.

EXERCISE 14-2 Reading and Writing: Understanding Claims

Directions: For each of the following issues, write a statement that takes a position on the issue. Write your claim in the space provided.

1. Issue: Minimum wage

   Claim: ____

   ____

2. Issue: Global climate changes

   Claim: ____

   ____

3. Issue: Air travel safety

   Claim: ____

   ____

4. Issue: Alternative medicine

   Claim: ____

5. Issue: Pop music

   Claim: ____

EXAMINING PROFESSIONAL WRITING

The following article, "Who Are the Animals in Animal Experiments?" appeared in 2014 in *The Huffington Post*. As you read, identify the parts of the author's argument (the issue, the author's claim about the issue, and the evidence she provides to support her claim).

Thinking Before Reading

1. Preview the reading, using the steps discussed in Chapter 1, page 4.
2. Connect the reading to your own experience by answering the following questions:
   a. Do you think that animals should be used for medical experimentation?
   b. Should there be laws and government agencies to protect animals subjected to experimentation?
3. Mark and annotate as you read.

Who Are the Animals in Animal Experiments?

Aysha Akhtar, MD, MPH

1 I once attended a neuroscience conference featuring a talk about spinal cord injury. The presenter showed a brief video clip that haunts me still to this day. The presenter showed a clip of his experiment in which he had crushed a cat's spinal cord and was recording the cat's movement on a treadmill. He had forcibly implanted electrodes into the cat's brain and she was struggling to keep upright, dragging her paralyzed legs on the treadmill. She repeatedly fell off the machine. At one point, the experimenter lifted her up to reposition her on the treadmill and the cat did something that was utterly unexpected. *She rubbed her head against the experimenter's hand.*

2 It's difficult for us to imagine what the lives are like for these animals. This is because these secretive experiments are hidden from public view and have been retreated to windowless, basement laboratories. We want to believe that those in the white coats are acting responsibly and that the animals are treated humanely; well, I have visited numerous laboratories and witnessed countless experiments on animals and I can tell you from personal experience that *nothing* is further from the truth.

3 As soon as you walk into a laboratory, you can't help but notice the rows and rows of barren cages holding sad animals living under the glare of fluorescent bulbs. Their bodies are burned, mutilated and scarred. Animals who have had their heads crushed grip their faces and convulse as blood pours out of their noses. You can smell and taste the stench of blood, feces and fear.

4 Animal protection guidelines and laws serve as smoke and mirrors. They give the impression that animals are protected from suffering when in fact, the guidelines actually serve as a cover for the protection of the experiments. Due to the lobbying efforts of the taxpayer-funded animal experimentation industry, the Animal Welfare Act (AWA) does not include upwards of 95 percent of all animals used in experiments: rats and mice. It also does not cover birds, reptiles, amphibians and animals used in agricultural experiments. Under the AWA, these animals are not considered animals. Even for the animals covered, the AWA provides minimal protection and leaves enforcement up to the notoriously incompetent U.S. Department of Agriculture (USDA). As explained by Mariann Sullivan, former Deputy Chief Court Attorney at the New York State Supreme Court (1):

> The standards set forth . . . require little more than that animals be fed, watered, vetted and kept in reasonably clean and safe enclosures that allow them to make species-appropriate postural adjustments. In other words, the AWA basically stipulates that animals be fed and be allowed to move about, if only a little, in their cages.

Vaccine test on laboratory mouse.

5 The AWA also requires that experimentation facilities set up so-called "Animal Care and Use Committees" to "consider alternatives" and "minimize discomfort, distress and pain to the animals." However, the AWA provides loopholes for even these standards and animal experimenters and their friends dominate the committees. Bottom line: any experiment, no matter how painful or how much suffering it causes, can be justified under the guise of "science."

6 Even when animal welfare violations are found, the fines charged rarely serve as a deterrent for future violations. In December, the USDA fined Harvard Medical School for repeated violations. Two monkeys died because they were not given access to water. One died from strangulation from a toy. The fine? $24,000. For an institution that receives hundreds of millions of our tax dollars to fund its experiments, the fine was a slap on the wrist. If these egregious violations can happen at Harvard, what do you think goes on in laboratories with far less visibility?

7 Surely we can do better than this. The animals used in experiments are much more than furry test tubes left over after years of living in fear. These animals, when given the opportunity, can experience joy, empathy, and affection. Watch a rat laugh as his belly is tickled or takes a bath and you can see how much joy they are capable of experiencing.

8 I often find myself thinking back to that cat I watched at the neuroscience conference. I said a quiet prayer that her spinal cord injury wiped out her ability to feel pain in her legs and I can't help but wonder if anyone else in the audience noticed what I did. Even at the peak of her suffering, the cat was seeking comfort from the very hand that caused it. Ten days later, she was killed and her brain dissected.

9 What does this say about us? Are we going to continue to turn a blind eye to the suffering we cause? Have we, to borrow a phrase from Pink Floyd, become comfortably numb? As Matthew Scully, a special advisor to President George W. Bush, wrote it in his book *Dominion*: (p. 382) When scientists abandon moral scruple in the treatment of animals, growing numb to the disfigurement and suffering before their eyes, regarding life itself as a mere instrument to be used and discarded, used and discarded, the habit is hard to shake.

10 Isn't it time we shake this habit, take a stand against this senseless suffering and pursue science that represents us at our best? We don't have to choose between helping animals or humans and we never did. And I say this as a medical doctor, neurologist and public health specialist: by ending the abuse of animals in experiments, not only do we save them, but we will also discover the most effective research methods that will save us.

11 Animal experiments don't represent the pinnacle of scientific achievement, but the basement. Unlike the naysayers, I believe that we are capable of so much more. All we need is the courage, vision and resourcefulness to make it happen. Let's make that our collective resolution for 2014.

Read an Argument Effectively

■ GOAL 3
Read an argument effectively

Count on reading an argument more than once. The first time you read it, try to get an overview of its three essential elements: *issue*, *claim*, and *support*. Then reread it more carefully to closely follow the author's line of reasoning, to identify and evaluate the evidence provided, and to analyze any counter-arguments.

Recognizing Types of Supporting Evidence

A writer supports a claim by offering reasons and evidence that the claim should be accepted. A **reason** is a general statement that backs up a claim. Here are a few reasons that support an argument in favor of more humane treatment of animals used in experiments:

- Animals suffer terribly when they are used in laboratory experiments.
- Animal protection guidelines and laws do little to protect animals used in experiments.
- Fines for violating animal welfare laws rarely serve as a deterrent.

However, for any of these reasons to be believable and convincing, they need to be supported with evidence. **Evidence** consists of facts, statistics, quotations, examples, personal experience, and comparisons that demonstrate why the claim is valid.

- **Facts** are true statements. For example, Aysha Akhtar states that Harvard medical School was fined for repeated animal welfare violations in December 2014. A quick search of the Internet shows that this is true, and this fact supports her argument. However, a conclusion does not always follow from the facts presented. For example, a writer may state that you will not get a cold if you eat a lot of oranges because oranges have vitamin C. It is true that oranges have vitamin C, but that does not necessarily mean that eating them will keep you cold free.
- **Statistics**—the reporting of figures, percentages, averages, and so forth—is a common method of support. For example, Aysha Akhtar states the Animal Welfare Act (AWA) does not include upwards of 95 percent of all animals used in experiments: rats and mice. However, these research animals may receive protection from other regulatory bodies such as the National Institutes of Health, which she does not mention. Statistics can be misused, misinterpreted, or used selectively to give other than the most objective, accurate picture of a situation.
- **Quotations and citations.** Writers often substantiate or confirm their ideas by including quotations or citations from experts or authorities

on the subject. For instance, Aysha Akhtar quoted Mariann Sullivan, former Deputy Chief Court Attorney at the New York State Supreme Court, to support the view that the animal protection provided under the AWA is minimal.

- **Examples.** Examples are descriptions of particular situations that are used to illustrate or explain a principle, concept, or idea. In "Who Are the Animals in Animal Experiments?" the author supports the idea that animals can experience joy by using the example of a rat having his belly tickled. Examples should not be used by themselves to prove the concept or idea they illustrate. The writer's experience may be atypical, or not representative, of what is common.
- **Personal experience.** A writer may use his or her own personal account or observation of a situation. For example, in supporting her claim about the mistreatment of laboratory animals, Aysha Akhtar described the suffering of a cat shown in a video at a neuroscience conference she attended. Although a writer's personal experience may provide an interesting perspective on an issue, personal experience should not be accepted as proof.
- **Comparisons and analogies.** Comparisons or analogies (extended comparisons) serve as illustrations. Their reliability depends on how closely the comparison corresponds or how similar it is to the situation to which it is being compared. For example, Martin Luther King, Jr., in his famous letter from the Birmingham jail, compared nonviolent protesters to a robbed man. To evaluate this comparison, you would need to consider how the two are similar and how they are different.

EXERCISE 14-3 Reading: Recognizing Support for Claims

Directions: Read each of the following sets of statements. Identify the statement that is a claim and label it *C*. Label the one statement that supports the claim as *S*.

1. ______ Year-round school is advantageous for both parents and children.

______ Continuous, year-round application of skills will prevent forgetting and strengthen students' academic preparation.

______ Year-round school may be costly to school districts.

2. ______ Many celebrities have been in trouble with the law lately because of their involvement with theft, drunk driving, violence, and even murder.

______ Celebrities do not act as positive role models for the people who admire them.

______ Acquiring fame and fortune does not automatically relieve a person of stress and suffering.

3. ______ Millions of students cannot afford to attend college because tuition costs and fees are so high.

   ______ States should find ways to control tuition costs at public colleges and universities.

   ______ Officials at private institutions of higher learning do not have to worry about budget issues since they have huge endowments.

4. ______ Drug companies should not be allowed to advertise on television.

   ______ Physicians do not provide all the necessary information patients need.

   ______ My grandparents are easily persuaded to buy expensive medications they do not need.

5. ______ Today's artists receive more media attention than in previous decades.

   ______ Modern art is confusing.

   ______ I am never sure what an abstract painting represents.

EXERCISE 14-4 Reading: Understanding Types of Evidence

Directions: Each item below begins with a claim, followed by supporting statements. Identify the type(s) of evidence used to support each claim. Choose from among the following types: personal experience (PE), examples (E), statistics (S), facts (F), quotations and citations (Q), and comparisons (C).

______ **1.** Library hours should be extended to weekends to make the library more accessible. My sisters have part-time jobs that require them to work late afternoons and evenings during the week. They are unable to use the library during the week.

______ **2.** Because parents have the right to determine their children's sexual attitudes, sex education should take place in the home, not at school. Teaching children about sex in school is like teaching them to sit in assigned seats and walk around quietly in single file at home.

______ **3.** It is more expensive to own a dog than a cat. According to the American Veterinary Medical Association, a dog visits the vet twice as many times as a cat.

______ **4.** Many married couples find that they need to set aside special times to be together. Some married couples find that planning a weekend retreat helps them focus on their special relationship.

______ **5.** Parents should read to their children to promote literacy skills. Children who were read to as preschoolers learned to read earlier than children who were not read to.

______ **6.** Dr. Samuel Rodriguez, a child psychologist, urges parents to read several books to their children daily (McGraw 71).

Use the following specific strategies for reading arguments:

NEED TO KNOW

Tips for Reading Arguments Effectively

1. **Read once for an initial impression.** Do not focus on specifics; instead, try to get a general feel for the argument.
2. **Read the argument several more times.** First identify the specific claim the writer is making and start to identify the reasons and evidence that support it. Read the argument again to examine whether the writer acknowledges or refutes opposing viewpoints.
3. **Annotate as you read.** Record your thoughts; note ideas you agree with, those you disagree with, questions that come to mind, additional reasons or evidence overlooked by the author, and the counterarguments not addressed by the author.
4. **Highlight key terms.** Often, an argument depends on how certain terms are defined. In an argument on the destruction of forests, for example, what does "destruction" mean? Does it mean building homes within a forest, or does it refer to clear cutting the land for timber or to create a housing subdivision? Highlight both the key terms and the definitions the author provides.
5. **Diagram or map to analyze structure.** Because many arguments are complex, you may find it helpful to diagram or map them. By mapping the argument, you may discover unsubstantiated ideas, reasons for which evidence is not provided, or an imbalance between reasons and emotional appeals.

Think Critically About Arguments

■ GOAL 4
Think critically about arguments

Not all arguments are reasonable and not all arguments are sound and logical. Thinking critically about arguments involves evaluating evidence, examining opposing viewpoints, considering emotional appeals, and identifying errors in reasoning.

Evaluating Evidence

When you evaluate evidence, consider whether it is relevant—in other words, does it directly support the claim?—and sufficient, which means it adequately supports the claim.

Is the Evidence Relevant?

Evidence that is offered in support of a claim must directly relate to that claim. For example, a friend may offer as a reason for being late for meeting with you that he had a flat tire, but this fact is not relevant if he would have had to walk only one block to see you. Writers may intentionally or unintentionally include information that may seem convincing but when analyzed more closely does not directly apply to the issue. Here is a possible earlier draft of paragraph 6 from the professional essay, "Who Are the Animals in Animal Experiments?". Can you identify the irrelevant information the paragraph contains?

Even when animal welfare violations are found, the fines charged rarely serve as a deterrent for future violations. In December, the USDA fined Harvard Medical School for repeated violations. Harvard Medical School, founded in 1782, attracts high caliber researchers from around the world, who should know better. Two monkeys died because they were not given access to water. One died from strangulation from a toy. The fine? $24,000. For an institution that receives hundreds of millions of our tax dollars to fund its experiments, the fine was a slap on the wrist.

In this paragraph, the sentence about the medical school's founding in 1782 and the quality of the researchers it attracts is not relevant because the argument is not about the history of the medical school itself or the quality of its researchers. To decide whether a statement is relevant, reread the claim and then immediately afterward reread the statement in question. Ask yourself, "Are the two logically connected?"

EXERCISE 14-5 Reading: Understanding Types of Evidence

Directions: For each of the claims listed, find three pieces of relevant evidence that support it. Write the letters of the evidence in the space provided. Not all pieces of evidence will be used.

Claims

_______ **1.** People are becoming ruder in our country.

_______ **2.** An increasing number of children need special education services, and it is often difficult for parents and students to obtain them.

_______ **3.** Parents and teachers should fight to keep art and music in the schools.

_______ **4.** Standardized tests do not accurately represent what American students know.

Evidence

A. Research shows that children need a variety of ways to express themselves.

B. The media bombard our children with images of violence.

C. Telemarketers just will not take no for an answer.

D. Celebrities live public lives of immorality, making promiscuity, drugs, reckless behavior, and divorce seem normal and even glamorous.

E. Incidents of road rage are increasing every year.

F. Some teachers do not fully understand the needs of students with learning disorders, and fail to refer them for needed services.

G. Not all school districts have the funds necessary to supply additional services that learning disabled students need.

H. Our society puts pressure on children to be consumers at a young age.

I. Learning to play an instrument helps with math skills.

J. Many students experience test anxiety, which can have a negative impact on their scores.

K. Many people have been storming out of stores because of insulting customer service.

L. In some schools there is tremendous pressure on teachers to boost test scores, forcing teachers to "teach to the test."

M. Studies have shown that learning to read music helps students with their regular reading skills.

N. Some teachers feel that students claim to be learning disabled when they are not.

O. Test writers understand education only in theory and do not write questions that are relevant to today's students.

Is the Evidence Sufficient?

There must be a sufficient number of reasons or pieces of evidence to support a claim. The amount and degree of detail of supporting evidence will vary with the issue, its complexity, and its importance. For any serious issue, it is not usually sufficient to offer a single reason or piece of evidence. For example, to say that our oceans are dying due to coastal development is not convincing because only a portion of the world's oceans are affected by coastal development. Other evidence to support this claim could include industrial waste dumping, oil drilling, ecosystem imbalance, and rising water temperatures.

The evidence a writer offers must also be sufficiently detailed to be convincing and believable. In "Who are the Animals in Animal Experiments?" the author might have written this first draft of paragraph 4:

> Animal protection guidelines and laws serve as smoke and mirrors. They give the impression that animals are protected from suffering when in fact, the guidelines actually serve as a cover for the protection of the experiments. Due to the lobbying efforts of the taxpayer-funded animal experimentation industry, the Animal Welfare Act (AWA) does not include some used in experiments: rats and mice. Even for the animals covered, the AWA provides minimal protection and leaves enforcement up to the notoriously incompetent U.S. Department of Agriculture (USDA).

To be convincing, more details were needed about the percentages and types of animals covered, why the requirements were inadequate, and confirmation that the author's information was accurate, which she provided by adding a quote from an expert source, Mariann Sullivan, former Deputy Chief Court Attorney. She also added specifics about the AWA's requirement that they "consider alternatives" and "minimize discomfort, distress and pain to the animals," loopholes in the AWA's standards, and the biased membership of the committees.

Examining Opposing Viewpoints

Many arguments recognize opposing viewpoints. For example, an author may argue that gay people should be allowed to marry. However, the author may recognize or admit that opponents believe marriage should only be allowed between a man and a woman.

Many arguments also attempt to refute the opposing viewpoint (explain why it is wrong, flawed, or unacceptable). For example, a writer may refute the notion that gay people will compromise cohesiveness in the military by stating that soldiers are unified against the enemy, not each other. Basically, then, refutation is a process of finding weaknesses in an opponent's argument.

When reading arguments that address opposing viewpoints, ask yourself the following questions.

- Does the author address opposing viewpoints clearly and fairly?
- Does the author refute the opposing viewpoint with logic and relevant evidence?

The author of "Who Are the Animals in Animal Experiments?" does not directly acknowledge or refute opposing viewpoints. Her argument would have been stronger if she had done so, and it may have been more convincing to those in her audience that hold opposing viewpoints. Indirectly, she does acknowledge the opposing argument that it is better that animals suffer than for people to suffer or die from diseases when she says "We don't have to choose between helping animals or humans and we never did." If she had explained why we are not forced to choose between animals and people, it could have served as a refutation of a counterargument.

Considering Emotional Appeals

Emotional appeals are ideas that are targeted toward needs or values that readers are likely to care about. Needs include physiological needs (food, drink, shelter) and psychological needs (sense of belonging, sense of accomplishment, sense of self-worth). An argument on gun control, for example, may appeal to a reader's need for safety, while an argument favoring restrictions on banks sharing personal or financial information may appeal to a reader's need for privacy and financial security.

Unfair emotional appeals attempt to involve or excite readers by appealing to their emotions, thereby controlling the reader's attitude toward the subject. Several types of emotional appeals are described below.

1. **Emotionally charged or biased language.** By using words that create an emotional response, writers establish positive or negative feelings. For example, an advertisement for a new line of fragrances promises to "indulge," "refresh," "nourish," and "pamper" the user, all positive terms that invite the reader to buy the product. In contrast, in paragraph 3 of "Who Are the Animals in Animal Experiments," the author's description of the plight of research animals is designed to evoke an emotional reaction of horror: "Animals who have had their heads crushed, grip their faces and convulse as blood pours out of their noses. You can smell and taste the stench of blood, feces, and fear."
2. **False authority.** False authority involves using the opinion or action of a well-known or famous person. We have all seen athletes endorsing underwear or movie stars selling shampoo. This type of appeal works on the notion that people admire celebrities and strive to be like them, respect their opinion, and are willing to accept their viewpoint.
3. **Association.** An emotional appeal also is made by associating a product, idea, or position with others that are already accepted or highly regarded. Patriotism is already valued, so to call a product All-American in an advertisement is an appeal to the emotions. A car being named a Cougar to remind you of a fast, sleek animal, a cigarette ad picturing a scenic waterfall, or a speaker standing in front of an American flag are other examples.

4. **Appeal to "common folk."** Some people distrust those who are well educated, wealthy, highly artistic, or in other ways distinctly different from the average person. An emotional appeal to this group is made by indicating that a product or idea originated from, is held by, or is bought by ordinary citizens. A commercial may advertise a product by showing its use in an average household. A politician may describe her background and education to suggest that she is like everyone else; a salesperson may dress in styles similar to his clients.

5. ***Ad hominem.*** An argument that attacks the holder of an opposing viewpoint rather than his or her viewpoint is known as *ad hominem*, or an attack on the man. For example, the statement, "How could a woman who does not even hold a college degree criticize a judicial decision?" attacks the woman's level of education, not her viewpoint.

6. **"Join the crowd" appeal.** The appeal to do, believe, or buy what everyone else is doing, believing, or buying is known as *crowd appeal* or the *bandwagon appeal*. Commercials that proclaim their product the "#1 best-selling car in America" are appealing to this motive. Essays in support of a position that cite opinion polls on a controversial issue—"68 percent of Americans favor capital punishment"—are also using this appeal.

EXERCISE 14-6 Reading: Understanding Emotional Appeals

Directions: Indicate the type of emotional appeal each of the following statements represents.

a. emotionally charged or biased language
b. false authority
c. association
d. appeal to common folk
e. *ad hominem*
f. join the crowd

_____ **1.** Michelle Obama recommends the book *Beloved*, by Toni Morrison; it must be very good.

_____ **2.** We must preserve our historic neighborhoods in order to save the memories of the hardworking men and women who built our cities with their sweat and blood.

_____ **3.** Don't go to that restaurant; the owner can't even keep her garden growing.

_____ **4.** Everyone who cares about education is voting for Proposition E.

_____ **5.** The mayor eats Mrs. Baker's pecan sandies; they must be the best.

_____ **6.** Mandatory collection of DNA samples from all criminals will stop brutal sexual assaults on our helpless women and innocent children.

_____ **7.** We provide quality service just like in the good old days.

_____ **8.** Join together with your brothers and sisters in the union; don't let rich managers and executives oppress you any longer.

_____ **9.** No one dresses like that anymore.

_____ **10.** My dentist is awful; he drives a Dodge Dart.

EXERCISE 14-7 Reading: Identifying Emotional Appeals

Directions: Reread the essay "Who Are the Animals in Animal Experiments?" on page 397 and identify the types of emotional appeals used by the author.

Identifying Errors in Reasoning

Errors in reasoning, often called *logical fallacies*, are common in arguments and they can invalidate arguments or render them flawed. Several common errors in logic are described next.

Circular Reasoning

Also known as *begging the question*, this error involves using part of the conclusion as evidence to support the argument. Here are two examples.

- Cruel medical experimentation on defenseless animals is inhumane.
- Female police officers should not be sent to crime scenes because apprehending criminals is a man's job.

In circular reasoning, because no evidence is given to support the claim—it is simply restated—there is no reason to accept the argument.

Hasty Generalization

This fallacy means that the conclusion has been derived from insufficient evidence. Here is one example: You taste three tangerines and each is sour, so you conclude that all tangerines are sour. Here is another: After observing one performance of a musical group, you conclude the group will never be a success.

Non Sequitur ("It Does Not Follow")

The false establishment of cause and effect is known as a **non sequitur**. To say, for example, that "Because my doctor is young, I'm sure she'll be a good doctor" is a *non sequitur* because youth does not cause good medical practice. Here is another example: "Arturio Alvarez is the best choice for state senator because he is an ordinary citizen." Being an ordinary citizen does not necessarily mean someone will be an effective state senator.

False Cause

The **false cause fallacy** is the incorrect assumption that two events that occur close to each other in time are causally related. Suppose you walked under a ladder and then lost your wallet. If you said you lost your wallet because you walked under a ladder, you would be assuming false cause.

Either-Or Fallacy

This fallacy assumes that an issue is only two-sided, or that there are only two choices or alternatives for a particular situation. In other words, there is no middle ground. Consider the issue of censorship of violence on television. An either-or fallacy is to assume that violence on TV must be either allowed or banned. This fallacy does not recognize other alternatives such as only showing violent material after 10 P.M., restricting certain types of violence from being shown on TV, and so forth.

EXERCISE 14-8 Reading: Identifying Errors in Reasoning

Directions: Identify the errors in reasoning in each of the following statements.

a. circular reasoning
b. hasty generalization
c. *non sequitur*
d. false cause
e. either-or fallacy

_____ **1.** All African-American students in my biology class earned A grades, so African-Americans must excel in life sciences.

_____ **2.** If you are not for nuclear arms control, then you're against protecting our future.

_____ **3.** My sister gets nervous when asked to do mathematical computations or balance her checkbook because she has math anxiety.

_____ **4.** A well-known governor, noting a decline in the crime rate in the four largest cities in his state, quickly announced that his new "get-tough on criminals" publicity campaign was successful and took credit for the decline.

_____ **5.** Carlos lives in a large house, so his father must have a high-paying job.

EXERCISE 14-9 Reading: Evaluating an Argument

Directions: Reread the essay "Who Are the Animals in Animal Experiments?" on page 397, and then complete the following.

1. Summarize the author's argument. Include the issue, the author's claim about it, and the main supporting points.
2. Indicate what type of evidence the author uses.
3. Determine whether the evidence is adequate and sufficient to support the author's point.
4. What other types of evidence could have been used?
5. How does the author attempt to win readers over to her viewpoint?
6. Evaluate the overall effectiveness of the argument. Was it convincing? Why or why not?

EXAMINING STUDENT WRITING

A good way to learn to read and write argument essays is to study a model. Throughout the rest of the chapter, we will use parts of Quinne Sember's essay to illustrate how to plan, organize, and write an argumentative essay.

Quinne Sember is a student at the State University of New York at Buffalo, where she is a pre-medical student majoring in political science and biomedical science. Quinne wrote this essay for a political science class. She was asked to choose an issue discussed in class and write an essay taking a position on the issue.

Sember 1

Quinne Sember

Dr. McCombs

Political Science 112

24 June 2014

Title indicates essay will argue for legalizing marijuana

Marijuana: An Argument for Legalization

Introduction compares alcohol, tobacco and marijuana

1 Marijuana is a commonly used drug in the United States. It is not as dangerous or addictive as alcohol or tobacco. Yet alcohol and tobacco are legal in every U.S. state, while marijuana is not. In fact, as of this writing, only 22 states (plus the District of Columbia) permit the medical use of marijuana ("State"). In addition, the recreational use of marijuana by adults is legal in only two states: Colorado and Washington. The situation is complicated by the fact that recreational marijuana use is still prohibited under U.S. federal law, which makes for inconsistent policies between states and the federal government. It costs the United States millions of dollars to prosecute and imprison people who possess marijuana when the government could be making money—and ensuring that marijuana is produced safely and without dangerous additives—by taxing the substance. The argument for the full and complete legalization of marijuana (for both medicinal and recreational uses) is a strong one, and many people support a law that would make this happen.

Thesis statement

Topic sentence states first supporting reason

2 The economic effect of the criminalization of marijuana use in the United State is astounding. We create a large number of criminals by sentencing people for nonviolent acts, including possession of marijuana. The United States holds 25% of the world's prisoners, but the country is home to only 5% of the world's total population. By some estimates, in 2010 the states spent about $3.6 billion enforcing marijuana laws (Bradford). For a nation that is in so much debt, that is a large amount of money that could be spent elsewhere. Shouldn't we improve

Statistical evidence

Sember 2

the roads or health care before we spend so much money on people who are not committing violent crimes? Shouldn't we invest in education, poverty reduction, and employment training instead of prosecuting people for possessing marijuana?

Topic sentence states second supporting reason

3 In addition to saving the country money, legalization of marijuana could also help us to make money. Taxation of the drug already produces considerable tax revenue. For example, tax revenues from the sale of marijuana in Colorado alone are expected to bring in $98 million in 2014 ("Moody's"). If all 50 states and the District of Columbia brought in the same amount of tax revenues from the sale of marijuana, the total would be close to $5 billion per year. Combine this with the annual cost of enforcing existing drug laws, and the country could be about $8.6 billion per year richer with the legalization of marijuana. The government could make even more money if it required a license to grow the plant. That is an astonishing amount of money that could be spent on health care, schools, or infrastructure. Obviously, regulation of and education about marijuana are more logical than the criminalization of its users. For example, the legalization of marijuana does not give people the right to break the law as far as driving under the influence is concerned. This practice is still illegal and a punishable offense.

Facts and statistics

Topic sentence states third supporting reason

4 As many states have already acknowledged, marijuana can have an effect on health, and it is not always a negative one. Many people use the drug to assist them with medical conditions. Cannabis can help to alleviate the symptoms of multiple sclerosis, Crohn's disease, and other inflammatory diseases. It can also increase appetite in people who are struggling with chemotherapy. Fortunately, in about half of the states, doctors can prescribe medical marijuana for these conditions. However, people in states where medical marijuana is illegal are

Examples support topic sentence

Sember 3

out of luck. It is also very difficult for people without a specific disease who have other problems for which marijuana could be helpful to get medical marijuana. The American Medical Association has recognized that marijuana can have a positive effect on nausea, glaucoma, extreme muscle tension, and pain (Cloud). With the full legalization of marijuana, people could buy the drug on their own accord to treat whatever symptoms they may have without having to battle with a doctor to get a prescription.

Citation of expert opinion as evidence

Topic sentence states fourth supporting reason

5 Maybe the most convincing argument for the legalization of marijuana is that people support it. A Gallup poll from 2013 shows that a majority of Americans—58% in 2013—favored legalizing the drug (Swift). This is a marked increase from 1969, when the Gallup poll first asked the question and only 12% were in favor of legalization. The number is even higher among the Millennial generation, 69% of whom favor legalization. A Pew Research Center poll recently reported that 76% of respondents believed that people convicted of minor possession of marijuana should not serve jail time, and that almost 70% of respondents believed that alcohol is more harmful to a person's health than marijuana (Motel). The question implied by these survey results is clear: Why should alcohol be legal while marijuana is not?

Statistical evidence

Topic sentence states fifth supporting reason

6 If this is not enough evidence, even a former U.S. Surgeon General, Joycelyn Elders, supports legalization. She told CNN, "What I think is horrible about all of this, is that we criminalize young people. And we use so many of our excellent resources . . . for things that aren't really causing any problems. It's not a toxic substance." Elders says that we have the "highest number of people in the world being criminalized, many for nonviolent crimes related to marijuana" ("Former Surgeon General"). She strongly believes that our resources can be put to better use. There is also a good deal of support among

Quotations from experts

Sember 4

politicians for the legalization of medical marijuana. New York's governor, Andrew Cuomo, has expressed support for medical marijuana, stating that it would "provide benefits to people who need it, which can be significant. Even for children, children with epilepsy" (Ferrigno and Assefa).

Topic sentence recognizes and refutes opposing viewpoint

7 Marijuana legalization is opposed by some who claim it has a negative impact on health; however, marijuana is actually much healthier than tobacco or alcohol. No one has ever died of THC (the active chemical in marijuana) poisoning or overdose (Cloud). People die every day from the effects of tobacco and alcohol, and these drugs are legal. Tobacco is proven to cause cancer, and while there has not been any evidence to show that smoking marijuana does cause cancer, there have not been any conclusive studies to show that it does not. Others argue that marijuana is an addictive substance. However, while one-third of tobacco users get hooked and fifteen percent of drinkers become addicted to alcohol, only nine percent of people using marijuana become addicted.

Conclusion: Quinne recaps her reasons and makes a final statement

8 The legalization of marijuana would help a lot of people. It would directly help people who suffer from symptoms of illnesses that can be treated with the drug such as chronic neuropathic pain (Ware et al.). It would also indirectly affect children who go to poor schools or people who can't afford health care because of the amount of money that is tied up in the courts, prisons, and police activity regarding marijuana. The government could use this money for much more serious and useful things. Many people believe that the legalization and use of marijuana is risky. With education and regulation, this practice would not be any more risky (probably less risky, in fact) than the use of tobacco and alcohol, legal substances in our country.

Sember 5

Works Cited

Bradford, Harry. "Marijuana Law Enforcement Cost States an Estimated $3.6 Billion in 2010: ACLU." *The Huffington Post*, 4 June 2013, www.huffingtonpost.com/2013/06/04/marijuana-arrests-cost-racially-biased_n_3385756.html.

Cloud, John. "Is Pot Good For You?" *Time*, 4 Nov. 2002, content.time.com/time/magazine/article/0,9171,1003570,00.html.

Ferrigno, Lorenzo, and Haimy Assefa. "New York to Be Next State to Allow Medical Marijuana." *CNN*, 20 June 2014, www.cnn.com/2014/06/20/health/new-york-medical-marijuana.

"Former Surgeon General Calls for Marijuana Legalization." *CNN*, 18 Oct. 2010, www.cnn.com/2010/HEALTH/10/18/former.surgeon.general.marijuana.

"Moody's: Colorado's Tax Revenues from Legalized Marijuana Exceeding Expectations." *Moody's Investors Service*, 11 Apr. 2014, www.moodys.com/research/Moodys-Colorados-tax-revenues-from-legalized-marijuana-exceeding-expectations--PR_297013.

Motel, Seth. "6 Facts about Marijuana." *Pew Research Center*, 14 Apr. 2014, www.pewresearch.org/fact-tank/2015/04/14/6-facts-about-marijuana.

"State Medical Marijuana Laws." *National Conference of State Legislatures*, 20 June 2014, www.ncsl.org/research/health/state-medical-marijuana-laws.aspx. Accessed 22 June 2014.

Swift, Art. "For First Time, Americans Favor Legalizing Marijuana." *Gallup*, 22 Oct. 2013, www.gallup.com/poll/165539/first-time-americans-favor-legalizing-marijuana.aspx.

Ware, Mark A. et al. "Smoked Cannabis for Chronic Neuropathic Pain: a Randomized Controlled Trial." *CMAJ: Canadian Medical Association Journal*, vol. 182, no. 14, 5 Oct. 2010, pp. E694–E701, doi: 10.1503/cmaj.091414.

Write Argument Essays

■ GOAL 5
Write argument essays

Being able to construct a solid and effective written argument is important in the classroom and in the workplace. Writing argument essays requires paying close attention to your audience and their position on the issue. An argument essay needs a clear and strong thesis statement that identifies the issue and states your claim and must be supported by adequate supporting evidence that is accurately documented.

Analyzing Your Audience

Analyzing your audience is a crucial step in planning a convincing argument. There are three types of audiences:

- **Audiences who agree with your claim.** These are the easiest to write for because they already accept most of what you will say and are likely to have positive feelings toward you because you think the way they do about the issue. For this audience, state your claim and explain why you think it is correct.
- **Neutral audiences.** These readers have not made up their minds or have not given much thought to the issue. They may have questions, they may misunderstand the issue, or they may have heard arguments supporting the opposing viewpoint. An essay written for a neutral audience should be direct and straightforward, like those written for an audience in agreement with your point of view. However, a fuller explanation of the issue is necessary to answer questions, clear up misunderstandings, and respond to opposing arguments.
- **Audiences who disagree with your claim.** These are the most difficult to address. Some members will have thought about the issue and taken a position that opposes yours. Others who disagree may not have examined the issue at all and are making superficial judgments or are relying on misinformation. Both types think their position is correct, so they will not be eager to change their minds. They may also distrust you, because you think differently from them. For such an audience, your biggest challenge is to build trust and confidence. Before writing, carefully analyze this audience and try to answer these questions:
    - Why does your audience disagree with your claim?
    - Is their position based on real facts and sound evidence, or on personal opinion? If it is based on evidence, what type?
    - What type of arguments or reasons are most likely to appeal to your audience? For example, will they be convinced by facts and statistics, or by statements made by authorities? Would personal anecdotes and examples work well?

Once you understand how your audience thinks, you can plan your essay more effectively.

Writing a Thesis Statement

Your thesis statement should identify the issue and state your claim about it. It may also suggest the primary reasons for accepting the claim. Place your thesis statement where it will be most effective. There are three common placements:

a. Thesis statement at the beginning

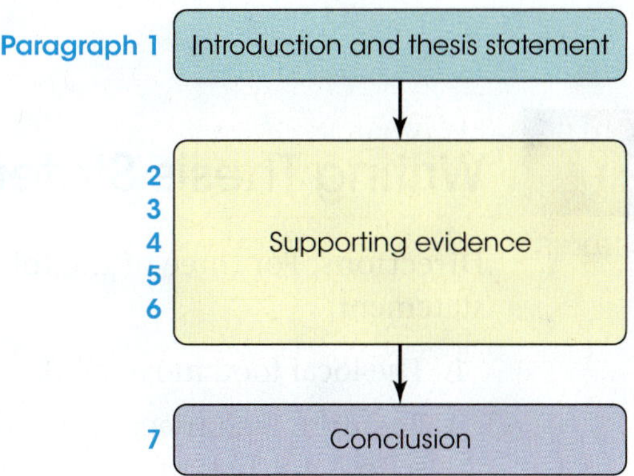

b. Thesis statement after responding to objections

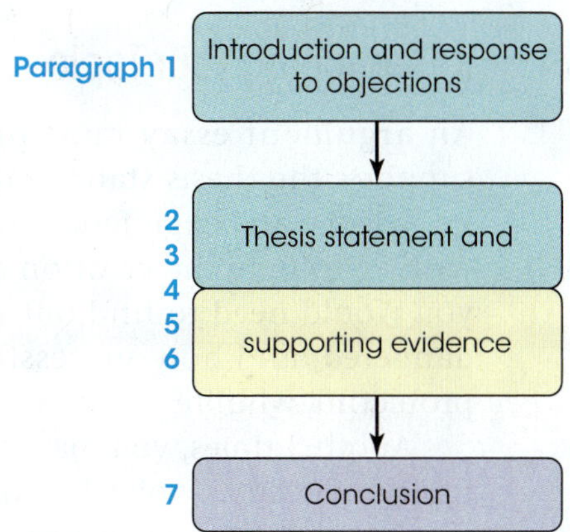

c. Thesis statement at the end

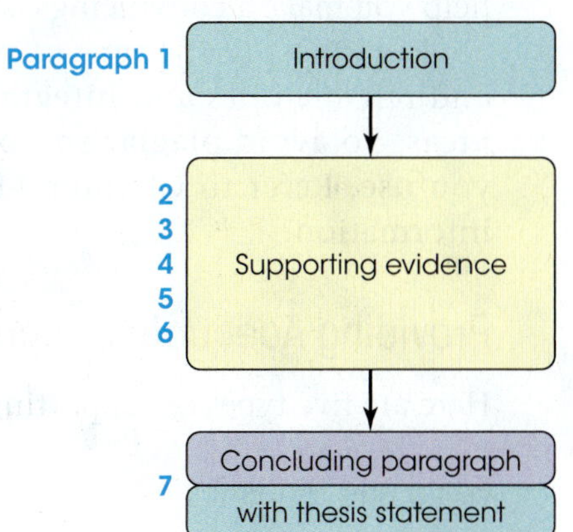

In general, placing the thesis at the beginning is best when addressing an audience in agreement with your claim or one that is neutral about the topic under discussion. For an audience that does not agree with your argument, a later placement gives you the opportunity to respond to the audience's objections before you present your thesis.

Writing Thesis Statements

Directions: For three of the following issues, take a position and write a thesis statement.

1. The local food movement
2. Requiring volunteer hours for high school graduation
3. Gay marriage
4. American involvement in foreign wars
5. Single-payer insurance
6. Paying college athletes
7. Gun control in the wake of mass shootings
8. Athletes and the use of steroids

Researching Your Topic

An **argument essay** must provide specific and convincing evidence that supports the thesis statement. Often it is necessary to go beyond your own knowledge and experience and research your topic. For example, if you were writing to urge the creation of an environmentally protected wetland area, you would need to find out what types of wildlife live there, which are endangered, and how successful other protected wetland sites have been in protecting wildlife.

At other times, you may need to interview people who are experts on your topic or directly involved with it. Suppose you are writing a memo urging other employees in your department to participate in a walk-a-thon. It is being held to benefit a local shelter for homeless men and women. The director of the shelter or one of her employees could offer useful statistics, share personal experiences, and provide specific details about the clientele the shelter serves that would help you make a convincing case.

Regardless of the type of sources you use, be sure to consult trustworthy and reliable ones and integrate and synthesize them to support your own ideas. To avoid plagiarism, be sure to cite and document all the sources you use. Refer to Chapter 11, "Writing Essays Using Sources," for more information.

Providing Adequate Supporting Evidence

Here are five types of supporting evidence you can use to develop your thesis.

Facts and Statistics

As in writing any other type of essay, you must choose facts that directly support the position you express in your thesis statement. Here is paragraph 6 from

Quinne's essay where she uses facts and statistics as evidence to argue in favor of legalizing marijuana:

Maybe the most convincing evidence for the legalization of marijuana is that people support it. A Gallup poll from 2013 shows that a majority of Americans—58% in 2013—favored legalizing the drug (Swift). This is a marked increase from 1969, when the Gallup poll first asked the question and only 12% were in favor of legalization. The number is even higher among the Millennial generation, 69% of whom favor legalization. A Pew Research Center poll recently reported that 76% of respondents believed that people convicted of minor possession of marijuana should not serve jail time, and almost 70% of respondents believed that alcohol his more harmful to a person's health than marijuana (Motel). The question implied by these survey results is clear: Why should alcohol be legal while marijuana is not?

It is usually more effective to present more than one statistic. Suppose you are writing to convince taxpayers that state lotteries have become profitable businesses. You might state that more than 60 percent of the adult population now buy lottery tickets regularly. This statistic would have little meaning by itself. However, if you were to state that 60 percent of adults now purchase lottery tickets, whereas five years ago only 30 percent purchased them, the first statistic would become more meaningful.

Tips for Selecting Statistics

In selecting statistics to support your position, be sure to

1. **Obtain statistics from reliable print or online sources.** These include almanacs, encyclopedias, articles in reputable journals and magazines, or other trustworthy reference material from your library. Online sources include databases, online journals, and scholarly Web sites.
2. **Use up-to-date information, preferably from the past year or two.** Dated statistics may be incorrect or misleading.
3. **Make sure you define terms and units of measurement.** For example, if you say that 60 percent of adults regularly play the lottery, you should define what "regularly" means. Does it mean daily, weekly, or monthly?
4. **Verify that the statistics you obtain from more than one source are comparable.** For example, if you compare the crime rates in New York City and Los Angeles, be sure that each crime rate was computed the same way, that each represents the same types of crimes, and that report sources were similar.

Quotations or Citations from Authorities

You can also support your claim by using expert or authoritative statements of opinion or conclusions. **Experts or authorities** are those who have studied a subject extensively, conducted research on it, or written widely about it. For example, in "Marijuana: An Argument for Legalization," Quinne cites the opinion of former U.S. Surgeon General Joycelyn Elders as a health expert in support of legalization.

Examples

Refer to Chapter 4 for a review of how to use examples as supporting details. In a persuasive essay, your examples must represent your claim and should illustrate as many aspects of your claim as possible. Suppose your claim is that many people use marijuana to assist them with medical conditions. The evidence you choose to support this claim should be clear, specific examples of medical conditions and symptoms that can be relieved through the use of marijuana.

The examples you choose should also, if possible, relate to your audience's experience. Familiar examples are more appealing, convincing, and understandable. For Quinne's essay on legalizing marijuana, the audience included her political science professor, so she focused on examples of economic benefits such as improved health care, education, and infrastructure.

Personal Experience

If you are knowledgeable about a subject, your personal experiences can be convincing evidence. For example, if you were writing an essay in favor of the legalization of marijuana, you could discuss your family's experiences obtaining a prescription for medical marijuana to treat a relative's glaucoma.

Comparisons and Analogies

Comparison and analogies (extended comparisons) are useful especially when writing for an audience that lacks background and experience with your subject. By comparing something unknown to something that is known and familiar, you can make your readers comfortable, non-threatened. For example, you could discuss the legalization of marijuana by comparing its effects to the effects of alcohol and tobacco. Be sure to make it clear what characteristics or features are similar and which are not.

EXERCISE 14-11

WRITING IN PROGRESS

Writing: Drafting an Argument Essay

Directions: Generate reasons and evidence to support one of the thesis statements you wrote for Exercise 14-10. Evaluate the evidence, and research your topic further if needed. Then write a first draft of your essay.

EXERCISE 14-12

WRITING IN PROGRESS

Writing: Revising Your Essay

Directions: Carefully read through your essay. Have you considered your audience and what they need to know in order to follow and understand your argument? Evaluate your argument and the support for it. Do you have relevant and sufficient evidence? Have you noted and refuted counterarguments? Have you correctly cited your sources (see p. 334)? Use your answers to guide your revisions. Then edit and proofread your paper (see checklists on p. 288), and format it using MLA (see p. 335) or APA (see p. 337) style.

READ AND RESPOND: A Student Essay

Marijuana: An Argument for Legalization

Quinne Sember

The questions and writing assignments below refer to the student essay "Marijuana: An Argument for Legalization" on page 409 that has been used in this chapter to illustrate aspects of writing an argument essay.

Examining Writing

1. For what type of audience does Quinne seem to be writing—neutral, in agreement, or not in agreement?
2. Did you find her argument convincing? Why or why not?
3. What other reasons could Quinne have included?
4. Does Quinne rely too heavily on statistics? Why or why not? What other types of evidence could she have included?

Writing Assignments

1. You are taking an ecology class. You have been asked to select a type of environmental pollution and develop an argument urging steps be taken to control it in your community. Write an essay fulfilling this assignment.
2. You are taking a political science class and you are studying voter registration and participation. Your instructor has asked you to write an editorial for your local newspaper urging that either more citizens become registered voters or more voters use their voting privilege. Write an argumentative essay that could be submitted to the newspaper's editor.
3. You are taking a zoology class and are studying the function of zoos. You are considering such questions as: Do zoos protect animals or put them on display? Do they preserve endangered species or do they sacrifice animal needs for those of humans? Write an essay that takes a position on zoos. Develop an argument that supports your position.

READ AND RESPOND: A Professional Essay

Who Are the Animals in Animal Experiments?

Aysha Akhtar, MD, MPH

Earlier in the chapter (p. 397), you read "Who Are the Animals in Animal Experiments?" and examined the basic structure of an argument essay. Now it is time to take a closer look at the reading by responding to the questions that follow and then writing a paragraph or essay.

Writing in Response to Reading

Checking Your Comprehension MySkillsLab®

Answer each of the following questions using complete sentences.

1. How did the cat with a crushed spinal cord respond to the experimenter's touch?
2. What is the purpose of the Animal Welfare Act?
3. Who wrote the book *Dominion*?
4. According to this article, what two animals make up 95% of the animals used in experiments?
5. What resolution does the author propose for her readers to adopt in 2014?

Strengthening Your Vocabulary MySkillsLab®

Identify at least five words used in the reading that are unfamiliar to you. Using context, word parts, or a dictionary, write a brief definition of each word.

Examining the Reading: Drawing an Idea Map

Create an idea map that shows the structure of the argument in this reading. Begin by stating the issue that the reading addresses, and then list the claim and the evidence presented to support it.

Reading and Writing: An Integrated Perspective MySkillsLab®

Get ready to write about the reading by discussing the following:

1. Do you think that mice and rats should be protected in the same way that dogs and cats are? Why or why not?
2. Why do you think the author says that animal protection guidelines and laws serve as smoke and mirrors?
3. The author asks if we have become "comfortably numb." What does this term mean?
4. Evaluate the author's introduction. What impression did her description create? Write a journal entry giving your response to the story of the cat.
5. Why is the photograph a useful addition to the reading? What details about the photograph seem to support the author's argument?

Thinking and Writing Critically MySkillsLab®

1. Examine the author's credentials. How qualified is she to write about this issue? How qualified and reliable are her sources?
2. Highlight words in the reading that have strong positive or negative connotations. How do these words enhance or detract from the author's argument? Do they indicate bias?
3. What assumptions does the author make?
4. What is the tone of the reading?
5. What, if anything, could the author have included to make her argument more convincing? What other information did you want to know about the subject?
6. Who is the author's intended audience?
7. What inferences can you make about the author? What actions does she ask of the reader?

Writing Paragraphs MySkillsLab®

1. Assume you will be participating in a debate on the topic of using animals in medical and agricultural experimentation. Write a "pro" paragraph and a "con" paragraph that summarizes each side of the argument.
2. In paragraph 9, the author asks if we have become "comfortably numb." Can you think of some practices in our society that might suggest that we have become comfortably numb? In a paragraph, discuss these practices and our response to them.
3. Have you ever encountered animal abuse? Write a paragraph describing your experience and your response to it.

Writing Essays MySkillsLab®

4. After reading this article, what changes do you think need to be made to animal experimentation practices and the government agencies that oversee the entities that conduct these experiments? In an essay, discuss the proposed changes.
5. In the final paragraph, the author claims that "animal experiments don't represent the pinnacle of scientific achievement, but the basement." Research the topic of animal experiments and find additional evidence to support the author's claim; then write a paragraph or an essay in which you present the claim and support it with evidence from the research you conducted.

SELF-TEST SUMMARY

To test yourself, cover the Answer column with a sheet of paper and answer each question in the left column. Evaluate each of your answers as you work by sliding the paper down and comparing your answer with what is printed in the Answer column.

QUESTION	ANSWER
■ GOAL 1 Understand the use of argument What is an argument?	An argument is a line of reasoning intended to persuade the reader or listener to agree with a particular viewpoint or take a particular action.
■ GOAL 2 Recognize the parts of an argument What are the essential parts of an argument?	An argument has three essential parts: an issue (the problem or controversy that the argument addresses); a claim (the writer's viewpoint on an issue); and support (the details that demonstrate a claim is correct and should be accepted). Some arguments may also include a refutation, which attempts to disprove opposing viewpoints.
■ GOAL 3 Read an argument effectively How do writers support a claim?	Writers support a claim by offering reasons and evidence that the claim should be accepted. A reason is a general statement that backs up a claim.
What types of evidence are used to support a claim?	Evidence consists of facts, statistics, quotations, examples, personal experience, and comparisons that demonstrate why a claim is valid.
■ GOAL 4 Think critically about arguments How do you think critically about arguments?	Think critically about arguments by evaluating evidence, examining opposing viewpoints, considering emotional appeals, and identifying errors in reasoning.
■ GOAL 5 Write argument essays How do you write argument essays?	Determine what type of audience you have (one who agrees with your claim, disagrees, or is neutral). Write a thesis statement that identifies the issue and states your claim. Place the thesis statement at the beginning, at the end, or after responding to objections. Research your topic and provide adequate support for your claim.

MySkillsLab®

Visit **Chapter 14 "Critical Thinking: Reading and Writing Arguments,"** in MySkillsLab to test your understanding of chapter goals.

PART FIVE THEMATIC READER

WRITING IN RESPONSE TO READING

Theme 1 Crime in the 21st Century: Technology and Trafficking 424

Reading 1: (Textbook) Technology and Crime 424

Reading 2: (Article) Why Human Trafficking is Called Modern Day Slavery 436

Reading 3: (Article) Human Traffic: Exposing the Brutal Organ Trade 442

Read and Respond to the Theme 455

Synthesizing Ideas 455 ■ Writing About the Readings 455

Theme 2 Journalism: A Changing Field in a Digital Age 456

Reading 1: (Textbook) An Inside Look at Today's News Media 456

Reading 2: (Article) The Media Need to Stop Inspiring Copycat Murders. Here's How. 462

Reading 3: (Article) Photojournalism in the Age of New Media. 467

Read and Respond to the Theme 474

Synthesizing Ideas 475 ■ Writing About the Readings 475

Theme 3 Sports and Society 475

Reading 1: (Textbook) Drug Abuse Among Athletes 476

Reading 2: (Article) The National Brain-Damage League 481

Reading 3a: (Opinion Piece: PRO) Should College Football Student Athletes Get Paid? 485

Reading 3b: (Opinion Piece: CON) College Athletes Already Have Advantages and Shouldn't Be Paid 490

Read and Respond to the Theme 494

Synthesizing Ideas 494 ■ Writing About the Readings 495

Theme 4 Issues Facing College Students (These readings appear in the chapters indicated.) 495

Reading 1: (Textbook) Secrets for Surviving College and Improving Your Grades, Chapter 1 5

Reading 2: (Article) Among Dorms and Dining Halls, Hidden Hunger, Chapter 4 117

Reading 3: (Article) Students Vulnerable to Computer Gaming Addiction, Chapter 7 232

Read and Respond to the Theme 496

Synthesizing Ideas 496 ■ Writing About the Readings 496

MySkillsLab® Visit **Part 5, Thematic Reader** in MySkillsLab to test your understanding of each of the readings.

Theme 1

Crime in the 21st Century: Technology and Trafficking

For many, the word *crime* connotes violent or headline-worthy criminal acts like bank robbery, murder, or rape. But crime defies easy classification. At one end of the spectrum are completely nonviolent crimes like shoplifting; at the other end are extremely violent crimes like mass shootings or terrorist incidents. Some crimes have only one victim, while others (such as the theft of data) may have thousands or even millions of victims. And there is also crime that flies under the radar, illegal practices that do not receive much attention in the media. In the following readings, we examine several types of crimes that are often underreported. These include not only the various types of technology-related crimes but also crimes that involve the illegal trafficking in human organs or even human beings themselves.

Reading 1: (Textbook) Technology and Crime, by Frank Schmalleger

Reading 2: (Article) Why Human Trafficking is Called Modern Day Slavery, by Phillip Martin

Reading 3: (Article) Human Traffic: Exposing the Brutal Organ Trade, by Nancy Scheper-Hughes

Technology and Crime

The following excerpt, "Technology and Crime," was originally published in a textbook, *Criminal Justice Today*. As you read, note how the author uses examples and quotes various experts or authorities to support his key points.

Thinking Before Reading

1. Preview the reading, using the steps discussed in Chapter 1, page 4.
2. Connect the reading to your own experience by answering the following questions:
   a. Have you ever copied a CD, a computer program, or a DVD from a friend or relative?
   b. Have you ever been the victim of a phishing, malware, or identity-theft scam?
3. Mark and annotate as you read.

Technology and Crime

Frank Schmalleger

1 Rapid advances in the biological sciences and electronic technologies during the past few decades, including genetic mapping, nanotechnology, computer

networking, the Internet, wireless services of all kinds, artificial intelligence (AI), and global positioning system (GPS) devices, have ushered in a wealth of new criminal opportunities. Crimes that employ advanced or emerging technologies in their commission are referred to as **technocrimes**.

2 New York State Police Captain and law enforcement visionary Thomas Cowper says that "it is important for police officers and their agencies to understand emerging technologies" for three reasons: (1) to anticipate their use by terrorists and criminals and thereby thwart their use against our nation and citizens, (2) to incorporate their use into police operations when necessary, and (3) to deal effectively with the social changes and cultural impact that inevitably result from technological advances. According to Cowper, "Continued police apathy and ignorance of nanotech, biotech and AI, and the potential changes they will bring to our communities and way of life, will only add to the turmoil, making law enforcement a part of the problem and not part of the solution."

Biocrime

3 In 2005, the World Health Organization raised alarms when it said that some samples of a potentially dangerous influenza virus that had been sent to thousands of laboratories in 18 countries had been lost and could not be located. Bio-kits containing the influenza A (H2N2) virus, which caused the flu pandemic of 1957–1958, were sent to 4,614 laboratories for use in testing the labs' ability to identify flu viruses. Meridian Bioscience Inc. of Cleveland, Ohio, sent the kits on behalf of the College of American Pathologists and three other U.S. organizations that set testing standards for laboratories. Although most of the laboratories were in the United States, some were in Latin America, and a few were in the Arab world—raising fears that Islamic terrorists might use the viral material, against which most people living today have no immunity, to create a pandemic. The H2N2 scare ended on May 2, 2005, when the U.S. Centers for Disease Control and Prevention (CDC) issued a press release saying that the last remaining sample of the virus outside the United States had been found and destroyed at the American University of Beirut in Lebanon. The Lebanese sample had been misplaced by a local delivery service but was discovered in a warehouse at the Beirut airport. Although the incident came to a successful conclusion, it heightened concerns about the spread of highly pathogenic avian influenza viruses and the possible appropriation by criminals of reverse-genetics research on the 1918 pandemic flu virus that killed millions worldwide.

4 Biological crime, or **biocrime**, is a criminal offense perpetrated through the use of biologically active substances, including chemicals and toxins, disease-causing organisms, altered genetic material, and organic tissues and organs. Biocrimes unlawfully affect the metabolic, biochemical, genetic, physiological, or anatomical status of living organisms. A major change in such status can, of course, produce death.

5 Biocrimes can be committed with simple poisons, but the biocrimes of special concern today involve technologically sophisticated delivery and dispersal systems and include the use of substances that have been bioengineered to produce the

desired effect. Biocrime becomes a high-technology offense when it involves the use of purposefully altered genetic material or advanced bioscientific techniques.

6 Although many people are aware of the dangers of terrorist-related biocrimes, including biological attacks on agricultural plants and animals (agroterrorism) and on human beings, many other kinds of potential biocrimes lurk on the horizon. They include the illegal harvesting of human organs for medical transplantation, human cloning, and the direct alteration of the DNA of living beings to produce a mixing of traits between species. Stem cell harvesting, another area that faces possible criminalization, is currently the subject of hot debate. The situation in the United States with regard to stem cell harvesting is one of funding restrictions, not legal or criminal restrictions. Although the federal government has yet to enact comprehensive legislation curtailing, regulating, or forbidding many of the kinds of activities mentioned here, there are a number of special interest groups that continue to lobby for such laws.

Cybercrime

7 The dark side of new technologies, as far as the justice system is concerned, is the potential they create for committing old crimes in new ways or for committing new crimes never before imagined. In 2013, for example, two sophisticated operations involving people in more than two dozen countries acting in close coordination hacked their way into a database of prepaid debit cards and then used the card numbers to drain $45 million in cash from ATM machines around the world. Seven people were arrested in the United States, some with backpacks stuffed with hundred dollar bills, and charged with using bogus magnetic swipe cards at teller machines in Japan, Russia, Romania, Egypt, Colombia, the U.K., and Canada.

8 Similarly, a few years ago, technologically savvy scam artists replicated the website of the Massachusetts State Lottery Commission. The scammers, believed to be operating out of Nigeria, sent thousands of e-mails and cell phone text messages telling people that they had won $30,000 in the Massachusetts State Lottery. People who received the messages were told to sign on to an official-looking website to claim their prize. The site required that users enter their Social Security and credit card numbers and pay a $100 processing fee before the winnings could be distributed.

9 A person's online activities occur in a virtual world comprised of bits and bytes. "True" computer criminals engage in behavior that goes beyond the theft of hardware. Cybercrime, or computer crime, focuses on the information stored in electronic media, which is why it is sometimes referred to as *information technology crime* or *infocrime*. Two decades ago, for example, the activities of computer expert Kevin Mitnick, then known as the Federal Bureau of Investigation's (FBI's) "most wanted **hacker**," alarmed security experts because of the potential for harm that Mitnick's electronic intrusions represented. The 31-year-old Mitnick broke into an Internet service provider's computer system and stole more than 20,000 credit card numbers. Tsutoma Shimomura, whose home computer Mitnick had also attacked, helped FBI experts track Mitnick through telephone lines and computer networks to the computer in his Raleigh, North Carolina, apartment, where he was arrested. In March 1999, Mitnick pleaded guilty to seven federal counts of computer and wire fraud.

He was sentenced to 46 months in prison but was released on parole in January 2000. Under the terms of his release, Mitnick was barred from access to computer hardware and software and from any form of wireless communication for a period of three years. In an interview after his release, Mitnick pointed out that "malicious hackers don't need to use stealth computer techniques to break into a network. . . . Often they just trick someone into giving them passwords and other information." According to Mitnick, "People are the weakest link. . . . You can have the best technology, firewalls, intrusion-detection systems, biometric devices . . . and somebody can call an unsuspecting employee . . . [and] they [get] everything."

10 Neil Barrett, a digital crime expert at International Risk Management, a London-based security consultancy, agrees. "The most likely way for bad guys to break into the system is through **social engineering**. This involves persuading administrators or telephonists to give details of passwords or other things by pretending to be staff, suppliers or trusted individuals—even police officers. They could be even masquerading as a computer repair man to get access to the premises." Social engineering is a devastating security threat, says Barrett, because it targets and exploits a computer network's most vulnerable aspect—people.

Types of Cybercrime

11 In 2005, a novel form of cybercrime made its appearance in the form of computer ransomware that installs itself on users' computers through an insecure Internet connection and then encrypts the users' data files. When the machines' owners try to access their own information, they are presented with a message telling them to provide their charge card number to a remote server, which then sends them an unlock code. According to the FBI, this high-tech form of extortion is still rare but on the rise. Particularly targeted are financial institutions and other businesses that stand to lose large amounts of money if their data is corrupted or irretrievable.

12 Peter Grabosky of the Australian Institute of Criminology suggests that most cybercrimes fall into one of the following broad categories: (1) theft of services, such as telephone or long-distance access; (2) communications in furtherance of criminal conspiracies—for example, the e-mail communications said to have taken place between members of Osama bin Laden's al-Qaeda terrorist network; (3) information piracy and forgery—that is, the stealing of trade secrets or copyrighted information; (4) the dissemination of offensive materials such as child pornography, high volumes of unwanted commercial material such as bulk e-mail (spam), or extortion threats like those made against financial institutions by hackers claiming the ability to destroy a company's electronic records; (5) electronic money laundering and tax evasion (through electronic funds transfers that conceal the origin of financial proceeds); (6) electronic vandalism and terrorism, including computer viruses, worms, Trojan horses, and cyberterrorism; (7) telemarketing fraud (including investment fraud and illegitimate electronic auctions); (8) illegal interception of telecommunications—that is, illegal eavesdropping; and (9) fraud involving electronic funds transfer (specifically, the illegal interception and diversion of legitimate transactions).

13 The 2010/2011 Computer Crime and Security Survey, conducted by the Computer Security Institute (CSI) and the FBI, found that the most expensive

computer security incidents were those involving financial fraud. Forty-six percent of the 351 information security professionals responding to the survey reported that their companies or organizations had been subjected to at least one targeted attack during the survey period (July 2009 to June 2010). "Targeted attacks" were defined as malware attacks aimed exclusively at the respondent's organization. Eighteen percent of respondents stated that they notified individuals whose personal information was breached. Sixteen percent said that as a result of attacks they provided new security services to users or customers. An overview of the Computer Security Institute's survey results can be found online at **http://gocsi.com/survey**.

Computer Viruses, Worms, and Trojan Horses

14 **Computer viruses** are a special concern of computer users everywhere. Computer viruses were first brought to public attention in 1988, when the Pakistani virus (or Pakistani brain virus) became widespread in personal and office computers across the United States. The Pakistani virus was created by Amjad Farooq Alvi and his brother, Basit Farooq Alvi, two cut-rate computer software dealers in Lahore, Pakistan. The Alvi brothers made copies of costly software products and sold them at low prices, mostly to Western shoppers looking for a bargain. Motivated by convoluted logic, the brothers hid a virus on each disk they sold to punish buyers for seeking to evade copyright laws.

AP Photo/Nick Ut

Luis Mijangos, 32, of Santa Ana, California. Mijangos was sentenced to six years in prison in 2011 for sextortion (digital extortion) after he pleaded guilty to computer hacking and wire-tapping. Mijangos used file-sharing networks to infect the computers of women and teenage girls, searching them for sexually explicit pictures. He'd then contact the victims demanding that they provide more photos or videos or he'd post what he had on the Web. In some cases he was also able to turn on victims' computer microphones and cameras to record their personal activities. How can you tell if your computer is immune to attacks like those perpetrated by Mijangos?

15 A more serious virus incident later that year affected sensitive machines in National Aeronautics and Space Administration (NASA) nuclear weapons labs, federal research centers, and universities across the United States. The virus did not destroy data. Instead, it made copies of itself and multiplied so rapidly that it clogged and effectively shut down computers within hours after invading them. Robert Morris, creator of the virus, was sentenced in 1990 to 400 hours of community service, three years' probation, and a fine of $10,000. Since then, many other virus attacks have made headlines, including the infamous Michelangelo virus in 1992; the intentional distribution of infected software on an AIDS-related research CD-ROM distributed about the same time; the Kournikova virus in 2000; and the later Sircam, Nimda, W32, NastyBrew, Berbew, Mydoom, and Code Red worms.

16 Technically speaking, most of today's malicious software falls under the category of worms or Trojan horses—called **malware** by technophiles. Malware (also called *crimeware*) has become increasingly sophisticated. Although early viruses were relatively easy to detect with hardware or software scanning devices that looked for virus "signatures," new malicious software using stealth and polymorphic computer codes changes form with each new "infection" and is much more difficult to locate and remove. Moreover, whereas older viruses infected only executable programs, or those that could be run, newer malware (such as the Word for Windows Macro virus, also called the *Concept virus*) attaches itself to word-processing

documents and to computer codes that are routinely distributed via the World Wide Web (including Java and Active-X components used by Web browsers). In 1998, the world's first HTML virus was discovered. The virus, named HTML Internal, infects computers whose users are merely viewing Web pages. Later that year, the first Java-based malware, named Strange Brew, made its appearance, and in 2004 malware capable of infecting digital images using the Joint Photographic Experts Group (JPEG) format was discovered. Evolving forms of malware are even able to infect cell phones and other wireless-enabled handheld devices.

Phishing

17 One form of cybercrime that relies primarily on social engineering so succeed is *phishing* (pronounced "fishing"). Phishing is a relatively new form of high-technology fraud that uses official-looking e-mail messages to elicit responses from victims, directing them to phony websites. Microsoft Corporation says that phishing is "the fastest-growing form of online fraud in the world today." Phishing e-mails typically instruct recipients to validate or update account information before their accounts are canceled. Phishing schemes, which have targeted most major banks, the Federal Deposit Insurance Corporation, IBM, eBay, PayPal, and some major healthcare providers, are designed to steal valuable information like credit card numbers, Social Security numbers, user IDs, and passwords. In 2004, Gartner Inc., a leading provider of research and analysis on the global information technology industry, released a report estimating that some 57 million adult Americans received phishing e-mails during the spring of 2004 and that 11 million recipients clicked on the link contained in the messages. Gartner estimated that 1.78 million recipients actually provided personal information to the thieves behind the phishing schemes.

Software Piracy

18 Another form of cybercrime, the unauthorized copying of software programs, also called **software piracy**, appears to be rampant. According to the Software and Information Industry Association (SIIA), global losses from software piracy total nearly $12.2 billion annually. The SIIA says that 38% of all software in use in the world today has been copied illegally. Some countries have especially high rates of illegal use. Of all the computer software in use in Vietnam, for example, the SIIA estimates that 97% has been illegally copied, whereas 95% of the software used in China and 92% of the software used in Russia are thought to be pirated—resulting in a substantial loss in manufacturers' revenue.

19 Software pirates seem to be especially adept at evading today's copy-protection schemes, including those that involve software "keys" and Internet authentication. Similar to software piracy, peer-to-peer Internet file-sharing services (which directly connect users' computers with one another via the Internet) have been criticized for allowing users to download copyright-protected e-music and digital video files free of charge. Lawsuits involving the music-sharing service Napster resulted in the site's near closure, and similar websites, such as KaZaA, Morpheus, and Grokster, are the targets of ongoing music industry lawsuits. In 2003, however, a U.S. district court in New York held that many music-swapping services and their operators could not be held accountable for the actions of their users, although individual users who download copyrighted materials *can* be held liable

for copyright infringements. That same year, a federal judge in Los Angeles ruled that peer-to-peer network software providers Grokster and StreamCast Networks could not be held liable for the copyright infringements of their users. In 2004, the 9th U.S. Circuit Court of Appeals upheld that ruling, but in 2005, in the landmark case of *MGM* v. *Grokster*, the U.S. Supreme Court found that online file-sharing services may be held liable for copyright infringement if they promote their services explicitly as a way for users to download copyrighted music and other content. The *Grokster* decision contrasts with the 1984 case of *Sony Corporation of America* v. *Universal City Studios, Inc.*, in which the Court held that a distributor/operator of a copying tool cannot be held liable for users' copyright infringements so long as the tool in question is capable of substantial noninfringing uses.

Spam

20 Nearly a decade ago, federal legislators acted to criminalize the sending of unsolicited commercial e-mail, or **spam**. The federal CAN-SPAM Act (Controlling the Assault of Non-Solicited Pornography and Marketing), which took effect on January 1, 2004, regulates the sending of "commercial electronic mail messages". The law, which applies equally to mass mailings and to individual e-mail messages, defines commercial electronic mail messages as electronic mail whose *primary purpose* is the "commercial advertisement or promotion of a commercial product or service." The CAN-SPAM law requires that a commercial e-mail message include the following three features: (1) a clear and conspicuous identification that the message is an advertisement or solicitation, (2) an opt-out feature, allowing recipients to opt out of future mailings, and (3) a valid physical address identifying the sender.

21 Some experts estimate that 80% of all e-mail today is spam, and many states have enacted their own antispam laws. Virginia's 2013 antispam statute, for example, imposes criminal penalties of from one to five years for anyone convicted of falsifying electronic mail transmission information or other routing information during the sending of unsolicited commercial bulk e-mail (UCBE). The law applies to anyone sending more than 10,000 UCBEs in a 24-hour period and to anyone who generates more than $1,000 in revenue from a UCBE transmission. The law also applies to anyone who uses fraudulent practices to send bulk e-mail to or from Virginia, a state that is home to a number of large Internet service providers, including America Online. In 2005, in the nation's first felony prosecution of a spammer, Jeremy Jaynes, age 30, one of the world's most active spammers, received a nine-year prison sentence under Virginia's law after he was convicted of using false Internet addresses and aliases to send mass e-mailings to America Online subscribers. Prosecutors were able to prove that Jaynes, a Raleigh, North Carolina, resident, earned as much as $750,000 a month by sending as many as 10 million illegal messages a day using computers operating in Virginia.

Crime, Terrorism, and Technology

22 The technological sophistication of state-sponsored terrorist organizations is rapidly increasing. Handguns and even larger weapons are now being manufactured out of plastic polymers and ceramics. Capable of firing Teflon-coated armor-piercing hardened ceramic bullets, such weapons are extremely powerful and impossible to uncover with metal detectors. Some people have also raised

concerns over the new technology represented by 3-D printers, capable of cranking out complex shapes that could be assembled into weapons—including handguns and other weapons; and in 2013 the State Department ordered the removal of what are believed to be the world's first printable gun blueprints from a Website called Defense Distributed. The do-it-yourself instructions had already been downloaded more than 100,000 times before the site was able to take them down.

23 Evidence points to the black market availability of other sinister items, including liquid metal embrittlement (LME), a chemical that slowly weakens any metal it contacts. LME could easily be applied with a felt-tipped pen to fuselage components in domestic aircraft, causing delayed structural failure. Back-pack-type electromagnetic pulse generators may soon be available to terrorists. Such devices could be carried into major cities, set up next to important computer installations, and activated to wipe out billions of items of financial, military, or other information now stored on magnetic media. International terrorists, along with the general public, have easy access to maps and other information that could be used to cripple the nation. The approximately 500 extremely-high-voltage (EHV) transformers on which the nation's electric grid depends, for example, are largely undefended and until recently were specified with extreme accuracy on easily available Web-based power network maps.

24 It is now clear that at least some terrorist organizations are seeking to obtain **weapons of mass destruction (WMDs)**, involving possible chemical, biological, radiological, and nuclear threats. A Central Intelligence Agency (CIA) report recently made public warned that al-Qaeda's "end goal" is to use WMDs. The CIA noted that the group had "openly expressed its desire to produce nuclear weapons" and that sketches and documents recovered from an al-Qaeda facility in Afghanistan contained plans for a crude nuclear device.

25 The collapse of the Soviet Union in the late 1980s led to very loose internal control over nuclear weapons and weapons-grade fissionable materials held in the former Soviet republics. Evidence of this continues to surface. In 2003, for example, a cab driver in the Eastern European nation of Georgia was arrested while transporting containers of cesium-137 and strontium-90, materials that could be used to make a "dirty" bomb (a radiological dispersal device, or RDD) that would use conventional explosives to spread nuclear contamination over a wide area. A month later, officials arrested a traveler in Bangkok, Thailand, who had a canister of cesium-137 in his possession. Although the Thai traveler told police that he had acquired the cesium in Laos, scientists were able to determine that it had originated in Russia.

26 A study by Harvard University researchers found that the United States and other countries were moving too slowly in efforts to help Russia and other former Soviet-bloc nations destroy poorly protected nuclear material and warheads left over from the cold war. The study also warned that most civilian nuclear reactors in Eastern Europe are "dangerously insecure." Experts say the amount of plutonium needed to make one bomb can be smuggled out of a supposedly secure area in a briefcase or even in the pocket of an overcoat.

27 Biological weapons were banned by the 1975 international Biological weapons Convention, but biological terrorism (or bio-terrorism), which seeks to disperse destructive or disease-producing biologically active agents among civilian or

military populations, is of considerable concern today. **Bioterrorism**, one form of biocrime, is defined by the Centers for Disease Control and Prevention as the "intentional or threatened use of viruses, bacteria, fungi, or toxins from living organisms to produce death or disease in humans, animals, or plants." The infamous anthrax letters mailed to at least four people in the United States in 2001 provide an example of a bioterrorism incident intended to create widespread fear among Americans. Five people, including mail handlers, died, and 23 others were infected. Other possible bioterror agents include botulism toxin, brucellosis, cholera, glanders, plague, ricin, smallpox, tularemia Q fever, and a number of viral agents capable of producing diseases such as viral hemorrhagic fever and severe acute respiratory syndrome (SARS). As mentioned earlier, experts fear that technologically savvy terrorists could create their own novel bioweapons through bioengineering, a process that uses snippets of made-to-order DNA, the molecular code on which life is based. Visit the Institute for Biosecurity at **http://www.bioterrorism.slu.edu**, and read the CDC's overview of bioterrorism at **http://www.justicestudies.com/pubs/biochemcdc.pdf**.

Technology and Crime Control

28 Technology, although it has increased criminal opportunity, has also been a boon to police investigators and other justice system personnel. In one example from 2013, the Omaha Police Department hosted the eighth Social Media Internet Law Enforcement (SMILE) national conference (also known as SMILECon 8) at Omaha's Old Market District. Conference organizers noted that police departments can both benefit as well as suffer from recent developments in social networking, and said that the adoption of social media by law enforcement agencies "is in a stage of exponential growth."

29 In a practical example of the use of social media in policing, the Bergen County (New Jersey) Sheriff's Office launched "FaceCrook" in 2012, which includes public information on outstanding warrants tied to a Google Maps app, including an anonymous tip feature that allows people to provide anonymous tips via computer and telephone (**http://www.facecrook.net**).

30 In another example, the Dunwoody, Georgia, Police Department recently experimented with using Twitter to help the city's 46,000 residents better understand the nature of police work. For 24 hours the department tweeted about each significant activity undertaken by its officers—beginning with an early morning traffic stop and concluding the next morning with a 6 a.m. report of a suspicious person.

31 Other police departments are jumping on board the social media bandwagon. In 2011, for example, the California Highway Patrol created Twitter pages—one for each of its divisions; and the Modesto, California, Police Department set up an active Twitter account to notify followers about major incidents and to provide links to ongoing investigations and newsworthy events. The department also uses Twitter to steer people away from accident sites, to coordinate the activities of searchers during Amber Alerts, and to warn people to stay inside during potentially dangerous situations. "It's a valuable tool that allows us to get out message out," says Stanislaus County Sheriff's Department spokesperson Deputy Luke Schwartz.

"You're going to see a lot more law enforcement agencies get on board with social networking sites like Twitter and Facebook," says Schwartz.

32 Schwartz points out, however, that social networking technologies don't always benefit the police. "The element of surprise is everything, and social media is taking away the element of surprise that we need to keep people safe when we have tactical situations," Schwartz said.

33 One of the best examples of the use of social media in law enforcement today is TheDailyOfficer. Follow TheDailyOfficer on Twitter **@DailyOfficer**, from which you can access an ever-changing compilation of current police news and blogs from around the world. Concerned citizens can provide tips to law enforcement agencies via the Web-based Crime Stoppers International tipline at **http://www.facebook.com/CSIWorld**. Another website, Connected Cops, describes itself as "law enforcement's partner on the social web," and can be visited at **http://connectedcops.net**. Connected Cops is international in scope, and provides a blog populated with messages from law enforcement social media visionaries on how to leverage technology in the service of law enforcement.

34 Similarly, access by law enforcement to high-technology investigative tools has produced enormous amounts of information on crimes and suspects, and the use of innovative investigative tools like DNA fingerprinting, keystroke captures, laser and night-vision technologies, digital imaging, and thermography are beginning to shape many of the practical aspects of the twenty-first-century criminal justice system. Today, some laptop computers and vehicles are programmed to contact police when they are stolen and provide satellite-based tracking information so authorities can determine their whereabouts. Many rental car companies, for example, now have cars equipped with systems that can send and receive from a central location. Security employees at those companies can send instructions to vehicles to prevent the car from starting and thus being stolen. The system can also track the car as it moves. Likewise, some police departments are using high-technology "bait cars" to catch auto thieves. Bait cars can signal when stolen, send digitized images of perpetrators to investigators, radio their position to officers, be remotely immobilized, and lock their doors on command, trapping thieves inside.

35 Another crime-fighting technology making headway in the identification of stolen vehicles is automatic plate recognition (APR) technology. In December 2004, for example, the Ohio State Highway Patrol completed a four-month evaluation of an APR system using infrared cameras mounted at strategic points along the state's highways and connected to computers to alert troopers to the possible presence of stolen vehicles or wanted persons. During the four-month test period, the system led to the apprehension of 23 criminal suspects and the recovery of 24 stolen vehicles.

36 Car thieves, however, have made some technological advances of their own, including the "laundering" of vehicle identification numbers (VINs), which allows stolen cars to be sold as legitimate vehicles. Stolen cars with "cloned" VINs are usually not discovered until an insurance claim is filed and investigators learn that there are two or more vehicles registered with the same VIN to people in different locations. As these stories indicate, the future will no doubt see a race between technologically sophisticated offenders and law enforcement authorities to determine who can wield the most advanced technical skills in the age-old battle between crime and justice. Have a look at how the FBI sees crime fighting's future at **http://www.justicestudies.com/pubs/futuretech.pdf**.

Jason DeCrow/AP Wide World Photos

The New York City Police Department's Real Time Crime Center, where police work can seem like science fiction. At the center, where about a dozen analysts work, information on suspects is displayed on huge screens and can be relayed to detectives' laptops instantly. What do you imagine the future of police work will be like?

37 One of the best examples of the use of contemporary technologies in the service of crime fighting can be found at New York City's Real Time Crime Center. The center is staffed by specially trained data analysts who pore over enormous multiple-screen monitors that feed streams of information to them from video cameras, human intelligence gatherers, detectives and police officers, and computer programs searching for links between diverse bits of information. The center has been described as "a round-the-clock computer-data warehouse that can digitally track down information, from a perpetrator's mug shot to his second former mother-in-law's address." Kenneth Mekeel, a former captain of detectives, now runs the center. "It used to take us days to find a number or an address." Mekeel says. "Now we send stuff to detectives who are literally standing [at the crime scene]."

Getting Ready to Write

Checking Your Comprehension MySkillsLab®

Answer each of the following questions using complete sentences.

1. What is a technocrime?
2. List three reasons that Thomas Cowper gives to explain why police officers and police agencies need to understand technology.
3. What is the current status of stem cell harvesting in the United States?
4. What are two synonyms for the term *cybercrime*?
5. According to Luke Schwartz, which vital component of crime fighting does social media take away?

Strengthening Your Vocabulary MySkillsLab®

Identify at least five words used in the reading that are unfamiliar to you. Using context, word parts, or a dictionary, if necessary, write a brief definition of each word.

Examining the Reading: Drawing an Idea Map

Create an idea map of "Technology and Crime." Start with the title and thesis and include the main points of the selection.

Reading and Writing: An Integrated Perspective

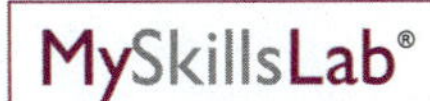

1. Think about the way you live and work with computers. Based on this selection, to which types of crimes do you feel most vulnerable? Explain your answer in a journal entry.
2. Paragraph 9 talks about criminal hackers. How might a hacker work for the good of society instead of against it?
3. Check your e-mail's spam filter. Approximately how many spam messages do you get a day? Typically, what are these spam messages trying to sell you or get you to do?
4. This selection originally appeared in a textbook. Does the author carefully define the key terms that he introduces? Consider, for example, the definitions of *biocrime* (paragraph 4) and *social engineering* (paragraph 10).
5. Why has the author divided the reading into numerous sections, subsections, and headings? How might these help you prepare for a quiz or test on the topics covered?
6. Evaluate the author's use of photos in this reading selection. Are they useful? What key points do they reinforce?
7. Why does the author quote Kevin Mitnick in paragraph 9?

Thinking and Writing Critically MySkillsLab®

1. Is this selection primarily fact based or opinion based? That is, is the author seeking primarily to convey information, or he is making a strong argument for or against something? *Hint*: Consider the source in which "Technology and Crime" was originally published. (For more on identifying facts and opinions, see Chapter 12.)
2. Identify at least two opinions in the reading. (*Hint*: One opinion can be found in paragraph 10.) Do the people whose opinions are quoted in this reading appear to be experts on the topic? How can you tell? (For more on opinions, see Chapter 12.)
3. How does the author feel about his subject? Does he seem rather bored with it, or is he highly interested in it? How would you describe the author's tone? (To learn more about tone, see Chapter 12.)

4. Do you see any bias in this reading? If so, would you describe the bias as light, moderate, or heavy? (For more on identifying and evaluating bias, see Chapter 13.)

5. It might be argued that textbooks are composed mostly of generalizations. Do you agree with this statement? Does this reading, which is taken from a textbook, make frequent use of generalizations? (For further information on generalizations, see Chapter 13.)

6. Explain the connotations and denotations of the following words and phrases from the reading: "the dark side of new technologies" (paragraph 7); "dangerously insecure" (paragraph 26); "technology in the service of law enforcement" (paragraph 33). (For more on connotation and denotation, see Chapter 13.)

7. What types of evidence does the author provide to support his claims? Has he provided enough evidence? If not, what types of evidence might help make the reading stronger? (For more on evaluating evidence, see Chapter 14.)

Writing About the Reading MySkillsLab®

1. The issue of file-share Web sites has been very contentious legally, particularly for publishers of books and music, who argue that the sites permit and encourage piracy of intellectual property. Do you think that, in the Internet era, everything should be free? Or should intellectual property continue to be protected? Write an essay in which you craft a solid argument.

2. Write an essay in which you explain how to protect your identity in an age of cyber-fraud and hacking.

3. Suppose someone writes a computer virus that crashes 10,000 computers. Another person sends spam e-mails to 1,000,000 people, asking them to send him $1 because he really needs the money. Both of these acts are crimes. Should the perpetrators be punished equally? Why or why not? Which types of cybercrime should be punished the most harshly? Which types should result in a stern "warning" to stop the behavior? Write an essay exploring these questions.

Why Human Trafficking is Called Modern Day Slavery

The following article, "Why Human Trafficking Is Called Modern Day Slavery," appeared in the October 1, 2013 edition of the *Huffington Post*. The author, Phillip Martin, is a Senior Fellow for The Schuster Institute for Investigative Journalism, an independent reporting organization focused on social justice and human rights. Through investigative reporting, The Schuster Institute hopes to inform those who make our laws about the plight of the "the poor, the voiceless, and the forgotten." As you read, note Martin's frequent reference to public policy makers and the difficulties associated with controlling this criminal activity.

Thinking Before Reading

1. Preview the reading, using the steps discussed in Chapter 1, page 4.
2. Connect the reading to your own experience by answering these questions:
   a. Do you think slavery ended with the Civil War?
   b. Have you ever encountered the terms "sex trafficking" and "human trafficking"? What do they mean?
3. Mark and annotate as you read.

Why Human Trafficking is Called Modern Day Slavery

Phillip Martin

1 If you think slavery ended in 1865 with passage of the 13th Amendment, think again. Human traffickers have picked up where slavery, brutal racial-based penal laws, sharecropping and Jim Crow left off. If that seems far-fetched, just listen to Luis CdeBaca at the U.S. State Department. "In the wake of the Civil Rights Movement, there was a perception that the problem of slavery, of share-cropping, was a thing of the past," CdeBaca said. "And, quietly, the abusers were bringing in immigrants to replace the African American community." Years before he became U.S. Ambassador-at-Large to Combat Human Trafficking, CdeBaca was with the Justice Department investigating slavery in the U.S.

Farms, Nail Salons and Shipyards

2 "The involuntary servitude and slavery program had been a little bit on the back burner during the '70s and '80s because of the gains of the Civil Rights

Movement," said CdeBaca. "And, then, by the '80s and '90s, we were starting to see—whether it was Guatemalans, or Mexicans or others—suffering often in the same farms in the American South picking tomatoes, cucumbers, onions. So, when I had a chance to work on a farm worker slavery case, I didn't shy away from it."

3 Farm work is just one occupation subject to super-exploitation. In August, the Southern Poverty Law Center (SPLC) filed new human trafficking lawsuits against Signal International LLC alleging that the shipbuilder and recruitment firm and its agents cheated foreign workers from South Asia out of their hard earned money. The lawsuits further allege that the guest workers assigned to Signal's shipyards in Pascagoula, Miss., and Orange, Texas, endured overcrowded and unsanitary conditions in racially segregated labor camps. The men were told that they had to pay back money that was used to "recruit" them, which amounted to tens of thousands of dollars. These individuals toiled for little or no compensation and, according to the SPLC, "they also were threatened with financial ruin and deportation if they balked".

Trafficked To The USA

> In the wake of the Civil Rights Movement, there was a perception that the problem of slavery, of sharecropping, was a thing of the past and, quietly, the abusers were bringing in immigrants to replace the African American community
>
> —*Ambassador Luis CdeBaca*

4 About 18,000 people are trafficked to the U.S. each year, according to the State Department. What do they have in common? Most are indebted to smugglers and traffickers. According to the Polaris Project, a national anti-human trafficking group, victims have also been pressed to work in factories, nail salons, strip clubs, begging and peddling rings and as domestic workers—for little or no money.

5 Matt Friedman, formerly of the United Nations Inter-Agency Project on Human Trafficking said those coercive conditions have always existed. "To kind of engender people into the sex industry, or objectionable jobs like fisheries, or sweat shops and so forth—that's never stopped," Friedman said

6 In Boston, San Francisco, New York and other American cities, immigrants have found themselves working in restaurants. A kitchen is where an ambitious, middle-class 19-year-old woman from Fujian province in China ended up– a long way from her dreams. I'll call her "Ming-Wei." This is one woman's story of labor trafficking.

Smuggled and Then Trafficked

7 Years ago, she stood in line at Bangkok's modern airport waiting to board a flight to the U.S., as I'm standing here now. "When I transferred Hong Kong to Thailand, they gave me a fake passport, but the picture is of myself," Ming-Wei said.

8 She entered into an agreement with a smuggler. To take you from China to the U.S., smugglers charge as much $75,000 per person. In Mexico, they're called coyotes. In East Asia, they're known as snakeheads. They help get you across rivers, under fences, over mountains and through deserts. But sometimes they just put you on a plane. Per the instructions of her snakehead, Ming-Wei pretended to be a citizen of Thailand and was provided a fake passport. "Nothing information matched with me," Ming-Wei said. "But the only thing is the picture of me. But they trained me to look like the person. Actually, I'm Chinese."

9 Once on board, both her Chinese passport and fake Thai papers were confiscated by the snakehead. She landed at JFK without documentation. Ming Wei, as instructed by the smuggler, then filed for political asylum based on religious persecution. "They, the snakehead, told me [to claim asylum] because of religion, like I believed in Buddha or Jesus," Ming-Wei said. "Actually, I don't believe anything."

10 What she did believe was that she had arrived in a place where dreams come true.

11 "And you could live in a big house," she said. "You could buy your own car. You could buy a very nice good car, something like that, education, or a lot of beautiful things—a good job."

12 Officials at the airport gave her a date to show up for an immigration hearing. And what happened after she cleared customs has been repeated for many trafficked immigrants arriving to America, according to the Polaris Project. Outside the international terminal, she was met by a driver, someone she didn't know. "I just followed him, stayed there for one night," she said.

13 That was in New York's Chinatown.

Indentured in a Chinese Restaurant

14 The next day she was driven to a restaurant in Pennsylvania. And then another restaurant, and then another: all belonging to the same wealthy Chinese family. Ming-Wei was told that she had to pay back the smuggler who brought her here

from China via Bangkok; a cost of $8,000 that quadrupled when room and board were later added. "I can't ask [how much money I'm paid], I can't ask," she said. "I'm not allowed to ask. And I get whatever they pay me."

15 That often came to less than $100 per month, working in the restaurant from 8 a.m. to 1 a.m. the next morning, for two weeks straight and one day off. "The underground restaurant network is very amazing," said immigration attorney Lauren Burke.

16 Burke manages the legal department at the New York Asian Women's Center, (NYAWC), the group Ming-Wei eventually turned to for help. She says many of the center's 600 clients they help annually are vulnerable to the extreme labor exploitation that forms the basis of human trafficking. "There's a street in Chinatown called Eldridge Street and there's all these job agencies . . . you go to one and they give you a ticket," she said. "And I have clients that are shipped to North Carolina, to Ohio, to Boston, to Florida, and they are working in these little side of the road buffet restaurants across the country."

17 The distance between Boston and New York until recently was bridged by growing numbers of Chinatown-based bus companies. Two of those firms are currently out of commission pending mechanical and administrative improvements mandated by the federal government. But the companies in question may soon be back in business. Burke says the low fare carriers that are popular with Boston-area college students are also vehicles of choice for hustlers in the underground trade.

18 "There will be recruiters on the buses who look for young vulnerable kids and say, you know, you should work at this massage parlor," Burke said. "So I know that the recruiters do work on those routes." Burke says the budget buses were set up originally to ferry lowly paid workers between New York and Massachusetts before they were geared to the general public.

19 Massachusetts Attorney General Martha Coakley said she has seen scattered reports of domestic laborers held against their will or having their wages withheld. "Women in other countries are told we'll provide transport for you to the United States, and once they get here they're told you owe us money for that," Coakley said. "And they will be put to work. Sometimes, it's in a factory or in a particular industry, and sometimes it's sex trafficking, but they are made to believe, you know, that they're going to have a job here, that they'll have a new life. But there's a little piece of the contract left out that you have to pay off your expenses, and it's really the whole idea of involuntary servitude that's the other side of labor trafficking that we worry about."

20 But proving it is difficult. And a report published last year by the Urban Institute and Northeastern University suggests why: a lack of law enforcement resources, legal guidance and cooperation from victims. But Burke said if what victims have experienced cannot be proven, she at least hopes that public awareness will put pressure on those who profit from exploited laborers.

21 "I have clients with cuts on their arms and have been burned by pans, and they sleep with bugs biting them all night long," she said. "If you are an employer who knows those are the conditions, and continue to pay somebody and use exploitation as a form of fear, I believe you're just as much culpable as any trafficker."

22 As for Ming-Wei, who arrived here from China via Bangkok at age 19, she is still working in the restaurant business at age 38, and still paying off debt to snakeheads and traffickers. Though she is safe, her family in China may not be. And she takes the threat of violence against them quite seriously.

Getting Ready to Write

Checking Your Comprehension MySkillsLab®

Answer each of the following questions using complete sentences.

1. What do the 18,000 people trafficked to the U.S. each year have in common?
2. What types of occupations are subject to exploitation in the United States?
3. Why is it difficult to prove involuntary servitude cases?
4. What is a snakehead? How did a snakehead "help" Ming-Wei?
5. How are people lured into the human trafficking trap?

Strengthening Your Vocabulary MySkillsLab®

Identify at least five words used in the reading that are unfamiliar to you. Using context, word parts, or a dictionary, if necessary, write a brief definition of each word.

Examining the Reading: Drawing an Idea Map

Create an idea map of "Why Human Trafficking Is Called Modern Day Slavery." Start with the title and thesis and include the main points of the selection.

Reading and Writing: An Integrated Perspective MySkillsLab®

1. Were you aware of the extent of human trafficking before you read this article? Write a journal entry explaining what facts in this article you found most surprising or shocking.
2. What can the news media in the United States do to help make people more aware of the vast extent of human trafficking?
3. Why does the author reference the Civil Rights Movement?
4. Why does the author include the story about Ming-Wei? What effect does this example of human trafficking have on readers?
5. Evaluate the article's concluding paragraph. Do you find it effective? How might it be improved, if at all?
6. How effective are the photographs that accompany the reading? Write captions to accompany them

Thinking and Writing Critically MySkillsLab®

1. How does the author feel about his subject? What words would you use to describe the author's tone? (To learn more about tone, see Chapter 12.)
2. This reading is very heavy on facts and statistics. However, it does contain opinions. Identify at least one opinion found in the article. (For more information on identifying and evaluating opinions, see Chapter 12.)

3. Do you see any bias in this reading? If so, would you describe the bias as light, moderate, or heavy? (For more on identifying and evaluating bias, see Chapter 13.)

4. Discuss the connotations and denotations of the following words and phrases used in the article: "brutal racial-based penal laws" (paragraph 1); "papers were confiscated by the snakehead" (paragraph 9); "extreme labor exploitation" (paragraph 16); "involuntary servitude" (paragraph 19); " they sleep with bugs biting them"(paragraph 20). How do these phrases help convey the author's tone? (For more on connotation and denotation, see Chapter 13.)

5. Often a writer uses figurative language as a way of describing rather than telling. Provide two examples of figurative language that the author could have used to enhance the description in the essay. (To learn more about figurative language, see Chapter 13.)

6. What assumption underlies this entire article? (To learn more about identifying and evaluating assumptions, see Chapter 13.)

7. What types of evidence does the author provide to support his claims? Has he provided enough evidence? If not, what types of evidence might help him better support his argument? (For more on evaluating evidence, see Chapter 14.)

Writing About the Reading MySkillsLab®

1. The reading discusses human trafficking as exploitation that is difficult to prove because of a lack of law enforcement resources, legal guidance and cooperation from victims. What other types of exploitation do you think are equally difficult to prove, and why? Write an essay exploring this topic. For example, some people think that date rape is underreported and thus hard to prove.

2. Watch the movie *12 Years a Slave*. Write an essay summarizing the plot and explain how watching the movie affected you.

3. Ambassador Luis CdeBaca suggests that "In the wake of the Civil Rights Movement, there was a perception that the problem of slavery, of share-cropping, was a thing of the past and, quietly, the abusers were bringing in immigrants to replace the African American community." Write an essay in which you explain Ambassador CdeBaca statement and then discuss why you agree or disagree with the statement.

Human Traffic: Exposing the Brutal Organ Trade

The following excerpt, "Human Traffic: Exposing the Brutal Organ Trade," was originally published in *The New Internationalist*, a magazine that calls attention to various issues of social inequality and injustice. The author is a professor of medical anthropology at the University of California, Berkeley. As you read, note how the author is part of the story she is telling. How does this fact relate to the selection's credibility and believability?

Thinking Before Reading

1. Preview the reading, using the steps discussed in Chapter 1, page 4.
2. Connect the reading to your own experience by answering the following questions:
   a. Do you know anyone who has received a donated organ? Do you know anyone who is on the waiting list for an organ?
   b. Have you signed up to be an organ donor upon your death?
3. Mark and annotate as you read.

Human Traffic: Exposing the Brutal Organ Trade

Nancy Scheper-Hughes

1 The slide on the screen showed several skinny, dark Filipino men lined up, displaying their sacred wound, the kidney scar, long as a saber slice across their convex torsos. More than 150 representatives of scientific and medical bodies from 78 countries stared solemnly at the photo during the Istanbul Summit of 2008, the defining moment in the global recognition of human trafficking for "fresh" kidneys. "Is this why we began as transplant surgeons?" one of the convenors, U.S. surgeon Francis Delmonico, asked. "Are we comfortable with this? Is this fair? Do we want to participate in this?"

2 The man sitting next to me, a Hindu surgeon in white robes, reminiscent of Hippocrates, was moved. When I asked what he was thinking, he replied: "This is too late. Kidney selling is no longer a strange or exotic act. It is normal, everyday, and entrenched. We in the South can agree that it is a tragic turn of events, but the demand comes from outside."

3 In the early 1980s a new form of human trafficking, a global trade in kidneys from living persons to supply the needs and demands of "transplant tourists," emerged in the Middle East, Latin America, and Asia. The first scientific report on the phenomenon, published in *The Lancet* in 1990, documented the transplant odysseys of 131 renal patients from three dialysis units in the United Arab Emirates and Oman. They traveled with their private doctors to Bombay (now Mumbai), India, where they were transplanted with kidneys from living "suppliers" organized by local brokers trolling slums and shantytowns. The sellers were paid between \$2,000 and \$3,000 for a "spare" organ. On return, these transplant tourists suffered an alarming rate of post-operative complications and mortalities resulting from mismatched organs, and infections including HIV and Hepatitis C. There was no data on, or discussion of, the possible adverse effects on the kidney sellers, who were still an invisible population of anonymous supplier bodies, similar to deceased donors.

4 In 1997, I co-founded Organs Watch, specifically to draw attention to the then invisible population of kidney "suppliers."[1] Today human trafficking for organs is a small, vibrant, and extremely lucrative business that involves some 50 nations.[2]

No Cadavers Wanted

5 In the summer of 2009 I received a phone call that unnerved me. "Are you the Organs Lady?" a young man I'll call Jim Deal* asked me with a slight tremor in his voice.

6 "Perhaps," I replied. "How can I help you?"

7 "I just found out that my kidneys are failing and my doctor wants me to start dialysis immediately."

8 "Yes?"

9 "Well, I can't attach myself to a machine three days a week. I've just started a new company and I can't lose a minute. I need a kidney now. Where can I go to get one? I have the resources. Money is not an object."

10 My suggestions to ask his relatives (who included several siblings) were rejected—they were all busy with their careers and families. Would he be willing to take the "Steve Jobs option," registering in multiple transplant centers in different regions of the United States, increasing the possibility that his number would be called—Bingo!

The Demand for Organs Outstrips Supply

11 Advances in medicine that keep us alive longer, coupled with rising levels of type-2 diabetes and heart disease, mean that the pool of patients waiting for organs is growing. In any given year, fewer than 1 in 10 waiting for a donor organ will receive one. At the same time, there are fewer organs from young, healthy people—who make the best deceased donors—due to the life-saving influence of car seat belts. Prolonged end-of-life medical care can also mean fewer usable organs upon death. Nevertheless, the WHO believes national self-sufficiency through deceased donor organs is possible—efforts to retrieve usable organs from the deceased need to be maximized. Progress in stem cell research, the creation of workable artificial organs, and xenotransplantation could help towards meeting the demand in the future.

12 "No cadavers," Jim said. It would have to be a kidney purchased from a living stranger. Could I recommend a surgeon or a broker who could help? Given his family genealogy, which included a grandparent from Iran, I told Jim that he might be in luck. Iran had the only legalized and regulated kidney selling program, but it was reserved for Iranian citizens and diaspora. "I'm not going to go to Iran, if that's what you are saying," Jim countered. "I want First World medicine."

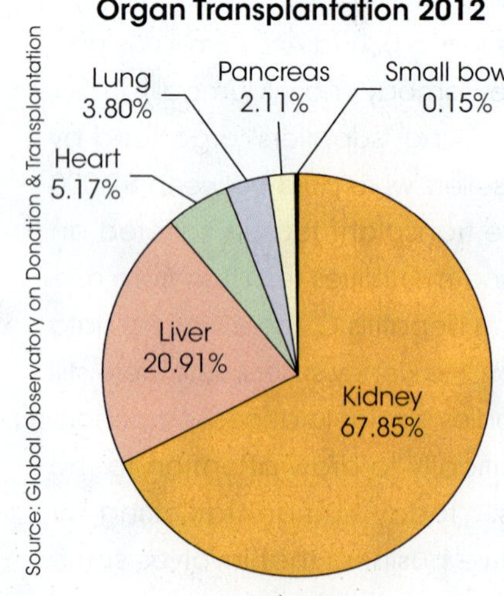

13 There was no use trying to convince Jim that Iran had "First World" surgeons. Some weeks later he called to tell me that his family had found several local, willing kidney providers online through Craigslist. He chose the least expensive "option": a kidney from 19-year-old community college student Ji-Hun*, an immigrant from South Korea who could not afford his tuition, books, room, and board, and who feared deportation if he dropped out.

14 The deal was secured for $20,000. The night before the transplant, two very nervous Korean brothers met with Jim's relatives in an upscale suburb of Los Angeles to count the kidney loot in crisp one hundred dollar bills.

An armed guard oversaw the encounter. The seller requested half in advance. The family refused, but they agreed to hand over the money to the seller's older brother as soon as both parties were under anesthesia but before they knew the outcome of the organ transfer.

15 By the time I arrived at the famous "hospital for the Hollywood stars" in Beverly Hills, the surgery was over and Jim was out of the recovery room and surrounded by well-wishers. His private room was festive with flowers, gifts, smiles, and prayers for Jim's recovery. Nurses popped their heads in and out to see if everything was going well.

16 It took some sleuthing to locate Ji-Hun, who was tucked away in a corner room several flights above the regular post-op recovery rooms. He was a delicate young man, weighing no more than 55 kilos. He was doubled over with pain, and blushed with shame when I introduced myself to him as an informal "kidney donor" advocate. The nurses tittered anxiously when I presented my calling card with its Organs Watch logo. They told me that Ji-Hun would be released that same day, although he had not yet seen a doctor following his kidney removal. He was worried about returning to his one-room bedsitter apartment in a dodgy section of Los Angeles. Before leaving the hospital Ji-Hun gave me his cell-phone number.

17 A few days later Ji-Hun reported that he was still in bed, immobilized with pain, and unable to eat, urinate, or defecate. His older brother, a surly young man who worked as a dish washer in a fast-food restaurant, was angry with him. He had no medical insurance, and the $20,000, which had been handed over to his brother in a public toilet on the surgical ward, was already all but gone after settling unpaid bills along with student tuition and remittances for their parents in Korea. After a few brief calls, Ji-Hun's phone went dead.

18 Jim, anxious about disclosure, emigrated to another country and on last report was married and able to work. The head of the surgical staff of the complicit hospital refused to discuss the case, citing patient confidentiality. The consulting nephrologist who worked shifts at the private hospital contacted me to say that he had seen many other instances of bartered kidneys, but was loath to be a "whistleblower."

19 While most illicit kidney transplants take place in the so-called developing world—India, Pakistan, Bangladesh, Egypt, the Philippines, and more recently Central Asia and Central America—future transactions are likely to resemble the above story. Facilitated by the Internet, organ "suppliers" will be drawn locally from the large pool of new immigrants, refugees, and undocumented workers. The transplants will be arranged in private hospitals where the transactions are reported as altruistic, emotionally related donations.

Organized Crime

20 That is the future. For now, transplant tours are more usual. They can bring together actors from as many as four or five different countries, with a buyer from one place, the brokers from two other countries, the mobile surgeons traveling from one nation to another where the kidney operations actually take place. In these instances, and the case of a private clinic in Kosovo is perhaps the best

example, the participants appear and disappear quickly, with the guilty parties, including the surgeons, taking with them any incriminating data. When the police finally arrive at the scene, they discover the bloody remains of a black-market clinic, with traces of forensic evidence, but the key players long since disappeared.

21 Over the course of more than 17 years of dogged field research, my Organs Watch colleagues and I had realized that we were not dealing with a question of medical ethics. Rather, we had gained entry into the world of international organized crime. Following fieldwork in Turkey, Moldova, the United States, Israel, Brazil, Argentina, the Philippines, and South Africa, it became apparent that organ brokers were human traffickers involved in cut-throat deals that were enforced with violence, if needed. Many of the "kidney hunters" who seek out new candidates in poor localities are former sellers, recruited by crime bosses.

22 The transplant and organ procurement traffic is far-flung, sophisticated, and extremely lucrative. Although trafficking in human organs is illegal in almost every nation, the specifics of the laws differ, making prosecutions that can involve three or more nations a judicial nightmare. In some countries it is illegal to sell a kidney but not to purchase one. In others it is illegal to buy and sell within the country but not to buy and/or sell abroad.

23 Organ trafficking made its début as a much-contested add-on to the 2000 United Nations Palermo Protocol on Human Trafficking, which recognizes that even willing participants in underworld illicit kidney schemes can be counted as victims. Indeed, most are coerced by need, not physical threats or force. Some even pay significant amounts of money to be trafficked.

24 As it is covert behavior, it is difficult to know with any degree of certainty how many people are actually trafficked for their kidneys, but a conservative estimate, based on original research by Organs Watch, is that at least 10,000 kidneys are sold each year. Human trafficking for organs is a relatively small and contained problem, one that could be dealt with efficiently with the political will to do so.

Complex Co-Ordination

25 Unlike other forms of trafficking that unite people from shady backgrounds, the organ trade involves those at the highest—or at least middle-class—levels of society: surgeons, doctors, laboratory technicians, travel agents, as well as criminals and outcasts from the lowest.

26 Transplant professionals are reluctant to "name and shame" those of their colleagues involved in the trade, thereby creating a screen that conceals and even protects the human traffickers who supply the surgeons. And because trafficking living donors for organs is a traffic in "goods" (life-saving "fresh kidneys") not traffic in "bads" (drugs or guns) there is reluctance, even on the part of the justice system, to recognize the "collateral damage" it inflicts on vulnerable bodies—and the harm to society and the profession of medicine itself.

27 Organ brokers are the linchpins of these criminal networks, which handle an onerous feat of logistics. They co-ordinate three key populations: (1) kidney patients willing to travel great distances and face considerable risk and insecurity; (2) kidney sellers recruited and trafficked from the urban slums and collapsed

villages of the poor world; (3) outlaw surgeons willing to break the law and violate professional codes of ethics. Well-connected brokers have access to the necessary infrastructure such as hospitals, transplant centers and medical insurance companies, as well as to local kidney hunters, and brutal enforcers who make sure that "willing" sellers actually get up on the operating table once they realize what the operation actually entails. They can count on both government indifference and police protection.

28 The complicit medical professionals perform expert teamwork—technicians in the blood and tissue laboratories, dual surgical teams working in tandem, nephrologists and post-operative nurses. There are "transplant tour agencies" that can organize travel, passports, and visas. In the Middle East and in the United States, religious organizations, charitable trusts, and patient advocacy groups are often fronts for such international networks.

Tactics of Persuasion

29 Some brokers in Moldova used underhand tactics that had already been honed in recruiting naïve Moldovan women into sex work. They offered the opportunity of work abroad to unemployed youth, or household heads in debt or in need of cash to support sick spouses or children. On arrival, the young men were kept in safe houses, had their passports confiscated, and were reduced to total dependency on the brokers (women were exceptions). A few days later, the brokers would break the news that it was not painting or ironing trousers that was needed from the illegal "guest workers" but their kidneys. Those who refused outright were threatened or beaten. One young man, Vladimir*, explained the stark "choice" that faced him in Istanbul: "If I hadn't given up my kidney to that dog of a surgeon, my body would be floating somewhere in the Bosporus Strait."

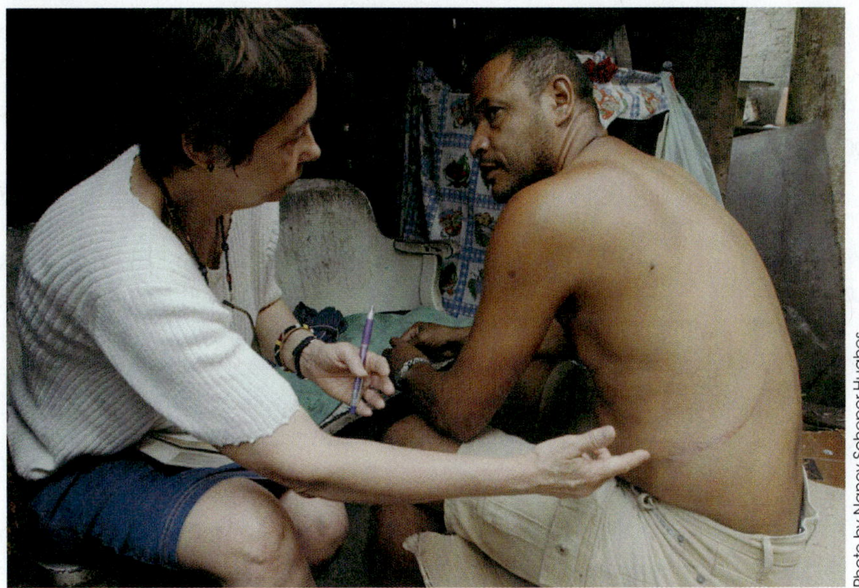

Photo by Nancy Scheper-Hughes

Nancy Scheper-Hughes with Alberty Alfonso da Silva, who was recruited from a Brazilian slum to provide an organ to an American woman from New York City.

30 Most brokers, however, offer themselves as altruistic intermediaries promising a better life to donors and recipients. The commonest scenario is of vulnerable individuals easily recruited and convinced to participate in the trade. The pressures are subtle; the coercion hidden.

31 In Baseco, a dockside slum and notorious "kidney-ville" in Manila, brokers recruit young men (and a small number of women) who are distant kin, related by blood or marriage or informal fosterage. Ray Arcella, a famous broker from the area, could often be seen with his arm slung loosely around the shoulders of his young recruits, some of whom referred to Ray as their uncle or their godfather. Ray's less than avuncular advice to his many "cousins" and "nephews" was that kidney selling was the best way of helping out one's family—since mechanized containers had rendered dock work, once Baseco's main source of employment, obsolete.

32 Brokers will hire local kidney hunters—often former sellers—to do the dirty work of recruiting their neighbors and extended family members. In these seemingly consensual transactions, controlling behavior, fraud, and manipulation are well hidden.

The Sellers

33 Kidney sellers are predictably poor and vulnerable: the displaced, the disgraced, or the dispossessed. They are the debtors, ex-prisoners, or mental patients, the stranded Eastern European peasants, the Turkish junk dealers, Palestinian refugees, runaway soldiers from Iraq and Afghanistan, Afro-Brazilians from the *favelas* and slums of northeast Brazil, and Andean Indians.

34 Most enter willingly into a "transaction" in which they agree to the terms, which are verbal, but only realize later how they have been deceived, defrauded, or cheated. Few are informed enough to give consent. They do not understand the seriousness of the surgery, the conditions under which they will be detained before and after the operation, or what they are likely to face with respect to the discomfort or immediate inability to resume their normally physically demanding jobs.

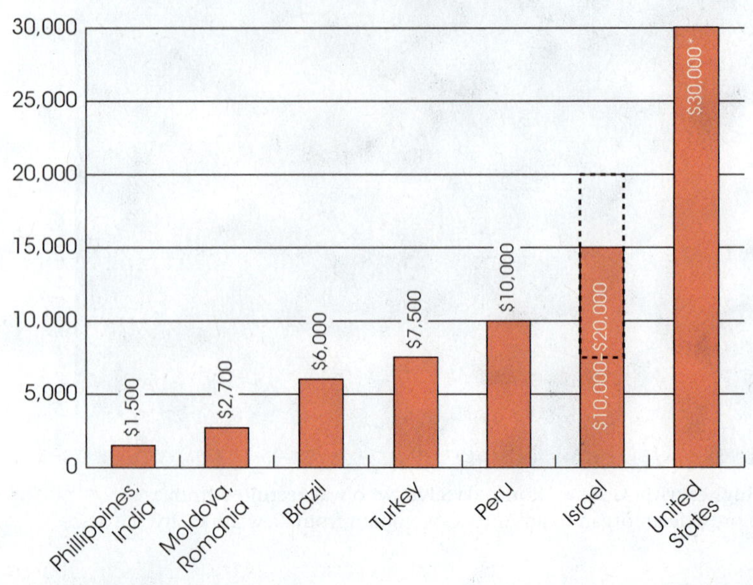

35 Some in the slums of Manila, as in the slums of Brazil, were underage teens who were counseled by brokers to fabricate names and add a few years to their age to make them "acceptable" to the surgeons. Many of those trafficked deny the "sale," saying that what they were paid was too small to constitute a sale for something as "priceless" as a non-renewable body part. In these unconventional transactions, the boundaries between gift, commodity, and theft are decidedly blurred.

36 Male kidney sellers tend to minimize the trauma they experienced to protect their pride. But their reserve often crumbles under gentle but probing questioning of how their lives have been affected. Some male sellers in Moldova denied that they were "trafficked" because the language of

trafficking made them sound like female "prostitutes," a stigma they could not live with. Others become obsessed with the kidney sale and attribute all the misfortunes that occurred before or since to that one act of "stupidity." Among a group of 40 Moldovan kidney sellers we followed from 2001 to 2009, there were deaths from suicide, failure of the remaining kidney, and even from battering by angry villagers who felt that the sellers had disgraced their village. Some were banished from their homes and disappeared.

The Brokers

37 The brokers, who may be transplant surgeons, or organized crime figures, co-ordinate transplant tour junkets that bring together relatively affluent kidney patients from Japan, Italy, Israel, Canada, Taiwan, the United States, and Saudi Arabia with the impoverished sellers of healthy organs.

38 Transplant brokers and organ traffickers are ever more sophisticated, changing their modus operandi, realizing that their engagements with public and private hospitals in foreign locations are severely time-limited. Israeli brokers, for example, recently confided that they either have to pay to gain access to deceased donor pools in Russia or Latin America (Colombia, Peru, and Panama in particular), or they have to set up new temporary sites and locations (Cyprus, Azerbaijan, and Costa Rica) for facilitating illicit transplants quickly and for a short period of time, already anticipating police, government, and/or international interventions. They are always prepared to move quickly to new locations where they have established links to clandestine transplant units, some of them no more sophisticated than a walk-in medical clinic or a rented ward in a public hospital.

The Buyers

39 Transplant tourists are a varied but determined and risk-taking population, willing to travel to "parts unknown" to purchase a stranger's kidney. They pay for a package deal; they do not know—nor do they want to know—the exact price that will be paid to the person who will deliver their fresh kidney. They *do* want to know whether the purchased organ will come from a healthy person, an educated person, a person of acceptable race and ethnicity. (Ethnicity matters to them because it might signify a "closer" or a "better" match.) They want a kidney that has not had to work hard for a living, and they want their surgeon to make sure they get access to the seller's healthiest kidney. There is a preference for male donors between the ages of 20–30 years. Transplant tourists are asked to pay a great deal of money—normally somewhere between $100,000 and $180,000—of which the sellers receive a mere fraction. Some buyers refuse kidneys from women, expressing a kind of old-fashioned chivalry, others an old-fashioned sexism. Men are by far the greatest purchasers.

40 In 2010, I was paid a visit by a sixty-something man from southern California who insisted on setting me straight on certain matters. David* wanted me to know what it felt like to be in his shoes. "Dialysis is like a living death," he said. "You get cataracts, problems in your gut, you can hardly eat. You lose your libido, you lose the ability to relieve yourself until finally you stop urinating altogether. You lose

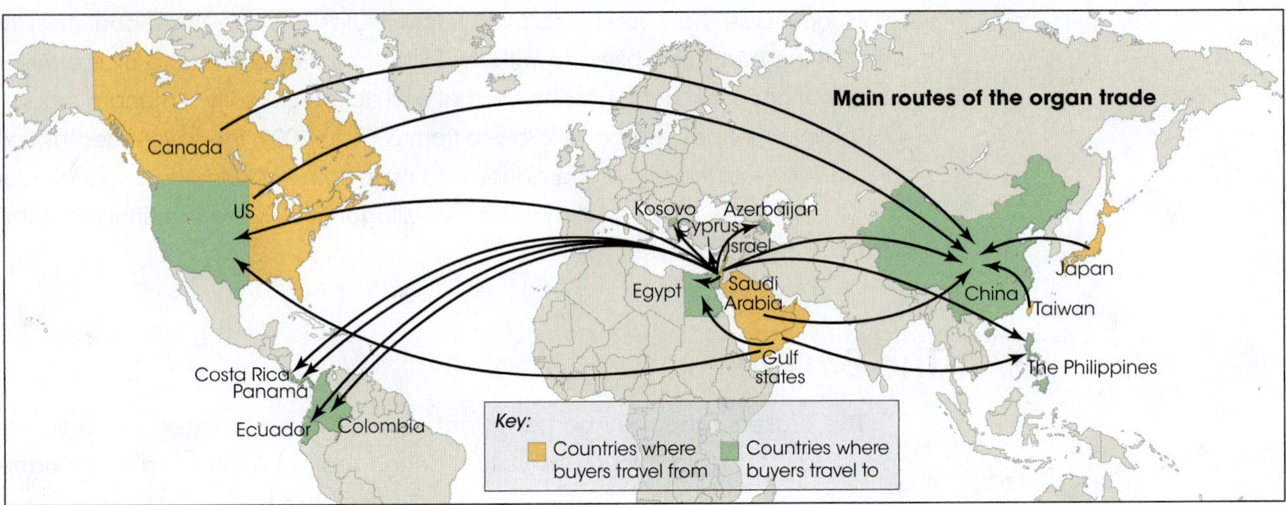

your energy, you become anemic, and you are cold all the time. You get deeply depressed."

41 He was put into contact with a surgeon and his broker in Tel Aviv, who required him to settle the entire package—$150,000—in advance for a transplant at an undisclosed location. Putting his fate in their hands, David travelled to Israel, and following cursory medical exams, he flew with the Israeli surgeon and his broker on to Istanbul where they picked up a second surgeon. "One takes out and the other puts in," was the simple explanation. Only in Istanbul was David told that his transplant would take place in Kosovo, a country he knew nothing about. The day before flying there, the broker announced that police had broken into the Medicus Clinic in Pristina, and that the planned transplant there was now unavailable. However, he was willing to offer, at a cut-price rate, another option that had opened up in Baku, Azerbaijan. And that is where David finally received his kidney, from a seller from Central Asia.

The New Generation

42 Following the Istanbul Summit in 2008, the Declaration of Istanbul Custodian Group was instituted. For the last eight years, it has been working closely with The Transplantation Society, the World Health Organization (WHO), and a vast network of transplant professionals to negotiate with public health and other government officials to create new laws to encourage deceased donor programs, promote transplant self-sufficiency within nations, and discourage transplant tourism. It has also exerted pressure on hospitals to stop sheltering the outlier surgeons who perform transplants involving foreign patients and trafficked kidney suppliers. But illicit transplant trafficking schemes remain robust, exceedingly mobile, resilient and generally one step ahead of the game.

43 The new generation of organ traffickers is also more ruthless. During the Beijing Olympics, brokers had their supply cut off after foreign access to organs harvested from executed Chinese prisoners was shut down. Undeterred, they began to pursue transplants from living donors, some of them trafficked Vietnamese, others naïve

villagers in parts of China where blood-selling programs had groomed people to accept kidney selling as another possibility.

44 The sites of illicit transplants have expanded within Asia, the Middle East, Central Asia, Eastern Europe, Central and Latin America, Europe, and the United States. As for the recruitment of kidney sellers, they can be found in almost any nation. One crisis after another has supplied the market with countless political and economic refugees who fall like ripe, low-hanging fruit into the hands of the human traffickers.

10-15 years
Life span of a kidney from a deceased donor

15-20 years
Life span of a kidney from a living donor

Source: Explore Transplant

45 Prosecutions are difficult. In most instances a few culprits, usually lower-ranking brokers and kidney sellers, are convicted. The surgeons, without whom no organ trafficking crimes can be facilitated, and the hospital administrators often escape, pleading ignorance. The famous Netcare case in Durban, South Africa, is a case in point. A total of 109 illicit transplants were performed at Saint Augustine's Hospital, including five in which the donors were minors. A police sting resulted in several plea bargains from various brokers and their accomplices. Netcare, the largest medical corporation in South Africa, pleaded guilty to having facilitated the transplants. The immediate result was the plummeting of Netcare stocks.

46 The four surgeons and two transplant coordinators who were indicted held fast to their not-guilty plea. Their defense was that they had been deceived by the company and its lawyers, who had stated these international surgeries were legal. In December 2012, they were given a permanent stay of prosecution and the state was ordered to pay their legal costs. It is fair to state that rogue transplant surgeons operate with considerable immunity. This is unfortunate because they constitute the primary link in the transplant-trafficking business.

114,690
organs reported transplanted in 2012

77,818
kidneys transplanted in 2012

≤10%
of global demand

Source: Global Observatory on Donation & Transplantation

A Victimless Crime?

47 Because human trafficking for organs is seen to benefit some very sick people at the expense of other, less visible or dispensable people, some prosecutors and judges have treated it as a victimless crime. When New Jersey federal agents caught Levy Izhak Rosenbaum, a hyperactive international kidney trafficker who had sold transplant packages for upwards of $180,000, the FBI had no idea what a "kidney salesman" was. The prosecutors could not believe that prestigious U.S. hospitals and surgeons had been complicit with the scheme, or that the trafficked sellers had been deceived and at times coerced. The federal case ended in a plea bargain in 2011 in which Rosenbaum admitted guilt for just three incidents of brokering kidneys for payment, although he acknowledged having been in the business for over a decade.

48 At the sentencing in July 2012, the judge was impressed by the powerful show of support from the transplant patients who arrived to praise the trafficker and beg that he be shown mercy. The one kidney-selling victim, Elhan Quick, presented as a surprise witness by the prosecution, was a young black Israeli, who had been recruited to travel to a hospital in Minnesota to sell his kidney to a 70-year-old man from Brooklyn. Although Mr. Cohen had 11 adult children, not one was disposed to donate a life-saving organ to their father. They were, however, willing to pay $20,000 to a stranger.

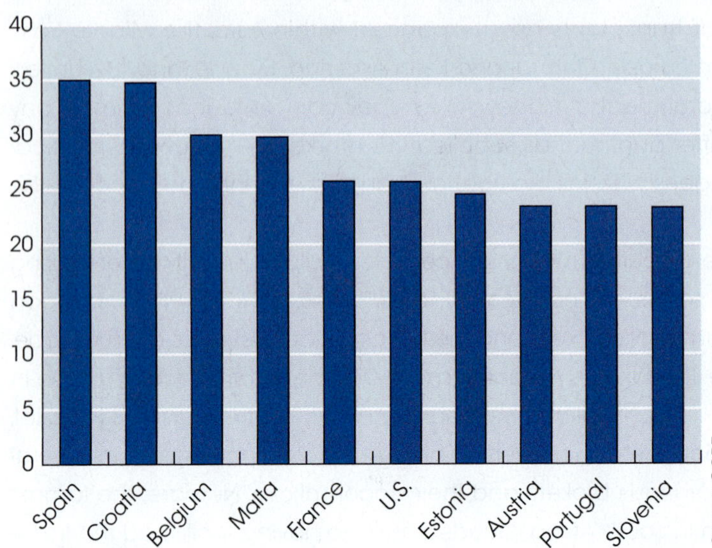

49 Quick testified that he agreed to the donation because he was unemployed at the time, alienated from his community, and hoped to do a meritorious act that would improve his social standing. On arrival at the transplant unit, however, he had misgivings and asked his "minder," Ito, the Israeli enforcer for the trafficking network, if he could get out of the deal as he had changed his mind. These were the last words he uttered before going under anesthesia.

50 His testimony had no impact. The judge concluded that it was a sorry case. She hated to send Rosenbaum to a low-security prison in New Jersey for two-and-a-half years as she was convinced that deep down he was a "good man." She argued that Elhan Quick had not been defrauded; he was paid what he was promised. "Everyone," she said, "got something out of this deal."

Closing Down the Networks

51 Convicted brokers and their kidney hunters are easily replaced by other criminals—the rewards of their crimes ensure that. Prosecuting transplant professionals, on the other hand, would definitely interrupt the networks. Professional sanctions—such as loss of license to practice—could be very effective. Outlaw surgeons and their colleagues cooperate within a code of silence equal to that of the Vatican. International bodies like the UN and the EU need to take concerted action on the legal framework in order to prosecute these international crimes.

52 Prosecutors look kindly on kidney buyers because they are sick and looking to save their lives. But buyers have no qualms about taking a kidney from deprived persons without any medical insurance, any future, and sometimes no home. They have to be made accountable.

53 Until we can revolutionize the practice of transplantation, a case needs to be made for a more modest medicine that realizes our lives are not limitless. This is a difficult message to convey when transplant patient advocacy groups and religious organizations have sprung up demanding unobstructed access to transplants and to the life-saving "spare" organs of "the other," as if this were a moral crusade.

54 The kidney is the blood diamond of our times. The organ trade is one of the more egregious examples of late capitalism where poor bodies are on the market in the service of rich bodies.

---

* Names marked by an asterisk are pseudonyms.

1. Organs Watch was co-founded with Lawrence Cohen. They are both professors of medical anthropology at the University of California, Berkeley, who had made initial anthropological forays into the various sites where illicit transplant operations were arranged. Over the years they have been joined by a number of independent medical human rights activists from the countries in which they have worked.
2. As identified by Organs Watch, WHO, The UN Office on Drugs and Crime and the Declaration of Istanbul Custodian Group.

Getting Ready to Write

Checking Your Comprehension MySkillsLab®

Answer each of the following questions using complete sentences.

1. Why is the number of patients who are waiting for organs growing? Why is the supply of organs provided by young, healthy people decreasing?
2. Who does the author believe will be the source of "donated" (actually sold) organs in the not-too-distant future?
3. In 2012, what was the most commonly transplanted organ? Approximately how many of these organs are trafficked each year?
4. In the United States, what types of organizations often act as fronts for organ-trafficking operations?
5. According to the author, why do men who sell their kidneys tend to underplay the consequences?

Strengthening Your Vocabulary

Identify at least five words used in the reading that are unfamiliar to you. Using context, word parts, or a dictionary, write a brief definition of each word.

Examining the Reading: Drawing an Idea Map

Create an idea map of "Human Traffic: Exposing the Brutal Organ Trade." Start with the title and thesis and include the main points of the selection.

Reading and Writing: An Integrated Perspective MySkillsLab®

1. Do you believe it should be legal in the United States for healthy people to sell their organs to those who wish to purchase them? Write a journal entry explaining your answer.
2. Does the author believe that some human lives are more important or more valuable than other human lives? Discuss.
3. Why does the author begin the article by discussing a slide of Filipino men displaying their "sacred wound"?
4. The author recounts two conversations with people who have sought kidneys on the black market: Jim Deal (beginning in paragraph 5) and David (beginning in paragraph 40). Why does she recount the details of her discussions with these men?
5. The author has included seven visual aids with this reading (six graphics and one photo). Write a one-sentence summary of the main point of each visual aid.
6. Why did the author include the story of Ji-Hun (beginning in paragraph 13)?
7. Are the last two paragraphs of the article—paragraphs 53 and 54—a good summary of the author's argument? As you finished reading the article, did you find yourself agreeing with the author in these last two paragraphs?

Thinking and Writing Critically MySkillsLab®

1. What inferences can you make from the author's recounting of her conversation with Jim Deal? In other words, what can you infer about Jim Deal that is not explicitly stated in the article? What can you infer about Ji-Hun that is not explicitly stated in the article? (For more on making inferences, see Chapter 12.)

2. This article is predominantly factual, but it does contain some opinions. One example is "Human trafficking for organs is a relatively small and contained problem, one that could be dealt with efficiently with the political will to do so" (paragraph 24). Identify at least two other opinions in the reading. Do you agree with each of these opinions? (For more on opinions, see Chapter 12.)

3. How would you describe the author's feelings about her topic? Point to some sentences or paragraphs where the author's feelings about organ trafficking are evident. Use three words to describe the author's tone. (To learn more about tone, see Chapter 12.)

4. Is the author qualified to write about this topic? Why or why not? (For more on assessing an author's qualifications, see Chapter 12.)

5. Do you see any bias in this reading? If so, where, and would you describe the bias as light, moderate, or heavy? (For more on bias, see Chapter 13.)

6. Explain the connotations and denotations of the following words and phrases: "First World medicine" (paragraph 12); "count the kidney loot in crisp one hundred dollar bills" (paragraph 14); "hospital for the Hollywood stars" (paragraph 15); "outlaw surgeons willing to break the law and violate professional codes of ethics" (paragraph 27). (For more on connotation and denotation, see Chapter 13.)

7. The author uses figurative language in the last paragraph of the selection: "The kidney is the blood diamond of our times." What type of figurative language is this? What does the author mean? (To learn more about figurative language, see Chapter 13.)

8. What is the author's main argument in this selection? What types of evidence does she provide to support her claims? How strong is this evidence? (For more on evaluating evidence, see Chapter 14.)

Writing About the Reading MySkillsLab®

1. Write an essay in which you argue for or against the position that everyone should check the "organ donor" box on his or her driver's license.

2. There are many people on waiting lists for organ donation. What criteria should be used to determine who receives an organ transplant? Should the rule be "first requested, first given"? Should a 20-year-old person receive preference over a 90-year-old person? Should a healthy person be given preference over someone who is sick and has a limited life expectancy? Write an essay in which you explore some of these questions and offer some guidelines.

3. Write an essay in which you outline some ways that nations can increase their supply of organs so that the black market for organ transplants can be eliminated.

Read and Respond to the Theme

Synthesizing Ideas

1. Of the crimes discussed in these selections, which do you find the most upsetting or serious? Which do you find the least upsetting or serious? Why?
2. All of these readings use data to support their key points. In what other ways are these readings similar? How are they dissimilar?
3. Two of the readings in this section use the word "trafficking." What exactly does this word mean in relation to crime? What other types of illegal trafficking exist?
4. Why are you unlikely to become a victim of human trafficking or organ trafficking? How does your country of residence play into your answer?
5. Compare the writing style in each of the readings. Which did you enjoy reading the most? The least? Why? Which do you think provides the best model to follow if you need to write an essay for your criminal justice or sociology class?

Writing About the Readings

1. Suppose someone asks you for a brief summary of two of the following topics: computer crime, human trafficking, and organ trafficking. Write one paragraph summarizing each topic. Your goal is to provide a broad overview of the crime, its perpetrators, and its victims.
2. To which of the crimes mentioned in these readings do you personally feel the most vulnerable? Why? Write an essay in which you explore why you are at risk of these crimes and what you can do to minimize this risk.
3. All of the readings in this section emphasize the international aspects of crime. In other words, crime is not simply a U.S. phenomenon. However, the United States has the highest rate of imprisonment in the world. Write an essay in which you explore some ways to decrease the U.S. prison population while controlling crime.
4. Suppose you could work at a nonprofit organization that advocates for human rights. Which type of organization would you work for? For example, would you work to get the death penalty abolished? Would you work to feed the poor and hungry? Would you work to increase the minimum wage? Write an essay explaining your choice.
5. The authors argue for the criminalization of trafficking. What types of behavior should be criminalized and punished? Write an essay explaining your reasons.

Theme 2

Journalism: A Changing Field in a Digital Age

Journalism has been an important force in society since the invention of the printing press. In fact, journalists are often called the "fourth estate" because of their role in bringing news to the public, uncovering facts, investigating crimes and cover-ups, and keeping politicians honest. There is no denying, however, that journalism is changing as the world moves from paper-based media (such as newspapers and magazines) toward online and video-based news sources. The readings in this section examine some of the challenges facing journalists in modern society, outlining the changes that are affecting today's news media, looking at some of the moral questions that journalists face, and proposing rules for the effective use of photos in a visual age.

Reading 1: (Textbook) An Inside Look at Today's News Media, by John Vivian

Reading 2: (Article) The Media Need to Stop Inspiring Copycat Murders. Here's How, by Zeynep Tufekci

Reading 3: (Article) Photojournalism in the Age of New Media, by Jared Keller

An Inside Look at Today's News Media

The following excerpt, "An Inside Look at Today's News Media," was originally published in a textbook, *The Media of Mass Communication*, 11th edition. The fact that the book has gone through eleven editions hints that it is a widely used and highly respected resource for the college classroom. As you read, note the features the author has used to engage student interest. How does the author make his opinions known about various topics?

Thinking Before Reading

1. Preview the reading, using the steps discussed in Chapter 1, page 4.
2. Connect the reading to your own experience by answering the following questions:
   a. How do you tend to learn about the news? For example, do you read Web sites, magazines, or newspapers? Do you prefer to watch TV news or Web broadcasts? Do you listen to news reports on the radio?
   b. Do you think the news media cover all the stories they should? What types of stories would you like to see more often? What types of stories would you like to see less often?
3. Mark and annotate as you read.

An Inside Look at Today's News Media

John Vivian

Variables Affecting News

STUDY PREVIEW

1 The variables that determine what is reported include things beyond a journalist's control, such as how much space or time is available to tell stories. Also, a story that might receive top billing on a slow news day might not even appear on a day when an overwhelming number of major stories are breaking.

MEDIApeople

CLEVER, SMART, DORKY?

Rachel Maddow Rachel Maddow broke into the old boys' club of cable television, dominated by Bill O'Reilly at Fox, Larry King at CNN and Keith Olbermann at MSNBC, with a distinctive take on political news.

2 Rachel Maddow was no ordinary kid. At 4, her mother remembers little Rachel would perch on a kitchen stool as her mom fixed breakfast and, still in pajamas, read the newspaper. At 7, during the 1980 presidential campaign, Maddow remembers an Intense repulsion to Ronald Reagan on television.

3 Maddow, now a leading political commentator on the political left, can't explain her Reagan-loathing as a grade-schooler. Noting Reagan's political conservatism, Maddow quips that some kind of "reverse engineering" must have set in. It's a self-deprecating line typical of Maddow's quick humor that draws audience chuckles and then double takes as the irony settles in.

4 The fact is that Maddow is hardly a slouch intellectually. She roots what she says on premises, not on whatever instinctive gut reactions may have been playing on her when she was 7. Maddow holds a degree from Stanford University in public policy. Then she won a Rhodes scholarship for an Oxford doctorate in political science.

5 Maddow has a common touch that goes beyond her trademark 501 baggy jeans and sneakers. Yes, that's how Maddow showed up for work at the radio network Air America, where she started a talk show in 2004. Maddow didn't change her style when, at age 35, the MSNBC television network gave her a show during the 2008 heated presidential campaign. The button-down MSNBC culture in Manhattan hasn't affected Maddow. She says she's still comfortable

dressing like a 13-year-old boy. Before going on the air nightly at MSNBC, however, she pulls a pantsuit from a closet of identical suits. She calls her style "butch dyke."

6 The common touch is more than wardrobe. Maddow earned money in college heavy-lifting. For a while she unloaded trucks. She also did yard-clearing for a landscaper. Then there was a job putting stamps on coffee packets. For reading she's as at home with Malthus and Machiavelli as with graphic novels.

7 At MSNBC in the intensive 2008 presidential campaign, Maddow quickly doubled the 9 p.m. Eastern audience to 1.9 million. Among viewers 25 to 54, she outdrew the CNN icon Larry King 27 of 44 nights in her first two months.

8 Her work ethic from college has carried into her career. Her days run 16 hours. She admits to getting only a couple hours of "drunk sleep" some nights.

9 Maddow's drive is contagious. Her crew at MSNBC, political junkies in their 20s and 30s, uses the same term "drunk sleep" and concedes to crankiness as they show up at mid-afternoon to brainstorm themes with Maddow for the night's show. The sessions harken to those all-night free-form college dorm jams on imponderables.

10 Maddow, Lanky and 6 foot, flops on the floor however she's comfortable at the moment. Bubbling through the give-and-take is a rich mixture of optimism for the future and skepticism about politicians—and bedrock patriotism. The session is heavy on the day's events and questions that need to be asked and on guests to line up to address the issues. Maddow twirls and lobs a foam basketball. Shifting her body on the floor, she scribbles ideas in a notebook.

11 The loosely structured planning is all rehearsal for Maddow—a kind of free-form cerebral internalizing. On air there is focus, although an informal feel that has attracted the young audience that the major television networks covet. There's a practiced sneering, her sarcasm punctuated with a trademark "Duh." Cliches, none. There is no doubt of Maddow being bright, authentic and original.

12 To be sure, Maddow has detractors. Her innuendos and nudge-nudge, wink-wink comments have been called theatrical and biased. Others see Maddow as finding a flavorful balance that is substantive and distinctly refreshing. For sure, Maddow resonates with a mass audience that finds the old boys' club that has dominated cable television suddenly stuffy.

News Hole

13 A variable affecting what ends up being reported as news is called the **news hole**. In newspapers the news hole is the space left after the advertising department has placed all the ads it has sold in the paper. The volume of advertising determines the number of total pages, and generally, the bigger the issue, the more room for news. Newspaper editors can squeeze fewer stories into a thin Monday issue than a fat Wednesday issue.

14 In broadcasting, the news hole tends to be more consistent. A 30-minute television newscast may have room for only 23 minutes of news, but the format doesn't vary. When the advertising department doesn't sell all seven minutes available for advertising, it usually is public-service announcements, promotional messages and program notes—not news—that pick up the slack. Even so, the news hole can vary in broadcasting. A 10-minute newscast can accommodate more stories than a five-minute newscast, and, as with newspapers, it is the judgment of journalists that determines which events make it.

15 News hole, of course, is a non-issue on the Internet.

News Flow

16 Besides the news hole, the **news flow** varies from day to day. A story that might be displayed prominently on a slow news day can be passed over entirely in the competition for space on a heavy news day.

17 On one of the heaviest news days of all time—June 4, 1989—death claimed Iran's Ayatollah Khomeini, a central figure in U.S. foreign policy; Chinese young people and the government were locked in a showdown in Tiananmen Square; the Polish people were voting to reject their one-party communist political system; and a revolt was under way in the Soviet republic of Uzbekistan. That flow of major nation-rattling events pre-empted many stories that otherwise would have been considered news.

18 Heavy news days cannot be predicted. One would have occurred if there had been a confluence on a single day of these events: Hurricane Katrina, the BP Deepwater Horizon oil platform explosion, the death of Osama bin Laden, the conviction of Michael Jackson's physician, the Japanese tsunami nuclear disaster, the shooting of Congresswoman Gabby Gifford, and the 3,000th U.S. combat death in Afghanistan.

19 In a broader sense, an issue like global warming with the future of the planet at stake can end up neglected. In 2012, for example, coverage of health-care reforms, war in Afghanistan and the presidential election squeezed out climate change as an issue in U.S. news media.

News Staffing

20 Another variable affecting news is **staffing**. News coverage is affected by whether reporters are in the right place at the right time. A newsworthy event in Nigeria will receive short shrift on U.S. television if the network correspondents for Africa are occupied with a natural disaster in next-door Cameroon. A radio station's city government coverage will slip when the city hall reporter is on vacation or if the station can't afford a substitute reporter at city hall.

Perceptions About Audience

21 How a news organization perceives its audience affects news coverage. The *National Enquirer* lavishes attention on unproven cancer cures that the New York *Times* treats briefly if at all. The *Wall Street Journal* sees its purpose as news for readers who have special interests in finance, the economy and business. The Bloomberg cable network was established to serve an audience more interested in quick market updates, brief analysis and trendy consumer news than the kind of depth offered by the *Journal*.

22 The perception that a news organization has of its audience is evident in a comparison of stories on different networks' newscasts. CNN may lead newscasts with a coup d'état in another country, while Bloomberg leads with a new government economic forecast and Comedy Central with the announcement of a comedian's tour.

Competition

23 Two triggers of adrenaline for journalists are landing a scoop and, conversely, being scooped. Journalism is a competitive business, and the drive to outdo other news organizations keeps news publications and newscasts fresh with new material. Competition has an unglamorous side. Journalists constantly monitor each other to identify events that they missed and need to catch up on to be competitive. This catch-up aspect of the news business contributes to similarities in coverage, which scholar Leon Sigal calls the **consensible nature of news**. It also is called "pack" and "herd" journalism.

24 In the final analysis, news is the result of journalists scanning their environment and making decisions, first on whether to cover certain events and then on how to cover them. The decisions are made against a backdrop of countless variables, many of them changing during the reporting, writing and editing processes.

Getting Ready to Write

Checking Your Comprehension MySkillsLab®

Answer each of the following questions using complete sentences.

1. Is the "news hole" more consistent in newspapers or in broadcasting? Why? Does the "news hole" apply to the Internet?
2. What effect does the news flow tend to have on news coverage of broader social issues in the United States?
3. How does the news flow affect coverage of broader societal issues such as health-care reform?
4. Why is it impossible to predict heavy news days?
5. In paragraph 23, the author discusses the concepts of "landing a scoop" and "being scooped." What do these terms mean?

Strengthening Your Vocabulary MySkillsLab®

Identify at least five words used in the reading that are unfamiliar to you. Using context, word parts, or a dictionary, if necessary, write a brief definition of each word.

Examining the Reading: Drawing an Idea Map

Create an idea map of "An Inside Look at Today's News Media." Start with the title and thesis and include the main points of the selection.

Reading and Writing: An Integrated Perspective MySkillsLab®

1. How do you like to read or hear your news delivered? Do you like it to be just the facts, or do you like a mix of fact and opinion? Do you tend to engage with media or stations that support viewpoints you already hold? (For example, many people who are politically conservative prefer

Fox News, while many who are less conservative prefer NPR.) Write an journal entry answering these questions.

2. Many of the major Internet sites have a news feature. Examine several of the sites, looking for similarities in the stories covered. Write a summary of one of the major news stories that has been covered within the last day or two. What happened and who was involved?

3. This selection originally appeared in a textbook. Why does the author include the "Study Preview" in paragraph 1?

4. The selection offers a special-interest box about Rachel Maddow titled "Media People" (paragraphs 2-12). What is the purpose of this box?

5. This selection includes just one image: a photo of journalist Rachel Maddow. What other types of photos or visual aids would you have found useful? Describe at least two additional visual aids that would be helpful to readers.

6. The author occasionally uses informal language in the selection. For example, in paragraph 14, he says that public-service announcements can "pick up the slack." Identify at least two other examples of informal language in the selection. How does the use of informal language affect the selection's readability?

7. Think about the links between reading and writing in TV journalism. In what ways are news broadcasts "written"? Which components of the news are written, and which are not? Explain.

Thinking and Writing Critically MySkillsLab®

1. Describe the author's opinion of Rachel Maddow. Do you think he is a fan? What would the author consider Maddow's strongest points? Her weakest points?

2. Identify at least two opinions in the reading. One example comes from paragraph 11: "On air there is focus, although an informal feel that has attracted the young audience that the major television networks covet." (For more on opinion, see Chapter 12.)

3. How would you describe the author's feelings about his topic? Point to some sentences or paragraphs where the author's feelings about journalism are evident. How would you describe the author's tone? (To learn more about tone, see Chapter 12.)

4. The author states that "news is the result of journalists scanning their environment and making decisions." What exactly does the author mean by "scanning the environment"? If you were a journalist, what would you do to scan the environment?

5. Explain the connotations and denotations of the following words and phrases in paragraph 12: "nudge-nudge, wink-wink comments," "theatrical and biased," "flavorful balance," "substantive and distinctly refreshing," "old boys' club," and "suddenly stuffy." (For more on connotation and denotation, see Chapter 13.)

6. Paragraphs 21-22 discuss the term "perceptions of audience." Choose two or three broadcasts (whether TV-, radio-, or Internet-based) and discuss the intended audience for each. Which elements of the broadcast signal the targeted audience?

7. How would you evaluate the author's use of evidence in this selection? Has he provided enough evidence to support his claims? Do you find any pieces of evidence particularly helpful? If not, what types of evidence might he cite to make his argument stronger? (For more on evaluating evidence, see Chapter 14.)

Writing About the Reading MySkillsLab®

1. Suppose you are the programming director of a half-hour news broadcast. Write an essay in which you describe the types of stories you would run and why.
2. Suppose a news agency has hired you to prepare a report. The agency is looking for ways to bring the news to students of your generation. That is, they want advice on how to present and broadcast the news in a way that appeals to people your age. Write an essay in which you explore some of the advice you would give the news agency.
3. Watch or read a soft-news broadcast or publication, and then write an essay describing and critiquing the content. Some question you might consider: How accurate is the information presented? How useful is it? Would your time have been better spent doing something else? Why do you think people like watching soft news? How might soft news be made more "serious" while still being entertaining?

The Media Need to Stop Inspiring Copycat Murders. Here's How.

The following article, "The Media Needs to Stop Inspiring Copycat Murders. Here's How," was originally published in *The Atlantic*, a highly respected magazine that often features in-depth articles on topics of current interest. As you read, note the format the author has used. Why has she chosen to use boldfaced type and a numbered list in the second half of the article?

Thinking Before Reading

1. Preview the reading, using the steps discussed in Chapter 1, page 4.
2. Connect the reading to your own experience by answering the following questions:
   a. Can you provide an example of a recent murderous rampage? Do you know the name(s) of the alleged or proven killer(s)?
   b. Do you think the media should immediately seek interviews with the friends of families of people who have been murdered?
3. Mark and annotate as you read.

The Media Need to Stop Inspiring Copycat Murders. Here's How.

Zeynep Tufekci

After a wave of teen suicides in the 1980s, news outlets began reporting on these deaths more cautiously. Similar guidelines could help prevent more shooting sprees.

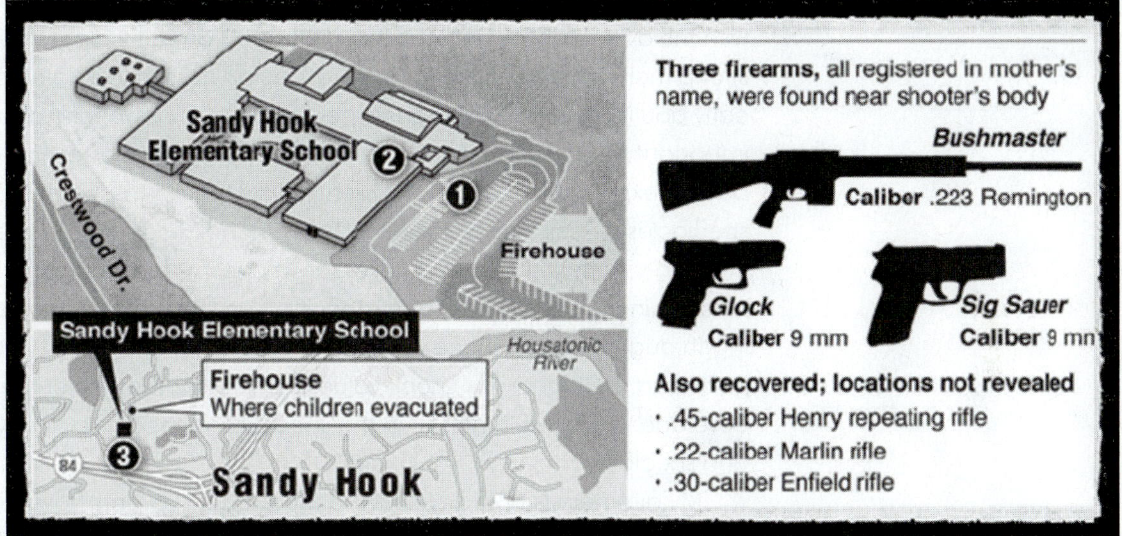

After the Newtown shootings, newspapers printed detailed information about the killer and his methods. (McClatchy Papers)

1 You might not have noticed, but the mass media rarely reports on suicides, particularly teen suicides. When it does, the coverage is careful, understated, and dampened. This is no accident: Following guidelines endorsed by the Centers for Disease Control and National Institutes of Mental Health, the media carefully and voluntarily avoids sensationalizing such deaths especially among teenagers. They almost never make the news unless the person is a public figure; methods of suicide are rarely mentioned; suicide pacts are not reported upon.

2 This is for good reason: Suicide, especially among teens, is contagious. It's a morbidly attractive idea that offers an established path of action for a troubled youngster. And we know from research in many fields that establishing a path of action—a complete narrative in which you can visualize your steps and their effects—is important in enabling follow-through. This, for example, is exactly why political campaigns ask people about where and how they plan to vote—imagined events are more likely to be carried out in real life. If you have a full story in your head, you are more likely to enact it, step by step. We also know such "contagion" effects are especially strong in adolescence and young adulthood—an especially turbulent time for mental health.

3 As a sociologist, I am increasingly concerned that the tornado of media coverage that swirls around each such mass killing, and the acute interest in the identity and characteristics of the shooter—as well as the detailed and sensationalist reporting of the killer's steps just before and during the shootings—may be creating a vicious cycle of copycat effects similar to those found in teen and other suicides.

4 Indeed, the rate of mass public shootings in the United States has been accelerating. In 2012 alone, there were at least a dozen of them. Seven dead at an Oakland college in April. Five killed at a Seattle coffee shop in May. Twelve killed in an Aurora, Colorado, movie theater in July. Six murdered at a Wisconsin Sikh temple in August, and six more killed in Minneapolis in September. Three dead in the Milwaukee spa shootings in October. And most recently, and unimaginably, 20 children as young as six, along with six adults, murdered at Sandy Hook Elementary School. The trend is disturbingly clear.

5 As many have pointed out, these mass public rampages are inextricably linked with the availability of high-capacity guns and ammunition, as well as with lack of strong mental health infrastructure—especially for those in late adolescence and early adulthood, the typical onset period for major psychotic disorder. But it's also important to recognize that while mental illness plagues every society, the ways people express it are heavily influenced by the norms, heroes, anti-heroes, and spectacles of their own places and times. In the Middle Ages, psychosis may have involved visions of the devil, snakes, or witches. In the 21st century, it can involve dressing in pseudo-combat gear, donning numerous high-powered rifles, and walking through a public place in a blaze of violence. The shock value is part of the goal–and the higher the shock value, predictably, the higher the ensuing media coverage, which fuels interest in the shooter and creates a whirlwind of attention and spectacle.

6 My aim here is not to blame the media: such events have undeniable news value, and there is intense public interest in uncovering their details. But it's important to recognize that such incidents are not mono-causal, and sensational news coverage is, increasingly, part of the mix of events that contributes to these rampages. We need to figure out how to balance the public interest in learning about a mass shooting with the public interest in reducing copycat crime. The guidelines on reporting on teen suicides were established after a spate of teenage suicides in the United States, some through suicide pacts, in the 1980s. Those who created the guidelines looked at examples from other countries—for example, the subway suicides in Vienna in the 1980s, which decreased after the media changed its coverage—and provided specific recommendations: Don't refer to the word suicide in the headline. Don't report the method of the suicide. Don't present it as an inexplicable act of an otherwise healthy person.

7 With that as a model, here are some initial recommendations.

8 **1. Law enforcement should not release details of the methods and manner of the killings, and those who learn those details should not share them.** In other words, there should be no immediate stories about which guns exactly were used or how much robo-cop gear was utilized. There should be no extensive timelines—no details about which room was entered first or which victim was killed second. In particular, there should be no reporting of the killer's words or actions before or during the shooting. Yes, I am a scholar of social media and I understand that these things will leak. But there is a big difference between information that can only be found if you really look for it and news stories that are blasted by every television station and paper in the country. At a minimum, we can and should greatly delay the release of these details by weeks, if not months.

9 **2. If and when social media accounts of the killers are located, law enforcement should work with the platforms to immediately pull them**. Yes, there will be screenshots, and again, I am not proposing that such information can be entirely shut out. But by making it harder to find, we can dampen the impact of the spectacle.

10 **3. The name of the killer should not be revealed immediately**. If possible, law enforcement and media sources should agree to withhold it for weeks. The identity can be released later during trial (if there is one) or during the release of the investigative report. Once again, merely delaying the release of information may greatly reduce the spectacle effect. The name may "leak," but that is very different from the full blast of attention that currently surrounds the perpetrators immediately after each incident.

11 Similarly, the killer should not be profiled extensively, at least not at first. There should not be an intense search for clues or reasoning beyond "troubled person commits unspeakable act; wish he had gotten help earlier," in as flat a reporting style as possible. We know that the killers tend to be young men, and they tend to have mental health issues. We do not need to know which exact video games they played, what they wore, or what their favorite bands were.

12 **4. The intense push to interview survivors and loved ones in their most vulnerable moments should be stopped**. This, too, may help reduce the sense of spectacle and trauma.

13 I don't claim that these are the only and best ways to deal with this issue. but I offer them as fodder for a conversation that I hope will be taken up by media and mental health experts. And we shouldn't be concerned that such guidelines will be impossible to follow. Just yesterday, news outlets revealed that Richard Engel of NBC had been kidnapped in Syria—and released. The information about his capture, though obviously newsworthy, was held back in order to aid the negotiations and rescue efforts. There are many such cases of media voluntarily acting to dampen coverage of certain events, especially when it involves one of their own. Let's entreat them to do it for the sake of potential shooting victims as well.

Getting Ready to Write

Checking Your Comprehension

MySkillsLab®

Answer each of the following questions using complete sentences.

1. Why do the news media rarely report on teen suicides? To which guidelines do most of the media voluntarily adhere when reporting on teen suicide?
2. According to the author, what is the connection between shock value and media coverage of a crime?
3. What recommendation does the author make regarding the social media accounts of those who have gone on murderous rampages?
4. Does the author believe that in-depth profiles of mass murderers should be published? Why or why not?

Strengthening Your Vocabulary MySkillsLab®

Identify at least five words used in the reading that are unfamiliar to you. Using context, word parts, or a dictionary, if necessary, write a brief definition of each word.

Examining the Reading: Drawing an Idea Map

Create an idea map of "The Media Need to Stop Inspiring Copycat Murders. Here's How." Start with the title and thesis and include the main points of the selection.

Reading and Writing: An Integrated Perspective MySkillsLab®

1. What does the author mean by "'contagion' effects" (paragraph 2)? What other types of social phenomena seem to spread by contagion? (One example might be videos that go "viral.")
2. The author states that mass public rampages are inextricably linked to "the availability of high-capacity guns and ammunition" (paragraph 5). Do you agree or disagree with statement? Explain your answer in a journal entry.
3. The topic of this article is how to stop copycat murders. So why does the author begin her essay (paragraphs 1 and 2) by discussing teen suicide?
4. In paragraph 4, the author lists the details of a number of mass public shootings in clear, simple language. Why does she do so? What is the effect of this technique?
5. Why does the author use a numbered list (points 1–4) in paragraphs 8–12? What purpose does this type of formatting serve? How does it help readers?
6. Why does the author close the essay by recounting the story of Richard Engel's kidnapping?
7. How does the graphic that accompanies this article (page 463) add to or detract from the author's message? What argument would the author make about this type of graphic when it is used in reporting about mass public rampages?

Thinking and Writing Critically MySkillsLab®

1. What is the author implying with the following statement from paragraph 8? "There should be no reporting of the killer's words or actions before or during the shooting." (For more on making inferences, see Chapter 12.)
2. How does the author balance facts and opinions in this article? Which paragraphs are primarily fact based? Which are primarily opinion based? (For practice in identifying facts and opinions, see Chapter 12.)
3. Keeping in mind that this article is a primarily an opinion piece, would you say that the author is heavily biased? What does she favor? What is she against? Do you agree with her primary argument? (For more on bias, see Chapter 13.)
4. On what generalization is this article based? Evaluate how accurate this generalization is. (*Hint*: Look closely at the title. For further information on generalizations, see Chapter 13.)
5. Identify the assumption in paragraph 11. (For more about assumptions, see Chapter 13.)

6. Look closely at paragraphs 8–12. How would you evaluate the author's use of evidence in these paragraphs? Has she provided enough evidence to support her opinions? If not, what types of evidence might she cite to make her argument stronger? (For more on evaluating evidence, see Chapter 14.)

Writing About the Reading MySkillsLab®

1. Some people have argued that newscasts are no place for stories about celebrities or reality-show stars, and some news programs have begun refusing to air stories about particular celebrities who seem overexposed (and who make little contribution to society). What is your opinion of celebrity news coverage? Write an essay in which you argue for (pro) or against (con) widespread coverage of celebrities and their lives.
2. The author discusses two types of news stories—those reporting on teen suicides, and those reporting on murderous rampages—that the media should not report on. What other topics do you think the media should voluntarily refrain from reporting on, if any? Why? Write an essay expressing your opinion on this question.
3. The author ties mass public rampages to the easy availability of guns and ammunition. Suppose gun-control legislation is being considered in your state. This legislation would make it impossible for most people to obtain handguns. Would you support this legislation? Why or why not? Write an essay in which you argue one side or the other.

Photojournalism in the Age of New Media

The following article, "Photojournalism in the Age of New Media" was originally published in *The Atlantic*, a magazine founded in 1857. *The Atlantic* is considered a serious magazine for people who like to think deeply about political, governmental, and social matters. As you read, note how the author uses his own experiences and perceptions to argue his opinion.

Thinking Before Reading

1. Preview the reading, using the steps discussed in Chapter 1, page 4.
2. Connect the reading to your own experience by answering the following questions:
   a. When you read an article or textbook, how much attention do you pay to the accompanying photos?
   b. Have you ever uploaded an image to a social media account that has received a large number of "likes" or reposts? What made that image so popular?
3. Mark and annotate as you read.

Photojournalism in the Age of New Media

Jared Keller

Social media have given photojournalists a million extra eyes in conflict zones. But if a picture can say a thousand words, the trick is finding the right one.

1 An elderly woman kisses a riot soldier in the streets of Cairo. A building collapses in Tokyo. Bloodied bodies and dismembered limbs fill an infirmary in Benghazi. The images come to us through Twitter and Tumblr and Facebook, captured through mobile phones or Web-ready digital cameras. Far from the grit of revolutionary unrest or the tumult of a natural disaster, average people sit, transfixed.

2 This story is a familiar one. As new media tools and social networks have become more widely utilized, the powerful images of the world's crises are delivered directly to the laptops and smartphones of people around the globe. Since Iranian citizens filled the streets of Tehran in 2009 in defiance of President Mahmoud Ahmadinejad's regime, social media has allowed even the least tech-savvy people around the world to become bystanders to history.

3 While new media's value as an organizational tool during global crises has been much debated since the Iranian election protests in 2009, its role in the process of narrative storytelling is palpable. In places like Libya where journalists are outlawed—or disaster zones like post-quake Haiti where regular means of communication are interrupted—the linkages of social networks can be turned into a means of observing (or, in the case of a tech-savvy dictatorship, surveilling) the origins of political unrest or the makings of a world historical moment. But new media also comes with challenges for photojournalists: while a single snapshot may tell a thousand-word story, the trick is to get that story right.

4 The technical benefits of new media to photojournalists in crisis zones are equivalent to unrefined digital omniscience. A whole universe of photojournalists, both amateur and professional, is made available to the public through social networks, allowing news organizations to ferret out important stories using tools beyond their existing technical capabilities. "With regards to Twitter, it's a very useful tool in order to point journalistic organizations towards potential leads and potential developments in stories," said Santiago Lyon, director of photography for the Associated Press. The AP, alongside Reuters and Getty Images, provides the vast majority of editorial photos used by American news organizations. "When there's a breaking story, whether it's an ongoing crisis or a spot development—like a plane down in the Hudson—we're very actively trolling social media sites for imagery: performing searches, scraping Twitter and Facebook, soliciting information. There's a fairly robust mechanism within the AP to identify and capture citizen journalism . . . once we find something of interest, then it's incumbent on a specialist to take care of it. Content goes through a specific department for vetting. We look, apply, crosscheck, reference."

5 Since the camera phone has essentially turned any casual observer into a potential photojournalist, an extra pair of eyeballs in Libya could eventually become a temporary appendage of a larger news collecting organization. Lyon provides the example of Alaguri, a Benghazi resident who became the AP's sole set of eyes in Libya in mid-February as Western journalists were just entering the country. "We found a guy in Benghazi in Libya who had posted some pictures onto the Internet," Lyon said. "We tracked him down through his Facebook account. We made contact, had a conversation, asked relevant questions, ascertained that he was who he said he was, got permissions for his photos and retained him for a couple days of work. Because of that, we were able to have an exclusive look into the events in Benghazi last weekend when there was no other imagery coming out of Libya. Our customers were using that. It was a great journalistic scoop on the strength of good, virtual, shoeleather reporting and verification."

6 But verification can often be problematic, and the proper context and attribution are often lost in the space between retweets and Facebook shares. If they happen to make contact, how does a news organization know they're dealing with the photographer or copyright owner? How do we make arrangements to distribute the content? Is there a financial transaction involved? Even determining the original owner of a photograph becomes problematic. "It's very complicated because what happens on the social media becomes something of an echo chamber," said Lyon. "People scrape stuff off each others' accounts, or a contextual claim is far from good or solid."

7 If the original source of a photograph cannot be verified, the value of content is called into question. "We have to look at these things on a case-by-case basis. There's no general blanket approach other than 'they must be sure' that the content is what is says to be and the person is in a position to deal with it (the owner, or a proxy)," said Lyon. "Everything is assessed on its value . . . we see this at times when the material is superseded or overshadowed by our staff material (not as good, so we don't need it), or it's stuff that we absolutely need because we don't have it or it's from a hard-to-get-to location or whatever that may be."

8 The Agence France-Presse and Getty Images found themselves in hot water over copyright infringement shortly after the 2010 earthquake in Haiti. Photographer Daniel Morel managed to post exclusive post-quake images from the devastation in Port-Au-Prince on his Flickr and Twitter accounts. The images were stolen and re-distributed on Twitpic by a Dominican named Lisandro Suero. AFP and Getty licensed and distributed the photos with attribution to Suero to major news organizations—the *New York Times*, Time Inc, the *Washington Post*. In December 2010, Morel won a pre-trial victory in federal court against AFP and Getty for copyright infringement. "A news organization didn't do due diligence," said Lyon. "It's absolutely critical. No matter how compelling the content is, we always make sure to deal with the copyright owner."

9 While verification can be a technical or legal obstacle for photojournalists utilizing new media as a newsgathering resource, it lies at the heart of the ethical and aesthetic issues of photojournalism and crisis reporting. The

sudden influx of raw images from areas ravaged by political conflict and natural disasters may be a wealth of information, and news organizations with limited budgets may be more inclined to rely on citizen journalists on the ground, but they do not necessarily constitute the narrative storytelling at the heart of valuable photojournalism.

10 I spoke to the staff at the Pulitzer Center on Crisis Reporting, an independent organization that sponsors reporting on global affairs, about the evolving role of new media in photojournalism. Founded in 2006, the Pulitzer Center treats news coverage of systemic global issues as long-term media campaigns maintaining a spotlight on often-ignored topics, ranging from water and food insecurity to homophobia and stigma to fragile states and women and children in crisis.

11 "The Pulitzer definition of 'crisis' differs from the usual conception of the term," said Nathalie Applewhite, managing director of the Pulitzer Center. "It's not that crisis doesn't mean immediate crises, like earthquake and floods, but the perspective of the Pulitzer Center has to do primarily with systemic crises: what happens before, after, the underlying causes. New media is very significant in immediacy, but not totally in long term. It doesn't matter if there are a thousand cameras, it's the storytelling that's important. A photojournalist with an artistic vision that transcends superficial coverage. It's a different media space."

A Haitian woman awaits the results of an HIV test. (Andre Lambertson/Pulitzer Center on Crisis Reporting).

12 Applewhite points to the work of Andre Lambertson, a New York-based photographer, as an example of high-quality photojournalism. Lambertson traveled to Haiti following the 2010 earthquake to document the spread of HIV and AIDS in Port-au-Prince for the Pulitzer Center project After the Quake: HIV/AIDS in Haiti. "The Haitian government estimated that 24,000 Haitians were accessing ARVs before the earthquake; by mid summer, according to UNAIDS, fewer than 40 percent had access," wrote Lisa Armstrong, a print journalist accompanying Lambertson on the project, which launched on the Pulitzer Center's website in August 2010. "Hundreds of HIV positive people live in tent cities for internally displaced persons, where their weakened immunity, and the unrelenting heat and rain, make them more vulnerable to diseases. Sex in these IDP camps—both forced and consensual—will likely increase the spread of HIV"*. His work in Haiti exemplifies the qualities that define valuable photojournalism, according to Applewhite: "sensitive vs. sensational, images that really tell a story. "We want images that stand the test of time," Applewhite explained. "Snapshots and photos taken by camera phones are not things we can come back to learn from and understand something deeper. Images from Haiti and the Congo, these images are telling a much bigger story than what's in front of them that moment."

13 What happens to the traditional photojournalist in the new media landscape? "It could be a really negative thing," Applewhite said. "News agencies are often happy with random snapshots from Egypt and they don't necessarily need professional, thoughtful content all the time." Applewhite noted that crowd-sourced content can be complementary for professional photojournalists just as it is for the AP and Reuters, allowing photojournalists and news organizations to explore and gauge new networks. "Direct feeds are absolutely complementary from citizen journalists and bloggers can draw attention to an issue," she said, echoing the AP's Santiago Lyon. "But we would want to verify sources, make sure that information is telling the story that it's telling before it's publicized."

14 The staff at the Pulitzer Center is particularly sensitive to issues of verification. In crisis situations, verification often goes far beyond the copyright issues and associated legal ramifications that are a major concern for major news services like the Associated Press, Getty Images, and Reuters. An out-of-context photograph can prove disastrous in a post-conflict zone. "People take images as truth much more than words," Applewhite emphasized. "And images can be manipulated. They can be used by someone with a vested interest to frame things in a certain way. There's a certain caution that comes from a large news organization."

15 Senior editor Tom Hundley witnessed the effect of unverified or out of context images well before the advent of social media. During the NATO bombing in Kosovo and Serbia, the Serbian Ministry of War published an elaborate set of volumes, full of pictures and stories of civilians who had been killed, as part of a propaganda campaign. "It was full of gory pictures, people's grandmothers with bodies blown apart," Hundley recalled. "During much of that I was there along with 40 or 50 other reporters. We were basically prisoners at the Belgrade Hyatt except when we were trotted out to report on civilian casualties and collateral damage. The Croatian/Serbian governments all made horrendous use of radio, newspaper, and television."

16 Government manipulation of imagery is certainly an issue, but the high velocity of social networks that makes verification so problematic means that conflict imagery is often left open to misinterpretation and, subsequently, reactionary violence. "With images, there's a huge danger of producing false impressions or false information with bad analysis," said Jake Naughton, who does outreach and production at the Pulitzer Center. "Now it only takes 30 minutes to make a correction, but a lot can happen in a half hour in a conflict zone, especially with the speed that information travels."

17 Despite social media's drawbacks—the increasingly uncertain problem of verification and a shifting emphasis to raw, immediate photographs—new media technology affords professional journalists and news organizations the right tools to engage in the type of storytelling that makes for valuable photojournalism. Social media, like so many other tools, isn't inherently good or bad; it simply needs to be deployed in the appropriate manner to accurately tell a story. With regards to longer and less-immediate crisis stories—famine, environmental decay, or post-conflict reconstruction—social media can keep an audience engaged long after bloody images are dropped from the evening newscasts. "One of the things that helps us creatively is playing out content over a long period of time," explained Maura Youngman, a new media strategist at the Pulitzer Center. "Sometimes the things we produce may fall off the map after

a couple of weeks, and stories may not be as digestible. Using new media and social media to create creative inroads allows people to come in and digest and enjoy information."

18 Youngman points to Lambertson's work in Haiti as an example of social media's power to keep a story alive. "Eight months after Andre's project was completed, we're re-releasing photos along with poems in English and Creole. New media allows us to find additional channels to take these stories and keep them alive. With the systemic crises we're dealing with, we're not just running to stay on top of the news cycle but trying to keep things in people's minds. This is the power of our social media channels."

19 The real test for working photojournalists is to reconcile the technical realities of the new media landscape with the aesthetic and ethical requirements of practical journalism. "Never has there been a time when you needed a professional class of journalists more than right now," Naughton said. "There's a real resurgence in formal and aesthetic qualities in contemporary journalism, the idea of aesthetics and photographers as storytellers, not just people who are be able to break the news."

20 In the past three years, new media has essentially experienced a baptism in fire as a newsgathering tool. The goal for institutions like the Pulitzer Center is to merge new media tools with the traditional. Mainstream journalists tell a story while creating links with local journalists and local channels through social media, and use new media tools to effectively convey a narrative to readers around the world. Maintaining the aesthetic balance with the speed of social media and keeping technology alive is important for us to keep stories going.

*The post originally attributed writing by Lisa Armstrong from the After The Quake: HIV/AIDS in Haiti project to Andre Lambertson. The Pulitzer Center's Maura Youngman e-mailed to note that this was incorrect. We regret this error.

Getting Ready to Write

Checking Your Comprehension MySkillsLab®

Answer each of the following questions using complete sentences.

1. What does the author mean when he says that new media's "role in the process of narrative storytelling is palpable" (paragraph 3)?
2. What does the author mean by the phrase "citizen journalism" (paragraphs 4 and 9)? How does this phrase relate to crowdsourcing, as discussed in paragraph 13?
3. Why is it sometimes difficult to ascertain the original sources (or owners) of photographs that have been posted on the Internet?
4. According to Nathalie Applewhite, which qualities define valuable photojournalism?
5. Why may social media have longer-term effects on social awareness of important issues than, say, daily news reports?

Strengthening Your Vocabulary MySkillsLab®

Identify at least five words used in the reading that are unfamiliar to you. Using context, word parts, or a dictionary, if necessary, write a brief definition of each word.

Examining the Reading: Drawing an Idea Map

Create an idea map of "Photojournalism in the Age of New Media." Start with the title and thesis and include the main points of the selection.

Reading and Writing: An Integrated Perspective MySkillsLab®

1. In paragraph 14, Nathalie Applewhite says, "People take images as truth much more than words." Do you agree or disagree with this assertion? Explain your answer in a journal entry.
2. What specific social problems do you think would be best documented by photos? Explain.
3. Suppose you upload a video or a photo to a social media site. How important is it to you that you be credited as the creator of that photo or video?
4. Discuss some examples of photos that have been used to mislead you. For example, did you ever buy a product that didn't look anything like the photo shown on the package? Does the fast food you buy look as good as it does in TV commercials?
5. Why does the author focus so many of his examples on political struggles and social problems?
6. Why did the author choose to include the example about Daniel Morel in paragraph 8?
7. The author extensively quotes staff members of the Pulitzer Center on Crisis Reporting. Why?
8. In what ways does the photo on page 470 illustrate the qualities of effective photojournalism as described in the article?
9. Why is the example explaining the work of Andre Lambertson (paragraph 12) so important to this article?
10. Why is the example regarding the Serbian Ministry of War's actions (paragraph 15) important to understanding the arguments made in this article?

Thinking and Writing Critically MySkillsLab®

1. Inferences can be made from photos as well as from words. What inferences can you make from the photo on page 470? (For more information on making inferences, see Chapter 12.)
2. What inference can you make from the following statement in paragraph 3? "While a single snapshot may tell a thousand-word story, the trick is to get that story right." How is this sentence related to the thesis of the article? (Consult Chapter 12 for more on making valid inferences.)

3. What does the footnote that appears on page 472 imply about the credibility of this source and the publication in which it appeared? (For more on evaluating sources, see Chapter 12.)

4. In paragraph 11, Nathalie Applewhite refers to "a photojournalist with an artistic vision that transcends superficial coverage." Discuss the connotations and denotations of the following four words: *artistic, vision, transcends*, and *superficial*. (For more information about connotations and denotations, see Chapter 13.)

5. Paragraph 20 makes use of figurative language with the phrase "baptism in fire." What exactly does this phrase mean within the context of the paragraph? (For more on understanding figurative language, see Chapter 13.)

6. Identify the key generalization found in paragraph 19. (For further information on generalizations, see Chapter 13.)

7. Which types of supporting evidence does the author use to support his claims and support his thesis? (For more on identifying and evaluating evidence, see Chapter 14.)

Writing About the Reading

MySkillsLab®

1. The article refers to the narrative, or storytelling, qualities of photos. Select a photo (or a series of photos) and write an essay about it. Your essay should tell some sort of story about the scene or the people pictured in it. (Be sure to properly credit the source of the photo.)

2. If you could document one event, one social problem, or one movement with photos, which would you choose? Write an essay explaining your choice and the types of photos you would take. (For example, would you document an animal-watching safari in Africa? A political campaign in your town? The life of a famous figure?)

3. The article makes use of the term "citizen journalists." What role(s) do you see citizen journalists playing in society? What are some of the possible pros and cons of having untrained people reporting on events or posting photos? Write an essay in which you explore these questions.

Read and Respond to the Theme

Synthesizing Ideas

1. Consider the three readings in this section. Which offers the strongest criticism of the media? Which presents the media in the most favorable light? Explain your answers.

2. Describe the intended audience for each of the three readings in this section. Is there any overlap among these audiences? How does the tone differ by intended audience?

3. All of the readings in this section use the word "media." What exactly does this word mean? How has the meaning of the word evolved over, say, the last decade?

4. All of the readings in this section make use of expert opinion. Who are the experts quoted in each reading, and are they reliable? In what other ways are these readings similar? How are they different?

5. Each of the readings in this section is accompanied by at least one visual aid. List the three visual aids you found most interesting or useful. Why did you find these visual aids particularly useful? Did any visual aids seem less effective? If so, why?

Writing About the Readings

1. Some studies have shown that people are much more likely to read a community newspaper than a regional or national newspaper. Write an essay in which you explore some of the reasons why this may be the case.

2. Watch an episode of the evening news, and then write an essay describing the types of stories broadcast as news segments. Write an essay explaining which stories were you most and least interested in, and why.

3. Suppose you want to spread information about a cause that is important to you—for example, the problem of overfishing the oceans. How might you use social media and images to get the word out? Write an essay explaining a few of the techniques you would use.

4. Consider the following two words: *concrete* and *philosophical*. Which reading(s) in this section would you consider the most concrete and fact-based? Which would you consider the most abstract or philosophical? Explain.

5. The term "media," used in the title of all the readings in the section, includes social media, such as Facebook, Twitter, Instagram, and YouTube. Choose one of these social media (or another one of your choice) and write about at least two positive social effects and two negative social effects that come from the widespread use of this social network.

Theme 3
Sports and Society

It is easy to underestimate the role of sports in society. From a very young age, children are encouraged to participate in sports, and multiple sporting competitions or games are broadcast every day of the year. International sporting competitions such as the World Cup and the Olympics draw millions of spectators, and successful athletes are some of the most highly paid people in the world. This section explores some of the controversies surrounding sports, including the use of performance-enhancing drugs, the underreported injuries sustained by many football players, and the question of whether college athletes should be paid.

Reading 1: (Textbook) Drug Abuse Among Athletes, by Michael J. Johnson

Reading 2: (Article) The National Brain-Damage League, by Shankar Vedantum

Reading 3a: (Opinion Piece: PRO) Should College Football Student Athletes Get Paid?, by Zachary Fegely

Reading 3b: (Opinion Piece: CON) College Athletes Already Have Advantages and Shouldn't Be Paid, by Paul Daugherty

Drug Abuse Among Athletes

The following excerpt, "Drug Abuse Among Athletes" was originally published in a human biology textbook. It begins the chapter titled "The Muscular System." As you read, note how the author uses examples to help explain how drugs improve athletic performance through their effects on the human body.

Thinking Before Reading

1. Preview the reading, using the steps discussed in Chapter 1, page 4.
2. Connect the reading to your own experience by answering the following questions:
   a. Do you know anyone who has used steroids or performance-enhancing drugs (PEDs)? As you watch sports, what telltale signs hint to you that an athlete has used PEDs?
   b. What do you think motivates professional (and amateur) athletes to use performance-enhancing drugs?
3. Mark and annotate as you read.

Drug Abuse Among Athletes

Michael D. Johnson

1 Baseball slugger Barry Bonds was convicted for lying under oath about using performance-enhancing drugs. Sprinter Marion Jones confessed to her drug use and offered a tearful apology, but was stripped of her five Olympic gold medals. High school athletes are routinely being tested for performance-enhancing drugs. What is going on here?

2 The short answer is that many performance-enhancing drugs do enhance athletic performance. They work in ways that are predictable and understood, based on human physiology. In an environment where just a hundredth of a second can make the difference between an Olympic gold medal and relative obscurity, the temptation to use these drugs is high.

Anabolic Steroids

3 Anabolic steroids and related compounds such as dehydroepiandrosterone (DHEA) and androstenedione ("Andro") are the most widely abused drugs in athletics today. Although anabolic steroids are banned by sports federations and school systems, many of them are available over the counter as the result of a 1994 federal law that was written to ensure access to herbal remedies. In general, they are structurally and functionally related to the male sex steroid testosterone. And, like testosterone, they make it easy for the user to increase his/her muscle mass. Muscle strength improves as well, leading to improved athletic performance in sports that require short bursts of energy.

4 How common is anabolic steroid use? A study funded by the National Institute on Drug Abuse found that 2.5% of 12th-graders. 1.5% of 10th-graders, and 1.1 % of 8th-graders had tried them. Information on steroid use by college and professional athletes is unreliable because the athletes are reluctant to talk about it. A few well-known athletes, including Arnold Schwarzenegger, sprinter Ben Johnson, and wrestler Hulk Hogan, have admitted to using them at one time or another.

5 A recent trend is the increased use of sophisticated "designer drugs" such as THG (tetrahydrogestrinone), designed specifically to avoid detection. THG is known as "the clear" to athletes because allegedly it couldn't be detected. And for years it wasn't detected—until an anonymous tipster sent a sample of the drug to a sport federation for testing. THG is so potent that it doesn't even have to be injected—just a couple of drops under the tongue are enough. In 2007 sprinter Marion Jones finally admitted that she started using THG in 1999 as she prepared for the 2000 Olympic Games. She was stripped of her five medals from the 2000 Olympics and banned from participation in the 2008 Olympics in Beijing.

6 Aside from the obvious issue of fairness in athletic competition, anabolic steroids are banned by sports federations because of their side effects and possible health risks. Androgens have masculinizing effects in both sexes. Men may experience gynecomastia (enlargement of the breasts), shrinkage of the testicles, reduced sperm production, and impotence. In women, breast size and body fat decrease and the voice deepens. Women may lose scalp hair but gain

Marion Jones after winning the gold in 2000, and in 2007 after admitting to using performance-enhancing drugs.

body hair. Some of these changes are not reversible. Anabolic steroid abuse is also associated with irritability, hostility, and aggressive behavior ("roid rage"). Prolonged anabolic steroid abuse is associated with an increased risk of heart attack, stroke, and severe liver disease, including liver cancer. Although the number of cases of these diseases is fairly low (so far), the effects of steroid use/abuse may be underestimated because these diseases tend to come later in life. We just don't know what will happen to steroid abusers 30 years later.

Blood Enhancers

7 Marathoners and cyclists aren't interested in muscle mass; they're interested in maintaining a high level of sustained performance over long periods of time. For that, they need increased aerobic capacity. Their (banned) drug of choice is erythropoietin (EPO), a hormone produced by the kidneys that increases the production of red blood cells. EPO is available by prescription only for patients with *anemia* (too few red blood cells in the blood). But cyclists and marathon runners use it to improve their performance. It's all a matter of normal human physiology; EPO produces more red blood cells, which leads to a higher oxygen-carrying capacity, which in turn leads to a higher level of sustainable muscle activity and faster times.

8 But a health risk is associated with EPO abuse. Excessive production of red blood cells can raise the hematocrit (the percentage of the blood that is red cells) to dangerous levels. The blood becomes sludge-like, increasing the risk of high blood pressure, blood clots, and heart attacks. Statistically, one of the most common causes of death among professional cyclists is heart attack, although no deaths have ever officially been listed as having been caused by EPO.

9 It's hard to test for EPO abuse because EPO disappears from the blood within days, leaving behind an increased hematocrit and an improved endurance that lasts for a month or more. The cycling organizations are only able to curb EPO abuse by setting an upper limit for hematocrit of 50%; above that EPO abuse is just assumed and the athlete is banned from competition. It is widely suspected that cyclists who choose to abuse EPO measure their hematocrit shortly before a race and then remove blood cells to just meet the 50% rule!

Next Up: Gene Doping

10 Within decades, it will probably be possible to use genetic engineering techniques to modify an athlete's genes for improved athletic performance. It's called *gene doping*. What if you could tinker with the genes that lead to the production of natural erythropoietin or testosterone, so that an athlete just naturally produces more of these hormones? What if you could alter muscle biochemistry so that muscles used energy more efficiently or more rapidly? What if you could insert genes that caused muscle cells to store up more ATP? These ideas are not so far-fetched. Nearly all experts on the subject are convinced that if gene doping hasn't been tried already, it soon will be. Gene doping will be extremely hard to detect or to prevent.

11 Have we lost our perspective for the role that sports should play in our lives?

Getting Ready to Write

Checking Your Comprehension MySkillsLab®

Answer each of the following questions using complete sentences.

1. Why are DHEA and Andro commonly and legally available for purchase?
2. Which drug was sprinter Marion Jones found to have used, and why would Jones choose to use that drug rather than another one?
3. What are some of the short-term and long-term effects of anabolic steroid usage?
4. Why have some runners and cyclists chosen EPO to improve their athletic performance? (In other words, how does this specific drug help their performance?)
5. What is *hematocrit*?

Strengthening Your Vocabulary MySkillsLab®

Identify at least five words used in the reading that are unfamiliar to you. Using context, word parts, or a dictionary, write a brief definition of each word.

Examining the Reading: Drawing an Idea Map

Create an idea map of "Drug Abuse Among Athletes." Start with the title and thesis and include the main points of the selection.

Reading and Writing: An Integrated Perspective MySkillsLab®

1. Suppose you are an athlete and could legally use a performance-enhancing drug of your choice. Would you do so? Write a journal entry explaining your answer.
2. Should Olympic athletes who are found to have used performance-enhancing drugs be stripped of their medals? Why, or why not?
3. If you are an athlete or play sports, what are some techniques you use to be successful or to work within the system? (For example, some wrestlers try to stay at the very top of a particular weight class so that they are among the biggest/heaviest in that class. They diet so that they will not be the smallest/lightest of the next class.)
4. Why did the author choose to introduce his topic by providing examples about Barry Bonds and Marion Jones?
5. The author closes the selection with a *rhetorical question*, which is a question that asks readers to think more deeply about a particular issue or viewpoint. Why do you think the author closes his selection with a rhetorical question?

6. What might be a good alternate title for the final section of the article, currently labeled "Next Up: Gene Doping"?
7. How do the photos included with this reading help support the author's thesis?

Thinking and Writing Critically MySkillsLab®

1. In paragraph 4, the author states, "Information on steroid use by college and professional athletes is unreliable because the athletes are reluctant to talk about it." What inference(s) might you make from this statement? Why are athletes reluctant to talk about steroid usage? (For a review of inference skills, see Chapter 12.)
2. How would you assess the author's reliability and credibility? How does the source of the reading help you answer this question? (For more information on assessing sources and author qualifications, see Chapter 12.)
3. Although this reading is predominantly factual, it does contain some opinions. Indicate which statements in paragraph 10 are opinions. (For an overview of fact and opinion, see Chapter 12.)
4. The author introduces several slang terms in the reading, including "designer drugs" (paragraph 5), "the clear" (paragraph 5) and "roid rage" (paragraph 6). What are the connotations of these terms? Are they positive, negative, or neutral? (For more information on connotations, see Chapter 13.)
5. Within the article, what is the author's underlying generalization regarding the main reason that athletes use anabolic steroids and other drugs? Do you agree with the author's generalization that gene doping may become common? (For guidance on how to identify and evaluate generalizations, see Chapter 13.)
6. Evaluate the author's bias or lack of bias in this reading. Do you think he fairly presents information regarding athletes' use of performance-enhancing drugs? (For specifics on identifying and evaluating bias, see Chapter 13.)

Writing About the Reading MySkillsLab®

1. Do you think the organizations that oversee professional sports should be in the business of testing athletes for drug use? Why or why not? Write an essay stating and providing support for your opinion.
2. The reading focuses on only one aspect of professional sports: the use of performance-enhancing drugs. But sports are associated with many positive effects for both individual athletes and spectators. Write an essay in which you discuss some of these positive effects.
3. Many activities, not just sports, require a specific set of athletic skills. Consider a career or special interest that you may have. Which specific skills are required for success? (For example, if you want to become a clothing designer, you must have a sense of fashion, an eye for fabrics, awareness of color, and so on.) Write an essay about the skills required by your chosen activity or interest.

READING 2
Article

The National Brain-Damage League

The following article, "The National Brain-Damage League" was originally published on Slate.com, a Web-based magazine that features topics of general interest. As you read, note how the author cites experts and authorities to support his thesis.

Thinking Before Reading

1. Preview the reading, using the steps discussed in Chapter 1, page 4.
2. Connect the reading to your own experience by answering the following questions:
   a. Do you know anyone (including yourself) who has been injured while playing a sport? What types of injuries were suffered, and did they have long-term effects?
   b. When you take part in an athletic activity (such as touch football or bicycling), do you use any protective equipment? If so, what types? If not, why not?
3. Mark and annotate as you read.

The National Brain-Damage League

Shankar Vedantam

Two football players facing each other head on.

The epidemic of head injuries in football is even worse than you thought.

1 In collisions, "G" is a unit equal to the force of gravity. A low-speed rear-end crash causes an impact of 10G to 30G. A high-flying soccer ball lands on your head with a force of around 20G. Then there's the high-school football player who, according to a recent evaluation by Purdue researchers, received a blow to the head during a game that carried a force of 289G—nearly 300 times the force of gravity. The scary thing about the hit was not the size of the impact. It was that the young man had no visible symptoms of a concussion.

2 Newfound concern about the well-being of football players has focused on the tip of a very large iceberg. Parents, schools, and athletes worry that thousands of amateurs each year may be suffering head injuries similar to the ones that make us gasp during NFL games. But there's a worse possibility: The most serious brain injuries at all levels of the sport are going completely undiagnosed and undetected. It gives me no pleasure to say this. I am a fan who eagerly awaits game day and the ultimate redemption of my long-suffering team.

3 Today we worry more about high-impact strikes to the head than about repetitive blows of moderate intensity. We think the only players who suffer brain injuries during collisions are the ones who later look dazed, or who can't keep their balance, or who suffer from slurred speech and vision. The Purdue research changes all that. Many brain injuries suffered by football players do not produce the "shell-shock" symptoms we associate with concussions. The damage caused by these hits is just as evident when you study players in brain scanners or give them tests that measure sophisticated aspects of brain functioning, but are not picked up by trainers on the sidelines.

4 The finding about a new group of brain injuries came about, like many discoveries, by accident. Purdue biomedical engineering professor Eric Nauman and his colleagues were studying garden-variety concussions among high-schoolers. Nauman and his colleagues wanted to compare changes in the brains of football players who had suffered concussions with the "normal" brains of football players who were concussion-free. But when they scanned the concussion-free players a few weeks into the season and compared these pictures to the same players' preseason scans, they found that many had long-lasting brain changes. "At first we thought our scanner was broken," Nauman said during a recent presentation of his findings to a group of journalists. "Then we realized this was a new group of impaired players."

5 Nauman calculates there are about 1 million high-school football players in any given year in the United States. There are some 67,000 reported concussions, and probably about as many that go unreported because fans, coaches, and parents don't want a star athlete pulled from a game. But among the supposedly injury-free remainder, the Purdue researchers believe tens of thousands of athletes routinely suffer serious brain injuries from high-impact collisions intrinsic to the game.

6 Some of the high-schoolers Nauman studied suffered about 150 head impacts per week during the season, or about 1,500 impacts per year. On average, the hits carried a force of around 40G. (The force of impacts is measured by sensors within helmets.) These hits did not knock players out, but they caused systematic changes in their brain functioning. Unlike the violent helmet-to-helmet collisions in the open field that have drawn warnings and suspensions from the NFL, these blows usually involved routine blocks and tackles, often along the line of scrimmage. "Half the population we brought in had no obvious impairment whatsoever," Nauman said. But when the Purdue group compared the in-season scans with the preseason scans, "We saw even more significant neurophysiological changes than in the players diagnosed with concussions."

7 Nauman and other research aren't exactly sure what is happening to these players. But they believe that what we call concussions are only one of several kinds of head injury that affect players' verbal ability, memory, and "vestibular system," which controls spatial orientation and balance. Many of the hits that produce "shell-shock" concussions involve blows to the side of the head, as happens with helmet-to-helmet collisions in the open field. The new group of injured players—the ones without visible injury—had suffered damage to the frontal lobe, the part of the brain that controls high-end "executive functioning."

8 "These seem to result from repetitive blows to the top-front of the head," Nauman told me in an e-mail. "Most common when players lead with their heads to block or tackle. The challenge is that we don't really have sideline tests that can evaluate visual working memory or impulse control. So it is very hard to find the players in this group. Our fear is that they go undiagnosed, keep playing, and accumulate more and more damage." To avoid running afoul of physicians who believe that all football concussions can be diagnosed on the sidelines, the Purdue researchers are not calling the new kind of brain injuries concussions. They are calling them impairments. But medical turf wars aside, it seems obvious these injuries are concussions, too.

9 Nauman thinks that while football helmets are pretty good at protecting against skull fractures, they are not good at protecting against concussions. And overconfidence in the helmets' protective power prompts many NFL athletes to deliver and accept hits that would have killed the helmetless players of previous generations. "If you have traumatic brain injury and keep playing, you are at enormous risk for really serious damage later on," Nauman said. "Because these kids don't show any symptoms, they keep playing and exposing themselves to neurological trauma."

10 The neurological changes observed by the Purdue researchers did subside in the postseason. As good as brain scans are, they measure only indirectly what is happening at the neural level. And, as with all science, the findings of the Purdue team need to be expanded and independently verified. So we're likely to remain uncertain about the exact nature of this new class of injuries, their behavioral implications, and how they translate to measurable deficits later in life.

11 While acknowledging those uncertainties, Nauman told me he would never allow a child of his to play football. And now that I've seen the pictures of brain changes among "concussion-free" players, I would no more let a school-age child of mine play competitive football than I would let him or her start smoking. At least one prominent football commentator has said the sport is not for his own son. What does it say about us that we derive so much enjoyment from watching other people's kids take risks we would never accept for our own?

Getting Ready to Write

Checking Your Comprehension MySkillsLab®

Answer each of the following questions using complete sentences.

1. In collisions, what does the term "G" mean?
2. In general, are moderate head impacts while playing football (or other sports) less dangerous or worrisome than severe head impacts? Why or why not?
3. What key conclusion can be drawn from the study conducted by Eric Nauman?
4. About how many concussions occur in high school football players each year? Give a number that includes both reported and unreported concussions. Why would some concussions go unreported?
5. Are "concussions" and "impairments" the same thing? Why or why not?

Strengthening Your Vocabulary MySkillsLab®

Identify at least five words used in the reading that are unfamiliar to you. Using context, word parts, or a dictionary, if necessary, write a brief definition of each word.

Examining the Reading: Drawing an Idea Map

Create an idea map of "The National Brain-Damage League." Start with the title and thesis and include the main points of the selection.

Reading and Writing: An Integrated Perspective MySkillsLab®

1. The article repeatedly uses the term *concussion*. What exactly is a concussion?
2. Do you think the use of protective sports equipment, such as helmets, may give players a false sense of security or invincibility? Why or why not? Write a journal entry answering this question. (Feel free to use examples from your own experience.)
3. Why does the author choose to begin the article by defining "G"?
4. Do you agree or disagree with the following statement? "The purpose of this article is to examine the results of one specific research study." Explain your answer.
5. In conducting his research for this article, how did the writer go "above and beyond" reading the research conducted by Eric Nauman and his colleagues? In other words, how did the author get answers to the questions he had?
6. Look closely at the photo on page 481. Write a caption that better ties the photo to the content of the article.

Thinking and Writing Critically MySkillsLab®

1. In paragraph 4, the author quotes Eric Nauman as saying "At first we thought our scanner was broken." What can you infer from Nauman's statement? (For a review of inference skills, see Chapter 12.)
2. Does the article provide any information to help you assess the author's reliability and credibility? If not, how would you go about determining the author's qualifications for writing this article? (To learn more about assessing sources and author qualifications, see Chapter 12.)
3. How does the author critically assess the research study by Eric Nauman and his colleagues? (*Hint*: Reread the last few paragraphs. For more on analyzing evidence, see Chapters 12 and 14.)
4. Does the author see the term *impairment* (paragraph 8) as a euphemism for *concussion*? (For a review of euphemism, see Vocabulary Workshop 1.)
5. What assumption or generalization does the author make about the parents, coaches, and fans of high school football players in paragraph 5? Do you think this assumption is fair? (To learn more about identifying and evaluating assumptions and generalizations, see Chapter 13.)

6. Evaluate the author's bias or lack of bias in this reading. Do you think he fairly presents information? How does the author make his own feelings about football apparent in the article? (For specifics on identifying and evaluating bias, see Chapter 13.)

7. Do you think the author uses emotionally charged language in paragraph 11? Or is the language more neutral? Explain your answer. (For more about emotionally charged language, see Chapter 13.)

Writing About the Reading MySkillsLab®

1. The National Football League oversees professional football and provides certain protections for its players. Do you think an organization should be created to oversee high school sports and to protect players? Why or why not? Write an essay stating and providing support for your opinion.

2. Write an essay in which you describe at least four popular sports. Rank them from least dangerous to most dangerous and explain which you would be comfortable having your children play.

3. Is high school football popular in your town or area? If so, write an essay describing a typical day at the football field on the day of a big game. Some questions you might answer: Who is in attendance? Who is the local team's biggest rival, and why? Which players are most impressive and why?

Should College Football Student Athletes Get Paid?

The following excerpt, "Should College Football Student Athletes Get Paid?" was originally published on PennLive.com, a Web site that features news articles, information, and opinion pieces about life in central Pennsylvania. The author is a student athlete at Pennsylvania State University (Penn State), which is the home of a highly ranked college football team, the Nittany Lions. As you read, note how the author uses his own experiences and perceptions to argue his opinion.

Thinking Before Reading

1. Preview the reading, using the steps discussed in Chapter 1, page 4.
2. Connect the reading to your own experience by answering the following questions:
   a. Does your college or university have any highly ranked (or highly popular) sports programs? Do you follow (or are you a member of) any of these teams?
   b. Do you think college student athletes should be paid for playing sports? Why or why not?
3. Mark and annotate as you read.

PRO: Should College Football Student Athletes Get Paid?

Zachary Fegely

1 With so many college football scandals concerning players taking money or receiving additional benefits to play at a certain school, is now the time to open up the checkbooks and start paying these hardworking athletes?

2 Most people, including some athletes, will say that there is no way that athletes should be paid to play a sport since most of them are getting a full ride at that school anyway. While getting a scholarship is a great incentive to playing a varsity sport at a prestigious institution, most athletes do not get scholarships to play their sport and simply play for love of the game.

3 When you examine what goes into being a student athlete—the lifting, the meetings, the practices, the games, the study hall hours logged—that is all on top of the athletes going to class and having to excel in the classroom. Many of us college students have a tough time doing as well as we want to at Penn State with no other responsibilities other than going to class. When you compound this with the fact that most student athletes are not allowed to work (NCAA says you can only earn $2,000 an academic year) it becomes very tempting for athletes to take money, especially when they have a family to provide for. Most of these student athletes, unfortunately, come from underprivileged families and are parlaying their athletic talent into a better life for themselves and their families.

4 Every year, Penn State and the NCAA make millions of dollars off their student athletes. They sell their jerseys, their likenesses, and their autographs, with none of that money going to the players who are selling the product that is Penn State football. How many people reading this have bought a Penn State jersey? You did not buy it simply because it was Penn State but because of the athlete or athletes

that it represents. I will admit I have the #40, #31, and #2 jerseys for Dan Connor, Paul Posluszny, and Derrick Williams, but none of those players (who all made it into the NFL) saw a dime of that money and those jerseys cost about 100 dollars a pop. With all the merchandise and tickets that are purchased solely because of the players on the field, should the players not be entitled to some of the money that the school is making off of them?

5 Granted, the counter argument is that not every player on the field is making as much money for the university as others. I am sure the amount of money that Evan Royster made for Penn State far surpasses what someone like Tamba Hall made, even though on paper they were getting the same benefits and perks of being a student athlete. That is why if you were to pay student athletes, it cannot be done based on performance or by the amount of money that a particular player earns for the university.

6 When you add in the threat of injuries that ultimately occur that can have a drastic impact on the rest of that player's life, it starts to sink in that maybe these players should get some money for playing. Adam Taliaferro, who made a miraculous recovery from a paralyzing spinal cord injury he suffered in 2000 against Ohio State, could have spent the rest of his life paralyzed from an injury that occurred while playing a sport for a scholarship. I personally do not think that not being able to walk again, and thankfully Adam was able to make a full recovery, is worth getting a full/ride scholarship.

7 Now I know that this is the exception and most players do not sustain this serious of an injury while playing, but the threat is still there. As more and more research is being done on ex-football players' brains, science shows that playing football and getting hit in the head will have drastic impacts on that person later on in life. With that said, even if they do not get hurt while playing at Penn State, the physical and psychological damage may already be done. Unlike the NFL, there is not a pension program for athletes who get hurt while playing college football. All they get is an education that they may not be able to be use, especially if they suffer head injuries.

8 It can be said that those playing pee-wee football could also suffer the same debilitating injuries. While that is true, the speed of the game and the strength that these college football players possess are NFL caliber, but the protections that are in place for these players are far worse than those which the NFL provides. Now I am not saying we should pay college players millions of dollars to get a free education and play football, but there should be some stipend given to the players.

9 Last year, Penn State football made $33,017,893 off football alone. Combine that with the $36,925,949 that was earned from sponsorship, endowments, and other donations and you are looking at a total of $69,943,842. Now some of those sponsorships and endowments come from different sports, but the majority of that is from football. Much of that money goes to other varsity sports like women's volleyball and field hockey, which I think is a great idea. However, even with all the money spent on other Penn State programs, the university still brings in $14 million a year off of its athletics. That is more than enough money to create a stipend pool for these players.

10 I know Penn State is one of the biggest revenue generators in college football, but I am sure that all Division 1 schools can afford to pay their student athletes, especially those that play football, something. To keep it fair and to stop this

from turning into the NFL, where the highest bidder wins, all stipends would be the same. That incoming freshman 5-star recruit would get the same amount of money as the third-string kicker at another school. Now I am unaware of just how much money each school makes, so I am unable to put a total on the amount that student athletes should get paid, but I am sure a total could be reached that is fair to everyone. Smaller schools and those in weak conferences are always going to be at a disadvantage, which is nothing new in the college football landscape as the BCS has been discriminating against them since its inception.

11 Now I am not saying that this needs to happen tomorrow, but as a student athlete who did not get a scholarship, it would be nice to get something for playing a varsity sport other than two credits. I just wanted to examine this as a hypothetical because we all know that this most likely will never happen in college. With that said, I would still love to hear what everyone else thinks!

Getting Ready to Write

Checking Your Comprehension MySkillsLab®

Answer each of the following questions using complete sentences.

1. According to the author, what is the primary motivation of most college athletes?
2. At Penn State University, how much does it cost to buy a football jersey with a college athlete's name on it?
3. Does the author think that college athletes should get paid based on their individual performance? Why or why not?
4. How does Penn State spend most of the money it makes from its football team?

Strengthening Your Vocabulary MySkillsLab®

Identify at least five words used in the reading that are unfamiliar to you. Using context, word parts, or a dictionary, if necessary, write a brief definition of each word.

Examining the Reading: Drawing an Idea Map

Create an idea map of "Should College Football Student Athletes Get Paid?" Start with the title and thesis and include the main points of the selection.

Reading and Writing: An Integrated Perspective MySkillsLab®

1. Do you think a full scholarship to a college or university is enough compensation for student athletes? Write a journal entry that addresses this question.
2. Would you wear a jersey that has an athlete's name on it? Would you pay $100 for such an article of clothing? Why or why not?
3. The author begin his essay (paragraph 1) with a question. Is this effective?

4. Does the author acknowledge both sides of the argument (that is, the reasons for and against paying student athletes), or is his article completely one-sided?

5. How does the author use dollar amounts to support his argument?

6. How does the author's sense of "fair play" show itself in the article? That is, what suggestions does the author make for paying student athletes and ensuring that the best athletes don't all end up at a small number of schools?

7. Was this article written for a local, regional, national, or international audience? How can you tell?

8. How does the photo add to or detract from the content of this article? Write a caption to accompany the photo.

Thinking and Writing Critically MySkillsLab®

1. What inference can you make from this statement in paragraph 11? "As a student athlete who did not get a scholarship, it would be nice to get something for paying a varsity sport other than two credits." For more on making inferences, see Chapter 12.)

2. How qualified is the author to write on the topic? Is his perspective broad or limited? (For more information on assessing an author's qualifications, see Chapter 12.)

3. Use at least two words to describe the tone of this article. (To learn more about tone, see Chapter 12.)

4. On what generalization is this entire article based? Is this generalization accurate? (*Hint*: Look closely at the question in the title. For further information on generalizations, see Chapter 13.)

5. Look closely at paragraph 7. Based on the author's assertions, certain evidence seems to be lacking. What evidence should the author have provided in this paragraph? (For more on evaluating evidence, see Chapter 14.)

Writing About the Reading MySkillsLab®

1. The author focuses on students who play varsity sports. However, many schools also offer intramural sports (in which teams within the college or university play one another, or groups of students at that school play against other groups of students at that school). Write an essay in which you explain some of the similarities and/or differences between being a member of a varsity team and being a member of an intramural team.

2. Write an essay in which you agree or disagree with the following statement, providing evidence to support your argument. "Sports should be banned in college. The college experience should be about learning, not about playing games."

3. How do you think the profits from a college or university sports team should be distributed? Write an essay explaining how you would distribute this money if you were the president of your college or university.

READING 3b
Opinion Piece: CON

College Athletes Already Have Advantages and Shouldn't Be Paid

The following excerpt, "College Athletes Already Have Advantages and Shouldn't Be Paid," was originally published in *Sports Illustrated*, a popular sports magazine. As you read, examine how the author compares his own experiences (and compensation) to those of professional and student athletes. The author is a columnist for *The Cincinnati Enquirer*.

Thinking Before Reading

1. Preview the reading, using the steps discussed in Chapter 1, page 4.
2. Connect the reading to your own experience by answering the following questions:
   a. Have you received a scholarship or any financial aid from your school? If so, what does your school expect in return?
   b. Do you have any friends who are on a sports scholarship? Do they think that being on the team is the equivalent of having a full-time job?
3. Mark and annotate as you read.

CON: College Athletes Already Have Advantages and Shouldn't Be Paid

Paul Daugherty

1 For three years at the University of Cincinnati, I taught a Class in Advanced Reporting to juniors and seniors interested in writing about sports for a living. We met late in the morning, plenty of time for 20-year-olds to shake the cobwebs from their brains and show up ready to learn. So it was disconcerting to see a few of them every semester arrive in my classroom and nod off. "Don't you like what I'm teaching?" I'd ask. "Am I boring you? How can I help?" Adjunct professors actually care about such things. "No, the class is good," is what I'd hear. "I had to work late last night." They'd be stocking supermarket shelves until 4 in the morning. They'd be tending bar. One worked as a security guard at an apartment building. They'd fall into bed six hours before they had to be in my class.

2 I think about these kids now, whenever the siren sounds for college athletes to be paid. What about my students? What does it say to them? These were not people who asked to be paid to attend college. These were folks who paid for the privilege. And let's be clear: College is a privilege. It is earned, not bestowed. Some, in fact, are still paying. It's one thing to go to school for free and to leave free of debt. It's quite another to work your way through and depart with a five-figure yoke around your neck.

3 Should college athletes be paid? Why? At the highest levels, here is what they endure. Here's some of the hardship involved if you are an athlete, attending a university for free: A four-year audition for prospective employers. Or three years, or two. Or basically, whenever you and your pro league of choice agree you've passed the audition. I don't know about you, but when I was a college junior, schlepping to town council meetings on Tuesday nights for my Journalism 301 class, no newspaper editor was there to praise my fascinating reporting on zoning changes in a residential subdivision.

4 When you agree to a full, free ride at a university and you are a football or basketball player, you do so knowing that if you're good enough at what you do, you will get noticed. It's not as If you'll need to spend any time assembling a resume. Your game is your resume. You will burnish your resume while flying to away games, often in chartered jets, and staying in first-class hotels. If you play basketball, it's likely you will visit a tropical island at least once in your four, free years. If you play football, you could spend a week at a bowl site, where you will get nice gifts from the game's sponsors.

5 Meantime, if scholarship is among your goals, there will be no shortage of attendants at your beck and call. You will have tutors and study tables. You will have coaches who assign managers to act as human alarm clocks, on the off chance you accidentally sleep late. In some places, you will be enrolled in classes designed to keep you eligible. You will have compliant and complicit professors, interested in the same thing. I was not a college athlete. I did not have tutors or study tables or anyone to make sure I went to class. If I earned an F, I got one. Scholarship was expected. It was, after all, what I was there for.

A star like Duke's Jabari Parker is given a free education and the opportunity to audition for the NBA.

6 Did I mention costs? It costs $57,180 to go to Duke. It's $31,946 to attend Butler. The University of Cincinnati, a public, urban place with lots of commuters, costs $24,942 if you're from out of state, which describes the bulk of football and basketball players. If you want to go to the University of Texas, and you're not a Texan, its $35,776 a year. Many people who work full-time jobs don't make $35,776 a year. Some even have college degrees. This is a lot of money. It's the sort of outlay that keeps parents awake at 3 a.m. Unless, of course, you're the parent of an athlete on full scholarship, in which case you want to know why he or she isn't getting paid.

7 So many advantages. If you are, say, a member of the men's basketball team at the University of Kentucky, you will have a job waiting for you after you graduate, assuming you do, even if you never get off of John Caliparl's bench. Athletes have built-in connections non-athletes can only dream of. Athletes are not starving their way through four years of indentured servitude. They are not, god help us, "slaves." On most campuses, they're among the privileged classes.

8 Solutions are everywhere lately, for the tragedy of having to play a sport to attend college. A few months ago. *Sports Illustrated* suggested that one way to pay football and basketball players is to bust down to club status other sports, men's sports mostly. That is: A swimmer is not as worthy to the school as a basketball player is. Even if he works as hard in the pool as the basketball

player does in the gym. Swimmers routinely practice at 5 or 6 in the morning. John Chaney used to hold basketball practice at Temple at 6. He was regarded universally as an Old School martinet.

9 *SI*'s stance suggests college sports should be viewed entirely in an economic light: If you don't pay for yourself, you have to come up with money to finance the program. That devalues the effort of a non-revenue athlete. It also assumes football and basketball are universally profitable. That's not the case, especially with football. Not every school is Texas or Michigan or Ohio State. It also cuts against the grain of what we like to think college is about: Opportunity. We will give you the opportunity to play a sport. Unless it's football or basketball, that opportunity's going to cost you.

10 Bob Knight once said the best argument against paying players is that it diminishes the value of an education. That's as true now as it has ever been. For every athlete demanding a paycheck, there are 10 deserving non-athletes who can't afford to walk in the door to whom a college degree would mean more than a direct deposit every couple of weeks.

11 Of course, things are out of whack now. Coaches' salaries are ridiculous. The hours athletes put in eliminate any semblance of college life. Parents should be able to take plane tickets and hotel rooms to see their kids play, without fear of NCAA blowback. Players should be able to afford the proverbial Friday night pizza. I'm not suggesting being a big-time athlete should be any more of a challenge than being a big-time student. In some, very tangible ways, it's less of a challenge already. Just ask those kids in my class, trying to stay awake after working all night.

Getting Ready to Write

Checking Your Comprehension MySkillsLab®

Answer each of the following questions using complete sentences.

1. What course did the author teach, and at what school?
2. Why did the author think his students found him boring?
3. List at least three advantages that college athletes have that are not given to students who are paying their way through school.
4. What solution did Sports Illustrated magazine propose for paying college football and basketball players?
5. What does the author see as the primary thing that "college is about"?

Strengthening Your Vocabulary MySkillsLab®

Identify at least five words used in the reading that are unfamiliar to you. Using context, word parts, or a dictionary, if necessary, write a brief definition of each word.

Examining the Reading: Drawing an Idea Map

Create an idea map of "College Athletes Already Have Advantages and Shouldn't Be Paid." Start with the title and thesis and include the main points of the selection.

Reading and Writing: An Integrated Perspective MySkillsLab®

1. What does the author mean when he says "College is a privilege. It is earned, not bestowed" (paragraph 2)?
2. Some might consider playing on a college athletic team the equivalent of an "internship" in a company. Would you agree with this assessment? Explain your answer in a journal entry.
3. How does the personal vignette that opens the article (paragraph 1) point to the author's thesis?
4. In paragraph 6, the author provides many examples of the tuition at various colleges. Why does he provide these examples?
5. How and where does the author acknowledge other sides of the argument?
6. How does the last paragraph of the article come "full circle" to the content of the first paragraph? How effective is this technique?
7. Who is the intended audience for this article? How can you tell?
8. How does the photo on page 491 add to or detract from the content of this article? What other types of photos would be appropriate visual aids to accompany this article?

Thinking and Writing Critically MySkillsLab®

1. Identify at least two places in the article where the tone is ironic or sarcastic. (To learn more about tone, see Chapter 12.)
2. As used in paragraph 5, what are the connotations and denotations of the words *compliant* and *complicit*? (To learn more about connotation and denotation, see Chapter 13.)
3. The author makes frequent use of figurative language. What does he mean when he says "the siren sounds" for college athletes to be paid (paragraph 2)? What does he mean by "a five-figure yoke" (also in paragraph 2)? Identify at least two other examples of figurative language in the article. (For more on figurative language, see Chapter 13.)
4. In paragraph 1, the author states, "Adjunct professors actually care about such things." What assumption(s) is the author making? What generalization(s) is he making? (For further information on identifying assumptions and generalizations, see Chapter 13.)
5. Evaluate the author's use of evidence to support his argument. Do you think he provides enough evidence to support his case? If not, what other types of evidence might he have included in the article? (For more on evaluating evidence, see Chapter 14.)

Writing About the Reading MySkillsLab®

1. The author offers many examples of schools with expensive tuition. Write an essay in which you explore some of the ways to manage the cost of getting a college education.

2. The author believes that all sports should be equal, that no particular sport (such as basketball or football) should be given special preference or treatment. Do you agree or disagree with this statement? Write an essay explaining your position.

3. In paragraph 11, the author says, "Things are out of whack now." He is referring to college sports. In what other areas of life are things "out of whack"? Write an essay in which you explore an example in detail. (For instance, you might think that movie stars' salaries are completely out of whack; or you might think that social media is out of whack, because it can replace human interaction with computers.)

Comparing Two Viewpoints

After reading "Should College Football Student Athletes Get Paid?" and "College Athletes Already Have Advantages and Shouldn't Be Paid," select two of the following questions to answer.

1. Compare the tone of the two articles. How can you infer the relative age of each author from what he has written?

2. What was your opinion on paying salaries to student athletes before reading these two articles? Has it changed as a result of reading these articles? If so, why? If not, why not? If your opinion hasn't changed, have you seen any benefits from reading this pair of articles?

3. Based solely on the quality of the supporting examples and evidence in these articles, do you think one of the readings does a better job of making its case than the other? If so, which one?

4. On the basis of these two articles, summarize the pros and the cons of paying salaries to student athletes. Add at least one "pro" and one "con" not found in either article.

Read and Respond to the Theme

Synthesizing Ideas

1. Which of the readings included in this section are the most sympathetic toward athletes? Which seem more critical of athletes and sports in general? Explain.

2. Discuss the writing style of each of these selections. Which was written by a student? Which was written by an instructor? How can you tell, and how is each writer's biases reflected in the reading?

3. Suppose you are working on an assigned projects with classmates who are not interested in sports or athletics at all. Briefly summarize why each reading is important and relevant beyond the world of sports and sporting events.

4. To a greater or lesser extent, all of the readings in this section are based on opinions. Which are the most opinionated? Which are the least opinionated (or most fact-based)?

5. Of the readings included in this section, which contains the most humor? Explain your answer.

Writing About the Readings

1. Write an essay in which you respond to the question asked by the author in paragraph 11 of "Drug Abuse Among Athletes": "Have we lost our perspective for the role that sports should play in our lives?"
2. What roles do sports in general play in society? Write an essay in which you explore some of these roles. (For example, sports are often a way for people to express support for their hometown, school, or state.)
3. Why do you think athletes are so prized and valued in American society and on college campuses? Write an essay addressing this question.
4. The readings in this section focus on some of the more controversial or negative aspects of sports and athletic participation. Write an essay in which you explore the many *benefits* of sports for both players and spectators.
5. Two of the readings in this section take opposing viewpoints on one controversial topic: whether college student athletes should be paid. But there are many other controversial topics in sports, including such topics as player and coach salaries (at some colleges, football coaches earn more money than the university president) and the price of tickets for major sporting events. Write an essay in which you explore a sporting-related controversial issue of your choice.

Theme 4

Issues Facing College Students

The readings for this theme can be found in the body of the text (page numbers are listed below).

Enrolling in college is like taking the first step on a long road of opportunity. A college education opens many doors, helping you develop academically and socially while preparing you for a career in your chosen field. However, like most experiences that offer the opportunity for growth, college offers challenges that many students encounter somewhere along the way. At one end of the spectrum, some students simply are not prepared for the rigors of college, because they have not learned the best ways to study and are not good at managing their time. Some students may find themselves easily distracted by electronic media such as video games and social media, which can eat up hours a day and even lead to addiction. The high costs of college can lead to a lack of ready cash, which can make it difficult to afford good, healthy food. All of the readings in this theme explore some of the issues facing today's college students, providing background information as well as suggestions for overcoming challenges in these areas.

Reading 1: (Textbook) Secrets for Surviving College and Improving Your Grades, by Saundra K. Ciccarelli and J. Nolan White 5

Reading 2: (Article) Among Dorms and Dining Halls, Hidden Hunger, by Kate Robbins 117

Reading 3: (Article) Students Vulnerable to Computer Gaming Addiction 232

Read and Respond to the Theme

Synthesizing Ideas

1. Of the issues described and discussed in these three readings, which do you find the most serious and troubling? Which are the most easily addressed or solved? Which will be the most difficult to resolve? Why?
2. List at least three common challenges facing college students that are not discussed in this set of readings. Provide suggestions for some of the ways students might meet these challenges head-on.
3. How do these three readings differ in tone and approach? Which is the most positive? Which sounds the most alarmed and disturbed?
4. Compare the writing among the three readings. Which do you find most accessible, interesting, and relevant? Which is your least favorite, and why? In each case, what has the author done to hold your interest or lose your interest?
5. Choose two of the readings and provide suggestions to the author for how the content might be expanded or improved.

Writing About the Readings

1. Write a paragraph that summarizes the three key issues discussed in the three readings in this theme.
2. "Hidden Hunger" and "Students Vulnerable to Computer Gaming Addiction" both treat topics that many students are uncomfortable talking about or admitting. Write an essay in which you discuss another challenge faced by college students that they may be unwilling to talk about. Why might students have this reluctance?
3. "Hidden Hunger" talks about some steps that are being taken to address problems with student hunger. Does your college offer any support services for students? Suppose you have a friend who is suffering from two of the problems discussed in these readings. Write an essay in which you outline where your friend might go (on campus or in the community) to get help with these problems.
4. The readings in this theme often discuss the "telltale signs" of certain problems that students may be struggling with. Write an essay in which you outline what the telltale signs might be for a common problem faced by students (and people in general), such as relationship problems at home, an inability to balance the demands of work and school, or difficulties concentrating and getting assignments done on time.

PART SIX REVIEWING THE BASICS

A. Understanding the Parts of Speech 498

A.1 Nouns 498
A.2 Pronouns 499
A.3 Verbs 502
A.4 Adjectives 508
A.5 Adverbs 511
A.6 Conjunctions 513
A.7 Prepositions 514
A.8 Interjections 516

B. Understanding the Parts of Sentences 517

B.1 Subjects 518
B.2 Predicates 519
B.3 Complements 521
B.4 Basic Sentence Patterns 522
B.5 Expanding the Sentence with Adjectives and Adverbs 523
B.6 Expanding the Sentence with Phrases 524
B.7 Expanding the Sentence with Clauses 529
B.8 Basic Sentence Classifications 531

C. Avoiding Sentence Errors 534

C.1 Sentence Fragments 534
C.2 Run-On Sentences and Comma Splices 539
C.3 Uses of Verb Tenses 543
C.4 Active and Passive Voices 547
C.5 Subjunctive Mood 549
C.6 Subject-Verb Agreement 550
C.7 Pronoun-Antecedent Agreement 553
C.8 Pronoun Reference 555
C.9 Pronoun Case 557
C.10 Correct Adjective and Adverb Use 559

D. Writing Effective Sentences 563

D.1 Misplaced and Dangling Modifiers 563
D.2 Shifts in Person, Number, and Verb Tense 565
D.3 Coordination 567
D.4 Subordination 569
D.5 Parallelism 571
D.6 Sentence Variety 574
D.7 Redundancy and Wordiness 576
D.8 Diction 578

E. Using Punctuation Correctly 580

E.1 End Punctuation 580
E.2 Commas 581
E.3 Unnecessary Commas 583
E.4 Colons and Semicolons 584
E.5 Dashes, Parentheses, Hyphens, Apostrophes, Quotation Marks 587

F. Managing Mechanics and Spelling 591

F.1 Capitalization 591
F.2 Abbreviations 592
F.3 Hyphenation and Word Division 594
F.4 Numbers 595
F.5 Suggestions for Improving Spelling 596
F.6 Six Useful Spelling Rules 597

OVERVIEW

Most of us know how to communicate in our language, but many of us do not know the specific terms and rules of grammar, which describes how language is put together. There are several reasons why it is important to understand how grammar works: (1) it allows you to recognize errors in your writing and correct them so that your papers read more smoothly and convey your ideas more effectively; (2) it helps you to understand the comments of your teachers and peers, so you can correct problems in your writing; and (3) it enables you to impart your message without distraction or confusion.

The different areas of grammatical study are highly interconnected. The sections on parts of speech, sentences, punctuation, mechanics, and spelling fit together into a logical whole. To recognize and correct a run-on sentence, for example, you need to know both sentence structure *and* punctuation. To avoid errors in capitalization, you need to know parts of speech *and* mechanics. Grammatical terms and rules demand your serious attention. Mastering them will pay handsome dividends: error-free papers, clear thinking, and effective writing.

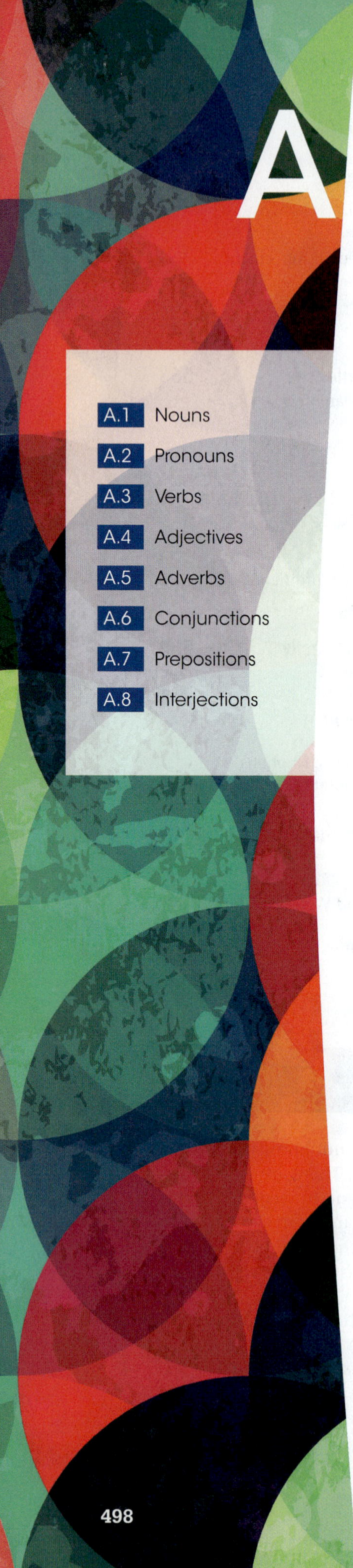

A Understanding the Parts of Speech

A.1 Nouns
A.2 Pronouns
A.3 Verbs
A.4 Adjectives
A.5 Adverbs
A.6 Conjunctions
A.7 Prepositions
A.8 Interjections

The eight parts of speech are **nouns**, **pronouns**, **verbs**, **adjectives**, **adverbs**, **conjunctions**, **prepositions**, and **interjections**. Each word in a sentence functions as one of these parts of speech. Being able to identify the parts of speech in sentences allows you to analyze and improve your writing and to understand grammatical principles discussed later in this section.

It is important to keep in mind that *how* a word functions in a sentence determines *what* part of speech it is. Thus, the same word can be a noun, a verb, or an adjective, depending on how it is used.

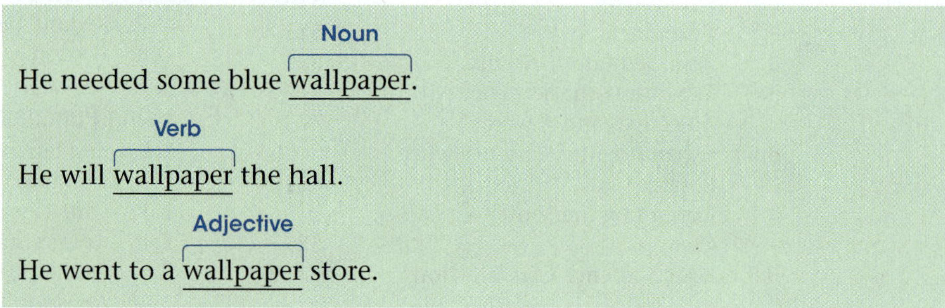

A.1 Nouns

A **noun** names a person, place, thing, or idea.

People	*woman, winner, Maria Alvarez*
Places	*mall, hill, Indiana*
Things	*lamp, ship, air*
Ideas	*goodness, perfection, harmony*

The form of many nouns changes to express **number** (**singular** for one, **plural** for more than one): *one bird, two birds; one child, five children.* Most nouns can also be made **possessive** to show ownership by the addition of *-'s*: *city's, Allison's.*

Sometimes a noun is used to modify another noun:

> Noun modifying diploma
>
> Her goal had always been to earn a college diploma.

Nouns are classified as proper, common, collective, concrete, abstract, count, and noncount.

1. **Proper nouns** name specific people, places, or things and are always capitalized: *Martin Luther King, Jr.; East Lansing; Ford Taurus.* Days of the week and months are considered proper nouns and are capitalized.

   Proper noun: September; Proper noun: Allen; Proper noun: Loyola University

   In September Allen will attend Loyola University.

2. **Common nouns** name one or more of a general class or type of person, place, thing, or idea and are not capitalized: *president, city, car, wisdom.*

   Common noun: fall; Common noun: students; Common noun: college; Common noun: education

   Next fall the students will enter college to receive an education.

3. **Collective nouns** name a whole group or collection of people, places, or things: *committee, team, jury.* They are usually singular in form.

   Collective noun: flock; Collective noun: herd

   The flock of mallards flew over the herd of bison.

4. **Concrete nouns** name tangible things that can be tasted, seen, touched, smelled, or heard: *sandwich, radio, pen.*

   Concrete noun: pizza; Concrete noun: freezer

   The frozen pizza was stuck in the freezer.

5. **Abstract nouns** name ideas, qualities, beliefs, and conditions: *honesty, goodness, poverty.*

   Abstract nouns: love, honor; Abstract noun: trust

   Their marriage was based on love, honor, and trust.

6. **Count nouns** name items that can be counted. Count nouns can be made plural, usually by adding *-s* or *-es*: *one river, three rivers; one box, ten boxes.* Some count nouns form their plural in an irregular way: *man, men; goose, geese.*

   Count noun: salespeople; Count noun: invoices; Count noun: files

   The salespeople put the invoices in their files.

7. **Noncount nouns** name ideas or qualities that cannot be counted. Noncount nouns almost always have no plural form: *air, knowledge, unhappiness.*

   Noncount noun: rain; Noncount noun: courage

   As the rain pounded on the windows, she tried to find the courage to walk home from work.

A.2 Pronouns

A **pronoun** is a word that substitutes for or refers to a noun or another pronoun. The noun or pronoun to which a pronoun refers is called the pronoun's **antecedent**. A pronoun must agree with its antecedent in person, number, and gender (these terms are discussed later in this section).

A. Parts of Speech

After the campers discovered the cave, they mapped it for the next group, which was arriving next week. [The pronoun *they* refers to its antecedent, *campers*; the pronoun *it* refers to its antecedent, *cave*; the pronoun *which* refers to its antecedent, *group*.]

The eight kinds of pronouns are **personal**, **demonstrative**, **reflexive**, **intensive**, **interrogative**, **relative**, **indefinite**, and **reciprocal**.

1. **Personal pronouns** take the place of nouns or pronouns that name people or things. A personal pronoun changes form to indicate **person**, **gender**, **number**, and **case**.

   Person is the grammatical term used to distinguish the speaker (**first person**: *I*, *we*); the person spoken to (**second person**: *you*); and the person or thing spoken about (**third person**: *he*, *she*, *it*, *they*). **Gender** is the term used to classify pronouns as **masculine** (*he*, *him*); **feminine** (*she*, *her*); or **neuter** (*it*). **Number** classifies pronouns as **singular** (one) or **plural** (more than one). Some personal pronouns also function as adjectives modifying nouns (*our house*).

	Singular	***Plural***
First person	I, me, my, mine	we, us, our, ours
Second person	you, your, yours	you, your, yours
Third person		
Masculine	he, him, his	they, them, their, theirs
Feminine	she, her, hers	they, them, their, theirs
Neuter	it, its	they, them, their, theirs

I called my manager about my new clients. She wanted to know as soon as they placed their first orders. "Your new clients are important to us," she said.

[I: First-person singular; my: First-person singular (pronoun/adjective); She: Third-person singular; they: Third-person plural; their: Third-person plural (pronoun/adjective); Your: Second-person singular (pronoun/adjective); us: First-person plural; she: Third-person singular]

A pronoun's **case** is determined by its function as a subject (**subjective** or **nominative case**) or an object (**objective case**) in a sentence. A pronoun that shows ownership is in the **possessive** case. (See p. 557 for a discussion of pronoun case.)

2. **Demonstrative pronouns** refer to particular people or things. The demonstrative pronouns are *this* and *that* (singular) and *these* and *those* (plural). (*This, that, these, and those* can also be demonstrative adjectives when they modify a noun.)

   This is more thorough than that.

   The red shuttle buses stop here. These go to the airport every hour.

3. **Reflexive pronouns** indicate that the subject performs actions to, for, or upon itself. Reflexive pronouns end in *-self* or *-selves*.

Tip for Writers

This, *that*, *these*, and *those* all refer to a thing, a person, things, or people within the speaker's sight, but *that* and *those* refer to things farther away. *This* and *these* refer to what is close to the speaker or writer.

Distance	Singular	Plural
near	this	these
far	that	those

	Singular	*Plural*
First person	myself	ourselves
Second person	yourself	yourselves
Third person	himself herself itself	themselves

We excused ourselves from the table and left.

4. An **intensive pronoun** emphasizes the word that comes before it in a sentence. Like reflexive pronouns, intensive pronouns end in *-self* or *-selves*.

   The filmmaker herself could not explain the ending.

   They themselves repaired the copy machine.

Note: A reflexive or intensive pronoun should not be used as a subject of a sentence. An antecedent for the reflexive pronoun must appear in the same sentence.

INCORRECT	Myself create colorful sculpture.
CORRECT	I myself create colorful sculpture.

5. **Interrogative pronouns** are used to introduce questions: *who, whom, whoever, whomever, what, which, whose*. The correct use of *who* and *whom* depends on the role the interrogative pronoun plays in a sentence or clause. When the pronoun functions as the subject of the sentence or clause, use *who*. When the pronoun functions as an object in the sentence or clause, use *whom* (see p. 559).

   What happened?

   Which is your street?

   Who wrote *Ragtime*? [*Who* is the subject of the sentence.]

   Whom should I notify? [*Whom* is the object of the verb *notify*: *I should notify whom?*]

6. **Relative pronouns** relate groups of words to nouns or other pronouns and often introduce adjective clauses or noun clauses (see p. 530). The relative pronouns are *who, whom, whoever, whomever*, and *whose* (referring to people) and *that, what, whatever*, and *which* (referring to things).

   In 1836 Charles Dickens met John Forster, who became his friend and biographer.

   Jason did not understand what the consultant recommended.

   We read some articles that were written by former astronauts.

7. **Indefinite pronouns** are pronouns without specific antecedents. They refer to people, places, or things in general.

   Someone has been rearranging my papers.

   Many knew the woman, but few could say they knew her well.

> **Tip for Writers**
>
> Be sure to use a *singular verb* after the *indefinite pronouns* that are grammatically singular: Everybody is here now. Let's eat! (Even though *everybody* means at least three people, it's grammatically singular.)

Here are some frequently used indefinite pronouns:

SINGULAR		PLURAL
another	nobody	all
anybody	none	both
anyone	no one	few
anything	nothing	many
each	one	more
either	other	most
everybody	somebody	others
everyone	someone	several
everything	something	some
neither		

8. The **reciprocal pronouns** *each other* and *one another* indicate a mutual relationship between two or more parts of a plural antecedent.

> Armando and Sharon congratulated each other on their high grades.

EXERCISE 1 Identifying Nouns and Pronouns

Directions: In each of the following sentences, (a) circle each noun and (b) underline each pronoun.

EXAMPLE (Jamila) parked her (car) in the (lot) that is reserved for (commuters) like her.

1. Shakespeare wrote many plays that have become famous and important.
2. Everyone who has visited Disneyland wishes to return.
3. Jonathan himself wrote the report that the president of the company presented to the press.
4. That desk used to belong to my boss.
5. My integrity was never questioned by my co-workers.
6. The class always laughed at jokes told by the professor, even though they were usually corny.
7. When will humankind be able to travel to Mars?
8. Whoever wins the lottery this week will become quite wealthy.
9. As the plane landed at the airport, many of the passengers began to gather their carry-on luggage.
10. This week we are studying gravity; next week we will study heat.

A.3 Verbs

Verbs express action or state of being. A grammatically complete sentence has at least one verb in it.

There are three kinds of verbs: **action verbs**, **linking verbs**, and **helping verbs** (also known as **auxiliary verbs**).

1. **Action verbs** express physical and mental activities.

Mr. Royce dashed for the bus.

The incinerator burns garbage at high temperatures.

I think that seat is taken.

The Web designer worked until 3:00 A.M.

Tip for Writers

A *direct object* answers the question *Who?* or *What?* about the verb.

Action verbs are either **transitive** or **intransitive**. The action of a **transitive verb** is directed toward someone or something, called the **direct object** of the verb. Direct objects receive the action of the verb. Transitive verbs require direct objects to complete the meaning of the sentence.

Amalia [Subject] made [Transitive verb] clocks [Direct object].

An **intransitive verb** does not need a direct object to complete the meaning of the sentence.

The traffic [Subject] stopped [Intransitive verb].

Some verbs can be both transitive and intransitive, depending on their meaning and use in a sentence.

INTRANSITIVE	The traffic stopped. [No direct object]
TRANSITIVE	The driver stopped the bus [Direct object] at the corner.

Tip for Writers

Be sure to use an adjective, not an adverb, after a *linking verb*. Use adverbs to describe other verbs: He seems nice. (but) He paints nicely.

2. A **linking verb** expresses a state of being or a condition. A linking verb connects a noun or pronoun to words that describe the noun or pronoun. Common linking verbs are forms of the verb *be* (*is, are, was, were, being, been*), *become, feel, grow, look, remain, seem, smell, sound, stay*, and *taste*.

Their child grew tall.

The office looks messy.

Mr. Davenport is our accountant.

3. A **helping (auxiliary) verb** helps another verb, called the **main verb**, to convey when the action occurred (through verb tense) and to form questions. One or more helping verbs and the main verb together form a **verb phrase**. Some helping verbs, called **modals**, are always helping verbs:

can, could	shall, should
may, might	will, would
must, ought to	

The other helping verbs can sometimes function as main verbs as well:

am, are, be, been, being, did, do, does

had, has, have

is, was, were

The verb *be* is a very irregular verb, with eight forms instead of the usual five: *am, are, be, being, been, is, was, were.*

Helping verb: will; Main verb: close

The store will close early on holidays.

Helping verb: Will; Main verb: close

Will the store close early on New Year's Eve?

Forms of the Verb

All verbs except *be* have five forms: the **base form** (or dictionary form), the **past tense**, the **past participle**, the **present participle**, and the **-*s* form**. The first three forms are called the verb's **principal parts**. The infinitive consists of "to" plus a base form: *to go, to study, to talk*. For **regular verbs**, the past tense and past participle are formed by adding *-d* or *-ed* to the base form. **Irregular verbs** follow no set pattern to form their past tense and past participle.

	Regular	***Irregular***
Infinitive	work	eat
Past tense	worked	ate
Past participle	worked	eaten
Present participle	working	eating
-*s* form	works	eats

Verbs change form to agree with their subjects in person and number (see p. 550); to express the time of their action (**tense**); to express whether the action is a fact, command, or wish (**mood**); and to indicate whether the subject is the doer or the receiver of the action (**voice**).

Principal Parts of Irregular Verbs

Consult the following list and your dictionary for the principal parts of irregular verbs.

BASE FORM	PAST TENSE	PAST PARTICIPLE
be	was	been
become	became	become
begin	began	begun
bite	bit	bitten
blow	blew	blown
burst	burst	burst
catch	caught	caught
choose	chose	chosen
come	came	come
dive	dived, dove	dived
do	did	done
draw	drew	drawn
drive	drove	driven
eat	ate	eaten
fall	fell	fallen
find	found	found

(continued)

BASE FORM	PAST TENSE	PAST PARTICIPLE
fling	flung	flung
fly	flew	flown
get	got	gotten
give	gave	given
go	went	gone
grow	grew	grown
have	had	had
know	knew	known
lay	laid	laid
lead	led	led
leave	left	left
lie	lay	lain
lose	lost	lost
ride	rode	ridden
ring	rang	rung
rise	rose	risen
say	said	said
set	set	set
sit	sat	sat
speak	spoke	spoken
swear	swore	sworn
swim	swam	swum
tear	tore	torn
tell	told	told
throw	threw	thrown
wear	wore	worn
write	wrote	written

Tense

The **tenses** of a verb express time. They convey whether an action, process, or event takes place in the present, past, or future.

The three **simple tenses** are **present**, **past**, and **future**. The **simple present** tense is the base form of the verb (and the *-s* form of third-person singular subjects; see p. 543); the **simple past** tense is the past-tense form; and the **simple future** tense consists of the helping verb *will* plus the base form.

The **perfect tenses**, which indicate completed action, are **present perfect**, **past perfect**, and **future perfect**. They are formed by adding the helping verbs *have* (or *has*), *had*, and *will have* to the past participle.

In addition to the simple and perfect tenses, there are six progressive tenses. The **simple progressive tenses** are the **present progressive**, the **past progressive**, and the **future progressive**. The progressive tenses are used for continuing actions or actions in progress. These progressive tenses are formed by adding the present, past, and future forms of the verb *be* to the present participle. The **perfect progressive tenses** are the **present perfect progressive**, the **past perfect progressive**, and the **future perfect progressive**. They are formed by adding the present perfect, past perfect, and future perfect forms of the verb *be* to the present participle.

The following chart shows all the tenses for a regular verb and an irregular verb in the first person. (For more on tenses, see p. 543.)

	REGULAR	IRREGULAR
Simple present	I talk	I go
Simple past	I talked	I went
Simple future	I will talk	I will go
Present perfect	I have talked	I have gone
Past perfect	I had talked	I had gone
Future perfect	I will have talked	I will have gone
Present progressive	I am talking	I am going
Past progressive	I was talking	I was going
Future progressive	I will be talking	I will be going
Present perfect progressive	I have been talking	I have been going
Past perfect progressive	I had been talking	I had been going
Future perfect progressive	I will have been talking	I will have been going

Mood

The **mood** of a verb indicates the writer's attitude toward the action. There are three moods in English: **indicative**, **imperative**, and **subjunctive**.

1. The **indicative mood** is used for ordinary statements of fact or questions.

    The light flashed on and off all night.

    Did you check the batteries?

2. The **imperative mood** is used for commands, suggestions, or directions. The subject of a verb in the imperative mood is *you*, though it is not always included.

    Stop shouting!

    Come to New York for a visit.

    Turn right at the next corner.

3. The **subjunctive mood** is used for wishes, requirements, recommendations, and statements contrary to fact. For statements contrary to fact or for wishes, the past tense of the verb is used. For the verb *be*, only the past-tense form *were* is used.

    If I had a million dollars, I'd take a trip around the world.

    If my supervisor were promoted, I would be eligible for her job.

    To express suggestions, recommendations, or requirements, the infinitive form is used for all verbs.

    I recommend that the houses be sold after the landscaping is done.

    The registrar required that Maureen pay her bill before attending class.

Voice

Transitive verbs (those that take objects) may be in either the active voice or the passive voice (see p. 547). In an **active-voice** sentence, the subject performs the action described by the verb; that is, the subject is the actor. In a **passive-voice** sentence, the subject is the receiver of the action. The passive voice of a verb is formed by using an appropriate form of the helping verb *be* and the past participle of the main verb.

Subject is actor — Dr. Hillel; Active voice — delivered

Dr. Hillel delivered the report on global warming.

Subject is receiver — report; Passive voice — was delivered

The report on global warming was delivered by Dr. Hillel.

EXERCISE 2

Changing Tenses

Directions: Revise the following sentences, changing each verb from the present tense to the tense indicated.

EXAMPLE I know the right answer.

PAST TENSE I knew the right answer.

1. Allison loses the sales to competitors.

   SIMPLE PAST ____________________

2. Malcolm begins classes at the community college.

   PAST PERFECT ____________________

3. The microscope enlarges the cell.

   PRESENT PERFECT ____________________

4. Reports follow a standard format.

   SIMPLE FUTURE ____________________

5. Meg Ryan receives excellent evaluations.

   FUTURE PERFECT ____________________

6. Juanita writes a computer program.

   PRESENT PERFECT ____________________

7. The movie stars Brad Pitt.

   SIMPLE FUTURE ____________________

8. Dave wins medals at the Special Olympics.

   SIMPLE PAST ____________________

9. Many celebrities donate money to AIDS research.

   PRESENT PERFECT ____________________

10. My nephew travels to Michigan's Upper Peninsula on business.

    PAST PERFECT ____________________

A.4 Adjectives

Adjectives modify nouns and pronouns. That is, they describe, identify, qualify, or limit the meaning of nouns and pronouns. An adjective answers the question *Which one? What kind?* or *How many?* about the word it modifies.

WHICH ONE?	The twisted, torn umbrella was of no use to its owner.
WHAT KIND?	The spotted owl has caused heated arguments in the Northwest.
HOW MANY?	Many customers waited for four days for telephone cable service to be restored.

In form, adjectives can be **positive** (implying no comparison), **comparative** (comparing two items), or **superlative** (comparing three or more items). (See p. 559 for more on the forms of adjectives.)

Positive
The computer is fast.

Comparative
Your computer is faster than mine.

Superlative
This is the fastest computer I have ever used.

There are two general categories of adjectives. **Descriptive adjectives** name a quality of the person, place, thing, or idea they describe: *mysterious man, green pond, healthy complexion.* **Limiting adjectives** narrow the scope of the person, place, or thing they describe: *my computer, this tool, second try.*

Descriptive Adjectives

A **regular** (or **attributive**) adjective appears next to (usually before) the word it modifies. Several adjectives can modify the same word.

The enthusiastic new hair stylist gave short, lopsided haircuts.

The wealthy dealer bought an immense blue vase.

Sometimes nouns function as adjectives modifying other nouns:

tree house, hamburger bun

A **predicate adjective** follows a linking verb and modifies or describes the subject of the sentence or clause (see p. 519; see p. 529 on clauses).

Predicate adjective
The meeting was long. [Modifies the subject, *meeting*]

Limiting Adjectives

1. The **definite article**, *the*, and the **indefinite articles**, *a* and *an*, are classified as adjectives. *A* and *an* are used when it is not important to specify a

particular noun or when the object named is not known to the reader (*A radish adds color to a salad*). *The* is used when it is important to specify one or more of a particular noun or when the object named is known to the reader or has already been mentioned (*The radishes from the garden are on the table*).

> A squirrel visited the feeder that I just built. The squirrel tried to eat some bird food.

2. When the possessive pronouns *my, your, his, her, its, our*, and *their* are used as modifiers before nouns, they are considered **possessive adjectives** (see p. 508).

   > Your friend borrowed my laptop for his trip.

3. When the demonstrative pronouns *this, that, these*, and *those* are used as modifiers before nouns, they are called **demonstrative adjectives** (see p. 499). *This* and *these* modify nouns close to the writer; *that* and *those* modify nouns more distant from the writer.

   > Buy these hot pink shoes, not those ugly black ones.
   >
   > This freshman course is a prerequisite for those advanced courses.

4. **Cardinal adjectives** are words used in counting: *one, two, twenty*, and so on.

   > I read four biographies of Jack Kerouac and seven articles about his work.

5. **Ordinal adjectives** note position in a series.

   > The first biography was too sketchy; whereas the second one was too detailed.

6. **Indefinite adjectives** provide nonspecific, general information about the quantities and amounts of the nouns they modify. Some common indefinite adjectives are *another, any, enough, few, less, little, many, more, much, several*, and *some*.

   > Several people asked me if I had enough blankets or if I wanted the thermostat turned up a few degrees.

7. The **interrogative adjectives** *what, which*, and *whose* modify nouns and pronouns used in questions.

   > Which radio station do you like? Whose music do you prefer?

8. The words *which* and *what*, along with *whichever* and *whatever*, are **relative adjectives** when they modify nouns and introduce subordinate clauses.

   > She couldn't decide which job she wanted to take.

9. **Proper adjectives** are adjectives derived from proper nouns: *Spain* (noun), *Spanish* (adjective); *Freud* (noun), *Freudian* (adjective); see p. 499. Most proper adjectives are capitalized.

   > Shakespeare lived in Elizabethan England.
   >
   > The speaker used many French expressions.

EXERCISE 3 Adding Adjectives

Directions: Revise each of the following sentences by adding at least three adjectives.

EXAMPLE The cat slept on the pillow.

REVISED The old yellow cat slept on the expensive pillow.

1. Before leaving on a trip, the couple packed their suitcases.

2. The tree dropped leaves all over the lawn.

3. While riding the train, the passengers read newspapers.

4. The antiques dealer said that the desk was more valuable than the chair.

5. As the play was ending, the audience clapped their hands and tossed roses onstage.

6. Stew is served nightly at the shelter.

7. The engine roared as the car stubbornly jerked into gear.

8. The tourists tossed pennies into the fountain.

9. Folders were stacked on the desk next to the monitor.

10. Marina's belt and shoes were made of the same material and complemented her dress.

____

____

A.5 Adverbs

Adverbs modify verbs, adjectives, other adverbs, or entire sentences or clauses (see p. 529 on clauses). Like adjectives, adverbs describe, qualify, or limit the meaning of the words they modify.

An adverb answers the question *How? When? Where? How often?* or *To what extent?* about the word it modifies.

HOW?	Lian moved awkwardly because of her stiff neck.
WHEN?	I arrived yesterday.
WHERE?	They searched everywhere.
HOW OFTEN?	He telephoned repeatedly.
TO WHAT EXTENT?	Simon was rather slow to answer his e-mail.

Many adverbs end in *-ly* (*lazily, happily*), but some adverbs do not (*fast, here, much, well, rather, everywhere, never, so*), and some words that end in *-ly* are not adverbs (*lively, friendly, lonely*). Like all other parts of speech, an adverb may be best identified by examining its function within a sentence.

I quickly skimmed the book. [Modifies the verb *skimmed*]

Very angry customers crowded the service desk. [Modifies the adjective *angry*]

He was injured quite seriously. [Modifies the adverb *seriously*]

Apparently, the job was bungled. [Modifies the whole sentence]

Like adjectives, adverbs have three forms: **positive** (does not suggest any comparison), **comparative** (compares two actions or conditions), and **superlative** (compares three or more actions or conditions; see also p. 560).

Julian rose early (Positive) and crept downstairs quietly (Positive).

Isaiah rose earlier (Comparative) than Julian and crept downstairs more quietly (Comparative).

Cody rose earliest (Superlative) of anyone in the house and crept downstairs most quietly (Superlative).

Some adverbs, called **conjunctive adverbs** (or **adverbial conjunctions**)—such as *however, therefore,* and *besides*—connect the ideas of one sentence or clause to those of a previous sentence or clause. They can appear anywhere in a sentence. (See p. 540 for how to punctuate sentences containing conjunctive adverbs.)

Conjunctive adverb

James did not want to go to the library on Saturday; however, he knew the books were overdue.

Conjunctive adverb

The sporting goods store was crowded because of the sale. Leila, therefore, was asked to work extra hours.

Some common conjunctive adverbs are listed below, including several phrases that function as conjunctive adverbs.

accordingly	for example	meanwhile	otherwise
also	further	moreover	similarly
anyway	furthermore	namely	still
as a result	hence	nevertheless	then
at the same time	however	next	thereafter
besides	incidentally	nonetheless	therefore
certainly	indeed	now	thus
consequently	instead	on the contrary	undoubtedly
finally	likewise	on the other hand	

EXERCISE 4

Using Adverbs

Directions: Write a sentence using each of the following comparative or superlative adverbs.

EXAMPLE better: My car runs better now than ever before.

1. farther: ____________________

2. most: ____________________

3. more: ____________________

4. best: ____________________

5. least neatly: ____________________

6. louder: ____________________

7. worse: ____________________

8. less angrily: ______________________________

____

9. later: ______________________________

____

10. earliest: ______________________________

____

A.6 Conjunctions

Conjunctions connect words, phrases, and clauses. There are three kinds of conjunctions: **coordinating**, **correlative**, and **subordinating**. **Coordinating** and **correlative conjunctions** connect words, phrases, or clauses of equal grammatical rank. (A **phrase** is a group of related words lacking a subject, a predicate, or both. A **clause** is a group of words containing a subject and a predicate; see p. 518 and 519.)

1. The **coordinating conjunctions** are *and, but, nor, or, for, so*, and *yet*. These words must connect words or word groups of the same kind. Therefore, two nouns may be connected by *and*, but a noun and a clause cannot be. *For* and *so* can connect only independent clauses.

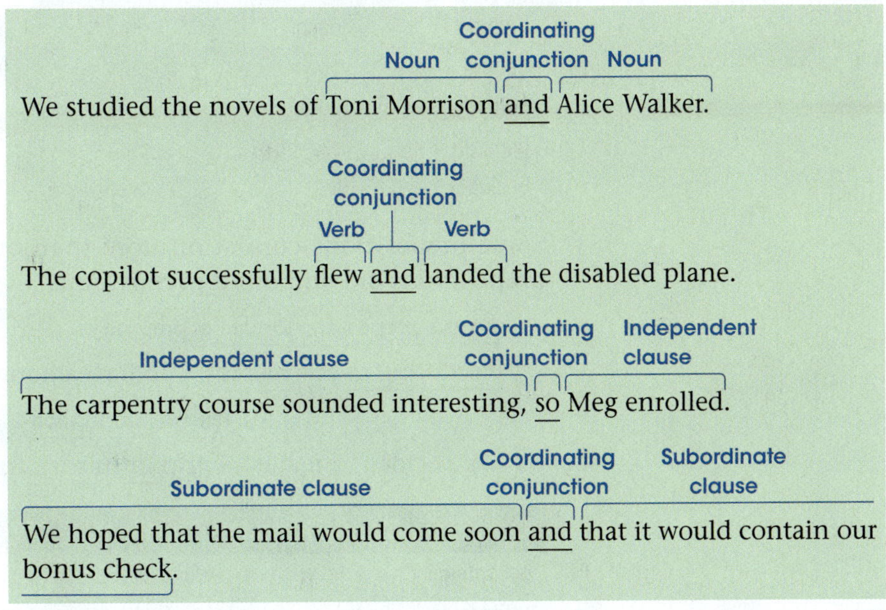

2. **Correlative conjunctions** are pairs of words that link and relate grammatically equivalent parts of a sentence. Some common correlative conjunctions are *either/or, neither/nor, both/and, not/but, not only/but also*, and *whether/or*. Correlative conjunctions are always used in pairs.

Correlative conjunctions

Either the electricity was off, or the bulb had burned out.

3. **Subordinating conjunctions** connect dependent, or subordinate, clauses to independent clauses (see p. 529). Some common subordinating conjunctions are *although, because, if, since, until, when, where*, and *while*.

Subordinating conjunction

Although the movie got bad reviews, it drew big crowds.

Subordinating conjunction

She received a lot of mail because she was a reliable correspondent.

A.7 Prepositions

A **preposition** links and relates its **object** (a noun or a pronoun) to the rest of the sentence. Prepositions often show relationships of time, place, direction, and manner.

Preposition / Object of preposition

I walked around the block.

Preposition / Object of preposition

She called during our meeting.

Common Prepositions

along	besides	from	past	up
among	between	in	since	upon
around	beyond	near	through	with
at	by	off	till	within
before	despite	on	to	without
behind	down	onto	toward	
below	during	out	under	
beneath	except	outside	underneath	
beside	for	over	until	

Some prepositions consist of more than one word; they are called **phrasal prepositions** or **compound prepositions**.

Phrasal preposition / Object of preposition

According to our records, you have enough credits to graduate.

Phrasal preposition / Object of preposition

We decided to make the trip in spite of the snowstorm.

Common Compound Prepositions

according to	in addition to	on account of
aside from	in front of	out of
as of	in place of	prior to
as well as	in regard to	with regard to
because of	in spite of	with respect to
by means of	instead of	

The object of the preposition often has modifiers.

Prep. / Modifier / Obj. of prep. / Prep. / Modifier / Obj. of prep.

Not a sound came from the child's room except a gentle snoring.

Sometimes a preposition has more than one object (a **compound object**).

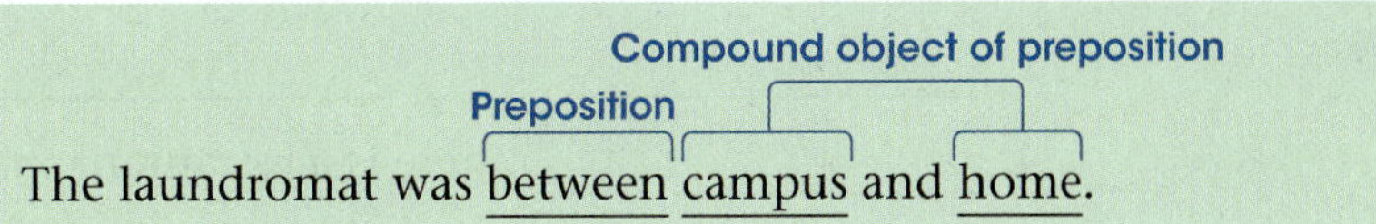

Usually the preposition comes before its object. In interrogative sentences, however, the preposition sometimes follows its object.

> Object of preposition — Preposition
>
> What did your supervisor ask you about?

The preposition, the object or objects of the preposition, and the object's modifiers all form a **prepositional phrase**.

> Prepositional phrase
>
> The scientist conducted her experiment throughout the afternoon and early evening.

Tip for Writers

Throughout means "all through." *Alongside* means "next to."

There may be many prepositional phrases in a sentence.

> Prepositional phrase — Prepositional phrase
>
> The water from the open hydrant flowed into the street.
>
> The noisy kennel was underneath the beauty salon, despite the complaints of customers.
>
> Alongside the weedy railroad tracks, an old hotel with faded grandeur stood near the abandoned brick station on the edge of town.

Prepositional phrases frequently function as adjectives or adverbs. If a prepositional phrase modifies a noun or pronoun, it functions as an adjective. If it modifies a verb, adjective, or adverb, it functions as an adverb.

> The auditorium inside the conference center has a special sound system. [Adjective modifying the noun *auditorium*]
>
> The doctor looked cheerfully at the patient and handed the lab results across the desk. [Adverbs modifying the verbs *looked* and *handed*]

EXERCISE 5 Expanding Sentences Using Prepositional Phrases

Directions: Expand each of the following sentences by adding a prepositional phrase in the blank.

EXAMPLE A cat hid under the car when the garage door opened.

1. Fish nibbled ________________ as the fisherman waited.

   ____

2. The librarian explained that the books about Africa are located ________________.

   ____

3. When the bullet hit the window, shards flew ________________.

____

4. ________________, there is a restaurant that serves alligator meat.

____

5. Polar bears are able to swim ________________.

____

6. Heavy winds blowing ________________ caused the waves to hit the house.

____

7. One student completed her exam ________________.

____

8. A frog jumped ________________.

____

9. The bus was parked ________________.

____

10. Stacks of books were piled ________________.

____

A.8 Interjections

Interjections are words that express emotion or surprise. They are followed by an exclamation point, comma, or period, depending on whether they stand alone or serve as part or all of a sentence. Interjections are used in speech more than in writing.

Wow! What an announcement!

So, was that lost letter ever found?

Well, I'd better be going.

Understanding the Parts of Sentences

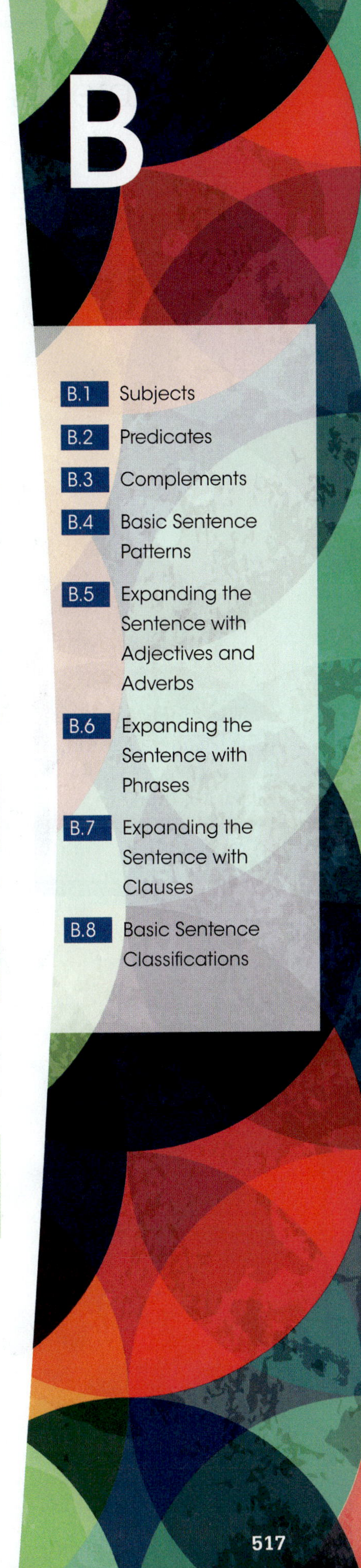

B.1 Subjects
B.2 Predicates
B.3 Complements
B.4 Basic Sentence Patterns
B.5 Expanding the Sentence with Adjectives and Adverbs
B.6 Expanding the Sentence with Phrases
B.7 Expanding the Sentence with Clauses
B.8 Basic Sentence Classifications

A **sentence** is a group of words that must expresses a complete thought about something or someone. A sentence contain a **subject** and a **predicate**.

Subject	***Predicate***
Telephones	ring.
Cecilia	laughed.
Time	will tell.

Depending on their purpose and punctuation, sentences are **declarative**, **interrogative**, **exclamatory**, or **imperative**.

1. A **declarative sentence** makes a statement. It ends with a period.

   Subject Predicate
   The snow fell steadily.

2. An **interrogative sentence** asks a question. It ends with a question mark (?).

3. An **exclamatory sentence** conveys strong emotion. It ends with an exclamation point (!).

   Subject Predicate
   Your photograph is in the company newsletter!

4. An **imperative sentence** gives an order or makes a request. It ends with either a period or an exclamation point, depending on how mild or strong the command or request is. In an imperative sentence, the subject is *you*, but this often is not included.

   Predicate
   Get me a fire extinguisher now! [The subject *you* is understood: (*You*) get me a fire extinguisher now!]

B.1 Subjects

The **subject** of a sentence is whom or what the sentence is about. It is who or what performs or receives the action expressed in the predicate.

1. The subject is often a **noun**, a word that names a person, place, thing, or idea.

> Adriana worked on her math homework.
>
> The rose bushes must be watered.
>
> Honesty is the best policy.

2. The subject of a sentence can also be a **pronoun**, a word that refers to or substitutes for a noun.

> She revised the memo three times.
>
> I will attend the sales meeting.
>
> Although the catsup spilled, it did not go on my shirt.

3. The subject of a sentence can also be a group of words used as a noun.

> Reading e-mail from friends is my idea of a good time.

Tip for Writers

The simple subject is *reading*, a gerund, a noun made from a verb. It takes a singular verb, in this case, *is*.

Simple Versus Complete Subjects

1. The simple subject is the noun or pronoun that names what the sentence is about. It does not include any **modifiers**—that is, words that describe, identify, qualify, or limit the meaning of the noun or pronoun.

> Simple subject
>
> The bright red concert poster caught everyone's eye.
>
> Simple subject
>
> High-speed computers have revolutionized the banking industry.

When the subject of a sentence is a proper noun (the name of a particular person, place, or thing), the entire name is considered the simple subject.

> Simple subject
>
> Martin Luther King, Jr., was a famous leader.

The simple subject of an imperative sentence is *you*.

> Simple subject
>
> [You] Remember to bring the sales brochures.

2. The **complete subject** is the simple subject plus its modifiers.

> Complete subject
>
> Simple subject
>
> The sleek, black limousine waited outside the church.
>
> Complete subject
>
> Fondly remembered as a gifted songwriter, fiddle player, and storyteller, Quintin Lotus Dickey lived in a cabin in Paoli, Indiana.
>
> Simple subject

Compound Subjects

Some sentences contain two or more subjects joined with a coordinating conjunction (*and, but, nor, or, for, so, yet*). Those subjects together form a **compound subject**.

Compound subject

Maria and I completed the marathon.

Compound subject

The computer, the printer, and the cable box were not usable during the blackout.

B.2 Predicates

The **predicate** indicates what the subject does, what happened to the subject, or what is being said about the subject. The predicate must include a **verb**, a word or group of words that expresses an action or a state of being (for example, *run, invent, build, know, will decide, become*).

Joy swam 60 laps.

The thunderstorm replenished the reservoir.

Sometimes the verb consists of only one word, as in the previous examples. Often, however, the main verb is accompanied by a **helping verb** (see p. 503).

Helping verb / Main verb

By the end of the week, I will have worked twenty-five hours.

Helping verb / Main verb

The training session had begun.

Helping verb / Main verb

The professor did return the journal assignments.

Tip for Writers

Did return is an emphatic past form. This form is often used (instead of the usual past, *returned*) when someone has made a mistake:

Alex said, "The professor didn't return our last essays."

Vera replied, "He did return them. He handed them back the day you were absent."

Simple Versus Complete Predicates

The **simple predicate** is the main verb plus its helping verbs (together known as the **verb phrase**). The simple predicate does not include any modifiers.

Simple predicate

The proctor hastily collected the blue books.

Simple predicate

The moderator had introduced the next speaker.

The **complete predicate** consists of the simple predicate, its modifiers, and any complements (words that complete the meaning of the verb; see p. 521). In general, the complete predicate includes everything in the sentence except the complete subject.

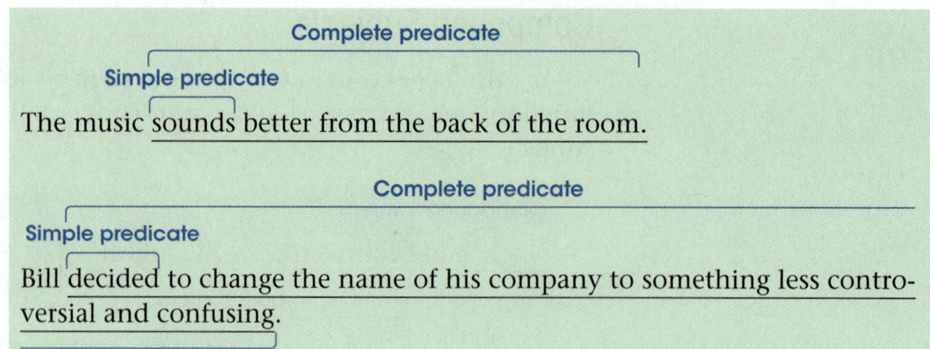

B. Parts of Sentences

Compound Predicates

Some sentences have two or more predicates joined by a coordinating conjunction (*and, but, or,* or *nor*). These predicates together form a **compound predicate**.

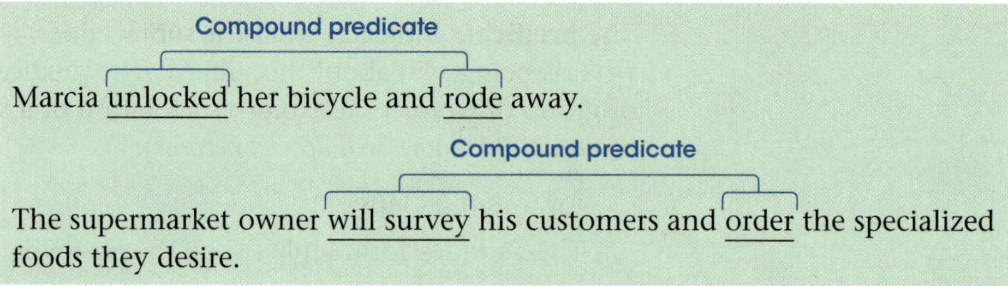

EXERCISE 6

Identifying Simple Subjects and Simple and Compound Predicates

Directions: Underline the simple subject(s) and circle the simple or compound predicate(s) in each of the following sentences.

EXAMPLE Pamela Wong photographed a hummingbird.

1. A group of nurses walked across the lobby on their way to a staff meeting.
2. The campground for physically challenged children is funded and supported by the Rotary Club.
3. Forty doctors and lawyers had attended the seminar on malpractice insurance.
4. Sullivan Beach will not reopen because of pollution.
5. The police cadets attended classes all day and studied late into each evening.
6. Greenpeace is an environmentalist organization.
7. Talented dancers and experienced musicians performed and received much applause at the open-air show.
8. Some undergraduate students have been using empty classrooms for group study.
9. A police officer, with the shoplifter in handcuffs, entered the police station.
10. The newly elected senator walked up to the podium and began her first speech to her constituents.

B.3 Complements

A **complement** is a word or group of words used to complete the meaning of a subject or object. There are four kinds of complements: **subject complements**, which follow linking verbs; **direct objects** and **indirect objects**, which follow transitive verbs (verbs that take an object); and **object complements**, which follow direct objects.

Linking Verbs and Subject Complements

A linking verb (such as *be, become, seem, feel, taste*) links the subject to a **subject complement**, a noun or adjective that renames or describes the subject. (See p. 503 for more about linking verbs.) Nouns that function as complements are called **predicate nominatives** or **predicate nouns**. Adjectives that function as complements are called **predicate adjectives**.

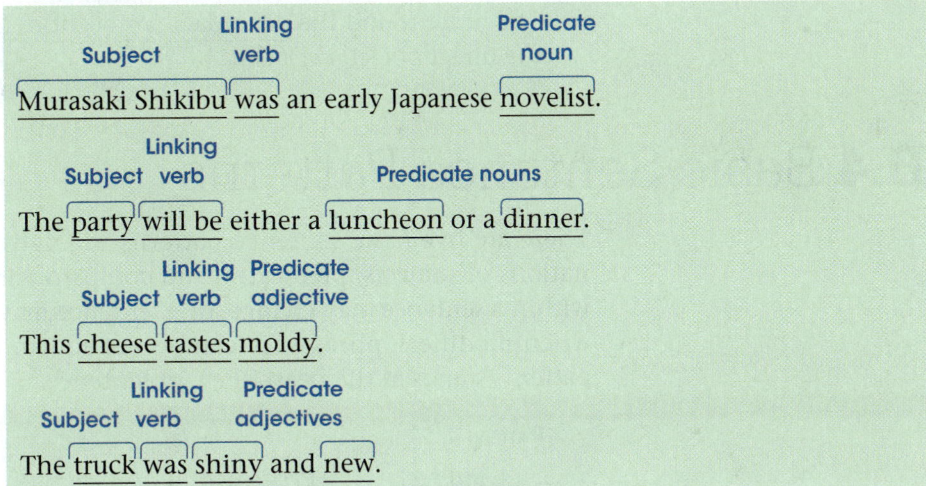

Direct Objects

A **direct object** is a noun or pronoun that receives the action of a transitive verb (see p. 503). A direct object answers the question What? or Whom?

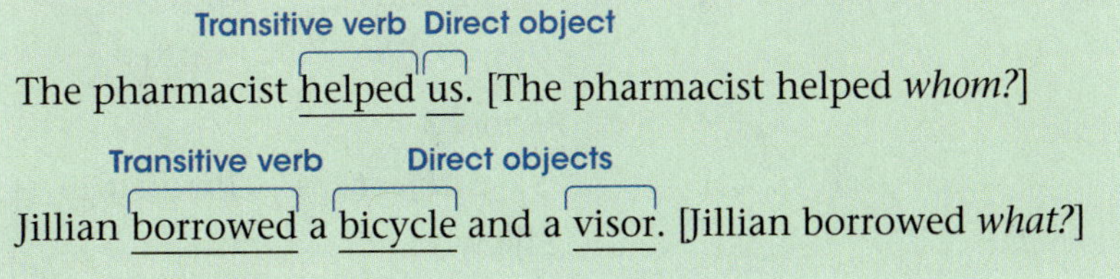

Indirect Objects

An **indirect object** is a noun or pronoun that receives the action of the verb indirectly. Indirect objects name the person or thing to whom or for whom something is done.

Transitive verb | Indirect object | Direct object

The computer technician gave me the bill. [He gave the bill *to whom?*]

Tip for Writers

In sentences that tell both *who* and *what* after the verb, follow the word order shown here:

Amir gave his sister a gift. (Do not use *to*.)

Amir gave a gift to his sister. (Use *to*.)

If you mention the person before the thing, don't use *to*.

Transitive verb — Indirect objects — Direct objects

Eric bought his wife and son some sandwiches and milk. [He bought food *for whom?*]

Object Complements

An **object complement** is a noun or adjective that modifies (describes) or renames the direct object. Object complements appear with verbs like *name, find, think, elect, appoint, choose,* and *consider*.

Direct object — Noun as object complement

We appointed Dean our representative. [*Representative* renames the direct object, *Dean*.]

Direct object — Adjective as object complement

The judge found the defendant innocent of the charges. [*Innocent* modifies the direct object, *defendant*.]

B.4 Basic Sentence Patterns

There are five basic sentence patterns in English. They are built with combinations of subjects, predicates, and complements. The order of these elements within a sentence may change, or a sentence may become long and complicated when modifiers, phrases, or clauses are added. Nonetheless, one of five basic patterns stands at the heart of every sentence.

Pattern 1

Subject	+	***Predicate***
I		shivered.
Cynthia		swam.

Pattern 2

Subject	+	***Predicate***	+	***Direct Object***
Anthony		ordered		a new desk.
We		wanted		freedom.

Pattern 3

Subject	+	***Predicate***	+	***Subject Complement***
The woman		was		a welder.
Our course		is		interesting.

Pattern 4

Subject	+	***Predicate***	+	***Indirect Object***	+	***Direct Object***
My friend		loaned		me		a laptop.
The company		sent		employees		a questionnaire.

Pattern 5

Subject	+	***Predicate***	+	***Direct Object***	+	***Object Complement***
I		consider		her singing		exceptional.
Lampwick		called		Jiminy Cricket		a beetle.

EXERCISE 7

Adding Complements

Directions: Complete each sentence with a word or words that will function as the type of complement indicated.

EXAMPLE The scientist acted ___proud___ as he announced his latest invention. predicate adjective

1. The delivery person handed ____________ the large brown package. indirect object
2. Ronald Reagan was an American ____________. predicate noun
3. The chairperson appointed Yesenia our ____________. object complement
4. Protesters stood on the corner and handed out ____________. direct object
5. The receptionist gave ____________ the messages. indirect object
6. Before the storm, many clouds were ____________. predicate adjective
7. The beer advertisement targeted ____________. direct object
8. The Super Bowl players were ____________. predicate noun
9. The diplomat declared the Olympics ____________. object complement
10. Shopping malls are ____________ before Christmas. predicate adjective

B.5 Expanding the Sentence with Adjectives and Adverbs

A sentence may consist of just a subject and a verb.

Linda studied.

Rumors circulated.

Most sentences, however, contain additional information about the subject and the verb. Information is commonly added in three ways:

- by using adjectives and adverbs;
- by using phrases (groups of words that lack either a subject or a predicate or both);
- by using clauses (groups of words that contain both a subject and a predicate).

Using Adjectives and Adverbs to Expand Your Sentences

Adjectives are words used to modify or describe nouns and pronouns (see p. 508). Adjectives answer questions about nouns and pronouns such as *Which one? What kind? How many?* Using adjectives is one way to add detail and information to sentences.

WITHOUT ADJECTIVES	Dogs barked at cats.
WITH ADJECTIVES	Our three large, brown dogs barked at the two terrified, spotted cats.

Note: Sometimes nouns and participles are used as adjectives (see p. 504 on participles).

People are rediscovering the milk bottle. (Noun used as adjective: milk)

Mrs. Simon had a swimming pool with a broken drain. (Present participle used as adjective: swimming; Past participle used as adjective: broken)

Adverbs add information to sentences by modifying or describing verbs, adjectives, or other adverbs (see p. 511). An adverb usually answers the question *How? When? Where? How often?* or *To what extent?*

WITHOUT ADVERBS	I will clean.
	The audience applauded.
WITH ADVERBS	I will clean very thoroughly tomorrow.
	The audience applauded loudly and enthusiastically.

B.6 Expanding the Sentence with Phrases

A **phrase** is a group of related words that lacks a subject, a predicate, or both. A phrase cannot stand alone as a sentence. Phrases can appear at the beginning, middle, or end of a sentence.

WITHOUT PHRASES	I noticed the stain.
	Sal researched the topic.
	Manuela arose.
WITH PHRASES	Upon entering the room, I noticed the stain on the expensive carpet.
	At the local aquarium, Sal researched the topic of shark attacks.

An amateur astronomer, Manuela arose in the middle of the night to observe the lunar eclipse but, after waiting ten minutes in the cold, gave up.

There are eight kinds of phrases: **noun**; **verb**; **prepositional**; **verbal (participial, gerund,** and **infinitive)**; **appositive**; and **absolute**.

Noun and Verb Phrases

A noun plus its modifiers is a **noun phrase** (*red shoes, the quiet house*). A main verb plus its helping verb is a **verb phrase** (*had been exploring, is sleeping*; see p. 503 on helping verbs.)

Prepositional Phrases

A **prepositional phrase** consists of a preposition (for example, *in, above, with, at, behind*), an object of the preposition (a noun or pronoun), and any modifiers of the object. (See p. 514 for a list of common prepositions.) A prepositional phrase functions like an adjective (modifying a noun or pronoun) or an adverb (modifying a verb, adjective, or adverb). You can use prepositional phrases to tell more about people, places, objects, or actions. A prepositional phrase usually adds information about time, place, direction, manner, or degree.

As Adjectives

The woman with the briefcase is giving a presentation on meditation techniques.

Both of the telephones behind the partition were ringing.

As Adverbs

The fire drill occurred in the morning.

I was curious about the new human resources director.

The conference speaker came from Australia.

With horror, the crowd watched the rhinoceros's tether stretch to the breaking point.

A prepositional phrase can function as part of the complete subject or as part of the complete predicate, but should not be confused with the simple subject or simple predicate.

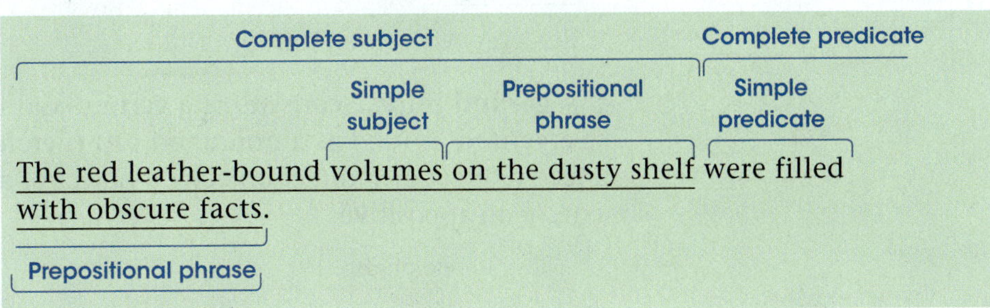

Complete predicate

Simple predicate Prepositional phrase

Pat ducked quickly behind the potted fern.

Verbal Phrases

A **verbal** is a verb form that cannot function as the main verb of a sentence. The three kinds of verbals are **participles**, **gerunds**, and **infinitives**. A **verbal phrase** consists of a verbal and its modifiers.

Participles and Participial Phrases

All verbs have two participles: present and past. The **present participle** is formed by adding *-ing* to the infinitive form (*walking, riding, being*). The **past participle** of regular verbs is formed by adding *-d* or *-ed* to the infinitive form (*walked, baked*). The past participle of irregular verbs has no set pattern (*ridden, been*). (See p. 504 for a list of common irregular verbs and their past participles.) Both the present participle and the past participle can function as adjectives modifying nouns and pronouns.

Past participle as adjective Present participle as adjective

Irritated, Martha circled the confusing traffic rotary once again.

A **participial phrase** consists of a participle and any of its modifiers.

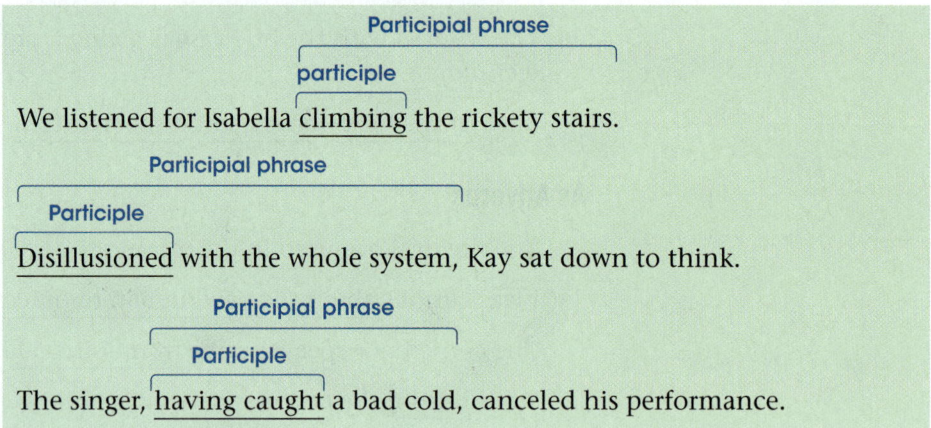

Gerunds and Gerund Phrases

A **gerund** is the present participle (the *-ing* form) of the verb used as a noun.

Shoveling is good exercise.

Rex enjoyed gardening.

A **gerund phrase** consists of a gerund and its modifiers. A gerund phrase, like a gerund, is used as a noun and can therefore function in a sentence as a subject, a direct or indirect object, an object of a preposition, a subject complement, or an appositive.

Gerund phrase

Photocopying the report took longer than La Tisha anticipated. [Subject]

Gerund phrase

The director considered making another monster movie. [Direct object]

Gerund phrase

She gave running three miles daily credit for her health. [Indirect object]

Gerund phrase

Before learning Greek, Omar spoke only English. [Object of the preposition]

Gerund phrase

Her business is designing collapsible furniture. [Subject complement]

Gerund phrase

Hana's trick, memorizing license plates, has come in handy. [Appositive]

Infinitives and Infinitive Phrases

The **infinitive** is the base form of the verb as it appears in the dictionary preceded by the word *to*. An **infinitive phrase** consists of the word *to* plus the infinitive and any modifiers. An infinitive phrase can function as a noun, an adjective, or an adverb. When it is used as a noun, an infinitive phrase can be a subject, object, complement, or appositive.

infinitive phrase

To love one's enemies is a noble goal. [Noun used as subject]

infinitive phrase

The season to sell bulbs is the fall. [Adjective modifying *season*]

infinitive phrase

The chess club met to practice for the state championship. [Adverb modifying *met*]

Sometimes the *to* in an infinitive phrase is not written.

Jacob helped us learn the new accounting procedure. [The *to* before *learn* is understood.]

Note: Do not confuse infinitive phrases with prepositional phrases beginning with the preposition *to*. In an infinitive phrase, *to* is followed by a verb; in a prepositional phrase, *to* is followed by a noun or pronoun.

Appositive Phrases

An **appositive** is a noun that explains, restates, or adds new information about another noun. An **appositive phrase** consists of an appositive and its modifiers. (See p. 584 for punctuation of appositive phrases.)

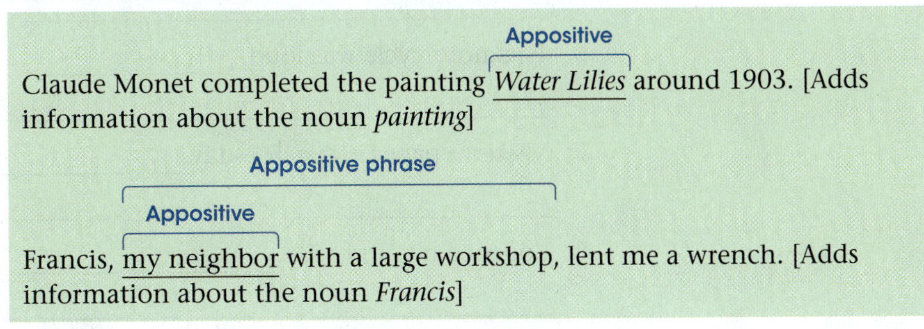

Appositive

Claude Monet completed the painting *Water Lilies* around 1903. [Adds information about the noun *painting*]

Appositive phrase

Appositive

Francis, my neighbor with a large workshop, lent me a wrench. [Adds information about the noun *Francis*]

B. Parts of Sentences

Absolute Phrases

An **absolute phrase** consists of a noun or pronoun and any modifiers followed by a participle or a participial phrase (see p. 526). An absolute phrase modifies an entire sentence, not any particular word within the sentence. It can appear anywhere in a sentence and is set off from the rest of the sentence with a comma or commas. There may be more than one absolute phrase in a sentence.

> Absolute phrase: The winter being over,
> The winter being over, the geese returned.
>
> Absolute phrase: his voice rising to be heard over the loud applause,
> Senator Arden began his speech, his voice rising to be heard over the loud applause.
>
> Absolute phrase: A vacancy having occurred,
> A vacancy having occurred, the hotel manager called the first name on the reservations waiting list.

EXERCISE 8

Expanding Sentences with Adjectives, Adverbs, and Phrases

Directions: Expand each of the following sentences by adding adjectives, adverbs, and/or phrases (prepositional, verbal, appositive, or absolute).

EXAMPLE The professor lectured.

EXPANDED *Being an expert on animal behavior, the professor lectured about animal-intelligence studies.*

1. Randall will graduate. ______________________________

2. The race began. ______________________________

3. Walmart is remodeling. ______________________________

4. Hillary walked alone. ______________________________

5. Manuel repairs appliances. ______________________________

6. The motorcycle was loud. ______________________________

7. My term paper is due Tuesday. ______________________________

8. I opened my umbrella. ______________________________

9. Austin built a garage. ______________________________

____

10. Lucas climbs mountains. ______________________________

____

B.7 Expanding the Sentence with Clauses

A **clause** is a group of words that contains a subject and a predicate. A clause is either **independent** (also called **main**) or **dependent** (also called **subordinate**).

Independent Clauses

An **independent clause** can stand alone as a grammatically complete sentence.

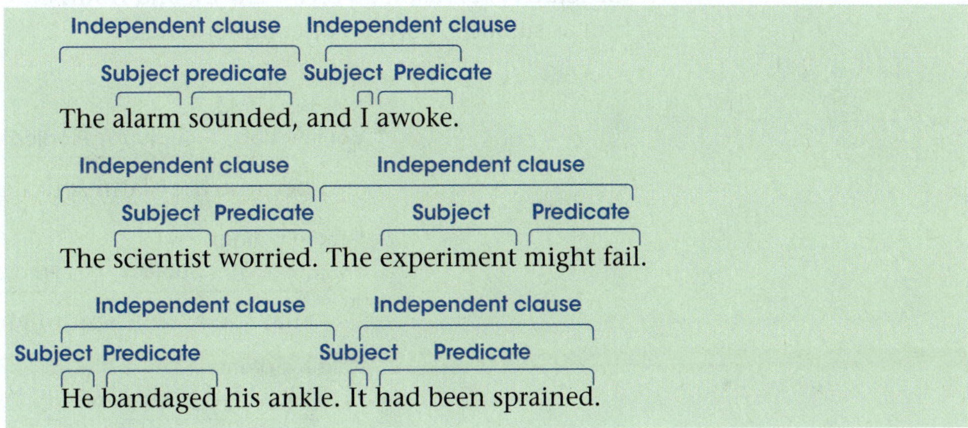

Dependent Clauses

A **dependent clause** has a subject and a predicate, but it cannot stand alone as a grammatically complete sentence because it does not express a complete thought. Most dependent clauses begin with either a **subordinating conjunction** or a **relative pronoun**. These words connect the dependent clause to an independent clause.

Tip for Writers

Remember that some of these words have two meanings. For example, *once* can mean "one time" or "after." *While* can mean "at the same time" or "but."

Common Subordinating Conjunctions		
after	in as much as	that
although	in case	though
as	in order that	unless
as far as	in so far as	until
as if	in that	when
as soon as	now that	whenever
as though	once	where
because	provided that	wherever
before	rather than	whether

(*continued*)

Common Subordinating Conjunctions		
even if	since	while
even though	so that	why
how	supposing that	
if	than	
Relative Pronouns		
that	which	
	who (whose, whom)	
whatever	whoever (whomever)	

These clauses do not express complete thoughts and therefore cannot stand alone as sentences. When joined to independent clauses, however, dependent clauses function as adjectives, adverbs, and nouns and are known as **adjective** (or **relative**) **clauses**, **adverb clauses**, and **noun clauses**. Noun clauses can function as subjects, objects, or complements.

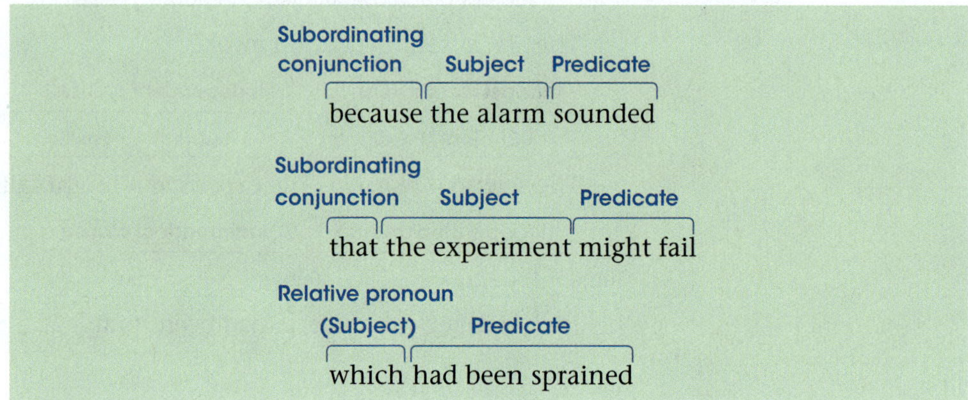

Adjective Clause

He bandaged his ankle, which had been sprained. [Modifies *ankle*]
(Dependent clause: which had been sprained)

Adverb Clause

Because the alarm sounded, I awoke. [Modifies *awoke*]
(Dependent clause: Because the alarm sounded)

Noun Clause

The scientist worried that the experiment might fail. [Direct object of *worried*]
(Dependent clause: that the experiment might fail)

Elliptical Clause

Sometimes the relative pronoun or subordinating conjunction is implied or understood rather than stated. Also, a dependent clause may contain an implied predicate. When a dependent clause is missing an element that can clearly be supplied from the context of the sentence, it is called an **elliptical clause**.

Elliptical clause

The circus is more entertaining than television [is]. [*Is* is the understood predicate in the elliptical dependent clause.]

Elliptical clause

Canadian history is among the subjects [that] the book discusses. [*That* is the understood relative pronoun in the elliptical dependent clause.]

Relative pronouns are generally the subject or object in their clauses. *Who* and *whoever* change to *whom* and *whomever* when they function as objects (see p. 559).

B.8 Basic Sentence Classifications

Depending on its structure, a sentence can be classified as one of four basic types: **simple**, **compound**, **complex**, or **compound-complex**.

Simple Sentences

A **simple sentence** has one independent (main) clause and no dependent (subordinate) clauses (see p. 522). A simple sentence contains at least one subject and one predicate. It may have a compound subject, a compound predicate, and various phrases, but it has only one clause.

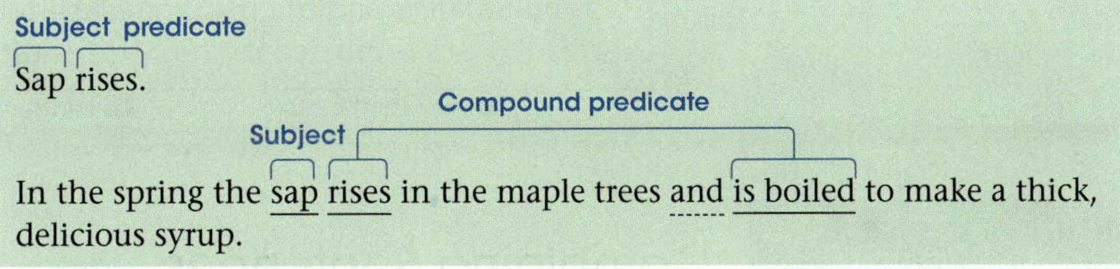

Tip for Writers

There is no comma before *and* because the subject (*sap*) is not repeated before the second verb (*is boiled*). The phrase after *and* is not a sentence; it is not a complete thought.

Compound Sentences

A **compound sentence** has at least two independent clauses and no dependent clauses (see p. 522). The two independent clauses are usually joined with a comma and a coordinating conjunction (*and, but, nor, or, for, so,* or *yet*). Sometimes the two clauses are joined with a semicolon and no coordinating conjunction or with a semicolon and a conjunctive adverb like *nonetheless* or *still* followed by a comma. (See p. 511 on conjunctive adverbs and p. 540 on punctuation.)

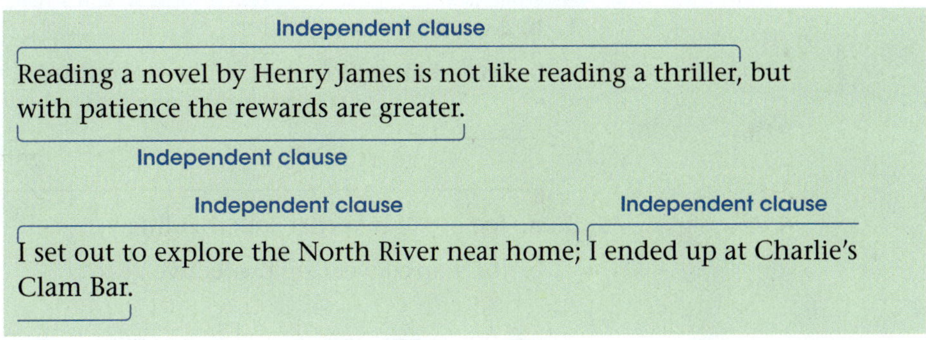

Complex Sentences

A **complex sentence** has one independent clause and one or more dependent clauses (see p. 522). The clauses are joined by subordinating conjunctions or relative pronouns (see p. 529).

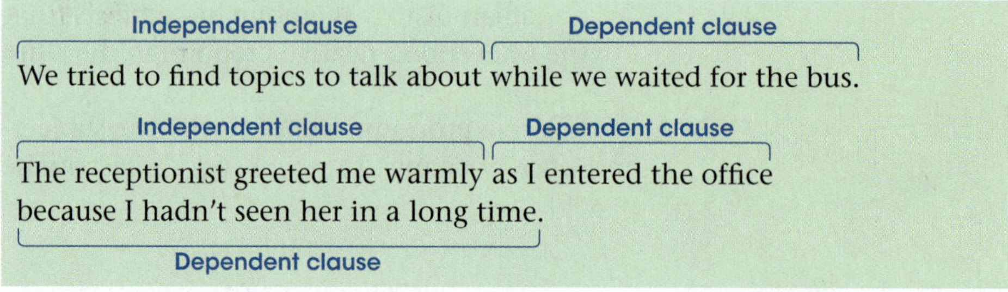

Compound-Complex Sentences

A **compound-complex sentence** contains two or more independent clauses and one or more dependent clauses (see p. 522).

Dependent clause | Independent clause

If students work part-time, they must plan their studies carefully, and they must limit their social lives.

Independent clause

Independent clause | Independent clause | Independent clause

It was mid-March, and the pond had begun to melt; I walked toward it expectantly as I wondered if I could go skating one last time.

Dependent clause | Dependent clause

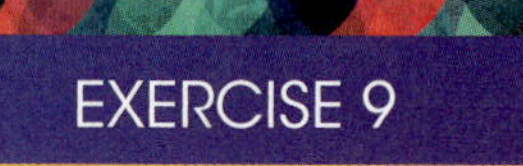

EXERCISE 9

Combining Sentences

Directions: Combine each of the following pairs of sentences into a single sentence by forming independent and/or dependent clauses. You may need to add, change, or delete words.

EXAMPLE **a.** The levee broke.

b. The flood waters rose rapidly.

COMBINED *After the levee broke, the flood waters rose rapidly.*

1. **a.** Margot is a picky eater.

   b. Ivan, Margot's cousin, will eat anything.

   ____

   ____

2. **a.** Joe broke his wrist rollerblading.

   b. Joe started wearing protective gear.

   ____

   ____

3. a. Rick waited in line at the Department of Motor Vehicles.
   b. At the same time, Aaliyah waited in line at the bank.

____

____

____

4. a. Beer is high in calories.
   b. Some beer companies now make low-calorie beer.

____

____

5. a. Keith says he is politically active.
   b. Keith is not registered to vote.

____

____

6. a. Miguel sprained his ankle.
   b. His friends drove him to the hospital.

____

____

7. a. The boat sped by.
   b. The Coast Guard was in hot pursuit.

____

____

8. a. The weather report predicted rain.
   b. I brought my umbrella.

____

____

9. a. Graffiti had been spray-painted on the subway wall.
   b. Maintenance workers were scrubbing it off.

____

____

10. a. Shoppers were crowding around a display table.
    b. Everything on the table was reduced by 50 percent.

____

____

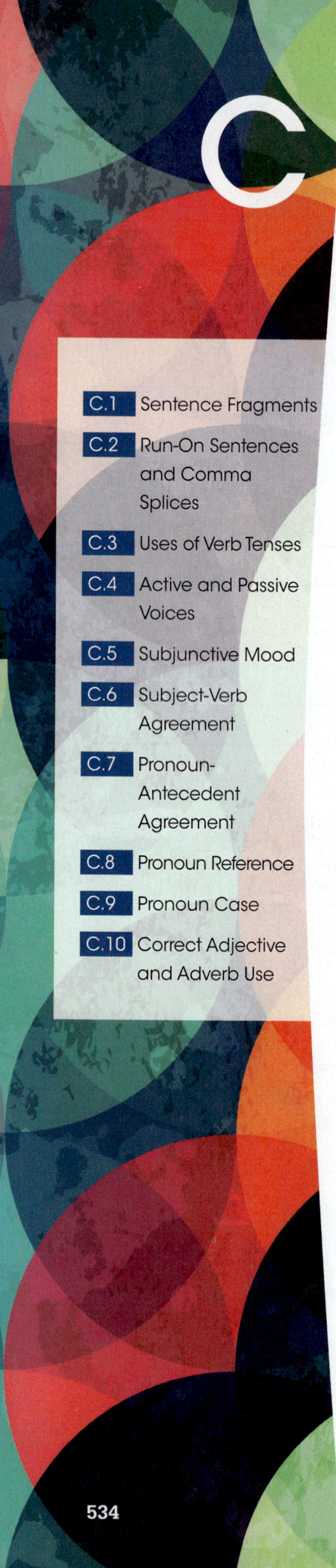

C Avoiding Sentence Errors

C.1 Sentence Fragments
C.2 Run-On Sentences and Comma Splices
C.3 Uses of Verb Tenses
C.4 Active and Passive Voices
C.5 Subjunctive Mood
C.6 Subject-Verb Agreement
C.7 Pronoun-Antecedent Agreement
C.8 Pronoun Reference
C.9 Pronoun Case
C.10 Correct Adjective and Adverb Use

C.1 Sentence Fragments

A complete sentence contains at least one subject and one verb and expresses a complete thought. It begins with a capital letter and ends with a period, question mark, or exclamation point (see p. 517). A **sentence fragment** is an incomplete sentence because it lacks either a subject, a verb, or both, or it is a dependent (subordinate) clause unattached to a complete sentence. In either case, it does not express a complete thought. Occasionally, a writer may knowingly use a fragment for effect or emphasis. This is known as an **intentional fragment**. However, it is best to avoid fragments in your writing; instead, use complete sentences.

FRAGMENT	Walked across campus this afternoon. [This group of words lacks a subject.]
COMPLETE SENTENCE	Pete walked across campus this afternoon.
FRAGMENT	The car next to the fence. [This group of words lacks a verb.]
COMPLETE SENTENCE	The car next to the fence stalled.
FRAGMENT	Alert and ready. [This group of words lacks a subject and a verb.]
COMPLETE SENTENCE	Juan appeared alert and ready.
FRAGMENT	While I was waiting in line. [This group of words is a subordinate clause unattached to a complete sentence.]
COMPLETE SENTENCE	While I was waiting in line, I studied the faces of people walking by.

How to Spot Fragments

To find sentence fragments in your writing, use the following questions to evaluate each group of words:

1. **Does the group of words have a verb?** Be sure that the verb is a complete sentence verb and not a verbal or part of a verbal phrase (see p. 526).

Complete sentence — Sentence fragment
Sentence verb — Verbal
Doug swam laps every night. To win the prize.

Complete sentence — Fragment
Sentence verb — Verbal
She felt very sleepy. Wanting him to leave now.

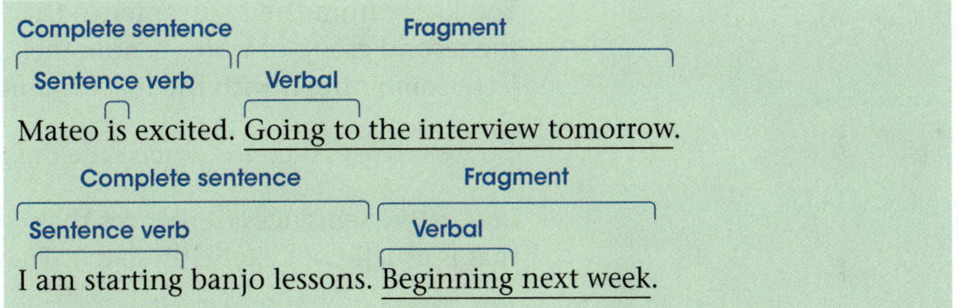

Each of the underlined phrases needs to be either (1) rewritten as a complete sentence or (2) combined with a complete sentence.

REWRITTEN	Doug swam laps every night. He practiced to win the prize.
REWRITTEN	She felt very sleepy. She wanted him to leave now.
COMBINED	Mateo is excited because he is going to the interview tomorrow.
COMBINED	Beginning next week, I am starting banjo lessons.

To distinguish between a complete sentence verb and a verbal, keep in mind the following rule: a sentence verb can change tense to show differences in time—past, present, and future. A verbal cannot demonstrate these shifts in time. You can change the sentence *I have a lot of homework* to *I had a lot of homework* or *I will have a lot of homework,* but the verbal phrase *riding a horse* cannot be changed to show differences in time.

2. **Does the group of words have a subject?** After you have found the verb, look for the subject. The subject is a noun or pronoun that performs or receives the action of the sentence (see p. 518). To find the subject, ask *who* or *what* performs or receives the action of the verb.

Subject Verb

The corner bookstore opens at noon. [*What* opens? The bookstore opens.]

Notice, however, what happens when you ask *who* or *what* about the following fragments:

Will study math with a tutor. [*Who* will study? The question cannot be answered; no subject exists.]

And walked away quickly. [*Who* walked away? Again, the question cannot be answered because there is no subject.]

Every sentence must have a subject. Even if one sentence has a clear subject, the sentence that follows it must also have a subject, or else it is a fragment.

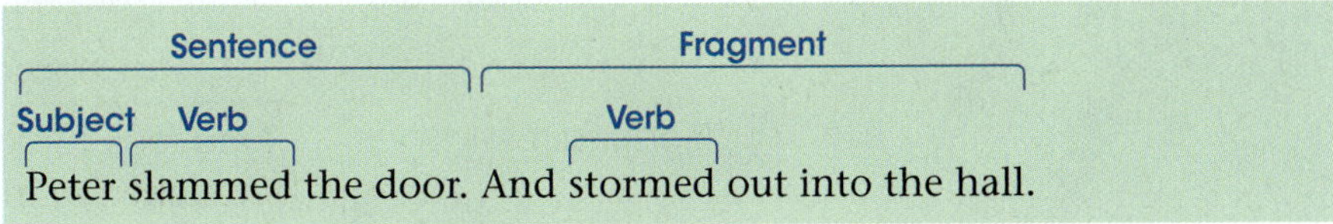

You know from the first sentence that it was Peter who stormed out, but the second group of words is nonetheless a fragment because it lacks a subject. Combining it with the first sentence would eliminate the problem.

COMBINED Peter slammed the door and stormed out into the hall.

Imperative sentences (sentences that command or suggest) have a subject that is usually not explicitly stated. They are not fragments.

Follow me. [The subject *you* is understood: (*You*) Follow me.]

3. **Does the group of words begin with a subordinating conjunction (such as *after, although, as, because, however, since,* or *that*)?** A group of words beginning with a subordinating conjunction is a fragment unless that group of words is attached to an independent clause (see p. 536).

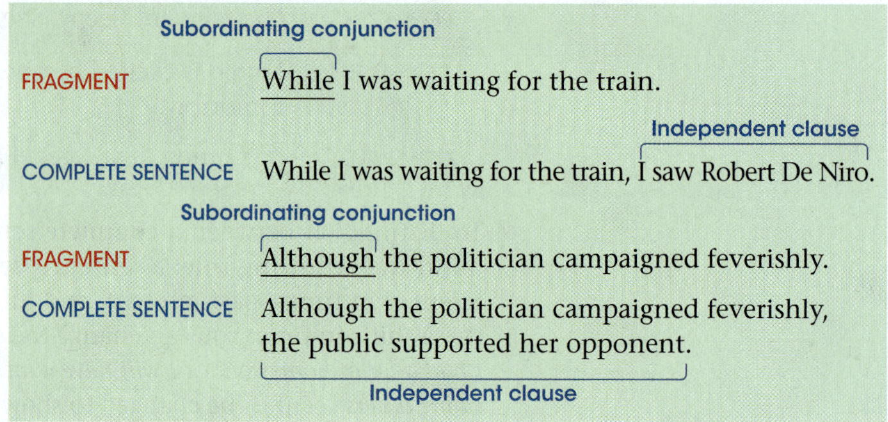

You can also correct a fragment that is a dependent clause by omitting the subordinating conjunction and making the clause into an independent clause, a complete sentence.

COMPLETE SENTENCE I was waiting for the train.

COMPLETE SENTENCE The politician campaigned feverishly.

4. **Does the group of words begin with a relative pronoun (*that, what, whatever, which, who, whoever, whom, whomever, whose*)?** A group of words beginning with a relative pronoun is a fragment unless it forms a question with a subject and a verb or is attached to an independent clause.

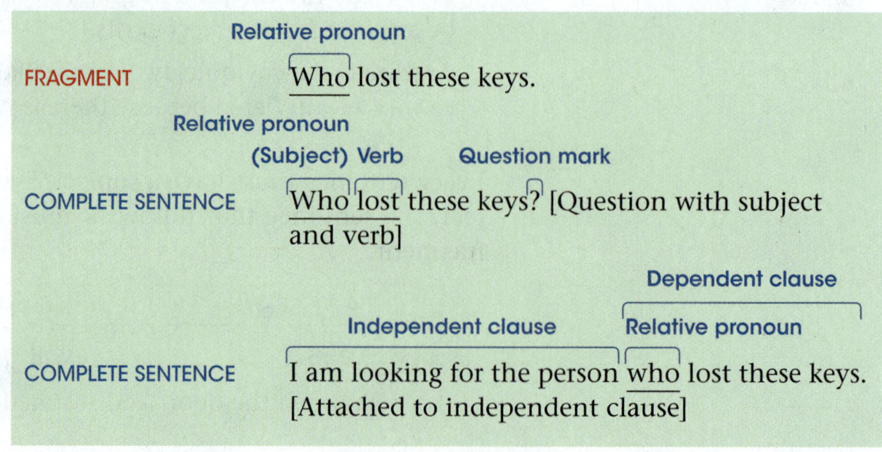

FRAGMENT	That we discussed after class. [Relative pronoun: That]
COMPLETE SENTENCE	This assignment is the one that we discussed after class. [Attached to independent clause] [Independent clause: This assignment is the one; Dependent clause: that we discussed after class; Relative pronoun: that]

Also check groups of words beginning with *how, when, where,* and *why*. If a clause beginning with one of these words neither asks a question nor is attached to an independent clause, then the word group is a fragment.

FRAGMENT	Where the meeting will be held. [Subordinating word: Where]
COMPLETE SENTENCE	Where will the meeting be held? [Question with subject and verb] [Verb: will; Subject: meeting; Verb: be held; Question mark: ?]
COMPLETE SENTENCE	We peeked into the room where the meeting will be held. [Attached to independent clause] [Independent clause: We peeked into the room; Dependent clause: where the meeting will be held]

How to Correct Fragments

1. **Attach the fragment to a complete sentence or an independent clause** (see p. 529).

FRAGMENT	While my boss was on the phone. She began to eat lunch. [Dependent Clause: While my boss was on the phone]
COMPLETE SENTENCE	While my boss was on the phone, she began to eat lunch. [Dependent clause: While my boss was on the phone; Independent clause: she began to eat lunch]
FRAGMENT	Students who missed five classes. They are ineligible for the final exam. [No sentence verb: Students who missed five classes]
COMPLETE SENTENCE	Students who missed five classes are ineligible for the final exam. [Subject: Students; Sentence verb: are]
FRAGMENT	Sabeen sketched portraits all morning. And read art history all afternoon. [No subject: And read art history all afternoon]
COMPLETE SENTENCE	Sabeen sketched portraits all morning and read art history all afternoon. [Subject: Sabeen; Compound sentence verb: sketched … read]

2. **Remove the subordinating conjunction or relative pronoun and make sure that the remaining group of words has a subject and a sentence verb—that is, that it can stand alone as a complete sentence.**

FRAGMENT	I did not finish the book. Because its tedious style bored me.
COMPLETE SENTENCE	I did not finish the book. Its tedious style bored me. (Independent clause: "Its tedious style bored me"; Subject: "style"; Sentence verb: "bored")

3. **Add the missing subject or verb or both.**

FRAGMENT	The patient refused to pay her bill. And then started complaining loudly.
COMPLETE SENTENCE	The patient refused to pay her bill. Then she started complaining loudly. (Subject added: "she")
FRAGMENT	The Summer Olympics were held in Beijing. Hot wind blowing every day.
COMPLETE SENTENCE	The Summer Olympics were held in Beijing. A hot wind blew every day. (Sentence verb added: "blew")
FRAGMENT	I had to leave the car in the driveway. The snow against the garage door.
COMPLETE SENTENCE	I had to leave the car in the driveway. The snow had drifted against the garage door. (Sentence verb added: "had drifted")

EXERCISE 10 Correcting Fragments

Directions: Make each of the following sentence fragments a complete sentence by combining it with an independent clause, removing the subordinating conjunction or relative pronoun, or adding the missing subject or verb.

EXAMPLE Many environmentalists are concerned about the spotted owl. Which is almost extinct.

COMPLETE SENTENCE *Many environmentalists are concerned about the spotted owl, which is almost extinct.*

1. Renting a DVD of the movie *Citizen Kane.* ______________________

____

2. Spices that had been imported from India. ______________________

____

3. The police officer walked to Jerome's van. To give him a ticket.

____

4. My English professor, with the cup of tea he brought to each class.

____

5. After the table was refinished.______________________

____

6. Roberto memorized his lines. For the performance tomorrow night.

____

7. A tricycle with big wheels, painted red. ______________________

____

8. On the shelf, an antique crock used for storing lard. ______________

____

9. Because I always wanted to learn to speak Spanish. ______________

____

10. Looking for the lost keys. I was late for class. ______________

____

C.2 Run-On Sentences and Comma Splices

Independent clauses contain both a subject and a predicate. When two independent clauses are joined in one sentence, they must be separated by a comma and a coordinating conjunction or by a semicolon. Failure to properly separate independent clauses creates the errors known as **run-on sentences** and **comma splices**.

A **run-on sentence** (or **fused sentence**) contains two independent clauses that are not separated by any punctuation or a coordinating conjunction (*and, but, nor, or, for, so, yet*).

A **comma splice** (or comma fault) contains two independent clauses joined only by a comma (the coordinating conjunction is missing). A comma by itself cannot join two independent clauses (see p. 529).

How to Spot Run-On Sentences and Comma Splices

1. **You can often spot run-on sentences by reading them aloud**. Listen for a pause or a change in your voice. That may signal that you are moving from the first clause to the second. Read the following run-on sentences aloud, and see if you can hear where the two clauses in each should be separated.

RUN-ON	We watched the football game then we ordered pizza.
CORRECT	We watched the football game, and then we ordered pizza.

RUN-ON	My throat feels sore I hope I am not catching a cold.
CORRECT	My throat feels sore; I hope I am not catching a cold.

2. **You can spot a comma splice by looking carefully at your use and placement of commas.** If you see a comma between two independent clauses but no coordinating conjunction after the comma, then you have probably spotted a comma splice.

COMMA SPLICE	The average person watches 15 hours of television a week, my parents allow my brother only 2 hours a week.
CORRECT	The average person watches 15 hours of television a week, but my parents allow my brother only 2 hours a week.

Coordinating conjunction

How to Correct Run-On Sentences and Comma Splices

There are four ways to correct a run-on sentence or a comma splice. Not every run-on sentence or comma splice can be corrected in the same way. The method you choose will depend on the meaning of the clauses.

1. **Create two separate sentences.** End the first independent clause with a period. Begin the next with a capital letter.

RUN-ON	We went for a walk in the woods we saw the leaves turning red and orange.
CORRECT	We went for a walk in the woods. We saw the leaves turning red and orange.

2. **Use a semicolon.** Use a semicolon when the thoughts expressed in the independent clauses are closely related and you want to emphasize that relationship. (The word immediately following the semicolon does not begin with a capital letter unless it is a proper noun.)

RUN-ON	It is unlikely that school taxes will increase this year citizens have expressed their opposition.
CORRECT	It is unlikely that school taxes will increase this year; citizens have expressed their opposition.

Note: An independent clause containing a conjunctive adverb (such as *finally, however, meanwhile, otherwise,* or *therefore*) must be separated from another independent clause with a period or a semicolon. (See p. 512 for a list of conjunctive adverbs.) In most cases, the conjunctive adverb itself is set off with a comma or pair of commas.

COMMA SPLICE	The road crew was repairing potholes, therefore traffic was snarled.
CORRECT	The road crew was repairing potholes; therefore, traffic was snarled.

C. Avoiding Sentence Errors

3. **Insert a comma and a coordinating conjunction (*and, but, for, nor, or, so, yet*).**

RUN-ON Americans are changing their eating habits they still eat too much red meat.

Coordinating conjunction

CORRECT Americans are changing their eating habits, but they still eat too much red meat.

4. **Make one clause subordinate to the other**. This method is especially effective when the idea expressed in one of the clauses is more important than the idea in the other clause. By adding a subordinating conjunction (such as *after, although, because,* or *until*), you can link a dependent clause to an independent clause. (See below for a list of subordinating conjunctions.) Be sure to use a subordinating conjunction that explains the relationship between the dependent clause and the independent clause to which it is joined.

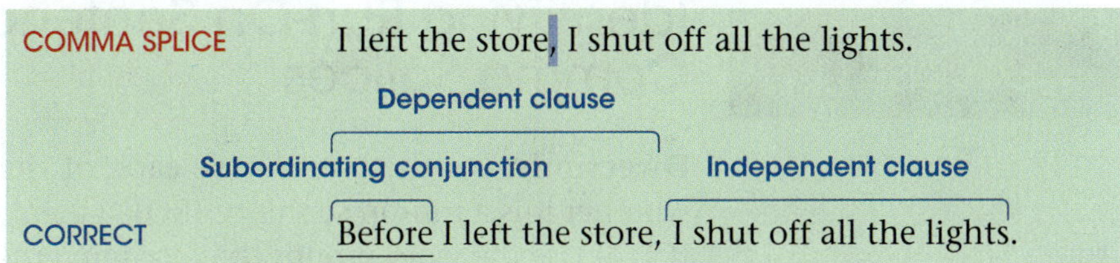

The subordinating conjunction *before* in the above sentence indicates the sequence in which the two actions were performed. In addition to time, subordinating conjunctions can indicate place, cause or effect, condition or circumstance, contrast, or manner.

MEANING	SUBORDINATING CONJUNCTION	EXAMPLE
time	after, before, when, until, once, while	After I left work, I went to the mall.
place	where, wherever	I will go wherever you go.
cause or effect	because, since, so that, that, as	I missed the bus because I overslept.
condition or circumstance	if, unless, as long as, in case, whenever, once, provided that	If I get an A on the paper, I'll be happy.
contrast	although, even though, even if, whereas, while	Even though I lost my job, I have to make my car payment.
manner	as, as if, as though	Ana acted as if she were angry.

The dependent clause can be placed *before* or *after* the independent clause. If it is placed before the independent clause, put a comma at the end of it. Usually no comma is needed when the independent clause comes first.

COMMA SPLICE I studied psychology, I was thinking about some of Freud's findings.

Dependent clause Independent clause

CORRECT When I studied psychology, I was thinking about some of Freud's findings.

	Independent clause / Dependent clause
CORRECT	I was thinking about some of Freud's findings when I studied psychology.

You may add a dependent clause to a sentence that has more than one independent clause (see p. 532).

RUN-ON	We toured the hospital we met with its chief administrator she invited us to lunch.
CORRECT	After we toured the hospital, we met with its chief administrator and she invited us to lunch. (Dependent clause: After we toured the hospital; Independent clause: we met with its chief administrator; Independent clause: and she invited us to lunch.)

EXERCISE 11 Identifying Run-On Sentences and Comma Splices

Directions: On the line beside each of the following word groups, identify whether it is a run-on sentence (RO), a comma splice (CS), or a correct sentence (C). Revise the word groups that contain errors.

EXAMPLE ___CS___ The children chased the ball into the street, cars screeched to a halt.

_____ 1. Inez packed for the business trip she remembered everything except her business cards.

_____ 2. A limousine drove through our neighborhood, everybody wondered who was in it.

_____ 3. The defendant pleaded not guilty the judge ordered him to pay the parking ticket.

_____ 4. Before a big game, Louis, who is a quarterback, eats a lot of pasta and bread he says it gives him energy.

_____ 5. Four of my best friends from high school have decided to go to law school, I have decided to become a paralegal.

_____ 6. Felicia did not know what to buy her co-worker for his birthday, so she went to a lot of stores she finally decided to buy him a gift certificate.

_____ 7. After living in a dorm room for three years, Jason found an apartment the rent was very high, so he had to get a job to pay for it.

_____ 8. The cherry tree had to be cut down, it stood right where the new addition was going to be built.

_____ 9. Amanda worked every night for a month on the needlepoint pillow that she was making for her grandmother.

_____ 10. Driving around in the dark, we finally realized we were lost, Dwight went into a convenience store to ask for directions.

C.3 Uses of Verb Tenses

The **tense** of a verb expresses time. It conveys whether an action, process, or occurrence takes place in the present, past, or future. There are twelve tenses in English, and each is used to express a particular time. (See p. 504 for information about how to form each tense.)

The **simple present tense** expresses actions that are occurring at the time of the writing or that occur regularly. The **simple past tense** is used for actions that have already occurred. The **simple future tense** is used for actions that will occur in the future.

SIMPLE PRESENT	The chef cooks a huge meal.
SIMPLE PAST	The chef cooked a huge meal.
SIMPLE FUTURE	The chef will cook a huge meal.

The **present perfect tense** is used for actions that began in the past and are still occurring in the present or are finished by the time of the writing. The **past perfect tense** expresses actions that were completed before other past actions. The **future perfect tense** is used for actions that will be completed in the future.

PRESENT PERFECT	The chef has cooked a huge meal every night this week.
PAST PERFECT	The chef had cooked a huge meal before the guests canceled their reservation.
FUTURE PERFECT	The chef will have cooked a huge meal by the time we arrive.

The six progressive tenses are used for continuing actions or actions in progress. The **present progressive tense** is used for actions that are in progress in the present. The **past progressive tense** expresses past continuing actions. The **future progressive tense** is used for continuing actions that will occur in the future. The **present perfect progressive**, **past perfect progressive**, and **future perfect progressive tenses** are used for continuing actions that are, were, or will be completed by a certain time.

PRESENT PROGRESSIVE	The chef is cooking a huge meal this evening.
PAST PROGRESSIVE	The chef was cooking a huge meal when she ran out of butter.
FUTURE PROGRESSIVE	The chef will be cooking a huge meal all day tomorrow.
PRESENT PERFECT PROGRESSIVE	The chef has been cooking a huge meal since this morning.
PAST PERFECT PROGRESSIVE	The chef had been cooking a huge meal before the electricity went out.
FUTURE PERFECT PROGRESSIVE	The chef will have been cooking a huge meal for eight hours when the guests arrive.

Writing all forms of a verb for all tenses and all persons (first, second, and third, singular and plural) is called **conjugating** the verb. Irregular verbs have an irregularly formed past tense and past participle (used in the past tense and the perfect tenses). (See p. 504 for a list of the forms of common irregular verbs.) Here is the complete conjugation for the regular verb *walk*.

Conjugation of the Regular Verb *Walk*

	SINGULAR	PLURAL
Simple present tense	I walk you walk he/she/it walks	we walk you walk they walk
Simple past tense	I walked you walked he/she/it walked	we walked you walked they walked
Simple future tense	I will (shall) walk you will walk he/she/it will walk	we will (shall) walk you will walk they will walk
Present perfect tense	I have walked you have walked he/she/it has walked	we have walked you have walked they have walked
Past perfect tense	I had walked you had walked he/she/it had walked	we had walked you had walked they had walked
Future perfect tense	I will (shall) have walked you will have walked he/she/it will have walked	we will (shall) have walked you will have walked they will have walked
Present progressive tense	I am walking you are walking he/she/it is walking	we are walking you are walking they are walking
Past progressive tense	I was walking you were walking he/she/it was walking	we were walking you were walking they were walking
Future progressive tense	I will be walking you will be walking he/she/it will be walking	we will be walking you will be walking they will be walking
Present perfect progressive tense	I have been walking you have been walking he/she/it has been walking	we have been walking you have been walking they have been walking
Past perfect progressive tense	I had been walking you had been walking he/she/it had been walking	we had been walking you had been walking they had been walking
Future perfect progressive tense	I will have been walking you will have been walking he/she/it will have been walking	we will have been walking you will have been walking they will have been walking

Following are the simple present and simple past tenses for the irregular verbs *have, be,* and *do,* which are commonly used as helping verbs (see p. 503).

Irregular Verbs *Have, Be,* and *Do*

	HAVE	BE	DO
Simple present tense	I have you have he/she/it has we/you/they have	I am you are he/she/it is we/you/they are	I do you do he/she/it does we/you/they do
Simple past tense	I had you had he/she/it had we/you/they had	I was you were he/she/it was we/you/they were	I did you did he/she/it did we/you/they did

Special Uses of the Simple Present Tense

Besides expressing actions that are occurring at the time of the writing, the simple present tense has several special uses.

HABITUAL OR RECURRING ACTION	She works at the store every day.
GENERAL TRUTH	The sun rises in the east.
DISCUSSION OF LITERATURE	Gatsby stands on the dock and gazes in Daisy's direction.
THE FUTURE	He leaves for Rome on the 7:30 plane.

Emphasis, Negatives, and Questions

The simple present and the simple past tenses of the verb *do* are used with main verbs to provide emphasis, to form negative constructions with the adverb *not*, and to ask questions.

SIMPLE PRESENT	Malcolm does want to work on Saturday.
SIMPLE PRESENT	He does not want to stay home alone.
SIMPLE PRESENT	Do you want to go with him?
SIMPLE PAST	Judy did write the proposal herself.
SIMPLE PAST	She did not have the money to pay professionals.
SIMPLE PAST	Did she do a good job?

Tips for Writers

The usual simple present tense form is this: Malcolm wants to work on Saturday. The *emphatic form* is sometimes used to correct a mistake:

Ivan says, "Malcolm does not want to work on Saturday."

Maria replies, "He does want to work on Saturday." (or) "Yes, he does."

The modal verbs *can, could, may, might, must, shall, should, will,* and *would* are also used to add emphasis and shades of meaning to verbs. Modals are used only as helping verbs, never alone, and do not change form to indicate tense. Added to a main verb, they are used in the following situations, among others:

CONDITION	We can play tennis if she gets here on time.
PERMISSION	You may have only one e-mail address.
POSSIBILITY	They might call us from the airport.
OBLIGATION	I must visit my mother tomorrow.

Common Mistakes to Avoid with Verb Tense

Check your writing carefully to make sure you have avoided these common mistakes with verb tenses.

1. **Make sure the endings *-d* and *-ed* (for past tenses) and *-s* and *-es* (for third-person singular, simple present tense) are on all verbs that require them.**

INCORRECT	I have walk three miles since I left home.
CORRECT	I have walked three miles since I left home.

2. **Use irregular verbs correctly** (see p. 504).

INCORRECT	I will lay down for a nap.
CORRECT	I will lie down for a nap.

3. **Use helping verbs where they are necessary to express the correct time.**

INCORRECT	I go to class tomorrow.
CORRECT	I will go to class tomorrow.

4. **Avoid colloquial language or dialect in writing**. Colloquial language is casual, everyday language often used in conversation. Dialect is the language pattern of a region or an ethnic group.

INCORRECT	I didn't get the point of that poem.
CORRECT	I didn't understand the point of that poem.
INCORRECT	The train be gone.
CORRECT	The train has gone.

Other common mistakes with verbs are failing to make the verb agree with the subject (see p. 550) and using inconsistent or shifting tenses (see p. 565).

EXERCISE 12 Correcting Verb Form and Tense Errors

Directions: Correct any of the following sentences with an error in verb form or verb tense. If a sentence contains no errors, write "C" for correct beside it.

EXAMPLE You ~~is~~ are next in line.

______ 1. Mercedes called and ask Jen if she wanted a ride to the basketball game.

______ 2. Eric went to a party last week and meets a girl he knew in high school.

______ 3. I cook spaghetti every Wednesday, and my family always enjoys it.

______ 4. A package come in yesterday's mail for my office mate.

______ 5. Louisa wears a beautiful red dress to her sister's wedding last week.

______ 6. Marni answered a letter she receive from her former employer.

______ 7. Rob waited until he was introduced, and then he run on stage.

______ 8. The audience laughed loudly at the comedian's jokes and applauds spontaneously at the funniest ones.

______ 9. The group had ordered buffalo-style chicken wings, and it was not disappointed when the meal arrived.

______ 10. Julie spends the afternoon answering correspondence when sales were slow.

C.4 Active and Passive Voices

When a verb is in the active voice, the subject performs the action of the verb. The direct object receives the action (see p. 521). The active voice expresses action in a lively, vivid, energetic way.

Subject (Actor): Carlos | Active-voice Verb: dropped | Direct object: calculator

Carlos dropped his calculator.

Subject (Actor): supermarket | Active-voice Verb: gave | Direct object: samples

The supermarket gave samples of prepared food.

When a verb is in the passive voice, the subject is the receiver of the action of the verb. The passive voice is formed by using an appropriate form of the verb *be* plus the past participle of the main verb. The actor is often expressed in a prepositional phrase introduced by the preposition *by*. Thus the passive voice tends to be wordier and to express actions in a more indirect way than the active voice.

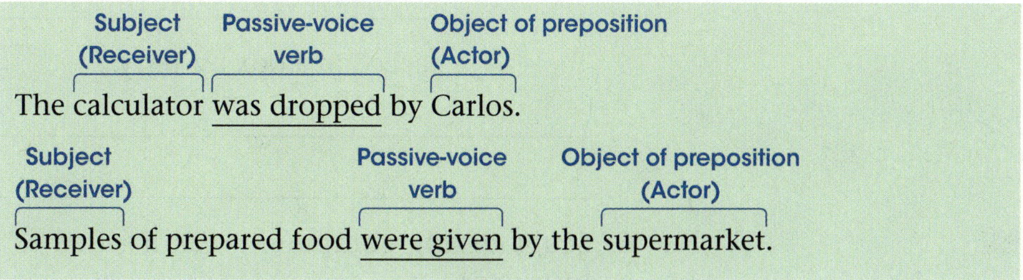

Sometimes the actor is not expressed in a passive-voice sentence.

ACTIVE	I did not remove the Halloween decorations until Christmas.
PASSIVE	The Halloween decorations were not removed until Christmas.

As a general rule, you should use the active voice because it is more effective, simpler, and more direct than the passive. In two situations, however, the passive may be preferable: (1) if you do not know who performs the action and (2) if the object of the action is more important than the actor.

PASSIVE The handle of the dagger had been wiped clean of fingerprints. [It is not known who wiped the dagger.]

PASSIVE The poem "Richard Corey" by Edwin Arlington Robinson was discussed in class. [The poem is more important than who discussed the poem.]

EXERCISE 13 Changing Verbs from Passive to Active Voice

Directions: Revise each of the following sentences by changing the verb from passive voice to active voice.

EXAMPLE The patient was operated on by an experienced surgeon.

REVISED *An experienced surgeon operated on the patient.*

1. The coin collection was inherited by Roderick from his grandfather.

2. A large stack of orders was delivered by the staff.

3. The presidential advisers were relied on by the president.

4. Ice cream was served to the children at the birthday party by one of the adults.

5. Tools were packed in a box by Terry.

6. Scuba-diving equipment was handed to the students by the licensed instructor.

7. Alaska was visited by my parents last fall.

8. A large order was placed by Wonderments Gift Shop.

9. The shipment was delivered by United Parcel Service.

____

____

10. Trash was collected and disposed of by the picnickers before they left for home.

____

____

C.5 Subjunctive Mood

Tip for Writers

In *subjunctive* (contrary-to-fact) present-tense statements, use a past tense verb in the *if* clause and a modal auxiliary plus an infinitive verb in the main clause:

If I lived in Minnesota, I would need a good pair of winter boots.

The **mood** of a verb conveys the writer's attitude toward the expressed thought. There are three moods in English. The **indicative mood** is used to make ordinary statements of fact and to ask questions. The **imperative mood** is used to give commands or make suggestions. The **subjunctive mood** is used to express wishes, requirements, recommendations, and statements contrary to fact (see p. 506).

INDICATIVE	Laurel lies in the sun every afternoon.
IMPERATIVE	Lie down and rest!
SUBJUNCTIVE	It is urgent that she lie down and rest.

The subjunctive mood requires some special attention because it uses verb tenses in unusual ways. Verbs in the subjunctive mood can be in the present, past, or perfect tense.

PRESENT	His mother recommended that he apply for the job. If truth be told, Jacob is luckier than he knows.
PAST	If she walked faster, she could get there on time. She ran as if she were five years old again.
PERFECT	If I had known his name, I would have said hello.

Here are several rules for using the subjunctive correctly:

1. **For requirements and recommendations, use the present subjunctive (the infinitive) for all verbs, including *be*.**

   Mr. Kenefick requires that his students be drilled in safety procedures.
   The dentist recommended that she brush her teeth three times a day.

2. **For present conditions contrary to fact and for present wishes, use the past subjunctive (the simple past tense) for all verbs; use *were* for the verb *be* for all subjects.**

   I wish that the workday began later.
   If Andrew were not so stubborn, he would admit that Adele is right.

3. **For past conditions contrary to fact and for past wishes, use the perfect subjunctive (*had* plus the past participle) for all verbs, including *be*.**

Tip for Writers

Note that in *contrary-to-fact statements*, the verb in the main clause usually begins with a modal auxiliary or *wish*.

If Roman had been at home, he would have answered the phone when you called.

When Peter told me what an exciting internship he had abroad last summer, I wished I had gone with him.

C.6 Subject-Verb Agreement

A subject and its verb must agree (be consistent) in person (first, second, third) and in number (singular, plural). (See p. 500 on the person of pronouns and p. 557 on verb forms in all persons and numbers.) The most common problems with subject-verb agreement occur with third-person present-tense verbs, which are formed for most verbs by adding *-s* or *-es* to the infinitive. (See pp. 504–505 for the present- and past-tense forms for certain irregular verbs.)

Agreement Rules

1. **Singular subjects.** For a singular subject (one person, place, thing, or idea), use a singular form of the verb: *I dance, he dances, Sally dances, the dog dances; I am, you are, Sally is.*
2. **Plural subjects.** For a plural subject (two or more persons, places, things, or ideas), use the plural form of the verb: *we dance, they dance, the girls dance, the dogs dance; we are, they are, children are.*

Common Mistakes to Avoid

1. **Third-person singular.** Do not omit the *-s* or *-es* for a present-tense verb used with the pronoun *he*, *she*, or *it* or any singular noun.

INCORRECT	She watch the training video.
CORRECT	She watches the training video.
INCORRECT	Professor Simmons pace while she lectures.
CORRECT	Professor Simmons paces while she lectures.

2. **Compound subjects.** Two or more subjects joined by the coordinating conjunction *and* require a plural verb, even if one or both of the subjects are singular.

INCORRECT	Anita and Mark plays cards.
CORRECT	Anita and Mark play cards.

When both of the subjects refer to the same person or thing, however, use a singular verb.

The president and chairman of the board is in favor of more aggressive marketing.

When a compound subject is joined by the conjunction *or* or *nor* or the correlative conjunctions *either/or, neither/nor, both/and, not/but,* or *not only/but also,* the verb should agree in number with the subject nearer to it.

Neither the books nor the article was helpful to my research.

Sarah or the boys are coming tomorrow.

3. **Verbs before subjects**. When a verb comes before a subject, as in sentences beginning with *here* or *there*, it is easy to make an agreement error. Because *here* and *there* are adverbs, they are never subjects of a sentence and do not determine the correct form of the verb. Look for the subject *after* the verb, and, depending on its number, choose a singular or plural verb.

Singular verb — Singular subject

There is a bone in my soup.

Plural verb — Plural subject

There are two bones in my soup.

4. **Words between subject and verb**. Words, phrases, and clauses coming between the subject and verb do not change the fact that the verb must agree with the subject. To check that the verb is correct, mentally erase everything between the subject and its verb to see if the verb agrees in number with its subject.

Singular subject — Singular verb

The new list of degree requirements comes out in the spring.

Plural subject — Plural verb

Expenses surrounding the sale of the house were unexpectedly low.

Phrases beginning with prepositions such as *along with*, *as well as*, and *in addition to* are not part of the subject and should not be considered in determining if the verb is singular or plural.

Singular subject

The lamp, together with some plates, glasses, and china teacups, was broken during the move.

Singular verb

5. **Indefinite pronouns as subjects**. Some indefinite pronouns (such as *everyone*, *neither*, *anybody*, *nobody*, *one*, *something*, and *each*) take a singular verb (see p. 502).

Everyone appreciates the hospital's volunteers.

Of the two applicants, neither seems well qualified.

The indefinite pronouns *both*, *many*, *several*, and *few* always take a plural verb. Some indefinite pronouns, such as *all*, *any*, *most*, *none*, and *some*, may take either a singular or plural verb. Treat the indefinite pronoun as singular if it refers to something that cannot be counted and as plural if it refers to more than one of something that can be counted.

Some of the ice is still on the road.

Some of the ice cubes are still in the tray.

All of the spaghetti tastes overcooked.

All of the spaghetti dishes taste too spicy.

6. **Collective nouns**. A collective noun refers to a group of people or things (*audience, class, flock, jury, team, family*). When the noun refers to the group as one unit, use a singular verb.

   The herd stampedes toward us.

   When the noun refers to the group members as separate individuals, use a plural verb.

   The herd scatter in all directions.

7. **Nouns with plural forms but singular meaning**. Some words appear plural (that is, they end in *-s* or *-es*) but have a singular meaning. *Measles, hysterics, news,* and *mathematics* are examples. Use a singular verb with them.

   Mathematics is a required course.

   Note: Other nouns look plural and have singular meanings, but take a plural verb: *braces, glasses, trousers, slacks, jeans, jodhpurs,* and *pajamas*. Even though they refer to a single thing (to one pair of jeans, for example), these words take a plural verb.

   His pajamas were covered with pictures of tumbling dice.

8. **Relative pronouns in adjective clauses**. The relative pronouns *who, which,* and *that* sometimes function as the subject of an adjective clause. When the relative pronoun refers to a singular noun, use a singular verb. When the pronoun refers to a plural noun, use a plural verb.

   Anita is a person who never forgets faces.
   [*Who* refers to *person*, which is singular.]

   The students who lost their keys are here.
   [*Who* refers to *students*, which is plural.]

EXERCISE 14 Identifying the Correct Verbs

Directions: Circle the verb that correctly completes each sentence.

EXAMPLE Everybody (like, likes) doughnuts for breakfast.

1. Physics (is, are) a required course for an engineering degree.
2. Most of my courses last semester (was, were) in the morning.
3. The orchestra members who (is, are) carrying their instruments will be able to board the plane first.
4. Suzanne (sing, sings) a touching version of "America the Beautiful."
5. Here (is, are) the performers who juggle plates.
6. Kin Lee and his parents (travel, travels) to Ohio tomorrow.
7. A box of old and valuable stamps (is, are) in the safety deposit box at the bank.
8. The family (sit, sits) on different chairs arranged throughout the attorney's conference room.
9. Elena and Erin (arrive, arrives) at the train station at eleven o'clock.
10. Directions for operating the machine (is, are) posted on the wall.

C.7 Pronoun-Antecedent Agreement

A pronoun must agree with its **antecedent**, the word it refers to or replaces, in person (first, second, or third), in number (singular or plural), and in gender (masculine, feminine, or neuter).

> Ronald attended the meeting, but I did not have a chance to talk with him. [The third-person, masculine, singular pronoun *him* agrees with its antecedent, *Ronald*.]
>
> We had planned to call our sister, but her line was busy. [*Our* agrees with its antecedent, *We*; *her* agrees with its antecedent, *sister*.]

Agreement Rules

1. **Use a singular pronoun to refer to or replace a singular noun.** (A singular noun names one person, place, or thing.)

   > Juanita filed her report promptly.

2. **Use a plural pronoun to refer to or replace a plural noun.** (A plural noun names two or more persons, places, or things.)

   > The shirts are hung on their hangers.

3. **Use singular pronouns to refer to indefinite pronouns that are singular in meaning.**

another	each	everything	no one	somebody
anybody	either	neither	nothing	someone
anyone	everybody	nobody	one	something
anything	everyone	none	other	

   > Singular antecedent: Someone; Singular pronoun: her
   >
   > Someone left her handbag under this table.
   >
   > Singular antecedent: Everyone; Singular compound pronoun: his or her
   >
   > Everyone in the office must do his or her own photocopying.

   Note: To avoid the awkwardness of *his or her*, consider rephrasing your sentence with a plural antecedent and plural pronoun.

   > Plural antecedent: workers; Plural pronoun: their
   >
   > Office workers must do their own photocopying.

4. **Use a plural pronoun to refer to indefinite pronouns that are plural in meaning.**

   > both few many several
   >
   > Both of the journalists said that they could see no violations of the cease-fire.

5. **The indefinite pronouns *all, any, most, none,* and *some* can be singular or plural, depending on how they are used.** If the indefinite pronoun

refers to something that cannot be counted, use a singular pronoun to refer to it. If the indefinite pronoun refers to something that can be counted, use a plural pronoun to refer to it.

> Most of the voters feel they can make a difference.
>
> Most of the air on airplanes is recycled repeatedly, so it becomes stale.

6. **Use a plural pronoun to refer to a compound antecedent joined by *and*, unless both parts of the compound refer to the same person, place, or thing.**

> Plural antecedent — Plural pronoun
>
> My girlfriend and I planned our wedding.
>
> Singular antecedent — Singular pronoun
>
> My neighbor and best friend started her book bindery at the local warehouse.

7. **When antecedents are joined by *or, nor, either/or, neither/nor, both/and, not/but,* or *not only/but also,* the pronoun agrees in number with the nearer antecedent.**

> Neither his brothers nor Sam has made his plane reservations.
>
> Neither Sam nor his brothers have made their plane reservations.

Note: Two or more singular antecedents joined by *or* or *nor* require a singular pronoun.

> Neither Larry nor Richard signed his name legibly.
>
> Eva or Anita will bring her saxophone.

8. **Collective nouns refer to a specific group *(army, class, family)*.** When the group acts as a unit, use a singular pronoun to refer to the noun. When each member of the group acts individually, use a plural pronoun to refer to the noun.

> The band marched its most intricate formation.
>
> The band found their seats in the bleachers but could not see the game because the sun was in their eyes.

EXERCISE 15

Correcting Pronoun-Antecedent Agreement Errors

Directions: Revise the sentences below that contain agreement errors. If a sentence contains no errors, write "C" for correct beside it.

EXAMPLE Somebody dropped ~~their~~ his or her ring down the drain.

_____ 1. Many of the residents of the neighborhood have had their homes tested for radon.

_____ 2. Each college instructor establishes their own grading policies.

_____ 3. The apples fell from its tree.

_____ 4. Anyone may submit their painting to the contest.

C. Avoiding Sentence Errors

_____ 5. All the engines manufactured at the plant have their vehicle-identification numbers stamped on.

_____ 6. No one requested that the clerk gift-wrap their package.

_____ 7. Either Professor Judith Marcos or her assistant, Maria, graded the exams, writing their comments in the margins.

_____ 8. James or his parents sails the boat every weekend.

_____ 9. Few classes were canceled because of the snowstorm; it met as regularly scheduled.

_____ 10. Not only Ricky but also the Carters will take his children to Disneyland this summer.

C.8 Pronoun Reference

A pronoun refers to or replaces a noun or pronoun previously mentioned, called the pronoun's **antecedent**. As you write, you must always make sure that a reader knows to which noun or pronoun a pronoun refers. The antecedent of each pronoun must be clear. Sometimes you may need to reword a sentence to solve a problem of unclear antecedent.

INCORRECT	Lois walked with Pam because she did not know the route. [Who did not know the route? The antecedent of *she* is unclear.]
CORRECT	Lois did not know the route, so she walked with Pam.

How to Use Pronouns Correctly

1. **A pronoun may refer to two or more nouns in a compound antecedent.**

   Mark and Dennis combined their efforts to fix the leaky faucet.

2. **Avoid using a pronoun that could refer to more than one possible antecedent.**

INCORRECT	Rick told Garry that he was right.
CORRECT	Rick told Garry, "You are right."

3. **Avoid using vague pronouns like *they* and *it* that often have no clear antecedent.**

INCORRECT	It says in the paper that Kmart is expanding the Williamsville store.
CORRECT	The article in the paper says that Kmart is expanding the Williamsville store.
INCORRECT	They told me that we were required to wear surgeons' masks to view the newborns.
CORRECT	The obstetrics nurses told me that we were required to wear surgeons' masks to view the newborns.

INCORRECT	On the message board, it says that there is a fire drill today.
CORRECT	The notice on the message board says that there is a fire drill today.

4. **Avoid unnecessary or repetitious pronouns.**

INCORRECT	My sister she said that she lost her diamond ring.
CORRECT	My sister said that she lost her diamond ring.

5. **Be sure to use the relative pronouns *who, whom, which,* and *that* with the appropriate antecedent.** *Who* and *whom* refer to persons or named animals. *That* and *which* refer to unnamed animals and to things.

   Mary Anne was the team member who scored the most points this year.

   Dublin, who is a golden retriever, barked at everyone.

   My sister gave me a ring that has three opals.

   Highway 33, which has ten hairpin turns, is difficult to drive.

6. **Use *one* if you are not referring specifically to the reader.** Use the second-person pronoun *you* only to refer to the reader. In academic writing, avoid using *you.*

INCORRECT	Last year, you had to watch the news every night to keep up with world events.
CORRECT	Last year, one had to watch the news every night to keep up with world events.

7. **Place the pronoun close to its antecedent so that the relationship is clear.**

INCORRECT	Margaux found a shell on the beach that her sister wanted.
CORRECT	On the beach Margaux found a shell that her sister wanted.

EXERCISE 16 Correcting Pronoun Reference Errors

Directions: Revise each of the following sentences to correct problems in pronoun reference. If a sentence contains no errors, write "C" for correct beside it.

EXAMPLE	It said that the grades would be posted on Tuesday.
REVISED	The professor's note said that the grades would be posted on Tuesday.

_____ 1. The puppy whom my sister brought home was quite cute.

_____ 2. Laverne and Louise they pooled their money to buy a new minivan.

_____ 3. They said on the news that the naval base will be shut down.

_____ 4. The street that was recently widened is where I used to work.

_____ 5. Ivan sat on the couch in the living room that he had bought yesterday.

_____ 6. You should highlight in your textbooks for higher comprehension.

_____ 7. Christina handed Maggie the plate she had bought at the flea market.

_____ 8. Bridget found the cake mix in the aisle with the baking supplies that she needed for tonight's dessert.

_____ 9. The multipurpose machine who scanned the document beeped several times.

_____ 10. It said in the letter that my payment was late.

C.9 Pronoun Case

A pronoun changes **case** depending on its grammatical function in a sentence. Pronouns may be in the **subjective case**, the **objective case**, or the **possessive case**.

Personal Pronouns			
SINGULAR	**SUBJECTIVE**	**OBJECTIVE**	**POSSESSIVE**
First person	I	me	my, mine
Second person	you	you	your, yours
Third person	he, she, it	him, her, it	his, her, hers, its
PLURAL	**SUBJECTIVE**	**OBJECTIVE**	**POSSESSIVE**
First person	we	us	our, ours
Second person	you	you	your, yours
Third person	they	them	their, theirs
Relative or Interrogative Pronouns			
	SUBJECTIVE	**OBJECTIVE**	**POSSESSIVE**
Singular and plural	who	whom	whose
	whoever	whomever	

Pronouns in the Subjective Case

Use the **subjective case** (also known as the **nominative case**) when the pronoun functions as the subject of a sentence or clause (see p. 499) or as a subject complement (also known as a predicate nominative; see p. 521). A predicate nominative is a noun or pronoun that follows a linking verb and identifies or renames the subject of the sentence.

C. Avoiding Sentence Errors

Subject

She has won recognition as a landscape architect.

Subject complement

Cathie volunteers at the local hospital. The most faithful volunteer is she.

The subjective case is also used when a pronoun functions as an appositive to a subject or subject complement (see p. 521).

The only two seniors, she and her best friend, won the top awards.

Pronouns in the Objective Case

Use the objective case when a pronoun functions as a direct object, indirect object, or object of a preposition (see pp. 521 and 522).

Direct object

George helped her with the assignment.

Indirect object

George gave her a book.

Objects of the preposition

George gave the book to him and her.

The objective case is also used when the pronoun functions as the subject of an infinitive phrase or an appositive to an object.

Subject of infinitive | Infinitive phrase

I wanted him to go straight home.

Direct object | Appositive to object

The district manager chose two representatives, Marnie and me.

Note: When a sentence has a compound subject or compound objects, you may have trouble determining the correct pronoun case. To determine how the pronoun functions, mentally recast the sentence without the noun or other pronoun in the compound construction. Determine how the pronoun functions by itself and then decide which case is correct.

Subjective case

They and Teresa brought the beverages. [Think: "*They* brought the beverages." *They* is the subject of the sentence, so the subjective case is correct.]

Objective case

Behind you and me, the drapery rustled. [Think: "Behind *me*." *Me* is the object of the preposition *behind*, so the objective case is correct.]

Pronouns in the Possessive Case

Possessive pronouns indicate to whom or to what something belongs. The possessive pronouns *mine*, *yours*, *his*, *hers*, *its*, *ours*, and *theirs* function just as nouns do.

C. Avoiding Sentence Errors

Subject

Hers is the letterhead with the bright blue lettering.

Direct object

I liked hers the best.

The possessive pronouns *my*, *your*, *his*, *her*, *its*, *our*, and *their* are used as adjectives to modify nouns and gerunds (see p. 509).

Our high-school reunion surprised everyone by its size.

Your attending that reunion will depend on your travel schedule.

Who and *Whom* as Interrogative Pronouns

When *who*, *whoever*, *whom*, and *whomever* introduce questions, they are interrogative pronouns. How an interrogative pronoun functions in a clause determines its case. Use *who* or *whoever* (the subjective case) when the interrogative pronoun functions as a subject or subject complement (see p. 521). Use *whom* or *whomever* (the objective case) when the interrogative pronoun functions as a direct object or an object of a preposition.

SUBJECTIVE CASE	Subject Who is there?
OBJECTIVE CASE	Object of preposition To whom did you give the letter?

Who and *Whom* as Relative Pronouns

When *who*, *whoever*, *whom*, and *whomever* introduce subordinate clauses, they are relative pronouns. How a relative pronoun functions in a clause determines its case. Use *who* or *whoever* (subjective case) when a relative pronoun functions as the subject of the subordinate clause. Use *whom* or *whomever* (objective case) when a relative pronoun functions as an object in the subordinate clause.

SUBJECTIVE CASE	The lecturer, who is a journalist from New York, speaks with great insight and wit. [*Who* is the subject of the subordinate clause.]
OBJECTIVE CASE	The journalist, whom I know from college days, came to give a lecture. [*Whom* is the direct object of the verb *know* in the subordinate clause.]

C.10 Correct Adjective and Adverb Use

Adjectives and adverbs modify, describe, explain, qualify, or restrict the words they modify (see p. 508 and p. 511). **Adjectives** modify nouns and pronouns. **Adverbs** modify verbs, adjectives, and other adverbs; adverbs can also modify phrases, clauses, or whole sentences.

ADJECTIVES	red car; the quiet one
ADVERBS	quickly finish; only four reasons; very angrily

Comparison of Adjectives and Adverbs

Positive adjectives and adverbs modify but do not involve any comparison: *green, bright, lively*.

Comparative adjectives and adverbs compare two persons, things, actions, or ideas.

COMPARATIVE ADJECTIVE	Michel is taller than Latoya.
COMPARATIVE ADVERB	Antonio reacted more calmly than Robert.

Here is how to form comparative adjectives and adverbs. (Consult your dictionary if you are unsure of the form of a particular word.)

1. **If the adjective or adverb has one syllable, add *-er*. For certain two-syllable words, also add *-er*.**

   cold ⟶ colder   slow ⟶ slower   narrow ⟶ narrower

2. **For most words of two or more syllables, place the word *more* in front of the word.**

   reasonable ⟶ more reasonable   interestingly ⟶ more interestingly

3. **For two-syllable adjectives ending in *-y*, change the *-y* to *-i* and add *-er*.**

   drowsy ⟶ drowsier   lazy ⟶ lazier

Superlative adjectives and adverbs compare more than two persons, things, actions, or ideas.

SUPERLATIVE ADJECTIVE	Michael is the tallest member of the team.
SUPERLATIVE ADVERB	She studied most diligently for the test.

Here is how to form superlative adjectives and adverbs:

1. **Add *-est* to one-syllable adjectives and adverbs and to certain two-syllable words.**

   cold ⟶ coldest   fast ⟶ fastest   narrow ⟶ narrowest

2. **For most words of two or more syllables, place the word *most* in front of the word.**

   reasonable ⟶ most reasonable   interestingly ⟶ most interestingly

3. **For two-syllable adjectives ending in *-y*, change the *-y* to *-i* and add *-est*.**

   drowsy ⟶ drowsiest   lazy ⟶ laziest

Irregular Adjectives and Adverbs

Some adjectives and adverbs form their comparative and superlative forms in irregular ways.

Tip for Writers

When writing *superlative statements*, always use *the*. Use *much* only in questions and negatives. In affirmative statements, use *a lot of* or *some*.

Do you have much time for painting now that you're going to school?

Yes, I still have a lot of time for painting. (or) No, I don't have much time.

Tip for Writers

Use *littler* and *littlest* for size; use *less* and *least* for amount (quantity). Use *little/less/least* before noncount nouns; use *few/fewer/fewest* before plural nouns:

The littlest of Lana's eight children is only two years old; Lana has less time to spend with her friends now that she has a big family. She has *fewer* friends now.

POSITIVE	COMPARATIVE	SUPERLATIVE
Adjectives		
good	better	best
bad	worse	worst
little	littler, less	littlest, least
Adverbs		
well	better	best
badly	worse	worst
Adjectives and Adverbs		
many	more	most
some	more	most
much	more	most

Common Mistakes to Avoid

1. **Do not use adjectives to modify verbs, other adjectives, or adverbs.**

INCORRECT	Peter and Mary take each other serious.
CORRECT	Peter and Mary take each other seriously. [Modifies the verb *take*]

2. **Do not use the adjectives *good* and *bad* when you should use the adverbs *well* and *badly*.**

INCORRECT	**Juan did good on the exam.**
CORRECT	**Juan did well on the exam. [Modifies the verb *did*]**

3. **Do not use the adjectives *real* and *sure* when you should use the adverbs *really* and *surely*.**

INCORRECT	Jan scored real well on the exam.
CORRECT	Jan scored really well on the exam. [Modifies the adverb *well*]
INCORRECT	I sure was surprised to win the lottery.
CORRECT	I surely was surprised to win the lottery. [Modifies the verb *was surprised*]

4. **Do not use *more* or *most* with the *-er* or *-est* form of an adjective or adverb.** Use one form or the other, according to the rules above.

INCORRECT	That was the most tastiest dinner I've ever eaten.
CORRECT	That was the tastiest dinner I've ever eaten.

5. **Avoid double negatives—that is, two negatives in the same clause.**

INCORRECT	He did not want nothing in the refrigerator.
CORRECT	He did not want anything in the refrigerator.

6. **When using the comparative and superlative forms of adverbs, do not create an incomplete comparison.**

INCORRECT The heater works more efficiently. [More efficiently than what?]

CORRECT The heater works more efficiently than it did before we had it repaired.

7. **Do not use the comparative form for adjectives and adverbs that have no degree.** It is incorrect to write, for example, *more square, most perfect, more equally*, or *most straight*. Do not use a comparative or superlative form for any of the following adjectives and adverbs:

ADJECTIVES				
complete	equal	infinite	pregnant	unique
dead	eternal	invisible	square	universal
empty	favorite	matchless	supreme	vertical
endless	impossible	parallel	unanimous	whole
ADVERBS				
endlessly	infinitely	uniquely		
equally	invisibly	universally		
eternally	perpendicularly			
impossibly	straight			

EXERCISE 17 Using Adjectives and Adverbs Correctly

Directions: Revise each of the following sentences so that all adjectives and adverbs are used correctly. If the sentence is correct, write "C" for correct beside it.

EXAMPLE I answered the question polite^ly.

_____ 1. Michael's apartment was more expensive than Arturio's.

_____ 2. When I heard the man and woman sing the duet, I decided that the woman sang best.

_____ 3. Flowers grow poorly in this soil.

_____ 4. The roller coaster was excitinger than the merry-go-round.

_____ 5. *The Scarlet Letter* is more good than *War and Peace*.

_____ 6. Susan sure gave a rousing speech.

_____ 7. Last week's storm seemed worst than a tornado.

_____ 8. Some women thought that the Equal Rights Amendment would guarantee that women be treated more equally.

_____ 9. Taking the interstate is the most fast route to the outlet mall.

_____ 10. Professor Reed had the better lecture style of all my instructors.

Writing Effective Sentences

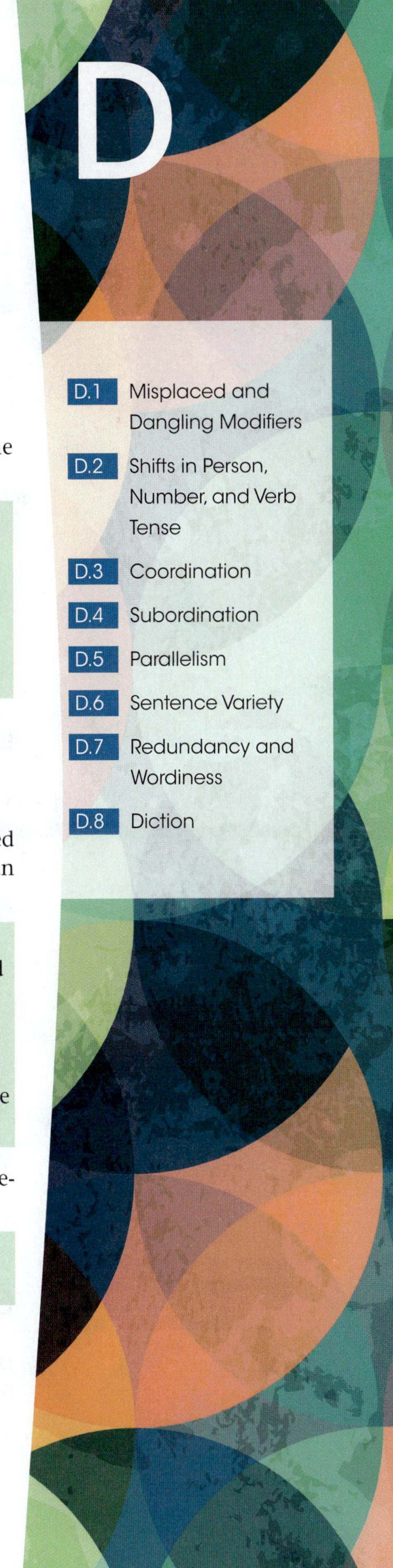

D.1 Misplaced and Dangling Modifiers
D.2 Shifts in Person, Number, and Verb Tense
D.3 Coordination
D.4 Subordination
D.5 Parallelism
D.6 Sentence Variety
D.7 Redundancy and Wordiness
D.8 Diction

D.1 Misplaced and Dangling Modifiers

A **modifier** is a word, phrase, or clause that describes, qualifies, or limits the meaning of another word.

WORD	She wore a red dress. [The adjective *red* describes the dress.]
PHRASE	I like the taste of vanilla ice cream. [The phrase "of vanilla ice cream" qualifies the word *taste*.]
CLAUSE	The boy who fell from the horse was hospitalized. [The clause "who fell from the horse" explains which boy was hospitalized.]

Modifiers that are not correctly placed can make a sentence confusing.

Misplaced Modifiers

Misplaced modifiers do not describe or explain the words the writer intended them to. A misplaced modifier often appears to modify the wrong word or can leave the reader confused as to which word it does modify.

MISPLACED	Max bought a chair at the used-furniture shop that was large and dark. [Was the chair or the furniture shop large and dark?]
MISPLACED	The instructor announced that the term paper was due on April 25 at the beginning of class. [Are the papers due at the beginning of class on the 25th, or did the instructor make the announcement at the beginning of class?]

You can easily avoid misplaced modifiers if you make sure that modifiers immediately precede or follow the words they modify.

CORRECT	Max bought a chair that was large and dark at the used-furniture shop.

CORRECT	Max bought a large, dark chair at the used-furniture shop.
CORRECT	At the beginning of class, the instructor announced that the term paper was due on April 25.

Dangling Modifiers

Dangling modifiers do not clearly describe or explain any part of the sentence. Dangling modifiers create confusion and sometimes unintentional humor. To avoid dangling modifiers, make sure that each modifier has a clear antecedent.

DANGLING	Rounding the curve, a fire hydrant was hit by the speeding car. [The modifier suggests that the hydrant rounded the curve.]
CORRECT	Rounding the curve, the speeding car hit the fire hydrant. [Modifies *car*]
DANGLING	Uncertain of what courses to take next semester, the academic advisor listed five options. [The modifier suggests that the advisor was uncertain of what courses to take.]
CORRECT	Uncertain of what courses to take next semester, the student spoke to an academic advisor, who listed five options.
DANGLING	Flood damage was visible crossing the river. [The modifier makes it sound as though flood damage was crossing the river.]
CORRECT	Flood damage was visible as we crossed the river.

There are two common ways to revise dangling modifiers:

1. **Add a word or words that the modifier clearly describes.** Place the new material just after the modifier, and rearrange other parts of the sentence as necessary.

DANGLING	While watching television, the cake burned.
CORRECT	While watching television, Sarah burned the cake.

2. **Change the dangling modifier to a subordinate clause.** You may need to change the verb form in the modifier.

DANGLING	While watching television, the cake burned.
CORRECT	While Sarah was watching television, the cake burned.

EXERCISE 18 Correcting Misplaced and Dangling Modifiers

Directions: Revise each of the following sentences to correct misplaced or dangling modifiers.

EXAMPLE Deciding which flavor of ice cream to order, another customer cut in front of Roger.

REVISED While Roger was deciding which flavor of ice cream to order, another customer cut in front of him.

D. Writing Effective Sentences

1. Tricia saw an animal at the zoo that had black fur and long claws.

____

2. Before answering the door, the phone rang.

____

3. I could see large snowflakes falling from the bedroom window.

____

4. Honking, Felicia walked in front of the car.

____

5. After leaving the classroom, the door automatically locked.

____

6. Applauding and cheering, the band returned for an encore.

____

7. The waiter brought a birthday cake to our table that had 24 candles.

____

8. Books lined the library shelves about every imaginable subject.

____

9. While sobbing, the sad movie ended and the lights came on.

____

10. Turning the page, the book's binding cracked.

____

D.2 Shifts in Person, Number, and Verb Tense

The parts of a sentence should be consistent. Shifts within a sentence in person, number, or verb tense will make the sentence confusing and difficult to read.

Shifts in Person

Person is the grammatical term used to distinguish the speaker or writer (**first person**: *I*, *we*), the person spoken to (**second person**: *you*), and the person or thing spoken about (**third person**: *he*, *she*, *it*, *they*, and any noun, such as *Joan* or *children*). A sentence or a paragraph should use the same person throughout.

SHIFT	If a student studies effectively, you will get good grades.
CORRECT	If you study effectively, you will get good grades.

Shifts in Number

Number distinguishes between singular and plural. A pronoun must agree in number with its antecedent, the word to which it refers (see p. 553 Section C.7). Related nouns within a sentence also must agree in number. (Sometimes you need to change the form of the verb when you correct the inconsistent nouns or pronouns.)

SHIFT	When a home owner does not shovel the snow in front of their house, they risk getting fined.
CORRECT	When home owners do not shovel the snow in front of their houses, they risk getting fined.

Shifts in Verb Tense

The same verb tense should be used throughout a sentence unless meaning requires a shift.

REQUIRED SHIFT	After my cousin arrives (Present), we will go (Future) to the movies.
INCORRECT	After Marguerite bought (Past) the health food store, she seems (Present) more confident.
CORRECT	After Marguerite bought (Past) the health food store, she seemed (Past) more confident.
INCORRECT	Emma heard (Past) the clock strike twelve, and then she goes (Present) for a midday walk.
CORRECT	Emma heard (Past) the clock strike twelve, and then she went (Past) for a midday walk.

D. Writing Effective Sentences

EXERCISE 19 Correcting Shifts in Person, Number, and Tense

Directions: Revise each of the following sentences to correct errors in shift of person, number, or tense. If a sentence contains no errors, write "C" for correct beside it.

EXAMPLE Boats along the river were tied to their docks.

_____ 1. When people receive a gift, you should be gracious and polite.

_____ 2. When we arrived at the inn, the lights are on and a fire is burning in the fireplace.

_____ 3. Before Trey drove to the cabin, he packs a picnic lunch.

_____ 4. The artist paints portraits and weaves baskets.

_____ 5. The lobsterman goes out on his boat each day and will check his lobster traps.

_____ 6. All the cars Honest Bob sells have new transmissions.

_____ 7. Rosa ran the 100-meter race and throws the discus at the track meet.

_____ 8. Public schools in Florida have air-conditioning systems.

_____ 9. Office workers sat on the benches downtown and are eating their lunches outside.

_____ 10. Before a scuba diver goes underwater, you must check and recheck your breathing equipment.

D.3 Coordination

Tip for Writers

Note the inverted (question) word order used with *nor*: She doesn't eat fish, nor does she eat chicken. (This means she doesn't eat either one.) The verb after *nor* is affirmative because *nor* is negative.

Coordination is a way to give related ideas equal emphasis within a single sentence. your readers will better understand the flow of your thoughts if you connect coordinate ideas.

How to Combine Ideas of Equal Importance

There are three ways to combine ideas of equal importance when those ideas are expressed in independent clauses (see p. 529).

1. **Join the two independent clauses with a comma and a coordinating conjunction (*and*, *but*, *nor*, *or*, *for*, *so*, *yet*).**

Independent clause: I passed the ball, Independent clause: but Sam failed to catch it.

You should choose a coordinating conjunction that properly expresses the relationship between the ideas in the two clauses.

Tip for Writers

The conjunction *for* is a more formal way to say *because*. Both are followed by a reason. Note the differences in punctuation:

Because I'm tired, I'm going home. (comma)

I'm going home because I'm tired. (no comma)

I'm going home, for I'm tired. (comma)

COORDINATING CONJUNCTION	MEANING	EXAMPLE
and	addition; one idea added to another	I went shopping, and I spent too much money.
but, yet	contrast	I wanted to grill fish, but Peter was a vegetarian.
or	alternatives or choices	Tonight I might go to the movies, or I might work out.
nor	not either	Julie was not in class, nor was she in the snack bar.
for	cause and effect	We went walking, for it was a beautiful evening.
so	result	I was early for the appointment, so I decided to doze for a few minutes.

2. **Join the two independent clauses with a semicolon.**

We decided to see the new Spike Lee film; it was playing at three local theaters.

Use this method when the relationship between the two ideas is clear and requires no explanation. Usually, the two clauses must be very closely related.

Note: If you join two independent clauses with only a comma and fail to use a coordinating conjunction or semicolon, you will produce a comma splice. If you join two independent clauses without using a punctuation mark and a coordinating conjunction, or a semicolon, you will produce a run-on sentence (see p. 539).

3. **Join the two independent clauses with a semicolon and a conjunctive adverb followed by a comma.** A conjunctive adverb can also be used at the beginning of a sentence to link the sentence with an earlier one.

CONJUNCTIVE ADVERB	MEANING	EXAMPLE
therefore, consequently, thus, hence	cause and effect	I am planning to become a nurse; consequently, I'm taking a lot of science courses.
however, nevertheless, nonetheless, conversely	differences or contrast	We had planned to go bowling; however, we went to hear music instead.
furthermore, moreover, also	addition; a continuation of the same idea	To save money I am packing my lunch; also, I am walking to work instead of taking the bus.
similarly, likewise	similarity	I left class as soon as I finished the exam; likewise, other students also left.
then, subsequently, next	sequence in time	I walked home; then I massaged my aching feet.

EXERCISE 20 Practicing Coordination

Directions: Complete each of the following sentences by adding a coordinating conjunction or a conjunctive adverb and the appropriate punctuation.

EXAMPLE Teresa vacationed in Denver last year; similarly, Jan will go to Denver this year.

1. Our professor did not complete the lecture; ________________ he did give an assignment for the next class.

2. A first-aid kit was in her backpack; ____________ the hiker was able to treat her cut knee.

3. An opening act began the concert; ____________ the headline band took the stage.

4. I always put a light on when I leave the house; ____________ I often turn on a radio to deter burglars.

5. Sue politely asked to borrow my car, ____________ she thanked me when she returned it.

6. My roommate went to the library; ____________ I had the apartment to myself.

7. Steve and Todd will go to a baseball game, ____________ they will go to a movie instead.

8. Serena looks like her father, ____________ her hair is darker and curlier than his.

9. Maureen took a job at a bookstore; ____________ she was offered a job at a museum.

10. Our neighbors bought a barbecue grill; ____________ we decided to buy one.

D.4 Subordination

Subordination is a way to show that one idea is not as important as another. When two clauses are related, but one is less important, the less important one can be expressed as a dependent (subordinate) clause (see p. 529). Dependent clauses do contain a subject and a verb, but they do not express a complete thought. They must always be added to a complete sentence or independent clause. If a dependent clause is used alone, it is a fragment and must be corrected (see p. 534).

How to Combine Ideas of Unequal Importance

1. **Introduce the less important idea with a subordinating conjunction.** Choose a subordinating conjunction that properly shows the relationship of the less important idea to the more important one. Common subordinating conjunctions are *after, although, because, before, unless, when,* and *while.* (See pp. 529–530 for a complete list.)

Dependent clause: After I finished revising my report,
Subordinating conjunction: After
Independent clause: I worked on my oral presentation.

After I finished revising my report, I worked on my oral presentation.

Dependent clause: Unless I win the lottery,
Subordinating conjunction: Unless
Independent clause: I will not be able to buy a new car.

Unless I win the lottery, I will not be able to buy a new car.

2. **Introduce the less important idea with a relative pronoun (such as *who*, which, *that*, or what).** A relative pronoun usually introduces a clause that functions as a noun when the clause is attached to an independent clause. (See p. 501 for more on relative pronouns.)

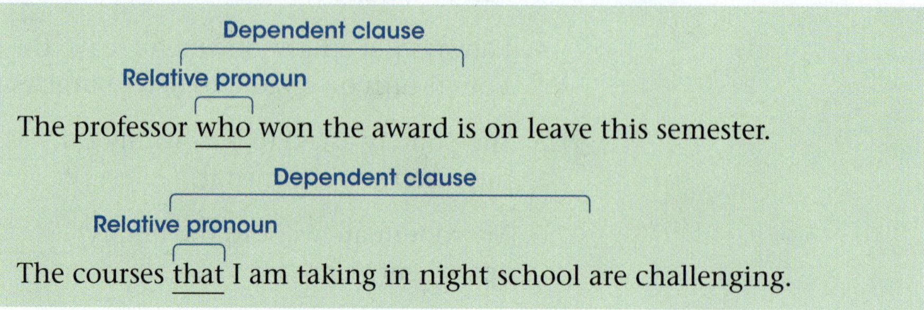

EXERCISE 21

Combining Sentences Using Coordinating Conjunctions and Relative Pronouns

Directions: Combine each of the following pairs of sentences by subordinating one idea to the other with a coordinating conjunction or a relative pronoun.

EXAMPLE **a.** One kind of opossum can glide like a bird.

b. The opossum lives in Australia.

COMBINED One kind of opossum, which lives in Australia, can glide like a bird.

1. **a.** Trina can get discount movie tickets.

   b. Trina's husband manages a movie theater.

   ____

   ____

2. a. Rob hit the ground with his tennis racket.

   b. Rob's tennis racket broke.

   ____

   ____

3. a. The car has satellite radio and a sunroof.

   b. I bought the car yesterday.

   ____

   ____

4. a. Visitors to the automobile museum can learn a lot about the mechanics of cars.

   b. Visitors enjoy looking at many old cars.

   ____

   ____

5. a. The sorority will hold its fall picnic next week.
   b. The picnic will be held if it does not rain.

____

____

6. a. Vicky went to the library to work on her term paper.
   b. Then Vicky went to pick up her son from the day care center.

____

____

7. a. Oprah Winfrey may run for public office someday.
   b. Oprah Winfrey is a popular public figure.

____

____

8. a. I will go shopping for a rain slicker tomorrow.
   b. I will not go if my roommate has one that I can borrow.

____

____

9. a. Linda and Pablo got divorced.
   b. They could not agree on anything.

____

____

10. a. The yacht sailed into the marina.
    b. The yacht is owned by the Kennedy family.

____

____

D.5 Parallelism

Parallelism is a method of ensuring that words, phrases, and clauses in a series are in the same grammatical form.

What Should Be Parallel?

1. **Words or phrases in a series**. When two or more nouns, verbs, adjectives, adverbs, or phrases appear together in a sentence connected by a coordinating conjunction (such as *and*, *or*, or *but*), the words or phrases should be parallel in grammatical form.

NOT PARALLEL	The dentist told me to stop eating so much candy and that I should floss my teeth. [Infinitive phrase: to stop eating so much candy; Relative pronoun: that; Subordinate clause: that I should floss my teeth]
PARALLEL	The dentist told me to stop eating so much candy and to floss my teeth. [Infinitive phrase: to stop eating so much candy; Infinitive phrase: to floss my teeth]
NOT PARALLEL	A well-rounded diet, exercising, and to get enough sleep are essential to good health. [Noun: diet; Gerund: exercising; Infinitive phrase: to get enough sleep]
PARALLEL	A well-rounded diet, exercise, and enough sleep are essential to good health. [Noun: diet; Noun: exercise; Noun: sleep]

2. **Independent clauses joined with a coordinating conjunction.** Independent clauses within a sentence should be parallel in tense and in construction.

NOT PARALLEL	The drivers waited patiently as the work crew cleaned up the wreck, but after an hour the horns were honked loudly by all the drivers. [Active voice: waited; Passive voice: were honked]
PARALLEL	The drivers waited patiently as the work crew cleaned up the wreck, but after an hour they honked their horns loudly. [Active voice: waited; Active voice: honked]
NOT PARALLEL	Carlos wanted to go to the concert, but Julia wants to stay home and watch a video. [Past tense: wanted; Present tense: wants]
PARALLEL	Carlos wanted to go to the concert, but Julia wanted to stay home and watch a video. [Past tense: wanted; Past tense: wanted]

3. **Items being compared.** When elements of a sentence are compared or contrasted, use the same grammatical form for each element.

INCORRECT	Mark wanted a vacation rather than to save money to buy a house. [Noun: vacation; Infinitive phrase: to save]
CORRECT	Mark wanted to take a vacation rather than to save money to buy a house. [Infinitive phrase: to take; Infinitive phrase: to save]

EXERCISE 22 Revising Sentences to Achieve Parallelism

Directions: Revise each of the following sentences to achieve parallelism.

EXAMPLE Rosa has decided to study nursing instead of going into accounting.

REVISED *Rosa has decided to study nursing instead of accounting.*

1. The priest baptized the baby and congratulates the new parents.

2. We ordered a platter of fried clams, a platter of corn on the cob, and fried shrimp.

3. Lucy entered the dance contest, but the dance was watched by June from the side.

4. Léon purchased the ratchet set at the garage sale and buying the drill bits there too.

5. The exterminator told Brandon the house needed to be fumigated and spraying to eliminate the termites.

6. The bus swerved and hit the dump truck, which swerves and hit the station wagon, which swerved and hit the bicycle.

7. Channel 2 covered the bank robbery, but a python that had escaped from the zoo was reported by Channel 7.

8. Sal was born while Bush was president, and Clinton was president when Rob was born.

9. The pediatrician spent the morning with sore throats, answering questions about immunizations, and treating bumps and bruises.

____

____

10. Belinda prefers to study in the library, but her brother Marcus studies at home.

____

____

D.6 Sentence Variety

Good writers use a variety of sentence structures to avoid wordiness and monotony and to show relationships among thoughts. To achieve **sentence variety**, do not use all simple sentences or all complex or compound sentences (see pp. 531–532), and do not begin or end all sentences in the same way. Instead, vary the length, the amount of detail, and the structure of your sentences.

1. **Use sentences of varying lengths.**
2. **Avoid stringing simple sentences together with coordinating conjunctions (*and, but, or,* and so on).** Instead, use some introductory participial phrases (see p. 526).

SIMPLE	There was a long line at the deli, so Chris decided to leave.
VARIED	Seeing the long line at the deli, Chris decided to leave.

3. **Begin some sentences with a prepositional phrase.** A preposition shows relationships between things (*during, over, toward, before, across, within, inside, over, above*). Many prepositions suggest chronology, direction, or location (see p. 514).

During the concert, the fire alarm rang.

Inside the theater, the crowd waited expectantly.

4. **Begin some sentences with a present or past participle (*cooking, broken*;** see p. 526).

Barking and jumping, the dogs greeted their master.

Still laughing, two girls left the movie.

Tired and exhausted, the mountain climbers fell asleep quickly.

5. **Begin some sentences with adverbs** (see p. 511).

Angrily, the student left the room.

Patiently, the math instructor explained the assignment again.

6. **Begin some sentences with infinitive phrases (*to* plus the infinitive form: *to make, to go*;** see p. 527).

To get breakfast ready on time, I set my alarm for 7 A.M.

7. **Begin some sentences with a dependent clause introduced by a subordinating conjunction** (see p. 529).

   Because I ate shellfish, I developed hives.

8. **Begin some sentences with a conjunctive adverb.**

   Consequently, we decided to have steak for dinner.

EXERCISE 23 Practicing Sentence Construction Techniques

Directions: Combine each of the following pairs of simple sentences into one sentence, using the technique suggested in brackets.

EXAMPLE **a.** The dog barked and howled.
b. The dog warned a stranger away.
[Use present participle (*-ing* form).]

COMBINED Barking and howling, the dog warned a stranger away.

1. **a.** Professor Clark has a Civil War battlefield model.
   b. He has it in his office.
   [Use prepositional phrase.]

   ____

   ____

2. **a.** Toby went to Disneyland for the first time.
   b. He was very excited.
   [Use past participle (*-ed* form).]

   ____

   ____

3. **a.** Teresa received a full scholarship.
   b. She does not need to worry about paying her tuition.
   [Use subordinating conjunction.]

   ____

   ____

4. **a.** Lance answered the phone.
   b. He spoke with a gruff voice.
   [Use adverb.]

   ____

   ____

5. **a.** The truck choked and sputtered.
   b. The truck pulled into the garage.
   [Use present participle (*-ing* form).]

   ____

   ____

6. a. Rich programmed his DVR.
   b. He recorded his favorite sitcom.
   [Use infinitive (*to*) phrase.]

____

____

7. a. The postal carrier placed a package outside my door.
   b. The package had a foreign stamp on it.
   [Use prepositional phrase.]

____

____

8. a. The instructor asked the students to take their seats.
   b. She was annoyed.
   [Use past participle (*-ed* form).]

____

____

9. a. Shyla stood outside the student union.
   b. She waited for her boyfriend.
   [Use present participle (*-ing* form).]

____

____

10. a. Bo walked to the bookstore.
    b. He was going to buy some new highlighters.
    [Use infinitive (*to*) phrase.]

____

____

D.7 Redundancy and Wordiness

Redundancy results when a writer says the same thing twice. Wordiness results when a writer uses more words than necessary to convey a meaning. Both redundancy and wordiness detract from clear, effective sentences by distracting and confusing the reader.

Eliminating Redundancy

A common mistake is to repeat the same idea in slightly different words.

> The remaining chocolate-chip cookie is the only one left, so I saved it for you. [*Remaining* and *only one left* mean the same thing.]
>
> The vase was oval in shape. [Oval is a shape, so *in shape* is redundant.]

To revise a redundant sentence, eliminate one of the redundant elements.

Eliminating Wordiness

1. **Eliminate wordiness by cutting out words that do not add to the meaning of your sentence.**

WORDY	In the final analysis, choosing the field of biology as my major resulted in my realizing that college is hard work.
REVISED	Choosing biology as my major made me realize that college is hard work.
WORDY	The type of imitative behavior that I notice among teenagers is a very important, helpful aspect of their learning to function in groups.
REVISED	The imitative behavior of teenagers helps them learn to function in groups.

Watch out in particular for empty words and phrases.

Phrase	***Substitute***
until such time as	until
due to the fact that	because
at this point in time	now
in order to	to

2. **Express your ideas simply and directly, using as few words as possible.** Often by rearranging your wording, you can eliminate two or three words.

the fleas that my dog has ⟶ my dog's fleas

workers with jobs that are low in pay ⟶ workers with low-paying jobs

3. **Use strong, active verbs that convey movement and give additional information.**

WORDY	I was in charge of two other employees and needed to watch over their work and performance.
REVISED	I supervised two employees, monitored their performance, and checked their work.

4. **Avoid sentences that begin with *"There is"* and *"There are."*** These empty phrases add no meaning, energy, or life to sentences.

WORDY	There are many children who suffer from malnutrition.
REVISED	Many children suffer from malnutrition.

D. Writing Effective Sentences

EXERCISE 24

Eliminating Redundancy and Wordiness

Directions: Revise each of the following sentences to eliminate redundancy and wordiness.

EXAMPLE Janice, who is impatient, usually cannot wait for class to end and packs up all of her books and notebooks in her backpack before the class is over.

REVISED Janice is impatient and usually packs everything in her backpack before class ends.

1. My co-workers are friendly, nice, and cooperative and always willing to help me.
2. Eva and Joe are returning again to the branch office where they met.
3. Lynn changed from her regular clothes into her shorts and T-shirt in order that she could play basketball.
4. Due to the fact that Professor Reis assigned 100 pages of reading for tomorrow, I will be unable to join the group of my friends at the restaurant tonight.
5. In my mythology class, we discussed and talked about the presence of a Noah's ark–type story in most cultures.
6. Darryl offered many ideas and theories as to the reason why humans exist.
7. There are many children who have not been immunized against dangerous childhood diseases.
8. Scientists have been studying the disease AIDS for many years, but they have been unable to find a cure for the disease.
9. The brown-colored chair was my father's favorite chair.
10. The briefcase that Julio has carried belonged to his brother.

D.8 Diction

Diction is the use and choice of words. Words that you choose should be appropriate for your audience and express your meaning clearly. The following suggestions will help you improve your diction:

1. **Avoid slang expressions.** Slang refers to the informal, special expressions created and used by groups of people who want to give themselves a unique identity. Slang is an appropriate and useful way to communicate in some social situations and in some forms of creative writing. However, it is not appropriate for academic or career writing.

SLANG	My sister seems permanently out to lunch.
REVISED	My sister seems out of touch with the world.
SLANG	We pigged out at the ice cream shop.
REVISED	We consumed enormous quantities of ice cream at the ice cream shop.

2. **Avoid colloquial language.** Colloquial language refers to casual, everyday spoken language. It should be avoided in formal situations. Words that fall into this category are labeled *informal* or *colloquial* in your dictionary.

COLLOQUIAL	I almost flunked bio last sem.
REVISED	I almost failed biology last semester.
COLLOQUIAL	What are you all doing later?
REVISED	What are you doing later?

3. **Avoid nonstandard language.** Nonstandard language consists of words and grammatical forms that are used in conversation but are neither correct nor acceptable standard written English.

Nonstandard	***Standard***
hisself	himself
knowed	known, knew
hadn't ought to	should not
she want	she wants
he go	he goes

4. **Avoid trite expressions.** Trite expressions are old, worn-out words and phrases that have become stale and do not convey meaning as effectively as possible. These expressions are also called *clichés*.

Trite Expressions		
needle in a haystack	sadder but wiser	as old as the hills
hard as a rock	white as snow	pretty as a picture
face the music	gentle as a lamb	

Practicing Correct Diction

Directions: Revise each of the following sentences by using correct diction.

EXAMPLE This here building is Clemens Hall.

REVISED This building is Clemens Hall.

1. Jean freaked out when I told her she won the lottery.
2. He go to the library.
3. The campus is wider than an ocean.
4. Marty sits next to me in chem.
5. Sandy's new stereo is totally cool and has an awesome sound.
6. We went nuts when our team won the game.
7. Them hybrid cars are expensive.
8. I think Nathan is as sharp as a tack because he got every question on the exam right.
9. Nino blew class off today to go rock climbing with his pals.
10. Dr. Maring's pager beeped in the middle of the meeting and she had to hightail it to a phone.

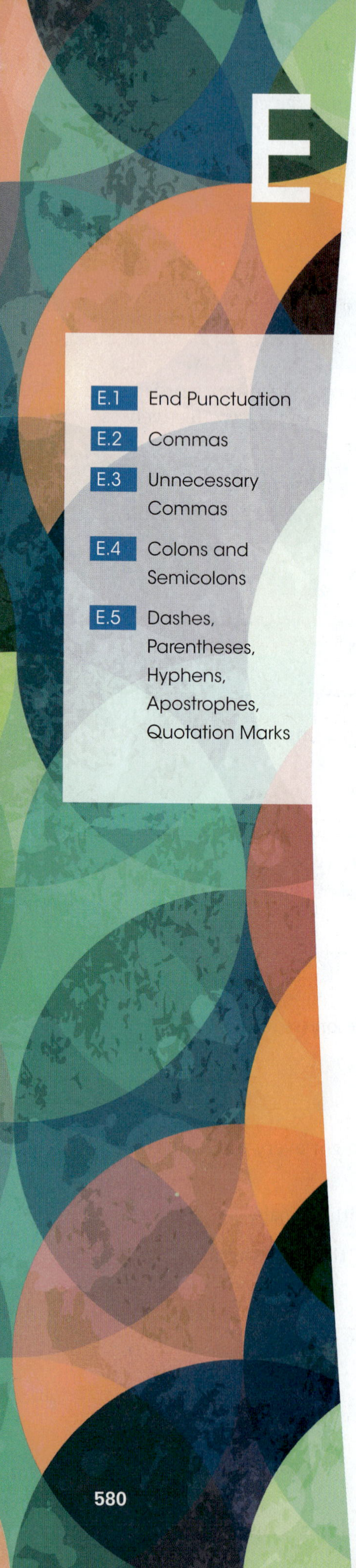

E Using Punctuation Correctly

E.1 End Punctuation
E.2 Commas
E.3 Unnecessary Commas
E.4 Colons and Semicolons
E.5 Dashes, Parentheses, Hyphens, Apostrophes, Quotation Marks

E.1 End Punctuation

When to Use Periods

Use a period in the following situations:

1. **To end a sentence unless it is a question or an exclamation.**

> We washed the car even though we knew a thunderstorm was imminent.

Note: Use a period to end a sentence that states an indirect question or indirectly quotes someone's words or thoughts.

INCORRECT	Samantha wondered if she would be on time?
CORRECT	Samantha wondered if she would be on time.

2. **To punctuate many abbreviations.**

> M.D. B.A. P.M. B.C. Mr. Ms.

Do not use periods in acronyms, such as *NATO* and *AIDS*, or in abbreviations for most organizations, such as *NBC* and *NAACP*.

Note: If a sentence ends with an abbreviation, the sentence has only one period, not two.

> The train was due to arrive at 7:00 P.M.

When to Use Question Marks

Use question marks after direct questions. Place the question mark within the closing quotation marks.

> She asked the grocer, "How old is this cheese?"

Note: Use a period, not a question mark, after an indirect question.

> She asked the grocer how old the cheese was.

When to Use Exclamation Points

Use an exclamation point at the end of a sentence that expresses particular emphasis, excitement, or urgency. Use exclamation points sparingly, however, especially in academic writing.

What a beautiful day it is! Dial 911 right now!

E.2 Commas

The comma is used to separate parts of a sentence from one another. If you omit a comma when it is needed, you risk making a clear and direct sentence confusing.

When to Use Commas

Use a comma in the following situations:

1. **Before a coordinating conjunction that joins two independent clauses** (see p. 567).

   Terry had planned to leave work early, but he was delayed.

2. **To separate a dependent (subordinate) clause from an independent clause when the dependent clause comes first in the sentence** (see p. 569).

   After I left the library, I went to the computer lab.

3. **To separate introductory words and phrases from the rest of the sentence.**

   Unfortunately, I forgot my umbrella.

   To pass the baton, I will need to locate my teammate.

   Exuberant over their victory, the football team members carried the quarterback on their shoulders.

4. **To separate a nonrestrictive phrase or clause from the rest of a sentence.** A **nonrestrictive** phrase or clause is added to a sentence but does not change the sentence's basic meaning.

   To determine whether an element is nonrestrictive, read the sentence without the element. If the meaning of the sentence does not essentially change, then the commas are *necessary*.

   My sister, who is a mail carrier, is afraid of dogs. [The essential meaning of this sentence does not change if we read the sentence without the subordinate clause: *My sister is afraid of dogs*. Therefore, commas are needed.]

   Mail carriers who have been bitten by dogs are afraid of them. [If we read this sentence without the subordinate clause, its meaning changes considerably: *Mail carriers are afraid of (dogs)*. It seems to say that *all* mail carriers are afraid of dogs. In this case, adding commas is not correct.]

Tip for Writers

Punctuation

Using punctuation incorrectly can sometimes change the meaning of your sentences. Here are two examples:

1. The children who stayed outside got wet. (Only some of the children got wet.) The children, who stayed outside, got wet. (All of the children got wet.)
2. Did she finally marry Roger? Did she finally marry, Roger?

5. **To separate three or more items in a series.**

   Note: A comma is *not* used *after* the last item in the series.

   I plan to take math, psychology, and writing next semester.

6. **To separate coordinate adjectives: two or more adjectives that are not joined by a coordinating conjunction and that equally modify the same noun or pronoun.**

   The thirsty, hungry children returned from a day at the beach.

   To determine whether a comma is needed between two adjectives, use the following test. Insert the word *and* between the two adjectives. Also try reversing the order of the two adjectives. If the phrase makes sense in either case, a comma is needed. If the phrase does not make sense, do not use a comma.

   The tired, angry child fell asleep. [*The tired and angry child* makes sense; so does *The angry, tired child*. Consequently, the comma is needed.]

   Sarah is an excellent psychology student. [*Sarah is an excellent and psychology student* does not make sense, nor does *Sarah is a psychology, excellent student*. A comma is therefore not needed.]

7. **To separate parenthetical expressions from the clauses they modify.** Parenthetical expressions are added pieces of information that are not essential to the meaning of the sentence.

   Most students, I imagine, can get jobs on campus.

8. **To separate a transition from the clause it modifies.**

   In addition, I will revise the bylaws.

9. **To separate a quotation from the words that introduce or explain it.**

   Note: The comma goes *inside* the closed quotation marks.

   "Shopping," Julia explained, "is a form of relaxation for me."

   Julia explained, "Shopping is a form of relaxation for me."

10. **To separate dates, place names, and long numbers.**

    October 10, 1986, is my birthday.

    Dayton, Ohio, was the first stop on the tour.

    Participants numbered 1,777,716.

11. **To separate phrases expressing contrast.**

    Jorge's good nature, not his wealth, explains his popularity.

E. Using Punctuation Correctly

EXERCISE 26 Adding Commas

Directions: Revise each of the following sentences by adding commas where needed.

EXAMPLE Until the judge entered, the courtroom was noisy.

1. "Hello " said the group of friends when Joan entered the room.
2. Robert De Niro the actor in the film was very handsome.

3. My parents frequently vacation in Miami Florida.
4. Drunk drivers I suppose may not realize they are not competent to drive.
5. Jeff purchased a television couch and dresser for his new apartment.
6. Luckily the windstorm did not do any damage to our town.
7. Frieda has an early class and she has to go to work afterward.
8. After taking a trip to the Galápagos Islands Mark Twain wrote about them.
9. The old dilapidated stadium was opened to the public on September 15 1931.
10. Afterward we will go out for ice cream.

E.3 Unnecessary Commas

It is as important to know where *not* to place commas as it is to know where to place them. The following rules explain where it is incorrect to place them:

1. **Do not place a comma between a subject and its verb, between a verb and its complement, or between an adjective and the word it modifies.**

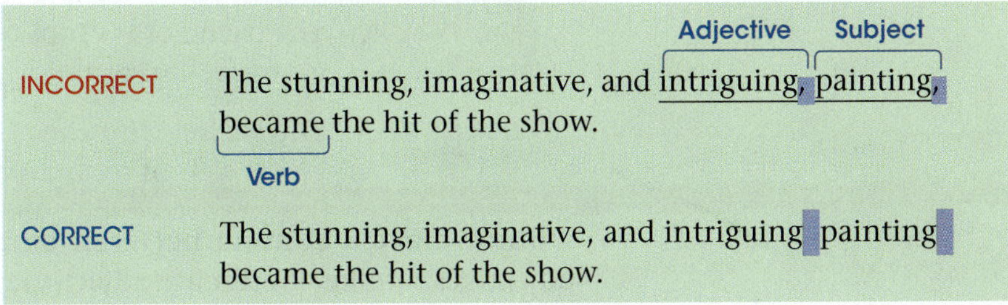

2. **Do not place a comma between two verbs, subjects, or complements used as compounds.**

Compound verb

INCORRECT Marisol called, and asked me to come by her office.

CORRECT Marisol called and asked me to come by her office.

3. **Do not place a comma before a coordinating conjunction joining two dependent clauses** (see p. 529).

Dependent clause

INCORRECT The city planner examined blueprints that the park designer had submitted, and that the budget officer had approved.

Dependent clause

CORRECT The city planner examined blueprints that the park designer had submitted and that the budget officer had approved.

4. **Do not place commas around restrictive clauses, phrases, or appositives.** Restrictive clauses, phrases, and appositives are modifiers that are essential to the meaning of the sentence.

INCORRECT	The girl, who grew up down the block, became my lifelong friend.
CORRECT	The girl who grew up down the block became my lifelong friend.

5. **Do not place a comma before the word *than* in a comparison or after the words *like* and *such as* in an introduction to a list.**

INCORRECT	Some snails, such as, the Oahu tree snail, have more colorful shells, than other snails.
CORRECT	Some snails, such as the Oahu tree snail, have more colorful shells than other snails.

6. **Do not place a comma next to a period, a question mark, an exclamation point, a dash, or an opening parenthesis.**

INCORRECT	"When will you come back?," Dillon's son asked him.
CORRECT	"When will you come back?" Dillon's son asked him.
INCORRECT	The bachelor button, (also known as the cornflower) grows well in ordinary garden soil.
CORRECT	The bachelor button (also known as the cornflower) grows well in ordinary garden soil.

7. **Do not place a comma between cumulative adjectives.** Cumulative adjectives, unlike coordinate adjectives (see p. 582), cannot be joined by *and* or rearranged.

INCORRECT	The light, yellow, rose blossom was a pleasant birthday surprise. [*The light and yellow and rose blossom* does not make sense, so the commas are incorrect.]
CORRECT	The light yellow rose blossom was a pleasant birthday surprise.

E.4 Colons and Semicolons

When to Use a Colon

A **colon** follows an independent clause and usually signals that the clause is to be explained or elaborated on. Use a colon in the following situations:

1. **To introduce items in a series after an independent clause.** The series can consist of words, phrases, or clauses.

   I am wearing three popular colors: magenta, black, and white.

2. **To signal a list or a statement introduced by an independent clause ending with *the following* or *as follows*.**

> The directions are as follows: take Main Street to Oak Avenue and then turn left.

3. **To introduce a quotation that follows an introductory independent clause.**

> My brother made his point quite clear: "Never borrow my car without asking me first!"

4. **To introduce an explanation.**

> Mathematics is enjoyable: it requires a high degree of accuracy and peak concentration.

5. **To separate titles and subtitles of books.**

> *Biology: A Study of Life*

Note: A colon must always follow an independent clause. It should not be used in the middle of a clause.

INCORRECT	My favorite colors are: red, pink, and green.
CORRECT	My favorite colors are red, pink, and green.

When to Use a Semicolon

A **semicolon** separates equal and balanced sentence parts. Use a semicolon in the following situations:

1. **To separate two closely related independent clauses not connected by a coordinating conjunction** (see p. 540).

> Sam had a 99 average in math; he earned an A in the course.

2. **To separate two independent clauses joined by a conjunctive adverb** (see p. 511).

> Margaret earned an A on her term paper; consequently, she was exempt from the final exam.

3. **To separate independent clauses joined with a coordinating conjunction if the clauses are very long or if they contain numerous commas.**

> By late afternoon, having tried on every pair of black checked pants in the mall, Marsha was tired and cranky; but she still had not found what she needed to complete her outfit for the play.

4. **To separate items in a series if the items are lengthy or contain commas.**

> The soap opera characters include Marianne Loundsberry, the heroine; Ellen and Sarah, her children; Barry, her ex-husband; and Louise, her best friend.

5. **To correct a comma splice or run-on sentence** (see p. 539).

EXERCISE 27 Correcting Sentences Using Semicolons

Directions: Correct each of the following sentences by placing colons and semicolons where necessary. Delete any incorrect punctuation.

EXAMPLE Samuel Clemens disliked his name; therefore, he used Mark Twain as his pen name.

E. Using Punctuation Correctly

1. The large, modern, and airy, gallery houses works of art by important artists, however, it has not yet earned national recognition as an important gallery.

2. Rita suggested several herbs to add to my spaghetti sauce, oregano, basil, and thyme.

3. Vic carefully proofread the paper, it was due the next day.

4. Furniture refinishing is a great hobby, it is satisfying to be able to make a piece of furniture look new again.

5. The bridesmaids in my sister's wedding are as follows, Judy, her best friend Kim, our sister, Franny, our cousin, and Sue, a family friend.

6. Mac got a speeding ticket, he has to go to court next Tuesday.

7. I will go for a swim when the sun comes out, it will not be so chilly then.

8. Carlos was hungry after his hockey game, consequently, he ordered four hamburgers.

9. Sid went to the bookstore to purchase *Physical Anthropology Man and His Makings*, it is required for one of his courses.

10. Here is an old expression, "The way to a man's heart is through his stomach."

E.5 Dashes, Parentheses, Hyphens, Apostrophes, Quotation Marks

Dashes (—)

The dash is used to (1) separate nonessential elements from the main part of the sentence, (2) create a stronger separation, or interruption, than commas or parentheses, and (3) emphasize an idea, create a dramatic effect, or indicate a sudden change in thought.

> My sister—the friendliest person I know—will visit me this weekend.
>
> My brother's most striking quality is his ability to make money—or so I thought until I heard of his bankruptcy.

Do not leave spaces between the dash and the words it separates.

Parentheses ( )

Parentheses are used in pairs to separate extra or nonessential information that often amplifies, clarifies, or acts as an aside to the main point. Unlike dashes, parentheses de-emphasize information.

> Some large breeds of dogs (golden retrievers and Newfoundlands) are susceptible to hip deformities.
>
> The prize was dinner for two (maximum value, $50) at a restaurant of one's choice.

Hyphens (-)

Hyphens have the following primary uses:

1. **To split a word when dividing it between two lines of writing or typing** (see p. 594).
2. **To join two or more words that function as a unit, either as a noun or as a noun modifier.**

> mother-in-law
> 20-year-old
> state-of-the-art sound system
> single-parent families
> school-age children

Apostrophes (')

Use apostrophes in the following situations:

1. **To show ownership or possession.** When the person, place, or thing doing the possessing is a singular noun, add *-'s* to the end of it, regardless of what its final letter is.

> The man's football tickets
> Aretha's best friend
> John Keats's poetry

Tip for Writers

Its, *your*, *his*, and *their* are *possessive* forms that go before nouns. Their meanings are possessive, so don't use an apostrophe in these words. On the other hand, *it's*, *you're*, *he's*, and *they're* are all contractions of pronouns with *is* or *are*, so an apostrophe is needed in each of these words.

With plural nouns that end in *-s*, add only an apostrophe to the end of the word.

the twins' bedroom	postal workers' hours
teachers' salaries	

With plural nouns that do not end in *-s*, add *-'s*.

children's books	men's slacks

Do not use an apostrophe with the possessive adjective *its*.

INCORRECT	It's frame is damaged.
CORRECT	Its frame is damaged.

2. **To indicate omission of one or more letters in a word or number.** Contractions are used in informal writing, but usually not in formal academic writing.

it's [it is]	hasn't [has not]
doesn't [does not]	'57 Ford [1957 Ford]
you're [you are]	class of '99 [class of 1999]

Quotation Marks (" ")

Quotation marks separate a direct quotation from the sentence that contains it. Here are some rules to follow in using quotation marks.

1. **Quotation marks are always used in pairs.**

   Note: A comma or period goes at the end of the quotation, inside the quotation marks.

   > Marge declared, "I never expected Peter to give me a watch for Christmas."
   >
   > "I never expected Peter to give me a watch for Christmas," Marge declared.

2. **Use single quotation marks for a quotation within a quotation.**

   > My literature professor said, "Byron's line 'She walks in beauty like the night' is one of his most sensual."

   Note: When quoting long prose passages of more than four typed lines, do not use quotation marks. Instead, set off the quotation from the rest of the text by indenting each line half an inch from the left margin. This format is called a **block quotation**.

   > The opening lines of the Declaration of Independence establish the purpose of the document:
   >
   > > When in the Course of human events it becomes necessary for one people to dissolve the political bonds which have connected them with another, and to assume among the powers of the earth, the separate and equal station to which the Laws of Nature and of Nature's God entitle them, a decent respect to the opinions of mankind requires that they should declare the causes which impel them to the separation.

3. **Use quotation marks to indicate titles of songs, short stories, poems, reports, articles, and essays.** Books, movies, plays, operas, paintings, statues, and the names of television series are italicized (or underlined to indicate italics).

   "Rappaccini's Daughter" (short story)

   60 Minutes [or 60 Minutes] (television series)

   "The Road Not Taken" (poem)

4. **Colons, semicolons, exclamation points, and question marks, when not part of the quoted material, go outside of the quotation marks.**

   What did George mean when he said, "People in glass houses shouldn't throw stones"?

EXERCISE 28

Adding Appropriate Punctuation Marks

Directions: To the following sentences, add dashes, apostrophes, parentheses, hyphens, and quotation marks where necessary.

EXAMPLE "You are not going out dressed that way!" said Frank's roommate.

1. My daughter in law recently entered medical school.

2. At the bar I worked at last summer, the waitresses tips were always pooled and equally divided.

3. Youre going to Paris next summer, aren't you?

4. The career counselor said, The computer field is not as open as it used to be.

5. My English professor read aloud Frost's poem Two Look at Two.

6. Frank asked me if I planned to buy a big screen television for our Super Bowl party.

7. Rachel the teaching assistant for my linguistics class spent last year in China.

8. Macy's is having a sale on womens boots next week.

____

____

9. Trina said, My one year old's newest word is bzz, which she says whenever she sees a fly.

____

____

10. Some animals horses and donkeys can interbreed, but they produce infertile offspring.

____

____

Managing Mechanics and Spelling

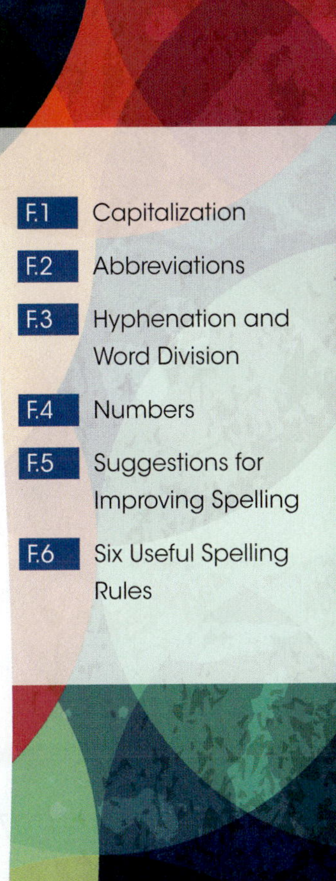

F.1 Capitalization
F.2 Abbreviations
F.3 Hyphenation and Word Division
F.4 Numbers
F.5 Suggestions for Improving Spelling
F.6 Six Useful Spelling Rules

F.1 Capitalization

In general, **capital letters** are used to mark the beginning of a sentence, to mark the beginning of a quotation, and to identify proper nouns. Here are some guidelines on capitalization:

What to Capitalize	*Example*
1. First word in every sentence	Prewriting is useful.
2. First word in a direct quotation	Sarah commented, "That exam was difficult!"
3. Names of people and animals, including the pronoun *I*	Aladdin Maya Angelou Spot
4. Names of specific places, cities, states, nations, geographic areas, or regions	New Orleans the Southwest Lake Erie
5. Government and public offices, departments, buildings	Williamsville Library House of Representatives
6. Names of social, political, business, sporting, cultural organizations	Boy Scouts Buffalo Bills
7. Names of months, days of the week, holidays	August Tuesday Halloween
8. In titles of works: the first word following a colon, the first and last words, and all other words except articles, prepositions, and conjunctions	*Biology: A Study of Life* "Once More to the Lake"
9. Races, nationalities, languages	African American, Italian, English
10. Religions, religious figures, sacred books	Hindu, Hinduism, God, Allah, the Bible
11. Names of products	Tide, Buick
12. Personal titles when they come right before a name	Professor Rodriguez Senator Hatch
13. Major historic events	World War I
14. Specific course titles	History 201 Introduction to Psychology

EXERCISE 29

Practicing Capitalization

Directions: Capitalize words as necessary in the following sentences.

EXAMPLE Farmers in the ~~m~~idwest were devastated by floods last summer. [M written above "midwest"]

1. My mother is preparing some special foods for our hanukkah meal; rabbi epstein will join us.
2. My american politics professor used to be a judge in the town of evans.
3. A restaurant in the galleria mall serves korean food.
4. A graduate student I know is writing a book about buddha titled *the great one: ways to enlightenment.*
5. at the concert last night, cher changed into many different outfits.
6. An employee announced over the public address system, "attention, customers! we have pepsi on sale in aisle ten for a very low price!"
7. Karen's father was stationed at fort bradley during the vietnam war.
8. Last tuesday the state assembly passed governor allen's budget.
9. Boston is an exciting city; be sure to visit the museum of fine arts.
10. Marcos asked if i wanted to go see the bolshoi ballet at shea's theatre in november.

F.2 Abbreviations

An **abbreviation** is a shortened form of a word or phrase that is used to represent the whole word or phrase. The following is a list of common acceptable abbreviations:

What to Abbreviate	*Example*
1. Some titles before or after people's names	Mr. Ling Samuel Rosen, M.D. *but* Professor Ashe
2. Names of familiar organizations, corporations, countries	CIA, IBM, VISTA, USA
3. Time references preceded or followed by a number	7:00 A.M. 3:00 P.M. A.D. 1973
4. Latin terms when used in footnotes, references, or parentheses	i.e. [*id est*, "that is"] et al. [*et alii*, "and others"]

F. Mechanics and Spelling

Here is a list of things that are usually *not* abbreviated:

What Not to Abbreviate	*Example* Incorrect	Correct
1. Units of measurement	thirty in.	thirty inches
2. Geographic or other place names when used in sentences	N.Y. Elm St.	New York Elm Street
3. Parts of written works when used in sentences	Ch. 3	Chapter 3
4. Names of days, months, holidays	Tues.	Tuesday
5. Names of subject areas	psych.	psychology

EXERCISE 30 Correcting Inappropriate Use of Abbreviations

Directions: Correct the inappropriate use of abbreviations in the following sentences. If a sentence contains no errors, write "C" for correct beside it.

EXAMPLE We live 30 ~~mi~~. outside NYC.
We live 30 miles outside New York City.

_____ **1.** Frank enjoys going to swim at the YMCA on Oak St.

_____ **2.** Prof. Jorge asked the class to turn to pg. 8.

_____ **3.** Because he is seven ft. tall, my brother was recruited for the high school b-ball team.

_____ **4.** When I asked Ron why he hadn't called me, he said it was Northeast Bell's fault—i.e., his phone hadn't been working.

_____ **5.** Tara is flying TWA to KC to visit her parents next Wed.

_____ **6.** At 8:00 P.M., we turned on NBC to watch *Dancing with the Stars*.

_____ **7.** Last wk. I missed my chem. lab.

_____ **8.** The exam wasn't too difficult; only ques. number 15 and ques. no. 31 were extremely difficult

_____ 9. Dr. Luc removed the mole from my rt. hand using a laser.

____

_____ 10. Mark drove out to L.A. to audition for a role in MGM's new movie.

____

F.3 Hyphenation and Word Division

Tip for Writers

A *syllable* is a group of letters with one vowel sound, such as *tall* or *straight*. In a dictionary, the first, bold-face listing of a world has dots to show where the word can be divided with a hyphen and continued on the next line:

trans•por•ta•tion

On occasion you must divide and hyphenate a word on one line and continue it on the next. Here are some guidelines for dividing words.

1. **Divide words only when necessary.** Frequent word divisions make a paper difficult to read.
2. **Divide words between syllables.** Consult a dictionary if you are unsure how to break a word into syllables.

   di-vi-sion pro-tect

3. **Do not divide one-syllable words.**
4. **Do not divide a word so that a single letter is left at the end of a line.**

   INCORRECT a-typical
   CORRECT atyp-ical

5. **Do not divide a word so that fewer than three letters begin the new line.**

   INCORRECT **visu-al**
   CORRECT **vi-sual**
   INCORRECT **caus-al [This word cannot be divided at all.]**

6. **Divide compound words only between the words.**

   some-thing any-one

7. **Divide words that are already hyphenated only at the hyphen.**

   ex-policeman

EXERCISE 31

Practicing Division

Directions: Insert a diagonal (/) mark where each word should be divided. Mark "N" beside it if the word should not be divided.

EXAMPLE every/where

_____ 1. enclose

_____ 2. house

_____ 6. disgusted

_____ 7. chandelier

_____ 3. saxophone

_____ 4. hardly

_____ 5. well-known

_____ 8. headphones

_____ 9. swings

_____10. abyss

F.4 Numbers

Numbers can be written as numerals (600) or words (six hundred). Here are some guidelines for when to use numerals and when to use words:

When to Use Numerals	***Example***
1. Numbers that are spelled with more than two words	375 students
2. Days and years	August 10, 2013
3. Decimals, percentages, fractions	56.7 59 percent 1¾ cups
4. Exact times	9:27 A.M.
5. Pages, chapters, volumes; acts and lines from plays	Chapter 12 volume 4
6. Addresses	122 Peach Street
7. Exact amounts of money	$5.60
8. Scores and statistics	23–6 5 of every 12

When to Use Words	***Example***
1. Numbers that begin sentences	Two hundred ten students attended the lecture.
2. Numbers of one or two words	sixty students, two hundred women

EXERCISE 32 Practicing Correct Number Usage

Directions: Correct the misuse of numbers in the following sentences. If a sentence contains no errors, write "C" for correct beside it.

EXAMPLE The reception hall was filled with 500 guests.

The reception hall was filled with five hundred guests.

_____ 1. At 6:52 A.M. my roommate's alarm clock went off.

____

_____ 2. I purchased 9 turtlenecks for five dollars and fifty-five cents each.

____

F. Mechanics and Spelling

_____ 3. 35 floats were entered in the parade, but only 4 received prizes.

____

_____ 4. Act three of *Othello* is very exciting.

____

_____ 5. Almost fifty percent of all marriages end in divorce.

____

_____ 6. The Broncos won the game 21–7.

____

_____ 7. We were assigned volume two of *Don Quixote*, beginning on page 351.

____

_____ 8. The hardware store is located at three forty-four Elm Street, 2 doors down from my grandmother's house.

____

_____ 9. Maryanne's new car is a 2-door V-8.

____

_____ 10. Our anniversary is June ninth, nineteen eighty-nine.

____

F.5 Suggestions for Improving Spelling

Correct spelling is important to a well-written paragraph or essay. The following suggestions will help you submit papers without misspellings:

1. **Do not worry about spelling as you write your first draft.** Checking a word in a dictionary at this point will interrupt your flow of ideas. If you do not know how a word is spelled, spell it the way it sounds. Circle or underline the word so you remember to check it later.
2. **Keep a list of words you commonly misspell.** This list can be part of your error log.
3. **Every time you catch an error or find a misspelled word on a paper returned by your instructor, add it to your list.**
4. **Study your list.** Ask a friend to quiz you on the words. Eliminate words from the list after you have passed several quizzes on them.
5. **Develop a spelling awareness.** You'll find that your spelling will improve just by your being aware that spelling is important. When you encounter a new word, notice how it is spelled and practice writing it.
6. **Pronounce words you are having difficulty spelling.** Pronounce each syllable distinctly.

7. **Review basic spelling rules.** Your college library or learning lab may have manuals, workbooks, or computer programs that cover basic rules and provide guided practice.
8. **Be sure to have a dictionary readily available when you write.**
9. **Read your final draft through once, checking only for spelling errors.** Look at each word carefully, and check the spelling of those words of which you are uncertain.

F.6 Six Useful Spelling Rules

The following six rules focus on common spelling trouble spots:

1. **Is it *ei* or *ie*?**

   Rule: Use *i* before *e*, except after *c* or when the syllable is pronounced *ay* as in the word *weigh*.

   i before *e*: believe, niece

   except after c: receive, conceive

   or when pronounced *ay*: neighbor, sleigh

Exceptions:	either	neither	foreign	forfeit
	height	leisure	weird	seize

2. **When adding an ending, do you keep or drop the final *e*?**

   ***Rules*:** **a.** Keep the final *e* when adding an ending that begins with a consonant. (Vowels are *a, e, i, o, u,* and sometimes *y*; all other letters are consonants.)

hope → hopeful	aware → awareness
live → lively	force → forceful

   b. Drop the final *e* when adding an ending that begins with a vowel.

hope → hoping	file → filing
note → notable	write → writing

Exceptions:	argument	truly	changeable
	awful	manageable	courageous
	judgment	noticeable	outrageous
	acknowledgment		

Tip for Writers

The final *e* must remain on a word (before adding an ending) if the *e* is needed to keep a "soft" *c* sound (like *s*) or a "soft" *g* sound (like *j*) on the preceding letter. Two examples are *noticeable* and *manageable*.

3. **When adding an ending, do you keep the final *y*, change it to *i*, or drop it?**

   ***Rules*:** **a.** Keep the *y* if the letter before the *y* is a vowel.

delay → delaying	buy → buying	prey → preyed

b. Change the *y* to *i* if the letter before the *y* is a consonant, but keep the *y* for the *-ing* ending.

defy → defiance	marry → married
→ defying	→ marrying

4. When adding an ending to a one-syllable word, when do you double the final letter if it is a consonant?

***Rules*: a.** In one-syllable words, double the final consonant when a single vowel comes before it.

drop → dropped	shop → shopped	pit → pitted

b. In one-syllable words, *don't* double the final consonant when two vowels or a consonant comes before it.

repair → repairable	sound → sounded
real → realize	

5. When adding an ending to a word with more than one syllable, when do you double the final letter if it is a consonant?

***Rules*: a.** In multisyllable words, double the final consonant when a single vowel comes before it *and* the stress falls on the last syllable. (Vowels are *a, e, i, o, u,* and sometimes *y*. All other letters are consonants.)

begin' → beginning	transmit' → transmitted
repel' → repelling	

b. In multisyllable words, do *not* double the final consonant (a) when two vowels or a vowel and another consonant come before it *or* (b) when the stress is not on the last syllable.

despair → despairing	ben'efit → benefited
conceal → concealing	

6. To form a plural, do you add *-s* or *-es*?

***Rules*: a.** For most nouns, add *-s*.

cat → cats	house → houses

b. Add *-es* to words that end in *-o* if the *-o* is preceded by a consonant.

hero → heroes	potato → potatoes

Note: *Zoos, radios, ratios,* and other words ending with two vowels are made plural by adding *-s*.

c. Add *-es* to words ending in *-ch, -sh, -ss, -x,* or *-z*.

church → churches	fox → foxes	dish → dishes

Credits

Photo Credits

Abstract background, used throughout: gudinny/Shutterstock; **Thinking Visually icon:** Kak2s/Shutterstock; **Visualize It icon:** iStockphoto, Shutterstock; **Need to Know icon:** Roman Sotola/Shutterstock; **Connections Box icons (t):** SuperStock; **©:** Jack Hollingsworth/Getty Images; **(b):** Radius/SuperStock; **1:** Asia Images/Getty Images; **7 (t):** imageegami/fotolia; **(b):** mrivserg/fotolia; **8:** blanche/fotolia; **13:** spotmatikphoto/fotolia; **19 (tl):** divvector/fotolia; **(tc):** divvector/fotolia; **(tr):** divvector/fotolia; **(bl):** mmmp/fotolia; **(bc):** kibsri/fotolia; **(br):** rawpixel/fotolia; **20 ©:** samarets1984/fotolia; **(r):** andrewgenn/fotolia; **37:** Monkey Business/fotolia; **38 (t):** Exactostock/Exactostock/SuperStock; **©:** Jack Hollingsworth/Digital Vision/Photolibrary; **(b):** Radius/Radius/SuperStock; **41:** Bst2012/fotolia; Mehmet Dilsiz/fotolia; Micromonkey/fotolia; Rob Byron/fotolia; michael spring/fotolia; **45:** Jake Frey; **61 (b):** cherezoff/fotolia; **68:** Tom Wang/Shutterstock; **70:** Bragin Alexey/Shutterstock; **71:** Jirsak/Shutterstock; **72:** ene/Shutterstock; **74:** Alfanso de Tomas; **76 (t):** Rido/Shutterstock; **©:** Moises Fernandez Acosta/Shutterstock; **(b):** Eky Studio/Shutterstock; **77:** Pozitiv Studija/Shutterstock; **78:** Steven Frame/Shutterstock; **80 (t):** DenisNata/Shutterstock; **(b):** Andreser/Shutterstock; **81:** Karuka/Shutterstock; **82:** Dja65/Shutterstock; **83:** Henrik Lehnerer/Shutterstock; **84:** Ingrid Prats/Shutterstock; **85:** AVAVA/Shutterstock; **87:** CREATISTA/Shutterstock; **88:** Monkey Business Imaging; **89:** Leonard Zhukovsky/Shutterstock; **92:** Brian Bohannon; **98:** Kate Atkinson; **115:** Tupungato/fotolia; **118:** woe/fotolia; **129:** Yesenia Dejesus; **151:** Sergey Skleznev/fotolia; **152:** Peter King/DK Images; **153:** age fotostock/SuperStock; **157:** Leila Kaji; **158:** Photographee.ee/fotolia; **168:** C. Jones/Shutterstock; **182:** Eugene Suslo/Shutterstock; **184:** imageBROKER/Alamy; **201:** Jessica Nantka; **215 (l):** Richard Hutchings/Corbis; **(r):** Richard Hutchings/Corbis; **217:** maron/fotolia; **232:** SanjMur/fotolia; **238:** Tony Law/Redux; **240:** alexmillos/fotolia; **249:** Ted Sawchuck; **270:** Terrance Emerson; **273:** Ted Sawchuck; **291:** Mathias Rosenthal/fotolia; **292:** igor/fotolia; **297:** Exotica.im 8/Alamy; **299:** Cal Vornberger/Alamy; **302:** ZUMA Press/Alamy; **304:** Ronen/Shutterstock; **306:** markcarper/fotolia; **321:** Joggie Botma/Shutterstock; **323:** mediterranean/fotolia; **342:** Gino Domenico/Bloomberg/Getty Images; **345:** Brian Eichhorn/Shutterstock; **361:** Chase Beauclaire; **363:** duncanandison/fotolia; **368:** zaretskaya/fotolia; **371:** WaterFrame/Alamy; **385:** Aurora Gilbert; **391:** a katz/Shutterstock; **397:** Vit Kovalicik/fotolia; **408:** Quinne Sember; **423 (t-b):** nithid18/fotolia; My imagine/fotolia; Olexandr/fotolia; Oleksiy Mark/fotolia; **428:** AP Photo/Nick Ut; **434:** AP Photo/Jason DeCrow; **437:** Miravision/fotolia; **438:** apops/fotolia; **447:** Nancy Scheper-Hughes; **457:** Chris Pizello/AP Photos; **463:** © 2012 The Atlantic Media Co., as first published in The Atlantic Magazine. All rights reserved. Distributed by Tribune Content Agency, LLC; **470:** arindambanerjee/Shutterstock; **477 (l):** INTERFOTO/Alamy; **(r):** AP Photo / Frank Franklin II; **481:** goce risteski/fotolia; **486:** Stephen Coburn/fotolia; **490:** Chris Minor/Shutterstock.

Text Credits

Chapter 1

5: Pearson Education; **12:** Ciccarelli, Saundra K; White, J. Noland, *Psychology*, 4th Ed., © 2015, PIA4-PAIA8. Reprinted and electronically reproduced by permission of Pearson Education, Inc., Upper Saddle River, New Jersey; **13:** Houghton Mifflin Harcourt; **25:** Pearson Education; **31:** Pearson Education.

Chapter 2

41: From *The New York Times,* April 22 © 2012 The New York Times. All rights reserved. Used by permission and protected by the Copyright Laws of the United States. The printing, copying, redistribution, or retransmission of this Content without express written permission is prohibited; **53:** Kathleen McWhorter; Kathleen McWhorter; **55:** Jake Frey; **60:** Jake Frey; **61:** Jake Frey.

Vocabulary Workshops

77: Pearson Education; **78:** Pearson Education; Pearson Education; **79:** Pearson Education; Pearson Education; **87:** Pearson Education; Pearson Education; **88:** Pearson Education; Pearson Education.

Chapter 3

91–93: Reprinted by permission of the author. John Robbins is the author of No Happy Cows, see www.johnrobbins.info; **96:** Pearson Education; **96:** Pearson Education; **96:** Pearson Education; **97:** Pearson Education; **97:** Pearson Education; **98:** Kate Atkinson. Reprinted by permission of the author; **99:** Kate Atkinson. Reprinted by permission of the author; **99:** Kate Atkinson. Reprinted by permission of the author; **103:** Pearson Education; **103:** Pearson Education; **103:** Pearson Education; **103:** Pearson Education; **104:** Pearson Education; **104:** Pearson Education; **104:** Pearson Education; **104:** Pearson Education; **104:** Pearson Education; **109:** Pearson Education.

Chapter 4

117: Katie Robbins, "Hidden Hunger," *The Atlantic.* (http://www.theatlantic.com/health/archive/2010/05/among-dorms-and-dining-halls-hidden-hunger/39766/); **121:** Pearson Education; **121:** Pearson Education; **121:** Pearson Education; **122:** Pearson Education; **123:** Pearson Education; **125:** Pearson Education; **126:** Pearson Education; **126:** Pearson Education; **126:** Pearson Education; **127:** Pearson Education; **127:** Pearson Education; **128:** Kathleen McWhorter; **128:** Pearson Education; **129:** Pearson Education; **130:** Reprinted by permission of the author; **133:** Kathleen McWhorter; **134:** Yesenia De Jesus; **134:** Yesenia De Jesus; **136:** Yesenia De Jesus; **136:** Yesenia De Jesus; **137:** Yesenia De Jesus; **138:** Kathleen McWhorter; **139:** Yesenia De Jesus; **144:** Pearson Education; **144:** Kathleen McWhorter; **145:** *Psychology: An Introduction,* 3e, p. 700. New York: HarperCollins College Publishers, 1996; **145:** *Child Development: Change Over Time,* 8/e, p. 354. New York: HarperCollins College Publishers, 1996;

145: Pearson Education; **145:** Pearson Education; **146:** Pearson Education; **146:** Pearson Education; **146:** Pearson Education; **147:** Pearson Education.

Chapter 5

153: Amanda Fields. Reprinted by permission of the author; **155:** Pearson Education; **155:** Kathleen McWhorter; **156:** Pearson Education; **157:** Pearson Education; **157:** Pearson Education; **157:** Leila Kaji; **159:** Pearson Education; **162:** Pearson Education; **162:** Pearson Education; **163:** Pearson Education; **163:** Pearson Education; **165:** Amanda Fields. Reprinted by permission of the author; **167:** Pearson Education; **171:** Amanda Fields. Reprinted with permission of the author; **172:** Pearson Education; **173:** Pearson Education; **174:** Pearson Education

Chapter 6

183: Pearson Education; **185:** Pearson Education; **188:** Pearson Education; **188:** Pearson Education; **190:** Kathleen McWhorter; **191:** Kathleen McWhorter; **192:** Pearson Education; **192:** *Introduction to the Human Body: The Essentials of Anatomy and Physiology,* 2/e, p. 56. New York: HarperCollins College Publishers, 1991; **192:** Pearson Education; **196:** Pearson Education; **197:** Pearson Education; **201–202:** Reprinted by permission of the author; **205:** Jessica Nantka; **206:** Pearson Education.

Chapter 7

220: Reprinted by permission of the author; **221:** Reprinted by permission of the author; **222:** Reprinted by permission of the author; **223:** Reprinted by permission of the author; **224:** Reprinted by permission of the author; **225:** Reprinted by permission of the author; **227:** Reprinted by permission of the author; **232:** "Students Vulnerable to Computer Gaming Addiction," *Inside Higher Ed,* Dec 12, 2012. Reprinted with permission.

Chapter 8

240: Simon L. Garfinkel, "How to Stop the Snoopers," *Technology Review,* March/April 2011. Reprinted with permission; **243:** From Sandra Parshall's blog *Poe's Deadly Daughters,* posted September 14, 2011. Reprinted by permission of Sandra Parshall, mystery writer; **249:** Ted Sawchuck; **249:** Reprinted by permission of the author; **256:** Kathleen McWhorter; **260:** Kathleen McWhorter.

Chapter 9

274: Reprinted by permission of the author; **277:** Reprinted by permission of the author; **290:** Julia Angwin, "You're Under Surveillance, Dragnet Nation: A Quest for Privacy, Security, and Freedom in a World of Relentless Surveillance" (Excerpted from pages 1-20 as appeared in The Week, April 4, 2014). Reprinted with permission of Zachary Shuster Harmsworth Literary Agency.

Chapter 10

299: © 2014 The Atlantic Media Co., as first published in *The Atlantic Magazine.* All rights reserved. Distributed by Tribune Content Agency, LLC; **307:** Pearson Education; **313:** Pearson Education.

Chapter 11

323: Reprinted by permission of the author; **329:** Reprinted by permission of the author; **331:** *Social Psychology,* 6/e, Boston: Houghton Mifflin, 2005; **332:** *Understanding Interpersonal Communication,* 7/e, New York: HarperCollins College Publishers, 1996; **333:** Pearson Education; **333:** Pearson Education.

Chapter 12

344: Ashley Womble, "The Homeless Brother I Cannot Save," Salon. Reprinted with permission of Salon Media Group, Inc; **348:** Pearson Education; **348:** Pearson Education; **355:** Kathleen McWhorter; **355:** Kathleen McWhorter; **355:** Kathleen McWhorter; **362:** Chase Beauclair.

Chapter 13

370: Virginia Sole-Smith, "Sweatshops at Sea," *Utne Reader,* Sept–Oct 2010. Reprinted with permission of the author; **376:** Excerpted from "Palm Springs in August: The Ducks Use Sunblock," *The New York Times,* August 9, 2002; **376:** Excerpted from "A Plot of Their Own," *Newsweek,* January 21, 2002; **376:** Excerpted from "Launching Kids to Independence," *Seattle Times,* August 17, 2002; **378:** Excerpted from Letter to the Editor: "School's First Week Provides a Few Bright Exceptions," *Toronto Star,* September 6, 2002; **379:** Excerpted from "Raising the Sept. 11 Generation," *Chicago Tribune,* September 8, 2002; **379:** Excerpted from "From the Hip; Gun Control," *The Economist,* November 23, 2002; **379:** Excerpted from "Steroids Should Be Tagged Out," *San Jose Mercury News,* June 3, 2002; **379:** Excerpted from "Sign of Civilization," *Providence Journal,* August 15, 2002; **383:** Excerpted from "A Climate of Fraud," *The Washington Times,* November 30, 2011, p. 2; **384:** Kathleen McWhorter; **384:** Excerpted from "Will All Hispanic Men Be Suspect?" *Seattle Post Intelligencer,* July 30, 2002; **384:** Kathleen McWhorter; **384:** Excerpted from "Burning Will Go; That's Not All Good," *Spokesman-Review,* July 24, 2002; **385:** Excerpted from "Logging Illogic," *World Watch,* September/October 2002; **385:** Aurora Gilbert.

Chapter 14

394: Kathleen McWhorter; **397:** Dr. Aysha Akhtar, "Who Are the Animals in Animal Experiments?," Huffington Post, March 14, 2014. Reprinted by permission of the author; **399:** Dr. Aysha Akhtar, "Who Are the Animals in Animal Experiments?," Huffington Post, March 14, 2014. Reprinted by permission of the author; **403:** Dr. Aysha Akhtar, "Who Are the Animals in Animal Experiments?," Huffington Post, March 14, 2014. Reprinted by permission of the author; **404:** Dr. Aysha Akhtar, "Who Are the Animals in Animal Experiments?," Huffington Post, March 14, 2014. Reprinted by permission of the author; **409:** Reprinted by permission of the author; **417:** Reprinted by permission of the author.

Part 5

424: Schmalleger, Frank J., *Criminal Justice Today: An Introductory Text for the 21st Century,* 13th Ed., © 2015, pp. 595–604. Reprinted and electronically reproduced by permission of Pearson Education, Inc., Upper Saddle River, New Jersey; **437:** Phillip Martin, "Global Human Trafficking: A Modern Form of Slavery," *Huffington Post,* October 1, 2013. Reprinted by permission of the author; **443:** Nancy Scheper-Hughes, "Human Traffic: Exposing the Brutal Organ of Trade," *New Internationalist,* May 1, 2014. Reprinted with permission; **457:** Vivan, John, *Media of Mass Communication,* 11th Ed., © 2013, pp. 213–219. Reprinted and electronically reproduced by permission of Pearson Education, Inc., Upper Saddle River, New Jersey; **463:** © 2012 The Atlantic Media Co., as first published in *The Atlantic Magazine.* All rights reserved. Distributed by Tribune Content Agency, LLC; **468:** © 2011 The Atlantic Media Co., as first published in *The Atlantic Magazine.* All rights reserved. Distributed by Tribune Content Agency, LLC; **476:** Pearson Education; **481:** From Slate, January 18 © 2011 The Slate Group. All rights reserved. Used by permission and protected by the Copyright Laws of the United States. The printing, copying, redistribution, or retransmission of this Content without express written permission is prohibited; **486:** Zachary Fegely, "Should college football student athletes get paid?," Pennlive.com. © 2013 Pennlive.com All rights reserved. Reprinted and/or used with permission; **490:** *Sports Illustrated.*

Index

A

Abbreviations, 592–594
Active reading, 2, 35
Adjectives, 508–511, 523–524
  correct usage, 559–562
  descriptive, 508
  irregular, 560–561
  limiting, 508–509
Adverbs, 511–513, 523–524
  correct usage, 559–562
  forms, 511–512
  irregular, 560–561
Akhtar, Aysha, MPH, 397–398
"Among Dorms and Dining Halls, Hidden Hunger" (Robbins), 117–119
Angwin, Julia, 289–293
Annotating, 11, 13–14, 247–248
Argument, 392–418
  ad hominem, 406
  appeal to the "common folk," 406
  association, 405
  audience, analyzing, 414
  biased language, 405
  circular reasoning, 407
  claim, 393
  defined, 392–393
  either-or-fallacy, 407
  emotional appeals, 405
  errors in reasoning, 407
  evidence, evaluating, 402–404
  false authority, 405
  false cause, 407
  hasty generalization, 407
  issue, 393
  "join the crowd" appeal, 406
  non seqitur, 407
  opposing viewpoints, 404–405
  reading tips, 402
  refutation, 393
  support, 393
  supporting evidence, 399–400, 416–418
  thesis statement, 414–416
  topic, 416
Associating ideas, 29
Assumptions, 377–379
Atkinson, Kate, 98–99
Audience for writing, 39, 44, 45, 53–54, 67, 219, 256–257
Author, 248
  technique, 369–370

B

Bar graphs, 19
Beauclair, Chase, 362–363
"Benefits of Joining the Military" (Nantka), 201–202
Bias, 381–385
Brainstorming, 47, 254
Branching, 47, 48, 254
Brennan, Scott, 183–184
"A Brother Lost" (Womble), 344–346
Building blocks of writing, 39

C

"Cairo Tunnel" (Fields), 153–154
Capitalization, 591–592
"To Catch a Liar" (Parshall), 242–243
Chapter
  opener, 21
  review quiz, 21
  summary, 21
Ciccarelli, Saundra K., 5–9
Circle graphs, 19
Citations, 248
Clauses, 529–531
  adjective, 530
  adverb, 530
  dependent, 529–530
  elliptical, 530–531
  independent, 529
  noun, 530
  subordinate, 541–542
Clue words, 252
"College Athletes Already Have Advantages and Shouldn't Be Paid" (Daughtery), 490–492
Colloquial language, 578
Conjunctions, 513–516
  coordinating, 513
  correlative, 513
  subordinating, 513–514
Connecting to prior experience and knowledge, 10, 35, 248
Connotation, 25, 73–74, 285–286, 373–374
Context, 24
Context clues, 74–80
  contrast, 75
  definition, 75
  example, 75
  inference, 75
  synonym, 75
Coordination, 567–569
Critical thinking, 30–34, 36, 67, 343–364
  as active thinking, 31
  benefits of, 30
  information in textbooks, 33–34

D

Daughtery, Paul, 490–492
De Jesus, Yesenia, 130–132
Denotative meaning, 373
Details, 52
Diction, 578–579
Difficult assignments, tips for understanding, 23, 36
"Drug Abuse Among Athletes" (Johnson), 476–478

E

Editing, 44, 45
"The End of the Road: A Guide to Break Ups" (Kaji), 157–159
Essay, 239–269. *See also* Multi-pattern essay
  assigned topic, 251–253
  audience, 256–257, 282
  body, 246–247
  body paragraph drafts, 272–273
  classroom instruction, connecting to, 252
  clue words in assignment, 251–252
  conclusion, 242, 247, 279, 282
  content and structure analysis, 282
  critical thinking about, 248–249
  draft, 271–272
  draft, tips for, 271
  editing, 286–288
  error log, 286
  evidence, 273, 275
  expressing ideas, 249
  introduction, 242, 245, 278–279, 283
  main point, 55
  mapping, 263–264
  organizing, 263–265, 283
  outlining, 263–264
  paragraph checklist, 288
  pattern of organization, choosing, 265
  planning and drafting tips, 251–252
  presenting, 287
  proofreading, 286–288
  purpose, 239, 257–258, 282
  reading, 242–249
  revision, 280–286
  revision checklist, 288
  revision map, 281
  revision strategies, 280–281
  structure, 242–247
  thesis statement, 282
  title, 279–280, 283
  topic, 251–254
  transitions, 283

Euphemism, 73
Evidence, evaluating, 356–358
"E-Waste and E-Waste Recycling" (Withgott and Brennan), 183–184

F

Fact vs. opinion, 354–356
Fair use, 57
Fegely, Zachary, 486–488
Fields, Amanda, 153–154
Figurative language, 74, 374–377
Final review, 28
Fine print, reading, 32
First draft, 40, 44, 45, 55–56, 67
"The Flight from Conversation" (Turkle), 41–44
Footnotes, in a visual, 20
Formality of writing, 52
Format for writing, 52
Freewriting, 47, 254
"From Bullet to Blue Sky" (De Jesus), 130–132

G

"Gang Life: Better from the Outside" (Harris), 307–308
Garfinkel, Simson L., 240–242
Generalizations, 380–381
Generating ideas, 44, 45, 47–50, 48, 66
Gilbert, Aurora, 385–387
Goals of what you read, 32
Good writing, 38–39
Grammar checker, 287
"Greed, Cancer, and Pink KFC Buckets" (Robbins), 91–93
Guide questions, 10–11, 40

H

Harris, Dejohn, 307–308
Highlighting, 11–13, 36, 247
"Human Traffic: Exposing the Brutal Organ Trade" (Scheper-Hughes), 443–452
Hyphenation and word division, 594–595

I

Idea expression in writing, 38
Idea map, 263–264. *See also* Mapping
Immediate review, 28
Implied main ideas, 119, 143–147, 150
Inferences, 346–349
"An Inside Look at Today's News Media" (Vivian), 457–460
Intent to remember, building, 28
Interjections, 516

J

Jargon, 74
Johnson, Michael D.,476–478

K

Kaji, Keila, 157–159
Keller, Jared, 468–472

L

Lawson, Elizabeth, 217–219, 225–226, 229–230
Learning and recall strategies, 28–29, 36
Legend, of a visual, 20
Line graphs, 19

M

Mapping, 14–16, 36, 51. *See also* Idea map
Marginal vocabulary definitions, 21
"Marijuana: An Argument for Legalization" (Sember), 409–413
Martin, Philip 437–441
"The Media Need to Stop Inspiring Copycat Murders. Here's How." (Tufekci), 463–465
Metaphor, 375
"Mind Your Own Browser" (Garfinkel), 240–242
MLA Style, 335–337
Mnemonic devices, 29
Modifiers, misplaced and dangling, 563–565
Muller, Gabriel, 299–303
Multimodal essay. *See* Multi-pattern essay
Multi-pattern essay, 298–316
- assignment, 309–310
- audience, 310
- body paragraphs, drafting, 314–315
- conclusion, drafting, 315–316
- introduction, 313–314
- primary pattern, 303–305, 309
- purpose, 310
- recognizing patterns when reading, 303–306
- secondary pattern, 305–306, 311–312
- thesis statement, 312–313
- topic, 308–309, 310
- transitions, 315

"My Unexpected Addiction" (Lawson), 225–226

N

Nantka, Jessica, 201–202
"The National Brain-Damage League" (Vedantam), 481–483
Neologisms, 74
Nonstandard language, 579
Nouns, 498–499
- abstract, 499
- appositive, 527
- collective, 499
- common, 499
- concrete, 499
- count, 499
- noncount, 499
- number, 498
- possessive, 498
- proper, 499

Number, shifts in, 565–567
Numbers, 595–596

O

Omissions, 357
Organizing and categorizing, 28–29, 66
Organizing ideas, 44, 45, 50–52, 51
Outlining, 16–17, 36, 263–264

P

Paragraph, 90, 93–95
- defined, 39, 90
- supporting details, 90, 113
- topic, locating, 95–97, 113
- topic sentence, 90, 94, 113
- using specific words, 138–140

Parallelism, 571–574
Paraphrasing, 24–26, 36
Parshall, Sandra, 243–244
Passive reading, 2
Passive voice, 357
Patterns of organization, 152, 154–176, 179–180, 182–211
- argument, 304
- cause and effect, 182, 203–210, 214, 304
- choosing for essay, 265
- chronological order, 152, 154, 155–157, 304
- classification, 182, 190–195, 210, 214, 304
- comparison and contrast, 182, 195–201, 196, 210, 214, 304
- and conclusion, 304
- definition, 182, 184–190, 210, 214, 304
- description, 152, 165–170, 304
- example, 152, 170–176, 304
- identifying, 248
- multi-pattern, 298, 304
- narration, 152, 154–155, 161–165, 304
- primary pattern, 304
- process, 152, 154, 155, 159–161, 304
- secondary patterns, 305–306
- and supporting details, 304
- time sequence, 154–155
- and transitions, 304

Peer review, 58–59
Periodic review, 28
Person, shifts in, 565–567
Personification, 375
Photographs and graphics, 21
"Photojournalism in the Age of New Media" (Keller), 468–472
Phrase, 524–528
- absolute, 528
- as adjective and adverb, 525
- appositive, 527
- gerund, 526–527
- infinitive, 527
- noun and verb, 525
- participial, 526
- prepositional, 525
- verbal, 526

Post-reading strategies, 23–30
Predictions, 9
Preface or "to the student," 21
Prepositions, 514–516
- compound, 514–515

Pre-reading strategies, 4–9
Previewing, 4–5, 35, 40
Pronouns, 499–502
- antecedent, 499–500
- demonstrative, 500
- indefinite, 501–502
- intensive, 501

interrogative, 501
personal, 500
pronoun-antecedent agreement, 553–555
pronoun case, 557–559
pronoun reference, 555–557
reciprocal, 502
reflexive, 500–501
relative, 501
who and whom, 559
Proofreading, 40, 44, 45, 59–60, 67
checklist, 286
tips, 60
Punctuation, 580–590
apostrophes, 587–588
colons, 584–586
commas, 581–584
comma splice, 539–542
dashes, 587
hyphens, 587
parentheses, 587
periods, 580
question marks, 580–581
quotation marks, 588–589
semicolons, 584–586
Purpose for writing, 39, 44, 45, 54, 67, 219, 248, 257–258
Purpose of assignment, 251

Q

Questioning, 47, 48. *See* SQ3R system

R

Reading
building retention and response skills, 247–248
process, 3–4, 35
speed, 32
strategies, 11–23
Reading and writing, connecting, 39–40, 66
Redundancy, 285, 576–578
References, 248
"Relationships 2.0: Dating and Relating in the Internet Age (Sawchuck), 249–251
Review, 40
Reviewing and writing after reading, 248
Review questions/problems/discussions, 21
Revision, 38, 40, 44, 45, 57–59, 67
checklist, 288
peer review, 58–59
tips, 58
Revision, paragraphs, 216, 217–230, 237
error log, 228, 237
proofreading checklist, 227
revision checklist, 224
Rewriting, 44, 45, 67
Robbins, John, 91–93
Robbins, Kate, 117–119
"The Role of Sports in Life" (Beauclair), 362–363

S

Sawchuck, Ted, 249–251
Scheper-Hughes, Nancy, 443–452
Schmalleger, Frank, 424–434
"Secrets for Surviving College and Improving Your Grades (Ciccarelli and White), 5–9
Selective reading, 32
Sember, Quinne, 409–413
Sensory modes, using a variety of, 29
Sentence, 517–533
comma splice, 539–542
complements, 521–522
complex, 532
compound, 531–533
compound-complex, 532
coordination, 567–569
declarative, 517
direct objects, 521
errors, 534–562
exclamatory, 517
expansion with adjectives and adverbs, 523–524
expansion with clauses, 529–531
expansion with phrases, 524–529
fragments, 534–539
imperative, 517
indirect objects, 521–522
interrogative, 517
object complements, 522
patterns, 522–523
predicates, 517, 519–520
predicates, simple vs. compound, 519–520
redundancy, 576–577
run-on, 539–542
shifts in person, number, and tense, 565–566
simple, 531
subject, 517, 518–519
subject, compound, 519
subject, simple vs. complex, 518
subject complements and linking verbs, 521
subject-verb agreement, 550–552
variety, 574–576
wordiness, 576–577
Sexist language, 286
"Should College Football Student Athletes Get Paid?" (Fegely), 486–488
Simile, 375
Simmons, Adam, 323–326
Slang, 578
Sole-Smith, Virginia, 370–372
Sources, 248, 322–339, 350
APA style, 337–338
author's credentials, 350–351
comparing, 331–332
MLA style, 335–337
plagiarism, 327–328
proper use guidelines, 329–330
recording, 327–328
synthesizing, 331–334
your own qualifications as a source, 353–354
Special interest inserts, 21
Spellcheck, 287
Spelling, improving, 596–597
Spelling rules, 597–598
SQ3R system, 22–23, 36
Standard American English, 286
"Students Vulnerable to Computer Gaming Addiction", 232–234
Subordination, 569–571
Summarizing, 26–28, 36
Summary note, 20
Supporting details, 90, 113, 116, 119–132, 150, 248
descriptions, 125
examples, 124
facts or statistics, 124
least/most arrangement, 138
major vs. minor, 119–123
organization, 135–138
reasons, 124–125
relevancy, 132–134
spatial arrangement, 137
steps or procedures, 125
sufficiency, 132, 134–135
time sequence, 136
Supporting information, 242
"Sweatshops at Sea" (Sole-Smith), 370–372
Synonym, 24

T

"Technology and Crime" (Smalleger), 424–434
Test yourself questions, 21
Textbook learning aides, 21–22, 36
"The Russian and U.S. School Systems" (Atkinson), 98–99
Thesaurus, 24
Thesis, 26, 273–274
Thesis statement, 55, 242–243, 246, 260–263, 281, 282–284, 304, 312–313, 414–416
Thinking and writing, 38
Title, 242, 244–245
Tone, 52, 258–259, 358–360, 361
Topic, 113, 143
brainstorming, 254
branching, 254
choosing your own, 253–254
freewriting, 254
generating, 49, 114
generating ideas, 254–256
narrowing, 255–256
questioning, 254
refining, 100–101
revision, 281
selecting, 49, 98
sources of ideas for, 253
Topic sentence, 55, 90, 94, 105, 109–110, 113, 114
cause/effect, 208–209
classification pattern, 194
comparison/contrast pattern, 198
definition pattern, 189
locating, 102
and main point, 107
placement of, 102–105, 108
tips for writing, 107
Transitional words and phrases, 277, 283
and multi-pattern essay, 315
and patterns of organization, 304
and secondary patterns, 305
Transitions, 116, 140–143, 150, 276–277
cause/effect, 141, 205, 210

Transitions (*continued*)
- classification, 210
- comparison, 141
- comparison and contrast, 196
- comparison/contrast, 210
- continuation, 141
- contrast, 141
- definition, 210
- description, 167
- enumeration, 141
- example, 141
- summation, 141
- time sequence, 141
- useful words and phrases, 277

Trite expressions, 579
Tufekci, Zeynep, 463–465
Turkle, Sherry, 41–44
"TV's Bloody Obsession: Why Vampire Television is Dangerously Appealing" (Gilbert), 385–387

U

"An Unexpected Addiction" (Lawson), 229–230
Unfamiliar words, figuring out, 17–18

V

Vedantam, Shankar, 481–483
Verbs, 502–507
- action, 503
- active, 285
- emphasis, 545
- forms, 504–505
- gerund, 526–527
- helping (auxiliary), 503
- infinitives, 527
- intransitive, 503
- irregular, 504–505
- linking, 503
- modals, 503
- mood, 506, 549
- negatives, 545
- participle, 526
- questions, 545
- subject-verb agreement, 550–552
- subjunctive mood, 549–550
- tenses, 505, 543–547
- tenses, shifts, 565–567
- transitive, 503
- verb phrase, 503
- voice, 507
- voice, active and passive, 547–549

Visualizing, 29
Visuals, 19–21, 36, 56–57, 249
- fair use, 57
- source, 57
- variable, 20

Vivian, John, 457–460
Vocabulary
- actively practicing, 70–71
- connotative meaning, 73–74
- electronic log, 72
- euphemism, 73
- expanding, 68–71
- figurative language, 74
- foreign words and phrases, 74
- index card system, 71–72
- jargon, 74
- neologisms, 74
- and reading, 69
- specialized vocabulary, 73
- words you already know, 69

W

Web site, 352–353
"Weighing the Consequences of Censorship in Media" (Simmons), 323–326
"What Is the High Art of Competitive Eating?" (Muller), 299–303
White, J. Nolan, 5–9
"Who Are the Animals in Animal Experiments?" (Akhtar), 397–398
"Why Modern Human Trafficking is Called Human Slavery" (Martin) 437–441
Withgott, Jay, 183–184
Womble, Ashley, 344–346
Wordiness, 576–578
Word parts, 80–88
- prefixes, 80, 81
- roots, 80, 81, 83
- suffixes, 80, 81, 84, 85

Writing and reading, 23–24
Writing process steps, 44–46, 66

Y

"You're Under Surveillance" (Angwin), 290–293